UFO
FAQ

UFO FAQ

All That's Left to Know About Roswell, Aliens, Whirling Discs, and Flying Saucers

David J. Hogan

Backbeat
Books

An Imprint of Hal Leonard Corporation

Published in 2016 by Backbeat Books
An Imprint of Hal Leonard Corporation
7777 West Bluemound Road
Milwaukee, WI 53213

Trade Book Division Editorial Offices
33 Plymouth St., Montclair, NJ 07042

The FAQ series was conceived by Robert Rodriguez and developed with Stuart Shea.

All images are from the author's collection unless otherwise noted.

Every reasonable effort has been made to contact copyright holders and secure permission. Omissions can be remedied in future editions.

Printed in the United States of America

Book design by Snow Creative

Library of Congress Cataloging-in-Publication Data

Names: Hogan, David J., 1953– author.
Title: UFO FAQ : all that's left to know about Roswell, aliens, whirling discs, and
    flying saucers / David J. Hogan.
Description: Milwaukee, WI : Backbeat, an imprint of Hal Leonard Corporation,
    2016. | Includes bibliographical references and index.
Identifiers: LCCN 2016016213 | ISBN 9781480393851 (pbk.)
Subjects: LCSH: Unidentified flying objects—Miscellanea.
Classification: LCC TL793 .H566 2016 | DDC 001.942—dc23
LC record available at https://lccn.loc.gov/2016016213

www.backbeatbooks.com

For Mark A. Miller,
who knows the secrets of the stars

Contents

Acknowledgments

Margaret and Ronald V. Borst/Hollywood Movie Posters

Len Brown, formerly of Topps, for insights into *Mars Attacks!*

Rachel Hogan, for visuals related to McMinnville, Oregon's annual UFO Festival

Roger Marsh, MUFON's director of communications, for insights into that wide-ranging organization

Marie and Joe Martin, Neatly Chiseled Features, for permission to reprint *Mr. Boffo*

Ted Okuda, for information about the geographic dispersion of U.S. sightings, 1990–2015, and early saucer references in Hollywood movies

Mark Turner, for special abduction information

Professor Wilhelm Steigg, for sharing his keen grasp of science

Chase Winstead, for opening his illustration archive

John Cerullo and Marybeth Keating at Backbeat Books, for patience above and beyond

Special thanks to Gordon Lore, for his participant's insights into NICAP. His generosity and knowledge have been invaluable.

I looked, and I saw a windstorm coming out of the north—an immense cloud with flashing lightning and surrounded by brilliant light. The center of the fire looked like glowing metal, and in the fire was what looked like four living creatures. In appearance, their form was human. . . .

—*The Book of Ezekiel*, 1:4-5 (NIV), c. 593 BC–562 BC

I think that nothing can be more important than interplanetary communication. It will certainly come someday, and the certitude that there are other human beings in the universe, working, suffering, struggling, like ourselves, will produce a magic effect on mankind and will form the foundation of a universal brotherhood that will last as long as humanity itself.

—scientist Nikola Tesla, 1931

What does all this stuff about flying saucers amount to? What can it mean? What is the truth?

—Winston Churchill, 1952

UFOs are as real as the airplanes that fly over your head.

—former Canadian Defence Minister Paul Hellyer, 2005

UFO
FAQ

Introduction
Marvels and Speculation

The Aliens Are Out There, but Are They Here?

Living Among the Stars

On a humid July night not long ago, at a house in the Smokies above Gatlinburg, Tennessee, I sat on an elevated deck and watched the stars. For a while, I perceived nothing but the familiar splash of stationary points of light against a cradle of black. But soon, Venus and Jupiter—appearing almost twinned above the horizon—presented themselves.

And then things up there began to move. My eye was caught by a tiny, winking light: an airliner, aloft five or six miles in the night sky, moving across my field of vision from left to right. People in the air. Remarkable.

A meteorite cut a quick diagonal across the star-splashed blackness, a needle-thin splash of brilliance with a hint of a tail. How far had it come?

Another airliner showed itself, but this point of light followed a parabolic course rather than the straight path of a plane. *Not* an airliner, I finally supposed, but a satellite, another technical marvel.

The dense woods that surrounded the house vibrated with the chatter of katydids, a choppy, harsh-pretty sound that said *life* as surely as it said *summer night*. A brief, hot breeze rustled the tree branches. From somewhere on the forest floor, a frog spoke. After a moment, another answered. The katydids continued to gossip, their sounds a raucous chorus of call and response. Far off, a dog barked. As I listened and *felt*, my unique identity seemed to melt away; I became a point of consciousness in a universe far too vast for easy comprehension. I was alive. Like the trees and insects, and the numberless animals and people on Earth, I was life.

I returned my gaze to the stars. The universe was there, not cold, but hot with possibility.

I knew that intelligent eyes other than mine watched the sky, and that not all of them were with me on Earth. I knew that although the distances between stars are vast, and I may never know those other eyes firsthand, the eyes are there.

UFOs and Us

Over the many centuries of human history, and particularly since the late 1940s, countless people around the globe have witnessed Unidentified Flying Objects that could not be explained in conventional terms. Not that the authorities haven't tried. Official explanations of recent decades have invoked conventional aircraft, cloud formations, stars, planets (Venus is frequently cited), ball lightning, and St. Elmo's Fire (glowing, ionized air). Many UFOs have been explained away as satellites, weather balloons, reflected light (particularly off windows, camera lenses, and eyeglasses), smog, and a perennial favorite, swamp gas (spontaneous combustion of methane). Because government and other official agencies can be obdurate about holding to their findings, a great deal of UFO discussion has roused emotion and become simplistic, holding that 1) UFOs are hoaxes or illusions, or 2) UFOs are real. Reasoning of this sort hardly encourages anyone to consider the many subtle aspects of arguments for and against UFOs.

Fabricated reports of UFOs exist, too, and although many of them scream *hoax*, a great many find people willing to accept them. For many, UFOs suggest adventure and wonder, the thrill of being witness to visits from a heretofore unimagined civilization. For the conspiracy-minded (see chapter eleven), unidentified flying objects connote underhanded American or "world government" activities based on extraterrestrial technology—technology that humans have reverse-engineered or that, alternatively, has been shared, to no good purpose, by the aliens that created it.

On the other hand, people with a more sanguine view of UFOs and the crafts' operators look to the phenomenon as an antidote to the horrors unfolding daily here on Earth. Perhaps, just perhaps, the alien visitors are made of nobler stuff. Perhaps they are willing to show us the road to peaceful fulfillment of our potential as human animals.

As we'll discover in chapter two, the existence of extraterrestrial life, particularly the sentient variety, depends on a specific confluence of events: a planet situated within its sun's "golden zone," with an atmosphere and water, where life was germinated by an energized chemical soup that . . . well, it's complicated. During the last forty-five years, exciting information about conditions in near space has been generated by crewed space missions and probes launched by many nations. Fabulous telescopes, like the Hubble Space Telescope (launched 1990) and the Fermi Gamma-Ray Space Telescope (launched 2008), bring knowledge of extrasolar planets, the nature of quasars, the electromagnetic spectrum, and possible origins of the universe.

Evidence of life remains elusive. A case might be made for microbial life on Mars; that possibility, though thrilling, does not satisfy our craving to learn of intelligent life. The search continues. In 2009, NASA's Kepler mission set off to locate planets similar to our own. Before 2010 was out, Kepler had discovered more than twenty-three hundred potential planets. One of those, Kepler-22, is the first that we know orbits in a star's habitable zone. What—or who—is on that planet? We don't know. In the course of a single day's research, we can be stimulated, encouraged, discouraged, and then encouraged all over again.

What Is a UFO?

The question posed above seems absurdly simple. A UFO is an unidentified flying object. Yes, but just what does that mean—and what does it imply?

The *meaning* is basic: a skyborne object (usually on the move) or phenomenon that cannot be immediately identified. In other words, it is not anything a witness can identify at a glance, such as a hot-air balloon, a Cessna 172, high-flying geese, quickly moving clouds, or a Frisbee.

The *implications* raised by the term "UFO" are more complex, involving secret military aircraft, abduction, horrific medical experiments, presumed human-alien hybrids, warring/colluding governments, secret bases on the dark side of the Moon, and a lot more.

Once, though, a UFO was just an unidentified flying object.

A secret October 28, 1947, memo by United States Air Force Brigadier Gen. George F. Schulgen, chief of USAF intelligence, established UFO-identification guidelines that remain valuable today. General Schulgen crafted the memo after reviewing the particulars of UFO reports that arrived as a torrent following the thoroughly reported account of businessman Kenneth Arnold's June 1947 encounter with "flying saucers" over Washington State. Schulgen and his staff looked at the Arnold account, and others, as well as at various burn areas and other physical evidence, radar records, and accounts of military and commercial pilots. Schulgen expressed interest in the materials used in construction of unidentified aircraft, and noted "retractable domes" and other features.

So what are UFOs? General Schulgen discussed eleven pertinent points, writing:

1. An alleged "Flying Saucer" type aircraft or object in flight, approximating the shape of a disc, has been reported by many observers from widely scattered places, such as the United States, Alaska, Canada, Hungary, the Island of Guam, and Japan. This object has been reported by many competent observers, including USAF rated officers. Sightings have been made from the ground as well as from the air.

2. Commonly reported features that are very significant and which may aid in the investigation are as follows:

   a. Relatively flat bottom with extreme light-reflecting ability.

   b. Absence of sound except for an occasional roar when operating under super performance conditions.

   c. Extreme maneuverability and apparent ability to almost hover.

   d. A plan form approximating that of an oval or disc with a dome shape on the top surface.

   e. The absence of an exhaust trail except in a few instances when it was reported to have a bluish color, like a Diesel exhaust, which persisted for approximately one hour. Other reports indicated a brownish smoke trail that could be the results of a special catalyst or chemical agent for extra power.

f.   The ability to quickly disappear by high speed or by complete disintegration.
g.   The ability to suddenly appear without warning as if from an extremely high altitude.
h.   The size most reported approximated that of a C-54 or Constellation type aircraft. [Author note: *The Douglas C-54 Skymaster* was a four-engine, prop-driven transport aircraft derived from a civilian airliner, the Douglas DC-4. The Skymaster's wingspan measured 117 feet 6 inches, Total length was 93 feet 5 inches, with a height of 27 feet 7 inches. The *Lockheed L-049 Constellation* was a four-engine, prop-driven airliner that was adapted for military use. The military variant of the *Constellation* was called the *Lockheed C-69 Constellation*. Its wingspan measured 123 feet. Total length was 95 feet 2 inches, with a height of 23 feet 8 inches.]
i.   The ability to group together very quickly in a tight formation when more than one aircraft are together.
j.   Evasive action ability indicates possibility of being manually operated, or possibly by electronic or remote control devices.
k.   Under certain power conditions, the craft seems to have the ability to cut a clear path through clouds—width of path estimated to be approximately one-half mile. Only one incident indicated this phenomenon.

Since 1947 and General Schulgen's memo (which was declassified in 1985 under the Freedom of Information Act), UFO sightings and investigation have grown enormously more varied and complex. Even the memo itself grew more complex over time: in 1997, an indefatigable UFO researcher named Robert G. Todd claimed that the Schulgen memo was faked by whomever obtained it in 1985. (General Schulgen died in 1955, too soon for him to comment on his memo's contents.)

Since 1947, the traditional flying saucer shape has been joined by cylinders, deltas, lenticulars, and so-called Saturn shapes with an obvious equatorial ring. Some photographs and videos show faceless cubes and rectangles. A minority of UFOs are as bright and decorative-seeming as Christmas ornaments. Luminosity is a commonly reported characteristic. Other reports suggest highly reflective surfaces that interact with ground light.

Most UFOs are symmetrical, and exhibit no wings, tail assemblies, or other obvious design concessions to avionics. Regardless, the craft fly, swoop, flip upside down, and reverse course with apparent effortlessness. Speeds are difficult to judge at distance, and without the near presence of other, recognizable objects, estimation of a craft's size are mere approximations or sheer guesswork. Still, enough experienced aviators have seen UFOs to suggest that in-flight atmospheric speeds as great as ten thousand miles per hour may be possible.

In classic UFO scenarios, the crafts are crewed. Another opinion is that many, if not all, UFOs are remote controlled via technology (much like our drone aircraft) or by long-distance mind control. A few UFOlogists suggest that the craft may be organic, or part organic, rather than wholly inorganic. Around 2010, researcher Trevor James Constable proposed that UFOs are what he called "biological forms"—"plasmic, living organisms *native to our atmosphere.*" [emphasis added] Under this model, UFOs are not merely alive, but are indigenous to Earth.

An alternative theory holds that the craft are not from space but from other dimensions, and can slip in and out of our reality at will.

Since the early 1950s, many unhappy witnesses have encountered UFOs at distances close enough to cause irritated eyes, a sunburn-like insult to exposed skin, and even trace radiation. Unpleasant chemical odors and intense, sometimes painful sounds assail some witnesses. And over about the past fifty years, a significant proportion of UFO experience and research has focused on abduction of witnesses—the most unnerving aspect of the UFO phenomenon.

Conspiracy theorists sometimes insist that UFOs are joint alien/human endeavors launched to dominate the Earth; others feel that the craft are of human design, and exist to serve the military and/or to frighten or distract the general population from faltering national economies and other pressing problems.

Acting in opposition to all of the above is the assumption that because humans haven't the technology to travel between stars, no one else does, either. Particularly hardheaded skeptics refuse to investigate claims of UFOs; they elect not to be empirical.

UFOs, then, are many things, and arouse a variety of reactions. They may be as real as the jetliner that takes you on vacation. Or they may simply be whatever individuals—believers and skeptics alike—want them to be. But we know this: by definition, unidentified flying objects exist.

Throwing Open the Doors

In January 2015, more than 130,000 pages of declassified documents related to Project Blue Book became available on the World Wide Web. Blue Book—set up by the U.S. Air Force in 1947 to investigate UFOs and terminated in 1969—had been declassified since the 1970s. The files had been transferred to microfilm, and were accessible. However, anyone interested in researching the files had to investigate them in person, at the Maxwell Air Force Base Air University Library, in Montgomery, Alabama; and, later, the National Archives in Washington, D.C.

After the millennium, an investigator calling him/herself Xtraeme turned the 130,000 microfilmed pages into jpeg files. The jpegs inspired a young TV-documentary producer named John Greenewald, who wanted to make Xtraeme's work easily accessible. Greenewald is a devotee of the Freedom of Information Act, a law he vigorously leveraged in the late 1990s, while still a teenager. In 1996 he created The Black Vault, a Web site containing more than 1.3 million pages of formerly classified government papers. Greenewald is particularly fascinated by UFOs, and was excited by the work done by Xtraeme. Greenewald told *Huffington Post* reporter Lee Spiegel, "I figured out a computer script that would actually convert 130,000 essentially pictures into a little over 10,000 PDFs. . . . I was then able to program the Web site and ultimately create a search engine that dives into those 10,000 PDFs."

Greenewald's Project Blue Book Collection can be searched by year or key word. At one's fingertips, then, are records of 12,618 sightings investigated by the Air Force and other agencies during a period of more than twenty years.

A complementary Web site, Project Blue Book Archive, is maintained by Project 1947, the Archives for UFO Research, the Sign Historical Group (SHG), and the Fund for UFO Research (FUFOR). Like Greenewald's site, the Project Blue Book Archive offers easy-search access. In addition, the site pursues the dissemination of documents held in private collections.

These valuable resources offer information on a scale that, to some, may be overwhelming. Preparation and judiciousness will help prepare users to interpret the documents wisely. The trove should encourage every UFO enthusiast—and skeptics, as well—to conduct independent research, look to the skies, and wonder.

How This Book Works

To put together a single-volume guide to UFOs is a daunting and perhaps foolish endeavor. Widespread interest in unexplained objects in the sky dates back centuries, of course, but ever since the UFO boom that kicked off in mid-century 1947, many factions—public, artistic, medical, academic, scientific, technological, biologic, military, political—have laid claim to one portion or another of the UFO phenomenon. Information is scattered in books, enthusiast magazines, every TV-delivery platform, and the Web.

Given the avalanche of UFO information—solid, spurious, and in-between— no single volume can hope to cover the entirety of the UFO story. Even the effort required to create a twenty-volume UFO encyclopedia would fall short. Still, optimists tend to remain optimistic, and although *UFO FAQ* does not tell it *all*, I aim for it to tell readers enough about many aspects of UFOs to become a useful, portable guide, as well as to inspire further, more specific study.

If you write in care of the publisher to let me know about people or events not discussed in the book, be advised that I'm likely already aware of them, and chose omission because of considerations of manuscript length, or because the essence of specific UFO events is represented by other accounts—accounts that *are* part of the book.

In sixteen chapters plus bracketing text, *UFO FAQ* offers narratives about the basic topics noted above, as well as UFO-centric takes on the occult, futurism, World War II, Kenneth Arnold's famed flight over Washington State, the crash at Roswell, hoaxes, friendly aliens, the likelihood of intelligent extraterrestrial life, and the people comprising the UFO community.

I urge readers to give special attention to chapter one, "The UFO Community," for in it are capsule profiles of notable UFOlogists, living and deceased, as well as profiles of American and international UFO organizations. A careful read of this material will give a useful overview not just of specific persons and groups, but of the great divergence of opinions and goals within the community.

This book's bibliography notes books, magazine articles, papers, Web sites, and other sources consulted by the author during research. "Consulted" does not

Unidentified *Fearsome* Object? For seventy years, that's how comic books and other entertainment media have typically treated UFOs. Well, fair enough, because that's where the salable drama is, but a more encompassing approach reveals people, events, and science no less fascinating than "alien attack." *Space Adventures Presents U.F.O.* No. 60, 1967. Art by Dick Giordano and Rocke Mastroserio

necessarily mean "endorsed" or "believed." UFO study overflows with source materials of variable authority, scholarship, and usefulness. But even sources that failed to be "valuable" in the conventional sense sparked ideas. Whatever my feelings about a discrete source—positive, negative, or undecided—that source is part of the bibliography.

My goal has been a steady, open-minded rationality. We will explore fabulous and fantastic things, many of which cannot easily be comprehended or explained.

I claim no special powers of knowledge or insight. My responsibility is simply to be fair-minded. Just know, however, that I was the kid who lived for TV screenings of *Earth vs. the Flying Saucers*; cherished *Spacemen* magazine; devoured Clarke, Heinlein, Adamski, and many others; and wowed the fourth grade with my oral report on the famed *War of the Worlds* radio broadcast.

Well, okay, then, maybe *absolute* objectivity is a little beyond my inclinations.

David J. Hogan
Arlington Heights, Illinois

1

The UFO Community

Experiences, Activities, and Agendas

Shaping a Community

T he structured UFO community can be traced to an individual, American writer Charles Hoy Fort (1874–1932), a habitual contrarian eager to scold scientists for "dogmatic" attraction to scientific fact. He also was an early collector and chronicler of UFO reports. A reclusive autodidact, Fort spent years at the British Museum and New York Public Library, poring over newspapers and accumulating thousands of pieces of scrap paper, each scribbled with his notes about a scientifically anomalous event and his annotation of the published source.

Two early, unpublished books by Fort, *X* and *Y*, concern Martian meddling in human affairs; and an unscrupulous civiliza- tion located at the South Pole, respectively. Those ideas are outside the mainstream, and some of Fort's followers are convinced that the writer wanted to arouse skepticism, particularly in younger readers. What Fort called "inter-planetary inhabitancy" led him to a discussion, in *The Book of the Damned* (1919), of historical sightings of dark objects passing across the Moon. Moving lights near the satellite, and white spots on its surface, also piqued Fort's interest. By way of explanation, Fort went from extraterrestrials (with mythic and religious descriptors) to the supernatural, within the space of two pages. "Worlds in hordes—" he wrote, "—or beings—winged beings perhaps— wouldn't astonish me if we should end up by dis- covering angels—or beings in machines—argosies of celestial voyagers—[.]" Mere paragraphs later, he wrote, "Dark bodies, floating, or navigating, in inter-planetary space—and I conceive of one that's the Prince of Dark Bodies: Melanicus. Vast dark thing with the wings of a super-bat, or jet-black super-construction; most likely one of the spores

The fascination of the indefatigable researcher and iconoclast Charles Hoy Fort with the odd and paranormal helped establish the thought processes of the later UFO movement.

of the Evil One. . . . He obscures a star. He shoves a comet. I think he's a vast, black, brooding vampire."

Besides challenging readers with his idiosyncratic diction and punctuation, Fort teased them with pendulum-like swings of speculation on single topics. But that was beauty of what he did: take information from many sources, collate it, and present it in the frisky manner of a quasi-intellectual game.

Following the 1923 publication of Fort's *New Lands*, reader (and noted writer) Ben Hecht coined the term "Fortean," as a synonym for "anomalous." At the beginning of 1931, Tiffany Thayer established The Fortean Society in New York City. Dedicated to thinking seriously about anomalous natural events, and a repudiation of constrained, "traditional" scientific thought, the society published an official organ, *Fortean Society* magazine, which took a name change in 1944, becoming *Doubt*. Although the society and *Doubt* went defunct with Thayer's death in 1959, Fort's influence has been felt ever since. In 1973, British publishers with no official link to the Fort legacy established *Fortean Times* magazine, which continues to this day. Like Fort himself, the magazine is intellectually cheeky, colorful, and wide-ranging—a publication for people skeptical of skeptics.

Post-Fort People and Activities

A significant portion of UFOlogy is scientific, and dominated by persons trained in astronomy, avionics, astrophysics, biology, and other pertinent disciplines. Such people are familiar with the scientific method, and when they write, it is for peer-reviewed journals. Some in this group dedicate themselves to investigatory activity and a careful recording of events. Alternatively, less-rigorous groups are preoccupied with government involvement with UFOs. Some of those links motivate subgroups devoted to conspiracy theory predicated on an inherent sneakiness of Washington, NASA, and other entities.

Baseless conjecture can be addressed. But nobody can turn back the clock, which is to say that traditional-mode UFO enthusiasts are aging. Here, "traditional" connotes a certain purity of interest: rooted in astronomy if not complex astronomical science, and an openness to the possibility of UFOs' extraterrestrial origins. Organized U.S. government interest in UFOs brought the subject some useful gravitas during about 1948–70, but when government investigatory agencies pulled back and abandoned their public face, general interest in UFOs began to fracture into subgroups. From the late 1960s forward, increased public interest in the paranormal profoundly affected the philosophical nature of UFO studies. First- and second-generation UFO enthusiasts that had been formed from the "hardware" nature of World War II placed value on the solid, empirical aspects of technology and evidence. These people shared a cast-iron-and-rivets orientation, and an understanding of technology (particularly avionics). They could make distinctions between the real, the likely, the possible, and the absurd.

But those first- and second-generation enthusiasts are now between about fifty-five and ninety, and have aged into irrelevance in a culture that worships the young, the new, and the bizarre. Even bright youngsters that developed an interest in UFOs as recently as the mid-1980s are now in their middle forties, and some may have failed to resist the sirens' songs of parallel dimensions, human-alien hybrids, astrology, Bigfoot, extraterrestrial demons, and healers from the stars.

People younger than forty haven't the shared memory needed to return to the unsentimental empiricism of the early UFO investigators. Indeed, memory is hardly needed at all in a 21st-century environment of ceaseless blogs, texts, Instagram, and Snapchat.

In 2013, UFOlogist and retired process design engineer Frank Purcell wrote to UFO Trail, a popular blog. "Conjectures [about UFOs] are fine," he said, "but they are not science." He went on to elaborate on the importance of controlled laboratory experiments to any exploration aspiring to be scientific study. Specific to UFOs, Purcell said,

> [W]hile UFOs haven't been experimented on in laboratories, what we do have are anecdotal reports, sometimes with physical evidence such as radar reports, photographs, film, and even, occasionally, medical information from people interacting with UFOs. But an important distinction needs to be made if we contrast ufology with, say, evolution and astrophysics. With UFOs there is no body of laboratory-based knowledge from which to draw reasonable theories. The best people can do is make conjectures.

Credibility vs. Amateurism

Today, UFO book publishing is defined by traditional houses (St. Martin's, Tor, Haynes, Schiffer, Little Brown, et al.); specialty small presses (Feral House, History Press, Disinformation Books, Adventures Unlimited Press, New Page Books, et al.); e-books (many issued by Amazon Digital Services); and self-published books (Amazon's CreateSpace Independent Publishing is the choice of many amateur and semi-professional writers).

UFO books discussed beyond the boundaries of the UFO community are the work of established writers (Whitley Strieber's clever, purportedly fact-inspired 2006 novel *The Grays* received fairly wide and enthusiastic critical coverage); or authors with points of view that demand to be discussed in the mainstream (such as investigative reporter Annie Jacobsen, whose 2011 book *Area 51* astounded critics with a jaw-dropping claim tucked into the book's final chapter. For more about the Jacobsen book, see chapter eight).

Other authors bring credibility based in rigorous scholarship and underscored with an objective tone. Thomas E. "Eddie" Bullard, a trained academic and onetime member of MUFON (Mutual UFO Network), published *The Myth and Mysteries of UFOs* with the University Press of Kansas in 2010, artfully negotiating a line separating a folkloric interpretation of UFOs (Bullard's area of special expertise) and the intriguing consistency of abduction accounts and other "real world" UFO activity. *The UFO Book*, a 1998 encyclopedia by UFOlogist Jerome Clark, is a thick A-to-Z bible of UFO study, lively and heavy with detail. Although a former editor of *Fate* magazine, and a board member of the J. Allen Hynek Center for UFO Studies, Clark crafted an objective tone that helped place the book on store shelves around the world.

UFO-pertinent academic credentials and informed objectivity reflect well on UFOlogy. Other qualified researchers, such as Stuart Appelle, Tom Carey, Kent Jeffrey, Mark Rodeghier, and Michael Swords, approach the subject with intelligence and clarity. But Swords—a retired Western Michigan University professor of natural sciences, and an authority on U.S. government studies of UFOs—made his feelings clear in a 1995 response to this question posed to him by CUFON (the Computer UFO Network): "[What is the] State of UFOlogy today/Goals today?" Swords answered,

> "UFOlogy": a serious, objective, scholarly study of the UFO phenomenon. [underlines in original] There is essentially no UFOlogy today, and rarely has there ever been. There is much pseudo-UFOlogy (lacking in objectivity or any sense of the history of the subject or the scope of previous research and other relevant disciplines), and even more UFOria (sort of a wide-eyed gee whiz fooling around with "wonders"). The few [legitimate] UFOlogists who are active . . . find themselves isolated in an intellectual desert filled with UFOric persons who are constantly jumping beyond the evidence, and insisting upon concrete answers. . . .

Richard Hall, author, USAF veteran, and an early member of the National Investigations Committee on Aerial Phenomena (NICAP), has been critical of UFOlogical methodology, and resigned in protest from MUFON in 2001. Speaking to Computer UFO Network, Hall bemoaned UFOlogy as "mainly a bunch of amateurs working in their spare time on a problem that would baffle senior scientists. . . ." Hall called for increased professionalism, better handling and documentation of evidence, improved public education, and the promotion of "serious interest among scientists and other important persons whose skills or resources are necessary for a resolution of the problem. That includes weeding out nonsense from the field."

Eyes Only: Some Notable UFOlogists of the Past

Persons noted below engaged in various aspects of UFO study in the postwar era. A varied group, these UFOlogists came from many worlds: finance, science, journalism, philosophy, aviation, and the military. A few were contactees; others told personal tales of extraterrestrial sightings or abduction.

A few were deeply skeptical of the ET theory of UFOs.

Each person is deceased, which is of no significance other than that particularly paranoid conspiracy theorists propose that many dead UFOlogists died too young, or too coincidentally, or too conveniently.

George Adamski (1891–1965): The most celebrated and persuasive of all UFO contactees, Adamski enjoyed modest success in the 1930s as leader of a California religious cult that melded benevolent Christianity and mysticism. He took up

UFOlogy in the late 1940s (coincident with Kenneth Arnold's 1947 saucer sighting), after witnessing flying saucers and subsequently meeting their beatific, human-appearing pilots. Adamski opened a small restaurant on land he owned near Mount Palomar, California, selling saucer snapshots and other souvenirs, and speaking about his alien friends and extraterrestrial travels. He became a minor celebrity after attracting the attention of mainstream book publishers, and turned up as a speaker at UFO gatherings and occasionally on television. By osmosis, or just the generosity of his followers, Adamski became "Professor" Adamski in the late 1950s. He continued to profitably lecture and write until his death.

To some in the UFO community, Adamski (eager to share his impressions of Jesus-like aliens and spaceships bristling with glowing glass bricks and clunky coils) is an old-school eccentric. To others, however, the professor represents the best, first flush of alien contact. Whatever one's opinion, and despite the fact that popular thought about ETs is now dark rather than hopeful, Adamski is the undisputed farther of the contactee movement.

For more on George Adamski, see chapter twelve.

Notable books: *Flying Saucers Have Landed* (with Desmond Leslie); *Inside the Space Ships*; *Pioneers of Space: A Trip to the Moon, Mars and Venus*; *Flying Saucers Farewell*.

Orfeo Angelucci (1912–93): Lockheed metal fabricator and amateur botanist who, like George Adamski, greeted benign extraterrestrials. Angelucci made his first sighting of a saucer in 1946, little knowing that (as he described things) he would be under alien observation for the next five years. During a 1952 saucer sighting, Angelucci drank from a "crystal cup" that materialized on the fender of his car. A "golden

Amateur California stargazer George Adamski led UFOlogy's "friendly contact" faction, and achieved worldwide celebrity. *Flying Saucer News*, 1961.

voice" explained that "for our first contact with the people of Earth, Orfeo, we have chosen you."

Angelucci later inhabited the body of a resident of Neptune, an experience that Angelucci experienced as a "missing time" episode. For more on Angelucci, see chapter twelve.

Notable book: *The Secret of the Saucers.*

Gray Barker (1925–84): American film booker and distributor of educational materials who parlayed early articles about UFOs—notably a 1953 piece about an alien monster doing mischief near Flatwoods, West Virginia—into a prolific career as an author and lecturer. Barker's ostensibly factual 1956 book *They Knew Too Much About Flying Saucers* introduced the "Men in Black"—intimidating government operatives that monitor UFO investigators and contactees, so that UFO information best kept secret is not released to the general public. The book's central figure is Albert K. Bender, a real-life saucer witness who claimed to have been intimidated afterwards by creepy strangers wearing dark suits and sunglasses. The MiB concept played well with paranoid readers during the Cold War, and went on to secure a firm grip on the national consciousness. A big-budget Hollywood film, *Men in Black*, prospered at the box office in 1997, and inspired two sequels.

In a 1998 article for *Skeptical Inquirer* magazine, journalist and onetime Barker protégé John Sherwood revealed that Barker regarded UFO investigation and other paranormal studies as a lark, even as Barker claimed to believe in order to exploit public interest and make a living. In a 1968 letter to Sherwood, Barker described UFO enthusiasts as obsessed neurotics.

In the late 1960s, Barker encouraged the teenaged Sherwood to present a fictional account of flying saucer time machines as fact. The young Sherwood did so, and the "article" was printed in Barker's magazine, *Saucer News.* Barker informed Sherwood, with evident satisfaction, that "the fans swallowed this one with a gulp."

In the end, Barker's legacy as a UFOlogist may come down to something he told his sister Blanch: "There's good money in it."

Notable books: *They Knew Too Much About Flying Saucers*; *Flying Saucers and the Three Men* (with Albert K. Bender); *The Silver Bridge.*

Leroy Gordon Cooper Jr. (1927–2004): Original "Mercury Seven" astronaut, USAF test pilot, and aerospace engineer. The youngest of the Mercury astronauts, he also was the last of that group to go into space. During his May 1963 mission, the final Mercury flight, Cooper spent more than thirty-four hours in space and orbited Earth twenty-two times. A potentially disastrous power failure near the scheduled end of the flight forced Cooper to take manual control of the capsule and perform quick calculations to adjust his re-entry, preserve the capsule, and save his life.

Cooper went into space a second time, as part of the Gemini project, in 1965.

Although folklore holds that "Gordo" Cooper witnessed a UFO during a flight in space, he confirmed that that was not the case. However, he (and other pilots) witnessed multiple UFOs during a flight over Germany in 1951. Six years later, Cooper made another in-flight sighting.

For more on Gordon Cooper's UFO experiences, see chapter ten.

Notable book: *Leap of Faith: An Astronaut's Journey into the Unknown* (with Bruce Henderson).

Milton William "Bill" Cooper (1943–2001): American self-published author, on-air personality with the World Wide Christian Radio shortwave network, lecturer, gun-rights advocate, and antigovernment tax scofflaw who investigated and exposed conspiracy theories.

UFOs were not Cooper's primary area of interest, but he wrote and spoke about them colorfully. Project Luna, he said, was a secret alien base on the dark side of the Moon. Further, the United States had established a Moon base in the mid-1950s (Cooper was vague about the precise year), and a base on Mars not long after the first manned landing there (a joint United States–Russia endeavor) in 1962.

Cooper expressed concern for victims of alien abduction, who were, Cooper said, being rounded up by the government and illegally interned. During a 1989 lecture at a UFO conference in Modesto, California, Cooper insisted that the aliens seen on the *Alien Nation* fictional television series were real extraterrestrials. Although Christian, Cooper believed that much of the Bible "is the result of alien manipulation."

Cooper viewed the world's political, economic, and scientific establishments as corrupted components of a new world order—an immensely powerful cabal of Illuminati that worked in collusion with extraterrestrials to dominate the planet's affairs. Cooper claimed that President Eisenhower met with an alien ambassador in 1954, and that JFK was assassinated by a "gas pressure device" given to the driver of the presidential limousine by aliens linked to the Trilateral Commission. Kennedy had to die because he planned to expose Washington-alien collusion.

With his self-published 1991 book *Behold a Pale Horse*, Cooper elaborated on his theories, ranging sufficiently wide to encompass the *Protocols of the Elders of Zion*, an alleged scheme to establish FEMA concentration camps, the international plot that created and spread the AIDS virus, Jewish-Illuminati links, Satanic Church collusion with U.S. Army Intelligence, alien implants, and alien theft of human fetuses.

Although Cooper served in the U.S. Navy during the Vietnam era, he probably was not, as he claimed, an intelligence officer. Nor did he have a "license to kill" or authorization to move freely between branches of the service, changing uniforms as he went.

Cooper was a founding member of a militia group called the Second Continental Army of the Republic, and coordinator of that group's Citizens Agency for Joint Intelligence.

When a pair of Apache County (Arizona) deputies (backed by some fifteen other officers) arrived at Cooper's home in Eagar, Arizona, to serve a warrant for aggravated assault, Cooper fired on them. One of the deputies suffered two shots to the head; the other returned fire and killed Cooper. Not unexpectedly, some conspiracy theorists with tenuous links to the UFO community claim that Cooper was "murdered" so that his alleged truth-telling would be silenced. But in the world of UFO studies, Cooper has become a footnote in just fifteen years, and UFOlogists now have little patience with his ideas.

Notable book: *Behold a Pale Horse*.

Philip J. Corso (1915–98): Distinguished U.S. Army lieutenant colonel who made waves in the mid-1950s with allegations of U.S. abandonment of American POWs following the Korean War, and later claims of having seen artifacts from the 1947 crash at Roswell.

In Corso's *Dawn of a New Age*, a manuscript unpublished at the time of his death, he wrote of his 1957 sighting, near the White Sands, New Mexico, test grounds, of a "shiny, saucer shaped object on the ground," and his subsequent encounter with a humanoid alien. Corso claimed that he and the alien established a telepathic link. (Very much in the manner of the 1953 movie *It Came from Outer Space*, the alien simply wished to lift off unmolested.) The alien ship, Corso wrote, was the counterpart of the one discovered at Roswell ten years earlier. The ships crashed into each other in 1947, but because they traveled through time (in order to negotiate the vast distances between stars), ten years passed before the one seen by Corso "entered" Earth's space a second time.

An intelligence staff officer and battalion commander of European Air Defense, Corso is best-recalled for his stance on Roswell, though his complaints about Washington's treatment of POWs probably were the central event of his career, and a reason why his career stalled short of full colonel.

See chapter eight for more on Philip Corso and Roswell.

Notable books: *The Day After Roswell* (with William J. Birnes); *L'Alba di una Nuova Era* (Italian publication of *Dawn of a New Age*).

Frank Edwards (1908–67): American radio broadcaster turned author who wrote two of the most widely read of all UFO books, *Flying Saucers—Serious Business!* (1966) and *Flying Saucers—Here and Now!* (1967).

Edwards began his radio career in the 1930s. His curiosity about flying saucers grew from the Roswell story, and became so intense that in a 1949 broadcast on the Mutual network, Edwards declared that flying saucers "actually exist," adding that "they are not of this world." He later became intrigued by Washington's Project Blue Book UFO investigation, and by all manner of hard-to-explain phenomena. Edwards's syndicated radio show of the 1950s, *Stranger than Science*, found success, and led to his 1959 book of the same name. Edwards joined the board of NICAP (National Investigations Committee on Aerial Phenomena), and segued into television in the mid-1950s, discussing flying saucers and other phenomena.

Late in 1966, the King Features syndicate picked up *Flying Saucers—Serious Business!* for ten-part serialization in newspapers across the country. Besides burnishing Edwards's celebrity, the syndication deal greatly increased general American interest in UFOs.

During the final decade of his life, Edwards was a vocal critic of government censorship of UFO documents and other information.

Notable books: *Stranger than Science*; *Flying Saucers—Serious Business!*; *Flying Saucers—Here and Now!*

Arthur Ernest Exon (1916–2005): Heavily decorated USAF brigadier general in active service during 1942-69. In World War II, Exon amassed 325 combat hours as a flyer on missions over Sicily, Italy, Corsica, Africa, and Southern France. Over Italy in the spring of 1944, Exon's aircraft took damage from an exploding ammunition depot; Exon had to bail out, and was held by the Germans as a prisoner of war until June 1945.

Exon involved himself in high-level maintenance and logistics during 1948–54, before assignment to the Pentagon and responsibility for ballistic missiles in Turkey and across Europe. Later, while a lieutenant colonel, Exon assumed command of Wright-Patterson AFB, Dayton, Ohio.

Exon's official Air Force capsule biography makes no mention of the claims that make him a person of great interest to UFOlogists: his insistence (inspired by the accounts of others) that Wright-Patterson became a repository for Roswell crash debris and corpses retrieved from the crash site. Perhaps the most intriguing of Exon's assertions is the existence of a secret USAF supervisory committee at Wright-Patterson, comprised of top military officers and people from the intelligence community. Exon labeled this group "The Unholy Thirteen," and claimed that it controlled the flow of UFO information that fell outside the purview of Project Blue Book and established military intelligence.

In the course of a 1990 phone interview with UFOlogist Kevin Randle, Exon firmly stated that President Truman, USAF chief of staff Gen. Carl Spaatz, and their subordinates kept a lid on Roswell evidence for fear of a public panic if the information were leaked.

Richard H. Hall (1930–2009): American technical writer, Civil War historian, and UFOlogist active in the National Investigations Committee on Aerial Phenomena (NICAP), a private UFO-investigations group established in Washington, D.C., in 1964. Hall eventually became the organization's assistant director, sharing that role with Gordon Lore and answering to NICAP co-founder Donald Keyhoe.

In 1964, Hall assembled an important collection of UFO-sighting reports that had come into the main NICAP office in D.C. and satellites offices in New York City, Los Angeles, Chicago, Kansas City, and Hartford. He called the book-length collection *The UFO Evidence*; it remains one of the earliest and most credible studies of UFO activity reported during 1947–62. That NICAP had been put together by scientists, military people, businesspersons, and people with links to the nation's intelligence community caused *The UFO Evidence* to earn serious attention—even from Congress (NICAP saw that every member of the House and Senate received a copy). Further, because Hall concentrated on reports made by pilots, military officers, and scientists, witness credibility was high.

Notable book: *The UFO Evidence* (ed.).

Roscoe Henry Hillenkoetter (1897–1982): American naval vice admiral (combat veteran of World War II and Korea) and Director of Central Intelligence (predecessor to the CIA) during 1947–50. As director, Hillenkoetter oversaw American intelligence efforts to block Communist political activity in Italy and counter Soviet propaganda around the world. Hillenkoetter also was a principal of the Majestic 12 (MJ-12) Roswell-investigations group authorized by President Truman in September 1947.

In the course of a 1960 interview with an unnamed UPI reporter, Hillenkoetter said that "behind the scenes, high-ranking Air Force officers are soberly concerned about the UFOs. But through official secrecy and ridicule, many citizens are led to believe the unknown flying objects are nonsense." Hillenkoetter added that "to hide the facts, the Air Force has silenced its personnel."

As a creature of the military and intelligence establishments, Hillenkoetter had concern about UFOs and "unidentified flying objects" that presented potential threats to U.S. security. Although he did remark that the craft appeared to be "under intelligent control," he did not assume the craft were of extraterrestrial origin.

(Elliott) Budd Hopkins (1931–2011): Important American abstract expressionist painter and sculptor (1976 Guggenheim Fellowship for painting) who cultivated a deep interest in UFOs and became a seminal figure in alien abduction studies.

Hopkins witnessed a silvery disc above Cape Cod in 1964, and although he never was abducted, he became an empathetic compiler of abductee accounts. He published an abduction article with the *Village Voice* in 1976, and thereafter devoted a great deal of his time to UFOlogy. He founded the Intruders Foundation in 1989 and conducted interviews (some aided by hypnotic regression) with victims of abduction. He concluded that alien species pursued an aggressive program of crossbreeding with humans. Tangled or partial memories of alien abductions are familiar elements of abductee accounts, and Hopkins startled many people by claiming that one in fifty Americans has been abducted, and that most do not know it.

Although Hopkins's university degree was in art history, he conducted New York group therapy sessions for abductees.

Notable books: *Intruders: The Incredible Visitations at Copley Woods*; *Art, Life, and UFOs*.

J. Allen Hynek (1910–86): American astronomer associated with Ohio State and Northwestern universities, and a leading proponent of UFO study. Hynek is probably best recalled for his groundbreaking 1972 classification table of UFO contacts—which Hynek called "close encounters"—by degrees of witness proximity.

In the mid-1950s, when Project Blue Book requested his expertise as a consultant, Hynek had been a professor and working astronomer for nearly twenty years. Research at the John Hopkins Applied Physics Laboratory during World War II involved Hynek in classified weapons work. Educated at the University of Chicago and Yerkes Observatory, he was wedded to the tenets of objectivity and the scientific method. Although skeptical of many UFO reports, Hynek had the flexibility of mind—and innate curiosity—to agree to Blue Book's request.

In 1966, following a weeklong series of dramatic, multiple-witness UFO sightings in Michigan, Hynek, under pressure from the Air Force, offered that some of the Michigan witnesses may have seen "swamp gas." As a partial explanation, Hynek's sincere invocation of swamp gas was not unreasonable. Regardless, the two words became instantly notorious, and Hynek felt the sting of ridicule—a kind of ridicule similar to that suffered by many past witnesses to UFOs.

As Hynek developed an open mind about UFOs, he understood that among "serious" scientists, he represented a minority point of view. In a 1966 *Newsweek* article he said that scientists are eager to explore the phenomenon, but are "so vastly afraid of ridicule" that they do nothing. As a partial response to that unfortunate attitude, Hynek founded the Center for UFO Studies (CUFOS), near Chicago in 1973. (The organization became popularly known as the J. Allen Hynek Center for UFO Studies.) The research center depended on private funding, and when that grew inadequate in 1981, Hynek moved the center to his home.

For more about Hynek and close encounters, see chapter ten.

Notable books: *The UFO Experience: A Scientific Inquiry*; *The Hynek UFO Report.*

Carl Jung (1875–1961): Swiss psychiatrist whose conception of the collective unconscious, cultural archetypes, and the soul revolutionized not just analytical psychiatry but notions about theology, folklore, art, literature, and popular culture. Jung explored two equal and (ideally) congruent forces at work in all people: the urge to learn and understand the outside world in relation to oneself (differentiation); and the drive to achieve a congenial personal "whole" from innate personality traits, and useful understanding of immature and mature experiences (integration).

Part of Jung's drive to study and learn came from the paranormal. A head injury he suffered as a boy negatively affected his ability to concentrate, but one day, when Jung was twelve, he felt an almost physical lifting of a mental fog. The boy viewed himself with fresh clarity—and also intuited

A SIGNET BOOK · T3757 · 75¢

THE MOST EMINENT PSYCHOLOGIST OF OUR TIME

Dr. C.G. Jung

published this prophetic UFO STUDY
ten years before the CONDON REPORT

Flying Saucers

A MODERN MYTH OF THINGS SEEN IN THE SKY

With a Foreword written especially for this edition by
MARTIN EBON
Fully illustrated with photographs and drawings

Renowned psychoanalyst Carl Jung linked the flying saucer phenomenon with group memory and folklore.

that another person was present with and *in* him: a wise old man who had lived a century before. The experience marked Jung's fascination with human archetypes; the "wise old man"—who recurs in numberless myths, folk tales, artworks, and motion pictures—is just one of those archetypes. Among the others are the mother, the father, and the healer.

Although not a "believer" in UFOs, Jung accepted the sincerity of people that had witnessed such craft. He was struck by a consistency of similarity among the reports and descriptions, particularly the disc; to Jung, the shape implied a circle, an ancient human symbol suggestive of the circle of life—a circle that, to Jung, never completed itself, but simply led to new existence after physical death.

Jung's interest in parapsychology and mysticism predisposed him to be non-judgmental about UFO accounts. He acknowledged (as in a famous 1957 letter to *New Republic* editor Gilbert A. Harrison) that UFOs had shown up clearly on radar, and that many had physical, real-world characteristics. Jung's true interest, though, was the mind, and it was in this regard that UFOs most intrigued him. It was with no small pleasure that he described UFOs as humanity's challenge to so-called proper science, and to what we presumed to be the limits of knowledge.

Notable relevant book: *Flying Saucers.*

John Keel (1930–2009): Influential and prolific American author, investigator, and lecturer whose conception of aliens as other-dimensional beings, rather than extraterrestrial, gives UFOlogists plenty to discuss.

Based in New York City by the mid-1950s, Keel was a working writer who traveled the Middle East and Asia before selling travel articles, men's magazine adventure stories, and a nonfiction travel memoir, *Jadoo*, "[t]he astounding story of one man's search into the mysteries of black magic in the Orient." Keel wrote scripts for local NYC television and became a co-founder and editor of an audiophile magazine, *Echo*, in 1959.

A 1966 freelance assignment to do an article about UFOs sparked Keel's interest in the subject. In his 1970 book *Operation Trojan Horse*, Keel abandoned the ET theory because of what he termed "an astonishing overlap between psychic phenomena and UFOs." He brought forth his "ultraterrestrial" theory, by which alien visitors are supernatural, and arrived from other dimensions to plague us. Much in the vein of H. P. Lovecraft's iniquitous Old Ones, the ultraterrestrials have visited us for eons, to shape human history while diverting attention from themselves by suggesting the outer-space origins of UFOs. In this sort of bleakly determinist scenario, humans are small indeed. Helpless before our secret masters, our destinies mapped out and controlled by malevolent Others, we pursue what Lovecraft described as "common human laws and interests and emotions [that] have no validity or significance in the vast cosmos-at-large." Worse, the ultraterrestrials view us with contempt and scorn.

Shortly after *Trojan Horse*, Keel turned his focus to Point Pleasant, West Virginia, where locals linked a terrible bridge collapse with UFOs and a dreadful alien called Mothman (see chapter ten). Keel spent considerable time in the area and interviewed scores of residents. His 1975 book *The Mothman Prophecies* turned Keel into a vigorous player in the UFO and paranormal worlds.

With a 1970 paperback original, *Strange Creatures from Time and Space*, Keel revisited Mothman and discussed accounts of Bigfoot, sea serpents, angels and demons, and Men in Black. Because Keel's interests encompassed so much, he may have spread himself thin as a writer. Nevertheless, his work is reliably literate and intriguing.

Notable books: *Operation Trojan Horse; Strange Creatures from Time and Space; The Mothman Prophecies; The Best of John Keel; Searching for the String: Selected Writings.*

Donald Keyhoe (1897–1988): Throughout the 1950s, this aviator, writer, and retired marine major gained fame as the public face of flying saucer studies. But Keyhoe had succeeded before then in other, quite different areas. His earlier successes gratified him, but invited harsh—and unwarranted—criticism of his saucer research.

THE FLYING SAUCERS ARE REAL

DONALD KEYHOE

Following pilot training and his first retirement from the Marines in the 1920s, Keyhoe accompanied aviator Charles Lindbergh on a forty-eight-state tour celebrating Lindy's acclaimed 1927 solo flight across the Atlantic. Keyhoe chronicled that adventure in articles for *Popular Science* and *National Geographic*, and then elaborated with a best-selling 1928 book, *Flying with Lindbergh* (a puff piece that Lindy vetted closely).

During the 1930s, Keyhoe worked for the department of commerce and the national geodesic survey, while continuing to pursue his career as a writer of pulp-magazine short stories. Those lusty and fantastic tales, many centered on aviation, appeared in *Flying Aces*, the already legendary *Weird Tales*, and elsewhere.

Private aviator Kenneth Arnold made his saucer sighting in 1947; two years later, a *True* magazine editor who had already worked with Keyhoe reached out to the newly retired major (Keyhoe had returned to active duty, in Washington, during World War II) for a consequential article about the flying

Retired USAF Maj. Donald Keyhoe headed the independent National Investigations Committee on Aerial Phenomena (NICAP) during the years of greatest American military-political interest in UFOs. Keyhoe's seminal book, *The Flying Saucers Are Real*, appeared as a mass-market Gold Medal paperback in 1950.   *Cover art by Frank Tinsley* saucer phenomenon. *True* tapped into public interest at a propitious time, and the article's enthusiastic reception inspired Keyhoe to write his first UFO book, *The Flying Saucers Are Real.*

Keyhoe's belief that saucers were of extraterrestrial origin—and that the truth was suppressed by the U.S. government—not only excited readers but provided a keystone for the saucer-conspiracy subgroup.

At the close of 1956, inventor and antigravity researcher Thomas Townsend Brown founded the National Investigations Committee on Aerial Phenomena (NICAP), and tapped Keyhoe to be a director. Deficient finance management shuttled a pair of directors in and out, and Keyhoe assumed leadership of the group in 1957. Finances remained weak, and Keyhoe devoted a great deal of his time to fund-raising.

By the mid-1960s, the USAF felt itself losing control of the flying saucer narrative, and commissioned the University of Colorado to put together a UFO study. Keyhoe shortly grew disenchanted with the university's so-called Condon Committee, and his involvement with NICAP lessened. Keyhoe's disenchantment increased early in 1969, when the committee's conclusions became public. In essence, the report declared that nothing in past UFO accounts suggested any scientific value whatever. Further, neither Washington nor the military should support further UFO research.

For the remainder of 1969, NICAP struggled with waning membership, weak finances and a tangled payroll, and the barely veiled presence of CIA agents that had become members. Former NICAP associate director Gordon Lore told this writer that Keyhoe's reputation as the UFO "gadfly" bothered the Air Force, which resented being publicly challenged by NICAP while USAF spokespersons insisted that UFOs amounted to nothing.

At the end of 1969, with Keyhoe given notice of just a day or two, NICAP's files and physical office space were taken over by the CIA. The new leadership began to dismantle NICAP, and in 1973 the organization ceased to exist. Keyhoe, by now seventy-five, briefly pursued something he called Project Lure, by which extraterrestrials might be encouraged to visit Earth.

In 1998, the Fund for UFO Research (FUFOR) announced plans to establish an extensive archive of Keyhoe's papers in Washington.

For more about Keyhoe and NICAP, see chapter nine.

Notable books: *The Flying Saucers Are Real; Flying Saucers from Outer Space; The Flying Saucer Conspiracy; Flying Saucers: Top Secret; Aliens from Space: The Real Story of Unidentified Flying Objects.*

Philip J. Klass (1919–2005): American electrical engineer, aviation journalist, and alien-abduction researcher who investigated victims' accounts for nearly forty years—and claimed never to have found one that could not be explained in conventional terms. He felt, in fact, that some victims of abduction had physically marked their bodies and inserted foreign objects in order to create "proof." He also claimed that vital elements of abductee accounts (such as the aliens' appearance) varied considerably, and did not, as proponents and media claimed, share many similarities.

Further, Klass insisted that he had seen no evidence to suggest alien visitation of any sort.

Shortly after investigating the famed Lonnie Zamora sighting near Socorro, New Mexico, in 1964 (see chapter ten), Klass stirred the pot with particular fierceness by offering what came to be called "The Phil Klass $10,000 Challenge." He explained it this way during a November 2000 interview for the PBS series *Nova*:

> I . . . offer to pay ten thousand dollars to any person who believes they've been abducted, to report it to the FBI. Let the FBI investigate it. If the FBI comes back and says, 'We believe this person's story,' I will then go into my life savings and present this check for ten thousand dollars to that person. And thereby, we will have alerted the federal government. We can enlist the defenses of this nation to defend our people. And if this is simply a cult where people are being needlessly manipulated, and alien abductions are fantasy, then we can free the public from worrying about a non-existent threat.

Klass never had to pay.

When the "secret" Majestic 12 documents (which supposedly confirmed a government cover-up of Roswell) surfaced in 1987, Klass went on record as doubting their authenticity. He famously argued against positons held by J. Allen Hynek, Stanton Friedman, Budd Hopkins, John Mack, and other high-profile UFOlogists, in a tone that veered between good-natured kidding and real animus. All of this naturally put Klass at odds with the abduction community, and the larger UFO culture, as well. Conspiracy theorists accused Klass of being a "disinformation agent" in the pay of Washington and/or the military-industrial complex, so that the USA might maintain its monopoly on alien technology.

As he approached eighty, Klass joked he hoped to be abducted, reasoning that alien medicine might restore his aging body to youthful health.

In addition to his activities as an author and lecturer, Klass published the *Skeptics UFO Newsletter*, and was a senior avionics editor at *Aviation Week & Space Technology* magazine (he is credited with coining the word *avionics*). Klass co-founded the Committee for the Scientific Investigation of Claims of the Paranormal (later called the Committee for Skeptical Inquiry). His 1971 book *Secret Sentries in Space* is an important early study of spy-satellite technology.

In 1999, the International Astronomical Union changed the name of Asteroid 1983 RM2/7277 to Klass.

Notable books: *UFOs—Identified*; *UFO Abductions: A Dangerous Game*; *Secret Sentries in Space*; *UFOs Explained*; *The Real Roswell Crashed-Saucer Coverup*.

Roger Leir (1934–2014): American podiatric surgeon, author, and alien-abduction researcher who performed at least fifteen surgeries between 1995 and the end of his life to remove alien implants from abductees. Leir was encouraged to do his first implant removal by abductee researcher Derrell Sims. Leir operated only on victims' feet; implants discovered in other parts of abductees' bodies were extracted by his "surgical team." Leir tested some implants on the spot, with gauss meters (which measure magnetic flux density) and radio frequency detectors.

Most implants removed by Leir came out of the victims encased within membranous sacs that were either parts of the alien implant process or immune responses by the victims' bodies. Leir sent the implants to independent labs, where tests invariably revealed what Leir described as "metallurgic anomalies."

Leir acted as a consultant to the now-defunct National Institute for Discovery Science, a paranormal-studies group established and funded by Las Vegas developer, aerospace entrepreneur, and space enthusiast Robert Bigelow. Leir's own organization, A&S Research, functioned as a nonprofit that investigated the physical and psychological implications of abduction and implantation.

Patient Seventeen, a documentary about Leir scheduled for 2016 release, became available for streaming in the fall of 2015.

Notable books: *The Aliens and the Scalpel*; *Casebook: Alien Implants*.

John E. Mack (1929–2004): American psychiatrist, tenured Harvard Medical School professor, and author who studied alien-abduction cases from a psychological perspective. Mack typically believed the sincerity of the many abductees he interviewed, and although he proposed that the abductors might be beings "from another domain," he could not say with certainty that UFOs or aliens are actual, physical things. Like some other academically inclined researchers, Mack linked UFOs to notions of myth, shared cultural consciousness, and a broadly spiritual and metaphysical world view.

In 1994, four years after publication of Mack's *Abduction: Human Encounters with Aliens*, Harvard Medical School began a secret investigation of Mack's abduction research and methodology. Conservative and "dignified," the medical school fretted that Mack had interviewed people that had not been checked for "psychosis." Mack's discovery of the investigation damaged his professional and personal relationships, and precipitated a fourteen-month struggle between Mack and Harvard—a struggle that soon spilled into the media. Embarrassed by the investigatory body's secrecy and presumption, the university ultimately affirmed that Mack was a faculty member in good standing, and free to pursue whatever research he wished.

John Mack died after being struck by a drunk driver in London. Predictably enough, a few voices suggest that he was killed to stop his abduction research.

Experiencers, a 2004 documentary that features Mack, is dedicated to his memory. At this writing, a feature film tentatively titled *John Mack* is in development.

Mack's 1976 book *A Prince of Our Disorder: The Life of T. E. Lawrence* won the 1977 Pulitzer Prize for Biography.

Notable UFO-related books: *Abduction: Human Encounters with Aliens*; *Passport to the Cosmos: Human Transformation and Alien Encounters*.

James E. McDonald (1920–71): American atmospheric physicist and academic (senior physicist at the Institute of Atmospheric Physics at the University of Arizona), whose devotion to a scientific investigation of UFOs earned him the scorn of his peers, and probably contributed to his suicide.

McDonald attracted attention as a meteorological expert while a young PhD; some of his early research made use of funding from the Office of Naval Research, the National Science Foundation, the National Academy of Sciences, and NASA. The 1966–71 period accounted for McDonald's most active and public work on behalf of UFO research, and he carried on even when the Office of Naval Research withdrew its funding. He maintained a close association with NICAP, where he was liked and respected. (McDonald declared NICAP chief Donald Keyhoe a key figure in responsible UFO investigation.)

A prolific writer of scientific papers, McDonald had published fifty by 1971, in such journals as *Nature, Science,* and *The Journal of Atmospheric Sciences.* His scientific pieces for lay readers appeared in *Scientific American, Saturday Review,* and other top magazines.

McDonald's professional interest in UFOs began in the early 1950s, when he and two meteorologists witnessed a lighted object in the skies above the Arizona desert. At about the same time, McDonald attended a meteorological conference in Italy, where UFOs came up in conversation. After that, McDonald began to amass information about UFOs and UFO sightings, maintaining and adding to voluminous files (kept extant by his family to this day) until his death.

As a scientist, McDonald placed a premium on responsible observation and fact collection. He had little interest in anecdotal UFO information, and was wary of "eyewitness" accounts. McDonald's biographer, Ann Druffel, reports that he was particularly "dismayed" by the friendly-aliens accounts of George Adamski, Gabriel Green (who ran for president in 1960 on the "Flying Saucer ticket"), George Van Tassel, and other contactees.

The USAF-commissioned Condon Report of 1969, which dismissed UFOs as having no scientific value as subjects of study, received outspoken criticism from McDonald. The committee, he complained, had looked at only a "minute fraction" of available cases, and conducted "sloppy research." He testified to that effect in 1969, before the House Committee on Science and Astronautics, describing the "scientifically ludicrous [Condon] explanations" that hampered UFO research. McDonald planned to set aside 1970 to write a book-length rebuttal to the Condon group, buttressed by a wealth of Project Blue Book files detailing ground-radar contact with UFOs. The book was never written.

Concurrent with McDonald's criticism of the Condon Report—which he expressed in a series of formal lectures—was an FBI investigation of his activities. His criticism of government laziness and apparent disinterest in UFO study struck a nerve; likewise, McDonald's open sympathy with America's student left, including the SDS. One secret FBI memo complained that McDonald had a "young hippy [*sic*] protégé." The FBI investigation ended after person after person informed FBI investigators about McDonald's sterling reputation and Americanism.

In 1971, when McDonald testified before Congress about deleterious climatic effects of proposed supersonic transport (SST) aircraft, politicians on the panel attempted to discredit his testimony by mocking his UFO research. His chief tormentor was Massachusetts congressman Silvio Conte, who steered the SST discussion into a wholly unrelated discourse on UFOs and power blackouts. Outwardly unbowed by the committee's attitude, McDonald carried on with his SST testimony. But by the time Conte and others were done, committee members—and many persons in the audience—were laughing out loud.

Soon after, McDonald's wife asked for a divorce. The failed marriage, the public humiliation, the disapproval of peers, all of it became burdensome to McDonald. He put a gun to his head on April 9, 1971, but only succeeded in taking his eyesight. With divorce plans suddenly suspended, McDonald returned to work. Slivers of his sight returned, and he felt a small optimism.

His wife was to pick him up at his office on Saturday, June 12, but she went on a sudden weekend getaway. Before his daughter could come for him, McDonald called a taxi. He purchased a revolver at a pawnshop and then directed the taxi to deliver him to an empty crossroads in the Arizona desert. Later, in a nearby wash, McDonald shot himself to death.

The circumstances of the death provoked the inevitable conspiracy talk, centered, of course, on UFOs, the government, and the military. None of the speculation bears up well under scrutiny.

Donald Howard Menzel (1901–76): American theoretical astronomer and astrophysicist with teaching experience at the University of Iowa, Ohio State, and Harvard. While director of the Harvard College Observatory from 1952 to 1966, Menzel played a key role in the development of radioastronomy. Fascinated by many things—particularly geology, chemistry, solar research, and radio technology—he observed the postwar interest in flying saucers with skepticism. He was an empiricist who insisted that virtually all UFO reports could be accounted for with real-world explanations, most often as clouds, reflections of light, temperature inversions, and other natural phenomena. Menzel cited aircraft and satellites as frequent culprits. Further, because few UFO witnesses had scientific training, they were, in Menzel's view, simply unable to usefully explain what they had seen.

This "establishment" view of UFOs fit neatly with explanations given by Washington and the military. When Menzel gave testimony before a House committee symposium looking into unidentified flying objects, his reasoned, unexcited rationales seemed as impressive as his credentials. He was well received on the Hill, but many UFOlogists, including noted atmospheric physicist James E. McDonald, called him out for ignoring compelling details about case after case.

Accomplished in astronomy, wave propagation, cryptanalysis, and quantum mechanics, Menzel was a precise, lucid writer who published widely in scientific journals and the popular press. He was a chess champion and ham radio operator. He played various musical instruments, collected neckties—and habitually made sketches of flying saucers and extraterrestrials. Throughout his career, he was an enthusiastic debunker of astrology.

For more about Menzel, and latter-day claims that he was in cahoots with the CIA to obscure the reality of unidentified flying objects, see chapter eight.

Notable books: *Flying Saucers*; *The World of Flying Saucers* (with Lyle G. Boyd); *The UFO Enigma* (with Ernest H. Taves); *Stars and Planets: Exploring the Universe*.

Edgar Mitchell (1930–2016): As part of a field that longs for respectable spokespersons, retired American astronaut Edgar Mitchell proved invaluable. He held a doctorate in aeronautical engineering from MIT, and as the Apollo 14 lunar module pilot in 1971 he became the sixth human being to walk on the Moon. He was an outspoken advocate of future manned missions into space, and believed we are not alone in the universe. The aliens that crashed at Roswell, New Mexico, in 1947, Mitchell said, had been observing American atomic testing at nearby White Sands. Today, the U.S. government likely hides evidence of alien technology, because that technology could adversely affect what Mitchell called "moneyed interests."

Although Mitchell never observed a UFO, he was receptive to reasonable accounts, and firm that mysterious craft have been observed throughout the years by U.S. military personnel, top-ranking people among them.

Notable books: *The Way of the Explorer: An Apollo Astronaut's Journey Through the Material and Mystical Worlds*; *The Space Less Traveled: Straight Talk from Apollo 14 Astronaut Edgar Mitchell*.

James (Jim) W. Moseley (1931–2012): Self-described American "skeptical believer" who published *Nexus*, *Saucer News*, and, later, the *Saucer Smear* newsletter, which focused on personalities and the UFO social scene. Writing in *The UFO Verdict*, author Robert Sheaffer described Moseley as "the Voltaire of the UFO movement, in light of his perceptive and witty satires." In 1957, Moseley and UFO writer Gray Barker collaborated on the elaborate "Straith letter" hoax (see chapter fifteen) intended to give mock encouragement to ET contactee George Adamski.

Over time, Moseley leaned toward a made-by-humans explanation of UFOs, displaying a low tolerance for flimsy accounts and credulous UFO enthusiasts that readily accepted them; he took apparent delight in puncturing weak stories. Still, Moseley remained sharply cognizant of UFO incidents that defied easy explanation.

As if to underscore his simultaneous sense of mission and mirth, Moseley identified himself on the masthead of *Saucer Smear* as "Supreme Commander"; and occasionally published *Saucer News* as *Saucer Booze* and *Saucer Jews* (to acknowledge a Jewish friend).

Beginning in the 1960s and for thirty years thereafter, Moseley organized UFO conferences, many under the aegis of his National UFO Conference (NUFOC) organization.

Notable books: *Shockingly Close to the Truth! Confessions of a Grave-Robbing UFOlogist* (with the empirically minded UFOlogist Karl T. Pflock); *Jim Moseley's Book of Saucer News*.

Ray Palmer (1910–77): Astute American magazine editor-writer who had equal, enormous influence on UFOlogy, science fiction and SF fandom, hollow-Earth speculation, and the conspiracy-theory subculture.

Hunched and startlingly diminutive—results of a road accident suffered at age seven—Palmer had antic eyes, an expansive smile, and a good brain sharpened by spending many of his early years in bed surrounded by books. By 1938, Palmer landed the editor's job at Ziff-Davis's *Amazing Stories*, a directionless SF pulp in need of a firm hand and consistent vision. Palmer—or "Rap," as he came to be known to readers—removed the "Every Story Scientifically Accurate" banner from the *Amazing* covers, while soliciting stories with strong character development and human interest. And mindful of reader demographics, Palmer commissioned sexy cover art for *Amazing*, and replaced back-cover advertisements with more art. Palmer soon inaugurated a new, "weird" title called *Fantastic Adventures*. Eventually, Ziff-Davis put him in charge of the company's western, adventure, and detective pulps.

Happily married by 1943 and earning a hefty $10,000 a year, Palmer took a shine to a Richard S. Shaver, a Pennsylvania steelworker who claimed to have deciphered a lost language Shaver called Mantong. As Palmer saw it, Shaver's turn of mind jibed well with *Amazing*'s turn from traditional SF and Palmer's eagerness to reposition the magazine as a mystical-SF publication. Shaver began to pepper Palmer with stories and story ideas about a malevolent race—the Deros (detrimental robots)—that inhabited Earth's hollow core and traveled the outside world via flying discs. Worse, the Deros schemed to rob humanity of its sanity *and* kidnap men and women for cultivation as food. How did Shaver come by this hollow-Earth information? As he informed Palmer, the Deros stories were relayed to him telepathically—that is, he heard voices.

Ray Palmer, though a lover of the fantastic, also had the commercial instincts of a good editor, and jumped into the Shaver mythology, massaging and heavily rewriting Shaver's stories, switching out Atlantis for Lemuria (aka Mu), and coyly suggesting that the "Shaver Mystery" tales just might be factual.

Amazing ran the Shaver stories during 1945–48, but from the moment in the summer of 1947 when Palmer read of the Kenneth Arnold flying saucer sightings over Washington State, *Amazing*'s editor prepared himself to move on. He had milked the Shaver mythos dry, and although he had boosted sales and stimulated discussion and debate among SF fans, a lot of the discussion carried a negative, sometimes angry tone. Readers were fed up with the unasked-for conflation of SF with the paranormal. Palmer resigned from Ziff-Davis and *Amazing* in 1949.

Inspired equally by the new flying saucer phenomenon and public interest in the occult,

"The Man Who Invented Flying Saucers": writer-editor-publisher Ray Palmer combined sharp commercial instincts with fervent personal interest in UFOs. Palmer established *Mystic* magazine in 1953, and put himself on a cover three years later.

Palmer and former Ziff-Davis aviation editor Chris Fuller founded *Fate*, a brisk, digest-sized magazine devoted to ostensibly true accounts of flying saucers, poltergeists, lost cities, angels, clairvoyance, faith healing, telekinesis, Lemuria, dowsing, astrology (Jeron King Criswell, future costar of *Plan 9 from Outer Space*, contributed an astrology column)—even "The Curse of the Hope Diamond." Issue number one (Spring 1948) set the tone with a dramatic, fictionalized cover illustration of the Kenneth Arnold "Flying Disks" (*sic*). Arnold himself wrote the cover story, "The Truth About Flying Saucers" (with copious rewrite help from Palmer).

Palmer's tenure at *Fate* was undone late in 1953, when Chris Fuller's unhappiness with Palmer's mystical bent moved Palmer to sell his share of the magazine to Fuller. Palmer went on to edit *Mystic* (later called *Search*), which trafficked heavily in tales of séances, witchcraft, quack cancer cures, first-person accounts of meetings with friendly aliens (*Mystic*'s first issue

Ray Palmer's interest in Richard Shaver's lively "hollow Earth" tales propelled Palmer's *Amazing Stories* for many issues, but readers finally tired of Palmer's coyness about whether the accounts were fiction or fact. This is the June 1947 issue, with a cover painting by Robert Gibson Jones, "illustrating a scene in the caves."

published Orfeo Angelucci's "I Traveled in a Flying Saucer"), and, drearily, story after story about Richard Shaver.

In 1957, Palmer founded another magazine, *Flying Saucers from Other Worlds*, which became *Flying Saucers* a year later.

Palmer returned to Milwaukee. During 1960–61, he published a sixteen-volume, subscriber-supported paperback-book series called *Hidden World*. The books chronicled the preoccupations of—who else?—Richard Shaver, including a new one: mystical messages hidden in ancient rocks.

Palmer continued to edit *Search* and *Flying Saucers* (which perpetuated hollow-Earth theory), and introduced a monthly newsletter called *Ray Palmer's Forum*. Although Palmer assumed the guise of an angry reactionary in *Search*, he offered a milder persona in the newsletter, a subscriber-supported publication with a pleasingly upbeat, proto-New Age feel (Richard Shaver was by this time dead, and thus out of Palmer's life). Palmer became fond of the naïve activism of the hippie movement, and cultivated an intense opposition to America's mischief in Vietnam. Gradually, his mind filled with dark conspiracies; as a physically small man, and one who made war with a typewriter rather than a gun, he felt personally vulnerable to the predations of the CIA and Nixon (who bombed Cambodia, Palmer wrote, partly to destroy evidence of a secret UFO observation base).

Palmer slipped into fear of a worldwide "Zionist World Government," and became an ardent supporter of race-baiting Alabama governor, and presidential candidate, George Wallace—ostensibly because Wallace vowed to get the U.S "out" of Vietnam.

Palmer's last great crusades caused him to take a hard look at what he dubbed "the hole in the pole," secret egress for flying saucers based beneath the North Pole. Palmer died of natural causes. No conspiracy, no perfidy, no saucer ride to the upper atmosphere—just the aftereffects of a blocked artery.

Palmer is still sometimes referred to as "The Man Who Invented Flying Saucers," an honorarium that isn't as hyperbolic as it may sound. He helmed professional, nationally distributed magazines that allowed saucer news to expand beyond the pages of mimeographed newsletters and after-hours discussions in hotel rooms at saucer conventions. Who wouldn't gamble thirty-five or fifty cents for a magazine peek at the saucer phenomenon? In that regard, then, Palmer brought flying saucers into America's homes, barbershops, and beauty parlors. Palmer made UFOs "big."

Notable book: *The Coming of the Saucers: A Documentary Report on Sky Objects That Have Mystified the World* (with Kenneth Arnold).

Hector Quintanilla Jr. (1923–98): USAF major (later lieutenant colonel) with a physics background who headed Project Blue Book during 1963–70, the group's final seven years of existence. Quintanilla may be best recalled today for his "Unidentified" judgment of the famed Lonnie Zamora UFO sighting of 1964 (see chapter ten)—an evidence-based judgment that Quintanilla felt was misinterpreted by many UFOlogists to mean an acknowledgment of the account's credibility. In fact, Quintanilla sensed that patrolman Zamora misinterpreted what he had seen or, possibly, perpetrated a hoax. But Quintanilla felt that the available evidence did not allow him to make either of those opinions official. (The CIA, in its own summary, characterized the Zamora case as "Unsolved.")

Major Quintanilla also is recalled for criticism levied against him, and against Blue Book, by Blue Book civilian consultant J. Allen Hynek, who said that during Quintanilla's tenure, "the flag of the utter nonsense school was flying at its highest on the mast."

The basis of Hynek's complaint is his belief that Quintanilla lacked the scientific qualifications to head the government's UFO-study group. Hynek further complained that Quintanilla simply ignored any evidence that ran counter to the major's own preconceived opinions. James E. McDonald—like Hynek, a distinguished scientist—flatly stated that Quintanilla was "not competent"—although

McDonald added (fairly enough) that the major had not lobbied for the Blue Book position, but had been appointed.

The January 1966 issue of *Popular Mechanics* displayed a kinder, and more reasonable, attitude toward Quintanilla, regarding him as a professional interested in hard evidence. "We're certainly not trying to hold anything back," the major told the unnamed *PM* interviewer. "We accept every report as valid, unless there is evidence to substantiate a report as a hoax."

In Quintanilla's 1974 book proposal—to which he gave two suggested titles, *UFOs: An Air Force Dilemma* and *UFOs: A $20,000,000 Fiasco*—Quintanilla expressed his long-abandoned hope for a "non-partisan scientific committee," sponsored by "a reputable university," to "objectively evaluate UFOs and thus clear Blue Book of 'whitewash' accusations by McDonald, Hynek, and the UFO hobby clubs."

Edward J. Ruppelt (1923–60): United States Air Force officer who headed America's official UFO investigatory body, Project Blue Book (previously Project Grudge) during 1951–53. Ruppelt is credited with coining "unidentified flying object" and "UFO" as replacements for "flying saucer."

In his 1956 book *The Report on Unidentified Flying Objects* Ruppelt recounted numerous UFO sightings, including many given by experienced military pilots. Although he believed that "good UFO reports cannot be written off" as weather balloons, mass hysteria, and other easily summoned explanations, he concluded that "[t]here have been no reports in which the speed or altitude of a UFO has been measured, there have been no reliable photographs that show any details of a UFO, and there is no hardware. There is still no real proof." Ruppelt went on to acknowledge that while the USAF never denied the existence of interplanetary craft, "UFO reports offer absolutely no authentic evidence that such interplanetary spacecraft do exist."

Some conspiracy buffs in the UFO community struggle to come to grips with Ruppelt's death, at thirty-seven, from a heart attack, as if young men never fall over dead with bad tickers. One blogger, posting on ufocon.blogspot.com in 2013, wondered, "Does it make sense[?]"

For more about Captain Ruppelt and Blue Book, see chapter nine.

Notable book: *The Report on Unidentified Flying Objects*.

Harley Rutledge (1926–2006): American physicist and academic recalled for his 1973 endeavor Project Identification, a real-time sky-scan study involving hundreds of nights of fieldwork by 620 scientists, students, and motivated amateurs, armed with binoculars, telescopes, cameras, and spectrographs, all watching for and charting anomalous objects. Although a UFO skeptic, Rutledge had been impressed by some five hundred UFO sightings reported from near Piedmont, Missouri, during February–April 1973. As head of the Physics Department at Southeast Missouri State University, Rutledge was uniquely positioned to investigate. During 1973–77, he and his volunteers used video and time-lapse photography to capture about seven hundred objects, charting size, velocity, and distance.

As the team compiled data, Rutledge investigated such ancillary issues as coincidence, chance, subliminal thinking, and premonition.

Rutledge, who claimed to have seen 140 UFOs himself during the study, finally concluded that so many of the objects appeared to be "intelligently controlled" that no responsible scientist could dismiss them.

Unlike some other scientists/academics that came to similar conclusions, Rutledge enjoyed general acceptance of his data, and carried on thanks to grants from Southeast Missouri State and the *St. Louis Globe-Democrat*.

Notable book: *Project Identification: The First Scientific Study of UFO Phenomena.*

Carl Sagan (1934–96): Leading American astronomer, academic, author, popularizer of science, and longtime consultant to the U.S. space program. The citation for his 1991 Masursky Award from the American Astronomical Society lauds his "extraordinary contributions" to study of planetary atmospheres and surfaces, the history of Earth, and exobiology.

Sagan's 1996 book *The Demon-Haunted World: Science as a Candle in the Dark* is a reasonable and decisive indictment of what Sagan regarded as the worrisome general acceptance of magic, demons, the devil, faith healing, channeling—and UFOs. Devoted to the tenets of serious science, Sagan argued, generally speaking, for an acceptance of simple explanations rather than the complex. He acknowledged the excitement that comes from interpreting a mysterious flying object as something from another world (a complex assumption), but he more enthusiastically noted the logic of the prosaic, such as a weather balloon (a simple conclusion).

Sagan expressed his disappointment with a question often put to him: "Do you believe in UFOs?"

"I'm always struck by how the question is phrased," he wrote, "the suggestion that this is a matter of belief and not of evidence. I'm almost never asked, 'How good is the evidence that UFOs are alien spaceships?'" Sagan felt that many people claiming to be open-minded about the UFO phenomenon actually entered into the discussion with "highly predetermined" attitudes. They ignored scientific facts that seemed dull, assumed that every eyewitness account is accurate, and neglected to consider the human propensity to spoof and hoax. Sagan developed a mild interest in crop circles, and frequently mentioned Doug Bower and Dave Chorley, British hoaxers who admitted to having created and executed complex "alien" crop circles across Britain.

Sagan conceded that the government may have covered up facts about UFOs of American or foreign (Soviet) origin—a tactic that, given issues of national security, struck Sagan as sensible, particularly in light of complex technical issues of avionics and propulsion associated with rapidly advancing missile technology in the late 1950s–early 1960s.

Despite being dubious about hard-core conspiracies, Sagan remained loath to dismiss the extraterrestrial hypothesis out of hand. He encouraged, and even facilitated, informed scientific debate about the matter. (Particularly sober-sided scientists criticized Sagan for his flexibility of mind.)

For some UFOlogists, Carl Sagan is a difficult figure to counter. Few scientists of the 20th century have been as lauded and honored, and few contributed as much practical knowledge to our understanding of Earth and the planets. (A heavenly body, Asteroid 2709, is named for him.) Sagan achieved widespread popular acceptance as a researcher, teacher, author, and television personality (estimates place total viewership of his *Cosmos* TV series of 1980 at one billion). The difficulty faced by detractors is compounded because Sagan's professional confidence and ingratiating personal manner captivated viewers and readers, who appreciated Sagan's willingness to give UFOs serious thought.

Notable books: *Cosmos*; *The Demon-Haunted World: Science as a Candle in the Dark*; *Dragons of Eden: Speculations of the Evolution of Human Intelligence* (Pulitzer Prize); *Pale Blue Dot: A Vision of the Human Future in Space.*

Frank Scully (1892–1964): American show business journalist and author of novelty humor books who struck gold in 1950 with *Behind the Flying Saucers*, a "ripped from the headlines" exposé that revealed details of saucer crashes in the American Southwest that left some three dozen alien corpses behind. The meat of the narrative is a purported 1948 saucer crash near Aztec, New Mexico, which by itself accounted for anywhere from a dozen to nineteen tiny bodies. Although clumsily overwritten, the book has the dramatic appeal of a colorful story, plus Scully's claims of a government cover-up of the truth (a theme that still resonates today). In his foreword, Scully positioned himself as a fearless truth-teller willing to defy the "faceless spokesmen" that misled the public. Scully added that he "never participated in a hoax on flying saucers."

But he had. He just didn't know it yet.

The Aztec, New Mexico, account had been fabricated by a pair of longtime con men, and when the scam was exposed in 1952, Scully publicly expressed disinterest in the whole thing, saying he had moved on. (And indeed he had, with such tomes as *The Blessed Mother Goose* and *The Best of Fun in Bed*.)

Behind the Flying Saucers sold more than sixty thousand copies in hardcover, and at least one million more when issued as a mass market paperback in 1951. Sales numbers alone place it among the most important of early UFO books.

For details of Scully's involvement with the Aztec hoax, see chapter fifteen.

Notable book: *Behind the Flying Saucers.*

Wilbert Smith (1910–62): Government-employed Canadian radio engineer who envisioned Earth's magnetic field as an important future source of the planet's energy needs. Smith became interested in flying saucers in the late 1940s, and eventually surmised that saucers harnessed magnetic energy for propulsion. Smith had partial responsibility for the technical integrity of Canadian radio broadcasting, and enjoyed friendships with members of Parliament. Late in 1950, after Smith reminded officials that the USA was outstripping Canada in magnetic-field research, the Defence Research Board granted approval of funds and laboratory space for a geo-magnetism study dubbed Project Magnet. Later, Smith was one of a few key government workers brought into a new program, Project Theta (shortly renamed Project Second Storey), to index and analyze Canadian UFO sightings.

By the summer of 1953, when Smith earned permission to install UFO-detection equipment near Ottawa, Canada's intelligence community had assumed a dominant role in Project Second Storey. After Smith claimed to have established contact with UFOs, the Canadian government took him less seriously. Still, after his death, Smith was lionized as a leading light of Canadian science.

More than one thousand pages of Smith's government documents are gathered in a 2008 book edited by David Crawford, *38 Messages from Space.*

Pedro Ferriz Santa Cruz (1921–2013): Mexican history teacher, general broadcaster, newsreader, quiz-show host, and author who got into radio in 1939 and made his mark with *Un mundo nos vigila* (*A World Is Watching Us*), an XEW-AM program that explored extraterrestrial life. A chronicle of Mexican UFO activity and a resource for accounts from other countries, *A World Is Watching Us* had an outsize influence because XEW was a "border blaster"—a 250,000-watt powerhouse that also broadcast on shortwave. Although based in Mexico City, XEW maintained relay transmitters in Guadalajara, San Luis, Veracruz, and Monterrey, providing programming to forty-three other Mexican stations. Santa Cruz's audience, then, came from the length and breadth of Mexico, and from much of the American Southwest, as well. In this, Santa Cruz stands as a significant figure in the popularization of UFO study.

Notable book: *Un mundo nos vigila* (*A World Is Watching Us*).

Leonard H. Stringfield (1920–94): American public relations and marketing executive who published the *Orbit* newsletter; founded Civilian Research, Interplanetary Flying Objects (CRIFO); and advised NICAP during 1957–72. Stringfield, who had seen a UFO while an Army intelligence officer in Occupied Japan, sharpened his focus in the 1970s, when he devoted himself to careful collation of eyewitness accounts of crashed UFOs. He had special interest in incidents involving deceased aliens.

Although Stringfield claimed a partnership with Air Defense Command (including a dedicated phone line into his house), the Air Force denied the relationship.

In 2012, MUFON announced that it had taken possession of sixty volumes of Stringfield's papers and research, containing details of U.S. presidential interest in UFOs and intimidation of UFO investigators.

Notable book: *Situation Red: The UFO Siege.* In addition, Stringfield self-published seven volumes of *UFO Crash/Retrievals: Status Report*; and *Inside Saucer Post . . . 3-0 Blue*, a pamphlet.

Brinsley Le Poer Trench (Earl of Clancarty) (1911–95): British-Irish flying saucer enthusiast who established a pair of UFO organizations during the 1950s and

'60s (International UFO Observer Corps and Contact International), and edited *Flying Saucer Review*. Trench's theories about the origin of humankind combined notions about ancient astronauts and hollow Earth; he claimed to have traced his own lineage back to extraterrestrials that arrived on Earth around 63,000 BC.

A portion of Trench's thoughts about ancient astronauts ran along familiar lines (long-ago alien visitation from outer space and subsequent emergence of the human race); he expressed the connection to hollow Earth more dramatically, claiming that some branches of humanity sprang from creatures inhabiting areas of the Earth's crust, and who tunneled to the surface to interact with humans. (Trench borrowed the tunnel idea from the most visible ancient astronaut proponent, Erich von Däniken.) Trench identified the main points of egress as the North and South poles. In time, Trench suggested that secret bases at the poles hid flying saucers.

Pondering the origins of tales recounted in the Bible, Trench concluded that Adam and Eve lived on Mars, and that their descendants traveled to Earth when the Martian polar ice cap began to melt.

More prosaically, Trench offered secondhand, anecdotal evidence of a secret meeting of President Eisenhower and aliens at Edwards AFB in April 1954.

After succeeding to his earldom in 1975, Trench became a Minister of Parliament, and agitated for government investigation of flying saucers.

Notable books: *The Flying Saucer Story*; *The Sky People*; *Secrets of the Ages: UFOs from Inside the Earth*.

George Van Tassel (1910–78): American flight engineer, religious existentialist, and self-described channeler of benign extraterrestrial philosophy. Having met friendly, suntanned aliens, Van Tassel organized the first Giant Rock, California, UFO convention in 1954, which became an annual event attracting hundreds into the Mojave Desert for lectures, displays, and books and other wares offered by dealers.

Van Tassel established the College of Universal Wisdom, spoke vaguely about Lucifer, and collected funds to construct an Integratron, an alien-engineered geomagnetic device designed to rejuvenate human cells and function as a time machine.

Van Tassel's work on the Integratron remained incomplete at his death, but the structure is extant, well maintained, and a popular destination for UFOlogists, tourists, and the curious.

For details of Van Tassel's activities, see chapter fourteen.

Notable books: *I Rode a Flying Saucer: The Mystery of the Flying Saucers Revealed*; *Into This World and Out Again*.

Colin Wilson (1931–2013): Celebrated British autodidact of working-class origin who pursued a long and successful career as a novelist and nonfiction author. Wilson rocketed to fame in the UK, quite out of nowhere, with his first book, *The Outsider* (1956), a nonfiction existential rumination on vapid societies' need of critic-prophets. Wilson later moved toward commercial novels, and found popularity with *The Mind Parasites*, *The Space Vampires* (filmed as *Lifeforce*), and the multivolume *Spider World* saga.

He returned frequently to the theme of social alienation, and also became a stimulating chronicler of the history and psychology of crime; poltergeists, telepathy and other facets of the paranormal; Atlantis and other ancient civilizations; the heroic tradition; sex and love; and analytic psychology. Wilson wrote biographies of people as diverse as Aleister Crowley and Mozart; Uri Geller and Hermann Hesse.

Although UFOs did not engage Wilson as fully as other subjects, he wrote enthusiastically about documented sightings and abductions, arriving at an interpretation similar to Carl Jung's—UFO events as manifestations of a long-established collective consciousness. However, Wilson freely connected UFOs to out-of-body experiences, mysticism, ghosts, and other familiar subsets of parapsychology and the paranormal.

Notable books: *The Unexplained Mysteries of the Universe*; *Alien Dawn: An Investigation into the Contact Experience*; *World Famous UFOs*.

Eyes Only: A Selection of Leading Living UFOlogists

Although one may be a UFOlogist (either self-described or identified as such by others), the term does not imply belief. Many UFOlogists do believe, but others are cautiously skeptical. Still others are firmly skeptical. Some, particularly radio hosts, function mainly as disseminators of UFO theory and information.

Here, arranged alphabetically, are notes on particularly prominent members of today's UFOlogical community. The list is not complete, partly because "complete" is meaningless and undefinable, and because judgments of importance are subjective.

Jan Aldrich (b. 1944): Director of Connecticut-based Project 1947, which studies the early flush of interest in UFOs and the immediate pre-1947 period. The organization is funded by MUFON, CUFOS, and FUFOR. Aldrich's establishment of electronic UFO-research resources has been useful to scholars, buffs, and serious investigators.

Stephen Bassett: Founder of Paradigm Research Group and executive director of the Extraterrestrial Phenomena Political Action Committee. Bassett lobbies for increased U.S. government transparency about human-extraterrestrial interactions. Although tireless, Bassett generates controversy because of his tolerance for UFO charlatans, insisting that *any* discussion of UFOs prods the government closer to disclosure. World Disclosure Day is a signature Bassett initiative.

Notable book: *UFOs and U.S. Presidents: The Secret History*.

Timothy Green Beckley (b. circa 1945): Founder of the UFO Investigators League (UFOIL) and a protégé of *Fate* magazine editor Raymond Palmer. A self-published

UFO writer while in his early teens, Beckley went on to establish a publishing company, Inner Light Global Communications, which maintains an aggressive schedule of titles devoted to UFOs and the paranormal. He has written many books about various UFO-related subjects; recurring Beckley subjects are Men in Black and government conspiracies, alien visitation, hollow Earth, demons, and "soul suckers." A bit of a nostalgist, Beckley (who modestly calls himself "Mr. UFO") has been a faithful chronicler of the early years of the postwar UFO community.

Art Bell (b. 1945): Libertarian radio personality who embraces an eclectic mix of conservative and liberal beliefs, and gained national (if cultish) fame as host of *Coast to Coast AM*, an eccentric syndicated show carried during overnights by five hundred stations reaching fifteen million listeners. Broadcasting from what he described as a trailer in the Nevada desert outside Las Vegas, Bell interviewed UFO contactees, Roswell historians, time travelers, Bigfoot witnesses, professional racists (who inevitably pushed Bell into fury), Satanists, predictors of the end times, Wiccans, and a variety of other ostensibly fringe characters. Bell sold his program to Clear Channel Media in 2003, voluntarily cut back on his airtime, and retired in 2010. (*Coast to Coast AM* continues, with host George Noory.) Bell's *Coast to Coast AM* maintains a solid core of admirers; vintage episodes can be heard in rebroadcast on stations around the country.

In 2008, Bell returned to broadcasting with *Midnight in the Desert*, heard on Internet radio's Dark Matter Digital Network

Although Bell has described himself as a reporter, he has also acknowledged his function as a traditional broadcaster, that is, a person looking for ratings. "Ratings equal money," Bell said, "I should know."

Don Berliner: Former staff writer for the National Investigations Committee on Aerial Phenomena (NICAP), and now chairman of the Fund for UFO Research (FUFOR), Berliner is an experienced science writer specializing in space exploration and aviation history. Attuned to the power of words and terminology, Berliner suggests that "UFO" be abandoned, as the acronym is essentially synonymous with "flying saucer," a concept taken seriously by neither the general public nor opinion makers. Berliner's suggested alternative: UAP (Unexplained Aerial Phenomena). Strict educational and training requirements of UAP investigators, as well as an insistence on quality photography and primary documents, also figure strongly in Berliner's point of view, particularly if UFOlogy (another term he dislikes) is ever to be taken seriously.

Notable books: *UFO Briefing Document* (with Marie Galbraith and J. Antonio Huneeus; this is the public version of the study commissioned by Laurance Rockefeller); *Crash at Corona: U.S. Military Retrieval and Cover-up of a UFO* (with Stanton T. Friedman).

Kim Carlsberg: UFO abductee and speaker. She talks freely of having been taken and physically examined many times. Notable quote: "Those tables are really cold." Carlsberg claims seven alien grandchildren.

Bill Chalker (b. 1952): Leading Australian UFO researcher educated in chemistry and mathematics, and with professional experience in industrial chemistry. In 1982, he became the first civilian researcher given access to UFO files held by the Royal Australian Air Force. He has written about events linking UFOs and Australian military activity.

Notable book: *The OZ Files: The Australian UFO Story*.

Jerome Clark (b. 1946): Writer, researcher, and editor once associated with *Fate* magazine, Clark may be UFOlogy's most thorough and fair-minded researcher. His two-volume, 1,178-page *The UFO Encyclopedia* is a carefully documented resource that covers a wealth of topics and issues, major and esoteric, related to the UFO phenomenon. (A single-volume abridgment, *The UFO Book*, is hardly less useful.) Clark impresses with a reasoned belief in extraterrestrial visitation and his objective reporting of views that are at odds with his own. Other books by Clark cover such topics as hidden civilizations, cryptozoology, goblins, and freakish behavior of nature. Clark is a board member of the J. Allen Hynek Center for UFO Studies (CUFOS).

Erich von Däniken (b. 1935): Swiss writer, ancient (alien) astronaut theorist, and founder of a pseudoscientific organization, the Archaeology, Astronautics, and SETI Research Association.

Däniken had professional experience as a hotel manager, and amateur interests in astronomy and UFOs when he began to research his first book around 1956. Following a ghosted rewrite, the book was published in 1968 as *Chariots of the Gods? Unsolved Mysteries of the Past*. Although his notions about ancient astronauts that seeded Earth centuries ago with alien technology and cultural influences was not wholly original, Däniken's version became a publishing phenomenon, particularly after mass-market-paperback publication of *Chariots* in the United States.

Däniken essentially gave voice to people unable to reconcile that human beings created, without help, the Egyptian pyramids, Stonehenge, the majestic sculpted heads of Easter Island, and other "mysterious" artifacts. According to Däniken, assistance was provided by extraterrestrials—long-ago visitors to various spots on Earth who, over a course of many centuries, shared construction technology, as well as scientific knowledge that imbues the artifacts with extra-planetary significance.

Erich von Däniken's tussles with the law go back to his teen years. Things grew serious in 1968, when he was accused of cooking his hotel's books in order to give himself more than $125,000 in loans needed to fund his research travels. He served a year of a three-year sentence; while imprisoned, Däniken wrote his second book, *Return to the Stars* (later republished as *Gods from Outer Space*).

Not surprisingly, established archaeologists, historians, and scientists take a dim view of Däniken's ideas, ripping him for inadequate, poorly documented research; numerous misapprehensions about history; and a tendency to play fast and loose with scientific fact. During a 1974 interview with *Playboy* magazine, Däniken complained that archaeologists appreciate neither "fantasy" nor "speculation," and that they are concerned only with facts. "Who cares about that?" he asked.

In 1968, he implicitly admitted to having borrowed from Robert Joseph Grugeau's 1963 book *One Hundred Thousand Years of Man's Unknown History*. Grugeau was a postal employee, comic strip writer, and amateur archaeologist whose book (published under the pseudonym Robert Charroux) claimed to reveal the secrets of the pyramids, the flying men of Zimbabwe, giants, magic, and the end of the world—most of it tied in with flying saucers, and the extraterrestrial pilots of long ago that visited Earth and left their influences. Grugeau's publisher objected to similarities discerned in portions of Däniken's *Chariots of the Gods* and threatened a suit. Subsequent editions of *Chariots*, as well as Däniken's *Return to the Stars*, include token acknowledgment of Grugeau's work.

Notable books: *Chariots of the Gods? Unsolved Mysteries of the Past; In Search on Ancient Gods: My Pictorial Evidence for the Impossible; Signs of the Gods; The Gods Were Astronauts; Odyssey of the Gods: An Alien History of Ancient Greece.*

Peter Davenport (b. 1948): Director of the National UFO Reporting Center (NUFORC) since 1994, Davenport has professional experience as a college instructor, translator (Russian), and biotech businessman. Although quick to note that many UFO sightings are of satellites and other mundane objects, he works to increase mainstream media interest in unidentified flying objects, and raise awareness of government efforts to limit information about the phenomenon. NUFORC, he says, takes some twenty thousand calls about UFOs every year.

In 2006, Davenport paid $100,000 to purchase Atlas Missile Site No. 6, part of a decommissioned and abandoned underground nuclear missile complex located near Harrington, Washington, fifty miles west of Spokane. The damp space is windowless and claustrophobic, and struck Davenport as ideal for the undisturbed pursuit of NUFORC business.

Lisa Davis: San Diego-based researcher who established the Foundation for Abduction Research and Support in 2003, and later became executive director of the National UFO Reporting Center (NUFORC). Davis has looked into hundreds of abduction cases, and the ways in which Christian faith—specifically, "redemption through Christ"—can help victims recover from their experiences. Davis doubts extraterrestrial-origin UFO theories, holding instead that the craft's origins and purposes are clearly described in the Bible as vessels for fallen angels controlled by Satan. She is concerned also with human-alien hybrids, creatures that are dangerous because they have no souls. Davis herself is not an abductee. Her professional background is in children's health and disability.

Richard Dolan (b. 1962): Author, lecturer, and radio host with a strong interest in the U.S. government's decades-long cover-up of incidents of alien contact. He is among the more effective UFO generalists—a researcher keen on all aspects of the phenomenon. His insights into social media's effect on UFO research and discussion are particularly useful. Dolan owns Richard Dolan Press, a publisher of books about UFOs, romantic love and the supernatural, secret military bases dug beneath the ocean floor, and alien virology.

Notable books: *UFOs and the National Security State, 1941–1973, 1973–1991* (two volumes); *UFOs for the 21st Century Mind.*

Vicki and Don Ecker: Editors and directors of research for the American edition of *UFO* magazine. Don Ecker frequently takes issue with numerous hoaxers, "frauds and clowns," and other charlatans. His crusade against poor research and outright nonsense received enough blowback that he and Vicki exited UFOlogy in 2007, via an open letter penned by Don.

George A. Filer III: Retired USAF major and intelligence officer associated with MUFON and NUFOC (National UFO Conference). His popular "Filer's Files" feature on the NUFOC Web site keeps readers abreast of the latest UFO and astronomy-related news. While aboard a converted B-50 bomber above the North Sea in 1962, Filer was a passive participant in the plane's unsuccessful chase of an unidentified flying disc. Attached to McGuire AFB (New Jersey) in 1978, Filer contributed to briefings about a disc-shaped craft that landed at nearby Fort Dix, and that disgorged an apparently extraterrestrial pilot shot by USAF ground personnel.

Notable book: *Filer's Files: Worldwide Reports of UFO Sightings* (with David E. Twichell).

Salvador Freixedo (b. 1923): Former Catholic clergyman who has been a powerful voice in UFO/paranormal studies in Spain, Cuba, and Puerto Rico since 1970. Freixedo subscribes to an ornate variant of the ancient astronaut theme, asserting that UFOs are one manifestation of interdimensional beings—some helpful, others influentially malevolent—with discomfiting Lovecraftian qualities. The entities have been controlling us, invisibly, for many centuries, out of motives that are beyond our ken. The creatures represent a variety of species and forms, and not all of them get along with the others. Some can disguise themselves as human, and walk among us. What we identify as religious miracles are the work of the visitors—a provocative notion because it implies that larger notions of morality are not entirely our own, and that the creatures may fill the role usually assumed to be filled by God. Though interdimensional, the creatures travel the physical cosmos, employing methods of propulsion that defy what we presume to know about physics. SETI and other government-funded scientific projects are, according to Freixedo, "deceits" intended to distract us from the truth.

Notable book: *Teovnilogia: El origen del mal en el mundo.*

Stanton T. Friedman (b. 1934): Retired nuclear physicist who is arguably the world's preeminent, and most respected, UFOlogist. Friedman's UFO credentials are deep, going back to 1958. A decade later, he was the first civilian to investigate the Roswell incident on-site. He concluded that the crashed craft was extraterrestrial and, further, that the U.S. government involved itself in a cover-up. (Contrary to many in the UFO community, Friedman is convinced that many—but not all—of the post-Roswell Majestic 12 documents that surfaced in the 1980s are genuine, and confirm the cover-up. For more on MJ-12, see chapter eight.) A close investigator of the Barney and Betty Hill abduction case (see chapter thirteen), Friedman gives credence to Betty Hill's intriguing "star sketch," and concludes that UFOs come from star systems relatively close to our own. Friedman also is convinced, by evidence, that the U.S. government retrieved a crashed extraterrestrial spacecraft at Aztec, New Mexico, in 1948. (For details of this case, see chapter fifteen.)

A tireless writer and lecturer since devoting his full time to UFO study in the 1970s, Friedman expresses great impatience with UFO debunkers who 1) are unfamiliar with science and/or 2) misinterpret or ignore scientific evidence.

Notable books: *Crash at Corona: U.S. Military Retrieval and Cover-up of a UFO* (with Don Berliner); *Captured! The Barney and Betty Hill UFO Experience* (with Kathleen Marden); *Top Secret/Majic*; *Flying Saucers and Science.*

John Greenewald Jr. (b. 1981): Government-transparency citizen-activist whose determined campaign to force release of classified U.S.-government UFO documents (and docs on many other subjects, as well) culminated in Greenewald's important Web site, the Black Vault. He began to leverage the Freedom of Information Act while in high school and wrote his first book at twenty. By 2013, documents unsealed at Greenewald's request gave the name "Area 51" to the government's top-secret research center in southern Nevada. The site now hosts an astonishing 1.4 million pages of previously classified documents. Among Greenewald's better insights is that the government stonewalls researchers because too many people making requests for information give up after the first negative response, or lack of response. In other words, stonewalling is the government's easiest and most fruitful course. But researchers' perseverance will pay. In addition to operating the Black Vault, Greenewald has produced television documentaries and pseudo-documentaries about the Freemasons, underground alien bases, Hitler and the occult, and end-of-the-world scenarios.

Notable book: *Beyond UFO Secrecy.*

Steven M. Greer (b. 1955): Retired North Carolina medical doctor and proponent of government truthfulness via-à-vis UFOs. He has founded two organizations dedicated to expanded knowledge about UFOs and their inhabitants: The Center for Study of Extra-Terrestrial Intelligence (CSETI; 1990) and The Disclosure Project. As the latter organization's name suggests, Greer pushes government agencies and officials to come clean on what they know about UFOs, particularly as the knowledge relates to national and world security.

Some UFOlogists accuse Greer of presenting the research of other people as his own, and propounding theories—for instance, that alien spacecraft surrounded Neil Armstrong when the American astronaut walked on the Moon in 1969—that don't bear up well to scrutiny.

Another Greer project, the Advanced Energy Research Organization (AERO), extols Greer's fist-sized "zero energy" device, which, he says, can power a small city.

Notable books: *Extraterrestrial Contact: The Evidence and Implications*; *Hidden Truth, Forbidden Knowledge*.

Robert J. Gribble (b. 1926): Retired American firefighter who founded the National UFO Reporting Center (NUFORC) in Seattle in 1974. Gribble provided the organization's financing, while fielding six to ten calls daily about UFO sightings, and cataloguing them. Gribble routinely recorded calls made to the center, and he conducted many follow-up interviews. His activity yielded more than forty hours of first-person audio recordings, which he donated to UFOlogist Wendy Connors in 2004, and which became available for Web downloads in 2013.

Gribble's interest was sparked in 1954, when he read Harold T. Wilkins's *Flying Saucers on the Attack*. Donald Keyhoe's *The Flying Saucers Are Real* further excited Gribble, and inspired him to establish the Space Observers League (later called Civilian Flying Saucer Intelligence) and begin publication of a UFO newsletter, *Flying Saucer Review*, in 1955. Gribble also began to compile an archive of UFO news reports, which eventually stretched back to the year 1800. He also worked as a MUFON investigator.

Although not a UFO witness, Gribble wants others to have a place to log reports of their sightings. Twenty years of fielding calls and networking took its toll; Gribble handed stewardship of NUFORC to biotech entrepreneur Peter Davenport in 1994. Davenport later moved the headquarters from Seattle to a refurbished missile silo outside of Spokane.

By the millennium, Gribble had shifted his energy to a fervent campaign against illegal immigration from Mexico (whose leaders, he claimed, had designs on control of the U.S. government).

Richard Haines (b. circa 1939): Former NASA scientist at Ames Research Center, 1967–88 (plus later contract work), with a PhD in experimental psychology. Haines did landing simulation research at NASA, and worked on Head-up Display design, the EVA (Extravehicular Activity) spacesuit and other astronaut habitability challenges, astronaut ergonomics, improvements to long-distance image transmission, and various issue of vision and optics. Later a psychology professor at San Jose State, Haines has a strong scientific orientation that encourages him to be an open-minded but cautious UFOlogist. He has made careful study of more than thirty-four hundred UFO accounts given by pilots, as well as reports made by astronauts.

Haines is now chief scientist for the National Aviation Reporting Center on Anomalous Phenomena (NARCAP). In a 1995 interview with CUFON, Dr. Haines lamented UFOlogy's "drift into entertainment media," and urged neophytes to avoid TV and "read only the highest-quality books."

Notable books: *UFO Phenomena and the Behavioral Scientist* (editor); *Observing UFOs*; *CE-5: Close Encounters of the Fifth Kind*.

Larry Hatch: Forced by ill health to assume a lower profile in 2006, UFO researcher-compiler Hatch devoted twenty years to the creation of the "* U *" UFO Database, an exhaustive, single-source DOS-based UFO case-study compilation of more than eighteen thousand incidents spanning most of humankind's recorded history. Persons close to Hatch enjoyed access to the database while it was a work in progress. Unfortunately, Hatch's outmoded technology meant that his completed database was accessible only to sophisticated and dedicated computer-tech experts. Things improved in 2011, when Hatch announced that his database was not as "lost" as some had assumed. The best, latest retrieval method, for use by people running Windows XP and Windows Vista Business, is available on ufoupdateslist.com.

Paul Hellyer (b. 1923): Since 2005, this former Canadian defence minister (1963–67) and transport minister (1967–69) has advocated sharply for the release of UFO-related documents held by governments around the world. Trained as an aeronautical engineer and well versed in reform-style economics, Hellyer claims that four discrete alien species have visited Earth for centuries, sharing technology that culminated in LEDs, Kevlar, and microchips. The aliens also observe that the world's poor are not well served. At least another dozen alien species are aware of our existence; most, Hellyer says, hold good intentions for us, and are loath to directly intercede in our affairs. One species though, whom Hellyer calls the "Tall Whites," works with the U.S. Air Force in Nevada.

Every alien race that is aware of us is concerned about man-made ecological damage to the planet, and our loose controls on atomic weaponry.

To date, Hellyer is the world's highest-ranking government figure to reveal alien activity, and lobby for government disclosure.

Notable relevant book: *Light at the End of the Tunnel: A Survival Plan for the Human Species.*

Linda Moulton Howe (b. 1942): Researcher, archivist, and filmmaker known for *A Strange Harvest*, a 1980 documentary about cattle mutilations and their link to UFOs. A Peabody-winning television writer and producer, Howe unwittingly set into motion a great deal of fevered extrapolation based on a belief that the mutilations are part of a larger, more sinister alien effort involving the forced mating of alien males and human females, human-alien hybrids, facilitated organ growth, and organ harvesting. Howe is a frequent "talking head" commentator seen in television episodes and documentaries devoted to ancient aliens, Bigfoot, the Roswell cover-up, and another of her favorite subjects (and a favorite of hoaxers, as well), crop circles.

Notable books: *Alien Harvest: Further Evidence Linking Animal Mutilations and Human Abductions to Alien Life Forms; Glimpses of Other Realities, Vols. 1 and 2; Mysterious Lights and Crop Circles.*

David M. Jacobs (b. circa 1943): Retired Temple University professor whose concentration on 20th-century American history and culture led him into UFOlogy.

Jacobs lectures frequently, maintaining a high profile in UFOlogy circles. He has particular interest in alien abductions, and confidence that memory regression via hypnosis brings reliable accounts from abductees. (Jacobs has regressed some 150 abductees, at no charge, since 1986.) Jacobs warns that abduction is a key component of an alien scheme to infiltrate Earth with human-alien hybrids. His belief in hybrids, because it invokes issues beyond the realm of known science, cannot be argued against persuasively. However, Jacobs's surety about the useful-ness of memory regression via hypnosis has brought considerable criticism levied by astrobiologists and cognitive psychologists.

In a break from his practice of in-person hypnotic memory regressions, Jacobs regressed a female abductee (who calls herself Emma Woods) by telephone during 2004–07. The relationship degenerated after about a year, and Jacobs claims that Woods instigated a campaign of threats and other harassment against him; Woods retorts that during phone sessions Jacobs "planted suggestions" (Woods's words) that she had Multiple Personality Disorder. At this writing, the argument goes on in the respective Web sites of Jacobs and Woods, and in numberless UFO forums.

Jacobs is presently director of the International Center for Abduction Research.

Notable books: *The UFO Controversy in America* (a consumer version of Jacobs's PhD dissertation); *The Threat: Revealing the Secret Alien Agenda*; *UFOs and Abductions: Challenging the Borders of Knowledge*; *Walking Among Us: The Alien Plan to Control Humanity*.

Kal K. Korff (b. 1962): American paranormal researcher and UFO debunker, variously based in the USA, the Czech Republic, and India, and more noted for his claims about himself than for his investigative work. Korff has devoted considerable energy to debunking the Billy Meier UFO case (see chapter fifteen) and the Roswell crash and subsequent alien autopsy film—and greater effort to a ceaseless enumeration of his credentials: counterterrorism agent, undercover operative, security analyst, colonel with the Israeli Secret Service, consultant to the CIA, consultant to the FBI, widely read journalist, JFK-assassination expert, consultant to the O. J. Simpson civil trial plaintiffs, think-tank chief, husband to an Indian princess, and more. Korff has had difficulty providing documentation, witnesses, or other proofs of his personal claims.

A familiar "talking head" and panel guest on CNN and other outlets during much of the 1990s, Korff took a hit from a highly critical 1994 *San Jose Mercury News* feature, and severely damaged himself in 1997 by falsely claiming that radio host Art Bell objected to the plans of three Bell-affiliate stations to schedule Korff on shows other than Bell's. Because Korff's claim involved Bell's alleged threat to yank his show from those stations, Bell insisted that Korff apologize, via live telephone, on *Coast to Coast AM*. Korff did so, and posted a printed apology on his Web site.

YouTube partially revived Korff's flagging career and provided an easy plat-form for him to carry on with his claims and activities. But his detractors, too, are on the Web and campaign against him there, with gleeful vigor that frequently shades into the vituperative.

Notable books: *Spaceships of the Pleiades*; *The Roswell UFO Crash: What They Don't Want You to Know*.

Barbara Lamb: Abduction researcher and psychotherapist who has performed, by her count, more than eighteen hundred hypnotic regressions on more than eight hundred UFO abductees. Memories recovered with Lamb's intervention suggest that multiple alien species campaign to have forced sex with human women and men. According to Lamb, three alien types dominate: reptilians, mantids, and grays. Their goal is to create hybrids that will integrate with the human genome, and perpetuate traits of the respective races. Lamb has cited the angular features of some fashion models as identifiers of hybrid status—though UFO blogger, and informed skeptic, Robert Sheaffer has noted, dryly, that "anorexia and heroin might produce the same effect."

Lamb has a seat on the board of the Academy of Clinical Close Encounter Therapists. Crop circles account for Lamb's other main area of research; enthusiasts flock to her annual tours across the British countryside.

Notable books: *Alien Experiences* (with Nadine Lalich); *Crop Circles Revealed: Language of the Light Circles* (with Judith Moore).

Michael Lindemann (b. 1949): Educator, hypnotherapist, and social analyst trained in psychology and political science. Lindemann's professional interest in UFOs dates to about 1990, when he became intrigued by the possible connection between them and covert weapons development—specifically, the ways in which American public funds are secretly funneled to the development and maintenance of secret weapons bases. He founded CNI News (to disseminate UFO information), the Global Situation Report (global politics and futurism), and a Web-based body, the Institute for the Study of Non-human Intelligence (ISCNI). As "Michael Paul," Lindemann writes futurist novels that he issues under his Chancellor Publishing imprint.

With his wife, Deborah Lindemann, Michael Lindemann operates the Lindemann Professional Group, which utilizes hypnosis to treat anxiety, general fears and phobias, smoking, and excess weight.

Notable book: *UFOs and the Alien Presence: Six Viewpoints*.

Bruce Maccabee (b. 1942): Active in NICAP and, later, MUFON, Maccabee is a physicist who worked at the Naval Ordnance Library from 1972 to 2008, developing defense-oriented laser technology. He has done extensive research into the 1947 Roswell case, and hundreds of UFO sightings that occurred in the ten years following. He is a founding member of the Fund for UFO Research.

Maccabee's 2000 article "Prosaic Explanations: The Failure of UFO Skepticism" (*Infinite Energy* magazine) has been a rallying point for many UFOlogists.

Notable books: *The FBI-CIA-UFO Connection: The Hidden UFO Activities of USA Intelligence Agencies* (with Stanton Friedman); *If UFOs Are Real* (with Larry Koss).

Jim Marrs (b. 1943): High-profile American UFOlogist, JFK-assassination con-spiracy theorist, and author with professional experience as a journalist. Marrs blends his UFO studies with his thoughts about a variety of invisible conspiracies involving the military-industrial complex, the "New World Order," Freemasons, the Trilateral Commission, "zombie banks," and others. He brings a conspiracy mindset even to the ancient astronaut theory, postulating that humans sprang from "space-faring overlords" that traveled here from the planet Nibiru; today, Marrs suggests, Nibiruians secretly control a small but hugely influential cadre of people around the globe, at the highest levels of power.

To his credit as a professional writer, Marrs has turned himself into a brand: HarperCollins, a major publisher, issues his books, and on some covers his name dominates the tops of the jackets, above the titles. To the publishing establishment, Jim Marrs is money in the bank.

Notable books about UFOs: *Alien Agenda: Investigating the Alien Presence Among Us*; *Our Occulted History: Do the Global Elite Conceal Ancient Aliens?*

Greg Meholic: Experienced in practical applications of aerodynamics and aerospace technology, this American project engineer with California-based Aerospace Corporation brings knowledge of propulsion systems to extensive professional activity in space-travel issues of interest to the federal government. In addition to research, Meholic teaches a graduate-level propulsion systems course at Loyola Marymount University.

Meholic's everyday work on gas turbines and other existing technology, though rife with possibility, is relatively straightforward. His curiosity, however, has led him to maintain another, separate line of research into faster-than-light theory based in particle physics (the study of the fundamental, subatomic particles that combine to create matter and radiation). Meholic's informed speculation on nuclear and antimatter ramjets suggests that the stars may one day be within our grasp.

Royce Myers: American editor and founder of ufowatchdog.com, a useful Web site devoted to rational study of UFOs, UFOlogists, and UFO claims. Trained in criminal justice, Myers has no patience with hoaxers, whom he views primarily as charlatans that are "UFO people" only secondarily. He is curious about the motivations of hoaxers, and the material and emotional needs such people wish to fulfill. Myers is famously skeptical about the Roswell alien autopsy film, and the Project SERPO conspiracy (see chapter eleven).

Perhaps the most notable of Myers's targets is Sean David Morton, an unac-credited PhD (therapeutic counseling) who calls himself "America's Psychic," and who objected to Myers's investigation of his claims about associations with NASA astronauts, his psychic powers, and insider knowledge of extraterrestrials. Morton sued Myers and ufowatchdog.com (he lost his case in 2003), only to be sued himself by the SEC in 2010 for multimillion-dollar investment fraud. In 2013, a U.S. district judge ordered Morton to pay $11.5 million to the SEC; and Morton's wife, a relief defendant, to pay more than $570,000.

So successful is Myers in his determination to expose and explain hoaxers that some in the UFO community brand him a pawn of Washington, paid to debunk the UFOs that the government wishes to obscure.

James "Jim" E. Oberg (b. 1944): Retired NASA engineer who devoted years to the space shuttle project, and to an understanding of the strengths and limitations of the Russian space program. Oberg is a founding fellow of the Committee for Skeptical Inquiry (CSI); he does not automatically dismiss UFO reports from credible witnesses, but is impatient with accounts that amount to what he refers to as "space folklore." Unlike some other UFOlogists, Oberg is not infatuated with UFO reports made by experienced professional pilots. This stance is mildly controversial, as it seems to discount the extensive training and flight time of such pilots.

In a 1979 article for *New Scientist* magazine, Oberg lamented that some in the UFO community ignore "data verification, theory testing, and the burden of proof." Though a portion of today's UFO community finds Oberg nettlesome, he remains a constructive voice of reason and care.

Notable books: *UFOs and Outer Space Mysteries: A Sympathetic Skeptic's Report*; *Space Power Theory*; *Red Star in Orbit*.

Nick Pope (b. 1965): British journalist, former Ministry of Defence employee, and onetime researcher with Britain's UFO Project who gained notoriety in 2012 when he predicted imminent alien invasion of Earth. News stories quoted Pope: "The [British] government . . . has planned for the worst-case scenario: alien attack and alien invasion. Space shuttles, lasers, and directed-energy weapons are all committed via the Alien Invasion War Plan to defense [*sic*] against any alien ships in orbit." When eyebrows were raised in government and elsewhere, Pope clarified, saying that he was describing a new video game he had helped develop.

When declassified Ministry of Defence UFO files began to be released in 2008, Pope developed a high-profile feud with David Clarke, an academic and British UFO Research Association member who was official consultant to the UK National Archives, and who helped shepherd more than fifty thousand pages of documents into the public eye. Pope claims that many documents were not declassified and released; Clarke begs to differ.

Notable books: *Open Skies, Closed Minds: Official Reactions to the UFO Phenomenon*; *Encounter in Rendlesham Forest: The Inside Story of the World's Best-Documented UFO Incident*.

Harold Puthoff (b. 1936): Graduate-degree electrical engineer with professional experience in fiber optics, microwaves, opto-electronic computers, and laser physics. He has worked for Sperry, General Electric, and the National Security Agency. Since the 1970s, Puthoff has studied alternative fuel sources and zero-point energy (the study of electromagnetic interactions, and the energy left after all other energy is removed from a system).

While with the Stanford Research Institute (SRI), Puthoff and fellow physicist Russell Targ coined the term "remote viewing" to describe a non-objective form of extrasensory perception that the SRI explored for possible intelligence-gathering applications.

In the mid-1980s, Puthoff established a business, EarthTech International, and an academic research organization, the Institute for Advanced Study in Austin (Texas). Never an active UFOlogist, Puthoff nevertheless stimulates UFO researchers who are aware of his work in theoretical physics, and his suggestion that interstellar travel may be feasible.

Puthoff joined the Church of Scientology in the 1960s and remained until the 1970s.

Notable book: *Fundamentals of Quantum Electronics* (with Richard H. Pantell).

Scott and Susan Ramsey: North Carolina-based researchers best known for their investigation of the generally discredited 1948 UFO crash at Hart Canyon, near Aztec, New Mexico. (For more on Aztec, see chapter fifteen.) The Ramseys claim that sixteen diminutive aliens perished in the crash, and that the U.S. government took pains to cover up the incident. A plaque installed at the site by the Ramseys describes the craft as having been one hundred feet in diameter and eighteen feet high. Leading UFOlogist Stanton Friedman has praised the Ramseys for their persistent and dedicated research.

Notable book: *The Aztec Incident: Recovery at Hart Canyon.*

Kevin Randle (b. 1949): Prolific American military historian and novelist with a degree in journalism and advanced degrees in psychology and military studies. Combat experience in Vietnam and Iraq gave Randle the "nuts and bolts" outlook that typified first-generation UFO researchers. Although mildly skeptical of abduction accounts, Randle gives credence to the basics of the famed Roswell, New Mexico, crash—asserting that something that was *not* a weather balloon crashed there, and that subsequent investigations have been bollixed and purposely hindered by the U.S. government.

An association with a researcher-writer named Donald Schmitt during a Roswell book project damaged Randle's credibility in 1995, when investigation by the U.S. Air Force and others discovered that Schmitt had not been truthful about his education and other credentials. (For more, see chapter eight.) Schmitt eventually admitted his deceptions, via open letter. Randle's *Roswell Revisited* (2007) displays no patience for spurious Roswell "evidence," which encompasses faked memoranda and other documents, unproved claims of Roswell crash-debris metal that is not of this Earth, and the faked Roswell alien autopsy film.

Notable books: *UFO Crash at Roswell* (with Donald R. Schmitt); *Roswell Revisited*; *The Roswell Encyclopedia*; *Case MJ-12: The True Story Behind the Government's UFO Conspiracies*; *The Abduction Enigma* (with William P. Cone and Russ Estes); *Reflections of a UFO Investigator.*

Jenny Randles (b. 1951): British researcher, author, and lecturer associated with the British UFO Research Association (BUFORA), and author of dozens of widely read books about UFOs, and many aspects of the paranormal, including time travel, life after death, and spontaneous human combustion. She claims to have had fifteen UFO sightings since childhood, adding that she has been unable to satisfactorily explain only two. Randles's academic training is in geology and media communications.

Since the millennium, Randles has grown less interested in UFOs as conveyors of alien beings and more intrigued with the energy fields UFOs may generate. She has noted the diminishment of "standard" alien reports since the 1990s and the dramatic increase since that time of abduction accounts. (Randles has, in fact, worked to ban hypnotic regression, a tool often employed to coax possibly spurious memories from abductees.) Her observation suggests that ET accounts simply change with fashion and may never have represented reality. Indeed, some in the UFO community were startled by Randles's 2013 article for *Fortean Times*, in which she noted the continually "frustrating" search for intelligent extraterrestrials, and wondered whether such creatures—at least insofar as they might visit Earth—are "a space age equivalent of the dragons and the fairies." Randles believes that intelligent extraterrestrials exist, but that they are likely to be discovered by scientists rather than UFOlogists.

Vis-à-vis her energy-field notion, Randles posits that discrete UFOs generate a "sphere of influence," a physical force that may explain differences in multiple-eyewitness UFO accounts: witnesses located a farther physical distance from a UFO might experience a lesser level of what Randles calls "distortion," while people situated closer appear to be more prone to internalized buzzing, humming, and other physical effects. This suggests to Randles that many, and perhaps most, UFOs are physical phenomena, possibly atmospheric in nature.

Notable books: *The Truth Behind Men in Black: Government Agents or Visitors from Beyond*; *UFO Retrievals: The Recovery of Alien Spacecraft*; *UFOs and How to See Them*.

Nick Redfern (b. 1964): Leading British UFOlogist and prolific freelance writer who campaigns for release of classified British UFO documents. As a result of Redfern's efforts, thousands of pages of previously classified British documents have been released.

One Redfern book, *Three Men Seeking Monsters*, diverges from UFOlogy to look at pursuits of werewolves, apemen, water serpents, giant cats, and "ghostly devil dogs." Other books by Redfern examine Bigfoot, Chupacabra, demons and fallen angels, NASA's Moon-landing "hoax," and the purported link between RH-negative blood and alien ancestors. This activity would seem to mark Redfern as a facile commercial writer rather than a serious scholar.

Notable books: *Close Encounters of the Fatal Kind: Suspicious Deaths, Mysterious Murders, and Bizarre Disappearances in UFO History*; *Body Snatchers in the Desert: The Horrible Truth at the Heart of the Roswell Story*; *Men in Black: Personal Stories & Eerie Adventures*.

Mark Rodeghier (b. 1953): American astrophysicist with a PhD in sociology, and a commitment to well-grounded scientific research. He became president and scientific director of the J. Allen Hynek Center for UFO Studies in 1986, concurrent with his software and consulting duties with Chicago-based SPSS Inc., a statistical analysis firm that is now part of IBM's Business Analytics Portfolio.

In interviews and elsewhere, Rodeghier has explained that UFO research has been slow to provide concrete results not because the subject is frivolous, but because of a lack of the kinds of resources that fund and otherwise support standard scientific research. Without the ability to conduct what Rodeghier calls "real-time research," UFO investigators must rely on eyewitness reports—and those, while often credible, are not "scientific." According to Rodeghier, UFOlogy will not gain mainstream approval until it attracts funding and many more legitimate scientists.

He remains hopeful. In 2008, he told interviewer Jason Plautz, "If I meet someone whose mind is open, even just a crack, I can sit and talk to them. I just try to present the best cases. In the end, they always say, 'Okay, I see at least why you're studying this. There might really be something there.'"

Notable book: *UFO Reports Involving Vehicle Interference.*

Michael Salla: Australian academic (PhD in government affairs), and a proponent of exopolitics, the study of political policy relevant to human interaction with extraterrestrials. Salla interprets biblical references to demigods as evidence of human-alien hybrids, and identifies the Flood as the event needed to rid Earth of unrepentant fallen angels. Salla maintains that sixteen alien races are now involved in earthly affairs, some independently, others in collusion with Earth governments.

President Eisenhower, Salla reports, met with extraterrestrials during the Cold War. Space probes launched later by the U.S. and other nations discovered livable atmospheres on Mars, Venus, and Earth's Moon—information that has been kept from the public. Like many UFOlogists, Salla takes particular interest in Nikola Tesla, suggesting that the brilliant scientist-inventor was "a Venusian baby" given to an Earth family to be raised as a human.

Notable books: *Exposing U.S. Government Policies on Extraterrestrial Life: The Challenge of Exopolitics*; *Kennedy's Last Stand: Eisenhower, UFOs, MJ-12 & JFK's Assassination.*

Rudolph "Rudy" Schild (b. 1940): Harvard astrophysicist and researcher who directs the 1.5-meter-telescope program at the Harvard-Smithsonian Cambridge Observatories. The author and co-author of nearly three hundred peer-reviewed scientific papers, Schild is founding editor-in-chief (2009) of the peer-reviewed *Journal of Cosmology.* He is well known for his investigations into the quantum hologram theory of physics; the ancient, natural "seeding" of Earth that allowed the planet to develop life (the panspermia theory); and so-called super-planets—giant bodies that, in Schild's view, are caught in supernovas and other cosmic collisions, becoming the progenitors of smaller planets. Earth, Schild ventures, may have spun off from a sundered super-planet.

Besides his credentials, Schild has popular appeal because of his confident manner, his marriage to mezzo-soprano Jane Struss, and his collection of vintage automobiles and motorcycles. UFOlogists are attracted by his innovative (and controversial) thoughts about the magnetic properties of black holes, and possible creation of wormholes that might provide "shortcuts" suited to interstellar travel. (For more on Dr. Schild's theory, see chapter three.)

Notable book: *The Discovery of Alien Extraterrestrial Life: Our Cosmic Ancestry & the Origins of Life* (editor/contributor, with Richard Hoover, Chandra Wickramasinghe, and R. Joseph).

John F. Schuessler: Retired director of general services for Boeing, this American aerospace engineer is a founding member of MUFON (established 1969). From 2000 to 2006, Schuessler served as that organization's international director. In 1976, he founded Project VISIT (Vehicle Internal Systems Investigative Team), to bring aerospace and other technical expertise to studies of Unidentified Space Vehicles (USVs).

Schuessler is, to date, the best and most sympathetic chronicler of the so-called Cash-Landrum UFO incident of 1980, in which two Texas women and a boy witnessed more than twenty military helicopters struggle to intercept a UFO. (For more, see chapter fifteen.) Schuessler related the story with care, establishing himself as a thorough, knowledgeable, and principled investigator. He won the admiration of the three principals, not least because he listened carefully to the adult witnesses, whose accounts were dismissed by some because they were "unreliable women." Recalling Schuessler more than twenty years after the fact, Colby Landrum said, "[H]e was on top of things. I mean he was a wonderful man."

Notable books: *The Cash-Landrum UFO Incident*; *A Catalog of UFO-Related Human Physiological Effects*.

Robert Sheaffer (b. 1949): American author and magazine journalist who co-founded (with Philip Klass and James Oberg) the UFO subcommittee of the Committee for Skeptical Inquiry.

Sheaffer's take on UFOs is culture based, with a nod to folklore and myth—communal elements deeply ingrained in people's minds and expressed, over centuries, as different things: fairies, ghosts, mythic heroes, and, according to Sheaffer, UFOs. (Carl Jung had a similar idea.) In a 2012 interview, Sheaffer implied that unidentified flying objects are just one part of an imaginative human tapestry, saying that "UFOs have evolved into this enormous richness as asocial phenomenon."

UFO accounts involving professional pilots are particularly intriguing to Sheaffer, who declares pilots unreliable witnesses. Why? Because, he says, they are (and are obligated to be) caught up in the exigencies of the moment (*I can't crash into that object*) rather than in cool analysis (*I wonder what that object is?*). Sheaffer has debunked, to his own satisfaction, absorbing accounts from professional civil and military pilots, as well as other military personnel.

Sheaffer's criticism of militant feminism, and his unwillingness to acknowledge human-generated climate change, make him controversial in an arena larger than the world of UFOs.

Notable books: *The UFO Verdict: Examining the Evidence; UFO Sightings: The Evidence.*

Michael Shermer (b. 1954): American science writer, academic, UFO skeptic, outspoken atheist, and retired professional bicycle racer. Shermer holds a master's degree in experimental psychology and a doctorate in the history of science. In 1992, he founded the Skeptics Society, a nonprofit that investigates controversial science and pseudoscience, and advocates critical and scientific thinking. The group's membership roll approaches sixty thousand. The organization publishes *Skeptic* magazine; every issue includes a bound-in supplement for youngsters, *Junior Skeptic.*

Shermer has written with great lucidity about what he calls "patternicity," an outgrowth of evolution-driven association learning, by which our brains are predisposed to "connect the dots and create meaning out of the patterns that we think we see in nature." This is why, as Shermer explains, people see the Virgin Mary on a grilled cheese sandwich; why UFOlogists see a face in a Martian boulder; and why paranormal investigators hear voices of the dead in electronic babble issuing from a radio.

Notable books: *Why People Believe Weird Things: Pseudo-science, Superstition, and Bogus Notions of Our Time; The Believing Brain: From Ghosts and Gods to Politics and Conspiracies—How We Construct Beliefs and Reinforce Them as Truths.*

Seth Shostak (b. 1943): American astrophysicist and astronomer who is senior astronomer at SETI Institute, which trolls for extraterrestrial intelligence by receiving and analyzing radio signals from space. (SETI is not designed to *send* messages, a decision with which Shostak disagrees.) Thus far, the signal chatter analyzed by SETI algorithms and software has been explainable. No aliens—though UFOlogist Steven Greer gets Shostak's dander up by insisting that SETI has indeed made contact.

Shostak has been intrigued by a relatively recent phenomenon: eleven fast radio bursts (FRBs) picked up in the southern sky by an Australian radio telescope since 2007. The power of the signals suggests a potent natural cause, such as the collision of stars. But some astronomers claim to have discovered a mathematical identifier shared by all eleven—an unlikely situation in nature. So are these FRBs the work of a far-distant alien intelligence? Shostak urges caution before declaring alien contact. Still, he is confident that SETI will locate intelligent alien life by 2040.

Notable books: *Sharing the Universe: Perspectives on Extraterrestrial Life; Confessions of an Alien Hunter: A Scientist's Search for Extraterrestrial Intelligence.*

Derrel Sims (b. 1948): American UFOlogist, hypnotherapist, and self-proclaimed "world's leading expert on alien abductions." A colorful figure in a cowboy hat and black leather duster, Sims reports that he is himself an abductee. He says that one in four people have been or will be abducted by aliens, and can expect to come away from the encounter with an implanted device. The assertion is tailor-made for getting attention, and indeed, Sims has found a TV audience as star of a jumpily photographed Discovery Science series called *Uncovering Aliens.*

Sims's resumé notes activity as a private investigator, process server, commercial real estate analyst, martial arts instructor, insurance liquidator, graphologist, self-published author, military police officer, and Vietnam-era CIA covert operative.

Notable book: *Alien Hunter: Evidence and Truth About Alien Implants* (with Patricia Gray).

Brad Sparks (b. circa 1955): American UFOlogist, document-release activist, and co-founder of BlueBookArchive.org. Sparks established the archive after cataloguing some fifteen hundred unexplained UFO accounts recorded in Project Blue Book documents of the 1950s and '60s. At this writing, more than fifty-six-thousand document pages are online. Sparks also is a co-founder of Citizens Against UFO Secrecy (established 1977), and a leading expert on the Scientific Advisory Panel on UFOs (the so-called Robertson Panel of 1953; see chapter nine).

Skeptical of standard conclusions offered about Roswell, Sparks insists that any UFO claim or other paranormal event be supported with documentation.

R. Leo Sprinkle (b. 1930): Retired University of Wyoming professor of psychology and guidance education, with practical experience in hypnotic regression. Although Sprinkle accepts the "spacecraft hypothesis" of UFOs, he did not begin his professional life as a believer. But in 1949, when he (and a companion) witnessed a UFO Sprinkle could not explain, his attitude changed from, as he put it, "'scoffer' to that of 'skeptic.'" A second encounter, in 1965, turned the skeptical Sprinkle into an "unwilling believer."

Sprinkle has studied thousands of UFO accounts, and interviewed hundreds of witnesses and contactees. His use of hypnotherapy has allowed him to discern a link between contactees, reincarnation, and past lives.

Like many other UFOlogists with relevant educational backgrounds, Sprinkle is an advocate of codified, structured UFO investigation; he has urged the establishment of an international and/or national study center, "for continuous formal investigation of the physical, biological, psycho-social, and spiritual implications of UFO phenomena." Ideally, such a center would harness the expertise of people trained in astronomy, medicine, military affairs, law, politics, theology, mathematics, and other disciplines.

Notable book: *Soul Samples: Personal Explorations in Reincarnation and UFO Experiences.*

Peter Sturrock (b. 1924): Retired Stanford professor of physics and applied physics who has high-level associations with the American Astronomical Society, the Society for Scientific Exploration, and the Royal Astronomical Society. Sturrock is British, and earned his doctorate at Cambridge University. During World War

II he worked on the development of radar. He subsequently participated in British atomic energy research, and began his teaching career at Stanford after coming to that school to do microwave research. Today, he heads the Sturrock Solar Research Group at Stanford, where he and international collaborators explore solar neutrino flux, and muon and electron neutrinos.

The beauty of Sturrock's presence in the UFO community is that he is neither believer nor non-believer; he functions as a scientist. His group's 1998 report did not satisfy every UFO enthusiast: the scientists concluded, in fact, that "there was no convincing evidence pointing to . . . the involvement of extraterrestrial intelligence." A few mainstream critics pointed out that the study's funding came from the Society for Scientific Exploration, an organization with a propensity to give credibility to a variety of paranormal claims.

Notable books: *The UFO Enigma: A New Review of the Physical Evidence; A Tale of Two Sciences: Memoirs of a Dissident Scientist.*

Michael Swords (b. circa 1941): Retired natural science professor (Western Michigan University) and editor of *The Journal of UFO Studies* (with Robert Powell). Swords writes and speaks persuasively about U.S. government response to UFOs in the immediate postwar years, when Washington's interest in "national security" withered into carelessness and disinterest, allowing government UFO research to fall into an intellectual desert, where it become isolated and trivialized. This, Swords believes, suggests a great opportunity squandered.

In 2014, Swords precipitated a minor ruckus when he posted to his blog, *The Biggest Study*, a 1977 letter written by famed UFO abductee Betty Hill to UFO and hypno-regression researcher Ted Bloecher. In it, Betty Hill expressed great doubt about the application and value of hypnotic regression. Swords absorbed some angry criticism. The negative response seems unwarranted because Swords added very little comment to the letter, noting mainly that he had previously questioned the motives and techniques of untrained "abusers" of hypnotic technique.

Notable book: *UFOs and Government: A Historical Inquiry.*

Jacques Vallée (b. 1939): French computer scientist, high-tech-sector investor and venture capitalist, and leading UFO researcher-author. Vallée distinguished himself while an associate of J. Allen Hynek, codifying alien-encounter types that expanded on Hynek's famed "close encounters" register. In the 1960s, working with his wife, Janine, Vallée built the first UFO database. He holds degrees in mathematics, astrophysics (master's degree), and computer science (PhD). He has worked as an astronomer for NASA at MacDonald Observatory in Austin, Texas.

Vallée's scholarly interest in folklore encourages him to regard the familiar "extraterrestrial hypothesis" (ETH) as just one aspect of a larger tapestry of paranormal phenomena that includes physical evidence of elevated levels of consciousness, as well as demons, angels, and visitors from other dimensions. Religion (particularly apparitions that may actually have been UFOs) and cults also capture Vallée's attention. Alternatively, he suggests that UFOs may be natural phenomena, or even artificial—and if the latter, they could be manifestations of a higher consciousness that may or may not be extraterrestrial.

All of this indicates the wide framing of Vallée's thoughts—a desirable quality that nevertheless causes upset in ET-only segments of the UFO community. Some who are wedded to the ETH object because Vallée's ideas suggest an inbred human predilection to "see" things and interpret them falsely, or to otherwise react in ways that reveal the limits of perception when weighed against long-standing cultural landmarks. Vallée responds that much of the cultural "weight" of the UFO-ET link comes from a self-perpetuating idea rooted only partly in empirical reality: because ET enthusiasts receive attention and approval for their claims, subsequent witnesses are encouraged to "see" and report things that are similar and even, essentially, identical. When popular culture picks up certain UFO-related tropes—the big-head alien is one—witnesses and purported witnesses "know" what to see and report.

Vallée insists that UFOlogy must cultivate credible researchers. He also is vehement in his opposition to hypnotic regression, feeling that the therapists "are *creating* abductees under hypnosis." [emphasis added] As one might expect, his opinion puts Vallée at odds with a segment of the abduction sub-community.

Vallée inspired the ET-skeptical French scientist played by Francois Truffaut in Steven Spielberg's 1977 film *Close Encounters of the Third Kind*.

Notable books: *Anatomy of a Phenomenon: Unidentified Objects in Space—a Scientific Appraisal*; *Passport to Magonia: From Folklore to Flying Saucers*; *Messengers of Deception: UFO Contacts and Cults*; *Wonders in the Sky: Unexplained Aerial Objects from Antiquity to Modern Times* (with Chris Aubeck); *Dimensions: A Casebook of Alien Contact*.

Jean-Jacques Velasco (b. 1946): French optics expert long involved with the state-run National French Center for Space Studies (CNES), and a key player in sober, government-sponsored investigation of UFOs. As early as 1977, when he joined the new group GEPAN (Group Study of Unidentified Air Phenomena, a subgroup of CNES), Velasco studied the optics at play in specific UFO sightings, and then designed an instrument that reconstituted the optic stimuli experienced by the witnesses—in effect, an early form of virtual reality. He finds particular value in credible witness accounts that can be mated to radar records, which is the case in about 20 percent of reports made by pilots. Velasco also studies physical traces left by UFOs: marked or otherwise disturbed earth; burns and other changes to trees and ground cover; and anomalous trace metals.

Leadership of GEPAN fell to Velasco in 1983, by which time the French government was already pushing for budget reductions. In 1988, GEPAN was superseded by another French project, SEPRA (Rare Aerospace Phenomena Study Department). SEPRA operated under the aegis of the CNES, only to be terminated in 2004. But the French government reactivated SEPRA in 2005, dissolving GEPAN and replacing that body with a new CNES subgroup, GEIPAN (Unidentified Aerospace Phenomenon Research and Information Group), headed by Jacques Patenet. Velasco shifted to the CNES and later retired.

Notable book: *Disorders in the Sky: UFO Evidence Provided by Radar*.

Fabio Pedro Alles Zerpa (b. 1928): Uruguay-born Argentinean stage, film, radio, and television actor, radio host, researcher, and entrepreneur. Zerpa is a colorful, confident figure whose interest in UFOs is one part of his broader preoccupation with the paranormal; he has lectured and written not only on unidentified flying objects but on Nostradamus, past-lives theory, government conspiracies, and hollow-Earth theory. Zerpa contends that pre-Columbian art reflects UFO activity in Latin America. He claims educations in psychology, anthropology, sociology, and parapsychology.

Zerpa saw his first UFO (which he describes as "an extraterrestrial ship") in 1959 while aboard an Argentinean Air Force plane above Morón, Argentina, a dozen miles west of Buenos Aires. Nine years later, Zerpa organized the first Argentinean conference on extraterrestrial life, at the University of Buenos Aires.

Since the late 1980s, Zerpa has operated the Fabio Zerpa Foundation, providing "experiential workshops" in self-awareness, dream interpretation, past lives, and general paranormal studies. Zerpa also offers personal counseling that utilizes what he calls Quantum Sophrology, to help clients concentrate, overcome fears, and balance their physical, mental, and spiritual lives. (Sophrology is the study of relaxed, focused consciousness and the mind's influence on physical health.)

Zerpa's Web site identifies him as "Prof. Zerpa."

The foundation has an offshoot created by Zerpa in 1990, the Argentine Center for the Study of Anomalous Phenomena (CAEFA). Local UFOlogists wishing to conduct field research must, according to Zerpa, join CAEFA.

Notable book: *UFOs and Underground Cities.*

UFO Organizations

At this writing, at least fifty UFO-study organizations are active in the United States. A few, like MUFON and CUFOS, have national and international reach, that is, they make use of active investigator-members on the ground abroad. Others, such as the Cleveland UFOlogy Project and Hoosier State UFO Research, are active locally or regionally. Membership numbers vary, from mere handfuls of people to thousands.

The Internet allows even the smallest group a virtual international platform, with online forums, interviews, book discussion, and other remote interaction. Still, the social, meet-and-greet aspect of membership—whether via informal get-togethers (a Baltimore UFO group cheerfully calls them "meet-ups") or structured conferences—is what gives UFO organizations their energy and ability to grow. Informal meetings and other small-group get-togethers allow members to relax and share stories and ideas.

MUFON and other large organizations sponsor annual, multiday conferences featuring guest speakers, discussion panels, seminars, book signings, film and video screenings, tech study, skywatching, activism tutorials, and opportunities for UFOlogists to meet and network. Dinners and cocktail parties are common.

UFO organizations based abroad, and of significant size and activity, number well over fifty.

Eyes Only: Key USA UFO Groups

Large UFO organizations with national reach, and smaller groups with significant resources, are noted here.

Narrowly focused UFO research is carried out by state, regional, and local UFO organizations. Miami Valley UFO Society, for instance, investigates sightings in Ohio's Miami Valley area from headquarters in South Vienna, Ohio. Some organizations, such as the UNO UFO Study Group, maintain Web- or brokered-radio broadcasts, and podcasts.

- **Center for the Study of Extraterrestrial Intelligence (CSETI)/The Disclosure Project**: These linked, semi-autonomous organizations founded in 1990 by Steven M. Greer focus on extraterrestrial activity, peaceful interaction with ETs, and issues of national and world security. As the "Disclosure Project" name suggests, the center presses governments, government agencies, and politicians for honest UFO information.

  CSETI has had semi-official interactions with Congress, though the group's calls for UFO hearings have not been acted on. The organizations' links to the CIA, or to past and present CIA agents, remain a point of discussion in the UFO community.

  A minor kerfuffle erupted in 2011, when Greer and CSETI were charged with "operating a commercial venture on a national wildlife refuge." The venture was a nighttime CSETI sky-watch and training session held at Cape Hatteras National Seashore on North Carolina's Outer Banks. CSETI responded by saying that it had done nothing to compromise its longtime status as a 501c3 nonprofit.

- **Florida UFO Network**: Florida "Big Bend"-region investigations group established in 1991, and based in the Tallahassee metro area, at Havana, Florida. The group emphasizes proper scientific investigation, and "condemns New Age concepts and UFO cults." It solicits accounts of UFO sightings while taking a dim view of the friendly-alien trope.

  Florida UFO Network has origins in the Long Island UFO Network, and devotes a portion of its Web home page to the Long Island group's former leader, John J. Ford. Ford has been held in a psychiatric facility since late 1997, after being declared unfit to stand trial for conspiracy to murder three Suffolk County, New York, officials that, Ford felt, covered up ET activity.

- **Fund for UFO Research (FUFOR)**: Since its establishment in 1979–80 by people formerly associated with NICAP, the nonprofit FUFOR has pursued scholarly research of "a phenomenon for which there is no conventional explanation." The group accepts an extraterrestrial explanation of the Roswell crash, and maintains that the U.S. government has an ongoing pattern of deception about that event and other UFO accounts.

  FUFOR regards abduction accounts as having physical, rather than psychological, underpinnings.

- **International Community for Alien Research (I.C.A.R.)**: Co-founded by engineering/avionics expert Joe Montaldo to fill gaps in existing UFO statistics and general information. I.C.A.R. maintains an active presence at UFO conferences in the USA and abroad; besides the United States, ten other nations are home to active I.C.A.R. members. (Some sources describe Montaldo as the group's founder rather than co-founder.)

Since the group's establishment, I.C.A.R. representatives have interviewed more than five thousand UFO contactees and victims of abduction. Information gleaned from those interviews is carefully collated and catalogued. I.C.A.R. also conducts research and publishes tables detailing contactee blood types, eye color, and other physical traits. It reports on the relationship of UFOs and civil defense, and is a proponent of the Drake Equation, formulated in 1961 by astronomer Dr. Frank Drake to estimate the existence of ten thousand "communicative civilizations" in the Milky Way.

Twenty-eight pages of the controversial *Majestic-12 Group Special Operations Manual* (see chapter eight) are available on the I.C.A.R. Web site. The site maintains a link to the Freedom of Information Act site. Montaldo's *UFO Undercover Radio* is regularly heard on Internet radio's LIVE 365 and SoundCloud.

Note: Another, more narrowly focused organization, The International Center for Abduction Research, also uses the ICAR acronym, but without the periods separating the letters.

- **International UFO Congress (IUFOC):** This Arizona-based organization dates to 1991, and is known for its elaborate annual conference-convention. Laughlin, Nevada, hosted the event until 2011, when Phoenix—a larger and more easily accessible city—became the venue.

  The event is known for its aggressive marketing and size—the *Guinness Book of World Records* recognizes the IUFOC get-together as the largest UFO conference in the world. The 2016 event stretched across five days in February at We-Ko-Pa Resort & Conference Center in Scottsdale, Arizona, with more than thirty speakers, panels, sky-watching, vendors, film screenings, cocktail parties, dinners, and a banquet.

  The owner-organizer, Open Minds Production LLC, emphasizes that the conference is attended by NASA scientists and other similarly credentialed people, and is not a sideshow event. Nevertheless, a writer with the snarky BuzzFeed news and gossip Web site prefaced his picture coverage of the February 2015 event with "I was on a mission to find me some aliens."

- **J. Allen Hynek Center for UFO Studies (CUFOS):** Chicago-area group dedicated to serious academic study of UFOs, founded in 1973 by the late Northwestern University astronomy professor Hynek. He disliked the fringe element involved in UFOlogy, and made clear time and again that the center's mission was "to end a quarter century of misrepresentation and buffoonery."

  From the day he founded the center, Hynek took pains to avoid mentioning CUFOS and Northwestern in the same breath; the university did not care to be linked to a "flying saucer" group, and never officially recognized the center's work. The center's office space is not on university property.

  Directed now by astrophysicist Mark Rodeghier, CUFOS depends on volunteers to keep the office open to researchers; some five hundred volunteer associates across the country work from their homes, gathering files and news stories, and doing physical investigation of promising sightings. The enormous CUFOS information archive goes back to the 1940s; scholars can access it on a computer database called UFOCAT.

A recent CUFOS mandate, the Abduction Monitoring Project, sends researchers to abduction sites, to measure magnetic fields and other, possible physical traces of UFOs. But that work, and the rest of the center's agenda, is compromised by modest funding, a continual problem. The center publishes a quarterly magazine, *The International UFO Reporter*, and an academic annual, *The Journal of UFO Studies*.

- **Mutual UFO Network (MUFON):** This very active California-based nonprofit, founded in 1969 by chemistry professor Allen Utke, Motorola operations manager Walt Andrus, and aerospace engineer John Schuessler, collects UFO data and conducts on-site investigations around the world. MUFON has a membership of about three thousand. Each of the fifty states has an active chapter, and chapters are also maintained in American Samoa, Guam, the Northern Mariana Islands, Puerto Rico, and the U.S. Virgin Islands. Chapters exist in thirty-six other nations. Many members are well established in astronomy, physics, metallurgy, and other hard sciences.

The present executive director is Jan Harzan, a nuclear engineer who worked more than thirty years in IBM's information technology business.

The organization has three stated goals: to investigate UFO reports, promote UFO research, and educate the public. Every month, MUFON receives five hundred to a thousand reports from around the world. The organization gives investigative training to aspiring field investigators, who become qualified to travel to sites, collect data, and help with later evaluation.

UFO JOURNAL

March 2016   No. 575 $5

Remote Canadian site

American hunters encounter multiple 'dumbell' UFOs

EDITOR'S NOTE: Indiana MUFON State Section Director Philip Leech was approached in late 2015 by Case # 74282 Reporting Witness #1 - an Indiana state resident who had a UFO experience during a 2013 Canadian bear hunting trip. Witnesses #2 and #3 declined to be interviewed – although Witness #3 did make a video statement for us. Director of Research Robert Powell also submitted questions for the video interview. Witness #1 tells the story here about what happened in his own words. The video interview between Leech and Witnesses #1 and #3 in silhouette to protect identities will be posted on our website at mufon.com soon. A few of Powell's questions are embedded into this story in bold type.

August 2013, Ontario, Canada
6:45 p.m.

Part One

Having sat in the hunting stand since 4 p.m. I was becoming restless and the bugs were starting to pester me significantly, yet I drew breath quietly and persisted against the bugs in hopes of seeing a bear tonight.

CGI rendition of UFO from Witness #1.

6:55 p.m.

Black bear sighted and comes directly into my bait site to feed. I video the bear with my Sony DSC-TX1 Cybershot camera for a total of 12 minutes and then dispatch the bear with my rifle. After waiting 10 minutes I climb down from my stand and confirm the bear's final location and condition, all the while snapping pictures and taking additional site video. I made a mental note that the battery level was indi-

cating 41 minutes of camera time left - enough to video additional footage should another hunter in our party be successful.

I climb back into the tree stand to wait the two hours until pickup by the outfitter of the hunt and owner of the resort.

I watch a beautiful sunset from the tree stand through the trees and snap a

Continued on page 11

FEATURED NEWS

MUFON Symposium 2016: Orlando

Orlando, Florida, is the destination city for the 2016 MUFON Symposium hosted by Florida State Director Morgan Beall with the theme, "UFOs: From our Oceans to Outer Space." Enjoy Hilton Lake Buena Vista Hotel at Disney August 26-28 with Field Investigator training August 25.

Watch for a dedicated website soon listing the Keynote Speaker and all speaker topics. Some speakers include: Richard Hoffman on the Aguadilla Puerto Rico USO Case; Richard Thieme on Why People Can't Think Seriously About UFOs; and Robert Powell with the Top 10 Cases of 2015.

STATS BAR - February 10, 2016 - UFO Report Totals		
World Wide = 687	United States = 502	Under 500 feet = 234
Entities Reported = 56	Highest Shape Reported = Sphere, 129	Highest Reporting Country = United States
Highest Reporting State = California, 65	2016 To-Date Worldwide = 900	2016 To-Date Cases Closed as Unknown = 51

Since its establishment in 1969, the Mutual UFO Network (MUFON) has been a dynamic force in UFO investigation, research, and public education. The glossy and interactive MUFON Web site offers daily UFO reports, historical information, and news about such ancillary subjects as Bigfoot, alien abduction, and implants. *Courtesy of MUFON*

The key investigative aim is to discern "what is truly an unknown." MUFON estimates that 75 to 80 percent of cases are resolved as IFOs—identified flying objects. Information on thousands of cases is available via easy online access to the group's vast database.

In relatively recent years, the parent organization, as well as state and local chapters, have expanded reportage and research of Men in Black, crop circles, ancient astronauts, time travel, Bigfoot, Chupacabra, animal mutilations, and alternate dimensions.

MUFON sponsors an elaborate and informative national annual conference, as well as local and regional gatherings. Organization members receive a monthly print-and-Web magazine, *MUFON UFO Journal.*

- **National UFO Reporting Center (NUFORC)**: Although modestly funded, this organization, founded in 1974 by firefighter Robert Gribble, is one of the premier repositories of up-to-date UFO sightings. In addition, NUFORC maintains a UFO clip file dating to the late 19th century. NUFORC data have provided invaluable insights into patterns of UFO sightings, such as location, density, time of day, topography, weather conditions, physical states of the witnesses, and more. Government knowledge of UFOs is also investigated.

  Reports of new sightings are welcome, though NUFORC warns that "funny" or obvious hoax reports will be discarded. Since its inception, the group has maintained a twenty-four-hour hotline to take initial information about sightings. In recent years, the hotline has fielded some twenty thousand calls annually.

  Gribble handed directorship of NUFORC to Peter Davenport in 1994. Originally based at Gribble's home in Seattle, NUFORC headquarters moved to a refurbished missile silo outside of Spokane in 2006.

- **Project 1947**: Although carrying a name suggestive of Roswell, this Connecticut-based, volunteer-driven UFO investigatory organization concerns itself with primary documents reflecting the full range of international UFO incidents from what the group calls "the 1947 wave"; and, secondarily, documents pertaining to UFO accounts from 1900 to 1946; and, thirdly, 1948 to 1965. Documents most desired by Project 1947 are official UFO memos and reports, newspaper accounts, and credible personal accounts. The group takes full advantage of the Freedom of Information Act.

  At this writing, Project 1947 is excited about fresh documentation of American pilots' encounters with UFOs during the Korean War.

  Many documents uncovered by Project 1949 are accessible on the organization's Web site. These come from various years between 1909 and 1928, and 1943–55.

- **Starborn Support**: Abductee-support group founded in Maine by twins Audrey and Debbie Hewins. A dozen chapters can be found along the East Coast, from New England to Florida. Chapters are also located in the United Kingdom and Latin America.

  The group reaches out not just to abductees, but to persons who have seen UFOs, and those who have had extraterrestrial contact of any sort.

A twenty-four-hour hotline is available for reporting and counseling.

Because "Experiencer" events can be isolating, Starborn Support sponsors an annual "Experiencers Speak" conference, and encourages discussion on its Facebook page.

Eyes Only: Key International UFO Groups

UFO organizations cover the world, from India to South Africa, and Latvia to New Zealand. In all, some forty nations are home to UFOlogy groups of consequence. Here are groups—some UFO-only in orientation, others more broadly focused—based outside the USA that have especially broad reach and useful mandates.

- **Aerial Phenomena Research Association of Ireland**: (Ireland) Research and investigation; special emphasis on Irish cases.
- **Anomaly Researchers UK**: (United Kingdom) Yorkshire-based investigatory group that studies all manner of skyborne anomalies: saucers, glowing lights, and black triangles, plus aliens, abductions, and cattle mutilations. Mounts regular field trips to notable UFO sites around the UK.
- **Associacao Pesquisa Ovni**: (Portugal) Studies latest sightings, abductions, and astronomy; special emphasis on Portuguese cases.
- **Association for the Study of Unidentified Aerospace Phenomena**: (Romania) Established 1989. Nonprofit, science-based investigatory body; special emphasis on Romanian cases.
- **Association Québécoise d'Ufologie**: (Canada) Photo and video analysis, UFO news, science news.
- **Astrotruth**: (India) Strongly science-based emphasis on astronomy, astrophysics, and space propulsion. No interest in the paranormal.
- **Australian Close Encounter Research Network** (ACERN; Australia) Research and therapeutics organization that provides counseling and health support for UFO contactees. Secondary interest in past lives, hypnotic regression, channeling, and government cover-ups.
- **Australian UFO Research Network**: (AUFORN; Australia) Nonprofit established 1998. Active investigative teams across Australia.
- **Beta-UFO**: (Indonesia) Established 1997 to study UFO accounts, abduction reports, and photographs.
- **British UFO Research Association**: (BUFORA; United Kingdom) Sightings-report clearinghouse that does investigations, investigator training, and photo analysis.
- **Centro Ufologico Nazionale:** (CUN; Italy) Investigations and conferences.
- **Committee of Studies of Anomalous Aerial Phenomena**: (CEFAA; Chile) Strongly science-based investigatory body that operates under the aegis of Chile's Directorate General of Civil Aeronautics.
- **Consciousness Development and Research Group**: (Australia) Personal-consciousness development as it relates to C-5 encounters with ETs (mutual, bilateral communication).

- **DEGUFO e.V.**: (Germany) Objective, science-based body that investigates UFO reports in Germany and other German-speaking parts of the European Union. Maintains global archives of UFO sightings and research.
- **Drustvo za Ufoloska i Astroarheoloska Istrazivanja Polaris**: (Croatia) Studies developments in astronomy, UFO cases past and present, and ancient astronauts.
- **Dubai Research Congregation**: (Dubai, United Arab Emirates) Wide-ranging pursuits include UFOs, crop circles, ancient civilizations, portals and gateways, telepathy, healing, secret societies, and meditation.
- **Exopolitics UK**: (United Kingdom) UFO study group with an exopolitical emphasis that incorporates a political and policy mindset into extraterrestrial studies. As with other exopolitical groups, Exopolitics UK assumes that ET life and contact are facts, at least until proof to the contrary surfaces. The organization is preoccupied with government conspiracies and cabals funded by so-called "black budgets."
- **Extra-Terrestrial Association**: (South Africa) Founded 1995 to "research extra-terrestrial activity in South Africa and the African continent."
- **Fundación Anomalía**: (Spain) First European foundation dedicated to UFO research; considerable group research involves disclosure issues related to the Spanish government and aerodynamics.
- **Groupe de Recherche et d'Etude des Phenomenes Insolites**: (GREPI; Switzerland) French-language Swiss group positioned to appeal to longtime UFOlogists as well as newcomers. The organization successfully reinterprets vintage UFO sightings. Secondary interest: UFOs and links to American presidents.
- **Grupo UFOlógico de Guarujá**: (GUG; Brazil) Established in the early 1980s as a self-described "grass roots investigation group." GUG has uncovered and studied UFO cases informed by direct involvement of the Brazilian military (local cases) and military branches around the globe—branches that have been slow to be candid about years of sightings.
- **Hong Kong UFO Club**: (China) Well-funded group, established in 1996 to investigate UFO reports via seminars, film viewings, and independent study. Particular interest in ancient astronauts and the United States' role in UFO reports. The group hosts the biannual HK International UFO Congress.
- **Independent Network of UFO Researchers**: (INUFOR; Australia) Established in 1989 as an outreach group that offers investigation and support to UFO witnesses. INUFOR develops researchers that work in concert with counterparts from other Australian groups, and groups located abroad.
- **International Development Research Centre**: (Ukraine) Investigatory group that studies declassified USSR and Ukraine government documents and accounts of abductees. Members have a special interest in accounts of past lives, particularly when the past lives are alien.
- **Klub Psychotroniky a UFO, o.s.**: (KPUFO; Czech Republic) Self-described "non-political" paranormal investigations group with a broad range of interests: UFOs, ancient astronauts, and alternative medicine. The group invites written UFO testimonials. Since 1994, KPUFO has sponsored more than

twenty UFO expeditions to France, Austria, Malta, Italy, England, Scotland, the Republic of Ireland, Peru, Indonesia, and Egypt. Publisher of the *ZAZ Journal.*

- **Klub Psychotroniky a UFO v Slovenskej Republike**: (KPUFO.SK; Slovak Republic) Studies UFO accounts past and present, ancient astronauts, "mysterious places," and crop circles. Publishes *Azimut Záhad* (*Azimuth Mysteries*).

- **Leicestershire Unidentified Flying Object Investigation Network**: (LUFOIN; United Kingdom) UFO research organization, established 1969 to focus on sightings in the Leicestershire and Warwickshire regions of the UK dating from 1706 to the present. LUFOIN maintains an impressive archive of relevant UFO reports from that considerable span of time. The group solicits new UFO reports from its own geographical bailiwick, and from abroad. Secondary areas of study: UK crop circles and international ghost reports.

- **London UFO Studies**: (LUFOS; United Kingdom) Established 1995 to "fully investigate and evaluate" UFO sightings across the UK. Much of the group's attention is commanded by abductions, human and animal mutilations, and, especially, "grays."

- **Nautilus Foundation**: (Poland) Photo and video analysis, and discussion of abductions and implants; plus ancient astronauts, astrology, numerology, conspiracy theory, antigravity, Nostradamus, ecology and climate change, Bigfoot, and Chupacabra.

- **NLO Srbija**: (Serbia) Investigates and discusses UFO sightings in Serbia dating to the 1970s. Reports also on close encounters of the fifth kind, and abductions.

- **The Phenix Project**: (France) aka The Phenix Project for Humanity, established to discover and understand ancient extraterrestrial artifacts on Earth. The organization's hope is that concerted research will lead to new energy sources. The group actively solicits money for "fundamental research" from individuals and businesses willing to be "investors, partners, sponsors, and donors."

- **Puerto Rico UFO Network**: (PRUFON; Puerto Rico) Established in 2009 to conduct "no nonsense" UFO investigation in Puerto Rico and across the Caribbean. The abduction phenomenon is a key area of interest.

- **Russian UFO Research Station**: (RUFORS; Russia) Founded in 1996 as a clearinghouse for news about UFOs and lost civilizations, and to encourage UFO-related scientific tourism. In 2002, the group urged President Putin to authorize the release of non-secret UFO-related government documents.

- **Sirius UFO Space Sciences Research Center**: (Turkey) Investigative organization established in 1998 to study witness reports, and UFO photographs and videos. The group remained very busy during 2001–02, when Turkey was swept by a wave of UFO sightings. Sirius founded the Istanbul UFO Museum in 2001.

- **SOS Ovni Belgique**: (Belgium) Interdisciplinary UFO data collection and analysis group that works with consultants schooled in astronomy, biology, acoustics, and materials analysis.

- **Strange Phenomena Investigations**: (United Kingdom) Founded in 1979, and active in government-disclosure efforts.

- **Study Group of Anomalous Aerospace Phenomena**: (GEFAA; Brazil) Investigative group with a Brazilian emphasis on UFOs; little or no activity pertaining to the paranormal. This is a science-based organization that maintains a unit of field investigators that utilizes spectroscopic technology to assist in study of discrete cases.
- **Skandinavisk UFO Information**: (SUFOI; Denmark) Established in 1957 to promote UFOs as extraterrestrial spaceships, SUFOI later altered its mission after questioning the accuracy of eyewitness accounts. The group now researches *explainable* UFO sightings. SUFOI published a magazine, *UFO-Nyt*, from 1958 to 2010, when it became Web-exclusive.
- **Suomen Ufotutkijat**: (FUFORA; Finland) The Finnish UFO Research Association has emphasized "critical thinking and open-mindedness" since its founding in 1973. The group has no predigested central opinion about UFOs; rather, it simply follows the evidence, case by case. FUFORA also educates and trains UFO researchers from across Finland.
- **UFO and Paranormal Research Society of Australia**: (UFO-PRSA; Australia) Founded in 2000 to follow "a multi-disciplinary approach covering everything possible under the Paranormal [*sic*] banner." Conducts field investigations of reported sightings and abductions. Interested also in psychic abilities, cryptozoology, and ghosts.
- **UFOBC**: (Canada) Nonprofit registered with British Columbia, dedicated to on-site investigation of local UFO sightings. Particular areas of interest: abductions, animal mutilations, crash retrieval, and crop circles.
- **UFOCUS NZ Research Network**: (New Zealand) Investigative and research body that offers support for contactees. The group's activities are informed by an objective, scientific approach. Special attention is given to UFOs that compromise the safety of New Zealand airspace and reports that coincide with volcanoes and other seismic activity.
- **UFO Experience Support Association**: (UFOESA; Australia) Research and support-group organization headed by a male abductee who encountered two humanoid women during an abduction and was sexually abused.
- **UFO-Finland**: (Finland) Helsinki-based research and investigation group founded in 1999 to encourage witness and contactee investigation, in Finland and abroad.
- **UFOlats**: (Latvia) Latvian-centric organization that looks at UFOs in the context of new developments in astronomy and aviation. Interested also in folklore and cryptozoology.
- **UFO-Norge**: (Norway) Established 1973 to "collect, process, and study all available information on UFOs in Norway." Although receptive to a variety of hypotheses, the group is dedicated to science and the scientific method.
- **UFO Report**: (Japan) Clearinghouse for UFO reports gathered from around the world.
- **UFO Research (NSW) Incorporated**: (Australia) Public group established in Sydney in 1991 to develop public-sponsored UFO investigation and "promote a greater understanding of all aspects of the UFO phenomenon." Sites in

Sydney's CBD (central business district) host monthly public meetings and film nights.

- **UFO Research of South Africa**: (UfoRSA; South Africa) Founded in 2011 to encourage mainstream discussion of South African UFO events.
- **UFO Research Queensland Inc.**: (Australia) Nonprofit organization established 1956 "to receive, record, and research UFO sightings." The group works from the premise that unexplained UFOs are piloted by extraterrestrials.
- **UFO-Sweden**: (Sweden) Sweden-wide group dating to 1970, with links to more than two dozen local and regional Swedish UFO organizations. UFO-Sweden maintains an active partnership with various official Swedish agencies, including the Swedish Defense Research Agency, and keeps the Archives for UFO Research. With thousands of books and more than thirteen thousand case histories, UFO-Sweden's UFO archive is the largest in Europe.
- **UFO Werkgroep Nederland**: (The Netherlands) Compiles the latest news, and maintains a UFO-news archive going back to 2000.
- **Victorian UFO Action**: (Australia) On-site investigative group, UFO-news clearinghouse, and abductee-support group, founded in 2010.
- **Welsh UFO Research Network**: (WUFORN; Wales) Disclosure-activist group that petitions the Welsh and larger UK governments to open UFO files, in order for the public to know the truth about UFO incidents in Wales and elsewhere in the United Kingdom. The group is presently working its way through some nine thousand pages of declassified Ministry of Defence UFO documents.

2

Possible Shapes and Forms of Intelligent Extraterrestrial Life

Well, You Look a Little Peculiar Yourself!

In 1951, the brilliant science fiction illustrator Edd Cartier created a remarkable gallery of extraterrestrials for presentation as color plates in a hardcover, multiauthor story collection called *Travelers of Space*. The anthology came from Gnome Press, one of the legendary postwar publishers of high-quality science fiction. The imprint was owned by David Kyle, and Cartier's illustrations accompanied a wry Kyle story called "The Interstellar Zoo." (The tale's premise, that intelligent extraterrestrials volunteer for limited stays at Earth zoos, to foster better understanding between species, unfolds like a museum catalogue expressed in dialogue, as a mother and her two young children tour the exhibits and remark on each creature.) The sixteen color plates illustrating "The Interplanetary Zoo" are truly, deeply alien: a bulge-eyed, upright worm with a serrated chest plate above an arched lower body edged with graceful, fin-like papillomata; a floating, bifurcated bag of gas suspending a closely massed cluster that looks like grapes but is, unnervingly, probably an array of sex organs; an ambulatory mushroom sporting an attractively contoured trunk and topside sense organs reminiscent of insect legs; a vaguely humanoid horror (complete with rakish cowl piece and quasi-military tunic) supported by reverse-jointed legs and arms, and an outsized head with angry, bulged eyes. The creature's combination nose-mouth is adorned with plump cilia. Cartier's imagination went on like this, one fanciful invention after another, the creatures incorporating all the rainbow's colors and looking as juicy and squeezable as water-filled soft rubber.

Cartier's aliens were uniquely his own, of course, but the artist was firmly grounded in the SF-pulp tradition of BEMs: bug-eyed monsters. Good-natured repulsiveness was integral to Cartier's bag of tricks, and that sort of approach has typified much of our speculation about the physical natures of extraterrestrials. For every winsomely slender, doe-eyed alien in the *Close Encounters* style, we have imagined whole armies of beings with angry mouths, insectoid bodies, and bulged brains.

Popularly accepted notions of alien physiognomy come from sources as diverse as stone-mask makers of pre-Columbian Mexico, EC Comics artist Wallace Wood, Dutch painter Hieronymus Bosch, moviemakers, and the aforementioned pulp artists of the 1930s and '40s. When illustrator Howard V. Brown painted the cover of the June 1933 issue of *Astounding Stories*, he depicted extraterrestrials with enlarged heads, oversized eyes, and small, slit-like mouths—what UFOlogist Michael Grosso characterized as anticipating the "fetus-like" conceptions popularized after World War II. Grosso has written smartly about what he calls these aliens, and their peculiar appeal: startling in their strangeness, yet sympathetic because they evoke starving children.

All Shapes, Colors, and Sizes

Among the most frequently reported alien types are **grays** (short, spindly, big-eyed creatures that have been the dominant ET form for some seventy years); **insectoids** (fictionalized most famously in the novel/film *Starship Troopers*); **reptilians** (an intimidating, shape-shifting form also called draconians, saurians, lizard people, and, less commonly, reptoids and reptoloids); **nordic** (friendly blond aliens, sometimes called Pleiadians; tall, handsome, and sturdy, they brim with wisdom); **Andromedans** (creatures of pure energy that can nevertheless assume roughly

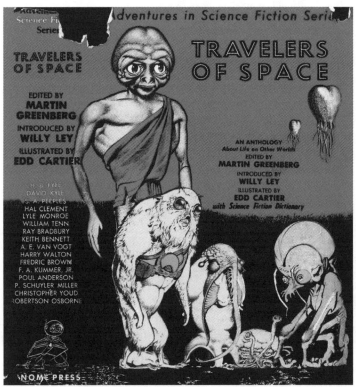

The fulsome imagination of science fiction and fantasy illustrator Edd Cartier culminated in compelling speculations about intelligent extraterrestrial life. This is Cartier's jacket art for *Travelers of Space*, a 1951 anthology from Gnome Press.

humanoid shapes); and the venerable **little green men** (pint-sized, bulge-brained visitors à la *Invasion of the Saucer-Men* and *Mars Attacks!*).

Some other, less common alien types are reported often enough to be noted here: the diminutive **hairy dwarves** (unpleasant and unprepossessing creatures, famously reported across Venezuela in 1954 and in Essex, England, in 1974); **sirians** (aquatic or amphibious types in humanoid form); **cryptids** (folkloric and quasi-folkloric creatures, particularly those of the Bigfoot variety [such as the "Missouri monster" Momo and the Australian Outback's Yowie] that encourage identification as extraterrestrial forms); and **dropa** (aliens that left small stone glyphs in China more than ten thousand years ago; the book *Sungods in Exile*, David A. Gamon's 1980 account of an expedition to locate and decipher the glyphs, was exposed as Gamon's little joke).

Variations and sub-classifications of major forms pop up as **Arcturians** (grays, except that they are blue); **sirian-human hybrids** (fashion-model beautiful); **essassani** (benevolent, physically attractive beings that are a complex hybridization of humans, grays, and reptilians); and **yahyel** (another hybrid species, described by one metaphysical Web site—and rather disappointingly—as a "gorgeous and graceful" species with "the appearance of an angelic anime character").

Of the countless comic book artists who have illustrated science-fiction stories, few have approached Wally Wood's vigorous and highly detailed concepts of extraterrestrial visitors. As is apparent on the 1951 cover of EC Comics' *Weird Science* No. 9, Wood reveled in the ET "ook factor," depicting the visitors as physically hideous and, usually, nefarious.   *Courtesy of William M. Gaines, Agent, Inc.*

Like Us? Not Likely

Biologists and other scientists frequently scoff at conceptions of intelligent extraterrestrial life that exhibit elements of the human form. The odds against alien life evolving along lines similar to our own are long, at best. It is more likely that intelligent extraterrestrial life looks nothing like us at all. The alien physiognomy may startle us. It may even repulse us, or trigger an atavistic urge to flee from it, or to destroy it. The familiar variations on the bilaterally symmetrical humanoid that walks upright—whether gray, scaly, or handsomely blond—invite charges of the narrow self-absorption that defines our fascination with monkeys and apes, and our representations of "ourselves" in dolls, puppets, and art. We are compelled to create those humanlike representations because of innocent arrogance, and because we need reassurance that our form is *the* form.

Because early humans had no conception of "star" or "planet," they had no impression of "other planets." When they thought about other intelligences, they thought of nonhuman things, such as rocks suffused with magical power, and unseen agents—particularly deities—that controlled the wind and the sea and other aspects of the natural world that were observed and experienced. The notion of extraterrestrial intelligence had still to evolve.

By the fifth century BC, the Greek philosopher Anaxagoras declared his belief that the Earth and Moon shared some physical properties. From there, the supposition of other Earthlike worlds was not a major leap. Because Anaxagoras had suggested the Moon had inhabitants, later thinkers wondered about intelligent, humanlike life on other planets.

In 165 AD, the Greek writer Lucian of Samosata issued *A True History*, a fanciful journey to the Moon via a violent whirlwind. The tale describes a universe filled with worlds populated by intelligent humans.

The Mars Craze

Fanciful tales about exotic-appearing Moon creatures found popularity with newspaper readers during the 19th century. The papers liked them as well, because they boosted circulation and encouraged readers to invoke the newspapers when discussing, for instance, the regal, bat-winged inhabitants of the Moon.

By the second half of the century, scientists had a better understanding of the kinetic nature of gases, and the particular properties that hold Earth's atmosphere in place. This knowledge put an end to scientific speculation about life on the Moon, a body with neither the size nor gravitational pull to maintain an atmosphere. In 1901, the estimable H. G. Wells sidestepped the atmosphere issue in his novel *The First Men in the Moon*, a hearty adventure involving intelligent beings that live in an atmosphere maintained *below* the Moon's surface.

Later, Wells's speculative magazine serial/novel *The War of the Worlds* (1897–98) diverted public attention to the planet Mars. It was from that planet, Wells wrote in the book, that Earth's affairs were "watched keenly and closely by intelligences greater than man's. . . ."

Wells's tales revived interest in Martian *canali* (channels), which had been claimed by Italian astronomer Giovanni Schiaparelli in 1877. Because Americans translated "canali" as "canals," laypersons eager to assume the existence of a great (or once-great) Martian civilization . . . assumed it. In 1926, American astronomers Carl Lampland and William Coblentz deduced that temperatures at Mars's equator rose as high as thirty-two degrees Fahrenheit, and even as high as seventy-seven. But Mars, they said, grew cold overnight, with equatorial temperatures at dawn as frigid as minus-150 Fahrenheit. Further, the thinness of the Martian atmosphere allowed fatal levels of ultraviolet light to reach the planet's surface. Despite this solid science, Mars and Martians continued to exercise a hold on the public imagination. If alien life was going to come from anywhere, it was going to come from Mars.

Partly because of Orson Welles's October 30, 1938, *War of the Worlds* radio broadcast (see chapter fifteen), popular interest in Mars ran high. Throughout the 1940s, comic books, radio plays, pulp magazines, and movie serials suggested Martian life. Ray Bradbury's elegant 1950 short story collection *The Martian Chronicles* crossed over into the literary mainstream, and helped spark popular notions about Mars exploration, a dying Martian race, and colonization of Mars by Earthlings—who become the new Martians.

American and Russian Mars probes undertaken beginning in 1962 reached a peculiar climax in the early 1990s, when British researcher David Percy studying Mars photographs was struck by an image of what appeared to be a five-sided pyramid located southeast of a cratered boulder field Percy called "the city." So that the pyramidal shape might be easily discerned, Percy overlaid the photographic image with a precisely drawn polygon, with five lines radiating from the pyramid's peak to the junctions of the five sides, creating a star within a polygon that looks like an elongated version of Chrysler Corporation's venerable Pentastar logo. Because he imposed order on the Martian pyramidal structure, Percy felt free to infer that the configuration was an intelligently engineered pyramid. Based on this and similarly manipulated evidence, Percy fell into some fallacies of weak inference, such as, "[I]t already seems established beyond reasonable doubt that Mars must once have been inhabited by sentient beings." Established by whom? Skeptics rightly pointed out that "pyramidal" is not the same as "pyramid," and that Percy's carefully drawn geometric lines amounted to calculated misrepresentation.

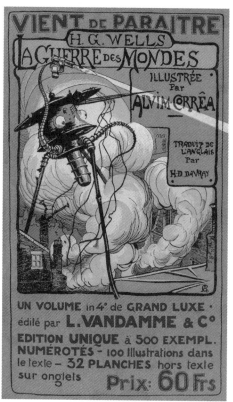

By the close of the 19th century, everyday speculation about the Moon had been superseded by curiosity about Mars. This French ad flyer for a 1906 full-text edition of H. G. Wells's 1897 serialized novel *The War of the Worlds* emphasizes the Martians' technology and violently acquisitive nature. Illustration by Henrique Alvim Corréa.

The Face

Discussion-provoking Martian news arrived via the successful American Viking 1 and Viking 2 orbiter-lander probes of 1976. In a photograph of Cydonia Mensae, a region peppered with mesas, there sat what appeared to be a mammoth, upturned humanoid face—with eyes deep in their sockets and a terse, implacable mouth. The effect of the sun on the Martian surface contributed to the eye-socket effect, and tiny black dots (visual evidence of unavoidable image dropout) seemed to express a hairline and a nostril.

Richard Hoagland, a science consultant temporarily associated with the Goddard Space Flight Center, claimed to be the first to see the face, which he identified (along with the pyramidal structures) as part of an enormous Martian monument. Because Hoagland lacked a university degree, and had pursued activities existing at the fringes of "legitimate" science, he was not taken seriously by the science establishment. Hoagland responded by naming NASA as party to a U.S. conspiracy to hide the truth about Mars. He subsequently turned the Martian face into a ticket to modest celebrity, which brought television and lecture appearances, and a book deal (*The Monuments of Mars*; 1987).

When support of the "face" theory came from the Yale-educated American astronomer Tom C. Van Flandern (who had a twenty-year professional relationship with the U.S. Naval Observatory), Hoagland's claim appeared to pick up some credibility. Van Flandern, though, was an inveterate controversialist, forever at odds with the astronomical establishment because of his alternative views on such things as the speed of gravity and the origins of the planets. Van Flandern persisted in his conclusion about the Martian face even after high-resolution photographs of the site became available in 2001.

Richard Hoagland built a small career on the Martian face and his theory of conspiracy, but lost steam in 1997, when the Mars Global Surveyor mapped the Cydonia region, and others, with unprecedented clarity. Photographs from the probe showed that the supposed pyramids were natural forms, and the famous face was an assemblage of rocks that had been massaged by shadows in 1976.

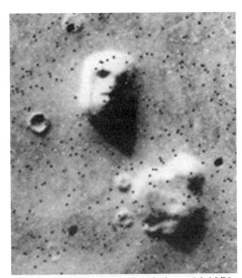

Wishful thinking continues, though. Early in 2015, a Mars rover photograph of Martian rock rubble purportedly revealed a Martian "book," a thick volume lying on its side amidst other rocks. Computer manipulation of random shadows by a person or group called the Mars Moon Space Photo Zoom Club "revealed" three neat columns of type on the book's "cover." This is how a random rock becomes a book. Despite acknowledging that the Zoom Club's computer manipulation "cleaned up" the image, altered colors, and *added detail* (emphasis added), a blogger on ufosightingsdaily.com enthused, "I bet the

NASA's Viking project of the mid-1970s sent back many fly-by photographs of Mars, including this image of the Cydonia Mensae region—complete with a mammoth, upturned humanoid face. Many laypersons, having come of age on such stuff as *Flying Disc Man from Mars* and *The Angry Red Planet*, eagerly embraced the image as proof of a Martian civilization. High-resolution photos of the site taken in 2001 show that the "face" had been a wishful interpretation of simple shadows.   *NASA* rover could drive right up to it and open that cover up easily as if it came right off a shelf."

Other recent claims about Martian rocks have invoked an ankh, a large dome, and "a little hut."

Modern Thoughts About Intelligent Life in Our Solar System

In order for life to establish itself and thrive, three things are necessary: free liquid (water is best); organic compounds; and energy, to build organic compounds from present molecules. Water (or water vapor) is a vehicle. Key organic compounds, and those that define all life as we understand it, are carbon, oxygen, and hydrogen, with lesser but significant amounts of sulfur, phosphorous, and nitrogen, plus trace amounts of dozens more. And what of the energy needed for life? The famed 1952 Miller-Urey experiment (conducted by University of Chicago graduate chemistry student Stanley Miller under the supervision of Harold Urey) placed a carefully considered mixture of water vapor, hydrogen gas, methane, and ammonia into a beaker. In a simulation of lightning coursing through the atmosphere of a primordial Earth, Miller sent an electric charge through the mixture. Within days, the beaker produced visible amino acids, which are essential to the creation of proteins. According to the Miller theorem, life begins, and continues, as a chemical process. Further, because the process can be started by things as common as lightning or element-rich volcanic eruptions, the beginnings of life are probably not unique to Earth. Although many—if not most—of the universe's planets have not produced life, the probability of extraterrestrial life is nevertheless high.

ALTRE SCOVERTE FATTE NELLA LUNA DAL SIG. HERSCHEL

Nineteenth-century speculation about life on the Moon inspired fanciful visualizations of what—and who—might reside there. This 1836 lithograph by Leopoldo Galluzzo reflects notions proposed by British astronomer John Herschel, and appeared in *Altre scoverte fatte nella luna dal Sigr. Herschel* (*Other Lunar Discoveries from Mr. Herschel*).

Molecules here on Earth developed from a coordination of amino acids, fatty acids, and sugars, which created nucleic acids that directed proteins to manufacture self-replicating cells. Although we understand the roles of the basic building blocks, the way in which proteins "got the message" remains a mystery. Further, human understanding of the specific types of early microorganisms is hazy at best. Still, we surmise that very simple forms of life, bacteria, evolved into other, more sophisticated forms. Assuming that bacteria developed and evolved on planets other than Earth, it is not unreasonable to suggest that sophisticated life forms exist (or have existed) elsewhere in the universe. Of course, a bacterium is a "sophisticated life form"; likewise an amoeba, a mold spore, and yeasts. There are no "simple life forms." Even the humblest-seeming form of life is incredibly complex. And when we turn our attention to plant life, marine life, animal life, and to ourselves, we are in realms of almost unimaginable complexity.

Other planets of our solar system hold only modest promise of any life at all, and virtually none for intelligent life. Although the giant planets of the outer solar system—Jupiter, Saturn, Uranus, and Neptune—are enormous contrasted to Earth (even the smallest of the giants, Neptune, is nearly four times the size of our planet), the giants have far less overall density, and are less massive than their sizes suggest. Little on these planets is solid. Jupiter, for instance, is mainly a swirl of liquid hydrogen. Because that liquid also contains water, ammonia, and methane, primitive bacteriological life could exist there. For more advanced life to germinate and take hold, however, a planet needs oceans (where life develops) and dry land (where life migrates and evolves). Even when we stretch the limits of speculation, and known science, to consider intelligent life on Jupiter and the other giants, the planets' lack of solid surfaces mandates the evolution of intelligent life quite different from ours—one, for instance, denied the capability to construct buildings or manufacture spaceships. Our solar system's other planets (including the dwarf planet, Pluto) are too hot or too cold to encourage life as we understand it.

Europa, a moon of Jupiter, has an ice-covered ocean that may support microbial life. Titan, the largest moon of Saturn, is the only satellite in our solar system to have a significant atmosphere. Life may have secreted itself there.

Perhaps the most compelling argument *against* intelligent life in our solar system is that the distances between planets are not great. (The enormous distance separating Earth from "Planet Nine" is another matter, and will be discussed in this book's afterword.) Communication from one party or another should already have been achieved. Instead, there is silence (other than random radio signals) from Earth's sister planets, and no visual evidence of agriculture, terraforming, or other intelligence-based alterations to the planets' surfaces or atmospheres. (Europa, its surface decorated with spidery red tracers, may be the exception.) The only possible sentient life is akin to the sort already discussed: a liquid, gaseous, or other form, lacking manufacturing capability. If such life exists in our solar system, evolution forces it to remain silent and unidentifiable, and almost certainly unaware that we are here.

Beyond Our Sun

The possibility of life of any sort appears more promising when we venture beyond our solar system. But consider: our galaxy is 100,000 light years across. A light year connotes distance: how far light travels in a year. As far as is known, nothing in the natural world is faster than light. And as we learn while young, light travels 186,000 miles per second, specifically, 186,282 mps. One light year, then, connotes a distance of 5,878,500,000,000 miles (5.9 trillion miles). Travel from one end of our galaxy to the other involves a distance of nearly six trillion miles *multiplied by 100,000*. The distance and time are unfathomable to human beings, frail creatures whose individual life spans run about eighty years.

Occasionally, Earthlike planets within our galaxy present themselves to us. In 2014, a 97.5-inch ground telescope at Spain's La Palma Island detected 55 Cancri e, an exoplanet with nearly eight times the mass of Earth, and twice its diameter. The continually sun-kissed side of 55 Cancri e develops temperatures as high as 3,000 degrees Fahrenheit—hot enough to melt iron. That's an unpromising environment for life, but if 55 Cancri e has hydrocarbons and organic chemicals, and if moderated temperatures outside the hot zone allow the planet to retain water, life there is not an impossibility. Future European and American study of 55 Cancri e will attempt to address those points.

NASA's Kepler spacecraft, as well as ceaseless study from the ground, suggests other Earthlike planets within our galaxy. But our Milky Way is not the only galaxy, of course. There are many others, and they are far away—so far away that the 100,000-light-year distance from one end of our galaxy to the other seems paltry by contrast. Andromeda, the galaxy closest to our own, is 2.2 million light years away. It is comprised of some 600 billion stars, but we have little hope of physically reaching any of them within a useful time span. If the expanse of our own Milky Way is, for now, physically closed to us, crewed journeys to other galaxies seem inconceivable.

In 2014, NASA's Kepler space observatory made a discovery of great significance: Kepler-186f, an exoplanet (a planet existing beyond our solar system) some 490 light years from Earth, orbiting red dwarf star Kepler-186. The planet has a radius just 10 percent larger than Earth's, suggesting that it is dense and rocky—a minimal requirement for the development of life as we know it. We will not be sure for a long time if life exists on Kepler-186f. In the meanwhile, the SETI program's Allen Telescope Array conscientiously sweeps that portion of the sky.   *NASA*

The Milky Way, Andromeda, a pair of Magellanic Clouds (dwarf, satellite galaxies of the Milky Way), and about twenty other systems comprise the so-called Local Group portion of the universe. The Local Group is home to about 1.5 trillion stars. Many galaxies exist beyond the Local Group. In the observable universe, there may be a billion trillion stars. Not every star is suited to have attracted planets, of course. And on stars that have, many factors come to bear on the possibility of life. A very small planet cannot sustain or hold an atmosphere. The distance separating a planet's sun from other suns is important, because close proximity invites annihilating collisions, chain reactions, and black holes. The biosphere (life-supportive) region around a star is relatively shallow, so a planet's distance from its sun is critical. The age and configuration of those suns matters, too, for an elderly sun will have begun to collapse upon itself, putting planetary life at risk. A sun that gives off continual blasts of ultraviolet light and X rays militates against planetary life. The particular gaseous makeup of stars is also important, given that helium and hydrogen are conducive to life (though those and other elements may be found in interstellar dust clouds).

Yet another factor to bear in mind is that *conditions ideal for life do not guarantee the creation of life.* On Earth, congenial combinations of proteins and amino acids came together to form life by creating reactions that built on one another, growing more sophisticated at every stage. The same or similar ingredients and combinations may not have appeared elsewhere. Despite Miller-Urey, the "somehow" aspect of the germination of life on Earth continues to intrigue and challenge laypersons, scientists, and theologians. What is it, exactly, that provides the spark that sets life's building blocks into motion? One theory cites "space spores" that drift to Earth (and other planets) from parts unknown. Once deposited on Earth, the spores generate life. The notion is captivating, but a nearly infinite collection of spores would have to make this journey in order for a probability of just *one* reaching Earth, or elsewhere. Equally discouraging is that while moving through space, such spores die from exposure to cosmic rays. Even assuming limitless spores that escaped radiation, solar gravity would repel them from our Sun (and any sun) long before they reached Earth or an Earthlike planet.

Another theory, spontaneous generation of life, is more mystical than empiric, and has no basis in known science.

Perhaps life's spark arrives in meteorites. Some examples that reach Earth's surface, called carbonaceous chondrites, carry amino acids—building blocks necessary to life as we know it. However, meteorites of this type are not robust; they do not travel well through space and fare even worse after hitting an atmosphere. The chemical properties of those few, over eons, that reached the Earth's surface quickly degraded, leaving them inert, and ill-suited to be spark plugs for life. Further, the amino acids carried by carbonaceous chondrites are evenly divided between those with links to simple life as we understand it and those that have no links at all. The life-in-a-meteorite theory has merit, but must be approached cautiously, at least if we remain wedded to the idea of amino acids being necessary for the generation of any kind of life at all.

The Drake Equation

The likelihood of intelligent life becomes a little more comprehensible because of the Drake Equation, an invention of leading American astronomer Frank Drake. The equation estimates the number of *communicating* technological civilizations in the Milky Way by taking seven factors into account: the formation rate of life-friendly stars; the fraction of those stars with planets; the average number of life-friendly planets per solar system; the fraction of those planets where life evolves; the fraction of those planets where intelligence evolves; the fraction of those planets where interstellar communications capability evolves; and the length of time those civilizations remain detectable from Earth. Although the equation seems to paint an unpromising picture (one can discern the numbers of planets growing fewer and fewer at each step), the outcome is realistic rather than hopeless, as it estimates the existence of between two civilizations and 280 million civilizations in the Milky Way with the ability to communicate. Even two is a wonder, and the possibility of some 280 million others is downright heartening.

Intelligence, SETI, and the Rise and Fall of Civilizations

Given the distances between stars, and thus between us and extra-solar planets, we can hardly be surprised not to have received indisputable knowledge of another intelligent civilization. Besides distance, other factors may militate against "us and them" getting together. Because animal species—and we are one—come and go, intelligent life on far-off planets may have developed, thrived, declined, and vanished hundreds of millions or even billions of years ago. In other words, some civilizations with the technological ability to travel to Earth might have gone extinct long before human life, or any life at all, developed here. Civilizations elsewhere could have perished from employments of nuclear weapons, local wars with deadly accumulative effect, or a global war. Worldwide pandemics might have destroyed alien civilizations; other disasters include climate change (natural or induced by the civilization), catastrophic volcanic activity, the worldwide incompetence of governments and subsequent collapse of alien systems, a superbug created by careless synthetic biology—even a malevolent artificial intelligence.

Of course, the death of one civilization, one era of civilization, or one species doesn't militate against the later rise of others on the same planet. A progression of that sort would require many millions of years, which certainly affects any calculations about the number of planets with technologically advanced life.

For about the past fifty years, variously focused and funded "search for extraterrestrial intelligence" (SETI) programs from around the world have tried to communicate with, or capture communication from, alien intelligences. This has been done by monitoring electromagnetic radiation, scanning for patterns in radio signals, launching space probes, creating physical messages (such as the gold-plated copper discs sent aloft with the 1977 Voyager missions), and radio-telescope arrays (such as the forty-plus dishes at Northern California's Hat Creek Radio Observatory, and the famous Mauna Kea setup on the big island of Hawaii). In August 1977, Ohio State University astronomer Jerry R. Ehman homed in on the "'Wow!' signal," a radio transmission some thirty times louder than competing, natural radio noise, and lasting seventy-two seconds—just the time needed for Earth to rotate out of alignment with the signal's presumed source, somehow near Tau Sagittarii, an orange star more than 122 light years away. In the years since, we have had no confirmation that the "'Wow!' signal" was intelligence- or nature-based. But we do know that it was anomalous. SETI work continues around the globe.

What Do *They* Think of *Us*?

If alien visitors travel to Earth in sophisticated spacecraft, the visitors possess a superior intelligence. To be sure, the whole UFO phenomenon is predicated on extraterrestrial intellects greater than ours is. (Only occasionally, as with Marvin Martian of the Bugs Bunny cartoons, are aliens portrayed as comic dunces.) Putting aside the issue of whether human beings possess the capability to decide what is "intelligent," there is the possibility that extraterrestrial visitors have observed us and decided we're just too dumb to bother with. That possibility worries astrophysicist Neil deGrasse Tyson, who reminded us in 2013 that we may appear to aliens the way earthworms appear to us: inconsequential.

Another possibility, one that has even more heft than the "too dumb" theory, has been posited by Stanton Friedman and others: aliens haven't formally revealed themselves because they perceive the danger we pose. Near the close of 2015, Paris was shocked by mass murder perpetrated by terrorists. The fact that the killers are of a particular ethnicity and pursue specific, purportedly religious goals hardly matters; the point is that this sort of brutality isn't an aberration but the very definition of human interaction here on Earth. Killing is what we do. Few of us could summon a rational reason for parachuting ourselves into the exercise yard of a penitentiary. Why, then, should extraterrestrials be eager to make themselves known in an alien landscape of inexplicable murder and other violence?

According to some UFOlogists and contactees, extraterrestrials are not corporeal creatures, but physically insubstantial things, such as a pair of atmospheric life forms a climber named Frank Smythe met on Mount Everest in 1933. He described them as dark, winged "balloons." A 1958 book, Trevor James Constable's *They Live in the Sky*, posited that such creatures live in Earth's upper atmosphere. Are such beings organic or semi-organic?

So extraterrestrials may be geniuses, or so far beyond our conceptions of genius as to be incomprehensible. Then again, they may be mere messengers or drones in the service of higher intelligences, motivated by rote learning, or even functioning on instinct. Or perhaps, as American scientist and electrostatics expert John M. Cage offered a half-century ago, *the creatures are the UFOs*, and keyed to follow human aircraft. Cage called these entities "life fields." The idea is hardly less reasonable than the notion of extraterrestrials that, in defiance of very long odds, look more or less like us. But Cage's idea never really caught on. Why should that be?

Because there is no comfort in it.

3

UFO Propulsion

Are We There Yet?

H ow do extraterrestrials deliver themselves to Earth? The superficial
concept of a spacecraft—that is, a conveyance with a protected enclosed
environment designed for space travel—is easy enough. If you have
materials, design sense, and a way with tools, you can build one in your backyard.
You can build a UFO-like craft that can . . . sit in your backyard. The issue, then, is
not the conveyance itself, but propulsion. How might an alien spacecraft generate
power sufficient to travel between stars?

Since the first powered human flight in 1903, propulsion research has been the
life's work of countless engineers, designers, and scientists. Here are some space-
propulsion systems that have piqued the interest of researchers—systems that
may already have been adopted, or tested and discarded, by other intelligences.

Ion Drive

In 2003, the European Space Agency's SMART-1 satellite mission to the Moon
utilized ion drive propulsion, harvesting electrical energy from solar panels to
accelerate ions and create thrust. Ion drive is newish even in theory, postulated
by American rocket researcher Robert Goddard and Russian rocket scientist
Konstantin Tsiolkovsky in 1906 and 1911, respectively. When SMART-1 demonstrated the system's practicality, scientists were particularly heartened because the
endless supply of harvested electrical energy means that relatively little traditional
fuel is needed.

On the debit side, though, is that ion drive, though efficient, is not speedy.
Standard velocity of a probe powered by an interplanetary ion drive is, like the
one that motivated SMART-1, about thirty-five thousand miles per hour. Because
interstellar ion drive engines do not yet exist, meaningful calculations can be based
only on existing engines. So, an interstellar craft powered by an interplanetary ion
engine would require eighty-one thousand years to reach Proxima Centauri. That
equates to the better part of three thousand generations—more time than human
beings are willing to contemplate. And until issues of ion-drive energy production
and carry-on fuel are addressed to allow interstellar drives, those eighty-one
thousand years from here to Proxima Centauri will stand.

The vast distances separating Earth and other solar systems are a commonly cited argument against the existence of UFOs. Naturally, such arguments reflect the present limits of human space travel—limits that may not be faced by other civilizations. One possible manner of ultra-long-distance travel, ion drive, exists already, harnessing solar energy to power spacecraft. The future ion-drive ship represented here will make far more efficient use of the technology than is now possible.   *Alamy*

Nuclear Pulse Propulsion

In 1947, an agency of the Department of Defense, DARPA (Defense Advanced Research Projects Agency), proposed a theoretical spacecraft propulsion system using the explosions of atomic bombs to thrust the craft into space. To prevent heat damage of engine components, the atomic explosions would be sited two hundred feet behind the craft, and directed against a large steel pusher plate, to pump liquid fuel through a nuclear reactor, expanding the fuel and producing thrust.

Because of practical limitations to the control of heat damage, as well as security issues, the idea languished. During the late 1950s, General Atomics envisioned a large, single-stage ship capable of traveling to Mars and back in four weeks. (Practical rocket technology of 2016 can deliver a crew to Mars in six months, for a one-year round trip.) Unfortunately, few people in authority had particular interest in going to Mars in the 1950s.

Russia's almost completely unanticipated 1957 launch of the Sputnik satellite made Americans feel inadequate and anxious. Partly because the USA felt a need to prove its technological prowess, a Moon-focused American space program got under way after 1960. Although emphasis was given to traditional rocket fuels and engines, atomic-pulse engines and other alternate technologies remained in the official "Maybe" file. The Air Force got a first look at all space agency programs, and the Air Force looked for military applications. Atomic-pulse engines might conceivably push a weapons platform into space, but the platforms would be vulnerable to Soviet missiles. So, to the Air Force, the propulsion idea had little merit. Further, the Partial Nuclear Test Ban Treaty of 1963 blocked atomic explosions in space.

Because the political and military landscapes are plastic and unpredictable, the U.S. Atomic Energy Commission (AEC; later called the Department of Energy) revived the nuclear-pulse idea in the late 1960s. The AEC sponsored a project called NERVA (Nuclear Engine for Rocket Fuel Application), which came close to a flight prototype before cancellation in 1972.

More than forty years later, nuclear-pulse propulsion remains theoretical. Conjecture about a future, practical system using electromagnetic energy created by induced nuclear fission suggests maximum attainable speeds of 5 percent of the speed of light, or just under fifteen million miles per second. At that rate of travel, a spacecraft would travel from Earth to Proxima Centauri in about eighty-five years—fewer than three generations, and thus conceivable and (reasonably) practical.

Einstein, Plus Other Theoretical Systems of Propulsion

Accepted wisdom is that the speed of light is the ultimate speed, and at the moment, we have no reasons to doubt that. But it is important not to get hung up on the speed of light, primarily because Albert Einstein's laws of relatively suggest that time slows down relative to an object traveling close to light speed. And as an object's speed increases and edges closer to the speed of light, space bends or curves, and time slows even more. In other words, the savings of time become greater.

Sophisticated experimentation has suggested that Einstein's "slow time" theory is correct. Additionally, exciting news from early 2016, the faraway collision of two black holes, seems to have confirmed Einstein's thinking. Interstellar travel may be possible *without* exceeding the speed of light. It is conceivable that other civilizations have devised technology that makes interstellar travel practicable. Here are some possibilities:

Antigravity: The pull of gravity is what tethers us to Earth, and prevents our lakes and oceans from disappearing into the sky. In that, and a lot more, gravity is a desirable thing. On the other hand, if you're five feet two and long to dunk a basketball, you're probably out of luck. Blame it on gravity. Gravity's pull also mandates that our aircraft carry their own power sources, to generate the thrust needed to send them aloft and achieve a useful speed. Antigravity—a force that opposes gravity—is appealing for frivolous reasons, such as the ability to hoist an engine block with the palm of your hand, and for serious ones, such as eliminating the force that wants to return aircraft to the ground.

In the early 1890s, the visionary American scientist and inventor Nikola Tesla deduced the underpinnings of what he later called a "dynamic theory of gravity." His ideas are at odds with Einstein's later theory of the curvature of space, and are thus considered radical: Tesla felt that the physical law of action and equivalent reaction "straightened" space, eliminating Einstein's vision of curved space and casting doubt on our understanding of the movement of bodies there. Tesla believed that space carries atomic and subatomic matter, and a field of "luminiferous ether," a force that influences gravity, momentum, and inertia. The ether, Tesla said, moves in whorl patterns at nearly the speed of light, creating ponderable matter (also referred to by Tesla as "gross matter": matter with measurable mass). When the force subsides, "the motion ceases and matter disappears."

Tesla dreamt of harnessing the power he had deduced. He said that if that could be managed, mankind would "have powers almost unlimited and supernatural." People could control the size of Earth and the planet's seasons, physically guide Earth through the universe, and *create and annihilate* material substance" [emphasis added]. Mated with what Tesla learned about electrostatic emissions and conductors, his gravitational theory suggested aircraft with sharply curved leading edges (where electrostatic emissions will concentrate), and with interior chambers of vacuum, and atmospheric pressure designed to create "free" power that allows the craft to work in opposition to gravity.

In the early 1920s, an American physics student named Thomas Townsend Brown discovered a relationship between the manipulation of positive and negative electric fields, and concomitant increases and decreases in mass of an X-ray vacuum tube. This relationship, he felt, suggested a way to control gravity by creating an ascendant "G-hill" wave and a descendant "G-well" wave on an imaginary horizontal. A mobile object designed to create those waves, and maintain them, could "defy" gravity. Brown eventually dubbed his field of study electrogravitics.

Forty years after Brown, aviation firms Northrop, Grumman (before the creation of Northrop-Grumman), and Avco experimented with high-voltage charges laid against the leading edges of experimental high-speed aircraft. Wind-tunnel tests showed that the voltage pushed the rush of air away from the planes' bodies. Although in no way suggestive of antigravity, the tests did display relationships between flight, aircraft bodies, and electrostatics, as Tesla and Brown had suggested.

Tesla's antigravity claims have been neither proved nor disproved. As for Brown, electrogravitics became a preoccupation of scientifically trained hobbyists, as well as of conspiracy theorists convinced that antigravity technology has been tested, proved, and then deep-sixed or otherwise concealed.

Around 1995, enthusiast claims of NASA experiments with antigravity surfaced, suggesting technology that utilized spinning, superconducting ceramic; liquid nitrogen; and solenoids that created and maintained magnetic fields, to allow levitation. Eight or ten years later, stories circulated about Boeing's Seattle "Phantom Works," where researchers in touch with Russia and Finland worked on Project GRASP (Gravity Research for Advanced Space Propulsion). Boeing claimed that the original Russian research was "plausible," but the project apparently yielded no useful results.

The allure of antigravity flight is no less potent today than it was in 1956, when interviewer William Gladych met visionary aircraft designer William Lear. Mr. Lear said,

All matter within the [antigravity] ship would be influenced by the ship's gravitation only. This way, no matter how fast you accelerated or changed course, your body would not feel it any more than it now feels the tremendous speed and acceleration of the Earth.

Gladych clarified: "In other words, no more pilot blackouts or any such acceleration headaches. The G[ravity]-ship could take off like a cannon shell, come to a stop with equal abruptness and the passengers wouldn't even need seat belts."

In just four sentences, Lear and Gladych explained the astonishing in-flight behavior of numberless UFO sightings.

Wormhole Travel: For all the eighty years of chatter about wormholes—those fabulous theoretical portals that transcend time and distance in deep space—the wormhole concept is hypothetical. A wormhole has two mouths connected by a passage called a throat. Science fiction suggests easy travel through the throat, but many factors relegate wormhole travel to theory. No wormhole has been observed, though physicists are reasonably confident wormholes exist. But wormholes are apt to be very small, even microscopic, and thus impractical for use by space travelers. The encouraging news is that the universe is expanding, and as it does, wormholes may expand too. If wormholes exist, interstellar flights of short duration are theoretically possible. A 1935 paper by Albert Einstein and Nathan Rosen proposed that, given Einstein's theories about gravity as having a warping effect on space and time, "bridges" (wormholes) might exist for very brief periods. The space-time bridges collapse before even light can escape from them, but if they could be kept "open," spaceships might pass through, overcoming the constraints of normal time to hop from one galaxy to another.

Harvard astrophysicist Rudolph "Rudy" Schild's thoughts about a magnetic variant of black hole theory—what he calls a magnetospheric eternally collapsing

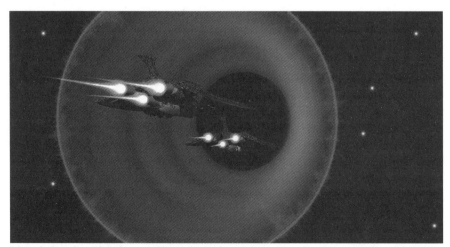

Wormholes, those fabulous and hypothetical portals across solar systems and even galaxies, may provide faraway alien civilizations with shortcut access to Earth—but precisely how such travel might work is presently unknowable.   *Alamy*

object (MECO)—bring fresh dimension to wormhole theory. During close study of a brilliant quasar located nine billion light years from Earth, Schild and his colleagues found evidence of a magnetic field. The discovery flew in the face of accepted notions about quasars, which had been understood to be "powered" by black holes. But a black hole prevents the escape of light, radiation, and matter from its event horizon (a black hole's theoretical boundary). Schild counters common belief by asserting that the magnetic properties of a MECO, in concert with quantum electrodynamics, *prevent* the formation of an event horizon. With the event horizon denied, a MECO's collapse is never completed, and goes on endlessly. Instead of becoming a black hole, the eternally collapsing MECO remains a hot ball of plasma.

If black holes are removed from the theoretical picture, the universe may not be shrinking. To the contrary, it may again be expanding, creating a negative gravity (colloquially known as dark energy) that enables wormholes. And wormholes are one way extraterrestrials might manage space travel to Earth.

Schild's theory has its supporters, particularly among UFO researchers and other enthusiasts, but has yet to be widely accepted by the scientific community.

American theoretical physicist Kip Thorne has suggested that exotic matter might prop wormholes open long enough for the passages to allow through travel. Exotic matter is repelled by gravity; until recent years, its existence was only theoretical. But quantum physics experiments since the millennium—notably the four-hundred-member Belle Collaboration and the Large Hadron beauty (LHCb) Collaboration—verify the existence of "the ghost particle": exotic matter.

A quark is a fundamental, subatomic particle. Ordinary matter is made from tightly knit composite particles called hadrons. Hadrons exist in two classifications: baryons and mesons. Baryons are created when three quarks combine. Two familiar building blocks of matter, protons and neutrons, are baryon hadrons.

Quarks have opposite numbers, called antiquarks. Quarks and antiquarks are identical in mass, but have opposite charges. When a quark and an antiquark pair up, the result is a meson. Like baryons, mesons are hadrons. However, mesons do not obey conservation laws; because they are composed of a quark and an antiquark, they are unstable. They are exotic matter.

Because exotic matter has been theoretically verified, its theoretical role in wormholes has not been disproved.

Wormholes lacking an exotic-matter bridge are unstable. Even one large enough to admit a spaceship might suddenly collapse. If travelers could introduce exotic matter to a wormhole, the stability challenge would be solved. That's good, but we don't know what will happen when the ordinary matter of the spaceship meets the exotic matter. Explosion? Disintegration? Or perhaps nothing violent at all.

Extraterrestrials that have mastered wormhole travel are technologically far ahead of us—so far ahead that we may not interest them at all, except as biologic footnotes.

Suspended Animation: In the opening sequence of the 1979 science-horror thriller *Alien*, the crew of the interstellar cargo ship *Nostromo* awakens after an unspecified period in hypersleep. Crew members have slumbered in discrete pods, and are awakened automatically when needed to resume tasks and continue the ship's commercial mission. Groggy for a few minutes, each quickly recovers. Wherever in space they are, it's a long way from Earth. Apparently lacking access to wormholes or other cosmic shortcuts (though "hypersleep" does imply "hyperdrive"), the *Nostromo*'s mission is feasible because during the period of suspended animation, the crew members require little food and water, and age relative to their immediate environment, rather than to Earth.

Long familiar in science fiction, suspended animation now may have a future in medical treatment of trauma victims. Researchers at Pittsburgh's UPMC Presbyterian Hospital began human trials in 2014, replacing portions of subjects' blood with chilled saltwater. With the body cooled to about fifty degrees Fahrenheit in fifteen minutes, bodily functions slow dramatically and give surgeons the time needed to make repairs.

Although akin to animal hibernation, the process does not yet have long-term applications. Still, it may be a signpost toward practical suspended animation of space travelers to Mars and elsewhere. NASA now works with SpaceWorks, an Atlanta company with technology that can shoot cooling liquid up an astronaut's nose and into the base of the brain. The process produces what NASA and SpaceWorks describe as "torpor," a sort of hibernation that will eliminate the need for galleys, exercise rooms, and full-dimension living quarters. And smaller quarters mean weight savings, less fuel, and increased long-journey practicality.

Granted, neither hibernation nor torpor is desirable for prolonged space travel. An induced slowdown of body systems is just that: a slowdown. Whether bear or human, the organism still ages; in other words, torpor will not prolong space travelers' lives. So even assuming that torpor could be maintained in space, the thirty-five-year-old astronaut that left Earth is going to be eighty-five after fifty years of hibernation-like travel. Besides saving on weight and stores, all that's been accomplished is that the astronaut didn't become bored during her journey. At eighty-five, even with scheduled muscle stimulation during the trip, the astronaut isn't going to be as spry—or as useful—as she had been fifty years earlier.

Alternatively (and strictly theoretically), infant astronauts could awaken as healthy middle-aged adults . . . with the mentalities of infants. Well, that's an obvious dead end.

Cryogenic suspended animation, by which bodies are frozen until a scheduled thaw, is unappealing because when ice crystals are thawed, migrating water can crush or dehydrate cell membranes. Cells might also be damaged by dissolved substances (solutes) that remained separate from the ice crystals.

Chemically induced hypoxia slows body functions, but may bring unavoidable brain damage.

Humans and extraterrestrials may share certain basic physical commonalities. If freezing damages human cells, the process may damage alien cells, as well. For this reason, wormhole travel, for all of the guesswork and theory attached to it here on Earth, may be more viable an option for interstellar travel than any form of suspended animation.

Photon Power: Photon propulsion, which has been discussed in scientific circles since the 1920s, may emerge during the next twenty to fifty years. Or it may not. Monumentally expensive and complex, photon power is a theoretical technology grounded in the nature of light.

All light is characterized by two qualities: electromagnetic waves and packets of fundamental subatomic particles called photons. All light is made of photons. Because photons—unlike those other familiar subatomic particles, electrons and quarks—have no mass, photons travel at, naturally enough, the speed of light. The speed is constant, regardless of whether the electromagnetic waves are manifest (as determined by wavelength) as visible light, X rays, infrared rays, ultraviolet rays, radio waves, or gamma rays. Optimum speed, though, is achieved only in a vacuum.

The energy of each photon varies according to wavelength: the shorter the wave, the more energy contained by each photon. But regardless of the apparent intensity of the light source, each photon contains the same amount of energy. Intensity is simply a function of the number of photons striking a given surface area during a prescribed time.

All rockets propel themselves forward by pushing a reaction mass (matter) out of an exhaust. The so-called "rocket equation" demonstrates that forward speed is directly proportional to exhaust velocity—that is, the speed at which the reaction mass leaves the exhaust. Maximum exhaust thrust produces, in theory, maximum velocity: the speed of light.

Speculation about photon propulsion's light or near-light speeds, which peaked in the 1970s and '80s, is certainly attractive: a journey of fifty light years (to, say, the star Mu Arae) would require just over fifty Earth years—while to the crew, fewer than ten would have passed (as posited by Einstein's Special Relativity).

More recently, velocity estimates have been scaled back to about 10 percent of the speed of light. Whatever the speed, how might photon propulsion be attained? In 1957, the German physicist Eugen Sänger proposed that a propulsion system bringing electrons together with positrons (antielectrons) would induce a matter-antimatter reaction as electrons and positrons annihilate each other and create gamma ray photons. According to Sänger, thrust is generated when the gamma photons are reflected rearward by a parabolic mirror. The theory is scientifically valid. However, positrons do not lie around in convenient heaps, and would have to be generated by the photon rocket's propellant. To generate sufficient energy is, at present, not possible, and even if it were, a photon rocket would have to be immense—perhaps two thousand miles in diameter—if it were to carry all the propellant needed to generate a matter-antimatter reaction. A ship of that size could not be easily moved at all, let alone brought up to near-light speeds. Acceleration to top speed could take years, even decades.

Further, the high heat involved in a matter-antimatter reaction is almost unimaginable, great enough so that the giant rocket's exhaust could seriously damage planets or other bodies that got in its way. (For an eye-opening narrative of such damage in a martial context, see Larry Niven's 1966 short story "The Warriors.") And unless the parabolic mirror was 100 percent perfectly reflective, the rearward blast of gamma ray photons would melt the mirror and destroy the ship.

The scientific, material, and economic feasibility of photon propulsion is debated, with more physicists than not feeling that the obstacles are too great to be overcome. Nevertheless, in a paper presented to the 2012 Space Technology and Applications International Forum II, American physicist Young K. Bae declared that photon propulsion is possible with development of accepted scientific principles. Bae suggested a twenty- to fifty-year development period, contingent on what he described as "consistent long-term world-scale economic interest and investment." In Bae's view, interest and investment would follow from "positive financial returns from routine interstellar commutes that can transport highly valuable commodities in a profitable manner." In other words, photon propulsion may be all about business.

If a proportion of UFOs are photon-drive extraterrestrial craft, the alien pilots may have been sent to Earth not by curious or aggressive intelligences, but by consortiums of dispassionate, off-world MBAs. Earth may be, for them, just one more potential profit center, one more bar chart in a financial portfolio or annual report.

Hyperdrive, Jump Drive, and Warp Drive: Each of these related terms is a sort of catch-all that suggests (but does not satisfactorily describe) various hypothetical faster-than-light (FTL) or "cosmic shortcut" propulsion systems. In conversation and casual, non-scientific writing, the terms are roughly equivalent, rendering them simultaneously colorful and meaningless. In more careful writing, such as studies of the employment of FTL drives by discrete television series, hyperdrive and jump drive remain roughly equivalent (and cluttered with impenetrable pseudoscience). As we'll see below, warp drive stands apart.

A spaceship running with *hyperdrive* has the capacity to take advantage of simultaneous, alternate dimensions of space and, frequently, time. Some definitions suggest that hyperdrive is a prepared "slip" or a "slide" into those dimensions, during which the journey from A to B is achieved in a sideways eyeblink. ("Slipspace" is, in fact, a sometime-synonym for hyperdrive.)

Jump drive (not to be confused with a synonym for a present-technology USB flash drive) is interstellar teleportation that allows instantaneous travel. The mechanics can be handled by computers or, in rare instances, by a human commander. Some sources establish that a ship must carefully coordinate itself in space-time prior to use of jump drive, an activity that requires hours or even days. Alternatively, in some instances the initial jump is made with little preparation, only to be followed by (for vague reasons) a time-consuming "after-drive" period in which the ship re-synchs itself with the universe. The science of all this is unavoidably vague; really, the word "jump" probably provides the clearest sense of what goes on.

Unlike hyperdrive and jump drive, *warp drive* requires a time expenditure to travel from here to there; its capabilities are not instantaneous. A special quality of warp drive is its ability to accelerate exponentially from Warp 1 (the speed of light) to Warp 10, the presumed maximum velocity. At Warp 10 (or perhaps Warp 9), the ship may bend the fabric of space, "double back" on itself, and travel into the future.

Sources suggest that any of these FTL systems may involve selective or mandatory wormhole travel.

We will again stress that these drive systems are stoutly hypothetical. If humans wish to master one anytime soon, the best hope is to capture and reverse-engineer an extraterrestrial craft that runs one of them.

Traditional-Propulsion Prototypes

Before we leave advanced and theoretical propulsion, a distinction should be made between those lines of research and speculation, and the real-life "flying saucers" and faux saucers created since circa 1939 to the present. The craft have been noodled with by national militaries, private companies, and individuals. The most notable, the Avrocar, came from Avro-Canada, under a commission to build saucer prototypes for the U.S. military. Avro-Canada began exploring the saucer concept with aeronautical engineer John Frost in 1953, before American sponsorship. Early "tease" information suggested rapid vertical climb and a flight speed of fifteen hundred miles per hour. A house organ, *Avro News*, promised that the saucer was "so revolutionary that it would make all other forms of supersonic aircraft obsolete." Initial prototypes showed a variety of flaws, but despite overheated engines that melted the steel frame, and violent shudder that popped rivets, the project intrigued the U.S. Army, which gave Avro the go-ahead for working prototypes in 1958.

The subsequent, disc-shaped VZ-9A Avrocar measured eighteen feet in diameter and weighed more than 5,600 pounds. Designers sited the cockpit nearer to one edge of the craft (at the "front") rather than at the center. Motive power came from three turbojets creating 927 pounds of static thrust apiece. A five-foot central fan on the saucer's underside generated upward thrust, sucking in air and forcefully expelling it around the craft's perimeter. By this time, estimates of maximum speed had been scaled back to three hundred miles per hour; anticipated ceiling, with a two-thousand-pound payload, was 10,000–15,000 feet. At landing, the saucer settled onto four hydraulically damped, wheeled legs.

During tests, the Avrocar prototypes (some with a tail fin, others without) struggled to remain level at low hover, and above just five or six feet, the saucer indicated it might like to flip over. But low, reasonably wobble-free flight was achieved in the Avro parking lot, between buildings and in and out of open hangars. During wintertime tests, the considerable thrust blasted great sheets of ice from the pavement and sent them pinwheeling. (For archival, color film footage of Avrocars in flight, see www.youtube.com/watch?v=cmPiZv4q4Ms.)

By about 1960 the USAF and the U.S. Army acted as joint sponsors. Although intriguing, the Avrocar had no future other than as a pricey novelty, and in the summer of 1961, the U.S. pulled its sponsorship.

The Avrocar and all other human-made saucer prototypes were motivated by traditional technology that encompassed, variously, two-stroke engines, gas turbines, and centrifugal-flow jet engines that provided power to internal rotors, contra-rotating external rotors, and rotating circumferences (to create compression

Filmed tests of prototype Avrocars that began in the late 1950s revealed a saucer-like craft capable of generating lift and forward motion—but not much of either. Wobbly and requiring a very careful hand on the stick, this U.S.–Canada tech collaboration was allowed to fade away by about 1961.   *USAF*

and gyroscopic stability). A few early examples had rocket-powered trolley takeoff systems. Saucers with multiple-engine setups arrayed the engines radially, usually around a central cabin. Jet-engine models sometimes added ramjets to let the craft transition from hover to level flight.

Lift came from swirled or blasted downward-directed air, though some designs created lift by downward-directed exhaust gases. The small size of these experimental craft created issues of heat buildup and dispersion, particularly when the design incorporated jet engines.

Designs accounted for stability and control with small fins, rudders, and central tails (standard elements of avionics that are noticeably absent on most UFOs); twin rotors (to eliminate torque); annular nozzles (to regulate pitch and roll); trailing-edge exhausts (to control yaw); electromagnetic rotor braking (yaw); louvered shutters; air intakes; and deflector vanes.

Leading-edge windows, wrapped viewing ports, or bubble canopies provided forward and side visibility. Some designs, such as Leroy Crookes's STOL (Short Take-Off and Landing) saucer, allowed downward visibility through transparent undercarriages. Two or three retractable legs or pods, usually wheeled, allowed smooth touchdowns.

Most prototypes were single-pilot craft, though a few made provision for two occupants. Pilots usually sat, though some lay prone on their stomachs.

Dreams of saucers capable of carrying machine guns, Gatling guns, cannon, rockets, missiles, and bombs shriveled because lift designs could barely raise unadorned aircraft, let alone those carrying burdensome armament. Because of this, notions of using saucers to deliver nuclear payloads came to naught.

Because all Earth-grown saucers struggled with lift, forward motion, and airspeed, possible commercial applications died right alongside the military ones. Saucer work continues, but the fact is that the design is probably not needed for practical use. (Why invent a flying saucer when you have a Beechcraft or an F-15 Eagle?) The novelty factor remains strong, of course, but hardly seems sufficient to justify significant expenditures of time, talent, and money.

At least here on Earth.

Paul Hill, Propulsion, and Practicality

Following the failed Avro-Canada craft, "official" interest in saucers didn't die, but it did diminish to a low simmer. Many experts grew skeptical. And then there was the American mechanical and aeronautical engineer Paul R. Hill (1909–90), who joined the National Advisory Committee of Aeronautics (NACA) in 1939. He rose through the ranks of research engineers, contributing to aerodynamic design during World War II and ramjet development following the war.

During 1953–55, Hill helped design the Hiller VZ-1 Pawnee, a VTOL craft named for the contractor, Stanley Hiller's Hiller Aircraft. The Pawnee looked like a circular platform with a railed, circular "dais" that steadied the pilot, who stood while manipulating the controls. A pair of forty-horsepower piston engines powered a pair of counter-rotating, twin-blade propellers that generated modest lift. Late prototypes had three engines, and provision for the pilot to sit. The Office of Naval Research and the U.S. Army shared an interest in this experimental craft.

Paul Hill witnessed UFOs twice, and was a proponent of the extraterrestrial hypothesis. The astounding speed and maneuverability of the objects challenged Hill's knowledge of physics and aeronautics; in particular, he wondered whether—contrary to popular scientific thought—the astonishing aerial behavior of UFOs did *not* violate laws of physics. Hall studied many UFO reports of the 1960s and '70s. Assuming that even a small proportion of anecdotal accounts were true, Hill reasoned that a broadly uniform technology allowed these craft to abruptly accelerate and suddenly stop, execute "impossibly" tight turns and other changes in direction, and exceed the sound barrier without creating a sonic boom. As he researched his posthumously published book *Unconventional Flying Objects: A Scientific Analysis*, Hill compiled accounts of UFO sightings. When he perceived what he called "UFO patterns," he refused to accept that the patterns could not be explained by conventional physics. Further, Hill knew that he must work from the evidence to create a hypothesis.

Hill worked backwards with UFO data, utilizing known science to eliminate explanations that could not pass the rigors of the scientific method. In sum, he proposed that UFOs act on repulsive, rather than propulsive, energy fields for their motion. The technology arises from what Hill termed a directed acceleration field, a force field that does not defy gravity but, rather, cancels it. And the field's effect is not limited to the craft. Because one data pattern in UFO accounts was the physical disturbance of water, ground matter, roof shingles, automobiles' electrical systems, and other things, Hill surmised that the UFOs' acceleration field is, like the gravity field, sufficiently strong to generate a sphere of influence.

The Hiller VZ-1 Pawnee VTOL, developed in the early 1950s by Stanley Hiller's Hiller Aircraft from designs by aeronautical engineer Paul Hill, piqued the interest of the U.S. military as a quick-hop offensive and recon device. The doctored U.S. Army photo seen here implies that the Pawnee could be easily flown by an infantryman—which is not the case at all. Paul Hill's greater contribution was his later research into the apparent aerodynamic capabilities of UFOs, which he called "unconventional flying objects."

U.S. Army

Objects (masses) within that area will exhibit physical reactions.

Without a gravity-canceling field, the first high-stress maneuver of a UFO would splatter its occupants against the bulkhead. But with gravity canceled, UFO interiors and occupants would not be subject to the accelerative g-forces that limit the ability of military pilots to mimic UFO maneuvers. Concurrent with accounting for g-forces, Hill's repulsive-force-field-propulsion model explains the particular maneuvers frequently noted in UFO witness accounts. Craft tilt forward to move forward, and dip backward to stop. Turns are achieved with banking, and the craft appear level when still (hover mode).

Although Hill performed his closest study of UFO maneuvers during the 1970s, he nevertheless had access to computer simulation—which he utilized, along with equational calculation and wind tunnel tests, during his research. To further test his ideas, Hill built and operated a variety of circular platforms capable of limited flight. Although powered by jet engines or rotor technology (the gravity-canceler naturally being unavailable to Hill), the platforms suggested that the directional maneuvers described above are ideal for execution of the desired final action.

Analysis of patterns of evidence led Hill to surmise that the optimal "unconventional flying object" weighed about thirty tons, and could reach nine thousand miles per hour in Earth's atmosphere. Acceleration produced a 100-g force effect that, as described above, was negated by the cancellation of gravity.

Why do UFOs appear to be unaffected by surface heat generated during rapid acceleration? This, too, can be accounted for by Hill's protective zone, which forces air to flow around the craft (allowing for maneuvering in atmospheres) but prevents air molecules agitated by the craft's rapid passage from splashing against the craft's surface.

Many UFO witnesses recall that the crafts' skins exhibited color changes, from, say, blue to red and then back again. Hill suggested that the protective sheath would show visible effects (color changes) on the craft's surface as the propulsion system powered up and cooled down. The sheath not only shows colors, but affects our visual perception of the craft itself. Witnesses frequently report that UFO surfaces, when viewed relatively close and head-on, appear firm and metallic. From a distance, however, and particularly when the craft presents the witness with an oblique view, the craft's outline appears indistinct, even fuzzy. Hill suggested that this phenomenon is another effect of the plasma sheath, which bends light rays at particular angles relative to a viewer.

Paul Hill held NASA's Exceptional Service Medal. He conducted and frequently led research that contributed significantly to aerodynamics and space science, particularly the dynamics of space stations and space laboratories. Because NASA officially frowned upon UFO research, Hill conducted his UFO work on his own time.

The scrupulous nature of Hill's exploration of UFO propulsion attracts scientists as well as laypersons. Hill's knowledge and research methods are well respected; inevitably, though, his acceptance of the extraterrestrial hypothesis inspires controversy that pushes his work to the margins.

EMH and EMR

One novel theory proposes that UFOs are not extraterrestrial but manifestations of electromagnetic radiation generated by natural or artificial sources. This electromagnetic hypothesis (EMH) is sometimes cited to explain other phenomena, such as poltergeists and hauntings. According to some EMH advocates, what may appear to be psychological disorders may be the result of electromagnetic radiation (EMR). In the presence of EMR, the human nervous system is disrupted, and the victim may experience a variety of hallucinations and visions, and may see Men in Black, as well as grays and other types of extraterrestrials. A portion of alien sightings may be real, but when EMR is at play, many of these manifestations are cued by culture. In other words, because grays are part of a shared consciousness, EMR may act as a trigger that propels the "idea" of a gray into an apparent physical manifestation.

In particularly unfortunate cases, EMR can induce heightened emotions, paranoia, time distortion, feelings of intense heat and cold, light flashes, and touches by invisible hands. EMR theorists are concerned because the waves are all around us, in radar, power lines, transformers, fused cutouts (a power pole's overload system), high-tension towers, power stations and substations—even junction boxes. Although scientific inquiry is ambiguous about links between EMR and cancer, EMH/EMR investigators warn that the hazard is real.

According to EMH thinking (archaeology writer Paul Devereaux, neuroscientist Michael Persinger, and UFOlogist Albert Budden were key developers), a significant proportion of UFOs go into a discrete group labeled Unclassified Aerial Phenomena (UAP). In quasi-mathematical form, then, EMH/EMR + UAPs = UFO reports.

Besides linking to paranormal objects and events, EMH links itself to Earth's geologic fault lines, to explain ball lightning, lights that accompany earthquakes, mountain-peak illumination, and other natural phenomena.

4

UFOs and Airpower Before the Age of Flying Saucers

Frogs, Wheels Within Wheels, Airships, and Comet Trouble

Questions and assumptions about peculiar objects in the sky have encouraged the human brain to ponder unidentified flying objects for a long time . . . and to regard such things with a certain dread. Although the term "UFO" was coined recently—around 1956, by U.S. military man and Project Grudge/Blue Book director (1951–53) Edward Ruppelt—the *idea* of UFOs is older than recorded history. Legends of Akakor, a mythical lost city located somewhere near the borders of present-day Brazil and Venezuela, hold that sometime between around 13,000 BC and 10,400 BC, fair-complexioned gods from the planet Schwerta landed in an enormous saucer to greet the indigenous Ugha Mongulala people. The Ugha accepted the knowledge offered by the aliens, and parlayed that into the later Mayan civilization. Another group located farther south, and also influenced by alien thought, became the Incas.

Besides ancient astronauts, the legend of Akakor invokes thirteen crystal skulls that will provide the aliens' message of salvation when mankind is on the verge of self-destruction. (Much of this is dramatized in the 2008 adventure film *Indiana Jones and the Kingdom of the Crystal Skull*. Ancient-astronaut proponent Erich von Däniken invoked Akakor [and other places] in his 1973 book *The Gold of the Gods*, and inspired some conversation until Däniken's sources proved not to be credible.)

The "end times" aspect of the Akakor narrative—complete with intercession by superior beings and superior wisdom—is very much in line with later Christian thought. As Christianity approached, accounts of unidentified objects in the sky entered legend around the globe. In 583 BC, the prophet Ezekiel wrote of a "wheel within a wheel" that he saw in the skies at the Cheber River in Chaldea (present-day Iraq). Did Ezekiel witness a UFO, or did he see (as some biblical interpreters insist) God's angels or cherubim? Or could it be that biblical invocations of angels and cherubim were inspired by UFOs and the crafts' alien operators? Did alien craft create the pillars of cloud and fire that led the Children of Israel through the wilderness? Is it possible that the star that guided the Three Wise Men wasn't a star at all, but an alien spacecraft?

Cicero reported that during battle between Locrians and Crotoniates at the Sagra River (present-day southern Italy) in 498 BC, warriors heard the disembodied voices of "Fauns," and saw deities so clearly that all but the "senseless" and "impious" acknowledged the presence of the Gods. Meanwhile, in India in 500 BC, witnesses were astonished by *vimanas*—piloted, and deadly, flying machines.

In China around 300 BC, an oversized jade "chariot" interrupted poet Chi Yuan's visit to the grave of an emperor, lifted the poet from the ground, and spirited him to distant mountains.

At Amiterno (present-day Italy) in 218 BC, the sun grew small, and white figures were seen in the sky. In areas nearby, witnesses saw phantom ships, a flying shield, two moons, and the sun "battling" the Moon. A few years later, at Hadria (present-day Adria, in northern Italy) in 213 BC, a shining altar manifested itself in the sky. Some witnesses reported seeing an imposing figure in white.

A "great fleet" was sighted in the skies above Lanuvio (southeast of present-day Rome), in 173 BC. An account from Pliny's *Natural History, Volume II* describes "celestial weapons from East and West meet[ing] in battle" above Ameria and Tuder (central Italy), where "the sky was on fire, and often seemed that the clouds had caught fire." The encounter dated to 104 BC. The same volume of Pliny notes an event at Tarquinia in 100 BC, where Roman consul Lucius Valerius Flaccus saw "a burning shield scattering sparks" move across the sky at sunset from east to west.

Accounts of ancient-era UFOs can be forceful, and are often expressed as elements of battlefield encounters. One possible inference is that the mysterious craft manifest themselves during periods of crisis. Perhaps the crafts' occupants objected to violent human behavior. Perhaps they wished to encourage a stronger moral code, or even warn us.

Wonders of the Bible

The Bible, a great moral arbiter of today's world, was set down by various hands between about 1400 BC and 95 AD, with a lengthy gap between 450 BC and the last half of the first century AD, during which little or no writing was done. (The gap is accounted for by a natural pause between the two books of the Bible, and known-world political upheaval caused by Alexander.) As empires of the period waxed and waned, the Bible's authors attempted to codify acceptable human behavior. Along the way, provocative descriptions of skyborne objects and wondrous creatures appear in many Books. **Genesis**, for instance, talks of the Nephilim: fallen angels, according to some interpretations, or perhaps the offspring of fallen angels and humans. Pillars of clouds and pillars of fire appear in **Exodus**, suggesting, to some, the landings and departures of extraterrestrial spacecraft. More clouds and flames appear in various **Psalms**.

A gout of flame that engulfs a sacrificial offering in **Leviticus** has been interpreted as alien high-tech, a heat ray or similar device. Similarly, a defiant Elijah and fifty of his men are "consumed" when "the fire of God fell from heaven" in

2 Kings. In the same Book, Elijah is lifted to heaven in "a chariot of fire," suggestive to some latter-day interpreters of a visit to a spaceship or even an alien abduction. Some translations use the word "chariots" as well as the singular "chariot," as if Elijah witnesses a mother ship and subsidiary craft.

Deuteronomy talks of the giant Og and "strong and tall" people called the Anakites. Some readings of the latter race describe the beings as "elongated"—to some minds, an alien physiognomy.

The Book of **Isaiah** describes "chariots," a "whirlwind," and other seemingly inexplicable upsets to the natural world, and the physical descent of (as some readers see things) mortal aliens that became worshipped as gods. **Zechariah** mentions "a flying scroll, thirty feet long and fifteen feet wide (5:1-2)—suggestive to some of the classic cigar-shaped UFO. Although verses three and four suggest that the scroll contains the Ten Commandments, some argue that "scroll" was Zechariah's best available word with which to describe a ship. But ancient Hebrew was rich language that translates well into modern Hebrew and modern English. In an instructive 2013 exercise, biblical scholar Michael S. Heisman examined the ancient Hebrew language to demonstrate a biblical writer's ability to accurately describe a UFO in then-contemporary terms, without recourse to words that (to some) open themselves up to controversial latter-day interpretation. (By using the word "scroll," for instance, Zechariah meant . . . a scroll.) Dr. Heisman found—and explicated—Hebrew equivalents for "round" and "disk"; "metallic" and "silver"; "bright," "shining," and "burning"; "black"; and a straight line, or "side."

Ezekiel contains many passages seized upon by UFOlogists and others holding a keen interest in extraterrestrial beings and unfathomable alien power. The "four living creatures" that assume center stage in 1:4-10 have faces unlike those of humans, which has allowed an extraterrestrial interpretation. The Book's repeated mention of "wheels" suggests alien technology to some. Likewise, "chrysolite," a blanket word for any number of semiprecious stones with which Ezekiel would have been familiar, is cited by some UFOlogists as Ezekiel's inadequate attempt to describe shininess and smoothness—such as the skin of a spaceship. The hotly glowing "figure like that of man" (8:2) means "angel" to some and "alien" to others. Later in Ezekiel, oddly featured "cherubim" appear on fabulous platforms showing wheels within wheels, and abilities to move easily in any direction. Surely, some feel, the words refer to advanced technology. But when Ezekiel wrote "wheels," wheels are what he meant. Some scholars suggest that "wheels within wheels" refers to wheels and their hubs. Others focus on the significance of the wheels themselves, specifically, that thrones of the ancient world often rolled on wheels. Thrones with wheels are

To some readers of the Bible, the prophet Ezekiel's visions of "wheels within wheels" and other phenomena suggest extraterrestrial visitation. Other readers are not so sure. German painter and draftsman Hans Holbein the Younger executed this woodcut for the Zurich Bible around 1538.

depicted in art from numerous ancient cultures. The notion was well known when the Book of Ezekiel was written; a unique sort of wheel, then, might metaphorically suggest the uniqueness of God's throne, and the unfathomable extent of his power.

In the New Testament, Jesus's Ascension in **Acts** 1:8-11 is observed by "two men dressed in white." Not surprisingly, many UFOlogists are excited by those men, regarding them as emissaries from an alien ship, and thus essential parts of the Resurrection narrative. They are present as Jesus ascends into a spaceship, and it is from a spaceship that Jesus will return—a notion seized upon by numerous quasi-religious UFO cults (as we will see in chapter fourteen).

The symbolic visions that comprise the Bible's last Book, **Revelation**, are the climax to the end of life on Earth, a final battle that comes as a response to the opposing poles—good and evil, Yahweh (God) and Belial (Satan)—that dominate human affairs. So intense does the tug of war for human souls become that all must be violently swept away, so that affairs on Earth may begin afresh later. Many things from earlier in the Bible that are often tied to UFOs recur in Revelation, including clouds, fire, angels, chariots, and horsemen. The book is among the best-written in the Bible; indeed, its imagery is frequently breathtaking. As religious-based literature, Revelation may have had no equal until Dante Alighieri's *Inferno* (written in the early 14th century as the first part of the author's *Divine Comedy*). Revelation pulses with strange beasts and demons; earthquakes, tidal waves, gigantic hailstones, and other violent natural upheavals; murder; famine and plague; deadly heat; agonizing boils and other sores; terrifying changes to the sun, Moon, and stars; peculiar numerology; Death personified; and a river of blood coursing 180 miles. It even describes "three foul spirits like frogs" central to Revelation 16: 12-21, and suggestive to some UFOlogists as a description of the aliens that we now categorize as grays.

UFOs in Christian Art

During the Renaissance, when religious belief drove much of everyday life, artists expressed Christian faith in exalted, often fanciful terms. Paintings and tapestries of the period bristle with details that strike us as provocative: flying half-moons with faces; radiant discs sending forth visible rays (as in Carlo Crivelli's 1496 painting *The Annunciation*); and airborne objects that we would today describe as "saucers." Hindsight suggests to us that Renaissance artists created stylized interpretations of UFOs, but hindsight is mistaken. What we see through the lens of our own time was viewed centuries ago through the twinned lenses of faith and commerce. Contrary to latter-day claims made by overeager UFOlogists, the artists' symbology invokes God, not visitors from space. Saucers, rays, cherubim, faces in the clouds—those are elements in a whole catalogue of Renaissance religious iconography dear to the wealthy patrons that supported artists. Like present-day commercial artists, Crivelli and others worked to please the people that paid them, knowing that their employers expected engaging symbols of the Divine.

Eyes Only: Selected UFO Sightings, 8th Century to 18th Century

Recorded accounts from this lengthy period easily number into the thousands, and would require a chronology-style book if most were to be noted. As well, there is an inevitable sameness to reports; the incidents noted below are especially novel.

As witness accounts approach the 17th and 18th centuries, visions based in Christian theology, such as flying men with swords, become more common. After about 1765, ground observers across Western Europe reported crewed and crewless hot-air balloons—novelties that encouraged sky-gazing.

742–814: During the rule of Charlemagne (King of France, King of Italy, and emperor of Western Europe), selected people were temporarily removed from Earth by spacecraft so that they could experience other worlds. Upon the travelers' return, however, many who greet them view them as sorcerers. **Note:** Reported in the Comte de Gabalis's *Discourses.*

776: In a battle of Franks and pagan Saxons at Castle Sigiburg, France, the latter panic and flee when "the likeness of two shields, red with flame" circle a church. **Note:** Reported in the *Royal Frankish Annals.*

839: Over the course of a few nights, "fiery stars" buzz various cities in Israel.

979: Saxons observing a night sky see "a bloody cloud in the likeness of fire." **Note:** Reported in the *Anglo Saxon Chronicles.*

c. 1055: A so-called "pearl" hovers above a wooded Chinese lake, illuminating the landscape and casting a shaft of bright light.

October 27, 1180: A flying "earthenware vessel" appears near a mountain summit in Kii province, Japan. **Note:** Some UFOlogists interpret "earthenware vessel" as "flying saucer," though the object could just have reasonably resembled a bowl, pitcher, cup, or vase.

1188: Witnesses report that "the heavens opened" over Dunstable, England, to reveal a cross bearing the figure of Christ.

1217: Three flying crosses traverse the skies above Nice, France.

1270: At Bristol, England, locals stone and burn a man who alighted from a flying ship. **Note:** Reported in Book I of Gervase of Tilbury's *Otto Imperialia.*

September 12, 1271: The execution of a Japanese priest at Tatsunokuchi, Nomi District, is interrupted by the sudden appearance of a bright, shiny disc or sphere.

November 4, 1322: Uxbridge, England, is overflown by a "pillar of fire" showing colors of varying intensity. Moments before speeding away, the object emits "fervent" red flames that look like "beams of light."

November–December 1387: Fiery revolving wheels, or perhaps barrels, are seen above Northamptonshire and Leicester, England.

January 5, 1433: At Ciudad Rodrigo, Spain, the assembled court of King Juan II witnesses "a great flame of yellow fire" move across the sky, showing a dark-colored center and emitting an ear-splitting roar that panics horses. The noise is emitted from the object's "end." **Note:** The account, attributed mainly to King Juan's physician, is controversial because the physician's presence at court has been difficult to discern. Further, some historians, UFOlogists, and literati suspect the physician's written account is a 17th-century forgery.

November 1, 1461: A fiery iron rod as large as a half-Moon is seen above Arras, France.

1543: As a comet roars over a German village, the body's tail removes all the water from a brook before consuming a field of grain. **Note:** Recorded by Conrad Lycosthenes.

February 1, 1554: Hundreds of witnesses watch a fiery-red cylinder fly an erratic course above Salon de Provence, France. **Note:** Chronicled by Nostradamus.

April 14, 1561: A substantial crowd sees various dark-colored flying balls emerge from flying cylinders above Nuremberg, Germany. The variously colored spheres appear to "fight" one another. **Note:** German artist Hans Glaser commemorated the incident in a 1566 woodcut.

The Italian Renaissance artist Carlo Crivelli painted this egg and oil altarpiece, *The Annunciation with St. Emidius*, in 1486. In all of his work, Crivelli concerned himself exclusively with Christian themes. The winged figure in the left foreground, for instance, is the Archangel Gabriel, who walks with St. Emidius. Mary (right foreground) is being informed that she will carry the Son of God. Contrary to the belief of some overeager UFOlogists, the saucer-shaped object at the upper left, which "connects" itself to Mary, is not a literal representation of what we now understand to be a UFO, but a metaphoric rendering of God's power and will.   *© The National Gallery, London*

May 1, 1606: A "flaming wheel" revolves in the sky above Nijo castle, Kyoto, Japan, for a quarter hour.

August 5, 1608: Three luminous, spinning objects descend from the skies above Nice, France, land neatly atop the waves of the Mediterranean, and disgorge a pair of humanoids with oversized heads. The craft rest on the sea for about an hour, turning the water "red" with emanations of heat.

January 18, 1644: In a diary entry, Boston governor John Winthrop says that according to a trio of fishermen, twin lights rose from the city's harbor and hovered in the sky for a quarter hour.

Late January, 1644: About a week after John Winthrop's January 18 diary entry (above), he describes a brilliant light that rose in the sky amidst a sparkling burst of light and flame.

August 15, 1663: An enormous flaming sphere at least 125 feet in diameter hovers over a lake in the Vologda region of Russia.

April 1639: A political funeral in Shansi province, China, is interrupted by a multicolored star that flies over the mourners before leaving to circle a nearby village.

1692: A triangular object in the sky above Harlech, Gwynedd, Wales, sets fire to "ricks of hay, corn, and barns."

circa 1700: Chippewa Indians in present-day Wisconsin encounter a "shining" man who says, "I dropped from the above." A few days later, the stranger enters a star that has descended to the ground, and returns with it back into the sky.

August 1700: An elderly man vanishes from Sahalahti, Finland, not long after a flying disc hovers above the village. **Note:** While searching nearby woods later, the victim's adult son encountered a creature that resembled a bear, and that verbally reassured him that his father had been taken to a better place, to live among "higher" beings.

December 18, 1707: An enormous cylinder moving lengthwise not far above the horizon at Northamptonshire, England, bursts into "flames of a pale-coloured fire."

May 11, 1710: A comet-like object above London travels just in front of "the likeness of a man in a Cloud of Fire, with a Sword in his Hand."

April 2, 1716: Over the Baltic Sea near Revel (present-day Tallinn, Estonia), rapidly moving dark clouds part to reveal, in turn, an "enormous shining comet" and a bright pillar of light. When one bank of clouds moves into the pillar, the sky is rent with arrow-like objects that quickly ascend even higher above the horizon.

January 15, 1721: An enormous pillar of fire hovers over the mountains west of Bern, Switzerland, and then moves toward the city. Three balls of light emerge from the cylinder and fly in different directions. **Note:** Some accounts describe four cylinders.

August 5, 1748: An unidentified craft flies toward about a dozen people in Aberdeen, Scotland. The craft's occupants are seen.

August 1783: A large ball of fire rises from the North Sea and travels above Ostend, Belgium. Briefly traveling north, the object reverses course and heads south, spitting "particles of fire of a bluish color."

November 2, 1730: In the night sky above Salmanica, Spain, two luminous columns that bracket "an amazing Globe of fire" display dramatic color shifts of red and green for five hours. **Note:** The display may have been the aurora borealis.

December 8, 1733: A male resident of Fleet, England, observes a silvery disc flying above the tree line.

1752: A man taken into a flying craft by a stranger garbed in white is removed from Earth and then returned, near Kazan, Russia.

May 10, 1760: Witnesses near Bridgewater, Massachusetts, report a morning sighting of a "sphere of fire," which casts a light so bright that the shadow overwhelms shadows cast by the sun. **Note:** Some UFOlogists cite this event as the world's first documented UFO report. Two centuries later, Bridgewater came to be identified as the center point of the "Bridgewater Triangle," a two-hundred-square-mile area that has produced an unusually high number of ghost sightings, accounts of grotesque animals, and UFOs.

September 8, 1767: A large, luminous pyramid rises from a loch near Perthshire, Scotland, and rolls along land and water, upending a man and a large cart, and destroying a house and a new bridge.

February 5, 1780: A flaming "dragon" hovers for fifteen minutes in the night sky above Bussieres, France. Local people and objects below are clearly illuminated.

October 12, 1796: Fifteen flying "ships" led through the sky by a flying man appear above the Bay of Fundy near New Minas, Nova Scotia. The ships pass close enough so that people on the ground can see portholes.

UFOs in the 19th Century

The 19th century brought a startling array of inventions and technical wonders, among them the telephone and filament lamp; the steam turbine and the automobile; radio and the cinematograph—even the electric chair. Powered flight was yet to come, but aviation science was growing, nevertheless. Beginning around 1880, Thomas Edison conducted nighttime wireless experiments involving illuminated balloons. Not surprisingly, people on the ground sighted his "electric balloons" many times, particularly during 1885 near the inventor's Menlo Park, New Jersey, laboratory. Most of the witnesses knew that the illuminated shapes belonged to Edison, but partly because of the technological innovations mentioned above, and increasingly sophisticated aviation, citizens were predisposed to the idea of other peculiar flying craft, and in fact continued to report airborne lights—sometimes called "electric stars"—long after Edison abandoned his balloon experiments. No matter: because of the new science created by Edison and others, the *idea* of flying lights acquired *plausibility*.

Eyes Only: Selected UFO Sightings of the 19th Century

April 5, 1800: A brilliant crimson object, described by witnesses as the size of a medium-size building, radiates heat onto observers, and passes low overhead at Baton Rouge, Louisiana. Shortly after the object disappears from view, witnesses hear the sound of an explosion.

September 7, 1820: "Strange objects moving in straight lines" cross the skies above Embrun, France. The objects are evenly spaced, and show what witnesses called a "military precision."

April 1, 1826: Gray, cigar-shaped objects are observed above the English Channel.

July 1836: People in Szeged, Csongrad, Hungary, have a close encounter with an unidentified craft and its occupants.

March 19, 1847: "Spherical craft" rise into clouds above London.

June 1, 1853: For thirty minutes, a pair of luminous objects appear over the campus of Tennessee's Burritt College; students and faculty observe that the larger object is a shape-shifter, changing from a globe to a cylinder. The smaller object disappears and then reappears, waxing and waning in size.

August 11, 1855: At Sussex, England, luminous circular craft "with spokes like a wheel" move across the sky, remaining visible for an hour.

April 6, 1856: A black or gray "aerial torpedo" seen above Colmar, France, traverses the sky while emitting a low-pitched hum.

August 8, 1863: A peculiar nocturnal light precedes a witness's close encounter with "inhuman beings" and the disappearance of mules, at Yale, British Columbia, Canada.

October 1, 1863: While seated with friends on his porch, a Lewisburg, West Virginia, man named Moses Dwyer observes odd, greenish clouds that touch the ground to disgorge "thousands and thousands" of marching men, carrying no weapons and dressed in identical white trousers and shirts. They march through a valley and finally disappear over a steep hill. The men are silent, and do not strike Dwyer as being either Union or Confederate soldiers. **Note:** Some sources date this incident to September 1, 1863. A similar sighting was made by Confederate troops at nearby Bunger's Mill (often incorrectly cited as Runger's Mill), West Virginia, on October 14, 1863.

Mid-September 1865: James Lumley, a trapper active near Cadotte Pass, Montana, witnesses a "bright, luminous body" streak across the sky and break up into "particles" shortly before a loud explosion fills the air with the scent of sulfur. The following day, Lumley comes upon a tree line split and broken by the apparent passage of a very large object. Beyond the trees, the tops of hills appear to have been "shaved off." Lumley subsequently discovers an "immense" stone carrying mysterious glyphs.

July 1868: Residents of Copiapo, Atacama, Chile, observe a flying craft with lights and engine noise; some witnesses describe the object as a scaly "giant bird." **Note:** A magical flying creature called the Chonchon, and a flying (sometimes feathered) serpent called the Peuchen, are staples of Chilean folklore.

July 6, 1873: An enormous object some three hundred feet across hovers over Bonham, Texas, startling residents and spooking animals. **Note:** This daytime sighting may be alcohol related. The date is sometimes given as summer, June, and November 20.

Mid-1878: Three German prospectors camping near Yuma, California, witness a flying "sailing ship" at sundown. One of the men is abducted, and turns up naked in the desert eight days later, dead of thirst. **Note:** Not clear whether this report originated in Yuma, Arizona, or nearby Fort Yuma, California. Other than a so-named neighborhood in California City, California, there is no Yuma in California.

July 29, 1878: A railroad crew working at Edwardsville, Kansas, observes an approaching train, with light and whistle, leave the track and disappear into nearby woods.

May 15, 1879: While sailing the Persian Gulf, crew aboard the HMS *Vulture* watch as a pair of large spinning wheels moves across the sky at an estimated forty-five knots (about fifty mph). Each wheel is approximately 130 feet in diameter. They slow and then land on the water; total time of the encounter is thirty-five minutes.

1880: Two military sentries at Aldershot, England, fire on a humanoid, wearing tight-fitting clothes and a helmet, as it flies over their heads.

November 17, 1882: England's Greenwich Observatory observes a "vast," mottled green disc, which is also sighted on the Continent.

1883: Cowhand Robert Reed Ellison observes mysterious flickering lights while driving cattle near Mitchell Flat, Texas, near Marfa. **Note:** The phenomenon has been regularly reported ever since, becoming known as the "Marfa Lights." Latter-day explanations include natural gases called "fool's fire": electric charges generated by rock beneath Mitchell Flat; light viewed at a distance through hot and cooler layers of air (a "superior mirage"); and, since about 1932, automobile headlights from nearby U.S. 67.

October 24, 1886: A family of nine is awakened in Maracaibo, Venezuela, by a loud hum and a brilliant light. **Note:** Within days, the people suffered vomiting, blackened skin, and hair loss. A week after that, nearby trees began to wither.

September 5, 1891: Two deliverymen and a minister see a swirling white apparition in the sky—for hours—near Crawfordsville, Indiana.

May 25, 1893: While cruising the Sea of Japan, the HMS *Carolina* observes an orderly formation of flying discs.

April 1897: In the countryside outside Baltimore, a whirring, hissing object descends from the sky, startling a witness and spooking a horse. The witness notes lights at each end of the craft, and two humanoid occupants, too. The occupants attempt to communicate with the witness, who does not recognize their language.

Early April, 1897: A farmer from Bethany, Missouri, tells a newspaper he witnessed a strange flying craft crash into a flagpole and leave two mangled corpses.

April 1, 1897: A witness in Galesburg, Michigan, is approached by the humanoid occupant of an unidentified craft, and senses that the creature wishes to communicate.

April 9–13, 1897: Unidentified airships and nocturnal lights figure in more than 150 reports from across Illinois, Indiana, Iowa, Kansas, Minnesota, Missouri, Nebraska, North Dakota, Wisconsin, and Manitoba, Canada. The sightings continue, with slightly decreasing regularity, into August 1897. **Note:** These sightings kicked off the so-called airship craze that produced hundreds of sightings in Europe and the USA between 1897 and the first few years of the 20th century. Explainable craft included gas and hot-air balloons, steam- and gasoline-powered dirigibles and zeppelins, and (after 1903 and the Wright Brothers) fixed-wing aircraft.

Mid–April 1897: A man in the hills outside Springfield, Missouri, witnesses the landing of an airship carrying two occupants. One of them is a woman, described as having "long golden hair" and a laughing voice "like silvery bells." She occupies

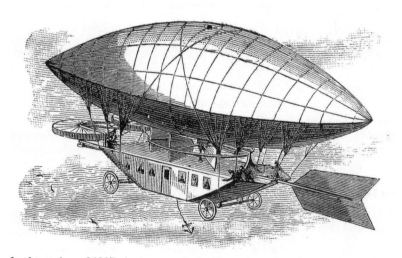

In the spring of 1897, during a period of keen American interest in airships, witnesses across the Midwest and Upper Midwest made more than 150 reports of mysterious unidentified aircraft. Because powered flight was coming closer to reality, the "airship craze" flowed almost seamlessly into sightings of unidentified winged craft in the early 20th century.

herself by picking flowers. **Note:** Whether or not this witness saw precisely what he thought he did, he almost certainly was in love.

April 17, 1897: Three men walk into a diner in Conroe, Texas, order dinner, and announce their intention to fly to Cuba. Bright lights and a mysterious airship are seen over the town an hour later.

April 18, 1897: People living near Aurora, Texas, witness an unidentified airship collide with a local windmill.

UFOs in the First Third of the 20th Century

General scientific and technological advances, showcased at world's fairs mounted beginning in the mid-19th century, helped turn facets of hard science into popular science. Citizens, armed with new knowledge, became more aware than before of technology and the natural world. The greatest of the pre-1900 world's fairs, the 1893 World's Columbian Exposition at Chicago, had a Westinghouse display with space devoted to the inventor Nikola Tesla (frequently invoked later in discussions of UFO propulsion); Tesla displayed an array of early AC devices that included motors, generators, visible high-frequency electrical discharges, and vacuum tubes illuminated by wireless transmission.

The Exposition's celebration of electricity—an essentially invisible power source—made a particular impact on fairgoers.

Eyes Only: Selected UFO Sightings, 1900–1913

Mid-1901: In a yard at Bournbrook, England, a ten-year-old boy discovers a small craft, about five feet across, and a living humanoid.

October 28, 1902: As the *Fort Salisbury* sails the Gulf of Guinea, three crew members observe a light-festooned object some 650 feet long settle onto the sea and then descend beneath the water line.

August 9, 1903: Five witnesses at Argenteuil, France, use binoculars to observe a skyborne red object travel more than four miles in twenty minutes—too fast for any known balloon or other airship.

February 28, 1904: Three red, blindingly bright objects pass over the USS *Supply* in the Pacific Ocean off San Francisco. The dominant object is egg shaped; the other two are smaller, and spherical. After being observed by crew members for a full two minutes, the objects suddenly ascend into the clouds. **Note:** Some accounts of the USS *Supply*'s sighting give the location at the Sea of Japan, off the eastern coast of Korea.

June 1904: Three members of a family observe a pair of blue-white objects hover six to ten feet above the ground near Rolling Prairie, Indiana. **Note:** Rolling Prairie is a well-known locus of ghost sightings.

1906: A "mystery meteor" performs elaborate aeronautical maneuvers above Syracuse, New York.

September 1906: Sackville G. Leyson, president of Emery County, Utah's Society for Psychical Research, reports that he has traveled to Mars with his mind, meeting two diminutive tribes with, variously, webbed feet, cyclopean eyes, huge ears, and copious hair.

June 30, 1908: A mammoth fireball explodes above Tunguska, Siberia, setting the night skies aglow, smashing eighty million trees flat in a radial pattern, and killing hundreds of reindeer over nearly eight hundred square miles of forest. Trees at ground zero remain standing, but are stripped of branches and bark. Forty miles from the site, at Vanavara, a man is tossed from his chair by a heat blast that makes him believe he is on fire. **Note:** Some UFOlogists regard the Tunguska event as the first recorded crash of an alien spacecraft. The more common, and generally accepted, conclusion is that the object was a 220-million-pound meteoroid (NASA's term), measuring some 120 feet across (estimates range as high as six hundred feet), which screamed into Earth's atmosphere at 33,500 miles per hour, heating the air around it to 44,5000 degrees Fahrenheit before exploding at an altitude of about 28,000 feet.

October 31, 1908: Men at Bridgewater, Massachusetts, see a black, spherical object fly over and then hover, to scan the ground with a brilliant beam of light.

April 24, 1909: Witnesses observe a light-colored ovoid fly over Florence Italy; two occupants are glimpsed inside.

June 16, 1909: At Dong Hoi, Vietnam, fishermen observe an illuminated cylinder hover above the village before it disappears into the sea. **Note:** Some accounts incorrectly give the place name as Dong Hui.

July 19, 1909: Residents of Oamaru, New Zealand, report strange flickering lights in the sky. **Note:** During July and August 1909, New Zealanders make nearly forty reports of mysterious flying objects; many accounts refer to "occupants."

July 23, 1909: An airship-like craft hovers for five minutes above a school in Kelso, New Zealand. One or more humanoids (accounts differ) is seen. **Note:** Drawings done later by the schoolchildren are similar in many details, but witness recollections cannot agree on whether the occupant(s) was seen on the ground or within the craft.

July 30, 1909: Two men witness the misty-morning descent of a domed disc near Gore, New Zealand. The craft gives off a yellow glow, and the clear dome allows the witnesses to discern two occupants. After executing a few low circles, the disc shoots upward and disappears.

July 31, 1909: A farmhand at Greenvale, New Zealand, observes a whirring, 150-foot-long airship fly rapidly through the early morning sky. The craft marks its passage with bright lights sited fore and aft.

January 12, 1910: A large, cigar-shaped object flying above Chattanooga, Tennessee, and Huntsville, Alabama, illuminates both towns with a powerful beam of light.

January 19, 1910: The mayor and other town officials at Invercargill, New Zealand, observe a loudly chugging, cigar-shaped ship that hovers overhead. A humanoid appears at a bulkhead door and speaks in an unknown language. After a few moments, the door slides shut and the craft rapidly accelerates beyond the witnesses' view.

May 29, 1910: At Sitges, Spain (near Barcelona), a photographer shooting a race car speeding around a curve during the Copa Catalunya (Catalan Cup) inadvertently captures a saucer-shaped object flying above and behind nearby trees. **Note:** This race is invariably misidentified in UFO literature as having taken place at an unidentified site in France, without month or day, or any hint of the driver's identity. The photograph has survived because it shows the winning car, No. 5, a Lion-Peugeot driven by Jules Goux.

June 29, 1913: People gathered at a racetrack watch as an oddly elongated craft flying "at great height" passes over Lansing, Michigan, ascending as it goes.

Aviation During World War I

During the European war of 1914–18, German zeppelins sent over London to drop bombs did damage but were no match for winged British aircraft fitted with Lewis machine guns, which chewed the bags of gas to pieces. Allied aerial-photographic reconnaissance that upended a great deal of German ground strategy impressed the public— and planted the idea that aircraft flying at an incredible twenty thousand feet could observe you without you even knowing.

Aviation advancements on both sides of the conflict spurred development of increasingly specialized aircraft; while the ground war seemed stalled during 1917–18, airplanes were undertaking air-to-air combat, recon, close air support, strategic bombing, tactical bombing, night bombing, and other dedicated tasks. At war's end, aviation showed promise as a carrier of mail

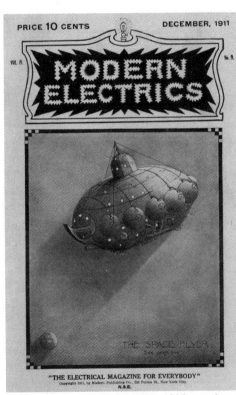

Modern Electrics magazine was a 1908 creation of editor-publisher—and American science-fiction pioneer—Hugo Gernsback. He intended the magazine for young men whose interest in SF had a firm grounding in real-world science and electronics. The "Space Flyer" dominates the cover of the December 1911 issue.

and supplies, but because it lacked practical passenger capability, lay observers regarded the science of flight as a primarily aggressive one.

Aviation During the Interwar Years

The seeming equivalency of death and aircraft grew stronger during the 1920s and '30s, when Great Britain turned the RAF against various British colonies in Africa and the Middle East; and in 1935, when Italian dictator Mussolini's *Regina Aeronautica* fielded nearly four hundred modern aircraft against an Ethiopian air defense consisting of four pilots responsible for about a dozen outmoded planes. To further drive home the aerial superiority issue, Italian planes dropped mustard gas onto hapless Ethiopian troops. During 1936–39, Germany's *Luftwaffe* sent a "volunteer" Condor Legion to strafe and bomb loyalist troops and civilians during the Spanish Civil War. So great was the horror that Spanish painter Pablo Picasso felt moved to create one of his most vivid and disturbing works, *Guernica*.

Aerial war in Asia unfolded in a similarly one-sided manner: when Japan began its fourteen-year war with China in 1931, it utilized airplanes in reconnaissance, ground support, and spotting for Japanese artillery. Chinese pilots were unskilled, and Russian aircraft and "volunteer" pilots did little to help. On December 12, 1937, Japanese bombers and fighters attacked and sank the USS *Panay*, a shallow-draft gunboat carrying American diplomats and other civilians up the Yangtze and away from Japanese mayhem in Nanking. Three people on board the *Panay* died, and Americans were both vexed and frightened. Japan claimed the attack was a mistake and paid reparations to Washington, but to people around the world, aircraft had become a synonym for "death from above." Beginning hardly more than ten years later, an evolution of that psychology caused witnesses to react with great alarm to UFOs.

Eyes Only: Selected UFO Sightings, 1914–1938

August 23, 1914: The retreat of British troops during the Battle of Mons (Belgium) is aided by glowing "angels" that send arrows at the pursuing German forces. **Note:** At the end of September, supernaturalist author Arthur Machen published "The Bowmen," a fictionalized version of the tale, based on survivor accounts.

Summer 1915: A six-year-old boy observes humanoids following the landing of a bell-shaped craft at Sulitjelma, Norway. The beings are about three feet tall and wear coveralls. They have long hair, gray skin, and oversized heads.

February 29, 1916: Three dockworkers witness the passage of an unidentified flying craft carrying three occupants at Superior, Wisconsin.

May 13 and October 13, 1916: Three small children and, later, thousands of adults see the Virgin Mary at Fatima, Lisboa e Vale do Tejo, Portugal. The Virgin's presence is announced in October by brilliant light, blue beams from the sun, and other skyborne phenomena. **Note:** Sources approach this famed event from various points of view: as a clear Christian-Catholic visitation; as an extraterrestrial visit mistaken for a religious apparition; as a natural event explainable by sunlight viewed through a layer of stratospheric dust, refraction of ice crystals in clouds (so-called sun dogs), or the distorting effects of direct sunlight on the human eye; and (somewhat less convincingly) as a prolonged instance of mass suggestion or mass hysteria.

Spring 1917: During aerial combat over Belgium, German pilot Peter Waitzrik witnesses fellow flier Baron von Richthofen shoot down a flying object covered in coruscating orange light. Both pilots observe the craft execute a shaky landing before disgorging two occupants, who dash into nearby woods. **Note:** Waitzrik waited until he was 105 years old to share this story with the press.

June 3, 1920: While fishing near Mount Pleasant, Iowa, a man named Clark Linch watches a translucent blue, egg-shaped object descend from the sky and silently settle just fifteen feet away. **Note:** Linch later doubted that the craft was inhabited, as it stood only as tall as a "five-gallon cream can."

February 22, 1922: A man living in Lincoln, Nebraska, is startled when a spherical object lands near his house and releases a humanoid standing almost eight feet tall. **Note:** UFOlogist Patrick Gross reports that this event has been conflated with another, less credible report made in Hubbell, Nebraska, some thirty-five years later. That account, also invoking the tall creature, came from a man named William Lamb, who claimed at other times to have seen God on photographs of the stars.

August 1922: Two silver hemispheres divided by a rotating ring are seen above Warsaw, Poland. The object releases a beam of light and then rapidly ascends out of sight.

July 1925: Before dashing off in alarm, a pair of men in Moora, Australia, get a good look at a silver, saucer-shaped object resting on four legs in a pasture.

January 1926: The plane of a stunt pilot performing above Wichita, Kansas, is surrounded by six "flying manhole covers"; each disc is about five feet in diameter.

August 5, 1926: While in mountains near Kukunor, Tibet, a party led by explorer Nicholas Roerich uses binoculars to track a silver, oblong UFO. **Note:** The year of this sighting is noted in some sources as 1927.

1927: Near Tamalpais, California, noted Irish poet and folklorist Ella Young observes a cigar-shaped craft make its way through the sky "by alternately contracting and elongating its body." **Note:** In 1946, Young and a friend witnessed a black, bat-like craft at Morro Bay, California.

April 1927: A delivery boy in West Frankfort, Illinois, sees a revolving, metallic sphere approach and then hover above a house about a hundred feet away. The sphere is some forty feet in diameter, with a gondola-like structure on its belly. After a minute or two, a wire-like filament is extended from the sphere toward the house, as if probing the structure. The gondola's windows close before the sphere ascends and disappears.

Mid-1929: A man is briefly abducted by occupants of a UFO near Spring Valley, New York. The witness describes the occupants as short, "very distorted" humanoids wearing outfits that resemble "a diving suit."

June 12, 1929: While on horseback near Fermeneuve, Quebec, a young man named Levis Brosseau is startled by something on the ground, a dark object about fifty feet in diameter and about sixteen feet high. The object has a yellow light that illuminates four or five minuscule figures standing nearby. After a few moments, the craft lifts from the ground and flies off. **Note:** Accounts do not make clear whether the craft left the tiny humanoids behind.

1930: A "little pink creature" about two feet tall walks into a rough-hewn camp shelter in Mandurah, Western Australia, and alarms a fifteen-year-old girl. Hairless and supporting an oversized head, the humanoid has a "slit of a mouth" and oversized eyes. The skin appears wet or oily. The girl's father scoops the creature in a net and puts it outside. **Note:** The unidentified witness related this story in 1982, after looking at a picture of Steven Spielberg's *E.T.*

Summer 1932: A snapshot of a man taken in St. Paris, Ohio, includes a domed saucer aloft in the background. **Note:** Apparently, neither the subject, George Sutton, nor the photographer noticed the object.

Summer 1933: After puzzling over odd lights occurring over a period of weeks, two men and a woman from Nipawin, Saskatchewan, Canada, observe a domed, saucer-shaped craft on the ground, attended to by small humanoids wearing silver clothes and helmets or caps. The witnesses, who secretly watch for about thirty minutes, get the impression that the humanoids are repairing the craft. **Note:** When the witnesses returned two days later, they found imprints of landing gear. Some sources date this incident to 1935. Also, some accounts misspell Nipawin as Nipawan.

July 5, 1933: A large flying sphere intrudes upon a nighttime formation of RAF fighters over Sussex, England. Sudden engine failure causes two planes to land. The pilot of another flies close to the sphere and suffers burns to his hands and face.

December 1933–spring 1934: Residents of Sweden report unidentified, luminous planes. The craft are never seen taking off or landing, and they fly even in the worst weather. Reports of planes are joined by accounts of unexplainable engine noise and searchlight beams. **Note:** These "phantom planes" may have resulted from war jitters; Hitler had taken charge of Germany in January 1933, and indulged in bellicose talk that made all of Europe nervous. Further, Germany and Russia were interested in Swedish and Finnish iron ore deposits, and may have conducted secret overflights. An official report issued by the Swedish government in April 1934 identified about 10 percent of the reports as credible, and admitted that "unauthorized air traffic has occurred." A similar scare, dubbed "ghost rockets," alarmed Sweden in 1946.

October 1, 1934: An elderly woman at Garganta la Olla, Spain, stumbles upon a short humanoid in shiny coveralls. Before the creature dashes off, it sends the woman a telepathic message about the impending birth of a grandson. **Note:** The woman later attested to the message's accuracy.

April 1935: A silver disc flying over Antwerp, Belgium, hovers so that "robots" in square helmets can exit the craft to examine it. The witness is a man named Aerts.

October 1936: Two men hitchhiking from Eklutna, Alaska, to Anchorage are buzzed by a UFO, and must dive into a snowbank to protect themselves.

January 1937: A private pilot flying over Van Buren, Missouri, chases an unidentified flying object.

Summer 1938: A Somerville, Massachusetts, man named Malcolm Perry observes a silent, blimp-like object dressed with portholes. Perry discerns moving silhouettes inside the craft, and feels he is being watched.

July 25, 1938: Two Spanish soldiers at Guadalajara observe a dark disc, about thirty-five feet in diameter, hovering six feet above a pasture. The object's upper and lower halves spin in opposite directions. A transparent column lowered from the belly of the object contains at least two moving figures. A blue beam is briefly aimed at the soldiers before the column retracts and the craft lifts off and disappears.

October 30, 1938: Orson Welles's *War of the Worlds* radio broadcast, a news-style account of an invasion from Mars, causes concern across the country and encourages small pockets of panic in New Jersey and New York. For more on the broadcast, see chapter fifteen.

5

UFOs and World War II

Gremlins, Balloon Bombs, and the World in the Balance

The story of flight during the Second World War (1939–45) is, of course, a mammoth one. Accounting for all belligerents, the United States included, air forces fielded 640 discrete models of *fighters* (with numerous subcategories related to wings, engines, weight, and roles), *bombers* (with numerous subcategories), *flying boats* and *float planes*, *observation* and *recon*, *photo recon*, *communications*, *light transport*, *cargo*, *passenger planes*, and *gliders*.

In addition, air forces of the world ran 144 *trainer* models (with subcategories); about ten *rotorcraft*; four *lighter-than-air craft*; and eight *missiles, rockets*, and *drones*.

Prototype aircraft that did not see combat nevertheless flew, and accounted for fifty-seven winged models; twenty-one glider models; nine rotor prototype models; nine missile prototypes; and thirty models of miscellaneous prototypes. Additionally, twenty-three models of *purely experimental prototypes* saw development and, in some cases, limited flight.

The most-produced combat plane of World War II, the Soviet Ilyushin IL-2 Sturmovik ground-attack plane, saw more than 36,000 units. The second- and third-most-prolific, the Soviet Yakolev Yak-1, -3, and -7 fighter; and Germany's Messerschmitt Bf-109 fighter, saw 31,000 and 30,500 examples, respectively.

The United States alone manufactured more than 275,000 aircraft of all types. During 1939–1945, then, skies around the world bristled with aircraft. Any attempt to detail them all is beyond the intention and scope of this book. However, salient points that relate to the later UFO phenomenon should be noted.

- Effective airpower enjoys support not just from the military but also government, scientists, engineers, logistics experts, manufacturers, workers, and civilians.
- Ample supplies of state-of-the-art aircraft, fuel, ordnance, and trained, motivated fliers can create a virtually unbeatable flying force.
- Significant losses in one or more of the areas mentioned above quickly degrade an air force's ability to survive and win.
- Lack of aerial preparedness (as with the Americans at Pearl Harbor) can be damaging or fatal.
- When evenly matched air forces face off, a spirited defense (as during the Battle of Britain) can turn back a determined attacker.

- Technological advances (such as drop tanks, incendiary bombs, aircraft carriers, radar, jet engines, rockets, and the atomic bomb) must be dramatic and continual.
- Tactical innovation (such as great naval battles conducted mainly by aircraft, and fighter support of bombers) is vital.
- Ceaseless, round-the-clock aerial attacks will wear down the enemy.
- Civilian areas should be freely bombed.

Allied adherence to the two final directives weakened Germany so that it could not resist Allied ground troops, and staggered Japan and set it up for the A-bomb. The directives also loom large in the minds of UFOlogists who wonder if our "first contact" will be with extraterrestrials that exhibit a "total war" mindset. This is a well-worn trope of science fiction. Still, we must prepare to accept that extraterrestrial visitors are or may become hostile.

Fairies, Gremlins, and Foo Fighters

As the world's air forces tangled during World War II, trained, alert pilots and air crews, functioning with a little luck, could complete their missions and survive to fight another day. But one in-flight obstacle encountered by fliers from many nations had a creepily perplexing aspect: the bothersome airborne objects called foo fighters.

The foo fighter notion is rooted in Pict lore dating from about 250 AD to 950 AD, specifically, magical creatures called fairies (sometimes spelled "faeries"). Some are handsome creatures resembling men and women; others are troll-like. Some are angelic while others look like demons. The fairies' otherworldy aspect encourages presumed links to gremlins, mischievous imps that figure prominently in Scottish and larger UK folklore. They came to the fore in UK popular culture during the world wars, when they displayed a keen—and often destructive—interest in aircraft. Biplanes' control wires were supposedly snipped by gremlins during 1914–18, and the creatures shouldered the blame for aviation mishaps during the Battle of Britain (1940) and other British air campaigns of World War II.

By mid-war, the gremlin figure had established itself in the United States, and American aircrews complained of the creatures' destructive mischief. Bugs Bunny met a clutch of mischievous gremlins in a memorable 1943 Warner Bros. animated cartoon, *Falling Hare*, and the Disney studio worked to develop British writer Roald Dahl's 1942 book *The Gremlins* as an animated feature or, alternatively, a short, during 1942–43. The studio abandoned the project, but a revised edition of Dahl's book became an international success when reissued, with Disney-studio illustrations, in 1943. (A replica reissue of the 1943 edition appeared in 2006.)

Foo fighters were even more mysterious than gremlins, and more closely related to the physical world. Initially unnamed, these illuminated aerial intruders bothered bomber and fighter pilots in all theaters of World War II. Many were spherical; others were disc-shaped, or configured like wedges. They usually moved parallel with combat planes, hanging behind in some instances, but sometimes keeping pace or zooming ahead. They were not aggressive, but they distracted

The pesky, inexplicable balls of light called "foo fighters" bedeviled Allied and Axis pilots during World War II. In this illustration, an American B-24 Liberator attracts some foos during a daylight bombing raid against Germany. *Everett Collection*

and annoyed pilots, who were busy avoiding ground fire and scanning the skies for enemy aircraft.

Foo fighters appeared first to British aviators, in the late summer of 1941. In time, German and Japanese flyers encountered them, too. American flyers began to complain of the peculiar lights late in 1944, and coined the "foo fighter" name to suggest the things' inexplicable nature. (The word "foo" came from Bill Holman's *Smokey Stover* comic strip, in which slapstick firefighter Smokey frequently proclaimed, "Where there's foo, there's fire!")

Although most wartime pilots accepted that the foos were not aggressive, some nevertheless fired bursts at them, mainly out of curiosity. On March 25, 1942, an RAF tail gunner over Holland spotted an illuminated flying object. The gunner fired from 150 yards, to no effect. That outcome may have been a common one, as there are no records of foo fighters displaying hits, damage, or destruction by gunfire.

Pilots snapped numerous photographs of foo fighters, but image quality is almost invariably poor. Skeptics explain foo fighters as many things, such as reflected light on canopies, visible "bounce" from the Moon or bodies of water, cloud formations, and defective or dirty cameras. Alternatively, pilots captured foo fighters in photographs snapped in clear airspace around the globe. Further, discrete pilot reports bear striking similarities.

A particularly aggressive foo revealed itself in December 1944, chasing an American fighter twenty miles down the Rhine River. By this time, the phenomenon was prominent on the metaphoric radar of U.S. military intelligence, where a consensus developed: the "phoo bombs" (as internal intelligence documents called them) had been developed by Germany; some in Allied intelligence suspected that Germany manufactured the foos in Austria. That conclusion isn't entirely unreasonable except that foo fighters continued to bedevil military and civilian aircraft after war's end in 1945. Although no convincing postwar document mentioning "phoo bombs" has yet surfaced, the things continued to preoccupy a segment of the U.S. military post-1945.

Military historians and UFOlogists with military orientations insist that the foo fighters originated in Germany. Some other UFOlogists opt for an extraterrestrial explanation. Whatever the truth, the fact is that secret investigation of unidentified flying objects took on robust life during World War II, and continued afterward—coinciding neatly with the epic UFO events of 1947: the Kenneth Arnold sighting and the saucer crash at Roswell, New Mexico. In other words, the military and military intelligence had UFO investigative apparatus in place long before 1947.

How a German Foo Fighter Might Have Functioned

Rudolf Lusar's 1959 book *German Secret Weapons of World War II* claims that *Luftwaffe* engineers developed small, pilotless aircraft late in the war. Lusar identified one of these as the *Kugelblitz* (Ball lightning) and another as the *Feuerball* (Fireball). He may have been on to something: a November 7, 1944, Associated Press story about "New Aerial Weapons" said, "The Germans are using jet and rocket propelled planes and various other 'newfangled' gadgets against Allied night fighters. . . ."

According to Lusar, the advanced German aircraft were more than idle experiments: they carried klystron tubes (vacuum tubes that contain an electronic gun) that emitted electrostatic discharges designed to foul Allied aircraft's vital electronic-control systems.

As the English translation of *Kugelblitz* might suggest, the electrical phenomenon known as ball lightning is another possible explanation for foo fighters. Ball lightning (sometimes referred to as ghost lights) is a rare form of lightning manifested as a bright, luminous sphere. It is probably composed of ionized gas, but the precise conditions that create it are unknown. Speculation of causation encompasses microwave radiation, nuclear energy, oxidizing aerosols, slowly burning particles of silicon left by a lightning strike—even exotica the likes of dark matter, antimatter, and black holes.

Ball lighting that manifested itself as green "fireballs" regularly visited the American Southwest during 1948–51. Some of the sightings were close to U.S. military bases. A theory propounded in 2012 by Australian scientist John Lowke (representing a research team) holds that ball lightning occurs when air molecules are excited by an accumulation of streaming ions on the outside of a glass window. The "ball" can even appear to pass through the glass. When encountered by aircraft, ball lightning often "rides" on wingtips or appears near the ship's nose. Occasionally, though, the phenomenon can be violent. Social historian Lee Krystek found just such a case for his online Museum of Unusual History, describing a literal explosion of light and electricity inside a cockpit of a USAF KC-135 Stratotanker flying near thunderheads above New Jersey in 2007. The pilot, copilot, and Krystek's witness, an Air Force Reserve master sergeant, looked on in alarm as a basketball-sized "globe" that rotated out of nowhere roiled above the plane's instrument panel. The witness described the sphere as yellow with blue and pink accents. After a few minutes, the thing "slithered" onto the deck and made its way to the aft portion of the ship, where it dissipated. The entire event lasted seven or eight seconds.

The Nazi Saucer Connection (with a Cameo by Imperial Japan)

An especially stimulating aspect of Nazi Germany's employment of airpower during World War II, and its place in the larger discussion of UFOs, revolves around German interest in flying discs. The notion that wartime Germany (and postwar German holdouts) filled the skies with flying discs began to take hold as soon as the war ended, and now permeates Western culture, in broad strokes if not in specific detail. It is well known that wartime Germany developed startlingly sophisticated avionics and aircraft. Further, because of an interest in the occult pursued by SS chief Heinrich Himmler and some others in the Nazi hierarchy, many latter-day saucer enthusiasts posit that German saucer technology is linked to "lost science," the secrets of ancient runes, and other occult things. The secret, and possibly apocryphal, Vril Society—introduced to American thought in 1935 by refugee German science writer, and rocket and spaceflight enthusiast, Willy Ley—supposed that mankind's origins were in the hollow Earth, with scientific and biologic connections to aliens. The substance Vril was described as a life-giving energy force, an "all-permeating fluid" that conferred unimaginable power on those that could be its master. Some writers and amateur historians wonder if the Vril Society had links to Germany's far-right Thule Society, an occult-based *volk*-and Fatherland group established in Munich around 1917. Thule sponsored *Deutsche Arbeiterpartei* (DAP), the small political group that Adolf Hitler—who chose Munich as the base for his formative political agitation—eventually spun off into the NSDAP (Nazi Party).

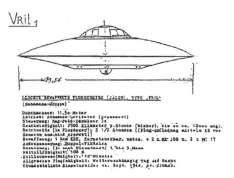

In 1935, Himmler sanctioned the establishment of the *Deutsches Ahnenerbe* (German Ancestral Heritage), a science-and-culture society. The group initially focused on German folklore and anthropological history (appropriating many private and institutional libraries along the way), linguistics, and classical philology. After 1939, *Ahnenerbe* activity shifted to explorations of genetics (hoping, for instance, to breed a horse capable of surviving the withering winters of Eastern Europe), and combat-related medicine, usually in cahoots with the heartless Institute of Applied Research, which experimented on unwilling human

Flying saucer technology linked to Nazi Germany has fascinated UFOlogists for more than seventy years. Although some latter-day claims are fanciful, Germany's advanced wartime work with rocket propulsion and unorthodox aerodynamics is well known. Tales of the "Vril Saucer" encompass science, fascist politics, and mysticism. The schematic seen here dates from September 1944.

subjects. Other wartime *Ahnenerbe* research explored astrology, ancient astronauts and hollow Earth, channeling, reincarnation, mass mind control, and the so-called Cosmic Ice Theory (by which titanic clashes of suns and "ice planets" account for earthquakes and other natural disasters on Earth, as well as provide a physical rationale for Atlantis and other lost civilizations).

This purported photo image of a German Vril saucer is from late 1942. An "urgent" November 7, 1957, FBI memo directed to J. Edgar Hoover discusses a former Polish POW who describes having seen a German flying disc, seventy-five to one hundred yards in diameter, in 1944.

Some UFO-centric sources claim that the *Ahnenerbe*'s ultimate function was as the framework supporting a two-part German goal: to contact extraterrestrials and mine alien technology; and locate ancient Earth technology—which may have been left by ETs in the first place. These undisciplined cultural correlations and wealth of odd notions combined to form a quasi-scientific Nazi stew of the Aryan "master race" and other crackpot eugenics, the durable hollow-Earth idea, and the demented 1939 journey of Himmler's SS into the mountains of Tibet to find the origins of the "Indo-Germanic" people. As the foolishness played out, Nazi occultists kept so firm a grip on the concept of Vril that the magic liquid, postwar, flowed into American and other Western pop culture right along with the swastika, the black-garbed SS, and iconic images of Hitler. Some people today are convinced that Germany used Vril to power its flying saucers.

Other present-day theorists are acolytes of Austrian naturalist and inventor Viktor Schauberger (1885–1958), who developed a special interest in the properties of water and air, particularly as those elements related to motive travel. He believed that fish, for instance, do not swim, but rather "are swum" by the water. Similarly, birds are "flown" by the air. In essence, the creatures do not push themselves along, but are pulled. Schauberger believed he found ancient references to this kind of propulsion: like some in Nazi government, Schauberger examined ancient Indian manuscripts, where he found what he believed to be lessons in the practical use of what he referred to as "flowing magnetism," a force that negated the effects of gravity. Original Sanskrit documents, Schauberger said, show flying craft called *vimanas*. Sometimes, the *vimanas* played roles in ancient aerial warfare.

Schauberger's innovation for powered flight involved what he called a biological vacuum, a dynamic field that, when manipulated with air directed through various chambers of a unique imploder motor, would create centripetal movement, and an implosive effect rather than the familiar explosive one. He felt that vertical takeoff and continual thrust were possible.

Schauberger and Hitler met in 1934, ostensibly to discuss challenges of irrigation; by 1944, Schauberger was working, possibly under duress, on his "Repulsine" engine. Objective: a flying saucer for German military use.

Surviving prototypes of the imploder engine survive. They are shaped like beefy saucers measuring about two feet across. When activated, they spin in place (to create the vacuum effect), inadvertently mimicking one "classic" style of flying saucer. Schauberger, though, simply intended his saucer-shaped motor to be mounted inside traditional vehicles, including submarines.

Riding the Rockets

World War II film footage of German V-1 rocket bombs and V-2 guided ballistic missiles, the experimental Me 163B *Komet* rocket plane, and the Horten brothers' "flying wing," as well as Allied pilots' startling aerial encounters with the remarkable Messerschmitt Me-262 jet fighter, has been widely seen and recalled for some seventy years. Because these rocket weapons existed—and led directly to American and Soviet successes in space—they suggest a plausible larger scenario involving Nazi flying saucers and (in even more expansive scenarios) secret German bases in Antarctica or on the Moon.

German tests of manned and unmanned experimental rocket fighters began early in 1944. Some, like the Bachem 8-349 A1, aka the *Natter*, were directed by remote control.

Because the Germans faced dramatic materials shortages as early as 1942–43, engineers designed the *Natter* on the cheap. Tools with low tolerances machined the *Natter*'s entirety, and final construction incorporated wood, inexpensive sheet steel, nails, and glue. Only one manned test of the *Natter* was made, and it was disastrous. At five hundred feet, the rocket plane lost its cockpit cover and headrest, assumed an unacceptable fifteen-degree angle of climb, and finally tilted over onto its back at five thousand feet before spiraling downward. Plane and pilot smashed into the Earth, leaving what historian Brian Ford described as "fragments."

Alexander Lippisch's stubby, swept wing Messerschmitt Me 163 *Komet* rocket fighter prototype was a piloted, climb-and-descend terror that touched six hundred mph during its first unfettered (non-towed) test flight in May 1941. The Walter HWK 509A rocket engine developed thirty-eight hundred pounds of continuous thrust, and sent the nine-thousand-pound Me 163 careening along the ground like a wobbly bullet. When the lightweight wheel carriage fell away, the rocket plane abruptly tipped back on its tail and accelerated straight up at some ten thousand feet per minute. Attainable top speed: 585–595 mph. Abrupt directional change and ferocious acceleration later became common elements of UFO reports from around the world.

Deltas and Discs

Mysterious, triangle-shaped craft, which comprise a significant portion of UFO accounts, have real-world antecedents in *Luftwaffe* research. The aforementioned Alexander Lippisch had a special preoccupation with delta-shaped "flying triangle" jet fighters, and designed a series of them. The Lippisch DM 1 had a vaguely delta-shaped fuselage, a classic "UFO" form that was considerably more pronounced on another German experimental aircraft, the Ho-IX Series rocket plane designed by brothers Walter and Reimar Horten. This fighter concept mounted a pair of Jumo

004 jet engines in twin nacelles that began at the leading edge of the fuselage, swept aft on either side of the tube-shaped cockpit, and culminated just forward of the plane's pointed, manta-like tail. Thrust from each Jumo engine was projected at 1,960 pounds. (The Horten ideal came to practical, if short-lived, fruition with the Northrop YB-49 "Flying Wing" heavy bomber of 1947.)

Extreme high altitude was another German fixation. At war's end, a dozen prototypes of the DFS-228 Mk 1 rocket plane existed; this was a reconnaissance aircraft designed to be towed to about twenty-five thousand feet and then released, whereupon it would climb to survey the battlefield from heights as great as sixty thousand feet. Test flights clocked the DFS-228 Mk 1 at 560 mph at level flight. The Germans destroyed every prototype, so the aircraft exists today only in drawings and test results.

Rocket-to-Saucer Evolution

The sophisticated, if doomed, German aeronautical activity still tickles the imagination today, partly as a "what if?" scenario (could the Germans have prevailed if they had had the resources to create such craft earlier in the war?); and partly as a presumed signpost on the road to working, practical German flying saucers. The SS allegedly maintained *Sonderburo* 13 (sometimes called SS–E IV) to collate, and keep secret, flying-disc research. Hitler may have hoped to send a manned disc into the stratosphere, or even for a brief flare into space. (*The Black Book of Flying Saucers*, a 1970 book by a French writer named Henry Durrant [real name, Didier Serres] first revealed the existence of *Sonderburo* 13; Durrant later claimed *Sonderburo* as a mischievous figment of his imagination.)

Although ignored, minimized, or dismissed by formally educated scholars of World War II, the German saucer program existed, and progressed well beyond wishful thinking. Much of the work culminated only in drawings, formulae, and small models, but some of the research went all the way to full-sized models and even working prototypes. The German rocket center at Peenemünde, for instance, functioned not only as the center of V-1 and V-2 development, but of flying-disc research. Nazi archives held in Europe have revealed schematics and strategic plans for a variety of disc-shaped aircraft. The *Haunebu*, for instance, is startlingly similar to the three-ball saucer photographed in the early 1950s by American contactee George Adamski. (Or perhaps Adamski's craft is similar to the *Haunebu*.) Another craft, the lightly armed prototype "Vril 1" disc (also known as the *Jager*), thirty-eight feet in diameter and fitted with a Schauberger imploder engine, may have flown in late 1942.

Hangars purpose-built to house enormous discs—some as large as 460 feet in diameter—are described in some historical sources; likewise a test of a Schauberger-powered disc, the Belluzzo-Schriever-Mietha, in Prague in February 1945. The B-S-M reportedly ascended above nine miles in three minutes, and achieved 760 mph. As the Allies closed in (Soviet troops liberated Prague on May 9), General Keitel (according to accounts) ordered the B-S-M destroyed, partly because some of its more sophisticated labor came from skilled inmates removed from the state-owned *Mittelwerk GmbH* underground factory in the Harz Mountains, near the Dora-Mittelbau concentration camp.

UFOs and the Battle of Los Angeles

The most astounding battle of World War II may not have been a proper battle at all, but just a bit of a misunderstanding. And although recognized as having occurred in and above Los Angeles on February 24–25, 1942, the real "battle"— such as it was—took place a day before, on February 23. That is when, shortly after 7:00 p.m., a lone Japanese submarine surfaced some twenty-five hundred yards off the coast of Ellwood, a tiny California crossroads located eight miles north of Santa Barbara. Onshore storage tanks kept by the Barnsdall Oil Company made a tempting target, and so the submarine's cannon devoted twenty minutes to shelling the tanks and beach. In the end, although nobody was hurt, and damage amounted to a paltry $500, the shelling was unusually brazen, particularly because the Coast Guard and other military—a mere ten weeks after the confidence-rattling Japanese attack on Pearl Harbor—were on the alert for suspicious activity in American waters. Whether the Japanese command timed this bad behavior to coincide with a presidential radio broadcast by Franklin Roosevelt is hard to say, but the fact is that just as FDR emphasized the danger facing the nation, an enemy sub surfaced, unmolested, and lobbed shells at a California beach.

When authorities became aware of what happened at Ellwood, Highway 101 was closed. Radio stations were ordered to suspend programming so that the authorities could make clear that a real alert, not a test, was underway. A few bombers went up to look for the sub, but they found nothing. Authorities lifted the alert after four hours.

Although the attack amounted to a gesture, the Japanese submarine had not been accounted for. People on the California coast wondered about that. *What if the sub hadn't come alone? Maybe enemy soldiers are lurking about. Maybe, somehow, the Japanese had sent planes.*

The remainder of the night and the daylight hours of the next day remained quiet, but then *another* evening alert went up, at about a quarter after seven on February 24. Someone had seen "unidentified objects" in the sky. Defense plants went on alert, but nothing further was reported, and city authorities lifted the general alert a little before 10:30 p.m.

Tick tock.

At 2:15 a.m. on February 25, coastal radar picked up an airborne object over the Pacific, about 120 miles from Los Angeles and moving toward the city. When a citywide blackout was ordered at 2:21, the nerves of Angelenos frayed all over again. Citizens began calling the police to report lights and other objects in the sky. Soldiers and sailors tensed. A few minutes past 3:00 a.m., ground watchers spotted a delta-shaped formation of bright objects flying at thousands of feet, apparently on their way to L.A. defense plants and munitions factories. The original object seen on radar had fallen off the screen, but that hardly mattered. Air raid sirens went off across the city. Civil defense workers grabbed their helmets and flashlights, and pushed into the streets, shouting at people to get inside and kill the lights. Some puzzled people looked at the sky from windows, rooftops, and balconies. Others tried to return to their families. Others just wanted to get indoors, now. The streets rang with screams and shouts. Cars that had doused their headlamps began to run into each other. Horns honked. *What a damnable mess.*

And then the batteries of antiaircraft guns opened up.

During the next hour and fifteen minutes, the largest city on America's West Coast was a bedlam. The reports from the hotly firing antiaircraft guns—thirty-seven-millimeter and three-inchers—shook buildings and rattled windows. The darkened streets and docks were flash-illuminated by shells exploding thousands of feet above. Stabbing, moving fingers of searchlights clawed the night sky. Shrapnel rained back onto the streets, panicking more people and encouraging the ack-ack gunners to fire more fiercely.

The gunners had targets, and civilians later insisted they'd seen moving balls of light periodically caught in the searchlights'

The February 24–25, 1942, Battle of Los Angeles is either a remarkable instance of American wartime vulnerability or one of the most fabulous military bungles of all time. Was Los Angeles attacked by flying discs? The soldiers that manned the roaring American antiaircraft guns said "yes."

Courtesy of Los Angeles Times

glare. People would talk about that for weeks. The gunners kept at their work, and citizens braced for something catastrophic.

Waning ammunition or a lack of targets or both finally had an effect, and by 4:15 a.m. the guns were mostly silent. Three hours later, the blackout imposed from San Obispo to the Mexican border was lifted. Nothing had been bombed or strafed, but in the violent confusion and, perhaps, the rain of shrapnel, five lives on the ground had been lost.

Washington quickly offered an explanation, but instead of reassuring people, "false alarm" only made them mad. *What the heck does that mean?* Secretary of the Navy Frank Knox—known afterwards as the "false-alarm" man—said that no planes had been aloft over Los Angeles. A day later, Secretary of War Henry Stimson explained that planes *had* been in the sky, fifteen American aircraft, flying over L.A. at between nine thousand and fifteen thousand feet. Despite the vigorous antiaircraft fire, no American planes had been damaged, and no airmen had been hurt.

Naturally enough, Angelenos who had seen aircraft concluded that if no American planes had been up, then enemy planes had been. The officers and enlisted men of the antiaircraft batteries saw, variously, planes, things "too big to be planes," and "meteorological balloons." Guesses at altitude ranged between eight thousand and thirty thousand feet. (Stimson's altitude estimate of nine thousand to fifteen thousand feet meant that the ack-ack guns, good beyond thirty-one thousand feet, should have brought down multiple aircraft—and they did not.) Gunners could not agree, either, on the numbers of planes: ten, ventured some; thirty, said others.

Knox and Stimson shortly came under pressure from local L.A. authorities and, worse, Congress. Charges of ineptitude rang out. The general disorder of the Battle of Los Angeles, and those five lost lives, loomed large. Some politicians wondered, along with California and the rest of America, if the Japanese had established secret bases in Mexico. (The Japanese had not.)

In their 1968 book *Mysteries of the Skies: UFOs in Perspective*, NICAP staffers Gordon Lore and Harold Deneault Jr. note that men's magazines and other pulps "explained" the activity as a response to a Japanese air raid. But those claims are spurious, as became clear during interrogation of Japanese command officers in the fall of 1945, after the war. No Japanese planes had been over Los Angeles on February 24. (And anyway, the very few Japanese planes that ever ventured close to American shores had to come singly, or perhaps as a pair, as they were collapsible aircraft carried by submarines.)

Lore and Deneault dismiss one theory that gained a bit of traction: the whole event had been staged by the U.S. military as a test of urban military and civil defense. No evidence to support that idea has emerged.

Although much about the Battle of Los Angeles defies logic, a mere moment of rational thought suggests that the official explanations are inadequate. Debate about what was in the sky that night continues—and almost nobody argues for Japanese or American airplanes.

Balloon Bombs, Plus Other Nastiness

Attack from the air is unnerving as well as potentially deadly. People, particularly civilians, do not cotton to the idea of harmful things dropping onto them from the sky. That's one psychological advantage held by purveyors of airborne warfare, and what drove the Japanese to pursue a strategically worthless but tactically clever air campaign against the United States in the final eighteen months of the war. Following study of Pacific air currents, a Japanese naval meteorologist named Sakyo Adachi confirmed that airborne incendiary-and-antipersonnel devices launched from Japan to float above the ocean—for days or weeks—would pass north of Hawaii and eventually reach America's west coast. Pacific trade winds blow from east to west, but above those winds is a west-to-east flow, the Japan Current. High explosives lifted above the trade winds would float eastward. In a test, Adachi attached an incendiary-filled canister to a simple paper balloon. The balloon was inflated with gas and released into the sky. A Zero fighter sent to track the flight confirmed the hoped-for ascension of the balloon into the Japan Current. The device was on its way east to, Adachi hoped, the United States.

The balloon bombs would ordinarily fall into a subsection of the UFO category, but because the balloons were so slow and small, they became UFOs of another sort: *unseen* flying objects. The scheme was clever, but Japanese naval aspirations for it were plainly incredible. The tacticians' dream was that a flurry of bombs wafting into the great pine forests that covered California, Oregon, and Washington would set off tremendous forest fires. America's timber industry would suffer, and, more crucially, civilians would be stunned into panic. Some Japanese meteorological projections anticipated explosive balloons floating as far east as Salt Lake City and even Chicago. The Japanese reasoned that if American timber, housing stock, and other civilian areas suffered regular damage, the USA might agree to a negotiated settlement to the war. That was a pipe dream, of course, especially given presidents Roosevelt and Truman's clarity on the issue of Japan's unconditional surrender.

Regardless, over a period of months some six thousand balloon bombs—known colloquially to their creators as *Fugo*—were lifted aloft into the Japan Current. They traveled east, but most were lost over the great expanse of the Pacific. Of the *Fugo* balloons that reached America's West Coast, one or two sparked small timber fires in Oregon and possibly Washington. Most of the devices lucky enough to make landfall dropped unnoticed onto desert areas of California and Nevada. The balloon-bomb program could never have forced a change to America's determination to end the war on its own terms, but would have created a stir if it could have duplicated its greatest—and most miserable—achievement: on May 5, 1945, a *Fugo* fell and exploded near Sunday School picnickers on Gearhart Mountain, near Bly, Oregon, killing a pregnant woman and five children.

An American attempt to send unseen flying objects to Japan was even more incredible than the *Fugo* scheme: President Roosevelt authorized Project X-Ray, which called for Japanese cities to be terrorized by millions of bats carrying tiny incendiaries. The small mammals were to be released from American planes. Trial runs in Texas, New Mexico, and California during 1942–43 showed an unpredictable kind of efficacy—a cadre of test bats accidentally incinerated a new U.S. airfield—but the bat-bomb campaign was terminated when American scientists made significant progress toward an atomic bomb.

The *Fugo* incendiaries and bat bombs are linked to (admittedly simple) technology, but most strongly to twisted notions of race. From the beginning of America's struggle with Japan, American propaganda, particularly illustrations, magazine cartoons, and animated cartoons, depicted Japanese as squalid, yellow, bandy-legged little creatures with fangs or, if the depiction was intended to be more "humorous," horsey buck teeth. Thick, round spectacles brought attention to squinted, "slanted" eyes above features twisted into perpetual grimaces. Sometimes, these cartoon Japanese had tails, like monkeys. (Arthur Szyk, a brilliantly talented Polish-American designer and caricaturist featured regularly in *Time, Collier's*, and other major magazines, was particularly skilled at creating these sorts of alien-seeming Japanese hobgoblins.) Much as the Nazi anti-Semitic cartoonist "Fips" (Philippe Rupprecht) depicted European and American Jews as subhuman in hundreds of drawings published in Jules Streicher's abhorrent rag *Der Stürmer*, Szyk and other American cartoonists established that Japanese were closer to vermin than human. We were encouraged to believe that against such creatures, the atomic bomb wasn't just justified but obligatory.

The Japanese exploited race hatred via cartoons of giant-sized, cucumber-nosed Americans, with red hair and an imperative to murder children and steal the virtue of Japan's women.

It is in such repugnant stuff that the war's belligerents developed a template reflected just half a decade later in such pop culture inventions as Hollywood's *The Thing from Another World*, a generation of horrific science-fiction comic books and aggressive SF toys, and, later still, accounts given by shaken victims of abductions engineered by brutal extraterrestrials. Like the Germans, these ETs have superweapons and other advanced technology; and like the imagined Japanese and the Americans, they are ugly, duplicitous, and vicious.

Some Important Sightings, 1939–45

Military pilots active during these years witnessed a variety of unidentified aircraft, and chased (or were chased by) some of them. Fliers attributed some incidents to foo fighters. Civilian sightings of the period are no less puzzling.

1939: During a professional visit to Washington, D.C., a Greenwich, Ohio, minister named Turner Hamilton Holt is taken to a Capitol Building sub-basement by his cousin, Secretary of State Cordell Hull, and shown large, chemical-filled glass "jars" containing the preserved corpses of four humanoids. The secret room also stores silver-metallic wreckage of a "vehicle." **Note:** When he related the story to his daughters, Reverend Holt described the humanoids as "creatures." At the scene, Hull explained to Holt that the creatures remained hidden in order to prevent panic. When invited by Hull to "lift" the wreckage, Holt was startled by the metal's unusually light weight. Around 2000, MUFON/CUFOS official William E. Jones contacted the Capitol Building's curator, who confirmed the 1939 existence of a sub-basement (since removed). But neither Hull's desk diary, memoirs, nor voluminous papers suggest the creatures' existence.

June 1940: The crew of an antiaircraft gun at Hoy Island, the Orkneys, Scotland, locks onto a flying sphere and tracks its course for ten seconds. **Note:** Calculations made from the gun's range-finder revealed that the object flew at thirty-eight thousand feet.

April 1941: Rev. William Huffman hurries to a plane crash outside Cape Girardeau, Missouri, and discovers three deceased humanoids near a badly damaged, seamless metallic disc. The bodies are about four feet tall and dressed in metallic coveralls. Reverend Huffman notes the creatures' gray skin tone and unusually long fingers. Local military removes bodies and craft.

February 24–25, 1942: Antiaircraft guns open up on a formation of discs flying high above war-nerved L.A., kicking off the noisiest portion of the Battle of Los Angeles. **Note:** Read the full story earlier in this chapter.

July 1942: In rural Kannaanpaa, Finland, a dark-haired woman leads a nine-year-old girl into a forest and to a metallic craft that sits on tripod landing gear. Outside the craft, two men hold tightly to a frightened thirteen-year-old boy. As the group prepares to enter the craft, the girl "hears" boarding instructions in her head, without audible sound. The woman asks the girl questions about Jesus, explains that there is no such thing as time, and suggests that the group is going to take a journey. Meanwhile, the boy sits on the floor, screaming. **Note:** The girl returned home safely but suffered stomach upset and seriously swollen eyes. She recovered after a month, but the boy was institutionalized at age seventeen.

October 28, 1943: A test of an American cloaking device at the Philadelphia Naval Yard goes awry, pushing some crewmen of the destroyer USS *Eldridge* into madness, and physically harming others. **Note:** One persistent rumor about this controversial event is that the cloaking technology had been acquired from extraterrestrials, or that UFOs above the Yard caused the mental and physical damage. For more on the so-called "Philadelphia Experiment," see chapter fifteen.

June 18, 1944: On an Oahu, Hawaii, beach near Kaneohe, U.S. Navy engineer Edward Langer sees a spherical craft on the sand and then encounters seven aggressive "dwarfs," about 4½ feet tall and dressed in green coveralls. Langer struggles with one of the little creatures and manages to snatch a belt with an attached black box. **Note:** Langer claimed later that the OSS confiscated the belt device. Then there is the "seven dwarfs" aspect of this story, which sounds too ripe to be true. Then again, the initial encounter is chronicled in Ted Bloecher and David Webb's useful Humanoid Catalog (HumCat) projects.

Summer 1944: While on his backyard swing in Meriden, Connecticut, five-year-old Bobby Luca sees a hovering, domed disc crewed by small, gray humanoids with oversized heads and eyes. The visitors temporarily paralyze the boy's body, and communicate with him telepathically. **Note:** The grown-up Bob Luca was abducted by aliens in 1967 and again in 1978, the second time with his wife, Betty. Like Bob, Betty had a 1944 childhood encounter with aliens.

September 10, 1944: Five hundred German troops at Epinal, France, are startled by a white disc hovering over railroad tracks. German small-arms fire is directed at the disc, to no apparent effect.

Mid-March 1945: The battleship USS *New York* is followed by a high-flying silver disc in the skies above the Admiralty Islands, Bismarck Archipelago (north of New Guinea). After thirty minutes the captain gives the order to fire, but the shells burst well below the disc, suggesting that the object is at twenty thousand feet or higher. Unharmed, the disc rapidly ascends and disappears. The incident is witnessed by sailors and Marines.

Mid-July 1945: Six Hellcat fighters assigned to the USS *Cowpens* are scrambled to pursue a fast-moving disc, tracked on radar as flying above the top-secret Hanford Ordnance Works at Hanford, Washington. The Hellcats chase the craft well above the planes' thirty-seven-thousand-foot ceiling, only to turn back when the object continues to ascend. **Note:** Mysterious flight activity above Hanford Ordnance caused grave concern because the site developed deadly plutonium necessary to the Manhattan Project. Hellcat pilot Rolan Powell later recalled the UFO's vaporous discharge, suggestive to him of a purposeful smoke screen. Hanford was home to Reactor B, the world's first full-scale plutonium-production reactor. The reactor became fully operational in February 1945, five months before the encounter described here. The Hanford facility expanded during the Cold War, and continued to produce weapons-grade plutonium. It attracted UFOs until 1987, when the final nuclear reactor was decommissioned.

Chaos in Antarctica

For nearly three generations, rumors have swirled around Operation Highjump, a 1946 U.S. Navy training exercise in Antarctica that supposedly failed because of troops' unexpected and disastrous encounter with advanced aircraft flying out of a secret Antarctic base. The precise nature of the claims varies, but two elements are constant: that the aircraft had been created and piloted by fugitive Nazis, aliens, or both.

Antarctica is the world's southernmost continent. Sealers probably encountered the landmass before 1815; Russian and American expeditions of 1819–20 made the discovery "official." Progressively more ambitious expeditions mounted by America, France, Britain, and Russia during 1820–42 made tentative attempts at mapping. Shipbuilding advanced over the next hundred years, but much of Antarctica remained a mystery in 1946. Operation Highjump was an immediate-postwar initiative to demonstrate American military prowess to the Soviet Union, and map "the bottom of the world" in advance of the International Geophysical Year scheduled for 1957–58. Washington had some apprehension (not shared with the public) about the *North* Pole, and the possibility of Soviet troops moving across Arctic ice to attack the United States from the north. (The U.S. military had put together a training exercise in the Arctic in the summer of 1946, but because the northern winter was coming on, no follow-up to that exercise was possible for 1946.) Highjump activities south in the Antarctic, scheduled for late 1946, would combine mapping with general evaluations of military operations in cold conditions.

The operation assembled thirteen ships, twenty-three aircraft, and some forty-seven hundred men. But most of the troops had no polar experience, and the expedition's flying leadership was, according to historian Dian Olson Belanger, "very thin." Further, Admiral Richard M. Byrd, the mission's ostensible leader, was not well, and functioned under the heavy thumb of the U.S. Navy. In the middle of a December 1946 blizzard, the crash of a Navy PBM Mariner (patrol bomber flying boat) carrying a crew of nine resulted in three deaths. The six survivors waited nearly two, bitterly cold weeks for rescue, and the bodies of the three dead men were buried where they had fallen.

Highjump's photo mapping was successfully carried out, and the crash was given appropriate press coverage. Interest in the PBM's fate intensified later, when UFO theorists downplayed the weather factor and focused on supposed alien or Nazi aircraft as the culprits. Although Admiral Byrd spoke publicly of future enemy aircraft able to fly "from pole to pole at incredible speeds," he had no reason to suspect such craft existed, and was simply hypothesizing.

Since 1959—beginning with *The Worlds Beyond the Poles*, a "hollow Earth" book by F. Amadeo Gianinni—and encompassing SF-fantasy novels from the 1990s to the present, as well as a questionable 2006 Russian documentary, various sources have suggested that the Byrd Antarctic mission was mounted to investigate hidden German airbases. What encouraged this speculation about Nazis? Some of the tales were fact-based. German pilots operating from an aircraft carrier had begun air exploration of the Antarctic shore and interior in 1939, focusing particularly on Queen Maud Land. Before February 1939 was out, German soldiers and explorers had established New Swabia. During 1941–42, German scientists, engineers, and troops arrived at a new outpost, Base 211. Although Hitler never used his navy to its capacity, the apparent German interest in Antarctica puzzled and worried some Allied observers. Many were perplexed by reports of the arrival at Base 211 of German tunnel-digging equipment, railroad tracks and ties, and rail-laying machines. Admiral Doenitz, the chief of the *Kriegsmarine*, was credited with saying this in 1939: "My submariners have found a true paradise on Earth." And Doenitz was alleged to have said this in 1943: "The German submarine fleet is proud, and at the other end of the world, we've made an impregnable citadel for our Führer." Speculation about warm Antarctic lakes and tunnels built wide enough for German submarines began during the war and continued into 1946. The Soviet Union claimed, nonsensically, that the American military had been unable to account for more than one hundred German subs, as well as thousands of top German rocket scientists, at war's end.

As Highjump unfolded, Admiral Byrd supposedly reported German fighter jets and unidentified craft that rose from beneath the water to confront his fleet. And according to a purported U.S. Navy witness named John Sireson, Byrd made a report on February 26, 1947, of "a mysterious, lethal ray" and silent "objects" that floated between his ships," firing rays from their noses." According to this account, a Navy destroyer, the USS *Murdoch*, was sunk. However, Navy records show no USS *Murdoch* active in the Antarctic at that time. The credibility of the claims is further undermined by confusing variations/contradictions of names and other facts: accounts cannot agree, for example, on whether the violent events took place in the Antarctic or the Arctic. Witness John Sireson is often referred to as "Sayerson," and the *Murdoch* is alternately identified as the *Murdock* and the *Maddox*. And in some accounts, the *Murdoch/Murdock/Maddox* is not a destroyer but a torpedo boat. In any event, no ship of any of those names was involved in Highjump; the name that comes closest is the USS *Merrick*, but that was a supply ship that returned to base in one piece.

A Germany-based Web site that is particularly vehement about the UFO aspect of Byrd's mission calls itself, in an amusingly *a priori* way, facts-are-facts.com. Another site, conspiracy-watch.org, describes the number of Highjump troops pretty accurately, but characterizes the mission as a U.S. "invasion."

The next paragraph begins, "This is fact. It is undeniable."

6

"The World of Tomorrow"

The Future Is Now—Don't Get Trampled

The Modernism that defined the 1893 World's Columbian Exposition in Chicago presaged a related yet fundamentally different philosophy, futurism. Less apprehensive about industrialization than the Modernists, Futurists celebrated industry's dynamism, and the sheer, aggressive joy of technology. In his 1909 "Manifesto of Futurism," Italian poet Filippo Tommaso Marinetti celebrated "a new beauty, the beauty of speed." He gloried in what he saw as a perfect symbol of the age and the movement: "[a] racing car with its trunk adorned by great exhaust pipes like snakes with an explosive breath, a roaring car that seems to be driving under shrapnel. . . ."

Futurism manifested itself most strongly in painting and poetry, and although much of it focused on the startle effect of a new visual aesthetic, it also was heavily philosophical. Marinetti's "Manifesto" expressed an overheated fondness for "the box on the ear, and the fisticuff," and for war, which Marinetti recommended as "the only hygiene of the world. . . . the fine Ideas [sic] that kill, and the scorn of woman."

This sort of distinctly male, essentially adolescent coffeehouse-and-garret rhetoric encouraged some dramatically fresh literature and visual art, but for everyday applications, futurism suggested only a way of thinking, rather than a material way of life. For the latter, we must turn to an offshoot of futurism, which can usefully be called Practical Futurism.

Practical Futurists found excitement in industry and cities—and speculated on how to remake our urban centers, our factories, our agriculture, and our homes. It is because of Practical Futurism that America and the larger industrialized world developed an openness about technology's possibilities—*the openness that allowed popular acceptance of a unique concept: unidentified flying objects.* By 1920, amateur and professional explorers had mapped the poles, the Amazon, "darkest Africa," and other points that had been inaccessible just a generation before. Technology to allow extensive undersea exploration had still to be developed, so Practical Futurists and exploration enthusiasts—cognizant, of course, of rocket technology—began to look seriously at places located beyond Earth.

The Technocracy movement of the 1930s posited that society could be made efficient and productive with rule combining production economics and technology, administered by elite technicians and engineers. So bloodless that it shortly came in for spoofing by W. C. Fields and others, Technocracy did not go easily: much of its love of order and high-tech autocracy manifested itself in the 1939 New York World's Fair, which was abuzz with robots and autogyros, and mechanistic visions of near-future highways, factories, cities, and homes. The Future had arrived.

Signposts on the Road to Practical Futurism and UFO Culture

Einstein's Theory of Relativity: Albert Einstein's famed theory is actually two: his *Special Theory of Relativity* (published 1905) and his *Theory of General Relativity* (1916). Together they encourage thoughts of practical, long-distance space travel.

The Special Theory is premised on the assumption that the speed of light is absolute. If you stand in place and switch on, say, a portable spotlight, the light will travel at 186,000 miles per second. Nothing can travel faster. But what happens if you switch on your spotlight as you run forward? Logic suggests that the beam will travel at the speed of light *plus* the speed at which you're running. However, because we've already accepted that light speed is the ultimate, our logic (which is, in this case, based in Newtonian physics) cannot lead to a true conclusion about the plus-light speed of the spotlight beam. Einstein said that space and time are interconnected, in a fabric or a continuum, called space-time. He thus postulated "time dilation," by which objects approaching the speed of light cause time to slow down, and scale objects' speeds to the speed of light. Speed and time are relative rather than absolute.

Einstein's Theory of General Relativity is a refinement and expansion of his Special Theory. It holds that gravity is a curved field created by the presence of mass. The mass of a great star or planet causes distortion in the space-time continuum. Here on Earth, we feel that distortion as gravity. Light moving toward a great mass appears to slow down; it also bends more than Newtonian physics predicts. Light moving *away* from a great object is stretched into longer wavelengths (which is why light from stars in a strong gravitational field manifest closer to the red end of the electromagnetic spectrum).

Einstein's theories suggest that distance and time need not be restrictors of space travel. Assuming a method of propulsion suitable to generate sufficient sub-light speed (see chapter three), spacecraft from Earth, or elsewhere, could travel enormous distances without prohibitive aging of the crew.

Speculative Magazine Fiction: Science-based adventure stories appeared in periodicals that encompassed the whimsical super-science of the *Frank Reade Weekly Magazine*, the Tom Swift adventures, Hugo Gernsback's *Amazing Stories* (with colorful and imaginative future-oriented cover paintings by Frank R. Paul), John W. Campbell's *Astounding Science Fiction* and other science-based story magazines; plus *Air Wonder Stories*, *Thrilling Wonder Stories*, *Planet Stories*, *Startling Stories*, *Captain Future*, and numberless other "space opera" SF pulps.

Air Wonder Stories is one of numerous pulp magazines that specialized in science-based tales of the future. The remarkable airship on this March 1930 cover is the work of illustrator Frank R. Paul.

Science Fiction Comic Strips: Alex Raymond's *Flash Gordon*, Dick Calkins and Philip Nowlan's *Buck Rogers,* William Ritt and Clarence Gray's *Brick Bradford*, and other SF newspaper strips offered lively, fanciful visions of technology and other worlds.

Science Fiction Comic Books: Four-color depictions of space adventure leapt from the pages of *Planet Comics, Fantastic Comics, Marvel Comics*, and superhero comics (many of which had SF elements) led by *Action* and *Superman.*

"How-to" Popular-Science Magazines: *Popular Science, The Electrical Experimenter, Mechanix Illustrated, Popular Mechanics, Modern Mechanix, Science and Mechanics*, and others gave "new science" a practical edge, giving equal space to sump pump installation and gaudily illustrated notions of future personal aircraft; rockets, airships, and atomic ocean liners; automated houses; atomic cannons; stereoscopic movies; and much more.

1939 New York World's Fair: Like the 1893 Columbian Exposition, this gala exhibition at New York thrilled visitors with technological achievements—existing and near-future—destined to make everyday life easier, more convenient, less stressful, and more enjoyable. In this, the Fair functioned as a trade show underwritten by Ford, General Motors, Westinghouse (showing the talking robot Electro and his robot dog, Sparko), Kraft, the American Tobacco Company, and many other highly visible sponsors. Many of the more popular exhibits, such as GM's Futurama, celebrated automobile culture with visions of roadways and other aspects of life in the scale-model City of 1960. Streamlined "future" cars, locomotives, airplanes, and other transportation suggested the rapid shrinking of the world. Special exhibits highlighted long-distance telephone technology, television, 3-D movies, and hydroelectric power. The Fair's signature buildings, the giant white Perisphere globe and its companion, the towering, slim obelisk called the Trylon, symbolized the promise of a fresh future—a future previewed just months before the world slipped into war.

Futurist-Oriented Industrial Designers: Led by Raymond Loewy (whose work could be seen at the World's Fair), Harley Earl, and Henry Dreyfuss, forward-looking designers brought streamlining and aircraft cues to lipsticks, automobiles, locomotives, appliances, furniture, and other elements of daily life.

Futurist-Oriented Urban Planners and Architects: Soaring, preplanned, multiuse skyscraper visions (often with provision for saucerlike commuter aircraft); and streamlined, functional single-family homes came from King Camp Gillette, Jules Guerin, Richard Rummell, Ludwig Mies van der Rohe, Le Corbusier, Richard Neutra, Francisco Mujica, Harvey Wiley Corbett, Wallace Harrison and J. André Fouilhoux (designers of the World's Fair Trylon and Perisphere), Hugh Ferriss, Frank Lloyd Wright, R. Buckminster Fuller, William Lescaze, and others. One of the greatest of these, Norman Bel Geddes, designed much of the 1939 World's Fair.

Detroit's Bohn Aluminum and Brass Corporation submitted patent drawings for a streamlined station wagon concept in 1944, and turned to illustrator Arthur Radebaugh for this sleek rendering. The futuristic wagon carries aerodynamic cues that would shortly characterize flying saucers.

Motion Picture Production Designers: Moving visions of futuristic urban life, often with unusual aircraft, distinguished German, British, and American work by Otto Hunte, Erich Kettelhut, and Karl Vollbrecht (*Metropolis*, 1927); Andrew Mazzei (*High Treason*, 1929); Stephen Goosson and Ralph Hammeras (*Just Imagine*, 1930); Erich Kettelhut (*F.P.1 antwortet nicht* [*F.P.1 Doesn't Answer*],1933); Otto Hunte (*Gold*, 1934); Ernö Metzner (*Trans-Atlantic Tunnel*, 1935); Laszlo Moholy-Nagy and William Cameron Menzies (*Things to Come*, 1936); and Ralph Berger (*Flash Gordon*, 1936). Why were rocketships real? Because they were there, twenty feet high, on movie screens.

The Future Comes Home

The pop-, design-, and tech-culture elements described above washed over America and the world like a wave, stimulating imaginations and opening minds to speculative ideas that would have seemed absurd just twenty years earlier. The World of Tomorrow took hold in the 1930s, and that world included notions of space travel, and what would shortly be called UFOs.

Founded in San Francisco in 1920, National Motor Bearing Company built its fortune with precisely machined laminated shims. NMB shortly offered oil seals, too, and became a major California defense contractor during World War II. Postwar, it joined the stampede of California tech manufacturers into sharply future-oriented advertising. The precise airbrush work on this 1951 "flying saucers" ad is by Art Radebaugh.

As discussed, technological innovations of World War II, particularly those related to flight, predisposed the public to a heightened awareness of aircraft. Postwar, German-influenced rocket development in America and the Soviet Union excited scientists and dreamers alike. Laypersons with "practical" turns of mind scoffed at the notion of a manned trip to the Moon until the mid-1950s, when rocketry achieved quick progress that culminated in the dramatic 1957 Soviet launch of the Sputnik satellite and the USA's simultaneous program of "catch-up." By the late 1950s, Americans felt at once threatened and heartened by rocket science. Nobody wanted enemy space satellites to drop things on their heads, particularly not atomic bombs.

On the other hand, America's accelerating military and industrial interest in rocketry and space encouraged citizens to feel patriotic and proud. America's notion of itself—clever, aggressive, forward-thinking—meshed well with the invigorated scientific atmosphere. Then, too, rocket and other space development promised enormous economic gains. Los Angeles had become a center of defense manufacturing and new aviation during the war, and moved easily from traditional aircraft to jets and rockets. Thousands of people, with varying levels of training and skill, would be needed to fill jobs that hadn't existed just a few years before. The inevitable ripple effect of job growth in and around postwar Los Angeles brought new homes and new jobs, many tied to L.A.-area defense contractors.

"Space Age" evolved from a child's notion to a way of life—and earning. The vaguely amorphous concept called "the future" brought tech and tech-support jobs not just to L.A. but Denver and San Diego; New York and Los Alamos; Sacramento and Detroit; Buffalo and Seattle; Ormond Beach, Florida, and Watertown, Massachusetts. Many companies—including Lockheed, Bosch Arma, Douglas, Martin, Bendix, Northrop, and Convair—already were well known, and nicely positioned to further define themselves via technological futurism. Others, such as Ball Brothers, Hydro-Aire, Kaylock, Electro-Tec, JPL, Lummus, Marquardt, Rocketdyne, Hallicrafters, and Ex-Cell-O, had kept lower profiles, or were new altogether.

The companies devoted themselves to communications systems and solar arrays; high-heat insulation and plasma thermionics; microwave antennas and missile-guidance systems; satellite mapping and solid-state electronics; nuclear engines and spacecraft navigation—an endless stream of systems, components, and concepts.

Print ads appearing in trade and consumer magazines during the 1950s and early 1960s could be especially telling. Because the essentially fanciful nature of advertising illustration had not yet been superseded by the literalness of commercial photography, postwar rocket-and-related ads did not restrict themselves to visualizations of the missiles and jet engines of the present day; artists were encouraged to depict many other wonders of tomorrow, and the day after tomorrow, too. Cultural historian Megan Prelinger has smartly discussed the colorful, aggressively modern Abstract Expressionist look of some tech ad art of the period. The unspoken message: *If you don't "get" this, you don't get the future.*

The Soviet Union's Sputnik satellite—the first such object ever launched from Earth—weighed 184 pounds and looked like a basketball festooned with antennae. By today's standards, Sputnik is a modest thing, but in 1957 it deeply frightened many Americans, who looked to the skies with new anxiety. Not everyone, though, felt terrified—as witness this young soda fountain customer, who enjoys a Sputnik sundae.

Getty Images

Most pieces, though, were considerably more literal. Many visualize graceful, finned rockets resting on the Moon. Others imagine revolving-wheel space stations, and nuclear-pulse rockets. Lockheed depicted a dramatically delta-shaped "Space Transport" rocket. An artist working for Bosch Arma rendered a titanic "lunar unicycle" on the Moon, a sophisticated gyroscope designed to carry a crew during lunar exploration. Another Bosch ad shows a graceful "solar wind ship" traveling in deep space without need for fuel. A Convair artist positioned a great, quadruple-sphere "fusion-proton intergalactic space vehicle" against the splendor of the Great Spiral Nebula. And a Douglas ad with a cheeky, rhetorical question about Moon vacations is dominated by an elliptical lander that is very like the classic flying saucer.

Most importantly, nearly every corporate tech advertisement depicted the endless sky, splashed with stars, meteors, and other planets. Whatever the wonders of the future, they would come from the sky.

7

Kenneth Arnold, the Eyewitness

He Saw What He Saw When He Saw It

Kenneth Arnold's Adventure of a Lifetime

If Kenneth Arnold had been a Hollywood actor registered with Central Casting, he would have been called for jobs playing police lieutenants, attorneys, Army majors, and businessmen. In 1947, he was handsomely masculine, with dark hair swept to one side in a sensible pompadour; and level, dark eyes set in a square face. Just thirty-two, Arnold had been a high school football star, and participated in swimming trials for the 1932 Olympics. He held a pilot's license, and yes, he owned a business, the Great Western Fire Control Supply Co. From his home in Boise, Idaho, Arnold pursued sales by flying forty to a hundred hours a month across five western states. June 1947 brought him to Washington State to oversee installation of fire-control equipment at Central Air Service, located in Chehalis.

On Tuesday, June 24, Arnold had completed his business and was flying alone in his three-seat, single-engine CallAir A-2 at about ninety-two hundred feet. (One or two sources identify Arnold's CallAir as an A-3.) With a bit of time on his hands, he decided to see if he could spot a Marine Corps C-46 transport plane that had gone missing in the area the previous January. The military offered a five-thousand-dollar reward, so Arnold diverted his flight path from his destination, Yakima, until he reached a spot some twenty-five miles away from Washington's Cascade Range, approaching the west faces of Mount Adams and Mount Rainier.

A few minutes before 3:00 p.m., Arnold's attention was captured by "nine peculiar-looking aircraft" flying in diagonal formation. His immediate thought had been geese—the big birds can fly as high as twenty-thousand feet—but Arnold dismissed the idea when he was momentarily blinded by "a tremendous bright flash" off the crafts' skins, and periodic flashes after that, as the objects heeled in the sky.

The objects moved in an odd, undulating unison that Arnold likened to the weaving "tail of a Chinese kite." The craft flying at point had a crescent shape with a pointed, delta-shaped aft portion; the eight that followed were disc-shaped and more fully rounded. (After returning to the sky above Mount Adams days later, to double-check on landmarks, Arnold estimated that the nine objects had been strung out for about five miles.) A uniform lack of tail assemblies perplexed Arnold, who removed his sunglasses and opened his port window for a clearer look. Sure enough, none of the craft showed tails, standard wings, or anything else required to maneuver a powered aircraft.

The CallAir flew in a clear, bright sky. Anyone aloft that day enjoyed visibility approaching fifty miles. While maintaining a steady hand on the controls, Arnold observed the nine objects for about two-and-a-half minutes. He was an experienced pilot with twenty-nine hundred flight hours and a clear grasp of precisely where he was in the sky, and the positions of the nine craft in relation to his own. He estimated that as he observed, the UFOs traveled forty-seven miles. (At one point, the craft passed behind a mountain peak located twenty-five miles from Arnold's position, giving the pilot a useful point of reference.)

Beginning at 2:59 p.m., and for the next minute and forty-two seconds, Arnold studied the objects, utilizing the peaks of Adams and Rainier, a cowling tool, and a DC-4 visible some fifteen miles off the port side of his plane as reference points. While trying to calculate the objects' approximate speed, he estimated the nine craft at twenty to twenty-five miles distant—considerably closer than the hundred miles when Arnold first saw them. The distances suggested that the UFOs maintained an arc of at least two degrees; anything less, and they would not have been visible to Arnold at all.

Although Arnold's initial report estimated the length of each craft as forty-five to fifty feet, a later look at Arnold's calculations suggested an individual length of 210 feet, and an astonishing speed of 1,200 miles per hour. (At the time of Arnold's sighting, the fastest piloted flight dated to July 1944, when German test

Idaho businessman and private pilot Kenneth Arnold saw "flying crescents" near Washington State's Cascade Range on June 24, 1947. Arnold, who had logged nearly three thousand hours of flight time, observed the craft for nearly two minutes. The Saucer Age had begun. *Alamy*

pilot Heini Dittmar took an experimental Me 163B *Komet* rocket plane to 700 miles per hour. The fastest American flight had been accomplished on June 19, 1947, by Col. Albert Boyd, who reached 624 mph in a P-80 Shooting Star, a U.S. jet fighter. In November 1947, five months after Edwards's sighting, an American X-1 rocket plane flown in a secret test by Chuck Yeager reached 891 mph.)

Arnold's last look at the nine craft came as they flew south and vanished behind the peak of Mount Adams.

What had Arnold seen? His first thought was camouflaged American bombers, or a phalanx of wholly experimental aircraft. (A helicopter pilot in the area saw the objects, too, and wrote them off as test-fired American missiles.) Arnold worried that disaster might result if the craft were somehow fitted with atomic bombs. He decided to talk with the FBI. After a quick stop at Yakima, he flew to the nearest local office, at Pendleton, Oregon. Because the office was closed, Arnold visited Pendleton's *East Oregonian* newspaper, where he found reporters Bill Bequette (who reported for UPI, as well as the *East Oregonian*) and Nolan Skiff.

Arnold gave his first press interview to Bequette. During the conversation, Arnold described the nine mysterious craft as "shiny, crescent-shaped plates," adding that they moved "like a saucer would if you skipped it across the water." The saucer image struck Bequette's imagination, and when the story ran on the front page of the *East Oregonian*'s June 26, 1947, edition, Arnold's crescents had become "saucer-like." It was from that description, of course, that reporters and others later derived "flying saucer." The "flying saucer" descriptor stuck immediately. For example, in the August 31, 1947, Sunday installment of the *Superman* newspaper strip—a continuity in which Superman tosses large plates into the sky as an advertising stunt—an astronomer at the eyepiece of an enormous telescope exclaims, "It looks like a flying saucer! It *is* a flying saucer!" Creators of comic strips worked four to six weeks ahead of publication, which means that *Superman* writers Jerry Siegel and Alvin Schwartz, and artist Wayne Boring, invoked "flying saucers" mere weeks after the Arnold story broke.

A tense world situation, apprehension that the craft belonged to a foreign government, and sheer novelty helped put the Arnold story on page one. Still, the *East Oregonian*'s headline writer struck a whimsical tone: "Impossible! Maybe. But Seein' is Believin', Says Flier."

By the time the *Oregonian* story appeared on the AP wire, Arnold's crescent-shaped craft had become "nine bright saucer-like objects." A follow-on story in the Norman, Oklahoma, *Transcript* quoted remarks Arnold made to a local businessman named Jack Whitman. Whitman had apparently absorbed the "saucer" remark, telling the *Transcript* that Arnold described the craft to him as "shaped like saucers."

Later in the week, Portland's *Oregon Daily Journal* quoted Byron Savage, an Oklahoma City man who had seen a single, silvery flying object on May 17, 1947, more than a month before Arnold's sighting of nine. Savage's wife and some skeptical friends suggested he may have seen lightning. "I kept quiet after that," Savage said, "until I read about that man [Arnold] seeing nine of the same things. I saw it and I thought it only fair to back him up."

By June 27, the term "flying saucer" appeared in a headline in a Boise, Idaho, *Statesman* story. The same day, a fresh Arnold description appeared in the *East Oregonian*:

> I saw them, weaving and ducking in and out as they came south not more than 500 feet over the plateau. They looked like they were rocking. I looked for the tails but suddenly realized they didn't have any. They were half-moon shaped, oval in front and convex in the rear. I was in a beautiful position to watch them. . . . I knew they were like nothing I had ever heard of before. There were no bulges or cowlings. They looked like a big flat disc.

Arnold had seen the craft just a half-week before, and his daily life was already taking some strange turns. Skeptics had lined up to take potshots at him, and a woman who spotted him in a Pendleton diner shrieked, "There's the man who saw the men from Mars!" Later, Arnold took a phone call from a Texas preacher, who informed him that the craft heralded doomsday. The preacher confided that he was preparing his congregation for "the end of this world."

During June 27–28, other people reported seeing UFOs. A man in Eugene, Oregon, snapped photos of unidentified craft flying in an "X" or "V" formation (lab workers shrugged off the UFOs as dust on the negative). In Bellingham, Washington, a man reported seeing three wingless flying objects traveling "real fast." In two separate incidents, a Kansas City carpenter and an Oklahoma City pilot saw nine discs, and in Yakima, Washington, housewife Ethel Wheelhouse rang authorities to say she'd seen "the whatzits."

The first nighttime sighting came from a Wenatchee, Washington, motorist named Archie Eden, who witnessed a large, wingless object descend rapidly toward the Earth and then explode about two hundred feet in the air.

In a short time, consensus among the American public was that Arnold had spotted secret weapons created by the USA or the Soviet Union. Despite the "men from Mars" idea familiar to fans of science fiction, the extraterrestrial angle had yet to catch fire. The American military did not routinely inform the FBI about secret American military projects, and the bureau had its doubts about Soviet capability to engineer flying saucers. Still, the Arnold story (or maybe just the news coverage it generated) piqued FBI interest, and led to an investigation of a possible Soviet campaign of disinformation. (Although the bureau gave Arnold himself no encouragement, it quickly began to assemble a file on him.) Because nothing in Arnold's background suggested itself as sinister, the FBI worried that American news media had set themselves up to be duped by phony reports of sightings and other mischief ginned up by Communist agents.

In the meanwhile, saucer sightings in the Pacific Northwest and Southwest blossomed like dandelions, giving local authorities and the FBI still more to think about. During the first week after Arnold's encounter, saucer reports came in from the Cascades (a prospector); the Grand Canyon (a medical doctor); Lake Meade, Nevada (a USAF pilot); and New Mexico (a rocket engineer). In addition, a sighting dated June 23, a day before the Kenneth Arnold event, was reported by a railroad engineer in Cedar Rapids, Iowa. (It is possible, though far from certain, that this witness backdated his sighting.) Excluding the nine craft witnessed by Arnold, these June 1947 sightings account for twenty-five flying discs.

UFOlogists with good antennae surmised that Arnold and the prospector at work in the Cascades had seen the same objects.

The pattern continued throughout July 1947, with another sixteen reports (accounting for as many as sixty objects, most of them disc-shaped) coming from Portland, Seattle, Boise, New Mexico, Texas, and Edwards Air Force Base (near Rogers Dry Lake in Southern California). Sightings from Wyoming, Massachusetts, and Ohio defied the intriguing geographical pattern. The witnesses included Air Force pilots and technicians, an astronomer, USAF intelligence officers, an interior decorator, and the crew of a Nevada-based B-25 bomber.

Meanwhile, the scientific community made an erroneous assumption about Arnold's sighting, reasoning that because Arnold was not a scientist, a serious investigation of his claim was pointless. And with that, Big Science relegated Kenneth Arnold to the fringe.

More Discs, Disaster, and the Army's Final Word

In July 1947, the Army Air Forces requested that Arnold prepare a report about his experiences, and send it to the commander of Wright Field (renamed Wright-Patterson AFB in 1948, following the establishment of the USAF), near Dayton, Ohio. Arnold complied, and even complemented his account with sketches of what he had seen. Not surprisingly, he felt "considerable disappointment" when the Air Forces did not reply. He was mystified that the military seemed unimpressed that his story had a corroborating account, from United Airlines DC-3 pilot Emil Smith and co-pilot Ralph Stevens. Just eight minutes after taking off from Boise, en route to Seattle, at about 9:00 p.m. on July 4, 1947, the DC-3 encountered five disc-like objects, followed shortly after by a separate group of four. Smith and Stevens flashed their landing lights at the first phalanx, assuming they were looking at other conventional aircraft. When both groups of discs exhibited unorthodox maneuvers, Smith and Stevens called the flight attendant, Marty Morrow, into the cockpit, so that she could function as a third witness.

The Army Air Forces were aware of the DC-3 case, as well as a June 21 incident at Maury Island, Washington (see chapter fifteen), when one of six unidentified flying objects dumped steaming slag into Puget Sound, astounding a witness and killing a dog.

The Air Forces' silence, and the other Washington State incidents, inspired Arnold to send a follow-up telegram to Wright Field. The message reiterated Arnold's belief that the mysterious craft "belonged to our government." Well, if that was the case, the USAAF wasn't going to admit as much to Kenneth Arnold, and not to anybody else, either. But even as the Army feigned disinterest, two of its own, Capt. William Davidson and Lt. Frank M. Brown, probed the sighting. They also looked into Arnold's background and personal life, and investigated the Maury Island event, too.

The officers met with Arnold and a Maury Island witness at a Tacoma hotel on the evening of July 31. Early in the morning of August 1, 1947, the B-25 carrying Davidson and Brown (who had departed the hotel clutching a bulging classified file) exploded and crashed near Tacoma, just minutes out of McChord Field. The smashup startled and discouraged Kenneth Arnold, and—not surprisingly—went on to encourage seventy years of speculation about conspiracy and cover-up.

Stung by media coverage of Arnold and Maury Island, plus the fiery deaths of Captain Davidson and Lieutenant Brown, the USAAF remained mum about the Arnold sighting for weeks more.

The explanation that finally came remains shocking in its uselessness: "mirage."

Arnold Presses On

Celebrity suited Kenneth Arnold reasonably well, but he pursued it on his own terms before finally allowing it to dissipate. Besides his photogenic looks, he had a pleasing, mid-range voice, free of accent and given to occasional, self-deprecating scoffs of laughter. Although responding to numberless phone queries and interviews, Arnold resisted attempts to paint him as quaint, amusing, kooky, or nuts. (Unknown to Arnold, a 1947 FBI report erroneously—or, perhaps, cleverly— claimed that "he is practically a moron in the eyes of the majority of the population of the United States.) Arnold knew what he saw when he saw it, and that was that.

Frustrated by apparently lukewarm official interest, Arnold told his story on radio programs and television shows, gave talks and made other personal appearances, and contributed a saucer article to the first issue (1948) of editor-publisher Ray Palmer's *Fate*. In 1950, Arnold self-published a booklet, *The Flying Saucer as I Saw It*.

The booklet is an unusual piece, sober rather than nakedly self-promotional, but sufficiently brave (or reckless) to identify the late Lt. Frank Brown as a "counterespionage agent" who operated out of New York's Mitchell Field. Arnold claimed that he had been contacted by Brown within days of the Mount Rainier sighting. Brown informed him that photographs of flying saucers were already held by the government. Accepting an invitation to visit Hamilton Field on San Pablo Bay, south of Novato, California, Arnold was met by intelligence officer Lt. Col. Donald Springer, who handed over prints of two of the saucer images, as a thank-you for Arnold's assistance in the official investigation of the Mount Rainier episode. Arnold's booklet includes both of those

After three years of interactions with the military, reporters, radio and TV interviewers, and a hugely curious public, Arnold set down his story in this self-published 1950 booklet, *The Flying Saucer as I Saw It*

photos. One page is devoted to the Maury Island incident, and another to a December 18, 1948, letter sent to Arnold by Velma Brown, widow of Lt. Brown. In it, Mrs. Brown wrote, "I have never thought that Frank's death was an accident."

In 1952, Arnold collaborated with Ray Palmer on a nonfiction saucer piece for *Other Worlds* magazine (February 1952 issue) and a book, *The Coming of the Saucers: A Documentary Report on Sky Objects That Have Mystified the World*. Despite the book's title, Arnold used the text to reiterate that the craft he saw were crescent shaped. But Arnold probably knew his fight against "flying saucer" was in vain. Regardless, as late as 1966, he again tried to repudiate the saucer trope, this time in a widely distributed news photo in which Arnold holds an artist's rendering of a crescent-shaped craft.

As the 1970s approached, public interest in Arnold had naturally declined. Arnold himself had grown tired of the familiar questions and government obfuscation, and he allowed his story to recede. But he pulled a surprise in 1977, when he traveled to Chicago to speak at the First International UFO Congress. As always, he expressed frustration with the lack of transparent government investigation of UFOs.

Arnold as a Cultural Marker

Iconographic status connotes neither competence nor ineptitude; honesty nor deception. Many unsavory persons and institutions are icons. The beauty of Kenneth Arnold as a seminal witness to a kind of phenomenon often not taken

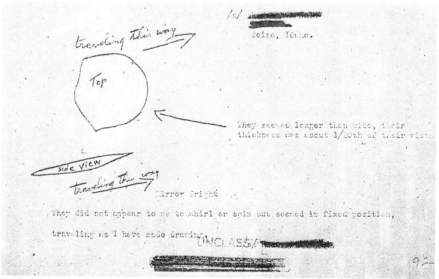

As the U.S. Army Air Corps negotiated its 1947 transition to the U.S. Air Force, Kenneth Arnold provided investigators with descriptions and sketches of the craft he had encountered. This sketch indicates direction of travel and a representative craft in top and side views. In his accompanying comments, Arnold said, "[A]s far as guessing what it is I observed, it is just as much a mystery to me as it is to the rest of the world." *USAF*

seriously is that he lived as "a solid citizen." He became an Eagle Scout at fourteen, and later competed successfully in sports and business. He supported a wife and two children. His neighbors liked him. Any UFO skeptic that hoped to paint Arnold as a dunce or a crank came away disappointed.

Arnold was a "type": sturdy, calmly confident, and comfortable in a sober suit. His public persona filtered into the back of America's group mind, and even without realizing it, Hollywood moviemakers riffed on Arnold to create another type: the straight, stolid SF-thriller hero that marshals facts, science, and the help of his associates to defeat alien invaders. Kenneth Arnold became the face of the first widely reported UFO event, and also suggested the sort of man qualified to deal effectively with the visitors. Other than astronauts and professional pilots, few eyewitnesses to UFOs surpass Arnold's aura of credibility.

Significantly, Arnold had no truck with the extraterrestrial hypothesis of UFOs. He remained convinced that the craft were of earthly origin, finding in that explanation a situation more fateful than any speculation about what he dismissed as "people from Venus." Ironically, then, Arnold's encounter turned out to be an enormous factor in the growth of the "little green men" notion, and helped encourage a later (and considerably more serious) study of extraterrestrials. Little of that, though, was clear during the fourth week of June 1947. It was enough that, for the briefest of periods, Kenneth Arnold's experience stood as the most exciting of all UFO sightings to date.

Then, in the New Mexico desert barely two weeks after the Arnold incident, a complex stew of things—aeronautics, the military, government secrecy, and questions of humankind's place in the cosmos—collided at a place called Roswell.

8

Always Roswell

Not Just Another Day in the Desert

Even the date of the onset of the Roswell mystery is a topic of debate. June 14, 1947, is the earliest among many. It was on that day—or perhaps three weeks later, on July 7—that ranch foreman William "Mac" Brazel, with his young son Vernon in tow, stumbled upon a debris field some thirty miles north of Roswell, New Mexico. Brazel worked for the J. B. Foster ranch, and was driving sheep on the day of his discovery. According to some accounts, the debris field was just a smidgen of a thing, hardly bigger than the footprint of an automobile. Other accounts say that debris lay strewn across a section of rough earth about two hundred feet in diameter. And still other versions describe the debris field as an impressive three-quarters of a mile long and about two hundred yards across. (The "big debris" theory is supported by claims that Brazel grew angry because his sheep refused to walk over the oversized area, forcing him to march the animals all the way around the debris to reach water.)

During the course of a newspaper interview Mac Brazel granted on July 8, he recalled the mess as "bright wreckage made up of rubber strips, tinfoil, a rather tough paper, and sticks."

A Possible Chronology

Despite the remoteness of the area, debris and other junk—at least in small to moderate amounts—was not uncommon. And anyway, no one paid Brazel to linger and speculate; the sheep and many other chores demanded his time. Whatever the extent of the debris, Brazel couldn't spare more than a few minutes to stare. When he finally went back for a second look nearly three weeks later, on the Fourth of July (according to the timeline that begins on June 14), he and his wife and young daughter gathered about five pounds of various pieces and left. The following day, July 5, Brazel went to nearby Corona, New Mexico, where chitchat informed him that some locals had seen "flying discs" in the sky. Brazel knew about the Japanese "balloon bombs" that had landed here and there on the Pacific coast in 1945, and he was aware (like everyone else in the area) that Roswell Army Air Field conducted secret flight experiments. Although the flying-disc reports caught Brazel's attention, he felt no particular urgency to find someone to talk to at the airfield, partly because Roswell was seventy-five miles from Corona. So Brazel waited until Monday, July 7, when he had business that was going to take him into Roswell anyway.

Roswell's sheriff, George Wilcox, took a look at what Brazel had brought into town, and sent a pair of deputies to locate the site. Wilcox also contacted the airfield. A pair of base personnel, Maj. Jesse Marcel and counterintelligence officer Capt. Sheridan Cavitt, came out to retrieve what Brazel had salvaged.

Nobody at Roswell Army Air Field (RAAF) could identify the stuff Marcel and Cavitt presented (members of the base's Balloon Group were at Alamogordo, unavailable to take a look). Although the pieces seemed earthly enough, even the small portion retrieved by Brazel included more rubber than would be found in a typical experimental weather-observation balloon.

A day later, July 8, the front-page headline of the *Roswell Daily Record* read, "RAAF Captures Flying Saucer on Ranch in Roswell Region." In its bid to attract readers, the paper obviously played on the two-week-old "flying saucer" phenomenon begun by the Kenneth Arnold story, but to this day, accounts of Mac Brazel's role in the headline and accompanying story differ. In some tellings, Brazel simply assumed he had found pieces of typical RAAF work—pieces that the Army would like to have back. But other accounts suggest that Brazel described to reporters the wreckage of a flying disc—not from another planet (that sort of speculation came from others, and much later) but from a foreign power. Although the USSR was still two years away from an atomic bomb, the postwar Cold War was already growing warm, making the U.S. military uneasy. Many secret tests occurred above the New Mexico desert. What if the Soviets had been monitoring that work?

Just hours after that day's *Roswell Daily Record* made its way to Roswell Army Air Field, RAAF public information officer, Lt. Walter Haut, issued a press release. Career-minded PI officers never act on their own; when Lieutenant Haut

What happened near Roswell, New Mexico, on a June day in 1947 remains a hotly debated piece of American history. Although the fanciful illustration seen here suggests that ranch foreman Mac Brazel discovered the remains of a craft of American origin, such a "fact" is far from a certainty.   *Alamy*

prepared the release, he did so at the request of the base commander, Col. William Blanchard. The release rather casually refers to the debris as a "flying disc" that "landed"—as opposed to "crashed"—on a local ranch. Haut, Blanchard, and many in-between caught hell for the "flying disc" angle, which was quickly walked back.

Although lame, the July 8 press release marked the beginning of official damage control. Step two became apparent on July 9, when the *Roswell Daily Record* meekly accepted the weather-balloon line. What became of the captured "flying saucer" of the previous day's headline? Well, the paper's editor, and perhaps its owner, as well, received communication from RAAF that essentially went like this: *Kill the saucer angle.*

Step three, as suggested above, mandated that "balloon" become the new word for "disc."

Intriguingly, the initial release dates Mac Brazel's discovery to "last week," or around July 1—more than two weeks *after* the foreman's first look at the wreckage. Questions persist as to why the Army wished to take mid-June off the table. One possible answer is that the thing that crashed had been American-designed to monitor nuclear testing. If that were the case, the Army would have been naturally inclined to describe the object in benign, knowable terms: a weather balloon.

Trouble is, a cover-up involving more than one person is almost invariably exposed. Unknown for forty years (until UFOlogist Kevin Randle began to locate witnesses and dig into Roswell documents) is that the RAAF's "first responders," Major Marcel and Captain Cavitt, visited the crash site on July 7, very shortly after visiting Sheriff Wilcox. This was a day before the *Daily Record* "flying disc" headline,

The Wednesday, July 9, 1947, edition of the *Roswell Daily Record* ran second-day coverage of the mysterious crash in the New Mexico desert. In direct contravention of Roswell Army Air Field's July 8 "flying disk" public-information release, Gen. Roger M. Ramey, commanding officer of the 8th Air Force, dismissed the debris, as the *Daily Record* paraphrased, as "a harmless high-altitude weather balloon." But other military officers close to the investigation felt otherwise. *Alamy*

and a day before the RAAF press release. The officers would not have done on-site investigation without clearance from the base. Such permission would have come from Colonel Blanchard, or someone very close to him.

When, in later years, Marcel described the crash site, he recalled seeing mainly metallic debris. The metal was, he said, thin but very strong, and could not be dented by a sledgehammer's blow. He was especially interested in nearly weightless metal members reminiscent of I-beams but shorter, and measuring just three-eighths-inch by one-quarter inch. He was unable to twist or bend them. Lying amidst the twisted metal were pieces of a parchment-like material that did not burn under direct flame. None of that is part of the official story.

Some sources claim that Marcel filled his staff car with debris.

In 1994, when the USAF decided to once again investigate the Roswell event, Col. Richard Weaver interviewed Captain Cavitt, who related impressions quite different from Marcel's. According to Cavitt, the debris was easily recognizable as pieces of a weather balloon, specifically, a destroyed radar deflector of the type commonly used with weather radar wind targets (RAWINs). A typical deflector shows multiple square corners, constructed from heavy paper and reflective foil, and hung below the balloon on a balsa wood stick frame attached to a triangular base. Cavitt's description of a RAWIN falls neatly in line with the military's "weather balloon" explanation of what came down near Roswell. (Indeed, as the Roswell story unfolded in 1947, the military released photographs of RAAF personnel kneeling next to the crumpled remains of a balloon with a RAWIN setup.) Weather balloons are tracked by radar, which utilizes waves that reflect back to the source from square corners. In other words, the square-cornered construction ensures continual radar monitoring.

The official 1947 explanation had grown threadbare by 1994, but Cavitt stuck to it.

Even from the beginning, RAAF personnel offered divergent stories. Some enlisted men recalled being sent to establish armed checkpoints on the main north-south route, U.S. Highway 285, to deter civilians. Other former soldiers recall that numerous *military officers* were halted at checkpoints. Civilians (including at least one located by Kevin Randle) remembered being stopped. Numerous dirt roads going east and west branched off from the highway, and every one, the civilian witnesses recalled, was blocked by soldiers in jeeps or other military vehicles. No civilians, and only selected military personnel, were going to be allowed to see the "weather balloon."

If all of that sounds like a lot of effort to prevent access to something very mundane, you may be on to something.

Ripening the tale further are accounts of non-military witnesses other than the Brazels. On July 2, a Roswell resident named Dan Wilmot observed an object cross the evening sky, headed northwest. The historian Randle notes that this sighting has encouraged many to believe that the Wilmot object is the one that crashed seventy-five miles away, and was discovered by Brazel. And multiple witnesses in and near Roswell described peculiar-sounding thunder on or about the second of July, climaxed by a distant "explosion."

In a 1993 affidavit, a man named William Woody recalled witnessing "something in the sky" during the summer of 1947, probably in early July. Woody was fourteen at the time, and lived on a farm three miles south of Roswell. (Woody still lived there in 1993.) Sunset had come and gone, and the summer sky was dark. As they stood outside, Woody and his father watched "a large, very bright object in the southwestern sky, moving rapidly northward." The object threw off an intense, white light, and was trailed by a long tail that Woody described as "a blowtorch flame fading down into a pale red." Father and son tracked the lighted object until it disappeared beneath the distant horizon. The younger Woody made a point in the affidavit to emphasize that the object did not "wink out" like a meteorite, but simply flew until obscured by the curvature of the Earth. Other witnesses claimed to have seen the object crash into the ground, but Woody said nothing like that in 1993.

The older Woody guessed that the object landed about forty miles north of Roswell. When father and son set out in the family truck to search a day or two later, they saw armed guards along Highway 285. Consistent with other eyewitness accounts, east-west egress off of 285 was blocked by random guards and more formal sentry posts. The important east-west route in the area, State Highway 247, had also been closed off by soldiers.

Near the end of his affidavit, William Woody said that his family, as well as neighbors, digested the weather-balloon story, which "seemed reasonable to us at the time."

So What's the Story, Really?

The accounts dating to mid-June 1947 inevitably interfere with the more common Mac Brazel timeline: did Brazel discover the debris on June 14 or two weeks later? At this juncture, there may no longer be an answer to that. Certainly, the "thunder" recollections of Dan Wilmot and others (including Brazel himself, who heard odd thunder early in July) are intriguing. William Woody's account is dramatic and reasonably detailed. The stories suggest that something anomalous—perhaps natural, perhaps not—occurred in that July sky. But how, then, do the July thunder incidents fit with Brazel's mid-June discovery of debris? If the June 14 date is accurate, Brazel's discovery, taken in concert with recollections by Brazel and others concerning early July, suggest that the crash was not a singular event, but part of a pattern that continued for weeks.

Substitute "ongoing research "for "pattern" and you are forced to consider that the Army had invested enough in its work that some quick subterfuge was called for. And in acting quickly, Army personnel inadvertently confirmed the deceptive nature of the official explanation. Let's think about Major Marcel. Under ordinary circumstances, he would not have touched the debris, let alone filled his staff car with it. Physical evidence pertinent to a military-related incident is very like the often-fragile physical evidence of a crime. One basic rule that first-responders must follow is *observe and record but do not touch*. And for heaven's sake, *don't move anything*. And if you're foolish enough to do that, *do not remove it to another location*.

But Marcel did the first two things, and, as we'll see, probably the third, too. Why would he have acted so recklessly? Because he acted under orders, and when he stood looking at the debris, recklessness didn't matter. Only an explicit order would have been sufficient for Marcel to lay a fingertip on any of the wreckage. Logic suggests that if he were ordered to do *that*, he also had been ordered to get rid of as much of the stuff as he could. (Otherwise, why touch it at all?) Someone back at RAAF—perhaps encouraged by Washington—wanted the crash debris to get "gone."

The early-period Roswell chronology is tangled, and some of the details curl back on themselves. If the seminal portion of the Roswell tale were a script or a novel, an editor would send it back for a lot of rewrite. What appears indisputable is that something (or things) fell to earth near Roswell in the summer of 1947. What appears possible, if not downright probable, is that things dropped from the sky over a period of days and even weeks. Chronological details are naturally very important, but today we are more concerned with the *what* than with the *when*.

In a bit of a twist that many casual Roswell enthusiasts are not aware of, the whole story dropped out of the newspapers and off the cultural radar very shortly after those first reports. The Army released an amended story, the local newspaper abandoned the saucer angle, and local folks just got on with their lives. But diminished public interest hardly means that Washington and the Army no longer paid attention to Roswell.

Three explanation scenarios are likely, and each rests on the assumption that the weather-balloon tale was intentional deception. Assuming further (as Mac Brazel did) that the debris was earthly in nature, the Army covered up an American mechanism far more unusual than a weather balloon—perhaps the aforementioned nuclear-monitoring device. Alternatively, the crashed object had been sent by a foreign power, to spy on test areas and, at the very least, embarrass the U.S. military.

The third possible explanation abandons the "earthly" mindset to invoke the cosmos, suggesting that the crashed object was neither American, Soviet, nor human. It was extraterrestrial.

It is the third explanation, of course, that has inspired some seventy years of ET talk, with tales of one or more disabled saucers taken virtually intact, and undersized alien corpses spirited off to secret labs. Extrapolated from that are claims of saucers secretly reverse-engineered by American tech experts, plus accounts of incredible weaponry, human collusion with aliens, human-alien breeding programs, and the notorious Roswell "alien autopsy" (see chapter fifteen).

A discussion of alien corpses brings us back around to the prominent UFOlogist Kevin Randle. Despite his unfortunate, later-severed collaboration with a fraudulent researcher (see chapter 1), Randle shook off the embarrassment and redoubled his efforts to get at the truth of Roswell. During the 1980s he interviewed many ex-military personnel and Roswell locals who claimed to have seen tiny corpses. Subsequent investigation by Randle revealed that those accounts were, in his words, "not based in reality."

Of course, the existence of a discredited witness, or even discredited multiple witnesses, says something only about the witnesses' spurious accounts, and nothing at all about whether the alien-body notion is true or false. So Randle kept at his research and found Frankie Rowe, a Roswell resident who had been a little girl in 1947. When Randle interviewed her in detail in 1993, Rowe recalled that her father, a firefighter, returned home from a call with a tale of a crashed "spaceship," small body bags, and one survivor, a child-sized humanoid with copper-colored skin.

Randle located other secondhand witnesses who, like Rowe, had been kids in 1947 and learned of the small bodies from parents. Firsthand accounts are always best, of course, and Randle eventually located a woman able to tell just such a story. Although elderly when Randle got to her in 1994, Anna Willmon recalled with reasonable clarity how she and her husband came upon wreckage near Pine Lodge Road, about twenty miles from Roswell. The Willmons discovered two corpses sprawled near a silvery disc. Anna Willmon recalled the bodies as being the size of small five-year-olds, with gray-brown skin.

Other civilians and former military personnel discovered by Randle and other researchers after 1990 spoke with varying degrees of credibility. The numbers of alien bodies varied (usually two, three, or four). Not every witness claims to have seen a living alien. Descriptions of skin color, eyes, attire, and other details vary. Employment logs and service records confirm that many of these witnesses were, or could have been, where they claimed. None of the people kept diaries or wrote letters describing their experiences, and the years had taken people that could have corroborated some of the stories.

"After-the-fact" eyewitnesses, such as people that studied metal fragments collected from the crash site, have been turned up, too. Documentation of their work often disappeared, or became classified and inaccessible. Many such witnesses agree that the military took special care to prevent leaks.

The Twining "Flying Discs" Memo

Publicity about the proximate Kenneth Arnold and Roswell incidents brought a pucker to the brows of many in Army Air Forces high command. Whether from a serious desire to discover the origins of "flying saucers" or to protect its own secret tests, the fact is that the AAF's heightened interest in unidentified flying objects created a receptive climate for what came to be called the Twining Memo. According to this memo—discovered, with other relevant documents, in the National Archives in 1985 by UFOlogists Stanton Friedman and William Moore— Gen. Nathan Twining had been dispatched to the AAF base at Alamogordo, New Mexico, in July 1947 to study the retrieved remains of a crashed object found twenty miles northwest of Socorro. The general arrived at Alamogordo on July 7, to look at the Socorro debris and meet with AAF Chief of Staff Carl "Tooey" Spaatz. On July 9, Twining traveled to White Sands Proving Ground, New Mexico, to view more wreckage. (Whether the wreckage Twining saw at Alamogordo and White Sands came from one or multiple crashes remains hazy.) Twining returned to Alamogordo on July 10 to observe new avionics and other classified work, and flew to Wright Field, Ohio, later that day.

Sample wreckage from one or multiple crashes went back to Wright with him.

Twining's September 23, 1947, report to AAF Gen. George Schulgen plainly invokes "flying discs." Twining described the crafts' elliptical shapes as typically "flat on bottom and domed on top." Although he acknowledged that many reports could be explained by weather, meteorites, and traditional aircraft, he asserted that the mysterious discs were legitimately unidentified, and of unknown origin.

There was a "possibility," he reported, that "some foreign nation has a form of propulsion [,] possibly nuclear, which is outside our domestic knowledge." Lacking evidence, however, the possibility had to remain just that.

Twining did not speculate about the existence of secretly produced American saucers, because he knew they existed and did not care to reveal them, or because his best information told him that such saucers did not exist at all. (Of course, Twining may not have been made aware of American saucer activity.) The memo suggests, however, that the United States would be well served by development of such craft, regardless of the fact that such an endeavor would be "extremely expensive" and "time consuming."

In the memo's subsection 2, Twining wrote, "It is the opinion that: a. The phenomenon reported is something real and not visionary or fictitious. b. There are objects probably approximating the shape of a disc, of such appreciable size as to appear to be as large as man-made aircraft."

Twining mentioned the objects' tendency to fly in formations of "three to nine objects" (a clear nod to the nine observed by Kenneth Arnold, and the United Airlines pilots Smith and Stevens). Twining had particular interest in the objects' ability to climb steeply and quickly, and their propensity to display startling evasive action. Mindful of physical stresses on crews during such maneuvers, Twining felt that, possibly, "some of the objects are controlled either manually, automatically, or remotely."

In subsection h., Twining said that, because of a "lack of physical evidence in shape of crash recovered exhibits," the origins of the flying discs must remain undetermined. People disinclined to believe in UFOs cite this remark as proof that nothing had crashed three or four months earlier at Roswell or elsewhere. That assumption, however, presumes that the memo's recipient, General Schulgen, had sufficiently high security clearance to be let in on the full Roswell story. No specific evidence to suggest the granting of that clearance has surfaced. Certainly, Schulgen was not part of the later Majestic 12 investigation (see below), and thus lacked UFO-specific information available to Twining and other key members of that body.

Twining closed his memo by suggesting that a secret, code-named investigatory body be established to uncover the truth of UFOs. He emphasized the desirability of cooperation between military intelligence, the Atomic Energy Commission (AEC), the National Advisory Committee for Aeronautics (NEPA), the RAND group, the Nuclear Energy for the Propulsion of Aircraft (NEPA) project, and the Joint Research and Development Board (JRDB). Because the Twining memo was forward-looking, it also was open-ended. It acknowledged the reality of UFOs and the mystery that surrounded them. Much more was still to be learned, and the military-intelligence establishment was obligated to pursue the truth.

Majestic 12

A significant addition to Roswell documentation arrived in 1984, when undeveloped photographs of documents related to a clandestine saucer-investigation project called Majestic 12 were mailed to Los Angeles-based television producer and UFO investigator Jaime Shandera. The package carried neither the sender's name nor address, but the postmark read Albuquerque, New Mexico. Shandera developed the photos and found documents that appeared to be briefing material prepared in late 1952 or early 1953 for president-elect Dwight D. Eisenhower. The key document was dated September 24, 1947 (a day after the Twining Memo); it was sent from President Harry Truman to Secretary of Defense James V. Forrestal. Via executive order, Truman instructed Forrestal to set up a secret UFO investigatory body, to get to the bottom of what had happened at Roswell earlier in the year, and to determine the credibility of other flying saucer reports. Further, the president wanted scientific information about flying saucers—particularly recovered weapons and propulsion systems that could be reverse-engineered.

This was bombshell stuff, not least because it established a link between flying saucers and Forrestal—who died in a fall, as an unconfirmed suicide, in 1949.

In 1986, two years after the mysterious delivery of the package, Shandera worked with author-researcher William L. Moore, who had published *The Roswell Incident* in 1980, to publicly release the documents. Not surprisingly, the papers

The controversial Majestic 12 project allegedly kicked off in 1947 to do secret investigation of UFOs. MJ-12 (the "12" indicated the dozen highly placed officials that comprised it) encompassed President Truman, the National Security Agency, the CIA, and, perhaps, completely clandestine elements of the U.S. government. Among the twelve was Truman's secretary of defense, James V. Forrestal. In the March 28, 1949, photo above, Truman (right) accepts Forrestal's resignation—a resignation demanded by Truman because of political disagreements. Just two months later, Forrestal fell sixteen stories to his death, an event that inspires robust speculation about an MJ-12/Truman/ military conspiracy to obscure the truth about flying saucers.   *Getty Images*

engendered excitement and argument. At last, apparent proof that Washington not only acknowledged saucers, but secretly investigated them.

Majestic 12 continues to inspire heated—and contradictory—controversy. Besides doubts cast on the veracity of the core documents (including the Twining memo discovered in the National Archives), MJ-12 is linked by some to the assassination of President Kennedy. According to this theory, the CIA (probably working through contractors) killed JFK because the president planned to disclose MJ-12's existence, and expose CIA involvement in it and the Roswell cover-up. The Kennedy assassination aside, we know that the FBI cast a jaundiced eye on the documents and convinced itself that MJ-12 never existed. The U.S. Air Force denied the past existence of any such body, and flatly declared the Shandera and National Archives documents to be fabrications.

Had MJ-12 been a true investigatory body, or just more disinformation created by Washington? Could the MJ-12 story have been a prank by saucer skeptics? Perhaps the documents were the work of a UFOlogist who wished to discredit Shandera, or take down UFOlogists and others likely to vouch for the documents.

Then again, perhaps the Majestic 12 documents, all of them, are dead true.

The Twelve

The Shandera papers identify a dozen leading American scientists, military men, and politicians as comprising MJ-12, an embarrassment of riches that caused skeptics to cry "fake" Surely, they reasoned, an assemblage of people so critical to national security could not possibly be connected to the schoolboy fancy of flying-saucer studies. Skeptics were particularly dubious about the inclusion of Dr. Donald Howard Menzel (see chapter one), a onetime child prodigy, a Harvard professor of astrophysics, and an outspoken critic of UFO claims. His useful 1935 book *Stars and Planets* became an oft-reprinted field guide to the heavens, and his 1953 study *Flying Saucers* established him as a prominent debunker of UFO claims. The title of a 1963 book Menzel co-wrote with Lyle G. Boyd, *The World of Flying Saucers: A Scientific Examination of a Major Myth of the Space Age*, suggested Menzel's stance more than fifteen years after Roswell.

Menzel dedicated himself to clarity in thought and writing. In the year 2000, however, UFO researcher James R. Lewis—echoing UFOlogist Stanton Friedman—suggested that Menzel's protestations may have been a blind; the professor had Top Secret, Ultra, security clearance and a long relationship with the National Security Agency. Further, he had had professional contact with the CIA. Not only did Menzel privately acknowledge the existence of UFOs, he reasoned that the craft had origins beyond our solar system.

Assuming that Menzel's secret opinion was shared by other scientific and military heavyweights, the early Cold War period might have easily (and *wisely*) involved America's top scientific and strategic thinkers in a formal evaluation of the UFO phenomenon. According to the political logic of 1947, God help an American president who ignored any aerial "phenomenon" that could be a threat.

Certainly, the beginning the U.S. government's fascination with UFOs, the 1947 incident at Roswell, was well documented. Whether to investigate further, or simply to control the flow of information from Roswell and future events, the establishment of Majestic 12 or a similar high-security body makes sense. So, having addressed possible motives behind the creation of MJ-12, we can profitably consider the backgrounds of the operation's principals. Alphabetical order is used here.

- **Dr. Lloyd V. Berkner**, executive secretary of the Joint Research and Development Board. The board was established by the U.S. military in late September 1947. Its purpose was to work within and without the military establishment to formulate strategies based on military R&D, based, in part, on *"recent and ongoing scientific developments"* (emphasis added). Berkner's special interest was the evaluation of weapons systems. Some people who have studied the so-called alien autopsy film footage insist that Berkner is one of the two surgeons visible on camera.
- **Dr. Detlev Bronk**, chairman of the National Research Council. He was a biophysicist and physiologist who served on Atomic Energy Commission's medical advisory board. Claims have been made that Bronk is the other surgeon seen in the alien autopsy footage.
- **Dr. Vannevar Bush**, whose National Defense Research Council and Office of Scientific Research and Development were essential to the USA's development of the atomic bomb.
- **James V. Forrestal**, American secretary of defense and the man who relayed President Truman's saucer-investigation order. A college dropout, Forrestal had professional experience in finance and naval aviation before becoming President Roosevelt's assistant, and later FDR's undersecretary of the navy, and secretary of the navy for Roosevelt and Truman during World War II. In 1947, Truman chose Forrestal to fill the newly created defense-secretary cabinet post. Conflicts with the Administration about the establishment of an Arab Palestinian state (Forrestal favored it), Truman's call for major cuts in defense spending (Forrestal opposed them), and the secretary's premature meetings with 1948 presidential-race front-runner Thomas Dewey caused Truman to demand Forrestal's resignation early in 1949. Forrestal handed over his letter on March 28, 1949. Eight weeks later he died in a fall from the sixteenth floor of the National Naval Medical Center, where he had been taken for treatment of depression. UFOlogists and others puzzled by Forrestal's death have proposed that the former secretary was murdered by parties eager to cover up Washington's awareness of UFOs. (Other theories point fingers at more obviously political forces.)
- **Gordon Gray**, assistant secretary of the army, and an assistant/adviser to President Truman on issues of national security. Gordon was named secretary of the army in 1949.
- **Adm. Roscoe H. Hillenkoetter**, whom Truman named as Director of Central Intelligence, and overseer of the Central Intelligence Group (CIG) in September 1947. When the Central Intelligence Agency (CIA) was established

in December 1947, Truman named Hillenkoetter as that agency's first director. The admiral fell into trouble two years later, when the CIA issued a top-secret report asserting that the USSR would not have an A-bomb until mid-1950 at the earliest, and more probably not until the middle of 1953. The report was dated September 20, 1949—nearly a month *after* the Soviets' successful, secret test of August 29.

- **Dr. Jerome Hunsaker**, chairman of the departments of mechanical and aeronautical engineering, MIT. Near the close of World War I, Hunsaker was a key figure in the development of U.S. air forces. He also did pioneering work with wind tunnels and airships.

- **Dr. Donald Howard Menzel**, professor of astronomy and astrophysics at Harvard, and an internationally regarded authority on the sun and the solar atmosphere. During World War II, he was a naval cryptologist. His public stance on UFOs was a skeptical one; his private opinion may have been the reverse.

- **Gen. Robert M. Montague**, onetime deputy commander of Fort Bliss, Texas, and later posted to Albuquerque to command the Atomic Energy Commission's Sandia Missile Base. Because Montague's work at Fort Bliss brought New Mexico's White Sands Missile Range under his purview, an assumption shared by many UFOlogists is that Montague was intimately aware of the 1947 incident at Roswell.

- **Sidney W. Souers**, a retired rear admiral who wrote the Intelligence section of the 1945 Eberstadt Report, a paper that recommended the creation of a National Security Council, and closer alignment between the U.S. intelligence community and people that shape foreign policy. During the first half of 1946, Souers directed Central Intelligence. At the time of his appointment to MJ-12, Souers was executive secretary to the National Security Council.

- **Gen. Nathan E. Twining**, posted to Wright-Patterson AFB, commander of Air Materiel Command. Because of his access to classified information, Twining shortly suggested the formation of an even more focused UFO study group. Such a group, called Project Sign (see chapter nine), was established during the first weeks of 1948.

- **Gen. Hoyt S. Vandenberg**, Air Force chief of staff who had been a key planner of the 1944 Allied invasion at Normandy. On October 1, 1947, virtually simultaneous with the establishment of MJ-12, General Vandenberg was appointed vice chief of staff of the newly established U.S. Air Force.

More Revelations

A popular 1997 book, Philip Corso and William J. Birnes's *The Day After Roswell*, explicitly ties MJ-12 to government-sanctioned study of other planets and extraterrestrials. Among proponents of the ET/MJ-12 relationship, Corso (who died in 1998) had particular credibility, as he was a retired U.S. Army lieutenant colonel who had worked in counterintelligence during World War II and the Korean War. Corso, who made special efforts throughout his career to look after the interests of

American POWs and displaced Jews, claimed to have had a key role in the disposition of physical evidence left by the Roswell crash. He also claimed to have had
telepathic contact with an extraterrestrial outside the White Sands missile base.

On July 7, just three days after ranch foreman Mac Brazel returned for a closer
look at what was later determined to be "Roswell debris," and just one day before
the crash was reported by the *Roswell Daily Record*, military officials (according to
the MJ-12 papers) began to gather crash wreckage—and four small, decomposed
bodies. MJ-12 documents reveal that group member Detlev Bronk examined the
four corpses. His conclusion was that they were not *Homo sapiens*, but the result
of some other evolutionary path. Bronk called them "extraterrestrial biological
entities"—EBEs.

Two other members of MJ-12, General Twining and Dr. Bush, examined the
wreckage. Although the impact of the crash apparently pulverized the craft's
propulsion system, both men were satisfied that the system was not in keeping with
present-day Earth technology. In 1947, practical flying saucers from human sources
were possible only theoretically; issues of lift and airborne propulsion blocked
anything beyond small-sized prototypes. (For more on earthly experiments with
flying saucers, see chapter three.)

The MJ-12 documents reveal that after Twining and Bush's report, some
(unnamed) members of the group expressed the opinion that the Roswell ship
originated on Mars. (Some witnesses claimed that peculiar-looking inscribed
characters ringed the perimeter of the Roswell saucer. The Air Forces' official
counter was that their weather balloon had been covered with decorative Scotch
tape.) But Twining and Bush surmised that the captured saucer was a short-range
reconnaissance craft, an opinion that must surely have invited this question: *Where
is the mother ship, or other base?*

Regardless of his thoughts about the craft's range, Twining felt that the saucer
had originated from outside our solar system.

Because Twining and Bush examined wreckage, neither saw the saucer in
flight. Regardless, the MJ-12 documents from the National Archives report that
the men felt encouraged to speculate on the craft's engineering and aeronautical
aspects. In keeping with what Kenneth Arnold had seen the month before the
Roswell saucer, the latter lacked wings, a piston- or jet engine, tail, and any other
standard element of powered flight (other than the presumed streamlining effect
achieved by the leading edge of the short, rounded fuselage). Enough large pieces
remained for Twining and Bush to determine that the saucer had been designed
to accept internal components completely foreign to human aeronautics. They
found, for example, no evidence of wiring harnesses; this implied wireless controls
and, perhaps, *mind* control.

People skeptical of the National Archives MJ-12 documents are not without
a case. Certain dates don't jibe with dates commonly given for William Brazel's
interactions with the debris—but then, the Brazel dates are a confusion even
without the documents. Twining and Bush appear to have made a great many
assumptions about the saucer on badly damaged evidence. It is likely that nothing

at all suggested that the craft came from Mars, or from outside our solar system, either, so those assumptions have the character of wishful thinking.

And then there is the issue of the documents' very existence, which is the basic source of bother to skeptics. How convenient that these papers should reveal themselves when UFOlogists came calling.

Contrarily, an assumption that the skeptics are justified in their suspicions invites more questions: *Who inserted the documents into the files? What was the motive?* One possible answer is that the government wished (and wishes) to obscure the truth about Roswell. By allowing relative crumbs of information about the craft and its occupants, larger and more dangerous issues are skirted.

Perhaps to encourage thoughts of a postwar conspiracy designed to silence the Majestic 12 participants, or the government's bid to undermine the Roswell story, some proponents of the documents emphasize that in addition to the premature and ostensibly mysterious death of James Forrestal, General Vandenberg and General Montague were both dead by 1958, before either had reached the age of sixty. The death dates are accurate (1954 and 1958, respectively), but nothing sinister was afoot. Vandenberg died of prostate cancer, and Montague by cerebral hemorrhage precipitated by a severe intestinal ailment picked up during his travels in South America. No credible source, inside or outside the military establishment, has raised the specter of foul play with regard to either death, or to Forrestal's, either. With the exception of Lloyd Berkner (d. 1967), MJ-12 members other than Forrestal, Vandenberg, and Montague lived until the 1970s and '80s.

Roswell "Invents" the Aliens

Although most established scientists argue against the Roswell-ET notion, or ignore it altogether, skeptics must admit that the Army handled itself badly. Inept military-speak in the official press release and in remarks that came later did little except encourage public doubt about what happened. The "weather balloon" explanation is not impossible or even improbable, just weak and convenient. Similarly, an Army scenario concocted to explain away bulbous-head descriptions of the small corpses—that a serviceman fell and ended up with a swollen noggin—is nothing but risible.

Eyewitness accounts, and latter-day interpretations, cause the Roswell aliens to present themselves to us as what is now shorthand for "extraterrestrial": small, thin-limbed, hairless bodies, and those enlarged heads. Although necks are described as slender, the frontal and parietal portions of the skull are enlarged. The nasal aperture is often described as considerably smaller than its human counterpart. Mandibles are less well-developed than in humans, so chins are narrow. (Other familiar details, such as enormous black eyes, seem to have been added later by the movies and/or various eyewitness accounts not obviously connected to Roswell.) Some UFOlogists believe that the term extraterrestrial biological entity (EBE) was coined by military scientists whose first look at intelligent alien life happened at Roswell Army Air Field.

Big Secrets at Area 51

Area 51 is America's most famous—and mysterious—military test facility. The name is an unofficial one, likely reflecting the base's parcel number as determined by Nevada land grids; today's officially approved names are Groom Lake or, alternatively, Homey Airport. The U.S. military and intelligence communities established the base in 1955. Since then, government-approved (or tolerated) names and nicknames have included Paradise Ranch, Dreamland, Home Base, the Box, and Watertown. Although a CIA official let slip the "Area 51" designation during the Vietnam War era, no Area 51 "existed" until the CIA's 2013 release of previously classified documents.

Isolated 124 miles northwest of Las Vegas, the base is an important focus of avionics and weapons-system development. Many believe it houses the remains of the Roswell saucer(s), and even the bodies of the extraterrestrial pilots. Because Roswell sits about 890 miles from Groom—a distance not likely to deter military flights—a Roswell-Area 51 connection is not logistically impossible. But the U.S. government and military have steadfastly denied this, successfully putting across the notion that anyone who claims a correlation isn't quite right in the head. Nevertheless, and assuming that whatever crashed at Roswell was not made by humans, Groom Lake/Area 51 (still designated in 1947 as Indian Springs Air Force Auxiliary Field) is a quite logical place for wreckage and other evidence to be taken: geographic isolation, an established military presence and security protocol, availability of qualified scientists, engineers, and other researchers.

Officially partnered with Edwards Air Force Base and proximate to Nellis AFB, Area 51 is a high-tech facility squatting in ninety thousand acres of flat desert scrub. Visible portions of the base occupy a relatively small footprint, and consist of runways, various radar arrays, mobile buildings (to quickly hide experimental aircraft from satellite cameras), some offices, barracks, and a mess hall. It is likely that some of the base's research and test areas are hidden underground, though these are probably neither as enormous nor as complex as imagined by some UFOlogists, conspiracy buffs, and fans of *Independence Day*.

Taxpayers support the place but taxpayers are not welcome. The idle or curious that come too close are greeted by weathered metal signs that don't mince words: RESTRICTED AREA, NO TRESSPASSING BEYOND THIS POINT. PHOTOGRAPHY OF THIS AREA IS PROHIBITED. WARNING, MILITARY INSTALLATION, OFF LIMITS TO UNAUTHORIZED PERSONNEL. USE OF DEADLY FORCE AUTHORIZED. Restricted ground is littered with buried motion sensors. Surrounding off-highway roads are patrolled by truck, and entrances are protected by guards and surveillance cameras.

Since the 1940s, this secure site has attracted active interest from many: the Naval Weapons Center, Strategic Air Command, Tactical Air Command, the National Defense Agency, Air Force Systems Command, Air Force Flight Test Center, the CIA's Foreign Technology Division, and other bodies and groups, including various personnel contracted to the CIA and its predecessor organizations.

Extensive clandestine testing of captured Soviet MiG fighters and other foreign aircraft began at Groom Lake in 1966. Of even greater importance is that over the past sixty years the base has bred an impressive number of spy and stealth aircraft, including the U-2 (built by Lockheed's Advanced Development Programs section, best known to the general public as the Skunk Works). Other Groom Lake/Area 51 aircraft include the CIA's A-12 OXCART, the F-117A Nighthawk fighter (another Skunk Works success), the remarkably high-flying SR-71 Blackbird (Skunk Works), and the problematic F-22 Raptor fighter, plus various drones designed for spy and missile duty. Elements of the Strategic Defense Initiative (Star Wars) were developed at Groom.

"Practical" testing of aircraft and weaponry is possible because of the base's isolation, and nearness to the Nellis Air Force Range, the Tonopah Test Range, and the Nevada Test Site. The nearly three million acres that surround Area 51 bring enhanced privacy, as well as a wealth of dry lake beds ideally suited for takeoffs and landings.

The Roswell flying saucer idea is healthy in areas surrounding the base, in ways that are at once intentionally humorous and unintentionally desperate. The combination of Area 51 secrecy, and the public's imagination and inclination to farce, has brought numberless toys, decals, bumper stickers, shot glasses, model kits, mugs, neckties, and some amusing faked signage. AREA 51 NO TRESPASSING, one sign begins, VIOLATORS WILL VANISH WITHOUT A TRACE.

AREA 51, Nonexistent Area, It is unlawful to enter areas that do not exist without permission of illusory installation commanders.

AREA 51, DO NOT ENTER. Trespassers will be [. . .] forcibly removed via catapult. (A tip to collectors: any sign that says "Area 51" is not the real article, even if its language is sober rather than whimsical.)

The settlement closest to Area 51 is Rachel, a town of fewer than one hundred people, and marked by mobile homes, an all-in-one restaurant-bar-motel-souvenir shop, a small Baptist church—and no post office. There is a gas station but the station does not operate. Rachel sits on Nevada Highway 375, a flat, straight route designated by state signs decorated with flying saucers. A roadside "POPULATION" sign erected by the town reads "Human YES Aliens ?" Area 51/Groom Lake is about thirty-six miles north of town.

Rachel's all-purpose motel is called the Little A'Le'Inn. Out front, hoisted on the back of a permanently parked wrecker, is a flying saucer. Guests can snug in their rooms and watch VHS episodes of *The X-Files*. Although ranches are in the area, Roswell and Area 51 are the basic sustenance of Rachel, and of much of the rest of this remote region. Without the saucer speculation that surrounds the base, there would be nothing to attract tourists.

Or unauthorized researchers.

Lazar Blows the Lid Off

In the late 1980s, a Nevada man named Robert Scott Lazar owned a photo lab that developed pictures for real estate agents and appraisers. Lazar was technologically clever, having installed a small jet engine in a Honda CR-X sport coupe, and executing similar work on a dragster. He confessed to a friend, Gene Huff, that photo work bored him, particularly because he had worked as a physicist in Area 51's S4 section, a top-secret underground facility. Lazar claimed he had won the job because famed physicist Edward Teller, who had seen Lazar's resumé, recommended him.

According to Lazar, the Spartan S4 complex was located underground at the east end of Papoose Lake, a dry bed located about ten miles southwest of the main Area 51 facility. Lazar was just twenty-four years old at the time, a reedy fellow with a ready smile, who identified himself as a scientist. In the course of his duties at S4, Lazar explained, he became privy to information about what he called an "anti-gravity reactor," a fantastic device that figured in top-secret Area 51 study of propulsion systems. Lazar assumed that the reactor was of human design, and then altered his opinion after being allowed to study nine alien spaceships kept in an underground hangar. (The precise nature of the security rating that cleared Lazar to see the ships remains a little hazy.)

Lazar also described a small, gray extraterrestrial he happened to glimpse in a room as Lazar was escorted along an S4 hallway by security men. (In 1995, Atari released *Area 51*, a video-arcade game in which a Strategic Tactical Advanced Alien Response team—STAAR—fights to round up escaped ETs.)

The ships studied by Lazar and others utilized antigravity propulsion that made use of a so-called "Element 115," an element that does not exist on Earth. This Element 115 is—and is not—related to the Periodic Table's Element 115, Ununpentium (Uup), an artificial element lacking stable isotopes. The 115 described by Lazar is dramatically more stable—and thus more useful—than the 115 that is presently known.

After becoming aware of Element 115's potential for propulsion, Lazar was brought onto Project Galileo, a carefully guarded government project that reverse-engineered the nine ships. One early success was the fabrication of five hundred pounds of Element 115. Lazar claimed that the United States would shortly have access to practical antigravity technology.

Lazar and Luff drove to Groom Lake in the spring of 1989 to secretly photograph test flights of the discs that Lazar had helped reverse-engineer. During the pair's second expedition, Area 51 security men discovered them and escorted their car from government land. Lazar was subsequently reprimanded; that black mark, plus officials' fear that Lazar's emotional equilibrium was imperiled by his wife's infidelity, caused Lazar to be stripped of his security clearance.

During these years, Lazar married and divorced twice, scrimmaged with the IRS, twice declared bankruptcy, and invested in The Honeysuckle Ranch, a legal Reno brothel.

In November 1989, Lazar contacted George Knapp, a reporter with Las Vegas TV station KLAS. Lazar claimed sensational inside information about the S4 group. Knapp, intrigued, gave Lazar airtime. Lazar's claims went over well with the KLAS audience, and made good copy for Nevada newspapers. After the story jumped to the wire services and went national, journalists grew curious about Lazar's job title and credentials; unfortunately, those were as hazy as Lazar's security clearance, and even his educational background was called into question: Lazar claimed to have studied at Cal State Northridge, Cal Tech, and MIT, but none of those schools have a record of him.

Lazar's brain kicked into a higher gear. He became convinced that his phone was bugged, and that agents followed him as he went about his daily activities. A security official who asked Lazar to meet him at a casino showed up, but failed to acknowledge Lazar's presence. Lazar readily identified government security men stationed around the room.

In 1991, Lazar overlooked or ignored local law when he installed a computer system in a Clark County, Nevada, brothel (not The Honeysuckle Ranch) where he was a regular client. (Friend George Huff recalls that Lazar simply repaired "a stereo or something like that.") Although some Nevada counties allowed legalized prostitution, Clark County was not one of them. Lazar was arrested, convicted of pandering, and placed on three years' probation (some sources say six months).

What to make of all this? Details of Lazar's background, as well as some iffy science, will encourage many to doubt his claims. But if his accounts form a hoax, Lazar would probably have pursued them more aggressively, and profited more. Although he has appeared in eight television documentaries made between 1990 and 2015 (*Dreamland: Area 51* [1996] is the best known), payment for such participation by non-celebrities is negligible. Notable only within the UFO community, Lazar soldiers on, lecturing to believers and skeptics alike.

The Roswell Slide Debacle

In 1998, a box containing four hundred Kodachrome slides was discovered by a cleaning woman in an Arizona home being prepared for an estate sale. The home had belonged to a deceased couple, a former petroleum geologist named Bernard Ray and his wife, Hilda Blair Ray. The cleaning woman (variously identified as "Catherine" and "Cat") took a cursory look and then stored the box in her own garage. When she discovered the box again ten years later, she found two slides of particular interest: blurry but fascinating images of tiny dead bodies laid in careful repose. With help from her brother, "Catherine" contacted filmmaker Adam Dew, who wondered whether the diminutive bodies could be Roswell, New Mexico, aliens. Dew brought the slides to a pair of Roswell researchers, Donald Schmitt (who, in 1995, admitted to fabricating Roswell research and his own credentials; see chapter one) and Tom Carey. Schmitt and Carey worked with Kodak to confirm the slides' year of origin, which was determined to be 1945–50. The Roswell crash occurred in 1947.

In 2014, Schmitt and Carey announced that the pair of images were priceless additions to human understanding not just of Roswell, but to an understanding of our place in the universe. UFOlogists Richard Dolan and Jaime Maussan joined Schmitt and Carey to vouch for the slides.

Who were the Rays, and could they have had connections to the Roswell incident? In 1947, Bernard Ray pursued petroleum-exploration research near Roswell. In the community of petroleum geologists, he was well known and highly regarded. Hilda Blair Ray was an attorney and a private pilot. A combination of factors—the slides, Ray's work and his proximity to Roswell, and Blair's status as a flying attorney—has encouraged speculation about clandestine government work, secretive legal shenanigans, and the couple's ability to travel quickly. What looks like coincidence to some is regarded as cover-up conspiracy by others.

The story put forth by Schmitt and Carey interested journalists, who got good copy when Schmitt described the slides' discovery as "certainly . . . the most important event in our lifetimes, because we are demonstrating, not only photographic evidence, but we are also demonstrating what all of these witnesses have reported to is over all of these years."

Interested parties were invited to pay twenty dollars to log into the live Web "reveal" of the slides, on May 5, 2015. Of course, the reliability of Schmitt's assertion hinges on one's willingness to disregard Schmitt's erroneous past claims, and to accept that the Rays had special insights into Roswell. Then there is the quality of the images. To the untutored eye, the frames appear unacceptably fuzzy, dominated by a dark, indiscernible mass situated diagonally at the intersection of what might be machined latticework. Whoever made the shots was an inexpert photographer, or in a terrible hurry.

Independent postings that appeared later include digitally "cleaned up" versions of the two photos. The figure in the improved images reposes, belly up, on a thin glass shelf attached by brackets to a lightweight metal strip. The strip has graduated, punched spaces that allow shelf adjustment. Reflections reveal that the shelf is inside a glass case. The alien physiognomy conforms, in a basic "big head" way, to the original Roswell witness reports. However, the figure appears to be considerably smaller and lighter than the "standard" Roswell humanoids. The shelf appears capable of supporting a few modest knickknacks and pictures, and little more.

Propped against the tiny legs is a rectangle of paper, out of focus and undecipherable, but likely an identifier. (Defenders of the Roswell-slide theory claim that the "paper" is a reflection of an overhead light fixture.)

In the background at frame right we see the slightly out-of-focus lower legs of a woman and the hem of her dress. The presence of the woman, and the photos' downward visual perspective, add to the impression that the wizened brown figure is very small. Further, the woman faces in toward the glass case, as if observing a museum display.

An independent body calling itself Roswell Slides Research Group cleaned up the images further to get a read on the printed paper. The paper said:

MUMMIFIED BODY OF TWO YEAR OLD BOY
At the time of burial the body was clothed in a slip-over cotton shirt. Burial wrappings consisted of three small cotton blankets.

Loaned by Mr. S. L. Palmer, San Francisco, California

In a statement dated May 12, 2015, co-promoter Tom Carey insisted that the Roswell Slides Research Group's enhancement "was faked." But just a day after that, blackvault.com administrator John Greenewald quoted from a 1938 National

Park Service publication discussing the Mesa Verde Archaeological Museum in Mesa Verde, Colorado:

> A splendid mummy was received by the Park Museum recently when Mr. S. L. Palmer Jr. of San Francisco returned one that his father had taken from the ruins in 1894. The mummy is that of a two year old boy and is in an excellent state of preservation. At the time of burial the body was clad in a slip-over cotton shirt and three small cotton blankets. Fragments of these are still on the mummy. [*Mesa Verde Notes*, September 1938, Volume VIII, Number 1.]

Roswell Slides Research Group historian and self-described "armchair researcher" Nab Lator discovered that the mummy remained on display at Mesa Verde from 1938 to June 1947. At the latter date, and with the permission of S. L. Palmer, the mummy was sent for display to the Montezuma Castle National Monument Museum, in Camp Verde, Arizona. And that is fitting, because it was at Camp Verde, not Mesa Verde, that Palmer discovered the mummy.

Records confirm that the mummy was displayed at Montezuma Castle throughout the 1950s and remained at the facility until at least 1971. No documentation of further movement has been found.

On May 15, 2015, Don Schmitt issued his "sincerest apology" for being "overly trusting." In other words, Schmitt was not at fault. He was led astray by others.

Festivals, Stalin, and the Children

Amidst the souvenir shops and tourist museums in and around Roswell, city officials opened an official place of study, the International Museum and Research Center, in 1992. Four years later, vintage photographs of a deceased alien that were a highlight of the September 1996 issue of *Penthouse* magazine turned out to show a prop from the Roswell museum; the item appeared in the magazine without the museum's knowledge. This sort of foolishness gives the amiable town of Roswell some free, unasked-for publicity but does harm to UFOlogy, trivializing the discipline and suggesting that believers are dupes or dopes, or both. Roswell itself, though, seems invulnerable.

Today a community of fifty thousand people, it gaily hosts the summertime Roswell Festival, an annual, four-day flying saucer-ET celebration that is the recurring climax of the town's determination to link itself to events of 1947. Hotels and motels for miles around are booked solid. Locals rent rooms and coax paying visitors to park on their lawns. A literal parade of celebrants (pets included) dressed and painted as extraterrestrials personifies the American sense of fun. Festival organizers offer live entertainment, book signings, guest speakers (Stanton Friedman and the indefatigable Don Schmitt led those who showed up in 2015), and a 10K alien-chase run. Families enjoy craft tables, a bicycle parade, and a carnival. Vendors sell unimaginable numbers of sno-cones, cotton candy, and tacos; T-shirts, toys, balloons, and innumerable other *tchotchkes*. Roswell is all about moneymaking and fun.

In 2011, though, a particularly bold Roswell-Area 51 narrative emerged. While its essentials are earthbound rather than extraterrestrial, the story is unimaginably disturbing. At the close of World War II, Soviet dictator Joseph Stalin experienced an understandably bad reaction to the destructive power of the American atomic bombs. Although Soviet spies in the United States had given Stalin advance knowledge of the Manhattan Project, the dictator nevertheless struggled to reconcile America's potential for undreamt-of violence with his own nation's relative helplessness. As the U.S. and USSR jockeyed during 1945–46 to get their hands on the top German rocket scientists, notes, and prototypes, Stalin had an idea: lacking atomic weaponry, the USSR might be able to panic America with a demonstration of another sort of technology, a flying disc built with "electromagnetic frequency" (EMF) technology explored by Germany's Horten brothers during World War II. Even better, the craft would land on U.S. soil, with an extraterrestrial crew. According to investigative journalist Annie Jacobsen, the disc that crashed near the Roswell, New Mexico, airbase in July 1947 was Soviet, and even sported Cyrillic characters around its perimeter. Inside was a crew (perhaps three or four, Jacobsen does not specify), including two that were comatose but alive. Although the child-sized crew members were humanoids with queerly enlarged heads and eyes, their origin was *not* extraterrestrial.

Jacobsen elected to close her 2011 book *Area 51: An Uncensored History of America's Top Secret Military Base* with the tale summarized above. Coming at the end of a generally smart and very well researched study, the story feels tacked on and gratuitous. Its tone is certainly at odds with the feel of everything that precedes it.

The account of the Soviet saucer comes from a single witness—an unnamed American engineer employed by defense contractor EG&G, a company enlisted in 1947 to help reverse-engineer the captured Soviet craft. By the time Annie Jacobsen first spoke with the man in 2009, he was the last living EG&G engineer (of five) with direct knowledge of the project. The weight of the truth, Jacobsen says, motivated the man to speak to her, and while that's dramatic and even a little heart-tugging, the man's remarks are, unfortunately, uncorroborated. Not long after the book's publication, the Web vibrated with speculation about the identity of Jacobsen's witness. (Commonly invoked names were Ben Rich, Clarence "Kelly" Johnson, Boyd Bushman, and Don Phillips, former Lockheed Skunk Works engineers that claimed to have seen and even reverse-engineered alien spaceships at Area 51.)

Excitement in UFO circles over Jacobsen's claim grew not just because of the purported Soviet connection to advanced technology, but because of the nature of the saucer's crew. All of them were child-sized because, they were, in fact, children. Human children. How could this be? According to the witness, the fiendish German extermination-camp doctor Josef Mengele contacted Stalin as the war ground to a conclusion. Mengele told Stalin he had performed surgical experiments, based in gene research and eugenics, on camp inmates. Perhaps, Mengele slyly suggested, Stalin might be interested in similar work performed by Mengele in a sanctuary inside the USSR. As Jacobsen's witness told the story, Stalin agreed, and put Mengele to work on an "extraterrestrial" crew. Stalin's objective was to stun American officials with a demonstration of hugely advanced "alien" technology and precipitate a panic, à la the one that supposedly occurred following the 1938 Orson Welles *War of the Worlds* broadcast.

The United States did not accept the saucer's supposed extraterrestrial origin, so Stalin's scheme failed. According to Jacobsen, the craft's technology was nevertheless carefully studied and duplicated. Subsequent "alien UFO" tales from Roswell may have been concocted by the government to deflect attention from the Soviet ship.

The child crew (some may have been as old as twelve or thirteen) did not fly the saucer but were guided to New Mexico by remote control. The children's craniums and eye orbits had been surgically enlarged. The two survivors, clinically dead, spent their final days upright and insensate in gel-filled tubes at Edwards Air Force Base.

And here is the greatest shock of all: according to the former EG&G engineer, the "child" flyers' existence went unrevealed because the United States used them as templates for hideous surgical experiments conducted on children and convicts at Area 51 well into the 1980s.

Nazis, Stalin, Mengele, iron-era saucer technology, Roswell, violated children, subterfuge—what a tale. Even cursory consideration, though, reveals impossibilities. Although Mengele did surgical procedures and experiments on children (mainly twins) and other extermination-camp prisoners, he lacked the surgical skill necessary to do as the Soviets allegedly wished. Also, Mengele's immediate postwar whereabouts—when he supposedly traveled to the Soviet Union—are well known: disguised, he labored as a field hand at farms in Germany. (He settled in South America later.)

Also:

- If Stalin intended that the Americans mistake the saucer for an extraterrestrial craft, its rim would not have carried Cyrillic letters.
- In 1947, no nation had the technology needed to remotely pilot an aircraft, over thousands of miles, to a target.
- No solid evidence exists that Germany's Horten brothers, who made great strides with flying wing design, created a flying disc.
- Assuming that the USSR had created the disc, sharing its design and the secrets of its fuel/propulsion systems with the West would have been the last thing Stalin wanted.
- Although erroneous reports of mass panic caused by the Welles broadcast had filtered to the USSR, Stalin had no reason to hope that his faked alien saucer would precipitate another one—not least because the U.S. military would surely keep the craft under wraps.
- Numerous Area 51 veterans who met Jacobsen and spoke with her about secret (but standard) weapons and avionics development were blindsided by the Stalin-Mengele-Roswell story, and denounced it loudly.
- In a 2011 *Popular Mechanics* article, tech writer Earl Swift reminds us that the big-head, huge-eyed alien conception did not surface until long after 1947. Jacobsen's witness, then, probably worked backwards from latter-day notions of ETs to describe the disfigured children he claimed to have seen.

- Swift wonders what happened to the saucer's (vaguely noted) EMF technology; if it existed, the world would have given up long ago on "old-school, fuel-chugging planes."

Mr. Swift is a sharp cookie, and he gets a gold star for his thoughts. He gets *two* gold stars for this discovery: in "Tomb Tapper," a 1956 short story by famed science fiction writer James Blish, locals in upstate New York can't determine whether a crashed saucer is from outer space or the USSR; when they force open the cockpit in an attempt to find out, they discover the body of a little girl, blonde and not more than eight years old.

People inclined to believe Annie Jacobsen's anonymous witness may say that Blish somehow got wind of the real events at Roswell, and wove it into his story. Yes, they might say that.

Eyes Only: Selected UFO Sightings, 1947–49

June 14 or July 7, 1947: Ranch foreman Mac Brazel discovers unusual debris in a sheep field near Roswell, New Mexico. Military explanations given during the following week veer between "flying disc" and "weather balloon." **Note:** One of the foundational incidents of UFO study, Roswell involves government obfuscation, sensational official documents (possibly real, possibly forged), and allegations of an extraterrestrial spacecraft and recovered alien bodies.

June 24, 1947: While flying above Mount Rainier, Washington, Idaho businessman and private pilot Kenneth Arnold observes nine vaguely delta-shaped objects in the sky at nine thousand feet. Arnold's description of the craft is partially misinterpreted by the press, which coins the term "flying saucer." **Note:** See chapter seven for the story of this seminal UFO sighting.

July 4, 1947: The pilot and co-pilot of a United Airlines DC-3 flying at eight thousand feet in a cloudless, twilight sky eight minutes out of Boise, Idaho, witness five disc-shaped objects on approach angle toward the plane; followed by a second formation of four discs. Both groups quickly pass out of sight, at speeds beyond the limits of standard aircraft. Captain Emil (E. J.) Smith describes the craft as "flat on the bottom, rounded on top." **Note:** Captain Smith had previously been openly skeptical about flying saucers.

August 14, 1947: Artist R. L. Johannis hails a pair of child-sized humanoids that have stepped from a thirty-foot disc at Villa Santina, Italy—only to be enveloped in a dark vapor and sent sprawling, dazed, onto his back. The creatures—about three feet tall and dressed in blue coveralls with red belts—appropriate Johannis's easel and return with it to their craft.

January 7, 1948: A P-51 Mustang piloted by Captain Thomas Mantell out of Godman Field Army Air Force Base, Kentucky, crashes while in pursuit of an unidentified flying object. Ground contact with Mantell is lost when the P-51 is at fifteen thousand feet; the plane goes down shortly afterward. **Note:** The official causes of Captain Mantell's pursuit and death remain points of dispute.

January 7, 1948, was the last day on Earth for Kentucky Air National Guard pilot Thomas Mantell, who flew his P-51 Mustang in pursuit of a UFO above Fort Knox. Whether the highly experienced Captain Mantell pushed his plane beyond its capabilities or was suddenly confronted by the bogey is unknown. The fact is, Mantell crashed and died, placing military pilots in the crosshairs of unidentified aircraft, and ushering in new apprehension about UFOs.   *Alamy*

March 25, 1948: Two men discover a crashed, dome-shaped saucer near Aztec, New Mexico, and a clutch of tiny alien bodies. **Note**: The Aztec UFO tale is among the most famous UFO account from the early post-Arnold period. The witnesses, Leo GeBauer and Silas Newton, were not quite as they portrayed themselves, and although the case was investigated by numerous sympathetic UFOlogists, neither details nor the witnesses bear up well under serious scrutiny. Opinions, though, continue to differ widely. For details of the crash at Aztec, see chapter fifteen.

April 24, 1949: A weather-balloon crew observes a dull-white ellipsoid, with a yellow cast to the underside, in the daytime sky above the White Sands (New Mexico) Proving Ground. Because the crew has been releasing and monitoring balloons, the unidentified object is tracked by an ML-47 theodolite, which incorporates a twenty-five-power telescope mounted to record elevation (vertical attitude) and azimuth (horizontal bearings). After about sixty seconds of telescopic and unaided observation by crew leader Charles Moore and four Navy enlisted men, the object pauses in its angular movement before disappearing following a sudden, rapid ascent. **Note**: The presence of trained observers and the theodolite (which allowed quantifiable tracking) gives this sighting particular gravity. The object appeared in a cloudless sky, and emitted neither noise nor vapor trail or other exhaust. For details of the crash at Aztec, see chapter fifteen.

9

Project Blue Book, or How UFOs Took over American Culture

Government, the Military, and the CIA, Too

It Started with a Sign

T he United States government and military were naturally disposed to be curious about such things as the Arnold sighting and the Roswell crash. The September 1947 Twining memorandum (discussed in chapter eight) noted the peculiar avionics of unidentified flying objects, and acknowledged that not every question about them would be resolved easily. General Twining's thoughts circulated in the middle of a rash of "saucer" sightings that followed close on the heels of Arnold and Roswell. Throughout 1948, representatives of the military and academia (including Ohio State University astronomy professor J. Allen Hynek) studied the UFO phenomenon, looking at the Swedish "ghost rocket" reports of 1946 (see chapter 5), and particularly incidents from 1947–48, some of which occurred very near to U.S. military bases in California (Muroc Army Air Base—later renamed Edwards AFB—in the Southern California desert near Lancaster, was one). Eyewitness reports from technicians, pilots, and other ostensibly credible witnesses suggested circular or disc-shaped machines with propulsion and avionics sufficient to reach speeds and execute aerial maneuvers beyond the capabilities of known aircraft—as well as beyond the capability of the human body to withstand.

America's official UFO investigative body received a name, Project Sign, on January 22, 1948, and was attached to Wright-Patterson AFB, near Dayton, Ohio. Gen. Nathan Twining, commander of the Twentieth Air Force during World War II, and later chairman of the Joint Chiefs of Staff, assumed duties as Sign's chief. Project members included security-cleared military personnel and civilians with expertise in missiles, nuclear energy, and aeronautics. One participant, Alfred Loedding, had already done work on disc-shaped aircraft, and wings with a low aspect ratio (the ratio of the length of wings to their width). Loedding's interest in flying discs was an obvious asset; likewise his wing studies, because short wings allowed greater maneuverability than what is possible with longer-winged aircraft.

Nazi Germany's Horten Ho 229 "flying wing" light bomber first flew, in prototype form, in the spring of 1944; although prototypes test-flew into 1945, this advanced jet-powered wing never went into production. If it had, its design might have afforded aeronautic advantages similar to those exhibited by flying discs.

America's own "flying wing," the prop-driven Northrop YB-35 experimental heavy bomber, flew in 1946. Its jet-powered follow-on, the YB-49, arrived in 1947. Given the very recent reports of apparently wingless, unidentified aircraft, General Twining and other leaders of Sign grew concerned that the Soviet Union had achieved startling advances in wing ratio technology, and conventional or atomic propulsion. (The atomic angle carries weight because the concern arose even before the Soviets test-exploded—and later revealed—their first atomic bomb in late August 1949.) Even if such advances had been made by Great Britain or another friendly nation, the world balance of power would change, to America's detriment.

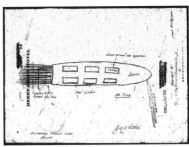

Project Sign collected UFO data, interviewed witnesses, and tried to explain discrete sightings. Above Montgomery, Alabama, on July 24, 1948, Eastern Airlines DC-3 pilots Clarence Chiles and John Whitted encountered a cylindrical UFO. First Officer Whitted made this drawing for Sign investigators two days later, indicating a finless craft about a hundred feet long, emitting a forty-foot "orange & red flame" exhaust. A simultaneous sketch by Captain Chiles also depicted the rocket-type shape and dramatic exhaust.   *USAF*

Sign realized that Alfred Loedding's work with flying-wing design became a particular asset just six months after the project's official startup. At five thousand feet outside Montgomery, Alabama, on July 24, 1948, Eastern Airlines DC-3 pilots Clarence Chiles and John Whitted got a good startle when a wingless cylinder with a taper to its leading edge approached head-on and streaked past their starboard wing, vanishing after executing a sudden ninety-degree ascent. Chiles and Whitted later estimated the craft's length at a hundred feet, with a diameter "twice B-29" (the wingspan of a B-29 Superfortress is 141 feet). The craft's fuselage exhibited rows of lights, which both pilots interpreted as illuminated windows or ports. At least one other professional pilot had encountered a rocket-shaped craft in the recent past (C-47; Tampa, Florida; August 1, 1946); that sighting gave additional credence to the Chiles-Whitted account, but here is the kicker: less than an hour before Chiles and Whitted's encounter over Alabama, a rocket-shaped object streaked across the sky above Robins AFB, located sixteen miles south of Macon, Georgia. It was observed there by Air Force ground personnel. The craft that came at the DC-3 shortly afterward was headed west (Chiles and Whitted were flying east, from Houston to Atlanta). The UFO sighted over Robins traveled west-southwest. Montgomery is 185 miles southwest of Macon.

Visitors had come to America's southeast.

The rocket shape that figures in the Montgomery and Macon sightings suggested human technology. Although "flying saucer" had already entered the popular lexicon, Washington was more concerned with the possibility of foreign (read: Communist) aircraft sporting heretofore unknown technology. An alternative possibility—that the saucers were experimental, super-secret aircraft designed and tested by the United States—was hardly less a concern than the Soviet one. Not every staff-level officer in every branch would necessarily know about such craft, and the general civilian population was not to know at all.

For a brief period, the possibility of extraterrestrial origin was not part of the official discussion—though many early U.S. investigators privately believed that otherworldly origins were not merely possible but likely.

Realpolitik

After seven months of investigative work, Project Sign startled the Pentagon (and perhaps itself, as well) by concluding that flying saucers were best explained by the extraterrestrial hypothesis. A number of persons and events helped cement that belief. Perhaps foremost was Capt. Thomas Mantell, who died over Kentucky on January 7, 1948, while flying in pursuit of a UFO. Although Mantell's propeller-driven P-51 could not keep pace with the airborne object Mantell pursued, the captain got close enough to radio that the thing "looks metallic and of tremendous size." Although some involved with Sign (particularly those more attuned to the Pentagon than to the USAF) remained wedded to the Soviet-aircraft theory (craft presumably engineered with assistance from German scientists captured after the war), others within Sign were not so sure.

The Soviet theory might have had more juice if Sign operated in a vacuum, ignorant of scientific, military, and political developments beyond the borders of Washington. But America had fielded assets sufficient to help win World War II. Of all of that conflict's many belligerents, the USA was the only one to come out of the war *stronger* than when it had gone in. Europe and the Soviet Union had been flattened, their infrastructures and economies badly mauled. The Japanese Imperial Empire had been destroyed, and Japan itself had suffered horrific physical and economic payback. An entire generation of Soviet and German young men had been lost. Millions of refugees and other dispossessed roamed the landscapes of vanquished and victors alike. Postwar, and particularly before the Soviet Union's successful A-bomb test in 1949, America bestrode the world like a colossus. The requirements of war had allowed it to become an economic powerhouse, and although the U.S. military was quickly drawn down after 1945, its tactical and strategic capabilities remained enormous. Further, a thriving, expanding intelligence community—although admittedly in the dark about the efficacy of Soviet spy activity—had a sharp sense of other nations' technologic capabilities. Even the Soviet atomic bomb, though ominous, had not been unexpected; Washington had realized that such a breakthrough was inevitable.

Conversely, Washington had a sense of high-tech that did *not* exist. If the USA had no flying saucers, the likelihood of the USSR or anyone else having them was very slight. America had gotten its hands on the cream of the German rocket scientists and avionics personnel. The identities and capabilities of German scientists spirited to the Soviet Union were well known to Washington. As a group, they were capable, but not more capable than those at work in the United States. Other relative issues, including access to natural resources, and economic and manufacturing capabilities (including the issue of an available workforce), favored America, and led some in U.S. intelligence to conclude—rightly, as things turned out—that the Soviets labored at tech levels inferior to levels achieved by the USA. Despite an ability to mount occasional surprises (such as the Bomb and the later Sputnik satellite), the Soviets were stuck in a perpetual game of catch-up. If no one in the Washington of 1947–48 predicted that the Soviets would one day spend too much and bankrupt themselves out of existence, some particularly canny American intelligence experts may have perceived the early indicators.

Then, too, came the issue of the wide geographic spread of saucer sightings. Objects spotted over Europe and the USA might be rationalized as Soviet on grounds of proximity and strategic interest, but what about sightings in Australia, Indonesia, Malaysia, and other remote corners of the globe? Why would the USSR spend its treasure to do faraway tests in areas of limited strategic and intelligence value? *How* would they send saucers over such great distances?

For all these reasons, many in Sign felt convinced that "flying saucers" were neither Soviet nor earthly.

Garrett Weighs In

In July 1947, six months before the establishment of Project Sign, the intelligence office of the Army Air Forces (shortly to become the U.S. Air Force) requested that other military services and the FBI contribute to a better understanding of the so-called flying saucers and other unidentified flying objects. The request came to Lt. Col. George Garrett, a USMC officer attached to the Pentagon. Garrett developed an interest in the Chiles-Whitted DC-3 account, and *three that predated* Kenneth Arnold: a May 19, 1947, account from Manitou Springs, Colorado, where three witnesses witnessed a hovering, motionless silver object before it finally streaked away; May 22, 1947, Oklahoma City, a ground sighting by a single witness; and June 22, 1947, Greenfield, Massachusetts, a small, silver-white sphere seen from the ground by one man, who estimated the object's altitude at one thousand feet. (The problematic aspect of the last account is not the sphere itself, but the witness's claims about the object's size and altitude, neither of which could have been anything other than a baseless guess.)

In all, Garrett worked from eighteen accounts (sixteen plus two added later)—some of which were Swedish "ghost rocket" sightings from 1946–47. Garrett's July 30, 1947, report to General Twining at Air Materiel Command concluded that the mysterious flying discs existed. That judgment may sound like a bombshell, but Garrett offered it honestly and easily, believing that the Pentagon and President Truman already knew that the discs were real. The real issue was the discs' origin, and to Garrett, the evidence gave "more than ordinary weight to the possibility that this is a domestic project, about which the President, etc. know."

Garrett had been encouraged in his "earthly" opinion by Gen. George Schulgen, who agreed that 1) the discs existed, 2) insiders already knew it, and 3) the best course was to say so, and let higher-ups decide whether to shut the door on further inquiry.

General Twining's office conducted independent research simultaneous with Garrett's. The Twining team relied more heavily on pilot accounts, feeling that the credibility of such witnesses was difficult to dispute. Although pilots frequently misidentify objects encountered in flight, the Twining team's response to the Garrett report nevertheless agreed that the flying discs existed. But unlike Garrett, the Twining people admitted to having no clue as to the objects' origins.

It is from this uncertainty that Project Sign developed.

"Estimate of the Situation"

The U.S. Air Force's Air Materiel Command (AMC) activated Project Sign on January 22, 1948, at Wright Field (later Wright-Patterson AFB) in Dayton, Ohio. Project director Robert R. Sneider worked closely with Air Force intelligence, as Sign investigated UFO reports from 1947 to September 1948. Sign investigators evaluated reports, flagging those of potential importance. Witness interviews, when deemed necessary, were conducted by AMC personnel. Witnesses filled out a standard questionnaire and gave verbal accounts of what they had seen.

In May 1948, Ohio State astronomer J. Allen Hynek came on board at Sign as a consultant, tasked mainly with looking at reports and determining which ones described meteorites, weather anomalies, and other things readily explained by science. However, some at Sign (Sneider included) leaned toward an extrater-restrial explanation, and were encouraged by the aforementioned Chiles-Whitted DC-3 encounter of July 1948. Two or three months later, Capt. Sneider completed an elaborate report—the Top Secret Estimate of the Situation—to explain Sign's work, conclusions, and advisements. (The report is best known as the Estimate of the Situation.)

Colonels attached to Sign gave approval for the report's slow march up the Air Force ranks, beginning with the chief of intelligence, Gen. Charles Cabell. The paper finally reached Air Force Chief of Staff Gen. Hoyt Vandenberg, who was alarmed by the report's conclusion: the best available evidence suggested an extraterrestrial origin for unidentified flying objects that could not be readily explained.

Even as Vandenberg struggled to absorb this, a contrarian document (pushed by Maj. Aaron Boggs) circulated at high levels. The Boggs report asserted that flying discs were *not* extraterrestrial. Vandenberg turned again to the Estimate of the Situation, which he finally regarded as informed guesswork. His interests and inclinations lay with things seen, felt, and documented. Because the Estimate cited no physical evidence in support of its ET theory, Vandenberg dismissed the paper and ordered all copies destroyed.

The Estimate's ET-centric orientation doomed it; the Air Force desired some-thing more easily digestible. In the years since, the Estimate of the Situation has achieved near-mythic status in UFO circles. For decades, the report's com-plete physical destruction seemed a certainty. Even the barest description of it—a thick sheaf of legal-sized paper bound beneath black covers stamped TOP SECRET—comes to us only from a claim by Edward Ruppelt, a heavily decorated flier attached in 1948 to Wright Field's Air Technical Intelligence Center. (As we will see, Captain Ruppelt later headed a follow-on to Sign, Project Blue Book.)

The general public had no knowledge of the Estimate until Ruppelt mentioned it in his 1956 book *The Report on Unidentified Flying Objects*. More recently, pages that apparently survived have been quoted, and posted to the Internet. Not unexpectedly, these pages provoke considerable debate. In the end, there seems no way to determine authenticity or fakery.

In the meanwhile, generals Cabell and Vandenberg coolly suggested that Project Sign try again. A subsequent paper handed in near the close of 1948 tip-toed around the extraterrestrial notion but did not abandon it. With that, Project Sign was suspended. Investigation of UFOs would continue—but then again, it wouldn't. Vandenberg realized that sharp observers in the press and scientific community might notice the sudden absence of an investigatory body looking into UFOs. Another was established early in 1949, but Vandenberg and people in USAF intelligence were clear that the investigation was to be theater, and nothing more. On February 11, the revived program received a code name calculated to suggest Air Force antipathy: Project Grudge. Although official USAF accounts deny that the word "Grudge" had any special significance, Edward Ruppelt was on the mark when he referred to Grudge as "the Dark Ages" of UFO investigation.

Politics and PR

Hobbled from the outset by the politics of disclosure and public relations, and "expected" to avoid the extraterrestrial hypothesis, Project Grudge ostensibly carried on with study of the saucer phenomenon. It relied heavily on astronomer J. Allen Hynek, who had consulted on Sign. Hynek was not "opposed" to the idea of unidentified flying objects, and he did not assume that witnesses had prevaricated. But he felt obligated to give weight to many witnesses' lack of scientific training, and the possibility of mistaken judgments even by pilots and other seemingly credible observers. Hynek examined various UFO cases objectively, making natural use of his expertise and training. His mindset did not allow for wishful thinking or leaps of logic. In his role as consultant to Grudge, he concluded, rather mildly, that many flying-disc reports had roots in explainable, everyday causes. He looked with particular interest at the Mantell P-51 crash, and suggested that the pilot probably chased the planet Venus. (Hynek later regretted his explanation: Venus was indeed in the sky when Mantell died, but, as Hynek realized, would not have been bright enough for the pilot to see.) In all, Hynek reviewed nearly 250 cases, and prepared a six-hundred-page report. He noted that although about a quarter of accounts appeared challenging, most of those could be explained by what Hynek called "psychological explanations." Of the other 75 percent, "there is no evidence that objects reported upon are the result of an advanced scientific foreign development; and therefore, they constitute no threat to the national security."

"Venus" and "no evidence" were just the sort of conclusions desired by military personnel eager to put the whole flying saucer business to rest. The subsequent Grudge Report recommended that the project files be made public via a standard press release. Why? The USAF and America's intelligence community wanted the public to believe that the American military had exhausted its interest in UFOs. Naturally enough, the unrestricted press release came to the attention of Moscow almost immediately—just as the Air Force and Grudge had planned. (The press release began with "Project Saucer Discontinued"; Project Saucer was the Air Force's public name for projects Sign and Grudge.)

In the spring of 1949, consecutive issues of the *Saturday Evening Post* carried a two-part article by Sidney Shallet. The journalist had been vetted by the Air Force, and allowed limited access to USAF saucer files. Probably because "Sign" was making the transition to "Grudge," Shallet's article referred to the Air Force investigatory body as "Project Saucer." The articles are essentially puff pieces—fluff that let the magazine run a flying saucer piece with an "official" imprimatur. In return for access, the Air Force insisted on final approval. Although the article notes a few intriguing, unsolved UFO cases, it is likely that the Air Force liaison was comfortable with the inclusion of such tidbits.

Grudge issued just one report (coded as Technical Report No. 102-AC-49/15-100), dated December 27, 1949. Although acknowledging that nearly a quarter of investigated sightings could not be explained, "Unidentified Flying Objects—Project Grudge" recommended that USAF investigation of UFOs be greatly curtailed. The report elaborated by suggesting that no further investigatory effort be put forth on sightings lacking "realistic technical applications." That phrase suggests that the Air Force had returned to the man-made/Soviet UFO mindset; the time and expense of scrutiny would henceforth be expended on sightings suggestive of real-world tech uses and consequences—which was one way of saying "military applications" and "foreign threats." Sightings with even a whiff of the fanciful seemed destined to be ignored and forgotten.

Key members of Grudge were not inclined to let go of all investigations. This was revealed long after the fact, in a declassified June 1968 report from the National Investigations Committee on Aerial Phenomena (NICAP; established in 1956 by a UFO enthusiast named Thomas Townsend Brown and shortly led by a retired USMC major, Donald Keyhoe). Publicly, Grudge had been declared finished; in reality, the project's work was, as the 1968 report put it, "permitted to exist in a kind of limbo of skepticism." What the 1968 NICAP papers describe as "several significant sightings in September 1951" were sufficient for Grudge's release from limbo just a month later. In March 1952, Grudge was officially resurrected, and with a new name, too: Project Blue Book.

Blue Book Mandates and Activities

A Grudge recommendation that was *not* shared with the public was that copies of the December 27, 1949, report be put on the reading list of U.S. military personnel studying psychological warfare. The intelligence community was apprehensive about Soviet exploitation of American fears of UFOs, and keen to devise ways to combat it. Increased UFO activity two years later spurred interest in psychological warfare: if Washington was to have a firm grasp of possible Soviet mischief, Washington had to have the best possible understanding of unidentified flying objects.

Capt. Edward J. Ruppelt, formerly of Air Technical Intelligence Center, Air Force, at Wright-Patterson AFB, headed Project Blue Book from September 1951 to September 1953. His tenure was marked by what NICAP described as "the great UFO sighting wave of summer 1952" (some of those sightings are described later in this chapter), and a largely successful effort to rectify the sins of the past. New sightings interested Blue Book, but Ruppelt also directed project energy to fresh study of UFO reports from 1947 to the establishment of Blue Book—reports that had been investigated inadequately by Sign and Grudge.

Ruppelt's instincts and intentions were good, but as soon as Blue Book reports suggested that UFOs might encompass more than Soviet activity, the Air Force—which had never desired that point of view—grew wary of Blue Book.

Wings, Lights, and a Black Eye at Lubbock

During the transition from Grudge to Blue Book, the Air Force investigated an unidentified "flying wing" reported on the evening of August 25, 1951, above east Albuquerque and near Sandia Base, a part of Kirtland AFB. Kirtland was home to Special Weapons Command; the base and surrounding area did research and tests of new weapons and delivery systems—atomic weapons included—particularly those with intercontinental capability. The Sandia witnesses were a security-cleared Sandia guard (off duty) and his wife. The guard estimated that the wing passed silently above his home at about eight hundred to a thousand feet, at three hundred to four hundred miles per hour. The width of the craft appeared to be about 350 feet (half again the width of America's enormous B-36 Peacemaker bomber). The wing's trailing edge showed what the witness described as "six to eight pairs of softly glowing lights."

FLYING SAUCERS: AN ANALYSIS OF THE AIR FORCE PROJECT BLUE BOOK SPECIAL REPORT No. 14

SECOND EDITION OCTOBER, 1957 PRICE $1.50

PREPARED AND PUBLISHED BY DR. LEON DAVIDSON

The USAF commissioned an analysis of Project Blue Book activity in 1955. The edition seen here is the 1966 edition; three years later, a USAF memo noted Blue Book's termination, claiming that nothing in Blue Book files characterized UFOs as threats to national security, creations of advanced technology, or extraterrestrial origin. Sightings that Blue Book designated as "unexplained" were conveniently ignored.   *USAF*

Retroactive investigation by Blue Book found that the skies that night carried broken clouds at seventeen thousand feet. Visibility was five miles. No Air Force plane was aloft at that spot or time. Further, Kirtland radar showed nothing out of the ordinary. Blue Book personnel determined that the guard was mentally stable. The report seemed credible, and investigators expressed curiosity about similarities between the arrangement of lights on the mysterious flying wing and a similar light formation reported above Lubbock, Texas, on August 25, 1951, the same day as the Sandia sighting.

The so-called Lubbock Lights figure in what may have been the beginning of the end of Blue Book. Although Blue Book carried on until January 1970, perception among the military and the public alike was set when Blue Book struggled to explain what had been sighted in Texas. Lubbock lies 290 miles southeast of Albuquerque, New Mexico. The August 25 sightings had been made by three Texas Tech professors relaxing in a backyard. The three saw twenty to thirty bright lights, flying in a U-shaped formation. Local authorities subsequently took a report of a separate August 25th sighting. After dark on August 30, a Texas Tech freshman named Carl Hart snapped four photographs of about twenty "lights," forming two lines, which moved across the sky in a V-formation.

Hart took his prints to Lubbock's daily, the *Morning Avalanche*. The photos appeared in the paper on September 1, and were shortly picked up by the Associated Press for wire distribution across the country. Professionals at the *Avalanche* and the AP found no evidence that the photos had been doctored or otherwise faked. The head of the Texas Tech biology department declared that the objects were not birds—a judgment that seemed to be confirmed when an *Avalanche* photographer took pictures of birds flying above the town's streetlamps, only to get images too faint to be publishable.

Excited by the photographs, the original trio of witnesses enlisted two colleagues and waited to see the lights again. They did, on September 5, 1951. The professors saw a bright light (or the lights of multiple objects; they couldn't be sure) just before the object(s) passed directly overhead. One of the professors, Grayson Mead, counted twelve to fifteen discrete, disc-shaped objects, each showing a green-blue color with a slight fluorescence. From the ground, and with no frame of visual reference, each disc seemed to Mead to be "about the size of a dinner plate." Mead and the others agreed that there had been no way to accurately estimate the discs' true sizes.

After the fact, friends and other locals suggested to Mead and his fellow witnesses that the lights had been ground illumination reflected from the bellies of passing birds. Mead, however, had considerable experience as a hunter. He was well familiar with the silhouettes of indigenous fowl, and insisted that the skyborne objects he saw were "absolutely circular." Another of the professors, W. L. Ducker, agreed that the group had not witnessed birds.

The five academics were not schooled in avionics, but they did hold between them advanced degrees in physics, mathematics, chemical engineering, petroleum engineering, and geology. All agreed that a wisp of cloud in the sky on September 5 likely hung at two thousand feet. The discs passed from clear sky to a spot above the cloud, and then back into the clear again. The professors calculated that the objects had been moving at about six hundred miles per hour.

The professors and others near Lubbock continued to witness nighttime lights until early November, coincident with Edward Ruppelt's investigative journey to Texas. While there, Ruppelt discovered more than he could comfortably absorb: a Lubbock man who observed flying lights on August 25 while driving; a Lubbock woman frightened by "an airplane without a body" that silently cruised over her house; and sightings by a pair of Air Defense Command radar stations of an unidentified object over Washington State, early in the morning of August 26. Radar indicated the object's altitude as thirteen thousand feet. An F-86 Sabre jet sent to investigate was not able to intercept before the blip vanished from the radar screens.

Ruppelt soon calculated that if the object sighted on radar was connected to the other objects seen on August 25–26, it had been traveling at about nine hundred miles per hour.

Despite the anomalous aspects of the August–November 1951 sightings, Blue Book finally suggested that the witnesses had seen birds, possibly plovers. As for Ruppelt, although he had been puzzled by many aspects of the sightings, particularly the speed that he himself calculated, he took the opportunity in his 1956 book to identify the Lubbock Lights as moths. Although Ruppelt had departed Blue Book three years earlier, his absurd explanation reflected badly on the project. Yes, the Air Force wanted Blue Book to dissuade the public from the whole idea of flying saucers, but the notion of supersonic moths just invited ridicule. The Air Force expected Blue Book to produce whitewashes, but not at the USAF's expense.

And though the explanation for Lubbock did not stand up to scrutiny, there was none at all for the "flying wing" sightings.

Good Grief, They're Going After the White House

As we've seen, Grudge issued just a single formal report. By way of contrast, between November 1951 and September 1953, Blue Book prepared and issued status reports at the end of every month (with a few exceptions). In addition, Blue Book staffers issued a "Special Report," dated December 28, 1951. Reports were variously designated as "Secret" or "Confidential."

The Special Report and first four status reports (November 30, 1951–February 29, 1952) were officially attributed to Project Grudge. The Blue Book name first appeared on Status Report No. 5, dated March 31, 1952. Fewer than four months later, events in Washington, D.C., pushed Air Force "explainers" to the wall, and gave Blue Book much more to grapple with.

Throughout 1952, nearly six hundred UFO reports were made to authorities around the world, with the vast majority coming from the length and breadth of the United States. The most dramatic sightings from that year occurred in July, and made one thing very clear: if you're piloting an unusual aircraft and crave attention, be sure to fly over the White House.

Late on the night of July 19, 1952, air traffic controllers from both radar centers at Washington, D.C.'s Washington National Airport picked up blips of rapidly accelerating aircraft some fifteen miles southwest of the capital. The same array was seen on radar at Andrews AFB, ten miles to the east. Tower sightings made by the naked eye confirmed the objects' rapid acceleration. And the pilot of a DC-4 awaiting permission to take off from National confirmed the fast-moving, glowing objects.

Not long after midnight, the objects took positions above the White House and the U.S. Capitol. People on the ground watched as the bright-orange objects wheeled in the sky, trailing fire. When two F-94 Starfire interceptors from New Castle AFB, Delaware, approached, the objects streaked away, only to return after low fuel forced the jets to retreat.

Sightings by radar and the naked eye continued until 3:00 a.m. July 20. An encore took place the following night, when radar operators estimated the objects' speed at nine hundred miles per hour. Additional sightings occurred throughout the following week; when a second pair of New Castle F-94s drew to within ten miles of the objects on the night of July 26–27, the odd craft sped away. One Starfire pilot never got a visual on the objects at all, but the other, Lt. William Patterson, not only saw them but found himself momentarily surrounded by what he described as "four glows."

The Air Force responded with a shoot-down order, to be in effect for any non-communicative unidentified flying objects in the area. The USAF shoot-down order is hardly surprising; authorities were legitimately concerned for the safety of President Truman and everyone one else in and near Washington, particularly following a failed assassination attempt on the president in November 1950, which caused the death of a Puerto Rican nationalist and a White House policeman. (Truman had been sleeping inside Blair House, and suffered no more inconvenience than being awakened from his after-lunch nap.)

Blue Book chief Edward Ruppelt happened to be in Washington on the night of July 19–20. When he learned of the incident the following day, he tried to investigate, only to be stonewalled by senior officers that did not want him around.

At a July 29 Pentagon press conference, Air Force representatives eager to undo the scare caused by the shoot-down order offered too many contradictory explanations: 1) the objects had not been solid (radar sightings

In July 1952, with Washington, D.C., already on edge because of Red atom spies, the Korean War, and a 1950 assassination attempt against President Truman, the capital jumped to attention after being buzzed by UFOs.   *Everett Collection*

notwithstanding), 2) pilots and ground observers had seen meteorites (they were solid again), and 3) the moving lights had been caused by temperature inversions (semi-solid). A later, official USAF explanation cited atmospheric mirages caused by stars viewed through the distorting effect of a "temperature inversion." Blue Book ultimately went along with that idea, over the objections of Capt. Ruppelt. He had finally gone back to Washington to interview various witnesses, including radar operators, all of whom scoffed at the weather theory. Further, one or two confided that their superiors had none-too-subtly tried to steer them toward that explanation.

Dr. James McDonald (see chapter one), a prominent atmospheric physicist and a dependable antagonist of glib explanations, conducted his own interviews, and then looked at July 1952 weather charts and declared that, given radar-propagation theory (which concerns itself with variations in the refractive index of the atmosphere), the temperature-inversion theory was impossible.

Putting on the Brakes

Early in 1953, the Air Force and CIA worked with Dr. H. P. Robertson—a Caltech physics professor who did classified consulting for the defense department—to convene the Scientific Advisory Panel on UFOs, a collection of scientists brought together to review existing UFO research, remark upon it, and recommend a future course for Project Blue Book. The panel (informally known as the Robertson Panel) was hurriedly assembled, and spent just four days, January 14–17, 1953, in review and discussion of Blue Book reports on a mere dozen sightings.

Because no evidence existed (according to the panel) to cast UFOs as threats to national security, Robertson and the others recommended that Blue Book activity be throttled back. Further, the UFO-related activity of military intelligence staff diverted resources from general intelligence work, compromising national security. Also, a continuation of high-profile UFO research might spark "hysterical mass behavior," and threaten the general order.

The panel added that no evidence existed to support the notion that UFOs were extraterrestrial in origin. Politics remained, however, and true to the nation's rapidly growing Cold War paranoia, the panel suggested that private UFO groups—such as Los Angeles-based Civilian Flying Saucer Investigators—be monitored for subversive activity.

Besides a cutback of Blue Book's activities, the nation would be well served, the panel said, by a public-education campaign designed to discredit UFO witnesses and the whole idea of unidentified flying objects. To that end, valuable contributions could be made by schools, chambers of commerce, and local radio and television stations. A particularly ambitious campaign to undercut saucer claims, the panel suggested, might be undertaken by Hollywood, and movies so fantastic that audiences would laugh out loud. Well, small chance of that, as moviegoers had already accepted the UFO idea in *The Flying Saucer* (1950); *The Thing from Another World* (1951); *The Man from Planet X* (1951); *The Day the Earth Stood Still* (1951); *The War of the Worlds* (1953); and *It Came from Outer Space* (1953).

At the close of 1953, what had been a Blue Book staff of about a dozen was reduced to Ruppelt and two others. Captain Ruppelt departed Blue Book in 1953; his successor, Capt. Charles Hardin, had virtually no interest in flying discs, odd lights, or the rest of the UFO phenomena. (And neither did the USAF, as witness the installation of consecutive captains—rather than majors or colonels—to head the project.) Hardin regarded Blue Book as a way station on his way to something better, so it served not only USAF interests but Hardin's if Blue Book cut paperwork, cut back investigations, and kept a low profile. In a report dated May 5, 1955, Blue Book's findings about earlier UFO cases were collated in "Project Blue Book Report No. 14," and released the following October. Although the report (designated Project Stork) was based on USAF research, the document was prepared by the Battelle Memorial Institute, an outside firm with no grounding in what Blue Book had been pursuing in the Ruppelt days. At 315 pages and supported by 240 tables, Report No. 14 was a sober, pedestrian effort that noted no "marked patterns or trends" that might lend legitimacy to UFO sightings. A simplified summation was prepared for journalists (who were not to share it with the public). Late in 1956, a private researcher obtained congressional permission to publish the reports, minus the tables, at his own expense. The documents and other research that provided the report's foundation were declassified in 1960 but not made available to the public until 1967, when interested parties were invited to view them at Wright-Patterson AFB.

Another Air Force captain, George Gregory, took over leadership of Blue Book in 1956. Like Hardin, he pursued a slowdown of Blue Book investigatory activity.

The Air Force, determined to make the press and public forget about peculiar objects in the sky, had failed to reckon with the Soviets. Russia's October 4, 1957, launch of the 184-pound Sputnik, the first artificial Earth satellite, was an embarrassing and worrisome blow to American prestige. What could be worse?

Practical Futurism, Part II

The Union of Soviet Socialist Republics. September 1959. That message is stamped on a metal pennant deposited on the Moon by the Soviet Union at the dawn of the space race. On September 14, 1959, forty-one hours after the pennant settled in Moon dust, Soviet premier Nikita Khrushchev arrived in Washington, D.C., eager to exploit his propaganda coup. His scientists had sent a rocket to the Moon and successfully landed an object on the surface. Meanwhile, in the States . . . well, since 1957 U.S. rockets had exploded on their launch pads, or shortly after liftoff, with dispiriting regularity. These disasters became staples of American newspapers, magazines, newsreels, and television. *Boom! Crash!* American journalists dedicated to the truth, as well as to what they imagined their readers wanted, publicly put two and two together. Their verdict was that Russia could strike New York City with atomic ICBMs, and America probably couldn't do much to prevent it.

UFO sightings increased.

Meanwhile, in Los Angeles in 1960, architect John Lautner earned fame with his saucerlike Chemosphere House—a structure that looked to be the limit of

America's space technology, because the Soviets one-upped the USA again on April 12, 1961, when cosmonaut Yuri Gagarin completed an orbit of Earth. Mercury 7 astronaut Alan Shepard became America's first man in space about three weeks later, on May 5, though he did not orbit. In any case, the space age had arrived, bringing with it a new kind of futurism and, as a cultural aside, increased interest in UFOs. News media gave breathless coverage to these events, and out-and-out space advocacy pushed the editorial agendas of major magazines. *Collier's* published a three-part space exploration feature by rehabilitated German rocket scientist Wernher von Braun, with eye-popping painted illustrations by Chesley Bonestell and Fred Freeman. *Life* became a fervent booster of the American space program and the original Mercury 7 astronauts. Tech- and science-focused periodicals the likes of *Popular Science* and *Mechanix Illustrated* also got in on the space action.

Public interest in modern aviation and other technology, as well as a preoccupation with UFOs, found its way into postwar advertising, particularly after 1950. Wichita's O. A. Sutton Corporation enjoyed marketplace success with its handsomely streamlined Vornado "air circulators." This circa 1954 ad standee invokes the Space Age and flying saucers, making alien craft seem, for once, amusing and unthreatening.

Los Angeles became a hub of next-generation American technology. Already heavy with infrastructure created to build warplanes and ships during World War II, L.A. had been active in rocket dynamics and other space-related technology since before Sputnik in 1957. Now it readied itself to refine the technology and build the rockets and propulsion systems that would literally vault the United States into space, and a new world of weather and communications satellites, intelligence gathering, military dominance from space, Moon and Mars landings, and long-term bases on those bodies.

Manufacturing and hard science came together, to make flying saucers and other UFOs plausible.

Things That Are Not There

During the 1960s, the "flying saucer" term persisted, connoting (variously) alien craft, flying discs created by other nations, and, possibly, discs controlled by the United States. When a noticeable bump in UFO reports occurred in 1965, popular publishing reacted with UFO/flying saucer magazines and comic books. Because most of the newsstand material exemplified the pulp publishing tradition, the Air Force felt secure that little of it would be taken seriously by the public. On the other hand, the extraterrestrial theory refused to die, and the military establishment wondered if Americans continually hammered by the idea might grow dissatisfied with official USAF explanations.

Over at Blue Book (led since 1963 by USAF Maj. Hector Quintanilla), tension was commonplace. Quintanilla had been appointed to the job. He had little affinity for UFOs one way or another, but he did try to establish an "every report is valid until proved otherwise" culture at the project. Although funding continued to dry up, Quintanilla, like Major Friend before him, felt some obligation to make his time at Blue Book useful. During the 1963–69 period of Blue Book activity, project officials grew increasingly savvy about the veracity of discrete reports; particular interest was paid to myriad things that often were innocently misidentified as alien spacecraft. In a 1968 memorandum sent to the "UFO Officer" at Kirtland AFB, Albuquerque, Capt. C. H. Van Diver, USAF, Blue Book cited such explainable things as optical mirages (issues of refraction or "simulation effects"; clouds and birds; radioactively charged gases emitted from the sun; and other heavenly bodies, including meteors, stars, and planets).

Identifiable man-made objects figured in what Blue Book placed in a "Miscellaneous" sighting category: missiles, planes and contrails, chaff, flares, satellites, reflections, flares, and fireworks. Incorrect radar analysis accounted for some of the sightings. And as expected, Blue Book made allowance for hoax sightings.

Research by Dr. Robert J. Low of the University of Colorado suggested other issues relevant to the veracity of UFO sightings. (Responding to public complaints about foot-dragging by the Air Force in 1966, the Department of Defense awarded the University of Colorado a grant to study, in conjunction with the Air Force, UFOs and UFO reports.) At the top of Low's list was "human perception," a factor weighted with physical, intellectual, and emotional facets. Fallible brains could make for inaccurate reports. Eyes could be mistaken, as well; Low cited "[d]ust on the cornea" as one culprit in misidentification. Fingertip pressure or "electrical means" on or near the eyes can conjure things that are not really there.

Light sources produce afterimages, and the apparent size of those afterimages cannot be estimated accurately. Gamma movement (the illusion that searchlights and other large sources of illumination fade away rather than vanish after being turned off) fooled numerous witnesses.

Anyone, particularly laypersons, has difficulty with "celestial angles" while attempting to determine an object's size, location, speed, and movement. The problem is exacerbated when objects are near zero degrees or near ninety degrees.

Autokinesis (which Low referred to, vis-à-vis UFO sightings, as "Auto kinetics") is a phenomenon of visual perception by which the eyes, when focused on an object discerned without a frame of reference (as in, say, an empty sky), exhibit very small movements. Psychologist Muzafer Sherif utilized the phenomenon during doctoral experiments on conformity he conducted at Columbia University in 1936. He sat test subjects, three at a time, in a dark room and asked them to look at a pinpoint of light on a wall. What he wanted, he explained to each threesome, was an account of how and how much the light moved. Although Sherif ensured that the light always remained stationary, subjects (unfamiliar with autokinesis) invariably described movement, arriving at an estimate of the nature of the movement that satisfied all three subjects. When the test was repeated later, subjects that had been part of threesomes went into the dark room alone. Despite the presumed lack of peer pressure and concomitant social obligation, the solo subjects still described movement. Sherif's principal idea was that social cues are not here-and-gone phenomena that are easily discarded when one is in solitude. To the contrary, those cues, as guides to "proper" social behavior, are internalized. The perception of each member of every threesome had been supported by the perceptions of the two other people. That support—mutual agreement that the light had moved—exemplified the kind of social cue that encouraged each subject to see movement while in the room alone.

Although Sherif's research was grounded in social psychology, his work had natural applications to investigations of UFO sightings. The purely physical nature of autokinesis might explain some UFO sightings; although Dr. Low did not use his memo to elaborate on the significance of autokinesis ("Auto kinetics" is all he wrote), one might infer that Low was alluding to Sherif's work. In that context, the social "confirmation" of UFO sightings by others probably encouraged sightings in situations where autokinesis was likely to occur.

In a bit of condescension that is nevertheless difficult to argue against, Low dryly observed that people who read about UFOs are more likely than other people to report them, and that "[n]on-scientific personalities are more likely to report UFO's [sic]." The memo dismissed all "personal recollection" (that is, eyewitness reports) as "very unreliable."

Low and the university also noted that quantifiable testing ("controlled experiments" in Low's words) had yet to be developed after nearly twenty years of Blue Book/Air Force activity. Valid photographic evidence was in short supply, a fact that Low implicitly attributed to lack of scientific method on the part of Blue Book researchers, rather than to an impossibility of such images.

Available investigative hardware, and people not adequately trained to operate it and interpret results, struck Low as another sticking point. Perhaps astronomers, weather observers, FAA personnel, and radar operators were hobbled by inadequate "instrumentation" and deficient instruction.

In a note about press coverage, Low pondered "an inter-connection or correlation" between that coverage and sightings. Further, he wondered "[t]o what extent do the reports of UFO's [sic] reflect the culture of the times."

Finally, in a vague and cryptic reference, Low asked about "Possible conspiracy. (Yes or no. If not, how do you convince the public?)" One assumption is that Low referred to government/military conspiracies to keep the truth about UFOs under wraps—but the government/military brought him into the investigation. If those institutions maintained a conspiracy, why would they risk the probing of Low and other outsiders?

Perhaps Low alluded to a conspiracy imagined by the UFO community, or one *maintained* by UFOlogists.

With Low's comments out of the way, Capt. Van Diver closed his four-page memo to Kirtland AFB by writing, "[W]e were instructed [by Blue Book superiors] to keep 'open minds' at all times during our investigations. Since we are now in a period in which space travel lies just ahead, it is within the realm of possibility that others (extra-terrestrial in nature) may also have the same capability."

That statement suggests a fair turn of mind, but if Blue Book had a fatal flaw, it is this: the committee was staffed mainly by skeptics.

The Condon Report

In 1966, as Washington readied to kick Blue Book to the curb, the Air Force invited University of Colorado physicist Edward Condon to investigate UFOs by enlisting other qualified people for the Colorado Project, which came to be known as the Condon Committee. What the government wished the committee to do (to the surprise of few close observers) was erase Blue Book's many ambiguities and replace them with a group more in synch with USAF propaganda. In this regard, Edward Condon's status as a UFO skeptic was hugely important. Privately, he felt the committee was pointless and without value. He used his position within the committee to repeatedly override the group's conclusions, and urged professional punishment for trained scientists and researchers who engaged in UFO study.

One committee member, University of Colorado psychology professor David Saunders, pushed for an objective report, and encouraged NICAP to send over its most credible accounts, many of them from astronomers, engineers, pilots, and military personnel.

Condon chose U of Colorado graduate school assistant dean Robert Low to be project coordinator. Despite Low's open mind (and his interest in the project's potential for his career), the final Condon Committee report of 1968, *Scientific Study of Unidentified Flying Objects*, declared that all UFO sightings are explainable in conventional terms. Of special significance is the report's conclusion that further investigation of UFOs could provide nothing of scientific merit. Naturally enough, this conclusion aggravated serious UFOlogists (including Dr. James E. McDonald; see chapter one), and encouraged conspiracy theorists' belief in government deception.

The report's conclusion, that Blue Book be closed, gave the Air Force the imprimatur it had longed for. Subsequent UFO investigation could be handed to a new, more malleable body.

It is important to note that some UFOlogists feel that Condon and Low were dupes, led by the government to declare the pointlessness of UFO study—*because the government knew UFO were real, and wished to deal with them secretly*. In any case, the Condon Committee was the last Washington-funded UFO-study group of any significance.

On December 17, 1969, the Secretary of the Air Force announced that Project Blue Book had been shuttered. CIA personnel took charge of Blue Book files, and closed the office on January 30, 1970—virtually simultaneous with the CIA's dissolution of NICAP.

The CIA handed Blue Book material to Edward Condon in 1973. The professor's 1968 report had prepared Blue Book's grave. Five years after that, Condon declared the UFO phenomenon a fraud or, in more nuanced cases, something based in hallucination.

NICAP and Keyhoe

Inventor and antigravity researcher Thomas Townsend Brown established the National Investigations Committee on Aerial Phenomena in Washington, D.C., at the end of 1956. As NICAP struggled to get its financial footing, Donald Keyhoe, a retired U.S. Marines aviator with a strong inclination to accept the reality of UFOs, accepted a 1957 offer to lead the group.

Gordon Lore, a journalist who worked as NICAP's assistant director, dedicated himself to well-documented, scientific investigation of UFO accounts. Lore's main responsibility was the coordination of some twenty-five investigating subcommittees across the United States, and in Canada, England, Australia, and elsewhere. NICAP mandated that the head of each subcommittee be a qualified scientist, and that subordinate members have UFO-investigatory experience. During the course of a typical investigation, witnesses were interviewed, and then asked to fill out a NICAP sighting report form standardized with a checklist and space for the witnesses' narrative accounts. Interviewers remained alert for witness descriptions of physical evidence, such as holes in the ground, burned areas, or other unusual marks. When accessible, physically altered areas were visited by investigators who, when possible, took soil and other samples. In a similar vein, unusual metallic or other objects were gathered for later study. Any objects or other evidence that had to be left in place were investigated later by scientists on the NICAP board of governors (James E. McDonald was one), or by those in a carefully assembled group of on-call alternates.

According to Gordon Lore, Keyhoe's "opinion right off the bat was that there was real possibility that Earth was being scrutinized by alien beings from space, and that it was time for the scientific community to start sitting up and taking notice." The

Flying Saucers Are Real (1950) and *Flying Saucers from Outer Space* (1953), popular books by professional writer and retired Marine Air Corps Maj. Donald Keyhoe, elevated his status as a credible UFO investigator. Keyhoe assumed leadership of the National Investigations Committee on Aerial Phenomena (NICAP) in 1957, bringing focus and structure to the activities of that nongovernment group. *Getty Images*

considerable numbers of sightings near military installations and nuclear power plants suggested to Keyhoe (who used the term "UFO" in conversation, and never "flying saucer") that the visitors had special interest in our arms and other technology. Keyhoe gave considerable importance to periodic rashes of UFO sightings, as happened in 1947, 1952, 1965, and 1973.

Keyhoe's ET orientation hardly made him a lone voice; Lore recalled an (unnamed) Lockheed vice president who believed, as Keyhoe did, that extraterrestrials were engaged in observation of Earth.

Go Down Together

NICAP staff naturally stayed abreast of Blue Book activity, and often collaborated with the USAF group via free exchanges of files. As a retired military man, the calm and methodical Keyhoe understood the value of shared intelligence, particularly when tepid Air Force support of Blue Book could mean an eventual end to NICAP access to Blue Book files. Keyhoe realized that his friends at Blue Book were working under increasingly less friendly conditions. But the nature of his NICAP group—a civilian organization, after all—suggested to Keyhoe more protective camouflage than NICAP actually had. Keyhoe made no secret of his disappointment in Air Force handling of UFO accounts. Further, because Keyhoe visited NICAP only once or twice a month, it was left to Gordon Lore and other day-to-day staffers to suspect that NICAP, too, may be on thin ice. Lore was particularly aware that the Air Force had labeled Keyhoe as a "gadfly"—a useful tag employed by those with real power. But neither Keyhoe nor NICAP held power.

After about 1966, a NICAP board member and, possibly, a rank-and-file investigator with CIA connections may have functioned as moles. On days when Keyhoe was absent, some members of the board sequestered themselves to examine NICAP case files. Over at Blue Book, the revolving door of mostly antipathetic directors did not suggest a bright future for that project. It was no stretch, then, for Lore and others at NICAP to imagine that their own organization was being observed by unfriendly eyes. NICAP's financials had stabilized around 1965, but now they were a mess. Memberships and contributions had dried up after the Condon Report. Because some level of financial reorganization was required, NICAP had made itself vulnerable. The real issue, though, is that the USAF simply got fed up with Keyhoe's insistence on pushing investigations of sightings for which the military and other authorities would have no plausible explanations. NICAP activity cast doubt on Air Force competence and credibility. As the Air Force saw it, NICAP had a bad attitude. Blue Book was going to go, and NICAP would go right along with it.

Despite having no formal warning of what was to come, NICAP staffers could read the bathroom walls. The 1968 Condon Committee report dismissed UFO investigation as useless. Blue Book was teetering. Thus motivated, three or four NICAP staff members devoted parts of NICAP's last weeks and months to copying as many particularly credible reports as possible, follow-up paperwork included. Those staffers removed the copies to secure locations.

Mid-December 1969 brought official USAF termination of Blue Book. Then it was NICAP's turn. No official rationale for the 1970 takeover of NICAP and immediate dismissal of staff was offered to anybody in the office. "One day we were operating as normal," Gordon Lore said. "The next day, the doors and desks were locked and employees were closely guarded while collecting their personal belongings."

Keyhoe, who lived about a hundred miles away in Luray, Virginia, was notified at his home. No member of the reorganized, "approved" NICAP board had the nerve needed to inform Keyhoe to his face, or even by phone. The message came to the major via telegram.

Of course, NICAP's civilian status prevented the Air Force/CIA from closing NICAP completely; with the CIA working from behind the scenes, the organization stumbled on for another ten years, shuffling files and publishing an occasional newsletter before departing the scene in 1980. NICAP's files are now held by the Center for UFO Studies (CUFOS). Another UFO group, the Fund for UFO Research (FUFOR), maintains an historical Web site, nicap.org.

Eyes Only: Selected UFO Sightings of the 1950s and 1960s

The plentitude of sightings dated 1952 and 1965 (below) reflect the dramatic increase in UFO reports during those years.

February 19, 1951: Crew and passengers aboard an East African Airways Model 18 Lodestar airliner observe an enormous, cigar-shaped object hover over Mount Kilimanjaro. The object—with dull silver skin periodically interrupted by dark bands—remains in sight for nearly twenty minutes, performing very rapid lateral moves and ascents when not hovering. One of the passengers attaches a telescopic lens to his movie camera and shoots thirty feet of color film. Pilot Jack Bicknell estimates the object's length as "over two hundred feet." **Note:** The USAF reportedly examined the movie footage, pronounced it an image of refracted light, and returned the film to the owner.

Spring 1951: A U.S. Army unit positioned near Chorwon, Korea (the so-called Iron Triangle), makes a nighttime sighting of what one soldier describes as a "jack-o-lantern." The thing floats serenely among artillery bursts before changing course to come at the soldiers. When its orange glow becomes a "blue-green brilliant light," the soldiers open fire with armor-piercing bullets, which strike the object with the sound of slugs against metal. A pulsing, tingling ray sweeps over the soldiers and causes them to dive into their bunker. **Note:** Various men in the group shortly exhibited dysentery-like symptoms, plus weight loss, disorientation, and unusually high counts of white blood cells. The account of the incident comes from former PFC Francis Wall, during a much later interview with researcher John Timmerman, representing the J. Allen Hynek Center for UFO Studies (CUFOS).

August–November 1951: Numerous witnesses in and near Lubbock, Texas, report precise formations of mysterious flying lights. (See the account earlier in this chapter.)

January 22, 1952: A pair of F-94 Starfire interceptors scrambled to meet fast-moving (fifteen hundred to twenty-four hundred mph) radar targets above Nenana, Alaska, are unable to keep up with the objects' speed and maneuvers. One F-94 pulls to within two hundred yards and has to pull up to avoid a collision.

February 2, 1952: Crew aboard the USS *Philippine Sea* sailing east of South Korea witness three objects trailing flaming exhaust perform complex maneuvers at great speed. Radar suggests 600 to 1,500 mph at about fifty thousand feet.

March 4, 1952: A C-54 Skymaster flying out of Ashiya AFB, Japan, establishes visual contact with an orange oval, a hundred feet long and fifty feet thick, flying at ten thousand feet. Visual contact is maintained for 90–120 seconds.

March 14, 1952: In flight above Hawaii, Navy Secretary Dan Kimball and others are twice circled by a pair of flying discs streaking at between 1,500 and 2,000 mph. The event is also witnessed by Adm. Arthur Radford, in a second plane.

May 12, 1952: A blue-green UFO flying at 30,000–40,000 feet forty miles west of Roswell, New Mexico, follows a precise triangular course three times before departing.

May 22, 1952: Near Falls Church, Virginia, a CIA official, a retired general, and others observe a red light in level flight at about five thousand feet that abruptly climbs almost straight vertical before leveling off and going into a vertical dive. The object levels off again and rapidly disappears.

May 28, 1952: In three discrete nighttime incidents, B-29 crews flying near Albuquerque, Tulsa, and Enid, California, observe green spheres at between 15,000 and 25,000 feet.

Summer 1952: An F-86 Sabre jet based at Wright-Patterson AFB, Dayton, dives and fires on a rapidly moving disc-shaped UFO from about five hundred yards. Apparently undamaged, the disc quickly accelerates and climbs out of sight. Wright-Patterson intelligence is ordered not to send a report to Project Blue Book, but an intelligence officer later shows the file to Blue Book chief Capt. Edward Ruppelt. **Note:** Ruppelt's is the best account of this incident. The file was later burned by the officer that revealed it to Ruppelt.

July 2, 1952: While driving near Tremonton, Utah, Navy photographer Delbert Newhouse and wife see twelve to fourteen shiny silver discs. Newhouse films the objects with his 16mm movie camera; after Navy and Air Force analysis, the footage is returned to Newhouse, without the frames showing the discs.

July 19, 1952: A Peruvian customs inspector snaps a photograph of a cigar-shaped object trailing heavy exhaust as it flies over Puerto Maldonado. The inspector, Domingo Troncoso, estimates the craft's length at more than one hundred feet. **Note:** Because the customs office sat along the border of Peru and Bolivia, some accounts of this incident claim that Troncoso photographed the object over Bolivia.

September 12, 1952: Schoolboys out at dusk near Flatwoods, West Virginia, run to investigate a UFO and discover a hissing, shiny-eyed creature enveloped in a noxious gas or mist. **Note:** For more on this, one of the most celebrated of all UFO cases, see chapter ten.

December 4, 1952: In the night sky above Laredo, Texas, USAF pilot Lt. Robert Arnold, flying a T-28 trainer, experiences numerous near misses with a glowing, blue-white object traveling at very high speed. The object approaches Arnold's plane from a variety of directions and attitudes: in rapid ascent beneath him; on an apparent head-on collision course; and on level course, keeping pace with the T-28 at six thousand feet.

November 23, 1953: An F-89 Scorpion scrambled from Truax Field, near Madison, Wisconsin, to intercept an "unidentified target" over Lake Superior disappears from radar at thirty thousand feet, after its on-screen blip merges with the blip of the UFO. The jet fails to return to base; neither debris nor the fliers, pilot Lt. Felix Moncla and radar operator Lt. Robert Wilson, are ever found. The USAF describes the "other" blip as a Canadian plane, until Canada explains that no Canadian aircraft had been over the lake during the pursuit. Then the Air Force suggested that Moncla suffered an attack of vertigo and crashed, directing his aircraft to avoid homes. The final USAF explanation is changed to say that the F-89 exploded in midair—leaving no wreckage. **Note:** Some latter-day accounts claim that the F-89 was scrambled from Kinross AFB in Michigan; in reality, Kinross tracked the object first and then notified Truax.

June 1954: Witnesses afoot past midnight at East Malvern and Carnegie, Australia, observe a flying object about the size of a rail car, and shaped like "a cross between an egg and a plate," that spits yellow fire and reveals "portholes." Visible behind the portholes are "vague shapes that looked like human busts."

November 1, 1954: As a woman named Rosa Lotti walks into Cennina, Italy, she encounters two diminutive, laughing humanoids that step from behind a doubled-coned craft (two cones joined at their bases). The little "men" approach her, snatching a carnation Lotti is carrying, and relieving her of one of her stockings.

August 21–22, 1955: Eleven people trapped in a farmhouse located between Kelly and Hopkinsville, Kentucky, spend a harrowing night besieged by two waves of mischievous, floating aliens. The men inside are armed with long guns, and blow the hell out of the house's walls and windows while firing for hours at the persistent little visitors.

October 4, 1955: While aboard a train in the Caucasus region of the USSR, Georgia Senator and Armed Services Committee chairman Richard Russell observes a disc-shaped craft, and then another, take off from a spot near the railroad tracks. Russell's interpreter also sees both craft. The "TOP SECRET" document pertaining to the sighting is dated October 14.

September 8, 1958: Officers and airmen at SAC command, Offutt AFB, Omaha, observe a red-orange "missile-shaped" UFO that tilts to forty-five degrees from

HOPKINSVILLE, KY
1955
CHASE '62

During the long night of August 21–22, 1955, people inside a house near rural Hopkinsville, Kentucky, marshaled a rifle and shotgun to battle aggressive aliens that scampered across the roof, flew between trees, and repeatedly popped up in windows. This 1962 illustration by Chase Winstead is based on eyewitness accounts.

Courtesy of Chase Winstead

horizontal while accompanied by "a swarm of black specks cavorting every which way"; after about a minute, the specks disappear. The primary object remains visible for from five to ten minutes, during which time the object slowly rotates back to horizontal and eases out of sight.

October 3, 1958: Numerous crew members aboard a passenger train on its way to Indianapolis observe four lighted discs flying in a V formation in the pre-dawn sky above Monon, Indiana. The objects traverse the train's entire half-mile length, moving from one side of the tracks to the other and then back again, so that crew in various sections of the train get good looks. At speed (perhaps seventy miles per hour) the objects glow bright white; as their speed decreases, the color changes to yellow and finally "dirty orange." The encounter lasts seventy minutes. **Note**: The conductor, Ed Robinson, estimated the discs as being about forty feet in diameter. (The other witnesses: engineer, fireman, head brakeman, and flagman.) A witness drawing done shortly after the sighting dates the incident at October 8 rather than October 3.

February 24, 1959: A DC-6 flying at eighty-five hundred feet in the night sky not far from Pittsburgh is approached and then paced by a trio of bright lights. The first inclination of the captain, Peter Killian, is that he's looking at Orion, but Orion is visible *above* the lights. The forty-five-minute encounter is corroborated by a pair of trailing airliners and tower personnel at Pittsburgh.

June 26 and 27, 1959: William Gill, an Anglican missionary in Papua, New Guinea, witnesses saucer-shaped craft and humanoid occupants on two successive nights. Missionary support staff and numerous locals gesture toward the craft and receive visual acknowledgment.

April 18, 1961: Three humanoids inside a flying disc hovering inches above the ground at an Eagle River, Wisconsin, chicken farm ask the farmer for water, and then reward him with "pancakes" cooking on a grill. The men are about five feet tall, attired in dark blue knit uniforms (some latter-day accounts say black) with turtlenecks and knit caps. After about five minutes, the ovoid craft lifts off at a forty-five-degree angle, bows nearby evergreens in its wake, and then disappears. **Note**: The Eagle River case is perennially popular and controversial, partly because the "pancake" claim of the farmer, Joe Simonton, seems risible. But Simonton meant *pancake-like*. (He said they tasted like "cardboard.") Alleged UFOlogist and/or Air Force analysis of the pancakes is difficult to verify, though accounts describe corn, buckwheat, soy, and other earthly ingredients. Simonton ended up rather worn out by the aftermath of his encounter, and finally said that "if it happened again, I don't think I'd tell anybody about it."

September 19, 1961: A New Hampshire couple, Betty and Barney Hill, are stopped and abducted by the operators of a UFO near Lancaster. A star map later drawn by Betty is remarkably accurate, and suggests a definite place of origin for the craft. **Note**: The most famous of all UFO abduction cases, the Hills' adventure is told in chapter thirteen.

April 24, 1964: In a desolate section of New Mexico desert, Socorro patrolman Lonnie Zamora investigates an overturned automobile that turns out to be an ovoid, three-legged craft that abruptly spits blue flame and flies away. **Note**: The integrity of Sgt. Zamora's record, and the trained eye that revealed many details to him, has caused this sighting to become both well known and, generally, highly regarded. For more, see chapter ten.

June 29, 1964: A Georgia businessman encounters a spinning, brightly illuminated UFO shaped "like a top" during a night drive near Lavonia. The amber-colored object keeps pace ahead of his car for at least a mile. Beauford E. Parham describes the object as large enough to hold a man, with the top section spinning clockwise and the bottom section spinning counterclockwise. The encounter ends when the top lifts and flies over the roof of Parham's car, leaving a stench like "embalming fluid." **Note**: A lively account, though one might struggle to explain why Parham's first instinct was to continue driving at sixty-five miles per hour, rather than jam on the brakes.

January 11, 1965: Six members of the Army Signal Corps observe twelve to fifteen rapidly flying white ovals, pursued by jets from Andrews AFB, Camp Springs, Maryland.

January 23, 1965: A lightbulb-shaped object, seventy-five to eighty feet tall and ten to twenty-five feet wide, causes cars to stall at the junction of U.S. Highway 60 and State Route 614, at Lightfoot, Virginia, north of Williamsburg.

January 28–February 1, 1965: UFOs are sighted across Alaska, at Anchorage, Cape Lisburne, Cape Newenham, Cape Romanzoff, Fairbanks, Fort Yukon, Indian Mountain, Northeast Cape, and Unalakleet.

February 1, 1965: Thirty to forty people observe a phosphorescent, domed UFO above Tallahassee, Florida, moving across the evening sky at one hundred to two hundred miles per hour. The same object is noted by an Eastern Airlines flight over Daytona Beach.

March 12, 1965: While camping in the Florida Everglades, a man named James Flynn gets a long-distance look at a large cone-shaped object some twenty-five feet high and seventy-five feet wide. Accompanied by his four dogs, Flynn approaches on his amphibious swamp buggy, watching as the craft lifts from the ground, hovers, and then settles back again. After observing from concealment for more than half an hour, Flynn brings his buggy closer, only to be halted by a tremendous blast of wind. When the cone lifts off again, Flynn leaves the buggy and steps into the open. Looking up at the thing at a ground distance of about seventy-five feet, Flynn is suddenly knocked flat—and unconscious—by a beam of light, "like a welder's torch." Flynn regains consciousness the next morning (his adventure had begun around 1:00 a.m. the previous night), and is blind. **Note**: Flynn saw an ophthalmologist on March 17; his left eye showed no obvious damage but the doctor could not even locate the retina of the right. Flynn's sight gradually returned, but imperfectly, and he waited for over a week for his reflexes to return to normal. When Flynn and some friends visited the site on March 26, they discovered an area seventy feet in diameter that had no vegetation, no twigs, nothing. Cypress trees that ringed the perimeter showed scorch marks. Although the Air Force encouraged Flynn to mark out the spot, Flynn never was told that his story had been investigated.

April 23, 1965: A Rivesville, West Virginia, a woman cleaning up after breakfast watches a flying disc land near her house and disgorge a small humanoid with pointed ears. The creature, who is apparently tethered to the craft, removes something from the ground and then returns to the disc. The object spins counterclockwise and ascends out of sight.

July 1, 1965: A French farmer named Maurice Masse notices two children in his field at Valensole. When he moves closer, he sees that the figures are humanoid but not human. Less than four feet tall, they have oversized bald heads and heart-shaped faces with large, oblique eyes and small mouths. Both creatures wear gray-green coveralls. When one of them points a tube in Masse's direction, he is frozen in place. Masse remains conscious, and watches as the creatures pick vegetation and then enter an egg-shaped craft that disappears into the sky. The effects of the immobilizer wear off in about fifteen minutes.

July 28, 1965: A USAF Reserve major based at Carswell AFB, Fort Worth, observes a silent, manta-shaped object, about forty feet long and showing flashing white lights, fly at about a thousand feet directly through the Carswell control zone. Personnel at the base's control tower also see the object. **Note**: Radar Approach Control (RAPCON) investigated, without making an identification. The RAPCON report said, "This sighting was a positive observation, under ideal circumstances, of a definite object of an unconventional nature, possibly of foreign origin, which could be a threat to national security."

August 3, 1965: In the early afternoon, an Orange County, California, highway inspector named Rex Heflin quickly snaps three black-and-white Polaroids of a flying disc topped with a squared-off dome. The craft apparently interferes with his truck's radio, as Heflin is unable to contact his garage as long as the disc is in sight. **Note**: Increasingly sophisticated photo analysis performed on the Heflin images as late as 1993 suggests that they are genuine. Although MUFON and

NICAP supported Heflin, the Air Force claimed that JPL analysis revealed fakery. Heflin absorbed unpleasant criticism for many years.

September 3, 1965: Two a.m. While walking along a rural highway three miles outside of Exeter, New Hampshire, an eighteen-year-old Navy recruit named Norman Muscarello is startled by movement above him: an enormous object showing blazing red lights. Muscarello tries to hide. When the object departs, Muscarello contacts the police, who have already taken a UFO call from a frightened woman two miles outside town, who says a red flying object chased her car along Highway 101 for ten miles. Exeter police officer Eugene Bertrand accompanies Muscarello back to the scene, where both watch an enormous illuminated object slowly rise from behind a stand of trees. The object makes no sound. As Bertrand and Muscarello retreat to the police cruiser, another Exeter officer, David Hunt, arrives on the scene. He, too, witnesses the object. Not long after, the police in nearby Hampton take a pay-phone call from an agitated male who claims he's been chased by a flying saucer. The call is cut off before the man can say more. **Note:**

The so-called Incident at Exeter (New Hampshire), of September 3, 1965, is among the most famous of all UFO close encounters, involving an eighteen-year-old local man and a pair of Exeter police officers. "Official" explanations struck many as laughably inadequate.   *Alamy*

Officer Bertrand later described the Muscarello object as "huge, shapeless," with five bright red lights that pulsed sequentially from left to right. The thing was, Bertrand said, "so bright you couldn't look at it." The sky above Exeter was clear that night, with unremarkable weather. Subsequent investigation by Blue Book was lackluster, and suggested that the witnesses had seen Air Force B-47s. The first gambit of the Air Force and the Pentagon was to enlist a parade of "expert witnesses" brought on to discredit Bertrand and Muscarello. The Pentagon/Air Force investigation suggested "weather inversion." But at the end of January 1966, after two letters sent by officers Bertrand and Hunt, the Air Force felt compelled to alter its position in a letter sent to the officers from the Office of the Secretary of the Air Force, conceding that "we have been unable to identify the object that you observed. . . ." This famed encounter is chronicled in the best-selling 1966 book by John G. Fuller, *Incident at Exeter.*

October 1965: The pilot of a small plane, and a passenger, observe three "bright objects" off the starboard wing, flying about a thousand feet above Lake Norman, North Carolina, near the McGuire Nuclear Station.

October 23, 1965: A radio announcer named James Townsend, driving west on State Highway 27 near Long Prairie, Minnesota, finds his way blocked by a silver, missile-shaped craft. After Townsend's car dies and coasts to a stop, three faceless humanoids emerge from the craft. A few minutes later, the "brownish-black" creatures return to the ship, and lift off.

March 14–20, 1966: Law enforcement officers in Washtenaw County, Michigan, investigate a seemingly unending rush of reports describing the aerial maneuvers of flying discs. They are seen over Lake Erie, over highways, and above a swamp. Most fly singly but others move in formation. Some are yellow; others are red and blue-green, or all three. Besides peace officers, some one hundred people witness the discs. **Note:** This is the case that Blue Book consultant J. Allen Hynek labeled "swamp gas," a description he gave hastily and lived to regret.

March 16, 1967: Illuminated UFOs cause worry and mechanical trouble at a missile-launch facility at Malmstrom AFB, Montana.

March 28, 1967: A motorist named David Morris sees an orange, cone-shaped UFO and then accidentally strikes and kills an extraterrestrial near Munroe Fall, Ohio. Morris stops the car and looks through his back window at three or four tiny aliens clustered around the body. Suddenly frightened, Morris drives away. **Note:** A pair of investigators from NICAP's Pittsburgh office carefully studied Morris's account, finding nothing to disprove it. The ET's death by automobile recalls a 1955 science fiction short story by Paul W. Fairman, "The Cosmic Frame," and the 1957 movie it inspired, *Invasion of the Saucer-Men.*

May 20, 1967: A Winnipeg man named Stephen Michalak at Falcon Lake, Manitoba, is left with a waffle pattern burned into his chest by the takeoff exhaust of an illuminated, domed saucer that sets his clothing on fire.

March 1968: The fiery crash of a UFO at Sverlovsky, Russia, leaves salvageable wreckage and at least one alien corpse. **Note:** This case is colorful but difficult to verify, because it came out of Cold War Russia, and was supposedly investigated by the KGB. A 1998 cable-television special purporting to chronicle the story includes film footage of a supposed alien autopsy.

January 9, 1969: Georgia peanut farmer Jimmy Carter (later Georgia's governor and President of the United States) and about ten other people witness a blue-red ball in the evening sky above Leary, Georgia. The sphere appears to move toward the group and then back away, maintaining distances of three hundred to a thousand yards. **Note:** Carter remained adamant that the object appeared "luminous, not solid." He has also remarked he has no reason to believe the object had on-board operators. Skeptics have suggested that Carter and the others were looking at Venus—but Venus was in the southwestern sky; Carter (a Navy man trained in the use of sextants and well familiar with the shifting locations of planets and stars) said the object floated in the western sky. Carter recounts his experience whenever asked, and has described it as "the darndest thing I have ever seen."

August 7, 1969: A teenage boy and girl working at a summer camp at Buff Ledge, Vermont, see a saucer-shaped UFO and are taken inside against their will. **Note:** During sessions of hypnosis around 1980, both people recalled medical examinations and a trip to a "mother ship."

October 24, 1969: A Chilean destroyer some 350 miles off the coast is buzzed by five UFOs sent forth from a dimpled "mother ship" at least 110 feet long. The vessel's power goes down and does not return until the largest UFO moves well beyond the bridge. **Note:** Claims of a subsequent Chilean cover-up are not unreasonable. Then again, the cover-up scenario conveniently explains why the name of the ship must remain a mystery.

Blue Book and Bubble Gum

And now, a brief detour into popular culture.

Although the Air Force and other Washington entities dedicated themselves to marginalizing Project Blue Book and dissipating its influence, Blue Book developed and sustained a hardy cultural presence. Generous newspaper and magazine coverage of project activity, plus occasional television documentaries, intrigued the public and cemented the connection between Blue Book and "flying saucers." Out of such stuff came a flood of accessible and fanciful interpretations of UFOs.

Aliens and flying saucers came to dramatic radio of the 1950s via *X Minus One*, *Dimension X*, *Beyond This World*, the BBC's *Journey into Space*, and numerous other anthology shows. Later, talk radio hosted by the likes of Long John Nebel and Art Bell turned UFOlogy into hyper burlesque. In a special moment, radio handled the UFO phenomenon with taste and intelligence in April 1950, with *The Case for the Flying Saucer*, a thirty-minute CBS radio documentary produced and hosted by Edward R. Murrow.

UFOs have been expressed in pop songs since the 1950s. A few highlights: "Flyin' Saucers Rock 'n' Roll" (performed by Billy Lee Riley); "Knocked-Out Joint on Mars" (Buck Trail); "(You'd Better Pray to the Lord) When You See Those Flying Saucers" (the Buchanan Brothers); "Have You Seen the Saucers" (Jefferson Airplane); "UFOs, Big Rigs and BBQ" (Mojo Nixon); "Rocket Ship" (Kathy McCarty); "Rosetta Stoned" (Tool). A good deal of this novelty material is collected on CD compilations; likewise vintage instrumental "space music" by composer-performers Harry Revel, Les Baxter, Ferrante and Teicher, and Esquivel.

Even Ella Fitzgerald, a sublime interpreter of the Great American Songbook, weighed in with "Two Little Men in a Flying Saucer." The kicker of that one is that the ETs catch a game at Ebbets Field, gape at women's hats, listen to a bloviating politician, and then decide we're all nuts.

Amusement parks regarded flying saucer rides as must-haves for many years. The most notable is Disneyland's Flying Saucers, which had a place in the park's Tomorrowland section during 1961–66. The attraction operated like an air hockey table, with sixteen single-rider saucers floating on a narrow cushion of forced air. (Ceaseless maintenance on the ride's plenum chamber, air valves, and retracting-disc floor spelled the attraction's doom.)

"Cook It!"

UFOs, aliens, and the movies were made for each other. *Keep Watching the Skies!*, historian Bill Warren's study of science-fiction movies from the 1950s *only*, runs a robust 1,004 oversized pages. So prolific has the genre become that UFO movies threaten to outpace UFOs themselves. Whether high-profile, B-grade, or pure underground, the films are accessible via streaming or DVD. (The same goes for television shows, from *The Twilight Zone* and *The Outer Limits*, to *Falling Skies* and *Colony*.)

One "saucer" movie that has endured for sixty-five years captured the "UFO moment" as that moment existed just a few years after Kenneth Arnold and Roswell. Howard Hawks's Winchester Films produced *The Thing from Another World* for 1951 release by RKO. This is a marvelous movie by any standard, with smart, crackling dialogue; intelligent male and female protagonists; and (mostly) cool-headed professional men that marshal themselves to battle a dangerous interloper. All of those are trademarks of Hawks (who eschewed on-screen credit in order to help his editor, Christian Nyby, get into the Directors Guild). *The Thing* is set inside an isolated Arctic base staffed by a few scientists and soldiers. The place is cold and claustrophobic, and thus hobbling to the humans, who can't just depart (the weather is punishingly frigid) or easily hide (the maze of buildings is small). The group quickly learns that the humanoid extraterrestrial they have released from an icy prison (after a long-ago saucer crash) isn't just ill-tempered and literally bloodthirsty, but more akin to plant life than animal. Leave it to the Hawksian heroine (Margaret Sheridan) to suggest how to deal with the monster: cook it.

That's witty, but *The Thing* has real historical importance, inviting Cold War audiences to "read" the alien as the Communist menace. Even more significant is

An early UFO movie, and arguably the best, Howard Hawks's *The Thing from Another World* (1951), establishes an uncomfortable equivalency between a murderous extraterrestrial visitor and its saucer-shaped spacecraft. In the photo above, men posted to an isolated Arctic base discover an aerodynamic fin protruding from the ice, and then startle themselves (below) by forming a perfect circle after assembling above the shadowed object beneath their feet.   *Photos courtesy of Ronald V. Borst/Hollywood Movie Posters*

that *The Thing* has a central image, a synecdoche that exploited current events and startled audiences: the alien's flying saucer. A bit of fin sticking from the Arctic ice is the first evidence. When a dozen or so men array themselves around the dimly perceived perimeter of the craft and link hands, we can see that the group stands in a perfect circle. "We've got one!" somebody shouts. "We've finally got one! A flying saucer!" UFO enthusiasts get chills because the Thing's saucer perfectly encapsulates the Kenneth Arnold era, and the chilly wonder of Cold War science and discovery.

UFO/film historian Bruce Rux mounts a thin argument about *The Thing from Another World* in his 1997 book *Hollywood vs. the Aliens*, claiming that because industrialist Howard Hughes—a man, Rux says, with ties to the CIA—owned RKO, *The Thing* is purposeful disinformation, an attempt to make the whole UFO phenomenon seem sufficiently ridiculous so that nobody who sees the movie will ever take UFOs seriously. Rux (who goes on in this possibly facetious vein while analyzing fifty years of UFO movies) fails to reckon with the cinematic power of *The Thing*. The film's signature line of dialogue, "Keep watching the skies!"—uttered by a broadcast journalist who has witnessed the whole adventure—inspires a *frisson* laced with awe. Nobody laughs at that cautionary declaration.

Years later, a benevolent alien temperament informed two of Steven Spielberg's most popular films, *Close Encounters of the Third Kind* (1977) and *E.T.* (1982). These beautifully crafted movies are rightfully popular, but the nasty little cabbageheads of *Invasion of the Saucer-Men* (1956, with classic bug-eyed-monster design by Jackie and Paul Blaisdell) are far more typical of Hollywood's notion of alien visitors.

Wrathful aliens in the Hawks mold have burst forth more recently in *The Puppet Masters* (1994), *Independence Day* (1996, and 2016 sequel), *Mars Attacks!* (1996), *Starship Troopers* (1997), the *Men in Black* series, *War of the Worlds* (2005), *Aliens vs. Predator: Requiem* (2007), *The Invasion* (2007, one of numerous remakes of the 1956 gem *Invasion of the Body Snatchers*), *Cloverfield* (2008), *Battle: Los Angeles* (2010), *Skyline* (2010), the *Transformers* series, *Cowboys & Aliens* (2011), and *The 5th Wave* (2016).

Despite breathless poster art and other promotional material calculated to exploit people's apprehension about UFOs, the 1956 quasi-documentary *Unidentified Flying Objects* delivered almost nothing in the way of saucer footage or thrills.
Photo courtesy of Ronald V. Borst/Hollywood Movie Posters

Dullumentary

By 1956, the UFO phenomenon was nine years old. Hollywood thrillers had been exploiting saucer-mania since 1950, and the time seemed right for a documentary treatment of the subject: *Unidentified Flying Objects* (1956), a ninety-one-minute slog that was (and remains) a test of one's patience rather than the vivid account saucer enthusiasts wanted. Voice-over narration sets a portentous tone, but nearly all of the film is comprised of stock footage of everyday military activity: jets taking off and landing; ground crews filling bomb bays with ordnance; radar techs staring at their screens. Grainy and unsatisfying footage of two UFO sightings, one in Utah and the other in Montana, shows up disappointingly late in the film. Saucer fans are far better served by another 1956 release, Fred F. Sears's fictional *Earth vs. the Flying Saucers*. That dynamic thriller, very loosely based on the Donald Keyhoe book *Flying Saucers from Outer Space*, has all the documentary-like verisimilitude that the real documentary lacks.

From Commercial to Lowbrow

UFO and extraterrestrial art made cultural heroes of illustrators such as Frank R. Paul (the first great SF illustrator), Edd Cartier (described in chapter two), Hannes Bok, Alex Schomburg (Deco airbrush), Chesley Bonestell (documentary futurism and planetscapes), Frank Kelly Freas (a master of luminous color), Ed Emshwiller, Jack Gaughan, Richard Powers (whose oddly organic images defined Ballantine paperback SF), Syd Mead (a sleek Futurist with keen interest in industrial design), Vincent DiFate, John Berkey (knife-edge tech), H. R. Giger (creator of the *Alien* universe); Ralph McQuarrie, the Brothers Hildebrandt, Debbie Hughes, Michael Whelan, and many others. Comic books have produced many ET-SF specialists, highlighted by artists as diverse as Joe Doolin (bug-eyed-monster cover-art maestro with *Planet* comics); Wallace Wood (a genius of EC Comics' *Weird Science* and *Weird Fantasy*); Al Feldstein (another EC artist, who wrote and edited, too); Osamu Tezuka (creator of Astro Boy); Jack Kirby (who took Marvel superheroes to boggling, eye-filling other worlds); Carmine Infantino (sleek, mid-century hardware, architecture, and planetscapes); Moebius; Philippe Druillet; and Masamune Shirow (epic science-cyberpunk).

So-called Lowbrow, or Outsider, Art—a calculatedly brazen commingling of pulp and comic art, fine art, illustration, and pin-up and hot rod aesthetics—has produced many luminaries, some of whom interpret the UFO/ET trope: Robert Williams (wrap your orbs around *Dr. Cinnabar's Cybernoid Art Ray: Beauty Is Best Expressed*); Tom Shropshire (see *UFO—A Scouting Party*, 2010); Fabrizio Cassetta (who has particular interest in grays); George Bryan Ward (homages to the box art of SF toys of the 1950s); John Robert Beck (see *Dancing Discs*, 2011); Keith Tucker (*Weird Tiki-Comics* and other mid-century retro); Dennis Larkins (genre-mixing mid-century; see *Abduction of the Innocent*); and others often featured in *Juxtapoz* and *Hi-Fructose* magazines.

Pulp and tabloid journalism has had fun with UFOs for sixty years. One of the greatest exemplars, the late, lamented *Weekly World News*, conjured some fabulous UFO headlines: "Titanic Sunk by Underwater UFO"; "Aliens Attack Vegas with Death Rays"; "Iran Launches Flying Saucer"; and "Your Spouse May Be an Alien." This sort of cynical yet joyous nonsense—as well as a great deal of UFO-oriented Outsider Art and other postmodernity—can be traced to a five-cent diversion for children.

Mars Attacks!

The company that created them hid its identity behind an alternate corporate name. Test distribution during 1962 was limited to the East Coast, where kids bought them furiously before parents raised the roof about gory violence and sexual suggestiveness. So great was the outcry that the gum-card set called *Mars Attacks!* was suspended, and never progressed to national distribution. In the many years since, pristine original examples of single cards run into hundreds, and even thousands, of dollars. Unopened packs are highly prized, and original counter displays designed to hold multiple packs are like gold. Auction houses traffic in once-forgotten concept sketches and finished paintings. If any flying saucer invasion can be termed "beloved," that invasion is *Mars Attacks!*

Created by Brooklyn-based Topps Chewing Gum Co. as a philosophical follow-on to a gory card set called *Civil War News*, *Mars Attacks!* comprises fifty-five cards developed by Topps creative director Woody Gelman and his young assistant, Len Brown. The pair took cues from the space race and science fiction movies of the previous ten years, and from the dark, sardonically funny EC horror and SF comics of the 1950s. Gelman's professional experience included cartooning, and he felt comfortable doing preliminary roughs, along with a pair of top SF cartoonists, EC veteran Wallace Wood; and Bob Powell, who had done handsome horror and SF work for Harvey Comics. When final subjects and compositions were agreed upon, Powell did tight pencils on illustration boards measuring barely more than three by five inches.

As he had done for *Civil War News*, illustrator Norm Saunders converted the pencils into paintings. Saunders brought a blunt, hysterically dramatic style to cards with such winsome titles as "Burning Cattle" (bovine terror when flying saucers light up stampeding cows); "Burning Flesh" (heat rays sear and filet astonished civilians); "Hairy Fiend" (incipient decapitation of a soldier by a gigantic spider set loose by the Martians); and the famed "Destroying a Dog" (Martian heat ray turns Fido into a skeleton right before the eyes of the kid that owns him).

Predistribution censorship came from high-level Topps executives who realized that this new set far exceeded the excesses of *Civil War News*. *Mars Attacks!* card #21, for instance, "Prize Captive," depicts a young beauty's struggle with a lecherous Martian; Saunders painted the woman with bare shoulders and a plunging neckline; in the printed version, the victim's blouse has short sleeves and a blue ribbon large enough to obscure any suggestion of cleavage. Card #17, a bedroom scene called "Beast and the Beauty," presented a similar challenge, with a beautiful girl wearing what Len Brown called "a small, revealing nightie." In Saunders's revision, the woman is buttoned up—wrist to shoulder, bodice to chin—in something that looks like white flannel. But she still struggles to avoid violation and death.

The preponderance of cards #1 through #15 focuses on the Martian flying saucers, and the high-tech mayhem they cause. Card #1, "The Invasion Begins," is the dramatic assembly of saucers preparing for lift-off from Mars, a Martian commander eagerly pointing the way to Earth. The craft are convex discs topped with broad, transparent domes—a design reported again and again by real-life UFO witnesses.

Card #2, "Martians Approaching," reveals a portion of the vast invasion fleet as viewed by Martians inside a command center. Other "saucer cards" from the first fifteen include "Attacking an Army Base," "Saucers Blast Our Jets," "Terror in Times Square," and "Washington in Flames." None of this reflected the friendly-alien paradigm; no, *Mars Attacks!* manifested the row-dier aspects of pop culture, as well as the concerns of the UFO community's menacing-aliens faction.

21 PRIZE CAPTIVE

Cited as a major influence by Stephen King and many other pop-culture writers and artists, Topps's *Mars Attacks!* gum-card set of 1962 not only stretched the limits of children's entertainment, but put a gleefully violent face on the UFO phenomenon. Card No. 21, "Prize Captive," anticipates real-life abduction incidents, and injects more than a little unwholesome sexuality.   *The Everett Collection*

The final card of the *Mars Attacks!* narrative is #54, "Mars Explodes." (Number fifty-five is a synopsis and checklist.) As illustrated, Mars goes blooey, like an oversized cherry bomb. In the foreground, American rocket fighters speed toward home; one rugged flyer harnessed beneath his bubble canopy looks over his shoulder at the sundered Red Planet and gives a hearty thumbs-up. Here, then, was the ultimate response to UFO threats real and imagined: resistance and absolute destruction.

Early sets distributed by Topps for test marketing (and credited to "Bubbles, Inc.") went out as *Attack from Space.* Buoyed by encouraging sales, the company quickly changed the name to the punchier *Mars Attacks!* Test sales continued on a robust course, but, inevitably, parents and educators soon involved themselves, spurring Topps to make still more revisions. The aforementioned "Beast and the Beauty," for example, came under such scrutiny that Topps did a hasty redo of the card's earlier in-house redo, with Saunders doing a self-portrait—a handsome, mustachioed gent in his fifties—to place over the figure of the frightened girl. The expense of alterations to a few other cards suggested that any further changes would be cost prohibitive. Topps decided to let *Mars Attacks!* expire.

But *Mars Attacks!* refused to die. Scarce and "forbidden," they became a cultural touchstone for two generations of kids and grown-up kids fond of the outré. Much-discussed, particularly by interested people who had merely glimpsed them or never seen any at all, the cards acquired a mythic status. Collector prices began to escalate in the 1970s, and licensed reprints appeared, from companies other than Topps, in 1984. When Topps reprinted the original set in 1994, the company created enough all-new cards (some based on theretofore unused 1962 concepts by Wood and Powell) to bump the *Mars Attacks!* total from fifty-five to ninety-eight.

Director Tim Burton's same-titled 1996 film adaptation perfectly captures the cards' comically outrageous fascination with UFOs. Although a box-office disappointment, *Mars Attacks!* found enduring life on DVD, so the Topps-Burton phenomenon remains a small, vivid part of the national consciousness. In 2012, Abrams published a handsome *Mars Attacks* art book (no exclamation point), with reproductions and backstories of every card (censored and uncensored), rare looks at *Attack from Space* wrappers and display boxes, and a tipped-in set of four collector cards. The book's waxy, yellow and red dustjacket mimics the gaudy original wrappers.

Why does *Mars Attacks!* attract so much devoted, quasi-historical attention? Although far from "forbidden" in this liberalized age, the cards nevertheless retain an aura of the cultural underground. They exploit and expand upon tropes from science fiction, but also from broader pop-entertainment conventions, particularly the fondness for violent challenges to human authority, and our equally violent responses. Because twenty-five of the original fifty-five cards explicitly reference the U.S. military, the storyline acquires an incidental layer of narrative, and a kind of authority, too, as if depicting secret, insider knowledge that the government does not want us to have. If Blue Book and other government investigations of UFOs were bungled, or purposely subverted, *Mars Attacks!* is the angry rejoinder.

The cards' preoccupation with humans as prey can hardly be overstated. The human fear of attack from above—by an animal or another, larger person who knocks us to the ground—is atavistic. Any institution or agency, human or extraterrestrial, that can send forth such destruction, is fearsome. "Slaughter in the Streets," a card from a follow-on *Mars Attacks!* set, depicts a scene of bloody urban warfare. Graffiti scrawled on the brick façade of a ruined building reads DEATH FROM ABOVE.

10

Close Encounters of the Unnerving Kind

Aggressive Aliens, Seven Degrees, and a Cop on the Front Line

Because the human imagination is essentially catastrophic—mayhem and mystery are, after all, more fun to contemplate than scenarios of peaceful certitude—documented UFO reports marked by varying degrees of physical interaction between craft and witness are inevitably engaging. "Friendly alien" scenarios (discussed in chapter twelve) are encouraging, and they certainly appeal to the hopeful aspect of our sense of wonder, but it is the essential conflict of perilous encounters that alerts our senses, and stimulates our innate craving for tales with clearly defined protagonists and antagonists. Angry aliens, aggressive aliens, imminent peril, the thrill of the dark unknown—it's like imagining an action movie, and you have fun. That is, unless you're in the middle of the encounter: shocked, confused . . . and maybe even fighting for your life.

The Seven Degrees of Close Encounters

For twenty-five years following Kenneth Arnold and Roswell in 1947, reports of UFOs were classified—by government agencies and UFOlogists alike—according to non-standard criteria. Basic information, such as size, speed, illumination, and distance from the witness, was noted, but no universal specification existed to codify encounters that had become increasingly intimate. As witnesses continued to report close physical proximity to UFOs, and even to the crafts' inhabitants, a need for a single system of encounter classification became increasingly apparent.

In 1972, astronomer J. Allen Hynek devised such a system, describing three levels of encounters. Hynek's experience as a consultant to Project Blue Book brought him serious regard. He had earned a doctorate in astrophysics at the University of Chicago in 1935. Teaching and administrative posts took Dr. Hynek to Ohio State and Northwestern. The high level of his research, and his willingness to advise Blue Book objectively—despite being a UFO skeptic—brought him more government work during the mid- to late 1950s, notably an assignment to train young astronomers to track man-made satellites as the United States prepared to send the first one into orbit.

Mr. Boffo, May 15, 2015: Every invasion brings upsides and downsides.

Courtesy of Joe Martin/Neatly Chiseled Features

Although invariably guided by the scientific method, Hynek had a flexible mind that rebelled in 1966, when the Air Force chose "swamp gas" as the official explanation for a series of intriguing UFO sightings in Michigan. That Hynek *himself* had offered the explanation during a press conference was galling to him, because he later realized he had spoken too quickly, and because the explanation inspired laughter.

Eager to put "swamp gas" behind him, Hynek advocated for serious scientific investigation of UFOs. His 1972 book *The UFO Experience* put the Air Force's feet to the fire, insisting that sloppiness and a predisposition to doubt characterized USAF investigations. Meanwhile, credible sightings mounted.

Here are Dr. Hynek's three degrees of "close encounters":

- **Close Encounter of the First Kind (CE1)**: Objects or lights are fewer than five hundred feet from witnesses, with no observable physical effect on objects or witnesses.
- **Close Encounter of the Second Kind (CE2)**: Because the witness has scientific expertise, hard scientific data are available. A physical effect from the UFO is apparent to the witness, and is observed in animate or inanimate matter. For example, engines of automobiles and other machinery become inoperable; or scorched or flattened grass is observed. A possibility of physical harm to the witness, and even death, exists.
- **Close Encounter of the Third Kind (CE3)**: The witness encounters an occupant of the UFO. (Hynek referred to such beings as "animated creatures.")

A UFOlogist named Ted Bloecher, among others, prepared CE3 addenda; these sub-classifications hinged on the physical relationships of the alien(s) to the UFO(s), such as whether the aliens are seen with the saucer or seen in isolation, and whether aliens entered or left the craft. Non-visual contact, such as a telepathic message, is another CE3 addendum. Finally, in instances where no craft may have been seen at all, the witness may encounter Sasquatch, Men in Black, or other non-standard UFO-related personages.

After 1990, Steven M. Greer and onetime Hynek associate Jacques Vallée created two additional CE classifications:

- **Close Encounter of the Fourth Kind (CE4)**: Abduction, physical harm, and/or physical examination of a witness.
- **Close Encounter of the Fifth Kind (CE5)**: Sexual contact with a UFO occupant(s).

Two more levels came later:

- **Close Encounter of the Sixth Kind (CE6)**: A UFO sighting is associated with the death of a human or an animal. Discrete cases of mutilated cattle may fall into this category.
- **Close Encounter of the Seventh Kind (CE7)**: An alien/human hybrid is created by sexual contact or technological/scientific means.

Hynek himself added classifications intended to clarify the nature of an object:

- **DD**: A discoidal object seen in the distant daytime sky.
- **NL**: Nocturnal light; an anomalous illuminated object viewed in the night sky.
- **RV**: Radar/visual; an object picked up simultaneously on radar and by an eyewitness(es).

Hynek's associate, Jacques Vallée, created additional standards focused on flight trajectories, evidence of life forms, witnesses' sense of altered reality, and instances of injury or death.

The Close Encounters table is a valuable tool that can recognize patterns of UFO reports (geographically, time of day, and so forth), as well as behavior of UFO occupants. On the other hand, the levels' specificity—particularly of CE4 through CE7—has provided blueprints for reports that, in time, prove to be

Astronomer and UFOlogist J. Allen Hynek in 1977, a few years after he devised a groundbreaking encounter-classification system to codify human-alien interaction. The utility of Hynek's invention is difficult to overstate.

Rex

spurious. Further, apparent patterns uncovered by CE classification can alternately support and undercut witness claims. If, for instance, a sole UFO encounter from Area A is shortly followed by a welter of Area A accounts from unrelated witnesses, skeptics will readily cite suggestibility and even hysterical reaction as reasons for the flurry of reports.

The Close Encounters classification system is at its most meaningful when utilized to codify contemporary UFO sightings, as the sightings occur. Not surprisingly, the system is frequently applied to sightings that predate Hynek's innovation. Much of this "postdating" is reasonable and, arguably, useful.

A few close encounters are sufficiently dramatic to warrant special mention below.

The Flatwoods Monster

Six West Virginia boys aged ten to seventeen observed a UFO descent near the village of Flatwoods at dusk on September 12, 1952. The thing came from the sky like a fireball, landing on a hill that was part of the nearby Fisher farm. The boys dashed to a nearby house and corralled a housewife, Kathleen May, who went with them to the point of impact, where flaming debris littered the ground. A noise caused the group to look up into the trees, where a hissing, shiny-eyed alien perched among the branches. Although a nauseating gas or mist emitted by the debris partially obscured the creature, the boys and Mrs. May were able to make out a heavy, pendulous body with no visible lower limbs, apparently draped in fabric, and with a face shaped like the ace of spades. In a heartbeat, the creature displayed what Mrs. May called "terrible claws," before gliding from the tree and toward the startled group. One of the boys dropped his flashlight, and the entire group scattered. Ever after, the creature has been called the Flatwoods Monster. (Because Flatwoods is in West Virginia's Braxton County, the creature is occasionally referred to as the Braxton County Monster.)

A sheriff's investigation a day later turned up nothing, but a day after that the editor of the *Braxton* (WV) *Democrat* discovered what may have been impact marks on the ground, and a peculiar gummy substance. On assignment from *Fate* magazine, UFO researcher Gray Barker arrived very soon after the incident, to interview witnesses and take a look at the site. Barker reported that the boys' sighting coincided with reports from other locals of "illuminated objects in the sky" over a twenty-mile radius.

The Flatwoods case is part of the 1952 "UFO explosion." That it has not become lost in the plethora of reports from that year marks it as unique. Admittedly, the narrative has been muddied by published accounts that draw upon—and embellish—earlier ones, and by some discrepancies among the witnesses. In some published accounts, the airborne object gave off a pulsing light, which is easily explained by a nearby trio of airplane beacons with flashing red illumination. Sometimes, all six boys belonged to Mrs. May, when only two, Eddie and Freddie, were hers. In certain retellings the creature's face is round and red, and topped by a pointed cowl (organic or possibly fabric; regardless, the detail is in line with

Along with five other West Virginians, Eugene Lemon and Kathleen May confronted a hissing, apparently extraterrestrial creature in trees near Flatwoods on September 12, 1952. On September 19, the two traveled to New York to appear as guests on *We, the People,* a human-interest chat show broadcast nationally by NBC-TV. Here, Lemon and May flank a network artist's conception of the creature they saw.   *Courtesy of Charleston Gazette-Mail*

the more precise "ace of spades" description). Some latter-day chroniclers note a green body that, green or not, ranges from "man-sized" to ten feet tall.

The witnesses' nausea is consistent among accounts, though historians cannot agree on whether the fumes emanated from debris or from an intact craft. Another possibility, though, is evening fog, which is common in the area in September.

During a trip to Flatwoods in 2000, researcher Joe Nickell uncovered locals that remembered the original stir from 1952–53. (A pair of plainclothes USAF investigators working on behalf of Project Blue Book visited Flatwoods early in 1953, to conduct routine research. Over the years, their presence has morphed— according to some sources—into a visit from Men in Black.) One longtime resident, ninety-five when Nickell spoke with him, recalled that the general consensus among townies was that the witnesses saw a meteor. Although some accounts from 1952 suggest that multiple objects were spotted that evening, Nickell intuited— probably correctly—that witnesses separated by geography simply saw a single object tracing a course across the sky.

More than one local felt that the gummy deposits and marks of ground impact reported by the *Braxton Democrat* are easily explained: leaked oil and skid marks from the ten-year-old Chevy pickup owned by a man named Max Lockard, who had driven to the site and found nothing, whereupon he executed a muddy U-turn and departed.

In later years, Kathleen May insisted that she and the others had not seen a monster at all, but an experimental aircraft. (Apparently eager to be disassociated with the "monster" story, neither Mrs. May nor son Fred agreed to be interviewed by Nickell in 2000.)

As for the creature itself, Nickell's research satisfied him that the creature in the branches was a barn owl, a large bird with a "cowled," heart-shaped white face and large eyes easily visible from the ground. The species has a variety of startling vocalizations that might easily be described as a hiss. Indeed, one common name for the barn owl is the hissing owl. The monster's gliding movement and claws also suggest a large bird.

Besides its publication by *Fate*, Gray Barker's account of the Flatwoods Monster dominated the first issue (September 1953) of his mimeographed *Saucerian*. Early in 2016, a bookseller in Cooperstown, New York, offered a "near fine" copy of that issue, *The Saucerian* Vol. 1 No. 1, for $1,250.

Mothman

Animals are prominent in an intriguing subset of encounters. Witnesses have reported the unexpected presence of deer, wolves, ravens, owls, butterflies, and bees. Animals that roam well beyond their usual habitat, such as black panthers seen near certain North American UFO encounters, are not uncommon. Are these familiar creatures attracted to something in UFO technology? Do alien visitors communicate with animals?

Other accounts revolve around *alien* animals, sometimes the peculiarly oversized. In some instances, witnesses see anomalous mixed-species creatures, such as humanoid reptiles and the insect-human hybrid popularly known as Mothman. This celebrated case began near Point Pleasant, West Virginia, in the Mid-Ohio Valley, on November 5, 1966. As sewing machine salesman Woodward Derenberger drove his small truck on I-77 near Mineral Wells, his way was suddenly blocked by a curvilinear craft sitting across the road. Although startled, Derenberger was able to have a conversation with one of the craft's occupants, a man in an overcoat who identified himself as Indrid Cold. Other UFO sightings in the Ohio River Valley (including a November 17 encounter that fueled the Mothman story) encouraged media interest in Derenberger, who later met another alien, named Carl Ardo.

By November 15, people in the Mid-Ohio Valley—an area that included Wood and Mason counties and the West Virginia towns of Mineral Wells, Parkersburg, Point Pleasant, and Huntington—had absorbed the ten-day-old accounts of Derenberger's adventure. For the next week, local authorities fielded many reports of strange creatures, including a tale told by four teenage boys. They had been startled in the night, they said, by a large, birdlike humanoid that glared at them with red eyes before unfurling its wings and taking flight. A local biologist named Duane Pursley suggested that the boys had seen a Canadian goose. Robert L. Smith, a wildlife biologist with West Virginia University, identified the creature as a sandhill crane, but the boys and people involved in other sightings insisted that the visitor was something unique—and frightening.

During the early morning of November 18, a pair of Point Pleasant volunteer firemen saw a "large bird of some kind." This encounter took place just north of Point Pleasant, near abandoned TNT storage bunkers built for use during World

War II. The TNT factory was long abandoned, and now the earth-covered concrete bunkers squatted on boggy ground amidst old-growth forest. Local kids and teenagers were naturally attracted to them, and hunters used them as reference points. Soon, speculation began that the creature—by now called "Mothman"—lived in one of the bunkers.

Within a week of the firemen's report, an unidentified reporter with the *Point Pleasant Register* interviewed another witness, a store manager named Tom Ury, for the paper's November 25 edition. Ury, who had his encounter in daylight, described the creature as humanoid, about six feet tall, with a modest bill and a wingspan of eight to ten feet. "It came up like a helicopter," Ury said, "and then veered over my car." Despite Ury opening his car up to seventy miles per hour, the flying creature kept pace.

Proper investigation of the various reports was difficult because the wooded areas that figured in the reports became overrun with curious hunters and other locals, who trampled the forest floor, damaged flora, and, inevitably, littered and vandalized the area. Near the end of the flurry of excitement, local and regional reporters arrived in the area, interviewing witnesses, neighbors, and the authorities, and generally putting local people on edge. (According to a U.S. Marine, the mysterious winged creature even showed up in South Vietnam.)

Circus

Meanwhile, Woodward Derenberger pursued his own story. UFOlogists Gray Barker and John Keel were among Derenberger's supporters, and in 1971, he collaborated with Harold W. Hubbard on a book, *Visitors from Lanulos.*

Derenberger's account inspired *The Mothman Prophecies*, a 1975 book by Keel, a popular writer who regarded UFOs as manifestations of ancient gods, rather than as craft piloted by present-day extraterrestrials. Aliens, according to Keel, are also manifestations of elder gods. Keel described the Mid-Ohio Valley as a UFO/supernatural hot spot—"window" is his term—that, for reasons unknown, attracts an inordinate number of UFO sightings and reports of aliens and peculiar, animal-like humanoids.

This provocative line of thought heightened buff and general-public interest in Mothman, but Derenberger's adventure came with a price. The flurry of television and newspaper coverage turned the salesman into a regional celebrity, and after people digested his story, many decided they wanted to see aliens themselves. In a 2011 interview with the *Parkersburg News and Sentinel*, Derenberger's daughter, Taunia Bowman, recalled that armed strangers planted themselves in trees outside the family's house, ready to deal with extraterrestrials. Other locals didn't like anything about Derenberger's claim. The entire family was harassed, and non-stop abuse prompted them to change their home phone number many times. After five or six moves to new addresses, Derenberger's wife finally wilted beneath the strain and left him in 1968, taking their daughter and two sons to new lives in Cleveland. She shortly married a Cleveland UFOlogist who had investigated her husband's story.

Woodward Derenberger suffered permanent estrangement from his sons. He passed away in 1990.

Mothman Disaster

Because Point Pleasant was among the Mid-Ohio Valley towns crawling with curious locals, reporters, researchers and other strangers during the last two months of 1966, some investigators and laypersons perceive a connection between UFOs, Mothman, and one of the worst-ever failures of American infrastructure: the December 15, 1967, rush hour collapse of the Point Pleasant Bridge connecting Point Pleasant and Gallipolis, Ohio.

Point Pleasant Bridge was known locally as the Silver Bridge, for the shiny aluminum paint that covered the steelwork. When construction ended in 1928, the 2,235-foot-long span was opened as a toll route (U.S. Highway 35). A thorough inspection made in 1951 found nothing seriously amiss, but did insist upon maintenance of concrete and metal parts, pilings, and other components; installation of new railings and bird screens; replacement of compromised concrete at anchorages and retaining walls; and other fixes. These and other improvements were made. Later inspections—in 1955, 1961, and 1965—were cursory; at least one was conducted from the ground, with the far-off inspector observing sections of the span with binoculars!

The bridge was suspended by a system of interlocked eye-bars held fast with thick pins. The system (as utilized on this bridge) had no redundancy; in other words, if the primary suspension component began to fail, there was no system to (literally) take up the slack. The eye-bars were made of carbon steel, a very strong alloy that is nevertheless vulnerable to weather corrosion. On December 15, a stress fracture one-eighth of an inch long gave way; the three eye-bars connected at that spot fell away, and in moments, the bridge's entire support system failed. Of the thirty-seven vehicles on the roadway at that instant, thirty-one fell into the frigid Ohio River. Forty-six people perished from, variously, crushing, drowning, and hypothermia.

As one might expect, the bridge failure was an enormous local, regional, and national story. The fact that the Point Pleasant span was about the same age of thousands of other bridges throughout the United States triggered a nationwide wave of bridge inspections. Although spans across the country got rigorous official attention, few motorists traveling bridges afterward did so without a small shiver of apprehension.

Opinion is divided as to Mothman's involvement with the bridge disaster. Some people speculate that the collapse was caused by a sonic boom generated by Mothman's wings; but others surmise that the creature arrived at Point Pleasant to warn of the impending collapse. The first "Mothman" book, Gray Barker's partly fictionalized *The Silver Bridge*, appeared in 1970.

Writer John Keel's investigative book from 1975, *The Mothman Prophecies*, spawned a 2002 movie of the same name. Despite good production values and the star presence of Richard Gere, the film flopped commercially. Regardless, Point

Pleasant was quick to cash in. Gunn Park became Mothman Park, and the town inaugurated the annual Mothman Festival. Boosters transformed a shuttered KFC restaurant into Mothman Visitors' Center. Today, Point Pleasant's tidy business district boasts a striking, twelve-foot Mothman statue in stainless steel, complete with red eyes. (The town was unable to afford the inner illumination needed to make the eyes glow.) Local merchants sell DVDs, posters, action figures, Christmas ornaments, and other souvenir merchandise. (Roadsideamerica.com, an online tourists' guide, notes that unnamed Point Pleasant daredevils had the temerity to create and sell pirated Mothman Beanie Babies.) September 2015 brought the fourteenth Point Pleasant Mothman Festival, a gathering that, according to mothmanfestival.com, offers "a wide variety of vendors and merchants, live local music, delicious food, and a family-friendly atmosphere."

All of this is amusing and uniquely American, but for those that witnessed what came to be called Mothman, or who wonder if rumors about the bridge collapse can be true, Mothman is a dark, intimidating figure. That sort of dread helped encourage conspiracy theories about events in the Mid-Ohio Valley, chiefly, that the strangers in the area during 1966–67 were participants in the disaster, and in collusion with 1) Mothman, 2) other aliens, 3) Men in Black, and/or other shadowy emissaries from government agencies.

Fear Under Pressure

"Hard" UFO evidence—things that can be touched and held—is scarce in the world of UFOlogy. Imagine the excitement, then, generated by a man named Bob White. While in Colorado near the Utah border in 1985, White observed as a UFO ejected a 7.5-inch metallic piece—thick and bulbous at one end, and tapered to a point at the other. The object's surface appearance evokes fish scales, as if the object had been carefully layered, one section over another. White, forty-six at the time, retrieved the object, only to spend the next decade and a half trying to understand it, and persuade other people about the truth of how the object came into his possession. He finally found an ally in the 2000s: Mark W. Allin, a UFOlogist who co-owns The Above Top Secret Web site. Allin has related that after he presented Bob White's metal object to a scientist at Los Alamos, the object picked up AM and FM radio signals, and heated and cooled with equal rapidity, which encouraged the scientist to pronounce the object as extraterrestrial. That judgment certainly backed up Bob White's story; Allin, though, was concerned because the Los Alamos scientist came under career-threatening pressure from his superiors, and recanted his findings. The bullying suggested to some in the UFO community that the scientist—and, by extension, White—was a victim of government conspiracy and cover-up.

Allin persevered. An independent metallurgist he hired in 2007 said the object was of terrestrial origin. A year after that, Allin took it to nuclear physicist Stanton Friedman, who examined it, considered the details of White's account, and classified the object as extraterrestrial.

Later in 2008, White and Allin found another ally, Franklin Carter, former president of the Institute for UFO Research, and later a member of MUFON (Mutual UFO Network). Mr. Carter spent time with the object. He believed White's story, and felt certain that the metal did not originate on Earth.

Bob White remained puzzled by the apparent cover-up at Los Alamos. Perhaps scientists there had seen similar objects before White showed up with his. In 2004, Bob White told his own story in a book, *UFO Hard Evidence*; and a DVD, *The Bob White Experience.*

Bob White's apparent sincerity aside, the nature of the object he retrieved suggests an alternative, and earthly, explanation with roots in old-style metallurgy. There may be no clearer explanation than one published more than seventy years before White's discovery: a 1914 issue of *American Machinist.* In a sub-article attached to a longer piece about the manufacture of shrapnel shells, technical writer W. T. Montague looked at the inevitable, and unwanted, accumulation of "grinding chips" on heavy-duty, foundry-rated grinders. As the grinding wheel turns against steel, white-hot flecks of metal collect behind the machine's wheel guard. A stalagmite-like (thick at one end, tapered at the other) combination of solid steel and minute pieces of the wheel's abrasive agent begins to form. The grinder's exhaust (for dust removal) generates a flow of oxygen that heats the stalagmite to the melting point of steel, 2,600 degrees F, sufficient for partial welding. An attentive operator will knock the stalagmite from the shield long before it has time to form into much of anything, but one left unattended will end up as "molten steel solidified into shiny solid masses of fantastic design."

Fantastic—like the metal piece discovered by Bob White.

Gordo Gets an Eyeful

U.S. aerospace engineer, Air Force test pilot, and astronaut Gordon "Gordo" Cooper went into space twice, as one of the original "Mercury 7" astronauts (1963) and as part of the Gemini project in 1965. Contrary to a long-standing erroneous assumption by some UFOlogists, Cooper did *not* witness UFOs during his space flights. However, while he and other USAF pilots flew their F-86 Sabre jets over Germany in 1951, scores of unidentified flying objects, grouped in what Cooper described as "fighter formation," flew above the jets. Although neither Cooper nor anyone else in his flight group could guess at the objects' size, the craft flew very quickly, performing aerial maneuvers that no jet could duplicate. Cooper and the unit made a report; when an official response came, the verdict was "flying seed pods."

In 1957, Cooper worked as a test-flight project manager at Edwards AFB. A USAF camera crew assigned by Cooper to fly above and film dry lake beds (before the surfaces were modified to become landing strips) witnessed a saucer-shaped object fly above their planes before extending a tripod landing assembly and coming to ground on one of the lake beds. When the jets swung back to approach, the saucer "lifted off, put the gear back in the [wheel] well and climbed out at a very high rate of speed and disappeared" (Cooper's account). Despite the saucer's quick departure, the Air Force camera crew captured the saucer and its maneuvers. Cooper contacted his superiors, who asked that the film be developed and prepared for pickup by courier. The courier arrived and left with the film—and Cooper never heard another word about it.

Although he had had no time to project the footage, Cooper unspooled a portion from the reel before the courier arrived, and examined it through the light from a window. "It was certainly good film," Cooper told an interviewer many years later. "Good close-up shots," he said.

Could the Edwards AFB saucer have been attracted by the dry beds' future role as landing areas?

Cooper got the distinct impression that the craft he saw in 1951, and the ones he glimpsed in film frames in 1957, were piloted. As an Air Force pilot-manager with privileged, classified access to the USA's top-secret U-2 spy plane, Cooper understood the current state of avionics. He remained adamant that neither the USSR nor any other nation had aviation technology of the sort exhibited by the saucers he saw. Further, Cooper felt that the U.S. government mishandled some of the saucer information that fell into its hands and purposely sat on other information that would have informed the public.

In a 1978 letter to the United Nations, Cooper wrote, "I believe that these extra-terrestrial [sic] vehicles and their crews are visiting this planet from other planets, which obviously are a little more technically advanced than we are here on earth." Cooper suggested that the best course would be to institute "a coordinated program to scientifically collect and analyze" UFO data from around the globe.

UFOs vs. Law Enforcement

As first responders, members of law enforcement are frequently involved in UFO incidents: investigating reports at the behest of local governments or military, taking down witness accounts, and scrutinizing apparent accidents or other anomalous physical conditions that may be linked to unidentified flying objects. Officers' physical encounters with UFOs carry special significance, because those men and women are servants of the larger population, dedicated to the protection of the public. An officer's negative encounter with a UFO, then, does not involve merely the officer, but all of us. An assault on an officer is an assault on everyone in the community.

Training helps officers develop watchfulness, self-discipline, and an active but objective attitude. Sometimes, though, even the best training has seemed inadequate.

Encounter in the Desert

Friday, April 24, 1964, near Socorro, New Mexico. 5:45 p.m.

Socorro patrolman Lonnie Zamora had picked up on the speeding black Chevy at the edge of town, just past the courthouse. The Chevy was new, and from the way the kid inside was pulling away south toward the desert, Zamora figured

Outside of Socorro, New Mexico, on April 24, 1964, Socorro police officer Lonnie Zamora witnessed the possibly unscheduled desert landing of an extraterrestrial craft, and got a clear look at two of the occupants. Zamora returned to the site on May 2, walking reporters through the event and pointing out depressions left by the craft's landing gear.   *Getty Images*

that the Chevy had the muscular 327 that pumped out three hundred horsepower. Zamora flipped his lights and punched his white '64 Pontiac Catalina. The cruiser had a police-package 389, and when the carb sucked greedily at the gas, Zamora's head snapped back as the big car leapt forward.

The Chevy had started three blocks ahead, but as the edge of town receded, Zamora rode the accelerator pedal hard and closed the gap. It was late afternoon, and the desert and surrounding Socorro Range were quickly filling in with purple shadow. Zamora was close, almost on the kid's bumper.

And then the sky to the southwest exploded in blue and orange. The concussive sound of a blast momentarily drowned out the roar of the cruiser's engine, and Zamora instinctively lifted his foot from the accelerator. He craned his neck for a better look at the flash as he reached for his radio. There was a dynamite shack in the desert outside of town, and now the damn thing had blown up. *And who blew up with it?* Zamora wondered.

The speeder in the Chevy was gone, out of sight, probably into Socorro's rodeo grounds. Zamora didn't care about that anymore. He brought the Catalina back up to speed and traveled about a mile, and then stood on the brakes to slew the cruiser off the macadam onto an unimproved dirt road that would bring him near whatever was left of the shack. The Pontiac's tail stepped out on the loose surface, but Zamora wrestled it back. He was thirty years old. He'd been with Socorro PD for five years, and had learned a long time ago how to handle a car on desert roads.

He continued on, slower now. Plumes of yellow dust rose from the sides of the cruiser, and small rocks pinged and thudded against the rocker panels. Zamora noticed that the blast fire's blue color had diminished; now it was mostly orange. And there was still a noise—like the blast, only less loud, and lower in register. Zamora scowled. *How could that be?*

Something about the flame seemed odd, too. It was unusually narrow at the base, like the controlled finger at the business end of an acetylene torch. The setting sun didn't help Zamora's vision, and he had to squint through his flip-down sunglasses. He was still two hundred yards from the blast, and now the road rose in a steep hill. Zamora blipped the accelerator, and the Catalina struggled to climb the dirt and loose rocks. Even with a light, steady foot, the rear wheels spun, and Zamora finally had to stop and try again. He got the same unsatisfactory result the second time, and he finally topped the crest only after rocking the car back and forth.

There was a car about 150 yards off-road. It lay on its side, or maybe on its roof, and two men in coveralls stood nearby. *Is this the shack? No, the shack is over there. It didn't blow up. And who are the jokers in the coveralls?*

Zamora pulled the cruiser onto the uneven desert scrub. When he looked again at the orange flame, the two men were gone. Zamora pulled to a stop and radioed in an accident report. The overturned car was in an arroyo, and when Zamora left his cruiser the low roar became louder, more like the first sound he had heard. The men in the coveralls were still nowhere to be seen.

Now Zamora could see that the object wasn't a car. It was car-sized or bigger, white—aluminum, maybe—and oval, without windows or doors, not even a seam. A peculiar, two-foot by two-foot insignia that Zamora couldn't identify was visible on the object's skin. Two slender support legs were visible at the base, but the coverall twins seemed to have vanished altogether. Something Zamora couldn't see thumped audibly once, twice, and then the flame beneath the object expanded and shifted to the blue tone Zamora had first seen. The object began to rise into the air. The roar was loud, like a jet engine, but Zamora knew it wasn't a jet. This was something else. The flame and noise were so great that Zamora was afraid the object was going to crash or explode. When he turned to crouch behind his cruiser his legs caught the front fender and he collapsed into the dirt. His glasses flew off. He could see all right without them, so he just ran. He wanted to get the car between him and the object, and he wanted some distance, too. He ran north, looking over his shoulder as the object rose to about ten feet. The blue flame had vanished, and now the oval just hovered. The thing made no noise at all, and Zamora was surprised that the sudden silence made his ears ring.

He locked his gaze on the object and slowly made his way back to the cruiser. He retrieved his glasses, and was surprised when the object took off laterally, in silence, clearing the dynamite shack by about three feet and continuing south at high speed. The thing cleared the distant peak of Six Mile Canyon Mountain and disappeared.

Zamora just stood there for a long moment. He rested his hand on the Pontiac's fender, and he thought how foolish and inadequate his fast car suddenly seemed.

He leaned through the window and got on the radio again. He told two colleagues, Chavez and Lopez, to get the hell out there, fast.

Patrolman Zamora didn't know it, but he had entered legend. He'd come as close to a UFO—an unidentified flying object—as anyone had yet reported. He was no longer simply Lonnie Zamora. Now he was Lonnie Zamora-who-got-within-spitting-distance-of-a-UFO-and-lived-to-tell-the-tale. Over the next fifty years, no one would be able to come up with a reasonable explanation for what Zamora had seen—and nobody could discredit his story, either. Although Air Force and other government investigators studied the scene, no details of their findings have ever been released.

Eyes Only: Ten Notable Police Run-ins with UFOs

The Lonnie Zamora case is the most dramatic and extravagantly studied of all UFO encounters involving peace officers. A touchstone of UFO studies, it is just one of many eye-opening accounts offered by law enforcement personnel.

1. **August 13, 1960**: Stan Scott and Charles Carson, two CHiPs officers on patrol near Corning, California, shortly before midnight observe a silent, airliner-sized object descend to within one hundred to two hundred feet above the ground before halting and reversing course, and halting again at about five hundred feet. As the object moves, it sweeps the ground with a broad red light. The presence of the ovoid, glowing object is confirmed by radar personnel at nearby Red Bluff Air Station. Officers Scott and Carson slowly keep pace as the object moves east, pausing whenever it moves closer to the patrol car. Oddly, the object retreats whenever the CHiPs officers flip on their cherry light. After nearly two hours, a second flying object joins the first. Both hover and emit periodic red beams before moving off, to disappear over the east horizon. The Air Force explains that Scott and Carson—as well as three deputies at the Tehama County sheriff's office—had seen light refracted from Mars and two stars, Betelgeuse and Aldebaran. (Other explanations suggest weather balloons, the Northern Lights, and smoke from a distant forest fire.) Later, when it becomes clear that Mars and the two stars had been below the horizon at the time of the officers' sightings, the Air Force alters its explanation, citing the star Capella.

2. **September 21 and 24, 1962**: During two nights at a quarry in Hawthorne, New Jersey, more than sixteen local police officers observe bright flying discs. Four officers and a watchman witness the first incident; and at least a dozen officers, plus a reporter, are present for the second. A pranksters' letter claiming that the objects are models launched from Bergenfield, New Jersey, is found to be the work of boys living in that town, which is located more than eight miles, as the crow flies, from Hawthorne. No models made by children could have traveled that far. Four area newspapers, including the *Newark Evening News*, support the claims of the officers.

3. **April 17, 1966**: At about 5:00 a.m., two deputies from the Portage County, Ohio, sheriff's office near Ravenna get an okay from headquarters to chase an

enormous, brightly lit ovoid UFO. The deputies drive for eighty-five miles at speeds up to a hundred, crossing into Pennsylvania to keep up with the smoothly gliding craft. Along the way, the deputies enlist an Ohio police officer and an officer from Pennsylvania for the pursuit. All four see the craft clearly, and hear the thing's steady hum, a sound that Portage County deputy sheriff Dale Spaur later describes as "like . . . an overloaded transformer." Moments after Spaur hears radio chatter about jets being scrambled to intercept the object, the UFO rapidly ascends "straight up" and disappears. A drawing done by Spaur depicts an egg-shaped craft with a sharply vertical tail. The Air Force later denies that any jets were scrambled, and says the officers had seen two relatively mundane objects, a satellite and the planet Venus. When the officers state they saw the UFO *as well as* the satellite and Venus, the Air Force has no comment. **Note**: This event is frequently cited as the inspiration for a vaguely similar, two-minute chase sequence that is a highlight of the 1977 film *Close Encounters of the Third Kind*.

4. **August 13, 1970 and July 14, 1973**: While on patrol near Hadersley, Denmark, on August 13, the cruiser driven by veteran officer Evald Maarup is suddenly bathed in blue light and stops dead. When the temperature inside the car rises, Maarup steps out and sees a metallic ovoid, about thirty feet in diameter, hovering overhead. The silent craft remains stationary for about five minutes, and then whisks itself away. Once the UFO has departed, Maarup's patrol car starts up and operates normally. In the same area almost exactly three years later, Maarup observes a similar craft—though the object shows no interest in Maarup, and does not interfere with his car.

5. **August 27, 1979**: During night patrol on Minnesota State Route 220 near the North Dakota border, Marshall County, Minnesota, deputy sheriff Val Johnson's Ford LTD is struck head-on by a ball of light moving rapidly northward from a tree line. Johnson loses consciousness, and awakes to find that his car has been flung across the road, and that he has mild burns around his eyes. A portion of his dental work is fractured. Although Johnson has no memory of applying the brakes, the highway shows a ninety-nine-foot skid track. The patrol car's roof and trunk antennae are bent back at sharp angles, with the latter peculiarly bent at ninety degrees just a few inches from the top. Although the car's inner-left headlamp is smashed, there is no damage to the rim or chrome trim. The center roof light is broken, and the casing shows a thick, vertical char. The windshield exhibits a pattern of cracks that, according to a Ford Motor windshield specialist, is the result of an unexplainable combination of forces simultaneously pushing and pulling on the glass. Of particular interest is that the patrol car's dash clock, *and* Deputy Johnson's wristwatch, run fourteen minutes slow. **Note**: The Val Johnson case is one of the most celebrated of all close encounters, because it involves an experienced police officer, well-documented physical evidence, and immediate police investigation. UFOlogist Guy Westcott, who investigated the case in 1979, returned to it in 2009, finally admitting that he had reached "a dead end," and that the case must be classified as "an unknown."

6. **November 28, 1980**: Shortly before dawn, Todmorden, West Yorkshire, England, police constable Alan Godfrey stops his patrol car to make a sketch of a rotating ovoid object flying low over a cow pasture—only to experience a hitch in time. When his senses return, fifteen minutes have passed and he is again driving. Significantly, other witnesses, including a constable from nearby Halifax, see an ovoid UFO at about the same time. **Note**: Under hypnotic regression later, Godfrey recalled the interior of the craft, and his meeting with a bearded man called Yosef. When a tabloid revealed Godfrey's identity, his department forced him to take a psychological test. Although he easily achieved a satisfactory result, he was encouraged to retire a few years later. Constable Godfrey is of further interest to UFOlogists: he helped investigate the June 1980 death of a local named Zygmund Adamski, a miner found dead on a coal pile five days after he had disappeared. Although nothing suggests that the crime is anything more than simple murder-robbery, several details, including Adamski's half-dressed state and minor burns on the back of his head, encouraged tabloids to claim that Adamski had been abducted by a UFO and later dropped atop the pile of coal.

7. **February 27, 1993**: Shortly before midnight, Jefferson County, Kentucky, flying officers Kenny Graham (pilot) and Kenny Downs (spotter) are on routine patrol when their helicopter is approached from below by a pear-shaped object the size of a basketball. Although the copter is moving at a hundred miles per hour, the object easily closes distance. As Graham takes evasive action, Downs pins the object in the copter's spotlight beam. The object rapidly ascends to the helicopter's altitude (about five hundred feet) and discharges three, fist-sized "fireballs" in the copter's direction, to no apparent effect. As Graham wheels away, the object disappears. **Note**: Graham and Downs, as well as two officers who observed the dogfight from the ground, agreed that the object reacted to the helicopter with intent, approaching and then backing off, executing tight loops, and exhibiting unexplainable bursts of speed and sudden stops.

8. **January 5, 2000**: Officers from multiple towns near Scott AFB (southeast of Shiloh, Illinois) investigate a civilian report of a large, flying object lined with rows of windows. Lebanon, Illinois, Officer Ed Barton is the first to respond; he observes a pair of bright lights that finally reveal themselves as components of a massive triangular-shaped craft some seventy-five feet long and forty-five feet across. On the object's underside, each corner is illuminated by a large, circular white light; the approximate center of the underside carries a smaller, blinking red light. The craft shows another red light at the center of its aft edge. The thing is noiseless, but Barton is more impressed by its ability to rotate without banking, as if on an invisible pivot. The craft's vertical midline is described by a single band of light with multiple, melded colors. Shiloh officer David Martin gets a similar impression a few miles away, and notes that the object's speed varies between fifteen and one hundred miles per hour. Not long after, two other Illinois officers, from the towns of Millstadt and Dupo, see the craft. **Note**: Although the triangular craft was at one point only two or three miles from Scott AFB, an Air Force representative asserted that Scott radar operators tracked nothing anomalous on January 5. Subsequent research by

NUFORC (National UFO Reporting Center) revealed that Air National Guard F-15 fighters may have been scrambled from nearby Lambert Field, at St. Louis.

9. **March 2002**: For about ten minutes between 7:30 and 8:00 p.m., Officer Brian Roberts and his wife observe a large, saucer-shaped object in the sky about 325 yards from their home in Trawsfynydd, North Wales. Viewed through binoculars, the object shows a brilliant perimeter of light moving in a circular pattern along its vertical midline. Roberts is concerned because the craft hovers near the decommissioned Trawsfynydd nuclear power station.

10. **December 26, 2003**: Three Huntington, Indiana, police officers make a mid-afternoon sighting of a silent, slowly "tumbling" UFO not far from the town's police station. The alternately black and orange object comes out of the north going northeast, and drops so close to a church steeple that Officer Randy Hoover expects it to get hung up there. After less than a minute, the object resumes a northerly course and disappears. **Note**: The three officers remarked that the object's shape was amorphous, suggesting a flat disc in some aspects, an oblong in others, and "wings" in still others. Although the object's size could not be precisely estimated, the officers agreed on a diameter of about fifty feet. Pressed by local media, the Huntington and Fort Wayne airports reported that nothing out of the ordinary occurred on December 26.

Conspiracies and Cover-Ups

The Government Tells Lies, Earth Is Hollow, the Men in Black Are Here— and Guess Who Killed Marilyn Monroe?

onspiracy proponent and radio host Alex Jones has said, "No one is safe, do you understand that? Pure evil is running wild everywhere at the highest levels." Jones's interests encompass the Twin Towers disaster (perpetrated by U.S. agents), the assassination of JFK (pulled off by the military-industrial complex), secret banking cartels (gripping the reins of a shadow world government), and more. Like numerous other conspiracy theorists, Jones accepts the existence of many conspiracies—some related to another, others not. The mindset suggests constant, and probably exhausting, vigilance. How, and why, do people comes to believe that invisible forces are conspiring against them? "Dead and Alive: Beliefs in Contradictory Conspiracy Theories," a 2011 paper by University of Kent psychologists Michael Wood, Karen Douglas, and Robbie Sutton, suggests that a preoccupation with conspiracies develops in layers, and that after the first foundational assumption (*This* was perpetrated by *them*), the mind is ready to add subsequent layers, even if some layers contradict earlier ones. What the researchers term the "cabalistic paradigm" is endlessly self-adjusting; once fixed in place, it adapts to suit itself. Once locked in place, conspiracies become "the default explanation for any given event—a unitary, closed-off worldview in which beliefs come together in a mutually supportive network known as a mono-logical belief system."

Tell Me a Story

Why is the mind ready to add those additional layers? Because we love narratives. We don't want unadorned facts, or even unadorned balderdash—we want a story. We *need* a story. We are story-loving and story-telling creatures by nature. And what is a story but a sort of explanation? We long to believe that inexplicable things happen for reasons. Stories engage us, and bring the satisfactions of resolution.

Conspiracy theories are, at their cores, intellectual and emotional muddles; the various parts don't really piece together. The components are bits of outrage, flecks of fear, chunks of confusion. But embedded into narratives, the untidy flotsam acquires the illusion of coherent structure, and encourages the forced, much-desired logic of *this caused that because of the other*—never mind that "this," "that," and "the other" might be plain absurdities or fancies that, in a sensible environment, would remain unrelated and unconnected.

On the other hand, conspiracies do happen, and no one will argue that our government tells us *everything*. We have no need to know certain things; other facts are dangerous for us to know, too complicated for us to make sense of, or so sensitive that to reveal them to the citizenry is tantamount to revealing them to the nation's enemies.

UFO-related conspiracy theories are elaborate and many. Enough of them exist to fuel the dissertations of whole nations of academics involved in the study of psychology, sociology, and anthropology. UFOs are, by definition, unidentified; is that ambiguity sufficient to assume they are sinister, as well? For some, the answer must be "yes." Theories linked to conjecture about UFO-related schemes devised and carried out by "invisible" powers are part of what some call dark side theories. The 1947 incident at Roswell has encouraged a particularly robust—and dark—conspiracy mindset. Has Washington told us everything about Roswell? It is impossible to say, but the fact that early official responses were weak and contradictory has encouraged people to feel that much of the truth about Roswell was covered up, and that government's role in the affair was purposely obfuscated. However, garbled early responses from officials may be just that, and indicative of lazy thinking and poor internal communication rather than part of a purposeful attempt to conceal or mislead. Then there is the possibility that Washington lied about Roswell in 1947 and continues to lie about it nearly seventy years later. Because conspiracy theories flourish on a presumed lack of honesty, they are predicated on voids, negatives. Sophisticated observers can analyze and, possibly, refute untrue things commonly accepted as facts. But purposeful misinformation, and a *lack* of information, are meaningfully examined only with difficulty, and may require knowledge and resources that are unavailable to most people, even in the Internet age.

Horror in New Mexico

Some observers cite the mid-1960s as the period when the National Security Agency (NSA) initiated secret contact with extraterrestrials. During the 1970s, Paul Bennewitz, a New Mexico businessman who had studied physics, aggressively argued for this idea, claiming that NSA perfidy allowed aliens to impose secret agendas on humans, via electromagnetic waves. Bennewitz operated a company called Thunder Scientific Corporation, which manufactured temperature and humidity controls for the U.S. military. Thunder maintained its facilities just outside the perimeter of Kirtland AFB, which is, by car, three hours northwest of Roswell. Bennewitz himself, he claimed in correspondence, bore physical scars left by the touch of an alien "surveillance sphere"—one of thousands operated by extraterrestrials to keep track of potential troublemakers. Further, aliens had free use of U.S. military infrastructure in return for advanced technology.

Bennewitz described the aliens as "vindictive" and "warlike," and dedicated to the creation of "mass unrest" and a principle of "total control or kill." He took pains to make clear that these extraterrestrials were not the familiar grays linked to everyday abductions, but another, more rapacious species. The alien ruling structure, Bennewitz explained, combined elements of monarchy and autocracy. Top leaders approached one thousand years of age. Domination of discrete generations of humans is a short-term tactic in the service of a long-term strategy. By the rules of UFO-alien conspiracy theories, the mind-control aliens are in it for the long haul.

In a dramatic stroke, Bennewitz identified a secret underground base at Dulce, New Mexico. Humans and extraterrestrials operated Dulce Base jointly, he said, for numerous purposes, but primarily for 1) the development and nurture of alien embryos, and 2) pursuit of unchallenged domination of Earth. In the minds of the Dulce aliens and their human collaborators, the greater human population exists to provide wombs and disposable slaves (many of the latter directed by implanted brain transceivers).

According to the "breeder" train of thought, generations of human-alien hybrids have cycled in and out of secret birthing hostels. Some breeder theorists describe alien activity with primates that existed before human beings—the ancient astronaut notion with a revolting twist. Many of these "hybridists" claim that human-alien breeding continues today. (Consider, however, that no reason at all exists to suggest that alien DNA would mesh with human DNA; a human-alien hybrid is impossible, just as the coupling of a spider with a centipede—assuming that that sort of romance were physically possible—would result in . . . nothing.) Claims of government-condoned vivisection and interspecies rape are not uncommon. Particularly sinister theories insist that unscrupulous humans allow extraterrestrials access to human children, for uses too awful to ponder.

In the late 1980s, Bennewitz prepared Project Beta, a quasi-military white paper describing strategy and tactics designed to render Dulce Base inoperable. Because alien body temperature normally runs ten to fifteen degrees higher than the human norm, the creatures require frequent hydration. Control of water to the base is thus critical. If an attack on Dulce was to succeed, nearby dams had to be secured first. But even thirsty aliens would have to be physically confronted and overcome. To that end, Bennewitz promised that a new company, Bennewitz Labs, Ltd., would research, develop, and manufacture startling new weapons designed to engage the aliens and disable their powerful flying discs. With this objective accomplished, conventional weapons would be sufficient to mop up any extraterrestrials that survived.

Plot and Counterplot

Bennewitz gleaned some of his background information, including photographs, from a USAF intelligence operative named Richard Doty, who was probably engaged in a disinformation campaign aimed at Bennewitz, to encourage claims that could be easily refuted. (Doty also led documentary filmmaker Linda Moultin Howe astray in 1983, promising her access to an extraterrestrial . . . but no ET ever materialized. It is alleged that sometime before the 1987 publication of Whitley's Strieber's alien-abduction blockbuster *Communion*, Doty gave Strieber calculatedly false information about aliens.)

If Richard Doty deceived Bennewitz, Doty wasn't alone. In the course of a July 1989 MUFON lecture in Las Vegas, travel writer and UFOlogist William Moore admitted feeding Bennewitz erroneous information, to encourage his activity. Discredited and neutralized, the hoodwinked Bennewitz would fall even further to the margins, allowing reasonable discussion of UFOs to continue without distraction.

We must add that many accounts of Bennewitz-Doty-Moore exist, and they do not always jibe. Character issues are especially variable: some accounts paint Bennewitz as a hopeless paranoiac, and Doty and Moore take roles ranging from deceitful villains to principled activists. The truth of all that cannot be determined here, though Bennewitz's relative silence after 1988—when he was briefly committed to a mental hospital—suggests that his activities turned out to be, for one reason or another, more dramatic than he could comfortably handle. Paul Bennewitz died of natural causes in 2003, at age seventy-five.

Others came forward to pick up where Bennewitz left off. A man named Thomas Edwin Castello claimed to have been a Dulce Base security officer—though precisely when he held that job is a little hazy. Castello explained that Dulce began as an ancient network of natural caverns that was later used, for centuries, by white or beige reptilian humanoids Castello called "the Draco." Much more recently (as Castello explained things), the RAND Corporation supervised a refit and enlargement of the caverns; this work took place early in the RAND Corp's existence (the think tank was established in 1948), when the only RAND client was the U.S. Air Force. A secret Washington "Black Budget" financed this early work, and funds continue to be drawn from that source today.

Additional aspects of the Dulce tale, invoked by Bennewitz, Castello, and others, include hapless grays in the employ of the Draco; secret bases on the Moon and Mars; the inevitable "world government" hanky-panky perpetrated by Masons, the Illuminati, the Trilateral Commission et al., and sponsored by aliens; ancillary bases at Los Alamos (where most of the alien and human-alien flying discs are stored), Salt Lake City, and Antarctica (with the familiar Nazi-saucer connection); and secret tunnel egress in states across the West, Great Plains, and Midwest. Dulce is also the focal point of internecine quarrels involving the Draco, reptilians, and aliens from an assortment of star systems across the Milky Way.

Rebellion

A poorly armed uprising of captive humans and rebel reptilian workers (green, rather than the white or beige varieties) at Dulce was crushed by American Delta Force troops working with the Draco; some sixty rebels died in the fight. As with the dates of Castello's employment at Dulce Base, the date of this uprising is impossible to pin down, though Philip Schneider, an American explosives engineer who claims to have worked at the base, gives the date as 1979. Unfortunately, Schneider cannot elaborate because he is said to have committed suicide.

In the late 1980s, a UK UFO-research group, Quest International, revealed the so-called Dulce Papers, which discuss the science and biology behind the Dulce disc and breeding programs. Included with the papers were about two dozen black-and-white photographs of the base interior, and a silent, six-minute videotaped "tour" of the facility.

Thomas Edwin Castello disappeared shortly after the appearance of the Dulce Papers. Some Dulce theorists claim he was murdered by the U.S. government; others claim that Castello went into hiding alone, without his immediate family, all of whom were killed. One UFO chat forum, alien-ufos.com, reports that Castello was alive in 2009, but had terminal cancer, and likely died sometime during 2010–2011.

Bennewitz's Dulce Base account has outlived him, and enjoys some life in pop culture. In "Dukakis and the Aliens," a 1992 alternate-history short story by Robert Sheckley, President Michael Dukakis has special interest in Dulce because Dukakis is an alien. (That may explain the ineptitude of Dukakis's real-world 1988 presidential campaign.) Elements of the fictional television series *V* (1984–85 and 2009) reflected (according to some sources) elements of the Dulce story. *Colony*, a 2016 series produced by USA Network, is predicated on human cooperation with ETs.

The Dulce story has received lightweight coverage on *Conspiracy Theory with Jesse Ventura*; *Ancient Aliens*; *Unsealed: Alien Files*; and other cable-TV infotainment programs. An April 2014 *Huffington Post* article about the purported rebellion and massacre, did not regard the rebellion, the public disclosure, or much else about Dulce Base with seriousness. The piece is cheekily titled "That Time Subterranean Aliens Killed 60 People in New Mexico." The unnamed writer closes the article with this: "The truth is out there . . . or is it? It is. Maybe. But, probably not. Or it could be."

Incident at Rendlesham Forest

Today, nearly forty years after the incident, this is the official stance of Britain's Ministry of Defence:

> No evidence was found of any threat to the defence of the United Kingdom, and no further investigations were carried out. No further information has come to light which alters our view that the sightings of these lights was of no defence significance.

And so the MoD writes off "Britain's Roswell," the December 26–27 and 28, 1980, sightings that, in the minds of many, resist easy explanation.

The Encounter

The United States Air Force established a tactical air wing at Royal Air Force Woodbridge (located in Suffolk County, England) in 1952. During 1952–80, the British-American venture brought various fighter-bomber wings and support aircraft to the base at a time when NATO was consolidating its activities in Western Europe. Besides hosting squadrons of fighter-bombers, Woodbridge provided access to USAF B-47 Stratojet bombers and KC-97 Stratofreighter refueling tankers. In 1958, USAF activity at Woodbridge expanded to encompass another RAF base, located nearby at Bentwaters. By 1970, Woodbridge and Bentwaters were available to C-130 Hercules transport aircraft and HH-53B "Jolly Green Giant" combat search-and-rescue helicopters. Nineteen eighty brought six squadrons of A-10 Thunderbolt II "Warthogs"—a fearsome close-support aircraft dreaded by enemy infantry and tank corps; the Thunderbolts were divided between Woodbridge and Bentwaters.

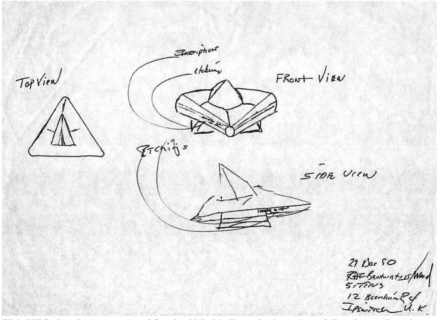

This UFO sketch was prepared for the U.S. Air Force by American S/Sgt. James Penniston, who was part of a USAF air wing posted to Royal Air Force Woodbridge. Early in the morning of December 26, 1980, when he and another American airman stepped into Rendlesham Forest to investigate a peculiar illumination, Penniston goggled at a black, delta-shaped craft, about ten feet by ten feet, that hovered close to the forest floor. "Rendlesham Forest" remains the most celebrated British UFO incident.   *USAF*

At about 3:00 a.m. on December 26, 1980, USAF personnel at Woodbridge reported unexplained lights in and above nearby Rendlesham Forest. Reports suggested that the illumination alternated between white, blue, red, and orange. USAF security police dispatched three men to investigate: S/Sgt. James Penniston, A1C (Airman First Class) Ed Cabansag, and A1C John Burroughs. As Cabansag remained with the truck to monitor the radio, Penniston and Burroughs entered the piney woods. Distant farm animals reacted to the lights (or possibly, just to the presence of the men) with lowing and other vocalizations. As Penniston and Burroughs stepped closer to the pulsating lights, the illumination retreated a bit, and then hovered at the tree line. Shortly, the object settled to the forest floor, where Penniston could clearly see its "triangular" (delta) shape and "smooth, opaque black glass" surface.

The air around Penniston and Burroughs seemed heavy with current, as if the forest were highly charged with static electricity. Though apprehensive, Penniston put out his hand and touched the peculiar glyphs etched onto the craft. The symbols had a rough texture that contrasted with the skin's general smoothness.

Penniston's hand rested on the craft for just a moment—but long enough for him to gain a sensation of missing or distorted time. When the craft suddenly flashed with brilliant illumination, Penniston was temporarily blinded; he and Burroughs retreated. Penniston regained his vision in time to see the craft lift off and depart.

Drawings prepared to accompany Penniston's witness statement depict a delta-shaped craft—noted by Penniston as about ten feet across and ten feel high—topped by a short obelisk. In his 2014 book *Encounter in Rendlesham Forest*, Penniston wrote, "I left the forest a different man. . . . I was in awe of the technology. . . ."

The Halt Tape, and a Conversation

USAF Lt. Col. Charles Halt, deputy base commander at RAF Woodbridge, felt skeptical about the December 26 sightings. On December 27, he entered Rendlesham Forest with an audio recorder, expecting to discover nothing at all, or something easily explainable. Instead, he was dazzled by a display of bright lights in the forest, and above the Woodbridge air base. The audio runs for eighteen minutes, and throughout most of Halt's running commentary, he refers to the lights as "it." And then comes this remarkable sentence: "[H]e's coming toward us now."

The lights had become "he"—evocative of a living thing or, alternatively, technology controlled by an unrevealed intelligence.

In a January 13, 1981, memo, Halt described the event with reasonable dispassion, but in a tone suggesting that he took the sightings seriously. In a notarized statement from 2010, Halt said,

> I believe the objects that I saw at close quarter were extraterrestrial in origin and that the security services of both the United States and the United Kingdom have attempted—both then and now—to subvert the significance of what occurred at Rendlesham forest [sic] and RAF Bentwaters by the use of well-practiced methods of disinformation.

Twenty-five years after the events, Halt claimed that British radar operating on December 27 picked up strange objects. Radar techs on duty that night remained mum for fear of ridicule, or worse, but once retired, they felt free to share their stories with Halt.

Lieutenant Colonel Halt's superior, Col. Theodore Conrad, commanded the twin bases near Rendlesham. Like Halt, he conducted a brief personal investigation immediately after the events of 1980. In 2009, Conrad agreed to speak with academic journalist and folklorist David Clarke. He remarked that Halt "should be ashamed and embarrassed" by his allegations of an international cover-up.

The Rendlesham Forest had still more to tell. After 11:00 p.m. on December 28, one or more trucks carrying British military men trundled to the forest edge. Larry Warren, a teenage enlisted man, witnessed what he called "disaster-preparedness officers" with Geiger counters, bending over an object on the ground near the tree line. And then a small red light—about the size of a basketball, Warren recalled—heralded the landing of a craft. Warren and another man, Sgt. Adrian Bustinza, observed as Wing Commander Gordon Williams subsequently engaged in quiet conversation with a humanoid kitted out in "bright clothing."

When superiors called Warren away at about 4:30 a.m. on December 29, Bustinza remained to witness the craft's queerly silent departure. After some moments of hover, the craft "went up and, like, took off at about a forty-five-degree angle." The thing disappeared in an eye-blink.

The next morning, radiation levels at the forest site registered unusually high.

Gen. Charles Gabriel, commander in chief of United States Air Forces in Europe at the time of Rendlesham, visited the bases not long after the initial reports. Some sources allege that the papers related to Gabriel's visits were snatched from the MoD files by the U.S. military.

In 1992–93, when the Cold War was presumed to have ended, the USAF departed Woodbridge and Bentwaters. The RAF closed both bases in 1993. Rupert Hawsley's 2014 article for London's *Daily Telegraph* revealed that since 1980 "nearly half" of all UFO correspondence and inquiries directed to the Ministry of Defence pertain to Rendlesham. Despite the high level of public interest, the MoD has not modified its stance.

Throughout the USAF presence at Woodbridge and Bentwaters, speculation arose that America secretly stored nuclear missiles there. If the USA had indeed sneaked another cache of missiles close to the European Continent, the MoD denials would have been equal parts military and political.

The Binary Code

Besides drawings, Sergeant Penniston later filled sixteen pages of a palm-sized, six-ring notebook with strings of zeros and ones—binary code. The sergeant wasn't "aware" of his pencil scribbles' meaning; he simply felt compelled to write down *specific patterns* of zeros and ones. Images of zeros and ones entered his mind, Penniston said, because he had touched the indecipherable glyphs. Years passed, and then, during a 2010 conversation with a retired computer systems engineer named Joe Luciano, Penniston mentioned the notebook pages he had filled with numerals. Luciano asked to analyze the pages. Penniston agreed, and following research conducted during 2011–12, Luciano arrived at what he called a "decoded and interpreted message." (Luciano did not transcribe Penniston's zeros and ones exactly as Penniston had written them; rather, Luciano made subjective allowance for "transmission errors" and "excess bit anomalies," adjusting some of Penniston's patterns and arriving at "logically and mathematically correct 8-bit binary ASCII." Luciano continued, "This has also translated to a mathematically consistent set of latitude/longitude geographic coordinates."

The message, as massaged and interpreted by Luciano, is a brief conglomeration of words and numerals, headed with, "EXPLORATION OF HUMANITY 666 8100." Sentence fragments with the words "PLANETARY" and "FOURTH COORDINATE" are followed by geographic coordinates (noted below) and these words:

EYES OF YOUR EYES

ORIGIN 52

ORIGIN YEAR 8100

It is impossible to know whether this text-and-numbers translation is an accurate reflection of the information relayed to Penniston; or merely a hopeful translation suggesting ideas that Luciano wished to see, or that he assumed others wished to see. Of course, the whole enterprise is pointless if Penniston had felt no compelling urge to write specific patterns of zeros and ones, and simply wrote zeros and ones at random. As with the nature of Luciano's translation, it is impossible to know how the ex-sergeant arrived at the sequences. At any rate, "EXPLORATION OF HUMANITY," as well as the phrase invoking eyes, seem swollen with significance; likewise "ORIGIN 52," which inevitably leads the layperson to ponder how the beginning of things relates to the number of weeks in a year. "PLANETARY" apparently confirms an extraterrestrial origin of the Rendlesham craft.

With "666," Penniston/Luciano facilitate the conversation's drift into the generally discredited superstitious aspect of apocalyptic Christianity. Did the alien visitors invoke 666 as a reflection of a human belief, and if so, is the invocation a taunt or a warning? Perhaps 666 has significance for the aliens, as well as for us. Or perhaps *our* ideas about 666 have no relation whatever to the aliens'.

"666" is immediately followed in the message by "8100"; the latter number reappears at the end of the message's text portion, and is suggestive of a year (to our minds). But which calendar is at play here? Does 8100 connote our future, our past, or a time that carries significance for the aliens only? Perhaps 8100 refers to something other than a date or time.

The aforementioned geographic coordinates cite, according to Luciano, Hy Brasil (a fabulous, and wholly mythic, super-civilization on a now-lost island off the coast of ancient Ireland, thought by some to be a portal to another world); as well as locations in Belize (Caracol); Arizona (Sedona); Peru (Nazca Lines); China

(Tai Shan Qu); Greece (the Portara at the unfinished temple to Apollo in Naxos); and, perhaps inevitably, the Great Pyramids at Giza, Egypt.

Each of the extant locations uncovered by Luciano is the site of notable and much studied UFO events. Is that dubiously convenient, or just unavoidable?

For Joe Luciano's exhaustive technical explanation of his translation methods and results, see Luciano's Web site, binarydecoder.info.

Despite—or perhaps because of—Luciano's labors, Britain's Ministry of Defence had nothing new to say about Rendlesham. As with the original MoD files, which showed no official interest or investigation at all—the latter-day reaction has been a nullity. If this suggests a cover-up, the tactics are maddeningly passive-aggressive. No hypervigilant denials, no labored alternate theories . . . just nothing.

Some persons outside the MoD surmise that the whole Rendlesham event was a hoax; or the headlights of a military vehicle; or the nearby Orford Ness lighthouse. Feel free to select one or add an explanation of your own. Britain's Forestry Commission decided to play along with the ET explanation, establishing a Rendlesham UFO Trail in 2005, complete with a UFO-inspired art installation.

The case inspired books other than Penniston's, including investigative journalist Georgina Bruni's *You Can't Tell the People* (2000), which levies the charge of deception against the CIA, and claims that that agency undercut witnesses by artificially inducing memories and amnesia. (The late Bruni, whose birth name was Linda Naylor, maintained a busy schedule as a private investigator and professional writer. Other than her Rendlesham book, she is best recalled for her online magazine *Hot Gossip*.) A 2012 "displaced detective" novel by Stephanie Osborn, *The Case of the Cosmological Killer: The Rendlesham Incident*, inserts a time-traveling Sherlock Holmes into the story.

Television adapted the Rendlesham event for episodes of the pseudo-documentary programs *Sightings* (1993), *Strange but True* (1994), *UFO Files* (2005), *Paranormal Witness* (2011), and *Alien Mysteries* (2013), plus various one-off quasi-documentaries, e.g., *Britain's Closest Encounters* (2003). A fictionalized TV-movie, *UFO Invasion at Rendlesham*, retold the story in 2003. *Close Encounters*, a fictionalized documentary series, handled the subject in an episode broadcast in 2014.

Did JFK Die for UFOs?

No other recent event has encouraged as robust a conspiracy industry as Lee Harvey Oswald's 1963 shooting of John Kennedy. Books alleging conspiracies of various motivations and complexities are almost literally numberless. Standard suspects encompass Lyndon Johnson, Fidel Castro, racist crackers, the John Birch Society, the international Jewish conspiracy, the CIA, the KGB, defense contractors, multiple shooters, Oswald impersonators, the Mob, and even a Secret Service agent detailed to the motorcade (as we'll see later in this chapter). Some of the conspiracy books are carefully researched and vetted, and raise challenging questions. Others are plainly absurd, hysterical, or the work of the unschooled or demented. (Although self-publishing platforms bring some of this material to [a tiny] market, much of the material is posted directly to the Internet, and never appears in book form.)

Inevitably, some JFK conspiracy theorists claim links between the Dallas event and UFOs. The connective tissues are a pair of memos, dated November 12, 1963 (ten days before the president's death), and sent by Kennedy to the CIA and NASA. At the time, Kennedy was exploring the possibility of space-program cooperation with the Soviet Union, and he wanted to see classified data about UFOs. He was interested in UFO reports that could not be attributed to traditional aircraft or tests of secret American aircraft. His concern reflects the value of standard risk assessment. Kennedy's concern was that the Soviets might misinterpret UFOs as breaches of the (proposed) partnership, or even as spy devices.

The memos are not unreasonable. Nor are they quite as interesting as assassination-UFO advocates believe. The White House made a request for esoteric, classified information. In that, the memos are little different from White House interest in, for example, American intelligence activity in Turkey, the speed with which Chrysler Corporation could ramp up tank production in case of renewed crisis in Berlin, the identities of KGB agents masquerading as diplomats around the Free World, or the true GNP of Bulgaria.

Regardless, conspiracy theorists made (and make) a leap of logic, insisting that because of a possible cover-up at Roswell, and because JFK wanted to know more about UFOs, it follows that the president was murdered by schemers anxious to protect the secret of human-alien connivance in the development of weapons systems (another leap); or the existence of alien bases on the dark side of the Moon (variously belonging to humans, humans and aliens, or aliens operating alone).

Long after the assassination, a USAF loadmaster assigned to Air Force One claimed to have asked the president what he thought about UFOs. According to the crewman (his name was Bill Holden), Kennedy took a long pause before gravely replying, "I'd like to tell the public about the alien situation, but my hands are tied." (This is an amusing echo of the frustrated airline pilot of Ed Wood's *Plan 9 from Outer Space*, who complains to his wife, "I saw a flying saucer. . . . Oh, it burns me up! These things have been seen for years. They're here, it's a fact. And the public ought to know about it. . . . But I can't say a word! I'm muzzled by army brass!")

Skeptics insist that Holden, as a loadmaster busy at the ass end of the aircraft, would have had no opportunity to interact with the president. (Holden claimed to have been an on-board steward as well as a loadmaster, an impossibility). Beyond that, the thought of Kennedy confiding top secret regrets to a crewman is risible. Yet this supposed encounter is a frequently cited part of Kennedy-UFO lore.

Some buffs claim that Kennedy planned to go "off speech" at the Dallas Trade Mart on November 22, putting aside his prepared remarks in favor of his own handwritten notes, to which he would refer when he revealed the truth about UFOs. (The notes have never been found.) Whatever the particulars, President Kennedy had to be eliminated. By signing off on the CIA and NASA memos, he signed his own execution order.

This kind of thinking has the grade-B fun factor of those splashy intrigue novels found at airport bookstalls. Sensible readers grasp (and happily accept) the inherent improbability of such tales. Conspiracy theorists, though, demand to be taken seriously, suggesting calamity if we fail to pay attention, and implicitly criticizing our supposed naïveté by defending their positions via liberal use of "certainly," "obviously," "of course," "There is no doubt," "naturally," and other certitudes that are nothing more than wishful assumptions.

Kennedy's presumed involvement with UFOs goes all the way back to the first days of Roswell itself. A supposed July 1947 MJ-12 memo dubbed "Interplanetary Phenomenon Unit Summary" reveals that Massachusetts congressman John F. Kennedy has been made privy to secret Roswell information—and was, in fact, the *only* House member to have the information. Given that Kennedy was just twenty-nine years old, a young man with little initial enthusiasm for politics, a freshman representative with barely a half year in office, and a rich kid whose father may have purchased the congressional seat he occupied, this level of insider status is remarkable. Preposterous, even.

In 1993, researcher Robert Wood got hold of what he described as a fire-scorched Majestic 12 memo supposedly written by CIA head John McCone thirty years before. (For more on Majestic 12, see chapter eight.) The memo reads, "As you must know, Lancer [the Secret Service's code name for JFK] has made some inquiries regarding our activities, which we cannot allow. Please submit your views no later than October. Your action to this matter is critical to the continuance of the group."

"The group" is an especially pungent pair of words, suggestive in this context of a cabal or a secret society. Because the memo's intended recipient is unknown, conspiracy buffs are free to speculate on precisely who and what "the group" might have been. A partnership of aliens and the CIA? The CIA and NASA? The government, arms makers, and aliens?

JFK-UFO speculation reached a particularly large audience during the 1996–97 run of *Dark Skies*, a fictional NBC-TV series in which Kennedy is killed after learning that the Hive—a malevolent, spiderlike alien race—conspires to take over Earth.

Some sources (exopolitics.org is one) work backwards from the Kennedy-UFO conspiracy to the August 1962 death of actress Marilyn Monroe, who was sexually involved with JFK (likely enough) and murdered by government operatives (most unlikely) a day or two before she planned to call a press conference and go public with UFO information gleaned from the president.

A proportionally insignificant number of Kennedy assassination books refute the standard conspiracy theories. The two best are Gerald Posner's *Case Closed: Lee Harvey Oswald and the Assassination of JFK* (1993) and Vincent Bugliosi's mammoth *Reclaiming History* (2007). Neither book mentions flying saucers, UFOs, extraterrestrials, or Roswell. Posner makes no mention of NASA; Bugliosi does, but only in discussions of the U-2 spy plane and the *Challenger* shuttle disaster. Are those omissions significant?

Those Dapper Men in Black

Black. This color—often described as the *absence* of color—connotes authority, competence, and sophistication. But over the centuries, black has also been the color of criminality, evil, fright, and death. Black mass. Black widow. Black plague and black lung. Crime's Black Hand society. Blackmail. The driver's hazard called black ice. Blacklist and black market. Black ops.

The last refers to military/intelligence operations built around secrecy. Anyone caught in the crosshairs of a black ops mission—as designated target or as someone who has revealed the operation's workings—can expect dire consequences. To many in the UFO community, black designates Men in Black—intimidating, anonymous figures that appear, seemingly from nowhere, to warn UFO witnesses to keep quiet about what they have seen. Usually, Men in Black (MiB) are variously thought to be representatives of 1) the American government and/or its intelligence agencies, 2) a secret hybrid government controlled by Washington and extraterrestrials, 3) a secret society of humans, antipathetic to Washington and other governments, that pursues world domination, or 4) aliens (probably malevolent) that wish to squelch chatter about their activities on Earth.

An early documented encounter with MiB occurred in Wales in 1905, when a young woman who saw a strange flying craft was shortly visited by a mysterious, dark-clad man. Sightings of peculiar aircraft (many were airships) had been common in Europe since the late 1800s, but the Wales story had the added fillip of the mysterious emissary. A local newspaper, the *Barmouth Advertiser*, reported, "In the neighborhood dwells an exceptionally intelligent young woman of the peasant stock, whose bedroom has been visited three nights in succession by a man dressed in black. This figure has delivered a message to the girl which she is too frightened to relate."

Little more than that is known of the encounter, although it is a certainty that *other* men in black were in Wales in 1905: the members of New Zealand's touring All Blacks rugby team. Named for their black uniforms, the All Blacks were informally called the men in black. Whether this spurred the young woman's imagination or is a simple coincidence is unknown.

MiB accounts more typically belong to the postwar era, when futurism and public awareness of the destructive abilities of science inspired people to be more aware than before of what was in the skies. Kenneth Arnold's 1947 saucer sighting, and news reports from Roswell the same year, further pushed peoples' gaze skyward. UFO sightings multiplied.

Intimidation and the "Weird" Factor

UFOlogist Albert K. Bender established the International Flying Saucer Bureau (IFSB) in the spring of 1952. He used the October 1953 issue of his magazine *Space Review* to warn his readers that they would place themselves in danger if they reported sightings of UFOs. (Magazines are advance-dated, so this issue went on sale in August.) Bender's piece was a peculiar, and anxious, bit of text, particularly because Bender said that although he had uncovered information proving the existence of flying saucers, he was afraid of being intimidated into silence. *Space Review* ceased publication immediately because (as he related later) a trio of mysterious men in black suits arrived in September 1953 to warn him to stop publishing saucer material *right now*. Bender also dissolved the IFSB.

Bender described himself as having been "scared to death" by his visitors (who threatened him with, among other things, summary transport to prison). Although he was sufficiently mindful of the threats to suspend much of his activity, Bender did give interviews later, claiming that the MiB had informed him that the government would reveal all about the aliens within four years, that is, by 1956.

Accounts of MiB came to an initial peak throughout the 1950s and 1960s with Gray Barker's 1956 book *They Knew Too Much About Flying Saucers*, an early and enduring classic. (*Not of This Earth*, a superior 1957 B-movie from director Roger Corman, is dominated by a sullen Man in Black, a burly businessman type who has come from the planet Davanna to harvest humans for "blood pasturing.") Gray Barker formalized the notion of dark-clad strangers, and filled his book with shakily verified stories of flying saucer publications intimidated into suspending operations. Although now dismissed by some as lightweight, even campy, Barker's volume captures a meaty portion of the distressed, sometimes paranoiac thought that crept across Cold War America.

The author's rough sketch of one of the three men. The eyes glowed like two flashlight bulbs.

In 1962, Albert Bender was back, with a book of great significance to MiB studies, *Flying Saucers and the Three Men*. In it, Bender asserted he had been abducted and flown to the South Pole. The aliens' goal, he explained, was extraction of vital elements from Earth's water. Bender further used his book to explain that MiB were not human agents, but extraterrestrials. He revealed that the MiB showed up in 1953 and revealed to him the source of flying saucers—information apparently so momentous that an intimidated Bender did not

Intimidated into silence in 1953 by what he described as ominous "men in black," UFOlogist Albert K. Bender nevertheless sketched one of his antagonists. In the sixty-plus years since, Men in Black have become familiar elements of UFO study and speculation.   *Alamy* require threats of imprisonment to hold his tongue. A clue to the nature of the situation, though, is Bender's stated conviction that "his" MiB had been sent by the U.S. government. Indeed, some in the UFO community are convinced that Bender was visited by CIA agents, not MiB. The thinking that supports this belief is that U.S. intelligence had been concerned with Bender's IFSB, particularly its attempts to plot the courses of UFOs and trace them back to their bases.

As MiB encounters multiplied during the 1950s, similarities became apparent, as if the mysterious men had all read the same employee handbook. Although some MiB appear from, seemingly, nowhere, they typically arrive in large, four-door sedans painted black. The cars are generally unadorned, sometimes with clear deliberation manifested in blacked-out trim and plain "dog-dish" wheel covers, or no wheel covers at all. Windshields may be grayed out, and side glass is often tinted or completely blacked out. Police-style whip antennas are occasionally seen. In keeping with the notion that MiB originate in Washington or are contracted by people who are professionally active there, the cars are almost invariably American. Although no longer produced, a pair of law-enforcement favorites, the Ford Crown Victoria and Mercury Marquis, still figure in MiB incidents. Of more recent automobile models cited in reports, Dodge Chargers and Chevrolet Impalas are particularly familiar. The MiB that visited UFOlogist John Keel arrived in a Cadillac. Witnesses with the means to trace license plates usually find that the ones on MiB vehicles are unregistered or phony.

MiB automobiles may be joined by hovering black helicopters. The "black" in that descriptor is a direct reflection of the previously mentioned "black ops." The U.S. military does not paint its copters that color, so black helicopters seen in conjunction with MiB are disguised or in the employ of civilian agencies. The Sikorsky UH-60 Black Hawk is frequently cited as a "black helicopter."

Thanks to the popular "Men in Black" and "Matrix" film series of recent years, public perception of MiB is one of carefully groomed, physically robust persons dressed in unimaginative but well-tailored black suits. The popular image also invokes sunglasses and, sometimes, fedoras. But during the 1950s and into the '60s, another, less hardy type came to the fore. Some UFO witnesses who received MiB noted that the visitors arrived wearing rumpled, ill-fitting suits that hung loosely on the men's slight frames. These MiB had a queerly deferential manner, as well: no strong-arm men, these fellows; no, they discreetly knocked on the doors of the people they had come to see, and did not enter home or apartment until they were invited inside. Many walked with a stiff or otherwise unnatural gait.

In normal light the MiB were very pale, even sickly. Some witnesses reported a slight Asian cast to facial features; others recalled "bug eyes." The men's skin was dry and fragile, causing John Keel to dub this breed of MiB "the cadavers." (Keel clarified his position by saying the MiB represent a paranormal entity that has meddled with people since the human race began.) The hats and sunglasses gave these undernourished MiB an unintended comic air—though all of that went out the window when the men began to speak, and gave their warnings. Speech might be halting, or monotone—and the warnings were intended to be taken seriously.

MiB Evolution

Relatively few American claims of MiB surfaced between 1970 and 1990, though the '70s saw increased MiB activity in Mexico, Brazil, and Spain. Alien visitors may have been intrigued (or troubled) by the Mexican government's brutal war against leftist students in the early '70s. As the conflict cooled later in the decade, and the Mexican government legalized progressive political parties, UFO and MiB activity there diminished. In a similar vein, Brazil's military dictatorship, and the fascist government in Spain during that country's often-violent transition to democracy, could have encouraged increased UFO and MiB activity in those countries, particularly during 1970–75, when tensions were at their highest.

By 1967, Men in Black had captured the attention of the USAF and Project Blue Book. The military's concern was the impersonation of government officials (black suits) or Air Force officers (uniforms the imposters were not entitled to wear). Col. George Freeman, Blue Book spokesman in 1967, acknowledged that the Air Force was eager to get its hands on any of these imposters. On March 1 of the same year, USAF Lt. General Hewitt T. Wheless sent a memo to numerous agencies in the Department of Defense. He seemed even more concerned about MiB than the people at Blue Book, expressing dismay that people passing themselves off as civilian agents of NORAD (North American Aerospace Defense Command) "demanded and received" UFO photographs belonging to private citizens. The memo went on to cite an even more brazen act of impersonation, in which a man wearing a USAF uniform "approached local police and other citizens who had sighted a UFO, assembled them in a school room and told them that they did not see what they thought they saw and that they should not talk to anyone about the sighting." Wheless closed the memo with instruction to civilian and military DoD personnel to be alert to such impersonations, and to report instances to the nearest office of the OSI (USAF Office of Special Investigations).

The Man with the Red Mouth

Activities of MiB in the USA did not shrivel to nothing in the '70s. Although frequency began to diminish, the decade produced one of the most detailed of all MiB encounter stories. In 1976, a sixtyish physician named Herbert Hopkins worked as a general practitioner in Old Orchard Beach, Maine. He had an interest in hypnosis, and had used hypnotherapy to help a pair of locals recall their UFO sighting and subsequent abduction. On October 27, 1975, Tripp Pond residents Danny Stephens and a friend now recalled only as Paul were taken aboard a UFO and examined by what the young men described as "a box." Although the abduction seemed brief, Stephens and Paul shortly realized that hours, and not minutes, had passed. Each was further disconcerted by a peculiar orange glow that surrounded—or perhaps originated in—their eyes. The next day, a burly man in a dark suit and sunglasses found the pair's trailer home. Consistent with such meetings, the MiB ordered the men to say nothing about their experience.

The bravado of youth (Stephens was just twenty-one) encouraged the pair to see Hopkins, who grew excited when hypnotic regression filled gaps in Stephen and Paul's memories. On the evening of September 11, 1976 (eleven months after Hopkins's session with Stephens and Paul), the doctor took a nighttime phone call at his home from a man who identified himself as a leader of the New Jersey UFO Research Organization. The caller requested a brief visit. Hopkins complied.

The caller showed up just moments later (cell phones did not exist at the time), and Hopkins naturally wondered where the call had originated. In his attire, the visitor conformed to some aspects of the MiB type: black suit, black shoes, white shirt with dark tie. But unlike some MiB, the man filled out his clothes well, and kept his suit and shirt carefully pressed. He eschewed sunglasses (a concession to the night) but covered his hands in gray suede gloves. The man removed his dark hat (whether out of deference or so Hopkins could see him clearly, Hopkins did not know), revealing a bald head. The penetrating aspect of the man's eyes was exaggerated by a lack of eyelashes and eyebrows. His red lips stood out starkly against his deathly white skin. (Later in the visit, the man absently brought a gloved hand to his mouth, and Hopkins was startled to see that the suede came away with a red smear of lipstick. One account claims that when Hopkins looked at his guest more closely, he saw a slit where a human mouth should be.)

The visitor was brusque but polite—though he gave Hopkins a chill when he blandly revealed that he knew how to remove human hearts without leaving a scar. Getting down to business, the man told Hopkins to erase the regression tapes from the previous year. Although the remark about hearts still hung in the air, the visitor expressed his request not as a threat, but as a simple order that the visitor expected to be obeyed. (Hopkins later did as the man instructed.)

And then the visitor performed an impressive parlor trick. He said Hopkins's pocket held two coins. Correct. Hopkins brought them out. The visitor put one aside, and left the other in Hopkins's palm. "Do not look at me," the visitor said, "but at the coin." Hopkins obeyed. In a moment, the coin blurred to blue and shimmered in Hopkins's gaze, as if, he said later, "it was going out of focus."

The coin vanished. Hopkins gave his hand an involuntary flex. He looked at his visitor, who said, "Neither you nor anyone else on this plane will ever see that coin again." (Some accounts substitute "planet" for "plane.")

The man suddenly appeared weary. He said something about his "energy" running low. The visit was over. Hopkins walked with his guest to the door, and felt compelled to close it the moment the man stepped outside. Through the drapes, Hopkins saw a moving, blue-white light in the driveway, but neither heard nor saw an automobile. Marks on the driveway (a dirt or gravel one, presumably) were not consistent with car tires. The next morning, the marks were gone.

For weeks afterward, Hopkins had trouble placing and receiving phone calls. When he reflected on his destruction of the Stephens and Paul tapes, he felt that he did it from compulsion rather than fear.

In a coda to many (but not every) account of Dr. Hopkins's adventure, the doctor's son John, and John's wife Maureen, agreed to meet a peculiar man and woman at a restaurant. The meeting eventually moved to John and Maureen's house, and the strange couple (attired in old-fashioned clothes) behaved more strangely than before. When the woman was inexplicably unable to step around her companion she complained, "I can't move him." John Hopkins went into the kitchen, and the strange man seized the opportunity: he asked Maureen, "What are you made of?" Then he inquired if she had nude photographs of herself.

Assuming this part of the Hopkins narrative is true, it appears that this "MiB" couple needed to brush up on their social skills—or were aliens with no knowledge or interest in such skills.

Manifestations of Folklore

On one occasion, an MiB encounter occurred because of the direction of scholarly research. It was November 1980, and University of Pennsylvania PhD candidate Peter Rojcewicz was investigating the folkloric aspects of UFOs (much in the manner of Carl Jung). Rojcewicz had a late-afternoon encounter in a library with a man in black who approached, as Rojcewicz recalled, "[w]ithout any sound." The stranger wore an oversized black suit, a black, Texas-style string tie, and scuffed black shoes. He walked around Rojcewicz's table, stared through a nearby window, and then sat down. His actions were "mechanical," his accent unorthodox and unidentifiable (though Rojcewicz later recalled it as "European"). Contrary to the nature of many other MiB encounters, the apparent purpose of this visit was to instruct rather than to threaten. Nevertheless, the man became agitated over Rojcewicz's inclination toward the abstract, and loudly said, "Flying saucers are the most important fact of the century, and you're not interested?" At this, Rojcewicz grew alarmed, and noticed—to his dismay—that the library was suddenly, inexplicably empty but for him and the stranger.

The man insisted to Rojcewicz that the central issue of UFO studies was the crafts' simple reality. Folklore, the scholar was told, was merely an interpretive sidelight—an intellectual diversion.

Rojcewicz was undeterred. His 1984 doctoral dissertation is called "The Boundaries of Orthodoxy: A Folkloric Look at the UFO Phenomenon." He went on to teach at the Juilliard School, and hold administrative positions with John F. Kennedy University and Antioch University Seattle. Today, Rojcewicz operates a consulting firm that tutors business executives in holistic leadership. He remains a noted folklorist.

Dr. Rojcewicz said nothing about the odd stranger for many years; indeed, in 1987, when he first published details of his MiB encounter, he wrote his paper in the third person, identifying the scholar as "Mark Elliott" (a name the article identifies as a pseudonym). Rojcewicz later admitted that *he* was Elliott. Regardless, Rojcewicz's published papers invoking the MiB phenomenon apprehend men in black as ancient archetypes, perhaps akin to the three mysterious men that visit Abraham in the Book of Genesis. In Rojcewicz's view, MiB "are part of the extraordinary-encounter continuum—fairies [in the malevolent mold of medieval belief], monsters, ETs, energy forms, flying saucers, flaming crosses," and other oddities. The devil, the professor says, is another MiB analogue. (Dr. Rojcewicz's thoughts about alien abduction are shaped along similar lines; he equates abduction claims to a belief in fairies, and warns that memories of abduction encounters can culminate in "severe depression" and "paralysis, burns, and disorientation.")

It is vital to note, particularly in light of the Rojcewicz/Elliott relationship, that a) Rojcewicz described Mark Elliott as a person who had "never heard or read about" MiB, and b) Rojcewicz's published works do not assume that encounters with MiB are invariably faked, or otherwise not real. To the contrary, he invoked his 1987 paper (called "The 'Men in Black' Experience and Tradition") to remind other folklorists to "seriously entertain the possibility that *a real experience* lies behind traditional belief" [emphasis added]. Personal experience is everything.

Watching the Skies with Hillary

By the 1990s, serious UFOlogists struggled to distance themselves from the conspiracy contingent, but the fact is that voluble fringe players inevitably attract media attention. In April 2015, shortly before Hillary Clinton announced her second run for the presidency, *Mother Jones* magazine blogger A. J. Vicens wrote a piece called "ETs for Hillary: Why UFO Activists Are Excited About Another Clinton Presidency." Vicens described President and Mrs. Clinton's relationship with the late philanthropist Laurance Rockefeller, who urged the president to open classified UFO files. The Clintons were fond of Rockefeller, but in the mid-1990s a White House staffer warned the president and First Lady to avoid prolonged public contact with the man. If they did not, the staffer warned, reporters would link Bill and Hillary with Rockefeller's avowed interest "in extra-sensory perception, paranormal phenomena, and UFOs."

The *Mother Jones* blog caught the eye of *Chicago Tribune* columnist Rex W. Huppke. He contacted a UFO conspiracy theorist named Michael Salla, whose blog, exopolitics.org, studies and reports on "key individuals, political institutions, and processes associated with extraterrestrial life." Salla elaborated on the Hillary tale, telling Huppke about documents "actually verifying that [Hillary Clinton] does have an interest in the UFO issue."

The antipathy held in some quarters for the Clintons—with recent animus directed more frequently at Hillary than at Bill—is expressed partly as conspiracy notions: Hillary's Wall Street connections and her scheme to enslave the world; Hillary's involvement in the murders of more than ninety enemies of the Clintons (see www.theclintonbodycount.com); Hillary's role—perhaps as a mistress—in the 1993 suicide of White House chief of staff Vince Foster; Hillary's penchant for decorating the White House Christmas tree with condoms and vulgar sex toys; her determination to turn America into a theocracy ruled by Scientologists. The rumors go on in this imaginative fashion, encouraging dead-serious conspiracy buffs and wisenheimers alike to concoct more tales.

Around 2010, a man named Tonio Cousyn (described on the Web as a "researcher") looked at 1995 photos of Laurance Rockefeller and Hillary Clinton, snapped at Rockefeller's Wyoming ranch. Hillary cradles a book in her arm as she walks with her host; just a portion of what appears to be the back cover is visible. Cousyn investigated and identified the volume as Paul Davies's 1995 book

Are We Alone? Philosophical Implications of the Discovery of Extraterrestrial Life. Davies is a celebrated physicist with an intense and rational interest in theology. *Are We Alone?* proposes that human discovery of intelligent extraterrestrial life would have rich and positive effects on theology as well as science. Such a discovery would confirm a theory held by Davies and many other scientists—that the universe and its structures tend toward complexity. Intelligent life other than our own would suggest that complexity and, as Davies sees it, "give us cause to believe that we, in our humble way, are part of a larger, majestic self-process of cosmic self-knowledge."

Davies's book was new when Hillary Clinton visited the Rockefeller ranch. Given Rockefeller's well-known interest in extraterrestrial life, we can hardly be surprised that Hillary arrived with (or, perhaps, that Rockefeller gave to her) a copy of *Are We Alone?* Regardless, conspiracy buffs inferred that Hillary Clinton possesses a fevered interest in extraterrestrial life, rather than casual curiosity. Consider this: if Hillary had visited Robin Burruss (president of Georgia's Tip Top Poultry, Inc.), she might have carried a copy of Mack North's *Commercial Chicken Production Manual.* Jumping to a conclusion, we might claim that Mrs. Clinton hoped to one day raise chickens in the White House back yard. Well, that's just dull; a suggested link between Hillary Clinton and extraterrestrial life is considerably more intriguing.

Blog chatter about the Hillary-UFO conspiracy continued throughout the Clinton presidential campaign.

Eyes Only: Fifteen UFO Conspiracy Theories That Won't Go Away

Whatever their preoccupations (JFK! Trilateral Commission! Faked Moon landing! Weather control!), conspiracy theories based in a belief in complex secrecy (to the detriment of society at large) are never easy to prove. Unsympathetic observers can be quick to insist that claimants are paranoid, but to glibly classify a belief as "paranoid" and leave it at that is a little lazy. It's certainly unenlightening. Further, the practice has an unintended leveling effect that makes all paranoia equal—a misstep, because some expressions of paranoia are considerably more reality-based than others.

Of all the conspiracy-oriented belief systems that have shown real endurance, UFO-related theories are among the liveliest. We look at familiar ones, such as Roswell, Men in Black, MJ-12, and Area 51, elsewhere in this book. Here are some others.

1. *J. Edgar Hoover's FBI clamped a lid on credible postwar UFO reports for fear of public panic and unwanted release of American atomic secrets.* A January 31, 1949, FBI memo prepared for Hoover and military intelligence services reports that airspace above the Atomic Energy Commission facility at Los Alamos, New Mexico, was breached by unidentified flying objects during nine mostly non-consecutive days in December 1948. The craft displayed dramatic aerial maneuvers above the high-security facility. The memo also describes near-misses of airliners and UFOs, the latter traveling at "a minimum of three miles per second and a maximum of twelve miles per second." And that, the

memo adds, amounts to a "calculated mean speed" of 27,000 miles per hour. Although the memo makes a token attempt to explain the objects in natural terms ("cosmic rays"), the text more firmly suggests that the objects were "man made," possibly by the Soviets. The memo adds that UFOs, "Unidentified Aerial Phenomena," "Flying Discs," "Flying Saucers," and "Balls of Fire" are regarded by U.S. military intelligence as "top secret." And if the FBI had anything to say about it, they would stay that way.

2. ***Earthlings are slaves to shape-shifting extraterrestrial lizards headquartered in the hollow Earth.*** This notion came to the fore in the early 1990s, when David Icke, a British soccer player cum television broadcaster, pulled together conspiracy notions about religion, finance, politics and governments, science, and media, shaking them into a gigantic Slushie of subjugation in which we sheeple (Icke's term) are duped, manipulated, and controlled by hidden, reptilian aliens. Apologists for hollow Earth acknowledge that the Earth is probably not hollow. But, they add, it is possible (according to them) that the inner Earth is composed of various electromagnetic dimensions and "frequencies" that are invisible to us. The denizens of the hollow Earth exist. We just can't see them. Icke wows receptive audiences at large, concert-style events he stages in Europe and New York.

3. ***President Kennedy and Vice President (later President) Johnson colluded with NASA to secretly send astronauts to the distant planet Serpo.*** Grateful to U.S. military doctors that saved its life at Roswell in 1947, an alien invited Earthlings to visit its people, the Eben, on Serpo—a trip that, according to the alien, would be technologically possible, with shared Eben wormhole technology, by 1965. Twelve American astronauts made the journey during 1964–65. After a visit lasting twelve years (some sources say thirteen or more), two of the astronauts elected to remain on Serpo and explore the planet's wonders; two more died of natural causes. Because Serpo has twin suns that give off radiation dangerous to humans, the eight astronauts that returned to Earth later died. The "Project SERPO" story surfaced in 2005, and had adherents ten years later. In 2013, Len Kasten, a writer interested in astrology and Theosophy (an occult belief system preoccupied with divine wisdom imparted by human messengers), found the Serpo tale sufficiently compelling and marketable to support a book, *Secret Journey to Planet Serpo: A True Story of Interplanetary Travel*.

4. ***Wise aliens representing the Star Nations provided information that allowed the USA to build and launch a secretly orbiting spaceship fleet, code-named Solar Warden.*** A variation on the true-but-shelved "Star Wars" missile-defense initiative, Solar Warden protects Earth from extraterrestrial invasion—which, apparently, is an ongoing threat. The SW spaceships are also on the lookout for terrorist mischief here on the ground. According to this belief, NACA and its follow-on agency, NASA, are mere dummy organizations designed to facilitate, maintain, and obscure the Solar Warden program. Further, the U.S. government works hand in glove with the United Nations (frequently cited as a villainous force behind a great variety of conspiracies) to perpetuate the program.

5. ***Malaysia Airlines Flight MH370 fell prey to UFOs, perhaps in collusion with humans.*** For reasons as yet unknown (at this writing), Malaysia Airlines' Boeing 777

crashed into a remote section of the Indian Ocean on March 8, 2014. What should have been an interlude of sober reportage became a sensationalized, non-stop media rave-up. The chief culprit, the CNN cable news network, regarded the accident as a potential ratings bonanza, and covered it to the exclusion of all other news—for weeks. Because hard facts were elusive, CNN put together endless panels of aviation experts for insights into what *might* have happened. On-air reporters planted themselves inside airliner flight simulators to demonstrate what *could* have brought the plane down. Staff meteorologists chattered endlessly about air currents and storms. Security analysts discussed the possibility of a terrorist act. Political operatives warned of possible international implications. When Malaysian officials stalled in their search for answers, CNN abruptly scaled back its coverage to almost none at all. Although the mass sensationalism had ended, failure to come to a neat resolution encouraged the impatient natures of some conspiracy fans. The UFO-snatch explanation, though marginal, maintains adherents because the notion of 239 souls at the mercy of meddling extraterrestrials is more exciting than a plain blank wall.

6. ***The dark side of the Moon is home to a secret alien base.*** Despite Apollo 20 and other NASA flybys that photographed and mapped the so-called dark side, the alien-base idea flourishes because, well, you can't see the dark side of the Moon from your backyard, or from anywhere on Earth. Clearly, then, something hinky is going on up there. The military/surveillance/world dominance purpose of the base is reasonably consistent from story to story, but the base's origin is attributed to numerous factions. One familiar claim is that the base is the creation of fugitive Nazis that utilized German rocket technology to flee Earth in 1945. Another theory credits the U.S. government, acting alone, with the base; yet another is that the base is a U.S. concern created with reverse-engineered alien technology captured at Roswell in 1947. Alternatively, the base is a joint U.S./alien endeavor, or (with sinister overtones) a joint project

Ongoing fascination with all things Nazi has led to rumors of secret bases on the dark side of the Moon, staffed by aged fugitive Nazis and their descendants. This swastika-shaped Moon base is a signature image from *Iron Sky*, a seriocomic science-fiction thriller released in 2012.

of the U.S. and Russia (or China); or the United Nations, with or without alien assistance. Familiar bogeys such as the Trilateral Commission (a nonpartisan think tank founded by David Rockefeller), world bankers (international Jewry, that is), the New World Order (super-rich and authoritarian power elite), the Illuminati (a secret society with mystical overtones and authoritarian ambitions), and other-dimensional demons are occasionally invoked in discussions of the dark-side Moon base.

7. *Humans walked on Mars in 1979, the culmination of a clandestine NASA space program established with technological assistance from aliens.* This flamboyant idea has roots in claims from a woman who called in to America's *Coast to Coast AM* radio program in 2006, identifying herself as "Jackie" and claiming to be an ex-NASA employee. A clandestine manned Mars program, she said, got underway in 1968 and achieved a remarkable, and very secret, Mars landing eleven years later. Jackie saw the astronauts walking and running on the Martian surface while she worked with a "downstairs" NASA team running telemetry from the astronauts' roving Viking lander. Even if we grant that Jackie meant "video feed" when she said "telemetry," the fact is that the Viking lander was not designed to send back video. Further, the Viking lander was just that, a lander, with no wheels. It could not have been roving about. (A possibly partisan add-on to this theory is that the NASA/alien cabal sent teenage Barack Obama to Mars around 1979.) Some critics that dismiss Jackie's claims say that she did not inadvertently see Mars but NASA footage of the faked 1969 Moon landing—a landing that, according to these theorists, never happened.

8. *A still-popular 1956 UFO thriller from Hollywood,* **Earth vs. the Flying Saucers,** *has hidden documentary and political underpinnings that Washington did not want discovered by the public.* On two occasions in July 1952, witnesses in and near Washington, D.C., reported formations of spherical or disc-shaped lights moving over the city—most famously, over the Capitol dome. Although the Air Force quickly credited the objects as tricks of light caused by "temperature inversions," interest in the sightings remained high for many years. In the mid-1950s, filmmaker Charles Schneer, a producer attached to Columbia's B-picture unit, sold the studio on what he described as a loose take on Maj. Donald Keyhoe's popular book *Flying Saucers from Outer Space.* Washington tolerated Keyhoe, but hardly wanted additional dissemination of his ideas about craft of extraterrestrial origin. (For more on Major Keyhoe, see chapters one and nine.) A resourceful and talented journeyman director, Fred F. Sears, brought a brisk hand to *Earth vs. the Flying Saucers*; stop-motion animator Ray Harryhausen (whose earlier professional work included the fabulous dinosaur that was *The Beast from 20,000 Fathoms*) provided startlingly believable special effects. Harryhausen's conception of the classically shaped flying saucers remains chilling, for although the craft are essentially featureless, they display rapidly rotating top parts, and extender arms that emerge from their bellies to send withering heat rays against tanks, ships, and troops. (In a sequence that exploits the paranoia caused by a handful of West Coast American deaths caused by fiery Japanese "balloon bombs" late in World War II, Harryhausen's saucers set an entire forest ablaze.) As part of his research, Harryhausen met

with Californian George Adamski, who claimed numerous, voluntary contacts with friendly aliens. Washington had seemed content to allow Adamski to exist on what it considered the fringes of UFOlogy, but the film's dark variation on the Adamski experience—the abduction, "brain drain," and murder of an Army general—cut too close to home. And in the script's climax (clearly inspired by Kehoe's interest in the 1952 D.C. sightings), the saucers mount an attack against Washington, panicking thousands, slicing through and toppling the Washington Monument, crashing into the Capitol dome, and setting down on the White House lawn. Although Schneer and Columbia geared themselves to promote *Earth vs. the Flying Saucers* as fiction, they received no preproduction cooperation from the U.S. government or military. The movie's Washington, D.C., sequences were cleverly cobbled together with miniature buildings, process plates, and street scenes filmed on the Columbia back lot in California. Only a handful of second-unit footage, most of it "establishing" material shot without sound, showed some of the cast in genuine Washington locations. The saucer's destructive interactions with the military combined process plates with stock footage of exploding ships and crashed military aircraft. In the story, the military is helpless, and the saucers are vulnerable only to a sound-wave gun, devised by a scientist working largely on his own, that disrupts the saucers' gyroscopic stabilizers. Given that the U.S. armed forces take a fall in *Earth vs. the Flying Saucers*, one cannot be too surprised that the military was disinclined to help facilitate the film's production. That refusal, and Washington's fondness for the "temperature inversion" explanation offered in 1952, suggests a "stonewall" action that some observers have tied to a conspiracy.

9. ***Cattle mutilations, although the work of terrestrial flying saucers, are falsely attributed to extraterrestrial craft in order to hide nefarious medical experiments conducted by American military doctors.*** According to this theory, flying saucer technology came to Washington via Nazi scientists and airmen relocated to the United States beginning in 1945, as part of Operation Paperclip and other quasi-secret government programs. Saucer technology that had been developed by the Nazis was effectively kept out of Soviet hands at war's end, and put to use by U.S. researchers interested in avionics, weapons systems—and eccentric disciplines the likes of cryogenics, radiation exposure, covert sterilization, and anti-coagulants. Adherents of this theory cite cattle as ideal study subjects—though one would think that, physiologically, pigs are a better match to humans. Regardless, the government's particular interests explain the ravaged state of cattle taken and then returned by saucers: animals left without blood, tongues, genitals, and various organs. To divert attention from its saucer and cattle program, the perpetrators spread rumors of extraterrestrials, murder cults, Satanists, and end-times ravers.

U.S. government dupes, in the thrall of takeover-minded extraterrestrials, murdered President Kennedy because the president planned to reveal the aliens' existence. Some proponents of this idea trace alien control of Washington to President Eisenhower, who made the mistake of dealing with extraterrestrials in return for advanced alien technology and government obfuscation of UFOs. Working through secret societies that included Skull and Bones, the Illuminati, and the

The best fiction film predicated on the UFO menace is *Earth vs. the Flying Saucers*, released by Columbia in 1956. Propelled by a sober script, remarkable special effects, and a climactic attack on Washington, D.C., the movie gets its UFO lore right—so well, in fact, that some people speculate that *Earth vs. the Flying Saucers* was developed for reasons other than simple entertainment.

Masons, Earth's hidden alien overlords control governments and economies around the world. JFK uncovered the plot while in the White House, and planned to expose it during (according to some accounts) a simultaneous three-network television broadcast in late 1963 or early 1964. (Yes, this theory is in direct opposition to the one that is number three on this list.) The identity (or identities) of the shooter are a little vague, but a violently Libertarian Arizona man named Milton William Cooper fingered JFK's limousine driver as the culprit. According to Cooper, William Greer killed Kennedy with an alien-engineered "gas pressure device." The Zapruder footage and still images reveal that Greer turned his head to look back at the President following the first shot; in Cooper's view, Greer was checking to see whether his alien weapon had done its work. Cooper broadcast his conspiracy and antigovernment views on his own shortwave radio program, and published a conspiracy book, *Behold a Pale Horse*, in 1991. He identified abduction-author Whitley Strieber as a CIA agent assigned to spread falsehoods about extraterrestrials. Cooper also outed mainstream UFO researchers Linda Moulton Howe and Stanton Friedman, as well as noted astronomer Richard Hoagland, as government/alien catspaws. During the last twenty years of his life, Cooper became preoccupied with the armed militia movement. Wanted for tax evasion, he retreated to a homestead in Arizona, where, in November 2001, he was shot and killed by Apache County sheriff's deputies after Cooper shot one officer in the head.

10. ***A violent 1979 clash of extraterrestrials and humans in New Mexico in 1979 resulted in the deaths of nearly four dozen human scientists.*** The secret base at Dulce, New

Mexico, is at the center of even more purported government cover-ups than are detailed earlier in this chapter. A 1962 government plan to repair and fly some of the dozens of alien spacecraft recovered since the late 1940s became the seed for a more ambitious project initiated in the late 1960s. The linchpin of that later program brought human scientists and aliens together at Area 51's S4 Nevada facility and at a base outside Dulce, New Mexico. At those places, aliens provided Earth scientists with advanced avionics and other technology in return for limited access to human beings selected by the aliens for abduction and biological study. U.S. military and intelligence insisted that the ETs prepare lists of names ahead of time, and that abductions had to be approved by S4 and Dulce officials. In the early 1970s, though, human officials discovered that the extraterrestrials had taken many more people than the relative handfuls whose names appeared on the lists. In fact, the aliens had abducted *thousands* of people, implanting some of them with mind-control devices before their release and killing others outright, carving away at their genitalia and other organs, to acquire the base materials needed for the creation of artificial, quasi-human organisms. The two factions reached an apparent rapprochement, but by 1979 (some sources say 1978), government officials had been pushed to the limit. Fearful of exposure, the U.S. officials demanded that the ETs cease unrestrained abductions. Subsequent alien intransigence led to the deaths—possibly by execution—of forty-four human scientists, and drove a stake into human/alien cooperation. Ever since, aliens have busily implanted mind-control devices in countless more humans, preparing them for use as fifth columnists.

11. *A 1996 sighting of an extraterrestrial by multiple witnesses inspired the Brazilian army to blame the whole thing on a corpse.* The most dramatic of all Brazilian UFO cases occurred in January 1996 in Varginha, a city of about 120,000 located in Brazil's upper southeast: three young women spotted a creature they described as "short, dark, with some sort of sticky liquid all over the body." The witnesses described three small horns on the creature's head, and a face dominated by large red eyes. Soldiers from the Brazilian army captured the creature—and then denied doing any such thing. The official explanation for the sighting wouldn't convince a nine-year-old: army troops had been in town to drop off a body at a local funeral home, and the women had simply glimpsed the corpse. On the inadequacy scale, the army's account is right up there with sticking your finger into a leak to hold back a bursting dam. Brazilians were disinclined to believe army claims about most anything, and the "corpse" explanation inspired a great deal of jaundiced laughter. The laughs vanished and the public grew cynical when news leaked that Brazilian authorities had been alerted to a UFO by NORAD (North American Air Defense Command) shortly before the creature sighting, and that the army had squelched farmers' eyewitness accounts of a silent, gliding craft. Despite the army's connivance and ineptitude, locals seem to have come to terms with the official obfuscation, for Varginha's centrally located municipal water tower is in the shape of a flying saucer. At night, it is variously bathed in pink and green light.

12. *Worldwide Islam fears UFOs because extraterrestrials are neither human nor angel, but demons.* Based on a gross simplification of Islamic ideas, this notion suggests an all-out Muslim war against aliens, specifically, an assault launched from Pakistan, the only Islamic nation (at present) with nuclear weapons. (Mainstream Islam, particularly as practiced in the West, emphasizes the importance of scientific inquiry in human affairs, and maintains an open-minded—and calm—attitude about intelligent extraterrestrial life.)

13. *Schemers in Washington manipulate UFO evidence and fabricate absurd disinformation of their own, and encourage conspiracy rants from the likes of radio host Alex Jones in order to discredit serious UFO investigators.* The most commonly cited reason for this scheme is Washington's desire (and the desire of other, faceless powers) to collude with extraterrestrials without worry of public awareness and the oversight of politicians.

14. *The only UFO conspiracy theory that matters is the one perpetuated by the U.S. government, in order to study citizen reactions to fabricated information about flying saucers.* According to this convoluted and sinister idea, visual sightings, radio signals, and other manifestations of UFOs are inventions of Washington's military and psy-ops communities. Some people who become obsessed with the spurious evidence fall into paranoia and other mental illnesses. The most extreme of such reactions become tailor-made case studies that Washington applies to larger issues of psychological warfare and national security. A 2014 documentary, *Mirage Men*, cites a memo (reportedly uncovered by Edwin Snowden) instructing spies on fruitful ways to manipulate citizens' minds in this and other ways. As with all conspiracy theories, this one depends on the unlikely ability of thousands of conspirators to keep their lips buttoned.

Dead Mountain

Some human tragedies are so unusual, so dramatic, that they persist for years despite perfectly reasonable explanations, and end up folded into UFO lore without proper oversight. A modern Russian conspiracy theory holds that early in 1959, nine experienced young Russian hikers camping on the Urals' Holatchahl Mountain were killed by UFOs. Some of that is fact. Seven men and two women from the Ural Polytechnic Institute, well trained in winter hiking and all but one between twenty-one and twenty-five years old (the oldest man was forty-eight), did indeed lose their lives on a semi-academic January–February 1959 hiking expedition into the Northern Urals. The hikers left Sverdlovsk (now Yekaterinbyurg) and traveled some 110 miles north; the group's final communication was sent from Dyatlov Pass, just east of Holatchahl, on February 1. When the bodies were finally discovered by army searchers on May 3, many questions presented themselves: Why was the back of the large communal tent neatly cut through? Why were shoes, boots, and even preparations for hot chocolate neatly laid out inside? How had the victims ended up in the frozen emptiness far from their tent? Why were the bodies in widely separated groups? Why were most not adequately dressed? What made some of the hikers venture into the snow without boots or even socks? Did they perish from exposure, or from something else? Though the scene presented no obvious signs of struggle, several of the hikers had suffered rib and skull fractures. One of the two women no longer had her tongue. Tests of the corpses discovered the presence of a radioactive substance, potassium-40. Family of some of the victims wondered about the peculiar ochre color of the facial skin. Rumors took flight. Some held that the group had been killed by nomadic locals. Others said that the hikers stumbled onto a Russian secret-weapons site, and were killed by the weapons, perhaps accidentally, or were murdered by soldiers. In 1990, one of the searchers claimed to have seen "flying spheres." Television documentaries in 2000 (from Russia) and 2011 (the History Channel) fastened hard onto the alien thesis. But in 2012, California documentarian Donnie Eichar retraced the hikers' final days. He learned that the levels of potassium-40 were normal. The woman whose tongue went missing had bitten it off herself, probably in a fall. Falls explained the broken bones. The peculiar skin tones came from normal decomposition in a cold but damp environment. No evidence suggested belligerent locals, UFOs, secret weapons, or even an avalanche.

Eichar's 2013 book *Dead Mountain* offers a plausible explanation: the hikers pitched their tents within proximity of Holatchahl's neatly shaped dome. Wind shear down the mountain coalesced into a horizontal roll vortex—a "flat" tornado that never touched the tent but produced an ear-splitting roar, and so much vibration that the young men and women could feel the force inside their chest cavities. Though experienced hikers, the wind phenomenon was something new to each of them. The group panicked, cutting through the tent and stumbling into the frigid blackness. The truth aside, filmmaker Renny Harlin produced a "found-footage" mockumentary, *Devil's Pass* aka *The Dyatlov Pass Incident*, for 2013 release; the thriller focuses on American college students that, like Eichar, retrace the steps of the original expedition, shooting with video cameras and iPhones as they go. Instead of a wind vortex, these students stumble onto a mélange of bloodthirsty ETs, teleportation, wormholes—even Yeti.

12

Making Friends

Beautiful, Ageless Visitors Who Share the Wisdom of the Universe

As saucer sightings became more common in the late 1940s, alien visitors grew bolder—or human eyewitnesses became more imaginative. Soon, some people did not simply see flying saucers, but received friendly greetings from the crafts' occupants and were sometimes invited inside. A lucky few enjoyed quick trips into space. A few others had the privilege of meeting the same amiable aliens multiple times, which allowed for the development of mutual understanding.

Contrary to the small body/big head alien that came to prominence after Roswell, aliens who make friendly overtures to witnesses are usually described in distinctly more human terms—much, in fact, like the so-called Aryan ideal: tall, slender and firmly muscled, with blond hair and light eyes. Sometimes, the eyes are subtly feline. This is an appealing conception which, though tied to Western ideals of race and beauty, are also the "Space Angel" type described by numerous contactees of the 1950s and '60s.

Professor Adamski

The sensei of all saucer contactees is George Adamski (1891-1965; see chapter one), a Polish immigrant who came to the United States at age two, pursued school through the eighth grade, and fought in the Great War. He settled in Southern California sometime in the 1920s, finding work as a house painter and a mason.

In the 1930s, Adamski established himself as a proto-New Age "teacher" in Laguna Beach, California. He accepted "students," and instructed them in elementary metaphysics. In 1936, Adamski relocated to Pasadena, where he established the Royal Order of Tibet, a benign, Jesus-oriented religious sect that gave him a forum to promulgate his thoughts about Christian ideals of brotherhood and harmony. A fringe player in California's proto-New Age scene, Adamski self-published a book in 1936 that combined Western and Eastern religious thought, *Questions and Answers: Wisdom of the Masters of the Far East*. The compilation is credited to Professor G. Adamski—an honorarium bestowed upon Adamski by himself and, one may assume, generous and indulgent followers.

Late in World War II (during which Adamski did duty as an air raid warden), he relocated himself and his students to Mount Palomar. He opened the Palomar

Garden Café and purchased a pair of telescopes—six and fifteen inches. He witnessed his first UFO, a cigar-shaped craft, in 1946. (Skeptics are amused that Adamski's initial sighting predates Kenneth Arnold's, and the Roswell incident, by a year, giving George an advantaged place in modern saucer lore.)

An official biographical sketch prepared in the 1950s describes the observatory-café setup in commune-like terms, with Adamski's followers helping him with maintenance of both enterprises. Some sources, though, characterize Adamski as a handyman who worked for the café's owner, a woman named Alice Wells. (Ms. Wells is sometimes identified as Adamski's "secretary.") After dedicating himself to the flying saucer phenomenon around 1946–47 (concurrent with the Kenneth Arnold sighting and the Roswell incident), Adamski refined his gift for self-promotion, cultivating hundreds, and then thousands, of followers. A pair of later books, *Flying Saucers Have Landed* (1953) and *Inside the Space Ships* (1955), detail the time he spent conferring and traveling with handsome, peace-loving extraterrestrials. His accounts attracted attention from *Fate* and other niche magazines, and eventually encouraged coverage by broader media. By the mid- to late 1950s, Adamski was a genuine—if marginalized—national celebrity. He granted radio and television interviews, promoted his books, and calmly explained that his dramatic accounts of personal travel in saucers, and the fuzzy photographs he snapped to document his journeys, proved the existence of kind, solicitous alien beings. Adamski became a fixture of UFO conventions and other conclaves, where he invariably enjoyed warm, enthusiastic receptions. He wrote two more books in 1961, *Cosmic Philosophy* and *Flying Saucers Farewell*, the latter (as its title suggests) an elegiac look back at Adamski's remarkable exploits and career.

Adamski met visitors from other worlds, had audiences with Queen Juliana of the Netherlands and with Pope John XXIII (more on the latter meeting shortly), and remained a popular speaker on the UFO circuit until his death from natural causes.

Although gulled by a particularly clever and mischievous hoax in 1957 (see "the Straith letter," chapter fifteen), Adamski's sincerity was difficult to doubt . . . or at least difficult to doubt with anger. If his claims are truthful, then he led a remarkable and privileged existence. If confabulations, the man behind them is hardly less remarkable. Adamski's story is peculiarly emblematic of the archetypal immigrant journey from hope to success: from humble beginnings, he made something of himself, in the Dale Carnegie fashion, by winning friends and influencing people. White-haired and ruggedly handsome during the apex of his fame, Professor Adamski appealed even to people whose first impressions of him were negative, and even hostile. Although not a thinker, Adamski possessed undeniable leadership skills.

The Meetings and the Books

Adamski's first contact with extraterrestrials occurred at Mount Palomar on November 20, 1952, when he met Orthon, a Venusian—a creature Adamski described as "a human being from another world." (This momentous meeting was purportedly witnessed by George Hunt Williamson, a second-rate anti-Semitic Fascist and self-described channeler of extraterrestrial messages. So taken was Williamson with the implications of Adamski's Mount Palomar encounter that he published a book in 1954, *The Saucers Speak*. Some sources suggest that Adamski absorbed and promoted Williamson's political views, though little or nothing exists to prove the claim, unless one wishes to focus on the "Aryanized" appearance of Adamski's ETs.)

Adamski established the International Get Acquainted Club in 1957. He embarked on a "world tour" two years later and established a formal publishing arm, Science Publications, in 1962. The George Adamski Foundation International followed in 1965.

The famous 1953 book, *Flying Saucers Have Landed* (published not by Adamski but by a "legitimate" house, New York-based British Book Centre), is a pastiche, with Irish Theosophist nobleman Desmond Leslie writing the book's first (and greater) portion and Adamski the second, which amounts to just 55 of the first edition's 232 pages. Leslie's approach is pseudo-scholarly and seemingly well researched. Adamski's take, however, is personal—a picaresque journey. Leslie documents many UFO sightings, creating a reasonable-sounding prelude to Adamski's more theatrical accounts. Much of Leslie's section derives from newspaper accounts, in the manner of Charles Fort's research for *The Book of the Damned*, a celebrated 1919 compendium of the unexplained. (For more on Fort, see chapter one.) Editor Clara Johns formatted Leslie's notes so that they appear to reflect the work of Adamski as well as Leslie—a subtle deception that gives Adamski's section of the book a greater scholarly heft than it deserves. Adamski historian Colin Bennett feels that the greatest value of *Flying Saucers Have Landed* is Leslie's bibliography, which lists a wealth of obscure and intriguing books about ancient Egypt, Noah's Ark,

"Professor" George Adamski poses proudly with a painting of Orthon, one of his beatific Venusian friends, around 1953. Adamski claimed to have established amiable relationships with aliens in 1952.   *Alamy*

human oddities, Atlantis, religious mysticism, and other topics that may or may not have true relationships to UFOs, helpful aliens, and the origins of the human race. Leslie and Adamski did not meet until 1954, a year after the book's publication.

Adamski shortly found himself at the center of the contactee phenomenon. Nineteen fifty-three brought the first Spacecraft Convention, an amiably informal gathering mounted at Giant Rock, California. The convention became an annual event, drawing its biggest crowds, and the most media attention, during the 1950s, partly because Adamski was a regular attendee. The convention ran through 1977.

Inside the Space Ships (handsomely published by New York's Abelard-Schuman) continues Adamski's adventures with Venusians, and with a new, late-arriving extraterrestrial group, too, Saturnians. Adamski's privileged rides on scout ships and a mother ship—intriguing machines that seem equal parts rivets and unimaginable high-tech—give the accounts a special, and frankly irresistible, luster. *Inside the Space Ships* was ghosted by Charlotte Blodget, sometimes identified (like Alice Wells) as Adamski's secretary—and even identified as a victim of CIA and INTERPOL harassment. Although some sources claim that Blodgett passed away in the 1960s, she is likely to have lived beyond those years—and is probably Charlotte Blob (rhymes with "globe"), an Adamski follower and the founder of UFO Education Center (UFOEC). Over the years, some former members of UFOEC complained that Blob turned the organization into a quasi-religious cult, from which escape was difficult. In that, Blob contrasts sharply with her mentor.

A late Adamski work, a thirty-page booklet titled *Answers to Questions Most Frequently Asked About Our Space Visitors and Other Planets*, appeared under Adamski's own imprint in 1965, the year Adamski died.

Objections

In 1957, UFOlogist Jim Moseley insisted that Adamski faked the saucer photos in the two books, and plundered easily accessible science-fiction literature for the aliens' "space messages." Other critics charged that the saucers in the photos were decorated with glyphs Adamski copied from published sources, and that he reworked his twenty-year-old Royal Order of Tibet material so that it had a "Space Brother" imprimatur. Particularly harsh critics claim that Adamski submitted his "contact" story, as fiction, to Ray Palmer's *Amazing Stories* magazine in 1944. The story, apparently rejected, put Jesus inside an alien spaceship.

The single most famous Adamski photograph, of a hat-shaped saucer (published in *Flying Saucers Have Landed* and *Inside the Space Ships*) that Adamski identified as a Venusian scout craft, has generated equal parts awe and skepticism. The ship's portholes and globular, tri-part landing assembly are marvelous; on the other hand, some doubters insist that the ship is a model constructed from (according to discrete accounts) a hat, a hat box, a lamp shade, a mechanical chicken feeder, and vacuum-cleaner parts. But the scout ship has demonstrated popular longevity, and remains available as a carved, Philippine-mahogany desk piece in various sizes, and as plastic model kits, usually in 1/48 and 1/60 scale. The kits are manufactured around the world, and are called George Adamski Flying Saucer or Adamski Type Flying Saucer. (A 1/48-scale kit from South Korea's Hand Hero company notes the Adamski connection in small type at the bottom of the box art; the main headline reads, "FLYING SAUCERS HAVE COME.")

Doubts and criticism aside, by 1959, Adamski's standing in the UFO community was so well established that the March–April 1959 issue of *Thy Kingdom Come*, the newsletter of the Amalgamated Flying Saucer Clubs of America, ran the following as a news item:

ADAMSKI SAVES TRAIN FARE WITH FREE SAUCER RIDE

After just finishing a lecture in Kansas City, Missouri, last November, George Adamski boarded a train for Davenport, Iowa, where he had another lecture engagement scheduled. About 20 minutes out of Kansas City, the train stopped for some reason. Mr. Adamski got off the train and met a man who took him to a nearby wooded area and they both teleported about 50′ up into a Spacecraft, where he spent about 8 hours before being delivered to Davenport in time for his lecture that eve.

During the latter part of Adamski's life, and concurrent with his international celebrity, Adamski grew faintly paranoid about "conspirators" and others that might wish to silence him. This may have developed because of his incidental association with a man named William Dudley Pelly, a self-educated metaphysician with grotesque Fascist leanings.

Yamski

Adamski's death in 1965 hardly diminished his appeal and influence. Later that year, a Brit named Ernest Bryant identified himself as a contactee. That sort of thing was familiar enough in the UFO community, but what caught the attention of UFOlogists was Bryant's insistence that the extraterrestrial he spoke with appeared to him on April 24, one day after Adamski's death. Further, the alien *looked like* Adamski as a young man—and called himself Yamski. The alien carried artifacts similar to ones Adamski had once described. Bryant's contention was that George Adamski's spirit lived on, restored and reconstituted as an extraterrestrial.

Some sources claim that Bryant was able to produce a medal Adamski received from Pope John XIII during an audience in 1963. Yamski himself, Bryant said, handed him the medal. However, skeptics describe Adamski's Vatican medal as a cheap plastic souvenir, available at the Vatican and in shops across Rome. In any event, hard evidence of Adamski's special audience with the pope is elusive.

Today, the George Adamski story is persuasively disseminated on a Web site, adamskifoundation.com. The site is an evolution of The Adamski Foundation, which dates to 1965.

In a 2001 book, *Looking for Orthon: The Story of George Adamski the First Flying Saucer Contactee and How He Changed the World*, author Colin Bennett proposes that Adamski's widely disseminated stories contributed significantly to counterculture thought. Although a pleasing tribute, the book overestimates Adamski's cultural influence, and even his influence within the UFO community. (Friendly aliens are difficult to find these days.) Further, Bennett offers an unnecessary compliment when he calls Adamski "a phenomenon" rather than simply a man, and ventures into the absurd with a tossed-off description of Adamski as a "Hero"—capital "H," as in hero figures of folklore and myth.

Another Adamski

Adamski's claims encouraged others to share their own tales of interaction with friendly aliens. One of these, Daniel Fry, enjoyed particular notoriety after coming forward in 1954 to reveal his 1949 meeting with ETs, and subsequent ride on a spaceship. Fry worked as an explosives expert and rocket instruments technician, and eventually co-founded a pair of tech companies that manufactured transducers and other parts. In the summer of 1949, Fry worked for Aerojet at the White Sands (NM) Proving Grounds. Night had fallen on the Fourth of July, when Fry observed a saucer-shaped craft move against the starry sky and settle to a landing. Although the craft was (according to Fry) remotely controlled, Fry

The cover of this British paperback edition of Adamski's 1953 hardcover suggests considerably more apprehension than Adamski felt during his first alien encounter. The spaceship duplicates Adamski's most famous photograph, a lampshade-shaped saucer with distinctive underbelly pods.

didn't hesitate when a disembodied voice invited him aboard. Aloft for thirty minutes (during which time the saucer traveled from White Sands to New York and back again), Fry accepted an offer to chat with a fellow named "Alan," a former Earthling who departed the planet centuries ago. Fry chronicled his adventure in a 1954 book, *The White Sands Incident*. Others by Fry, including *Atoms, Galaxies and Understanding* (the physics of space travel) and *Steps to the Stars*, followed.

Fry lectured, ran his companies, and became a land developer. In 1955, he established an international, nonprofit goodwill organization he called Understanding, urging members to become engaged in civic life and pursue positive contact with people in other nations.

The Understanding group faded not long before Fry's death in 1992. But neither Fry nor his ideals were forgotten; in 2005, the entire run of the Understanding newsletter—more than 240 issues—was transcribed and downloaded to the Web.

Coming to Grips with George

Why do I discuss George Adamski in this chapter, rather than in the chapter devoted to hoaxers? Nostalgia and affection play parts. *Inside the Space Ships* is the first UFO book I acquired. That happened in 1963, eight years after the book's publication, when Adamski was still living, and still famous, and when I was a boy. I do not recall reading news stories about him, nor do I recall how I obtained the book. I know it did not come to me as a gift, so I probably bought it used, or traded for it. *Inside the Space Ships* has been part of my library, and my past, for quite a while.

As I re-read the book while preparing the one you are reading now, I was struck not just by the text's astounding detail and scientific wonders (and anomalies), but by the benign tone. The prose is calm and positive. The aliens bring a hopeful message. They are patient with Adamski's questions. They are "superior" in many ways, but make little note of it. When Adamski absently reaches for his cigarettes, for instance, and discovers he has none, a female alien offers to provide him with some, as well as "a receptacle for your ashes." Smiling, she adds, "You see, only Earth people indulge in that odd habit!"

That's the remark of a kind aunt, or a longtime friend who is as comfortable as old slippers. These are not the deadly aliens that routinely inform darker, more prevalent UFO narratives. These aliens may not be saviors, but they are surely our friends.

If Adamski profited monetarily from his students and books, he did not earn enough to fund an ostentatious lifestyle. His first book, *Flying Saucers Have Landed*, sold fifty thousand copies, possibly more, in the United States. *Inside the Space Ships* also sold well. Each of those retailed for $3.50, so assuming a sale of fifty thousand units for *Flying Saucers Have Landed*, Adamski came away with $17,500—an upper-middle-class annual salary for 1953, and a tidy sum, but hardly sufficient to maintain anyone in luxury for long, particularly because royalties are paid out over the life of a book (that is, for as long as the publisher deems it "in print"). Royalties inevitably diminish sharply before being suspended altogether.

Paperback sales and foreign editions brought more profit to Adamski, but because he was selling in a niche corner of publishing (in other words, he wasn't James Michener, or another writer with similar mass appeal), Adamski wasn't getting rich. One can surmise that his students paid him something, and then there were the modest stipends or other fees from speaking engagements.

My point in detailing all of this is to suggest that Adamski wasn't "in it for the money." Many people that purchased his books wanted them as entertainment, or as novelties. The greater portion of sales did not come from people who had no money to spare. Adamski wasn't a shakedown artist.

And so what was he? I am unable to argue against claims that he was a hoaxer. Nor would I claim that his celebrity meant nothing to him. But because of the dollars-and-cents facts above, and my aforementioned sentiment, I regard "Professor" Adamski as a man who believed what he said. If his adventures are untrue, they came to his imagination guilelessly.

Happy Life on Meton

Once the kindly Venusians contacted Adamski, similar aliens began to contact many other people. In the mid-1950s, Elizabeth Klarer (1910–94) revealed that she had witnessed UFOs as early as 1917, and had continued to see them ever since. She observed the landing of a tremendously large saucer in Natal in 1954, gaining a glimpse of the "handsomest" man she had ever seen. The man returned on April 6, 1956, a particularly interesting day because Klarer traveled with the gentleman and other friendly extraterrestrials to the planet Meton, where she lived happily for nine years (a mere four months in Earth time). So friendly were the aliens, in fact, that Klarer became pregnant by the handsome standout, Akon. In 1958, she bore a human-alien son called Ayling.

Much later, Akon admitted to Klarer that he was a Venusian by birth—as well as Klarer's reincarnated soulmate. Although Klarer's descriptions of Akon's joyous demeanor, exotic gifts, and "electric" kisses have the naiveté of a romance novel (she wrote of their bodies "merging in magnetic union as the divine essence of our spirits became one"), Klarer never modified her tone or her enthusiasm.

Klarer likened the love given by aliens to the love offered by Christ—an affection that promised not simply an afterlife based in pure energy, but reincarnation on other planets. She wrote and spoke of the aliens' "sophisticated" technology which was based in "the electromagnetic wavelength of the universe." She described space as "out there," and said it existed in the fifth dimension.

Meton, Klarer said, was continually bathed in the light of three stars, and was thus a place untroubled by night. Health concerns on Meton were addressed by a fabulous "silver herb" that grew not just on that planet but on Earth as well, at the landing point of the Meton starship decades earlier.

Klarer was a native South African educated, purportedly, at Cambridge. In middle age, she was a handsome, elegant woman with a self-described meteorological background, a posh accent, and an interest in the military-political ramifications of human contact with aliens. (Like many people interested in UFOs, she linked the craft with secret Nazi files discovered in Berlin at the end of World War II.) She claimed to have worked at high levels of the RAF during the war and afterward, investigating foo fighters (see chapter five) and decoding intercepted German military communications. Starship technology, she said, was in the hands of various world governments, which suppressed it. She feared for her safety in the 1950s, when the Soviet Union keenly desired her insights into starship technology.

Elizabeth Klarer published an autobiography, *Beyond the Light Barrier*. (A second book, *The Gravity Files*, was unfinished at the time of her death.) A representative portion of her lectures is preserved on audio tape. She was a calm, steady speaker who showed patience with polite questioners. If there is a sour note to all this, it is that she did not come forward until after reading George Adamski's accounts in the mid-1950s. Skeptics label Klarer a copycat; her advocates explain that Adamski created a level of public acceptance that encouraged Klarer to finally reveal herself.

Klarer's pleasing public manner did not prevent her from contentiously engaging another contactee—and another South African—Ann Grevler, who claimed to have begun an intimate relationship with an extraterrestrial called Ashtar sometime in the 1950s (Grevler declined to be more specific), after her car died on a remote road in the Transvaal. For reasons that Grevler never explained, Ashtar turned her disabled car invisible—a good parlor trick with the unintended consequence of Grevler walking into the invisible license plate and slashing her leg. Apparently the forgiving sort, Grevler accepted the alien's friendly greeting and was taken aboard Ashtar's scout ship. Following an in-space rendezvous with a mother ship, Ashtar and Grevler traveled to Venus, where Grevler met university students who studied ESP and Venus's form- and color-based "cosmic language."

Ann Grevler's 1958 booklet *Transvaal Episode* details friendly encounters such as the one described above; she did note, however, that Men in Black—whom she identified as malevolent aliens—wished to disrupt friendly contact between humans and extraterrestrials. Perhaps wishing to conceal her identity from unsympathetic persons and organizations, Grevler published her booklet under a pseudonym, "Anchor."

Like Klarer, Grevler drifted into religious reverie, identifying the Venusians as honoring "the Creator" and living by a broadly accepted moral code. Also like Klarer, Grevler was enthusiastic but vague about alien energy technology, especially the spaceships' motive power; Grevler attributed the latter to a system that drew from "cosmic power" and "powdered quartz" to create the "ionized air" that sent the craft aloft.

Another woman encouraged to speak out after absorbing George Adamski's stories was Cynthia Appleton, a British woman who claimed to have met—and been seduced by—one of Adamski's blond alien friends. She identified the son that resulted as a human-alien hybrid.

Klarer and Appleton fall in line with certain devotees of Christianity, Theosophy, and other belief systems, as contactees that come to be regarded—or regard themselves—as prophets. They are among the familiar "chosen few." Sometimes, this distinction is made and then elaborated on minimally or not at all. The "prophet" is a benign presence who demands little from her followers besides their attention. But inevitably, prophet status can inflate egos and encourage "class distinctions" within groups. Soon, the leader has chosen favorites, and those who fail to make the cut are regarded as lesser creatures, who are insufficiently devoted to the prophet and the prophet's message. Sometimes, these lesser acolytes are surprised to find themselves on the outs not just with the prophet but also with the entire group. In extreme cases, the lesser members are abused psychologically or physically. (For much more on UFO prophets and cults, see chapter fifteen.)

Orfeo

Southern California amateur physicist and onetime Lockheed employee Orfeo Angelucci, who witnessed a circular flying object approach his test balloons in 1946, had an even more dramatic encounter on May 24, 1952: while he drove near Burbank, hovering green objects dropped onto the road and halted his car. A disembodied voice explained that the green craft were extraterrestrial, and that the operators had been monitoring Angelucci since that first encounter six years earlier. The voice went on to reassure Angelucci that the ETs loved human beings. He found that comforting, but one wonders how he felt two months later, on July 23, 1952, when he fell into a coma and awoke as a passenger on a spaceship. In time, he regarded the aliens as angelic, even mystical creatures that helped him journey to an awareness of his higher self. (Angelucci's description of a tiny dancer in a champagne flute is particularly intriguing). "As I listened to their gentle voices," he recalled, "I began to feel a warm, glowing wave of love. . . . For a wonderful moment, I felt infinitely greater, finer, and stronger than I knew myself to be." Angelucci wondered if he had "transcended reality."

By the mid-1950s, Angelucci held a spiritual view of UFOs, and was a contributor to F. E. Rogers's *Talk of the Times*, a semi-professional, proto-New Age magazine that described itself as a "scientific-religious publication"; Angelucci contributed "California Soul Rush Days" to the magazine's July 1958 issue. He recounted his experiences in more detail in two books, *The Secret of the Saucers* (1955) and *Son of the Sun* (1959).

The Truman Show

Mormon Mesa, Nevada, July 1952. After relocating to Nevada from Redondo Beach, California, fifty-five-year-old Truman Bethurum spent his nights performing truck maintenance at an asphalt plant. He had free access to the trucks, so after wrapping up a shift he drove to the dry seabed at Mormon Mesa (about sixty miles north of Las Vegas), to look for seashells and relax before sunrise. He fell asleep in the cab and was awakened an hour later by a low murmur of voices. Dawn had not broken over the mesa, so Bethurum had to struggle to see who was speaking. He put his head out the truck's window and then quickly pulled it back: eight to ten black-haired men, dressed in short jackets and blue-gray pants, surrounded the truck. They stood impassively, and Bethurum's first absurd notion was that they were Greyhound bus drivers—except that each one was less than five feet tall, and conversed in a language Bethurum was certain he had never heard.

He gingerly stepped from the cab, and was relieved when one of the men took his extended hand. One spoke to him in English and directed Bethurum to a silently hovering, stainless steel flying saucer that Bethurum later described as "monstrous . . . three hundred feet across and six yards deep in the center."

Inside, the alien males introduced Bethurum to the ship's female captain, who identified herself as Aura Rhanes. She wore a black beret over short black hair, and regarded Bethurum with bright, probing eyes. The Earthman admired Aura's "olive and roses" complexion, as well as her form-fitting black velvet blouse and brilliant red skirt. (These aliens have not only evolved along lines very similar to humans—or vice versa—the women look like pin-ups.) Bethurum took pains later to emphasize Aura's extraordinary attractiveness, saying she was "tops in shapeliness and beauty." After Bethurum went public and described Aura in detail, many saucer buffs revisited the old pulp magazine trope of exotic and voluptuous female aliens. In August 1954, a beautiful, black-eyed fashion designer named Dolores Barrios caused a stir at a saucer convention at Mount Palomar, California. She had striking, vaguely exotic good looks, and whispers suggested she was an extraterrestrial. Truman Bethurum, George Adamski, and other contactees were guests, and a few in the crowd (which included FBI agents) assumed that Barrios was Aura Rhanes herself.

In early meetings, Aura explained to Bethurum that she and her companions had journeyed to Earth from the planet Clarion, a body perpetually hidden behind the Moon, and thus unnoticed by Earth astronomers. Clarion spaceships, Aura freely explained, were variously powered by "antimagnetic or gravitational" science; plutonic technology (apparently related to pressures harnessed from magma deep inside Clarion); or nutronic forces (*sic*; probably Bethurum's innocent misspelling of "neutronic," which suggests a method of bombarding chemical elements with neutrons to produce radioactive atoms). The Clarionites' visit to Earth, Aura insisted, had peaceful intentions, but because a "retroscope" allowed Clarionites to observe the totality of Earth's history and technology, Clarion had grown concerned about Earth's burgeoning nuclear capability, and potential ability to disrupt the peace of the solar system, very much as in the 1951 SF-movie *The Day the Earth Stood Still*.

Bethurum remained hazy as to why the Clarionites chose him for contact, but he reasoned that his avocation as a spiritual adviser was a factor.

During subsequent audiences with Aura, Bethurum learned that the Clarion ship (which Aura referred to as the

This appealingly authoritative woman is Aura Rhanes, a starship captain from the planet Clarion and friend to a Nevadan named Truman Bethurum. Captain Rhanes and her subordinates introduced themselves to Bethurum in 1952, setting off considerable excitement in some UFO circles.   *Everett Collection*

Admiral Scow) was made of superb Martian metal—Mars being home to brilliant metallurgists. Despite her apparent youth, Aura had grandchildren. Time and distance were irrelevant to Clarionites. Illness, Aura said, was unknown on her planet, where the ethnically and philosophically homogeneous population attended church and believed in "a supreme deity."

Bethurum learned to pick out Clarion ships in starry skies, and came to expect the pre-landing "flashing light [that] followed the same color pattern—bluish-green, then greenish-yellow, then a yellowish red." Following each meeting, Bethurum recorded details in his journal. "If I am found dead in my bed," he wrote after the first encounter, it will be because my heart has stopped from the terrible excitement induced by seeing and going aboard a flying saucer!"

Whether because of his inexperience as a writer, or Aura's relative unfamiliarity with the nuances of English, some of the alien captain's remarks are puzzling, even confounding. After revealing that she expected to live to be a thousand years old, and that she was a Christian, Aura segued into non sequitur when she added, "the water in your deserts will mostly be tears." Aura informed Bethurum that Clarion and "other planets" were untroubled by "even minor controversies," and that the toys given to Clarion's children were wholesome, and quite unlike Earth's endless selection of toy guns and miniature soldiers. Despite these and other rather studied declarations of pacifism, Aura also let Bethurum know that "Our enemies fall and disappear before us. None of your Earth people have anywhere near the powers which we control."

The intimidating and contradictory undertone of that remark apparently did not bother Bethurum, but he was surprised and hurt later in the summer when he ran into Aura having lunch near his home, at a restaurant in Glendale, Nevada, where she took pains to ignore him. (She was munching on toast.) The friendship was on again a bit later, when Aura promised to take Bethurum and a few of his friends on a saucer ride to Clarion. Although Bethurum signaled with flares Aura gave him for that purpose, neither the saucer nor a trip to Clarion materialized. Aura had not seen the flares (unlikely, given Clarion technology), or simply elected to ignore them. Still, she left Bethurum with a precious memento: a letter written to him on Clarionite stationery. Understandably, Bethurum declined to release this prize for examination by UFOlogists or the media.

Bethurum's experiences highlighted the debut issue of *Saucers* (published by UFOlogist Max B. Miller) and led to Bethurum's 1954 hardcover account *Aboard a Flying Saucer*. He quickly followed that one with two more, *The Voice of Planet Clarion* (1957) and the defiantly titled *Facing Reality* (1958).

Like George Adamski (who was actively supportive of his fellow contactee), Bethurum enjoyed the attention his accounts generated, and became a guest at saucer conventions, on the mainstream lecture circuit, and even on NBC's *The Betty White Show* (a music-and-chat program; 1954). His wife Mary eventually became fed up with Truman's mooning over Aura and filed for divorce. Cut loose by Mrs. Bethurum and apparently persona non grata with Aura, Bethurum remarried in 1960. But Aura was not done with him. In a final visit via projected image, the Clarionite captain suggested that Bethurum shift his life to a new course. Bethurum obeyed. He left construction and maintenance for good and established a peace group, the Sanctuary of Thought, near Prescott, Arizona. He passed away in 1969; his final book, *The People of Planet Clarion*, appeared the following year.

Big Bo and Little Buck

Missouri farmer and contactee Buck Nelson was slender and rough-hewn, with an angular face and a strong jaw. Invariably dressed in coveralls, he owned and operated eighty acres in the Ozarks. Fifty-nine when he gained notoriety in 1954, Nelson had experienced a hardworking, peripatetic life: railroad worker, cowboy, security guard, and sawmill operator. A native of Colorado, Nelson managed just a sixth-grade education. Regardless, he was enterprising, astute, and well liked. He recounted his adventures in a 1956 pamphlet, *My Trip to Mars, the Moon, and Venus*.

When Nelson saw a UFO for the first time, he saw three of them, during the afternoon of July 30, 1954. Geographically isolated, Melson had not heard of flying saucers, so he later described the craft as "things." The size of the principal craft impressed him; he later estimated it to be fifty feet in diameter and about eight feet high. (In some accounts, Nelson says that two other ships hovered behind the principal one.) Later, he supposed that the ship was powered by some fabulous manipulation of "magnetic currents." When he waved a lighted flashlight in greeting, a mysterious (but harmless) ray knocked him to the ground. The craft left, and when Nelson regained his feet, his bothersome back no longer pained him. The ray had provided a cure.

When the aliens returned to Nelson on February 1, 1955, they spoke to him from within the hovering craft, and promised to return. They did, on March 5, 1955. This time, creatures emerged from the craft: a "385"-pound dog named Big Bo; a young Earthling called "Little Buck" (who teaches English on Venus); and two extraterrestrials: an unnamed trainee (who appeared elderly) and a younger man who identified himself as Bob Solomon. Solomon said he was two hundred years old. Inside the farmhouse, Nelson satisfied his visitors' curiosity by demonstrating his oil stove and explaining various pieces of furniture.

The visits continued deep into the spring of 1955. Twelve rocks the aliens had arranged on the ground, Nelson learned, represented the Twelve Laws of God. These directives mimicked the tone and many specifics of the Ten Commandments. This exchange of morality occurred during the aliens' fifth visit with Nelson, at midnight on April 24, 1955. That same day, in the wee hours of the morning, the aliens invited Nelson into the ship.

Nelson recalled the controls as models of simplicity. With the barest assistance from the visitors, he was able to elevate the craft and take it into space. "After I got the ship high into space I was told I could play with the controls." Nelson flew upside down and rocked the ship from side to side. Big Bo, the alien dog, enjoyed all the tomfoolery.

Cruising above Mars, Nelson observed the canals, and horses and cattle, too. The group visited "the ruler's home," and then took off for Earth's Moon. Lunch was served in a ruler's home on the illuminated side of the Moon. Nelson studied the landscape and surmised that snow atop Moon mountains provided the residents with water.

Back to the ship, and then more lunch, this time on the Moon's dark side. Nelson seems to have been feeling overstuffed by this time, but he remained genial and awestruck.

Two stops on Venus followed. Nelson visited the homes of two more rulers; mercifully, he did not have to eat again. He was impressed by Venusian cars, which hovered above the ground in lieu of wheels or fenders. A Venusian wall clock had seventeen "scratchings" instead of numbers, and a thirty-four-hour Venusian day-night cycle split evenly, seventeen/seventeen.

Two facts shared with Nelson are particularly startling: of the planets in our solar system, Earth is the only one not actively traveling through space; and numerous American government officials had visited Venus. Nelson speculated that those officials said nothing because of fear for their reputations.

In an inadvertent anticipation of New Age thought, Nelson described the Venusians as healthy people ("much better looking in general" than we) who favored fruits and vegetables. Venus had no doctors, as the people were well versed in self-healing and natural cures. Wars and crime are unknown on Venus. Although users of advanced technology, the Venusians kept no munitions.

Buck Nelson's first trip through space consumed three memorable days.

Buck's pamphlet is sprinkled with Nelson's simple freehand drawings of Venusian architecture, the ship's fuselage and control panel, and other light technology.

Three months after Nelson's adventure, on July 26, 1955, he described his experiences to a "saucer club" in Detroit. In Chicago not long after, he answered scientists' questions: "One astronomer drove from the west coast and asked me what it looked like in outer space. I told him that it was inky black. He thanked me, bid me goodbye and left."

In a greeting recorded at Nelson's farm on Christmas Day 1955, Little Buck urged Earth to give up its atomic weapons.

In the back of the booklet, Nelson provided a simple how-to drawing of a "saucer detector," a piece of magnetized metal suspended horizontally from a ceiling in a draft-free area of the user's house. "If there is a Space Craft over the house, the magnetic bar will be drawn upward. If the Space Craft circles the house, the bar will move in a circle."

Nelson's experiences brought minor fame sufficient for him to inaugurate an annual "Spacecraft Convention" at his farm in the late 1950s. (Locations varied in subsequent years.) These conventions were real Americana, patronized mainly by middle-aged and elderly day trippers. A few young families arrived with simple tents, for camping. The settings were rustic and dusty. You could buy a Coke from a vendor in a weathered outbuilding, enjoy a carnival ride, and purchase books, photos, and pamphlets from a variety of UFO enthusiast-dealers. Buck, growing white haired and more leathery with each passing year, was around to chat, and maybe sell you a bit of fur from the giant space dog.

Nelson negotiated the lecture circuit, and conducted a modest mail-order business selling tape recordings of lectures, space music, and gospel tunes. The tapes, plus the buck-fifty convention admissions, brought in a few dollars, but bad news came in 1960, when Nelson announced that he had lost his disability pension because he had ridden in a spaceship. To address that, and to spread the word about the "Space Brothers," Nelson urged contributors to fund a radio station.

In her foreword to *My Trip to Mars, the Moon, and Venus*, a Missouri homemaker and dressmaker named Fanny Lowery compared Nelson favorably to John the Baptist: "a great teacher." Nelson passed away in 1984, but because of attention paid him years later by graphic novelist Tim Lane, and the print-on-demand availability of his booklet, Nelson's modest notoriety continues.

Human Gods

Finally, a friendly-alien encounter situation that is not about extraterrestrials at all, but is a fundamental—and innocent—misunderstanding of one culture by another. The "cargo cult" phenomenon pivots on a belief among indigenous peoples of Melanesia, dating to the 19th century, that manufactured goods arriving with colonialist explorers were spiritual in origin. People in previously unmolested areas of Fiji, New Guinea, and other Melanesian regions neither needed nor developed manufacturing processes. A rifle, a greatcoat, or a can of meat, then, would seem to have come from the gods, or the gods' emissaries.

Two generations after World War II, some Melanesian islanders maintain "cargo cults" inspired by material goods brought to the islands during the 1940s by godlike airmen. This photograph from the 1990s shows a World War II bomb—inert, one hopes—displayed in Solomon Islands as an object of veneration.   *Rex*

Activity in the Pacific during World War II brought Japanese and Allied manufactured goods to many islands in the South Pacific. The greater proportion of this cargo arrived via airplane (when landing strips were available) or air drops. The arrival of goods from the sky seemed significant, and encouraged worship of the goods' creators. Local assumption was that continued veneration ensured further deliveries.

Naturally enough, islanders noticed the visitors' facial features and skin tones. That perception of "otherness" helped foster beguiling cargo cults with echoes of Western preoccupations with UFOs and extraterrestrials. On the Vanuatu island of Tanna, the light-skinned god was (and is still) called "John Frum." (The origin of this name inspires debate, but the most reasonable explanation holds that "John Frum" is a variation of "John from _____.") Because African American G.I.s frequently labored in military construction battalions, some worshippers depict John Frum as a dark-skinned creature. Whether light or dark, the images of John Frum are central to the islanders' worship—much as the immediate-postwar bug-eyed saucer man, and the later gray ET, became central to UFO culture. And John Frum, whatever the particulars of his origin, was real. Extraterrestrial visitors may be no less real.

Although cargo deliveries dribbled away in the Pacific and finally stopped after the summer of 1945, indigenous residents continued their worship across generations, often constructing rough approximations of airplanes, airstrips, rifles, and other things associated with the visitors, things calculated to coax the gods' return. Local men hefting bamboo "rifles" might march in formation. Others might regularly clear a long-abandoned airstrip of overgrown vegetation.

In the West, we maintain SETI radio-telescope arrays to monitor the skies for extraterrestrials. Like the Melanesians, we are patient, and we wait.

13

Abductions

Helplessness, Pain, and Fractured Memory

Since the 1990s, reported abductions of human beings by extraterrestrials have become increasingly common, and in a variety of ways: anecdotally (a wealth of isolated accounts); philosophically (what do they want with us?); sexually ("and then they inserted the probe . . ."); and institutionally (reflecting a common theory that aliens perform abduction experiments in collusion with the U.S. government). The fewest abduction reports come from Europe; the United States produces the most. According to researcher Mark Rodeghier, Australia and South America also account for significant numbers of abduction tales. Although UFO theory of very recent years has begun a shift from abductions and notions of UFOs as material, nuts and bolts spacecraft to thoughts of energy fields and parallel dimensions, the abduction narrative remains strong in UFOlogy and popular culture.

How did all this begin?

Just an Ordinary Drive

For a moment, confusion registered on the face of Betty Hill. When she lifted a hand, her husband Barney thought his wife had found a flaw in the windshield.

> "Hnnh?" he said.
> "That light."

Now Barney focused, and he saw it. A bright light in the midnight sky, near Lancaster, New Hampshire. He lifted his foot from the accelerator. All around the couple, U.S. Route 3 in central New Hampshire was dark and deserted. September 19, 1961, was almost done. September 20 was minutes away.

The Hills' car was moving south, and the light appeared to be headed north. "It's moving," Betty said.

Barney squinted and leaned forward. "Is it? Can't tell 'cause the car's moving too." With that, he touched the brake and brought the car to a halt. He and Betty looked hard through the windshield and agreed that the light was not stationary. It was in motion, and moving north.

Barney put the car in gear and drove, more slowly now, flicking his gaze between the dark road and the moving light. The illumination appeared to be more than just a light—it was an object, and what had been a subdued course of movement now became erratic, almost whimsical. The northward course was abruptly reversed—as no known aircraft could do—and the thing flew south, keeping pace with the Hills' automobile. The object passed in front of the Moon, and moved closer to the car. Colored lights—red, green, amber, and blue—winked in a band on the thing's surface. When the object began to keep pace with the car, the Hills knew that the thing was some sort of aircraft, and one capable of very tricky maneuvers.

The craft disappeared from view. Barney slowed even more, watching. And then the thing was back, now just three hundred feet to the car's right and looming very large. The craft stopped and hovered.

Barney crushed the brakes and left the driver's seat even before the car's nose stopped bobbing. He kept binoculars with him, and clutched them as he settled his position on the road. The object, he said later, was just fifty feet in front of him. The craft emitted no engine or exhaust sounds, and the Hills discerned no motor noise when V-shaped "wings" (as Barney Hill described them), with red lighted tips, extended from the craft's sides.

The object presented its wide, curved leading edge to Barney. Expansive windows dominated this surface. Barney gripped the binoculars tighter and adjusted the focus. He clearly saw humanoid figures: three that stood closely together, apparently piloting the ship, and two others that stood separately. One of those, to the immediate right (from the Hills' point of view) of the threesome, had a bearing that suggested leadership. Farther still to the right was the fifth and final figure, and this one gave Barney a chill because it appeared to be grinning.

Barney had seen enough. He leapt back into the car and punched the accelerator, throwing up gravel from the shoulder and leaving skid marks on the macadam. The craft began to move again and followed the Hills for miles, flying erratically and filling the car's cabin with audible vibration of the sort emitted by a tuning fork.

The Hills' first account to authorities had some specifics and a great many ambiguities. As they initially recalled events, they heard a beeping sound as Barney drove. Then there is an apparent blank, for the next time they heard the beep, there were still driving—thirty-five miles from where the beep had begun. They arrived at their Portsmouth, New Hampshire, home at about 5:00 in the morning. That was peculiar because they should have arrived at 3:00 a.m.

What happened to the two hours? How could they have no recollection of a thirty-five-mile drive?

The Hills immediately fell prey to anxiety caused by undefinable fear. The turmoil disrupted their sleep during that first night, and made their waking hours the next day an intellectual and emotional jumble. Acting on advice from Betty's sister, the Hills reported their odd experience to officials at nearby Pease (New Hampshire) AFB, a heavy bomber base then under the control of Strategic Air Command.

The Hills' call was taken by Maj. Paul Henderson of the 100th Bomb Wing. Henderson followed routine, recording the Hills' information on USAF Form 112, designating it Report No. 100-1-61. Henderson's transcription is dispassionate and unadorned. Many important points are expressed in numbered lists. "The weather and sky was clear at the time." "Continuous band of lights—cigar-shaped at all times despite change of direction." "Tail, trail or exhaust: None observed." "Angle of elevation, first observed: about 45 deg." [*sic*] "Length of observation: Approx 30 min's." [*sic*]

In the latter part of the report, Major Henderson wrote, "Mr. Hill is a Civil Service employee in the Boston Post Office and doesn't possess any technical or scientific training. Neither does his wife." Henderson noted Barney Hill's statement to the effect that he nearly did not make a report, as he found "the whole thing . . . incredible" and that Barney felt "somewhat foolish."

Major Henderson finished his report:

> Information contained herein was collected by means of telephone conversation between the observers and the preparing individual. The reliability of the observer cannot be judged and while his apparent honesty and seriousness appears to be valid it cannot be judged at this time.

In an odd turn, the Air Force dragged its heels about forwarding the Hill report to Project Blue Book at Wright-Patterson AFB in Ohio—a peculiar circumstance considering the following: six or seven hours before the Hills' sighting, radar at nearby North Concord (Vermont) Air Force Station picked up a UFO. And just two hours *after* the Hill incident, a UFO was tracked by precision approach radar at Pease AFB. (Remember that the Hills lost two hours of their personal timelines.) Despite the close proximities in time and distance of the air base sightings, and to the Hills' experience on that lonely stretch of New Hampshire highway, a report about the Concord sighting was not wired to Blue Book for three days. That decision directly contravened Air Force policy, which was to wire relevant reports to Blue Book immediately. Further, the complete Hill report, and an appended note about the Pease AFB sighting, wasn't wired to Blue Book at all. Instead, Pease AFB *mailed* the information to Blue Book on September 29, 1961—nine days after the Hill encounter and the Pease radar sightings. The packet could not have arrived at Blue Book before September 30 or October 1.

When the information of September 19–20 finally got to Blue Book, that body did only a cursory investigation. There is no evidence of special Blue Book research into weather balloon launches and tracking in the area on those dates. Nevertheless, the Blue Book summation of the North Concord AFS radar sighting ends with this: "Conclusion: Probably balloon."

Further, Blue Book failed to follow up on the Hill case and the Pease AFB sighting, despite this on page one of Major Henderson's form 112: "Time and distance between the events could hint of a possible relationship."

Despite that finding, Blue Book took the Hill sighting no more seriously than it did the North Concord event. The Blue Book Project 10073 Record Card is brief, and elucidates just twelve points about the Hills and the Pease radar. Point 11 is labeled "Comments," and reads:

> Both radar and visual sighting are probably due to conditions resulting from strong inversion which prevailed in area on morning of sighting. Actual source of light viewed is not known but it has all the characteristics of an advertising searchlight.

In other words, Blue Book hazarded an unsubstantiated guess.

The Project's conclusions about Hill/Pease AFB originally said, "Optical condition." Afterward, the conclusion was changed (on the same card) to "inversion" and later still to "insufficient data." Independent of Blue Book, official USAF explanations for Hill/Pease AFB included "optical conditions" (whatever that means) and the planet Jupiter. The Air Force also picked up on Blue Book's weather inversion, even though neither Blue Book nor the Air Force investigated atmospheric conditions that might have produced the sightings. The Air Force, like Blue Book, came up with" insufficient data," citing the Hills' failure to note a direction of the light's course. As we've seen, of course, the Hills *did* provide a direction of travel: north followed by south.

Whether the official obfuscation suggests a conspiracy or just professional lassitude can't be known for certain. (Betty herself wrote to Blue Book, and to Major Keyhoe at NICAP, on September 26.) At the least, official investigators felt like investigating very little about what was observed by Barney and Betty Hill.

Unwilling Trailblazers

During the first thirty years of the world's intense postwar interest in UFOs, the objects themselves absorbed the attention of most researchers and laypersons. But UFO investigation

Betty and Barney Hill's September 1961 encounter with a UFO escalated into more than a simple sighting—it became a disconcerting dual abduction that established the narrative of the most dramatic kind of close encounter. Authorities gave the New Hampshire couple's account short shrift in 1961, and it was not until the 1966 publication of John G. Fuller's *The Interrupted Journey* that the Hills became well-known objects of curiosity. In this March 8, 1967, photo, Barney Hill displays a sketch of the craft he and Betty saw six years earlier.   *Getty Images*

grew circular, going round and round with the same syllabus of sightings, close encounters, and unacceptable official explanations. Alien abduction was a long-time staple of pulp and Hollywood science fiction; in 1955's *This Island Earth*, for example, a small plane carrying prominent Earth scientists is held immobile by a green ray and then pulled up through the underside hatch of an enormous flying saucer. The Hills' account, though, suggested credibility, and coverage by major national magazines turned it from a fringe story into a mainstream one.

By the 1980s, restless UFO investigators had shifted much of their attention to abductions, looking hard at alien life forms, kidnapping, sexual assault, lost time—even vats filled with body parts (the 1980 New Mexico abduction of a woman named Myra Hansen and her young son). Years later, during the 1993–2002 TV run of *The X-Files*, alien abduction drove many episodes, and was a vital aspect of the backstory of one of the lead characters, FBI investigator Fox Mulder. (The abduction theme returned in a short-form *X-Files* reboot broadcast in 2016.)

If not for Barney and Betty Hill, agent Mulder may never have existed.

In 1961, the Hills had no cultural pillars to lean against. So disturbed were they by their 1961 experience, and so confused by their fragmented memories of it, that their anxiety progressed to nightmares and pure misery. As is well known, details of the couple's experience came out under hypnosis. Nothing in Barney or Betty's behavior suggests opportunism or a hoax, or any untoward eagerness to go public, particularly because the Hills endured their emotional upset privately for nearly thirty months. Finally, in February 1964, Barney Hill agreed to interviews and hypnotic-regression sessions with Boston psychiatrist and neurologist Benjamin Simon. A week later, Betty Hill did the same. The sessions were tape recorded. Blue Book's scientific consultant, Dr. J. Allen Hynek, participated in the sessions, though he was not doing so under the aegis of the Air Force.

Of the two, Betty was the most voluble, and although both Hills recounted their stories under hypnosis, some observers questioned the depth of Barney's recollections, and wondered if he simply modeled his story on Betty's. (In 1997, Betty Hill wrote to UFO researcher Ted Bloecher, to express misgivings about the regression sessions and question the integrity of hypnosis. She was particularly concerned that too many witnesses to "fairly good" UFO events fell in with regression therapists who coaxed false memories, and were thus transformed from witnesses into abductees.)

As the regression sessions continued, the Hills revealed that as the craft kept pace with them, Barney suddenly veered from the highway and onto a side road. He could not recall whether he made the turn of his own volition or if he felt commanded to do so. In any case, he brought the car to a stop. The Hills were physically removed from the car by two humanoids and wrestled into the craft. In separate rooms, Barney and Betty were physically examined. A needle was inserted into Betty's navel—a pregnancy test, one of the aliens told her. (Betty was able to make herself understood in English, and received thoughts that her brain interpreted as English. Barney had no experience of language, only what he called "a humming.")

An artist named David Baker sat in on the second Simon-Hynek hypnosis session with Barney Hill. After the interview, Baker prepared pencil or charcoal renderings of the aliens' heads, as Barney had described them. The carefully shaded sketches suggest a mug-shot set, with a left profile and a full-face view. The profile image is hardly a profile at all, for the alien's nose is defined only by a nostril; the nose has neither bridge nor tip. The forehead slopes back sharply above the eyes. No obvious hearing aperture is visible, though Baker's sketch incorporates a shadowed area in the spot where humans' ears are located. The jaw is long and, from the side, heavy. Full-face, the width of high cheekbones is maintained into the upper jaw; the jaw narrows sharply below the mouth, and the chin tapers to a point. Full on, the creature's very large, apparently lidless eyes are sited at the extremes of the face, giving an aspect that is at once comforting (the eyes of human babies and baby animals are large relative to their faces, and are often wide-set) and disconcerting.

The nose is comprised of two short, vertical slits. The small, open mouth is without lips.

The relative height of the forehead appears slightly greater than human.

Where did the Hills' abductors come from? Under hypnosis, Betty Hill sketched a rough star map (linked to existing star patterns by later research of Marjorie Fish), crisscrossed with solid lines indicating what the alien leader referred to as "trade routes"; broken lines in Betty's drawing showed various, far-flung expeditions across space. The star map encouraged astronomical researchers to prepare polished versions of Betty's drawing. The conclusion of some is that the craft encountered by the Hills originated in Zeta Reticuli, a shorthand way of referring to twin stars Zeta 1 Reticuli and Zeta 2 Reticuli. We have already discussed the great distances separating Earth from other stars, and the Zetas are far away indeed: 220 trillion miles. A light year is the time needed for light to travel about six trillion miles, which places the Zeta twins 35.7 light years away.

Because the present conception of light years is unavoidably a human one, its presumed obstacles to practical travel between stars reflects human technological capabilities. If the Hills' aliens originated near Zeta 1 or Zeta 2, the visitors managed the trip with a propulsion system that is, at present, impossible for human beings to duplicate.

Living Special Lives

Barney Hill was African American; at the time of the abduction, he was thirty-nine years old. Betty Hill, forty-one, was Caucasian. When Barney and Betty met in New Hampshire in the mid-1950s, both were nearing the end of what would be their first marriages. Barney and Betty wed in the late spring of 1960, and settled in Portsmouth, New Hampshire. People anxious to explain the Hills' abduction in "rational" terms have suggested that because of the racial aspect of their relationship, the Hills existed "apart" from mainstream American society. Because of this, the rational-explainers said, the Hills were predisposed to invent a situation that played on and reinforced their "outsider' status. (Bear in mind that this racialist rationalization of the Hills' encounter was offered just three years after Virginia authorities arrested a "mixed-race" couple, Richard and Mildred Loving, for "miscegenation," and a full six years before the U.S. Supreme Court ruled that state laws prohibiting interracial marriage are unconstitutional.)

Betty developed a progressive turn of mind two decades earlier, while pursuing friendships with black students at the University of New Hampshire. Barney grew up in Virginia, where he negotiated a segregated society and experienced the usual sorts of everyday slights. In the Army during World War II, his career followed the course usually reserved for black soldiers: a support job, driving a truck. Later, after marrying Betty in 1960 and settling in Portsmouth, Barney took the job with the post office.

Portsmouth was home to relatively few African Americans. Because the local black population had few advocates, Barney established a visible presence as a community civil rights leader. He maintained membership in the NAACP and was appointed to the New Hampshire Civil Liberties Commission. Plain and simple justice motivated him; for instance, local businesses that refused to serve blacks eventually got restrained but firm visits from Barney. Much of Betty's activity as a social worker aided people of color.

The Hills' activism, and Barney's frequent night-shift hours, made for long separations. The Hills encountered the spacecraft while on a long-delayed vacation trip.

Local media covered the Hill case in 1961 but it was not until 1966 that the couple's tale achieved national impact. A badly done 1966 *Boston Traveler* article prepared without the Hills' involvement misrepresented the couples' experience. Barney and Betty were bothered by that, and were receptive when approached by a writer named John G. Fuller. Fuller would shortly have success with *Incident at Exeter*, a book about another UFO experience (see chapter nine). The book he wrote with help from the Hills, *The Interrupted Journey*, enjoyed even more success, and helped transform Barney and Betty into important cultural figures. A sober TV-movie, *The UFO Incident*, aired on NBC in 1975. (The film is, regrettably, not presently available on commercial DVD.) Two important stage and film actors, James Earl Jones and Estelle Parsons, effectively portrayed Barney and Betty, and brought the Hills' story into millions of American homes.

The Hills' details of their kidnapping startled the broader public and effectively put an end to the "benevolent alien" scenario propounded in the 1950s by George Adamski and others. Although Barney Hill died suddenly, of a cerebral hemorrhage, at age forty-six in 1969, Betty continued to speak about UFOs, and made claims of many additional encounters, including a craft that seemed to "visit" her on the day of her husband's funeral. Betty Hill passed away in 2004, at eighty-five.

Reactions to Betty's ongoing UFO activism varied. Some observers felt she damaged the veracity of the original account; others became more inclined to write her off as a kook or a publicity hound. Many doubters, untrained in psychology, declared that the Hills had flat-out lied. But among people inclined to believe the tale, the abduction of Barney and Betty Hill inspired considerable speculation. People (usually white people) wondered: *Why did the visitors abduct a couple? Maybe aliens are curious about human sexuality. Were the Hills selected because of sexual qualities and experiences unique to them, or did they just happen to be the first couple the aliens encountered? What happened to the Hills during their time inside the ship? Did Barney and Betty Hill tell the whole story? Could they even* remember *the whole story?*

The common argument against the Hills—that they fabricated a story in order to make money—doesn't bear much scrutiny. The Hills approached their social activism with energy and seriousness. Far from looking to line their pockets, the Hills initially avoided talking about their experience in order not to compromise their community work. Inherent seriousness characterized them both. Neither was a frivolous person. Further, J. Allen Hynek and other trained observers were inclined to believe their story. Although the things that happened to Barney and Betty in September 1961 cannot be proved true, nothing in their story falls apart under careful examination. Their encounter was intensely personal rather than public. They did not seek fame. They became famous because of events quite out of their control.

The Alien War Against Personal Liberty

Accounts of alien abductions originated in the United States, and continue to come from there more frequently than from any other part of the world. In this, Barney and Betty Hill set a course for the future just as surely as they annihilated assumptions from the past. Because America is built partially on a self-created notion of God-given independence, *freedom*—an idea with numberless American definitions—looms large in the national psyche. Because we have nothing like war-shattered London, Berlin, or Tokyo in our recent past, we have no experience with the humbleness brought by an enemy's ceaseless campaign of destruction, and loss of personal freedom. (The heinous, isolated 2001 attack on the World Trade Center towers, executed by a dangerous group rather than an identifiable enemy nation, is another issue.)

Abduction means captivity and a revocation of freedom. Whether perpetrated by extraterrestrials, professional kidnappers, or the pervert on the next block, it is an idea that encourages Americans to recoil. Alien abduction, then, has as strong a hold on our sense of self as on our physical bodies. Little wonder that Americans have reported this repugnant idea more faithfully than people living outside the USA. Still, study by psychiatrists, sociologists, behaviorists, and other professionals suggests a commonality among accounts related by abductees, no matter the victims' nationalities. John E. Mack, an academic who examined the spiritual aftereffects of alien abductions among victims he interviewed said, "I take them [abduction tales] seriously. I don't have a way to account for them."

Who Are Abductees?

The UFO Contact Center International, established in Washington State by certified hypnotist Aileen Bringle in 1978, initially served two functions: as think tank and research center, and as a haven for traumatized abductees. The importance of support groups to survivors of trauma is obvious, and even more obvious when the trauma inspires disbelief in strangers, friends, and even family members. Although movies and television give us some familiar alien abductee "types"—usually toothless yokels or unusually attractive women—real-life people with accounts of abductions diverge not at all from the American mainstream. Results from the first wave of the ambitious Baylor Religion Survey, released in 2006 and conducted with help from the Gallup organization, show that people associated with the UFO Contact Center and with other abductee support groups across America were more educated and more apt to pursue white-collar occupations than the general U.S. population. The average abductee respondent's age was forty-four; the average age of all Americans was forty-six. Abductee marital status—55 percent married—paralleled that of the general population (53 percent).

A survey conducted by American sociologist Brenda Denzler in 2001 indicated that although males comprise 56 percent of the UFO community, females account for 58 percent of abductees.

Eyes Only: The Three Familiar Types of Abduction Narratives

1. **Extraterrestrial hypothesis (ETH)**, by which the aliens and spacecraft are real, physical objects that come from worlds other than our own.
2. **Psychosocial hypothesis**, by which behavior (the giving of an account) is cued by the dominant culture, and the biases of abductees. In addition, biases of hypnotists, hypnotherapists, and other outside investigators must be considered.
3. **Religious-spiritual hypothesis**, by which the abduction account is one aspect of a religious conversion. Accounts conforming to this hypothesis share points of similarity, including memories of past lives, near-death experiences, and reincarnation. Religious-spiritual accounts may also be rooted in an anticipation of a coming apocalypse.

Of the three abduction-story types, the first brings built-in mystery and drama, as well as the promise of compelling first-person accounts. Scenarios two and three are more subtle than number one, and thus generate less widespread public interest. Hypnosis, a key element of type number two, is discussed later in this chapter. The religious-spiritual hypothesis (explanation number three) forms the core of chapter fifteen.

Where Did the Time Go?

The notion of "missing time" is a standard abductee complaint. Subjects report, variously, that time seems truncated, compressed, or missing (in chunks) altogether. One normal-life parallel is so-called highway hypnosis, a fugue state caused by fatigue, boredom, daydreaming, or, especially, over-familiarity with one's route. Commuters often pull into their driveways following long drives and ask themselves, *How did I get here?* Although no time was really lost, the drivers' awareness of it was compromised. Physically present, the drivers were nevertheless absent.

The phenomenon is familiar to some epileptics, whose seizures "blank" portions of memory—and thus, of time. Accident victims, particularly those who are concussed, often emerge with little memory of the moments before and after the accident, and no recollection at all of the incident itself. In cases of concussion, memory can return as the brain heals itself. For UFO abductees, though, memory may never return naturally. Regression hypnosis administered by a competent medical professional (working with a willing subject) may return memory to subjects' consciousness. Occasionally, however, the missing-time conundrum, and the state of an abductee's consciousness, can be determined by conventional means, without hypnosis.

Trucker Harry Joe Turner was abducted from a lonely Virginia highway, truck and all, in 1979. Although the experience seemed to Turner to have taken almost no time at all, he realized later that he had been gone for nearly four hours. Turner's case is an intriguing combination of missing-time syndrome and a hint of extraterrestrial friendliness that didn't work out quite as Turner hoped. He described his kidnappers as humanoids whose faces were marked with numbers. One of the aliens, Alpha La Zoo Loo, offered Turner a trip to a planet located light-years away. Although the journey happened, and Turner and his truck eventually returned to Earth in one piece, his recollection of the event was fuzzy.

Local authorities that took a good look at the truck found it had been tampered with by conventional means, which is to say, with ordinary tools the likes of wrenches and hammers. Turner insisted that the truck (which carried a load of catsup and mustard) returned to Earth covered by a peculiar caul. Investigators found nothing unusual on or inside the vehicle.

Turner later fell into paranoia and tranquilizer dependency, fearful of a second abduction and tormented because the physical evidence did not support his story. Had he fabricated his account, or had he told the truth? If the latter, did his abductors cover for themselves by tampering with his truck? "The Cosmic Frame," a 1955 science fiction short story by Paul W. Fairman (cited in chapter nine), unfolds along just those lines, with a man framed by extraterrestrials for an auto-related crime that is not his fault.

The Betty Andreasson Story

South Ashburnham lies in the center of Massachusetts, fifty-eight miles northwest of Boston. In 1967, as today, the village had a Little League team, some small restaurants, and a homogeneous white population. Because a larger town, Ashburnham, lay directly to the north, residents made a point to stress *South* Ashburnham in casual conversation with outsiders. Residents felt relaxed in this village of tree-lined streets and attractive, white frame houses. They enjoyed quiet lives.

Betty Andreasson was one such resident, but her circumstances changed on January 25, 1967. The time was just after 6:30 p.m. Darkness had fallen, and as Betty stood in the kitchen washing dinner dishes, she listened to the usual living-room chatter from her seven kids, and her mother and father. She gave a small start when the kitchen lights flickered and went out. During the brief interval of darkness, Betty clearly saw a peculiar red glow from the yard. When the glow began to blink, Betty called for her father. He joined her at the kitchen window. People were out there. Little people. Her father laughed. *Just kids in leftover Halloween outfits.* Children?

No, not children. As Betty instinctively turned to gather her own kids, her father watched as five humanoids, ranging from three to five feet in height, *hopped* toward the house. He moved to secure the kitchen door, but reared back when one of the figures walked *through* the wood and into the kitchen.

For eight years, Betty blanked on what happened next, and it was only through sessions of regressive hypnotism conducted by researcher Dr. J. Allen Hynek that she began to remember. Betty and the other nine people in the house were put into what Betty described as suspended animation. Four of the five visitors established telepathic contact with Betty, who felt tentative rather than alarmed. Still, the early moments of telepathic discourse were a little rocky: Betty misunderstood a remark or question and began to cook meat, which gave the small visitors a fright.

The visitors took Betty outside, where a saucer-shaped ship about twenty feet in diameter sat on the slope of the yard. Her father had seen the hopping, but to Betty the strange visitors seemed to levitate. She fell under the telepathic contact of four of the five creatures.

Betty Andreasson described the aliens in terms later recognized as markers of classic "grays": the creatures' heads were dramatically oversized and "pear-shaped," and dominated by "large, dark, almond-shaped eyes." When she recalled "very little neck," Betty meant that the creatures' necks were unusually thin, and seemed inadequate to support the large heads. Mouths were mere slits; ears and noses were "tiny holes." Betty noted that the alien hands had three fingers.

The creatures dressed identically in blue coveralls, the sleeves adorned with an avian symbol that Betty ultimately described as an eagle. The aliens' chests were crossed, uniquely, with quasi-military Sam Browne belts. (In some accounts the belt is characterized as a sash.) All five creatures wore boots.

And then Betty was taken inside the ship. She was instructed to remove her clothing and slip into a plain white gown. She underwent a physical examination. When the examination ended, she was telepathically invited to dress herself again. Despite the intimate nature of the examination—physical violation is common to abduction accounts, and is something nearly always recounted with horror—Betty felt "love" and "comfort" in the aliens' presence. Because she is a committed Christian who accepted Christ when she was sixteen, Betty was inclined to regard the aliens positively. "I believed them to be angels," she said. She identified the group's leader as Quazgaa.

Betty's recollections of the ship's interior were detailed and precise. The saucer was multileveled, with a center section dominated by a crystal wheel revolving around a clear tube filled with gray liquid. The main deck was divided into plain cubicles, and some areas were obscured by walls. Betty recalled strange "red creatures" that crawled along the walls, eyeballing her with orbs mounted on stalks.

The craft gave no physical or audial sense of movement, but Betty nevertheless had an impression of travel to another place—a "sense," she called it.

Hypnotic regression helped Massachusetts abduction victim Betty Andreasson recall details of her 1967 experience. As this illustration suggests, Andreasson described extraterrestrials in the now-familiar "grays" mold.   *Everett Collection*

Quazgaa told her that she would leave the ship, but not before she was treated with an "amnesia block." However, the alien suggested that the block would eventually lift.

About three years after the encounter, Betty became mildly intrigued by Erich von Däniken's *Chariots of the Gods*. But she was not a UFO enthusiast, and her interest in the subject did not take firm hold until she answered J. Allen Hynek's call for interview subjects in 1975. In the course of fourteen regressive-hypnosis sessions, Betty produced details not just of her 1967 encounter, but of brief abduction encounters dating to 1944, when she was just seven years old.

Betty's key early experience happened on the family farm in 1950, when the teenage Betty was confronted by a spherical craft that she initially misidentified as the Moon. She was taken aboard the ship, where a tracking device the size of a BB was implanted in her brain. Betty's calm reaction to the events of 1967 suddenly made sense, because the 1950 event was, for her, a positive one: Betty was taken to "the world of Light" for an audience with "the One." The implant marked her as a person to be contacted again—which is precisely what happened in 1967. (The aliens retrieved the implant, through Betty's nose, at that time.)

The 1967 event generated additional interest because of Betty Andreasson's skill as an artist. Her ability is at the semi-professional level, with a good grasp of perspective and visual narrative. Her talent has allowed her to draw competent images of alien spacecraft, as well as images of extraterrestrials and even herself, as she appeared during the twenty-year span of encounters. In the late 1970s she worked with Massachusetts UFOlogist-writer Raymond E. Fowler. His book *The Andreasson Affair* was issued by Prentice-Hall, a major publisher, in 1979. (A follow-up, *The Andreasson Affair: Phase Two*, appeared in 1982.) Though college-trained in the liberal arts, Fowler is a competent amateur astronomer, and has established himself as a careful and diligent UFO researcher. In 2002, he self-published *UFO Testament: Anatomy of an Abductee*, his account of his own experiences as a person snatched by extraterrestrials.

Between 1967 and the mid-1970s, while the events of January 25 still simmered in Betty's unconscious, some odd and tragic things happened. Betty's ex-husband disappeared, and her father died. After both of her sons were killed in an auto crash, Betty married a local man named Robert Luca, who had had a UFO experience of his own. The Lucases regularly attend UFOlogist events, and Betty is a frequent guest on local and cable-access television, and on Internet radio and podcasts. She is an attractive woman with black hair and calm, wide-set eyes. Her voice is soft and modulated, with just a hint of a New England accent. For longevity in the public eye, and for her appealing demeanor, Andreasson must be regarded as one of the most significant of all UFO abduction participants.

Betty and Robert eventually fell victim to what they felt was government harassment and surveillance. As recently as February 2015, Robert Luca wrote to the local FBI office (Richmond, Virginia) to express displeasure at continuing hacks into his personal computer by computers registered to the Department of Defense network information center, in Vienna, Virginia. Over the years, various residences of Robert and Betty have been surveilled by black helicopters; in 1980, Luca snapped a photo of one that hovered above the Luca home in Cheshire, Connecticut.

Betty's earliest encounters with aliens suggested to her that grays work in concert with superior beings called the Elders. Humanlike and attired in white robes, and sometimes glimpsed in flaming chariots—in accordance with popular Christian notions about angels and redemption—the Elders guide events so that human beings can advance spiritually. Even illness and death are calculated to bring the sufferers and their survivors to a higher spiritual plane. Life is never-ending; death is simply a path to the next level of existence. As described by Betty, the Elder mindset seems distinctly Christian. Just as the Christian God has involved himself in human affairs, the Elders, too, are keenly aware of our activities and behavior. Raymond Fowler's 1996 book *The Watchers 2* quotes Betty as saying, "We are all constantly being monitored. Nothing that you do in your life escapes them."

Could the black helicopters have been sent by the Elders?

In 2007, Robert Luca's son, Robert Luca Jr., used his Web site to post an open letter to the UFO community. He insisted that the entire Betty Andreasson abduction case was a lie, a fraud that had been perpetuated for more than thirty years. Robert Jr. claimed that his father built electronic "gadgets" to tap his own phone. Son accused father of alcoholism, and described Betty as delusional and "far gone."

Luca Sr. responded to the claims by saying Robert Jr. had no special insights into the case, or access to any related materials. The younger Luca had been estranged from his father and stepmother since 2005, partly because of what Robert Luca described as his son's "irrational and untruthful manner" following the death of his grandfather (Robert Sr.'s father), and an implied tussle over the grandfather's will. Robert Sr. wrote his son out of his own will in 2005. He is convinced that his son challenged Betty's account out of spite.

Not long after this dustup, Luca Jr. died. He was forty-three.

Betty Andreasson's oldest child, Becky, has forged a life structured as a sort of coda to her mother's, establishing an Internet presence as a channeler, psychic, and abduction survivor. She has been trained, she says, since infancy in the interpretation of alien symbols. Her stories, especially those involving a "murky brown" creature she likens to a Chupacabra, are ingenious and detailed. She has spoken and written about her abductors (the human-appearing "Elders"), and grays. There are, however, red flags. Becky Andreasson's Web site is monetized—a long-distance psychic reading costs fifty-five dollars—and Becky employs the language of a person inclined to believe in conspiracies dedicated to the suppression of private thoughts. In the meanwhile, Becky podcasts on Supernatural Girlz Radio.

Becky Andreasson's status might confirm a commonly held theory of "lineage abductions," by which people of successive generations are taken, to ensure an effective transfer of alien genetic information.

For a variety of reasons, not all UFOlogists are on board with Betty Andreasson's story. Her earliest drawings of the visitors, dating from the mid-1970s, depict eyes that, though enlarged, have distinct whites and pupils. But (as has been pointed out by Internet skeptic Aaron Sakulich and others) drawings Betty did after the 1977 release of the film *Close Encounters of the Third Kind* show ebony-black eyes, with no discernable pupils. Similarly, the coveralls Betty describes are familiar from pulp covers and science fiction films (aliens in the movies *Killers from Space* [1954] and *This Island Earth* [1955] wear the outfits).

"The Fantastic Imagination"

In the 1970s and '80s, psychologists led by Josephine Hilgard, and closely followed by Cheryl Wilson and Theodore Barber, became intrigued by what they termed "the fantastic imagination." They found that as many as 4 percent of Westerners have vivid imaginative fantasies. Further, these people secretly conduct the business of their lives within those fantasies. The fantasies can seem real, and have vivid appeals to sight, touch, smell, and taste. Animals in fantasies often have personalities, even stuffed animals. Sexual fantasy is common. What Wilson and Barber described as the "fantasy-prone personality" encouraged later researchers to invoke the condition to explain alien abduction, as well as night terrors, psychic powers, false memory, out-of-body experiences, and more.

A 1983 study by UFO researcher Keith Basterfield, sociologist Robert Bartholomew, and psychologist George S. Howard looked at biographical information on 154 UFO contactees and abduction victims going back to the 16th century. Of the 154 (some of whom reported extraterrestrials as benevolent and spiritual), 132 had "key symptoms" characteristic of fantasizers. Other studies look at cases involving people who may imagine things more mundane than UFOs, such as fibromyalgia.

Intriguingly, physical aftereffects of alien contact or abduction often jibe neatly with symptoms described by fibromyalgia patients: fatigue, sleep disorders, depression, anxiety, headaches, sensitivity to light, foggy cognition, and pain, particularly in the lower back and neck.

Incubi and Succubi

Alien abduction inevitably encourages conjecture about extraterrestrial interest in human sexual behavior. Ordinary criminal abduction is an intimate crime: abductors manhandle their victims, deprive them of their liberty, and force them to submit to an unsympathetic agenda. Alien abduction heightens the intimacy factor, particularly insofar as the victim endures confinement to a small, peculiar area (a ship) and is at the mercy of "strange" captors with an interest in the design and functions of the human body.

In this, sexual study and abuse during alien abduction exists in the realm of the scarily fabulous, rather like those regularly reported outbreaks of shrinking and disappearing male genitals in Africa and Asia. Societies the world over preserve venerable tales of rapacious ghosts, goblins, and demons. But the awfulness of alien abduction is unimaginable to those that have avoided it. The shock forces some victims into mortified silence, but moves others to shout warnings. As tales of alien sexual terror spread, the numbers of reported incidents rise. Many among the general public scoff at such claims, and sometimes, even sympathetic sources have their fill of alien sex, and go for all-out sendup, as *Fortean Times* magazine did in May 1999, by devoting its cover to "ALIEN SEX: Probing Close Encounters of the Intimate Kind." An illustrated sidebar discusses "Alien Voyeurs." A call-out deck on one page reads "For a three year period[,] they stretched his penis each night."

Abductees often report that sexual abuse happened while their minds were in an induced twilight state, or during sleep. A scenario in which a human intruder enters a bedroom through an unlocked window and ravages a sleeping victim is familiar enough, and justifiably distressing to contemplate, for it combines rape with "night terrors." *The Nightmare*, a famed 1781 painting by John Henry Fuseli, conflates all of that into the mythic incubus that has (or is about to) sexually abuse a sleeping woman in her bedchamber. Fuseli's blocky, humpbacked incubus is perched on the midsection of an unconscious young woman who epitomizes the Western feminine ideal of long limbs, golden hair, and creamy skin. (*Le Cauchemar* [*The Nightmare*], a marble sculpture completed by Eugène Thivier in 1894, brings the incubus/sleeping nude situation to unnerving dimensionality. And Reynold Brown's poster art for a 1964 horror film, *The Night Walker*, directly references Fuseli.)

A similarly unwelcome sense of the sexually preoccupied "other" dominates numberless depictions of succubi, the female counterparts of incubi. Like an incubus the succubus dedicates herself to forced sexual intercourse. The victim is male, and he's no more pleased about the violation than the victim of an incubus.

Whether incubus or succubus, these are creatures with frightening, distinctly nonhuman faces and bodies. Batlike wings are common accessories; likewise elongated ears, fangs, goats' or rams' horns, hooves instead of feet, and sometimes a tail. (Incubi/succubi images from the late 20th century and after are usually blends of Outsider Art and the pin-up aesthetic, with succubi in traditional girlie poses.) Whatever the gender of violator and victim, the incubus/succubus depictions are akin to scenarios of sexualized alien abduction. And whether mythic or UFO-based, the situations reflect the common fear of sleep, and the even more frightening phenomenon of sleep paralysis, by which the victim can neither awaken nor resist.

Rape is an unconscionable violation. In some quarters, this kind of alien behavior is explained in the blunt terms of breeding (either as experimentation or as part of a vast, concerted effort to create a human-alien hybrid race). To some other observers, though, the alien violations suggest some not-unreasonable questions. Are sexually aggressive aliens plain criminals? Practical jokers? Imps of the perverse? Shape-shifters? (To clarify: just how does alien equipment adapt itself to human bodies?)

Might extraterrestrials have long ago inspired the incubus and succubus figures of folklore and dreams?

"We Wish to Mate with You."

The experience of Barney and Betty Hill quickly became a popular topic of public conversation. After the case became well known, abduction tales multiplied, and many of those stories had sexual aspects. On a summer night in Michigan in 1966, a woman named Jean Sheldon was removed from her parked car and taken to a silvery craft. Inside, three naked humanoid males approached; one gave her a rather blunt pickup line delivered via telepathy: "We wish to mate with you." Sheldon understood the alien's wish that she not resist, so she complied, having sex with all three of the males. She reported that the encounter was stimulating.

A vaguely similar 1966 case unfolded near Melbourne, Australia, and involved a woman named Marlene Travers. Startled by the landing of a silvery disc, Travers got a second surprise when a naked, handsome humanoid male left the ship to tell her that she had been selected to be the first Earth woman to have sex with an extraterrestrial. Fear encouraged Travers to comply, but she was adamant afterward that the spaceman had raped her.

Around 1970, a French farmer observed a pair of aliens, one male and the other female, emerge from a spacecraft and copulate in a field. Afterward, the pair returned to their craft and departed. Whether this tryst was for science or just for fun is unknown.

A 1973 encounter in Somerset, England, began when a robot stalled a woman's car and took her to a spacecraft. Inside, the woman was strapped naked to a table and examined by three male humanoids costumed like surgeons. A pinprick injection made to one thigh paralyzed the woman's entire body, enabling one of the humanoids to have emotionless sex with her. Understandably mortified,

The sexual aspect of alien abduction, particularly as it involves human females, is at once titillating and off-putting; too much emphasis on the issue is apt to encourage blanket dismissal of the whole abduction idea. But comic books (such as this example from 1968, with cover by George Wilson) and other entertainment media have trafficked in the idea since the 1940s.

the woman insisted that authorities preserve her anonymity; to this day, she is "Mrs. X."

Near El Banco, Colombia in 1976, a cattleman named Liberato Anibal Quintero met three tiny aliens that dragged him inside a spaceship and encouraged him to have sex with a trio of humanoid females. The first woman was so enthusiastic that Quintero wore himself out. Quintero did not resist when offered a liquid aphrodisiac, which allowed him to service the other two females—who were no less passionate than the first. Finished with him, the women injected anesthetic into Quintero's back and deposited his unconscious body right on his doorstep.

Hysteria

When a man, woman, or child reports being abducted by aliens, is that person exhibiting symptoms of hysteria? Is the person responding rationally to a real event or inventing an abduction scenario in order to "work out" complex, deep-seated psychological issues?

The etymological origin of the word "hysteria" is in the Latin *hystericus*: "of the womb," a concept popularized in ancient Greece, via some sketchy medical thought, as "the wandering womb." Women had few rights in the ancient world. Their concerns were rarely taken seriously by men. As men saw things, women overreacted or became ill because their bodies had a built-in flaw. Women couldn't help themselves. "Hysteria," then, denoted biological-intellectual-emotional impairment.

Thousands of years later, hysteria is still a feminized condition, and remained a legitimate medical/psychological diagnosis in women (as well as men) well into the 1950s. In 1980, the American Psychiatric Association (APA) formally—and finally—discontinued use of the term *hysteria* because the word primarily suggests "being hysterical," rather than "having" a condition, and is thus pejorative. Further (though not noted by the APA in 1980), "hysteria" had been an amorphous, catch-all term utilized by mental health-care professionals—mainly men—to character-ize any female behavior thought to be loud, unladylike, or immoral.

The *Diagnostic and Statistical Manual of Mental Disorders* (*DSM*), is the APA's unavoidably subjective handbook for mental-health professionals, to be used as an aid in diagnosis and treatment. The guidelines and standards are based on consensus about symptoms, and *not* on (according to National Institute of Mental Health director Thomas Insel) "any objective laboratory measure." Regardless, the APA carries a lot of weight, and the *DSM* is commonly utilized during judgments about public funding of mental health programs, insurance payouts, and issues of competence and legal standing.

The handbook's fourth edition, *DSM-IV*, appeared in 1994, and struck "hyste-ria" from its roll of psychiatric conditions. But laypersons continue the free use of "You're hysterical" to dismiss people who appear to be out of control, irrational, and female-like.

In very recent years, controversial efforts have been made by anthropologists, literary critics, sociologists, and other non-medical professionals to reclaim and rehabilitate "hysteria," while continuing to condemn (more or less) the condi-tion's trivialization as a "women's problem." In her 1997 book *Hystories: Hysterical Epidemics and Modern Culture*, Elaine Showalter (a professor of English and then-president of the Modern Language Association) defines hysteria as "a cultural symptom of anxiety and stress." People unable to cope with those and other pres-sures, Showalter writes, may exhibit multiple personalities, recovered memories of sexual abuse, alien abduction, and (most controversially) Gulf War syndrome and chronic fatigue syndrome. Flash forward to 2016, and one can easily include Iraq War syndrome and even PTSD (post-traumatic stress disorder) in that judgment.

Because Showalter is not trained in medicine, it was easy for her to ignore organic causes of PTSD and chronic fatigue syndrome. Her book gives alien abduction similarly short shrift, discounting post-abduction organic evidence by suggesting that every abduction account from a credible woman or man is essentially the same: a fiction rooted in individual sexual conflict. Showalter is particularly interested in female sexual fantasy, utilizing it, as some medical professionals do, to account for the sexual aspect of many accounts of alien abduc-tion. By this way of thinking, alien abduction is invented unreality with a twist of sexual longing.

Showalter also sees a political agenda at work in abduction stories and other hard-to-explain narratives. She notes that when "accounts grow and become self-sustaining, affected groups organize, become increasingly vocal, and become politicized." After that, "sufferers begin to ask for things: they want more money, they want insurance, they want disability, they want recognition, whatever."

Unfortunately, medical people resistant to the concept of UFOs are inclined to reflexively dismiss UFO-involved patients' physical symptoms, much as sufferers of fibromyalgia were, and sometimes still are, dismissed as psychological wrecks, or cranks. But today, some twenty-five years after diagnostic guidelines that attributed symptoms of fibromyalgia to mental conditions, a broader range of caregivers gives credence to physical reasons for the disorder. Similar open-mindedness will guarantee more sensible and respectful diagnosis and treatment of people who exhibit physical symptoms following encounters with UFOs.

Assaults on Masculinity

The Betty Andreasson case is dramatic, and like the Barney and Betty Hill incident, is particularly piquant because a woman is the focal point. Men, though, are no less apt to be abducted. On November 5, 1975, aliens removed Arizona forest ranger Travis Walton from Sitgreaves National Forest and held him against his will. He was found five days later, huddled near a convenience store. Walton claimed to be the victim of medical experiments, and later claimed that accounts of his experience given by others were inaccurate. Frustrated by bad reporting, as well as by the aliens' attack on his masculinity (forest rangers can be expected to be tough and self-possessed), Walton wrote a book, *The Walton Experience*, in 1978. That volume inspired *Fire in the Sky*, a reasonably popular 1993 film with D. B. Sweeney and James Garner.

Military men, another group with honed physical skills and internalized tendencies to be wary, can also fall prey to extraterrestrial abduction. While driving across the nighttime desert on August 13, 1975, Charles L. Moody, a sergeant attached to New Mexico's Holloman Air Force Base, was startled by an immense disc—fifty feet across and twenty feet high—that hovered above the ground. Moody's car abruptly died, and although the sergeant initially had no memory of what happened next, he came to his senses in time to witness the craft's departure. A glance at his watch told Moody that he had "lost" about ninety minutes.

Two weeks later, via meditation initiated by Moody and monitored by the Aerial Phenomena Research Organization, the sergeant recalled the following: He left his car and then struggled physically with two humanoids that emerged from the craft. Each creature wore a skin-tight black coverall, and stood about six feet tall. Moody was overpowered and then subdued with temporary paralysis. His mobility returned inside the ship, where he was greeted by another, shorter humanoid, with the outsized pale head and eyes typical of grays.

Because scent memory is strong, Moody clearly recalled the sickly sweet odor that permeated the ship. His captors revealed that the craft was now hundreds of miles above Earth, in the proximity of a mother ship. When Moody was given an unexpected tour, he took considerable interest in the craft's propulsion mechanism, a large device powered, apparently, by large crystals that mounted a central drive rod.

The aliens explained that, for now, they were simply curious about Earth and its inhabitants. A public visit would not occur, Moody was told, for twenty years or more. Not long after this conversation, the aliens again rendered Moody insensible, and then returned him to the desert.

Moody's adventure (at least as the sergeant recalled it) did not involve a physical examination. In this, the Moody story differs sharply from many abduction accounts; something other than human physiology seems to have captured the aliens' attention. Holloman AFB was an obvious point of interest, but the base's *location* may be even more salient than the base itself. Holloman was established in 1942, some six miles southwest of Alamogordo, a modest city bordered by New Mexico's Sacramento Mountains. In the darkness of early morning on July 16, 1945, the world's first atomic bomb—dubbed "the Gadget"—was successfully test-detonated on a tower erected in the desert about sixty miles northeast of Alamogordo. The concussion shattered windows in Silver City, New Mexico, 120 miles west of the explosion, and the light of the flash was visible on the horizon in Albuquerque, fifty miles north. Dangerous levels of radioactive dust contaminated the desert in a diameter thirty miles from ground zero. Cattle thirty miles from the tower suffered radiation burns. Although local ranchers had been moved from their property in 1942, so that the military could conduct "test bombing runs," some people remained. They received no advance warning of the blast—the explosion was, after all, a secret. Unsuspecting citizens were shortly contaminated by their water, vegetables, milk, and the air itself.

Trace radiation was recorded as far east as Indiana.

These consequences are serious, with negative, long-lasting implications for everything that breathes. The first atomic test, then, may be the event that brought Sergeant Moody into contact with curious aliens thirty years later.

Strieber's *Communion*

Professional writer Whitley Strieber found solid, early commercial success as a horror novelist, with *The Wolfen* (published 1978) and *The Hunger* (1981). *Warday*, a 1984 collaboration with James Kunetka, is a fictional account of America following nuclear war. Strieber's first book of nonfiction, *Communion*, appeared in 1987, and became an enormous best seller. The book also set the course for Strieber's subsequent career. *Communion* is based on Strieber's own abduction experience at his cabin in New York State late in 1985.

Strieber awoke during the night of December 26, 1985, to see a humanoid creature standing in his bedroom. His next memory, of sitting alone on the forest floor, did not account for "missing time," one of the classic symptoms of alien abduction. Under regressive hypnosis later, Strieber remembered being removed from his bedroom and taken aboard a craft resting in the woods. Inside, he saw non-human creatures representing a variety of body types, from squat to very tall. One of the creatures took a blood sample from Strieber's finger. And then there was this: a needle inserted into his brain, and a probe pushed into his rectum. (Strieber identifies the rectal device as an "electroejaculator.") Abduction, dread, sexual assault—all reflected in Strieber's working title for what became *Communion: Body Terror.*

Although Strieber refers to his abductors as "visitors," and never identifies them as extraterrestrials, he sat with BeechTree/Morrow cover artist Ted Jacobs to help the artist put together the painting that became the book's jacket: a portrait of an alien with the by-then-requisite narrow chin, generous cranium, and immense ebony eyes.

At once rational and sensationalized, the book begins this way: "This is the story of one man's attempt to deal with a shattering assault from the unknown."

The book's gaudy opening aside, much of *Communion* has an involving, documentary-like realism. Strieber's account is powerful, particularly his descriptions of the religious fervor he held during his childhood, and his startling later encounters with "visitors," including encounters that predate his cabin experience by more than thirty years. Specifics of the hypnosis sessions undertaken by Strieber and his wife, Anne, with Dr. Donald Klein (with occasional kibitzing from artist-UFOlogist Budd Hopkins), to recall buried memories, are no less compelling. Strieber admits to being not just unnerved and fascinated by his 1985 abduction experience, but perplexed. Reflective of that, *Communion* pointedly avoids giving "answers." (Strieber subsequently defined the visitors in dark terms, describing them as "profoundly evil" things "maneuvering us toward the earliest possible extinction. . . .")

Although *Communion* enjoyed huge sales, the ridicule aimed Strieber's way soon threatened to deep-six his career. According to the author, sales of books he wrote immediately after *Communion* amounted to *bupkis*, and he had to declare bankruptcy. But he persevered. Notwithstanding a rather embarrassing 2004 "novelization" of a brainless science fiction movie, *The Day After Tomorrow*, Strieber has pursued a busy and commercially successful career during the past twenty-five years, producing some two dozen books that encompass horror and science fiction, adventure thrillers, young adult fiction, and pseudo-religious introspection framed as self-improvement.

On the other hand, the great success of *Communion* has typecast Strieber as "that UFO guy"—a status that may not have been his hope as he wrote that book, but one that he apparently feels obligated to pursue. Strieber's 1989 novel *Majestic* is a fictionalized account of the Roswell crash and subsequent cover-up. *2012*, a novel published in 2007, links the Mayan end-times kerfuffle to reptilians eager to steal human souls. *Transformation, The Secret School, Breakthrough, Confirmation, The Communion Letters*, and *Solving the Communion Enigma* are transparently commercial follow-ons to *Communion*. Strieber also lends his name to a mass-market-paperback series with the umbrella title "Whitley Strieber's Hidden Agendas"; those books are done by writers other than Strieber, and are devoted to a variety of UFO themes and events.

About fifteen years after the publication of *Communion*, Strieber revealed that memory regression had allowed him to recall that, as a boy, he had been one of many American children subjected to mind-control tests secretly carried out by the CIA. That revelation, as well as his postmillennium claims about unchecked world-government conspiracies, have clarified Strieber's status as a chronicler of the secret and paranormal, even as it has relegated him—perhaps unjustly—to the fringes.

Above all, though, stands *Communion*. The book defines much of Strieber's personal and professional lives, and still has the ability to unsettle readers. The rectal probe is rape, pure and simple, and quickly became an abduction trope so familiar that a comic take on the procedure motivates "Cartman Gets an Anal Probe," the pilot episode (1997) of the satiric television cartoon series *South Park*. (Strieber has written about his devastatingly negative emotional reaction to the cartoon.) Cartman's dilemma isn't just that he runs afoul of grays and is probed, but that he's left with a backside implant, as well; implants figure prominently in Whitley Strieber's writings.

Is Strieber's violation the first of its type? "Skeptical xenoarchaeology" blogger Jason Colavito notes that Barney Hill claimed to have been rectally probed in 1961—a detail that Mr. Hill omitted from early accounts of his misadventure. (Colavito very perceptively cites "The Invisibles," a 1963 episode of ABC-TV's *The Outer Limits*, as another early masscult instance of [implied] rectal probing conducted by malevolent extraterrestrials.)

Working from a description provided by abductee-author Whitley Strieber, artist Ted Jacobs elaborated on the big-eyed gray concept for the jacket of Strieber's most celebrated book, *Communion*.

That Strieber arrived on the publishing scene as a genre novelist unjustifiably undercut his credibility as a victim of abduction and assault. Even reviewers who praised his gifts as a storyteller struggled to give Strieber the benefit of the doubt as to his tale's veracity. Undeterred, two years after publication of *Communion*, Strieber established the Communion Foundation, taking the position that human encounters with benevolent visitors are turned into negative ones by regression therapists, hypnotists, and untrained UFOlogists. Contrarily, though, the foundation offers magnetic-resonance imaging to abductees, to detect alien implants.

Because of Strieber's prolific output, and his skill as a writer, he is now a "brand," an "airport author." He brings slick novelistic technique to his nonfiction, and an appreciation for history to his fiction, blurring (unintentionally, perhaps) the line separating truth and speculation—a situation that undoubtedly pleases his publishers.

The jacket of Strieber's entertaining 2006 novel *The Grays* is dominated by a stunningly discomfiting portrait illustration of a big-eyed gray in the vein of the alien visage that is central to various editions of *Communion*. A terse phrase printed above the main title of *The Grays*, "They're Already Here," suggests neither fiction nor nonfiction, and invites interpretation as either. So the writing continues, because even famous writers must buy groceries.

They also must sometimes put up with cranks, such as Richard Doty, who claimed to have given false background information to Strieber when *Communion* was in preparation; and Milton William Cooper, a deranged conspiracy theorist and sometime UFOlogist who loudly identified Strieber as a CIA agent assigned to sow disinformation about UFOs.

Eyes Only: Familiar Elements That Precede and/or Follow Alien Abduction

- Personal sighting of a UFO
- Sudden desire to travel
- A newly developed interest in extraterrestrial civilizations
- A newly developed interest in UFOs and interstellar travel
- Sudden psychic ability
- Out-of-body experiences
- A sense that deep relationships with other people are distractions from something more important
- Hypervigilant behavior, such as moving the bed to one wall and taking care to lock all doors and windows
- Mild paranoia, particularly a feeling of being watched
- Insomnia
- Sudden illness, particularly headaches, sinus trouble, and rashes
- Long-standing tendency to nosebleeds, or recent nighttime episodes of nosebleeds
- Tapping, mechanical humming, and other unexplained, bothersome noises, particularly at bedtime and during the night
- Dreams of flying
- Dreams of flying or floating in bright light
- Dreams of long and significant travel
- Dreams of medical procedures performed by doctors or dentists
- Sleepwalking
- Aversion to medical procedures
- Sleep paralysis, or awakening to find oneself immobile and unable to move
- Disassociation; sense of a lost connection to one's home or forebears
- A conviction that your true origins are somewhere other than Earth

- A conviction that you are essentially different from other people
- Connectedness to the stars; a sense that fundamental information awaits you in the cosmos
- Sense of selection to undertake an important mission
- Unanticipated meetings with oddly attired or otherwise mysterious strangers
- Frequent car trouble
- General apprehension

Eyes Only: Familiar Elements of Alien Abductions

- Victims' ability to walk through walls and other obstacles
- Body brushed by rapidly moving alien fingers
- Concentrated eye-to-eye contact with alien examiner
- Physical torture (this seems to be uncommon, though sexual contact might certainly fit the bill)
- Unwanted sexual intimacy (aliens sometimes conduct sexual investigation psychically rather than physically)
- Body probes
- Harvest of eggs/sperm
- Body implants
- Women: Second abduction two to three months after implantation of alien egg
- Women: Onboard interaction with human-alien hybrid newborns and infants
- Women: Onboard interaction with human-alien hybrid toddlers and youngsters
- Captors inform victims of selection to undertake a mission or fulfill an important objective
- Task instruction carried out via screen or other information-delivery method
- Tests of abductee reflexes
- Tests of abductee memory

Eyes Only: Familiar Elements That Follow Alien Abduction

- Dreams that reveal fresh details of the abduction, or elaborate on existing memories
- Imprints of alien faces on windows and window screens
- A sense of having traveled
- Sleepwear or other clothing worn incorrectly
- Memories of head restraints, needles, or drills
- Thirst or dehydration
- Unexplained body implants
- Subdermal fluorescence
- Pain or other stress to back and neck
- Missing time; minutes, hours, and even days seem to have been compressed or eradicated

- Memory wipe
- Sensitivity to light
- Sudden inability to retain facts
- Increased sensitivity to the emotional state of other people
- New, already-healed scars
- A feeling of sexual well-being
- Evidence of rape or other sexual abuse
- Unexplained pregnancy
- Spontaneous abortion
- Chronic fatigue
- Unexplained small points of injury (bruises, scrapes, etc.)
- Unfamiliar symbols, tattoos, and other new bodily markings drawn or pressed into the flesh, particularly on arms and lower trunk
- Sudden agoraphobia; inability or unwillingness to tolerate cities and crowds
- Low or lower-than-usual body temperature
- Reduced tolerance for liars
- A conviction that you must not talk about certain things that are important to you
- Being followed by mysterious people who may dress in black
- Fresh appreciation of Native Americans and other indigenous people
- Fresh appreciation of bees, praying mantises, and other insects
- Flashbacks; vivid memories of UFOs, spaceship interiors, aliens, babies
- A conviction that some children and adults you meet are human-alien hybrids

Pain

From the 1970s into the 1990s, abduction investigators noticed a sharp uptick in accounts involving dire physical insult. In such cases, a victim's fright over loss of liberty is intensified by physical pain. Terry O'Leary, Sandy Larson, and Jackie Larson (Sandy's fifteen-year-old daughter)—three North Dakotans abducted in August 1975—recalled under hypnosis that they traveled to two planets, and were studied there by a robot with red eyes. The group endured harsh physical examinations. Indeed, Sandy Larson recalled that her brain felt as if it were being pulled from her head.

In Liberty, Kentucky, on the sixth of January 1976, three women that encountered a brightly colored object were abducted from their automobile while driving. Whatever happened to them while (presumably) inside the object was wiped from their memories, but a look at a clock revealed that their captivity lasted nearly five hours. Some details of the event came out under hypnosis: the women had suffered intrusive physical examinations and scaldings with a mysterious hot liquid.

In many cases involving physical pain, bodily paralysis induced by the aliens holds victims fast. Worse, victims often are conscious, and aware of every detail of the probes levied against their bodies. Psychologically, this is not far removed from the venerable terror of being buried alive, an unimaginable situation in which victims are awake, alive . . . but trapped and physically helpless, forced to consider slow death—if the sheer exertion of panic does not kill them first. Paralysis during painful abduction events, then, has a horrific metaphysical aspect every bit as potent and emotionally damaging as the accompanying physical torment. The abductors are not likely to be thinking in metaphoric terms, but to human victims—already buffeted by self-involved governments, unsympathetic bureaucrats, and laws that seem frankly adversarial—abduction and torture by aliens may seem just an extreme expression of the depredations of human systems that can neither be reasoned with nor controlled.

Tales of abusively painful alien abductions come from around the globe, and there may be no other more awful than an event that occurred in an isolated area in southern Brazil, near São Paulo, sometime in September 1988. On the 29th, two boys exploring near Guarapiranga Reservoir discovered a nearly nude male corpse showing signs of bizarre multiple trauma. A medical examiner declared that the victim's internal organs had been taken from his body by "suction devices" placed against neat holes carefully drilled or cut into the armpits. Other holes symmetrically arranged across the face, chest, limbs, and at the rectum suggested the strange suction action, as well, taking with it muscles and other tissue. The holes themselves, the examiner reported, appeared to have been created by precise, sharply focused beams of heat, akin, perhaps, to a laser.

The body contained no blood; it had been drained dry. The perpetrator(s) took away an odd assortment of body parts: the left jawbone, left ear, both eyes and eyelids, tongue, lips, and scrotum (the penis remained), plus the aforementioned internal organs and muscle groups. Two small holes in the cranium suggested that portions of the brain had been removed.

The cause of death is on the books as cardio-respiratory arrest caused by extreme and prolonged pain.

Because neither the body nor surrounding ground showed blood spatter or signs of struggle, and because the body was not left tied or otherwise restrained (indeed, no evidence of ligatures came to light), investigators surmised that the man had been dumped near the reservoir after being killed elsewhere.

Certainly, a case can be made that the hapless victim died at the hands of a particularly vicious, perhaps vengeful, criminal(s). Human beings have shown themselves to be capable of perpetrating such horrors. However, experienced UFOlogists recalled similar mutilations, particularly one that followed the 1956 abduction of USAF Sgt. Jonathan Louette near the White Sands (Nevada) Missile Test Range (a superior witnessed the man being dragged into a "silver disc"); and a nearly nude, neatly mutilated male corpse discovered by hunters in Idaho in 1976.

Further, UFOlogists experienced with cattle mutilations became very interested in the Brazilian case because the damage done to the man's body paralleled damage done to livestock found dead, all around the world, in the vicinity of strange lights or flying objects. In such instances, cattle are precisely, neatly mutilated and left without internal organs and, frequently, blood. Sensory and sex organs are frequently taken (as happened to the men in Brazil, Nevada, and

Idaho). Investigators of cattle mutilations frequently suggest that the large animals are victimized while being held fast in some fashion that leaves no trace, such as the induced paralysis that characterizes many cases of human abduction by aliens.

When UFOlogists warn that extraterrestrials must be approached with care—or, better yet, not approached at all—they give advice intended to save human lives.

Post-Abduction Torment

Imagine the distress of Charleston, South Carolina, resident William J. Hermann, who witnessed UFOs five times during 1977–78, and was then taken (via a blue-green beam of light) into a craft on March 18, 1978. Hermann was a sober young man of twenty-eight, a Sunday school teacher and deacon at his Southern Baptist congregation. He frequently considered infinity and other realms, but had no apparent history of fanciful thinking.

Although not harmed aboard the ship, Hermann did endure a physical examination. Afterward, small, pale aliens in red coveralls telepathically answered some of Hermann's questions. They came from Zeta 1 Reticuli, part of a binary star system nearly thirty-six light years from Earth. (The star map sketched by Betty Hill in 1961 suggested the Zeta Reticuli system.) The alien planet described to Hermann is, like Earth, third from its sun, and Earthlike conditions had evolved there. The Reticulans admitted their concern for human welfare, and told Hermann that they had visited Earth numerous times during the past fifty years. One visit, from eighteen years before, involved their abduction and study of an Earth couple. Hermann became convinced that the aliens were referring to Barney and Betty Hill.

After that, Hermann lost track of time and place. When he regained his senses, he was standing in an open field fifteen or twenty miles from Charleston.

Retired USAF Lt. Col. Wendelle C. Stevens, an investigator with the Aerial Phenomena Research Organization (APRO), looked into Hermann's story. Stevens arranged for the first of Hermann's sessions with a hypnotist. That, and hypnotism and psychological tests arranged later by others, suggested that Hermann was not lying. At the least, *he* believed that space aliens had taken him aboard their craft. (Stevens went on to write a book about the Hermann case, *UFO . . . Contact from Reticulum.*)

Between 1979 and 1982, aliens came to Hermann twice more. During one encounter, aliens (presumably Reticulans) left a glowing ingot, inscribed with the letters M-A-N, in Hermann's bedroom. Professional examination showed that the ingot was a common lead-based alloy; Hermann explained that the metal, though common on Earth, was valuable to the aliens. After local and national publicity, Hermann suffered a flurry of crank calls and some local derision. Officials from Charleston Air Force Base (now Joint Base Charleston) rudely demanded photographs he had snapped of the UFOs. Hermann wrote an essay titled "Inevitable Destruction," and was chided for his prediction of nuclear war.

By 1983, Hermann's experience had become an emotional agony. Insomnia and migraine headaches upset his health and peace of mind, and he lost his job as a diesel mechanic when his employer claimed a general need to make cutbacks. Worse, Hermann was removed as a Sunday school teacher because a few congregants worried he had a connection to Satanism. Perhaps because the charges preyed on him for more than twenty years, he finally claimed his experiences were demonic rather than extraterrestrial.

Hermann's decision to share his adventure brought negative consequences. He is a sympathetic figure, and it's easy to feel bad for him. On the other hand, some abduction stories have peculiar or unrealistically specific details, and become difficult to accept as truth or even as jokes. Take the experience of E. Carl Higdon, a Wyoming oil roughneck abducted by a UFO on October 25, 1974, as he hunted deer in snowy Medicine Bow National Forest. When Higdon pulled the trigger on a good-looking elk, the bullet emerged from the rifle barrel in slow motion and dribbled to the ground a few feet away. At that, a bristle-haired alien with cranial antennae, and an arm that ended in a sharpened cone rather than a hand, surprised Higdon. (The creature's other arm had neither cone nor hand.) The alien stood about six feet tall. It identified itself as Ausso One, and directed Higdon to a man-sized cube that had apparently landed in the woods. The craft—which was considerably larger inside than outside—traveled to a spot 163,000 "light miles" distant, with Higdon the unwilling guest of Ausso and another extraterrestrial—and accompanied by five deer!

Other human beings were in the craft, too: a little girl, three teenagers, and a middle-aged man. Although Higdon observed the people through the craft's transparent walls, he shared no communication with them. As the ship continued on, Higdon spied a foreign planet that he described as "shaped similar to a basketball"—a clunky way of saying "round." He looked around the control room and noticed an intriguingly low-tech alien device festooned with loose wires, and observed the ship's control levers, which Ausso manipulated without touching. (This encourages the question, *Why have levers at all?*)

By now tethered to a chair, Higdon struggled to shield his eyes against brilliant light pulsing from an immense tower on the planet's surface. Ausso fed him food pills before a bulkhead-mounted device scanned his body for a few minutes. The ship finally returned to Earth, and Higdon's captors released him soon after.

Time had got away from Higdon, who struggled to his truck and waited there until a sheriff's search party discovered him. Although bothered after his return by a sore neck and shoulders, Higdon did receive a pleasant surprise: x-rays showed that his lungs, once badly scarred from tuberculosis, were now pristine.

Under multiple sessions of professional hypnosis conducted the month following his abduction, Higdon recalled his journey in more detail. The other humans and even the deer on board the ship, he said, were unwilling participants in a breeding experiment. Higdon could not explain why he hadn't been selected for the program; perhaps the aliens were put off by his scarred lungs.

Higdon's local reputation was good. He came in for little teasing, and his wife stood by his account. Encouraged, he insisted on his story's truthfulness until the end of his life.

Why Does Memory Matter to Us?

In *UFOs and Popular Culture*, Scott Scribner notes that linear time (and its quirks) became central to human philosophical life following the establishment of Christianity; the faith was essentially a countdown to the End Time and Second Coming. Thus, missing time acquires religious significance for many. Religion is a faith-based proposition that attracts most people on Earth. Intensity of belief is naturally tied to a *willingness* to believe. Willingness suggests spiritual and intellectual desire.

Carl Jung regarded the human subconscious as a swirl of religious ideas and symbols. Because abduction accounts often unfold in the manner of dreams, with significant gaps in time and abrupt shifts in locale, religiously oriented abductees may unintentionally "fill in" detail with religious assumptions or symbology. Levitation, degrees of persecution and resurrection, suggestions of ultimate knowledge—these are not uncommon in abduction accounts. Jung said that religious ideas and symbols are common in dreams. The concept suggests that some abduction accounts are reinterpreted dreams, or articulations of spiritual aspiration.

Dr. Kenneth Ring, professor emeritus in psychology at the University of Connecticut and a credible researcher of near-death experiences, has described abductees as "encounter-prone personalities"—more specifically, people who are likely to have suffered childhood abuse or other trauma. (In the late 1980s, Australian UFOlogist Keith Basterfield and American grad student Robert Bartholomew described such persons as FPPs: fantasy-prone personalities.)

A battered human mind works tirelessly, and mysteriously, to repair itself. The repair work is occasionally antisocial, as with the victim of long-ago childhood abuse who wrestles with feelings of helplessness by abusing others. But with other people, repairs are worked out via symbolic events that suggest great journeys. Near-death experiences (usually described by subjects in positive terms) and UFO abductions (usually traumatic) may be two such events. In the aftermath of such events, Ring feels, new levels of consciousness are attained. To what end? Healing.

Ring acknowledges that his conclusions are speculative, and thus in line with many other aspects of psychological study. People disinclined to accept complex psychological factors as the roots of UFO abduction accounts sometimes offer simpler explanations. Skeptics frequently cite a desire for "publicity." Others enter psychological territory without being aware of it, offering meaningless descriptors the likes of "delusional" and "nutty." Science fiction, biblical accounts of unearthly visitors (see chapter four), myth, and folklore are other things cited as the basis for the various tones and specific events of abduction accounts. Indiana University folklorist Thomas E. Bullard, a onetime board member of J. Allen Hynek's Center for UFO Studies, explained,

> Folklore can mean nothing more than "unofficial" culture, the beliefs and practices of people that stand apart from—and perhaps in opposition to—standard norms of the official culture.

Bullard adds that "folk" can refer to any group of people—large groups and small—that share interests and beliefs.

He also offers two useful definitions of myth: "a sacred narrative about origins" and "a false or erroneous story." UFOlogists with interest in ancient astronauts are likely to acknowledge the first definition as legitimate; UFO deniers (or UFOlogists who have no patience with speculation about ancient astronauts) are apt to favor the second. In truth, not a great deal of cultural cues separate believers and deniers. All folklore, myth included, originated in a common cultural-historical pool. Twenty-first-century Westerners are familiar with, say, Zeus and Hercules because those personages are parts of an ancient culture that led directly to our own. The commonality of folklore is intense and impossible to avoid. Specific beliefs are separated not by issues of origin, then, but by variations of folkloric tales designed to suit the beliefs and needs of specific groups.

After studying more than seventeen hundred abduction accounts, Thomas Bullard remarked that not all abduction stories are "full"; a full account, he said, would include "capture, examination, conference, tour of the ship, journey or otherworldly journey, theophany [a physical manifestation of God, or a god], return, and aftermath." If we accept that few of us have recall sufficient to relate every detail of the hours comprising, say, our first day on the job, we can concede that few abduction accounts are likely to be "full." If typical accounts did have that level of completeness, in fact, no one would have trouble dismissing them as fabrications. The incompleteness of abduction accounts is an element that suggests credibility. (A mundane example of this concept: people who give false information to police give themselves away with the unwavering detail and precision of their accounts. No one has an infallible memory, and a traumatic event, such as witnessing a crime, isn't apt to improve it.)

The Memory Path of Leah Haley

Leah Haley was disturbed—not in the clinical sense but in the way that any of us are niggled at by peculiar memories we can neither explain nor fully recall. A native Alabaman, Haley had been flashing back to fragments of childhood memory suggesting that she had been abducted by a UFO. She found the memories disconcerting, and entered hypnosis therapy in 1991 with John Carpenter, a psychological therapist trained in clinical hypnosis and MUFON's director of abduction research from 1991 to 2000. Haley and Carpenter engaged in fourteen hypnotic sessions in 1991, and as Haley's memories grew clearer, she knew she had been taken by extraterrestrials. Just as startling as the abduction itself was Haley's now-restored memory of being aboard the UFO when it was shot down by—as she discovered later—jet fighters scrambled from Eglin Air Force Base, located south of Alabama in Florida's central panhandle.

The clarity of Haley's abduction memories, if not unique, surely marked her as a significant abductee, and thus an important figure in abduction study. Her 1993 book *Lost Was the Key* (published by Haley's own Greenleaf Publications) is widely read by UFO enthusiasts and scholars. Initially able to investigate only her own story and forced to ignore others, Haley plunged into general abduction research. Her zeal was such that her past threatened to overtake her present. The intensity of her effort to get at the truth triggered family dissension and led, Haley is sure, to the failure of her marriage. She also began to feel that Carpenter had let her down, and finally accused him of exploiting his secondhand link to the CIA by selling her case file. This struck Haley as sinister, and she became convinced that something more than just her long-ago abduction was in play.

In a disquieting turn, Haley's abduction memories began to assume new forms. Elements other than aliens entered her thoughts. *There must be a reason*, she thought. She noted during research that the general UFO-abduction timeline corresponded to dramatic advances in the application of electromagnetic frequencies (EMFs). In time, Haley became convinced that she, and other abductees—perhaps *every one*—had not been abducted at all, but subjected to government-mandated EMF mind control. Haley pointed out that exposure to the frequencies alters the victim's consciousness, and can even implant voices in the brain.

Assisted after 1993 by her second husband, a UFOlogist named Marc Davenport, Haley continued to research her past, and the experiences of other abductees. Her 2003 book *Unlocking Alien Closets: Abductions, Mind Control and Spirituality* introduced her followers to her revised, conspiratorial turn of mind.

Physical discomfort dogged Haley in June 2000, when she heard voices in her head, and entered what she felt was an altered state of consciousness. Soon, she was temporarily paralyzed. Not long after, a helicopter hovered near her house.

In 2005, Haley's husband and collaborator, Marc Davenport, died of cancer—cancer that Haley feels was induced by the government.

During a 2011 interview with UFO Trail blogger Jack Brewer, Haley said that after spending thousands of dollars and years in alien-abduction research, "the only evidence I found was of human-instigated mind control. . . ." Haley and other abductees had been guinea pigs. "That's where the evidence pointed," she told Brewer. "I didn't find any concrete evidence—no absolute concrete evidence—of aliens, but *plenty* of evidence of human intervention" [emphasis in original transcript].

Despite her awareness of having been physically tortured by military personnel, Haley perseveres with her story, becoming the central figure in one of the most convoluted of all UFO abduction cases.

Taken . . . and Taken Again

A familiar aspect of nightmares is the exhausting repetition of unpleasant situations. The dreamer feels pursued and trapped. Some abductees experience similar discomfiture because they suffer alien abduction not just once but multiple times. One of the more celebrated of those unfortunates is Debbie Tomey, who was taken near Indianapolis on June 30, 1983. She later recalled the insertion of probes into her nose and abdomen, and although she had not been in good health before this ordeal, she showed no obvious ill effects after her release. But on October 3,

1983, Debbie Tomey was abducted again. This time, her alien captors informed her that during her earlier visit male aliens impregnated her nine times. As Tomey struggled to absorb that, her abductors brought an alien child into the chamber. As Tomey stared, the kidnappers declared that the child was a hybrid—and that it was hers.

As the pseudonymous Kathie Davis Tomey, Debbie Tomey became a central figure of *Intruders: The Incredible Visitations at Copely Woods*, a popular 1983 book by UFOlogist, artist, and Guggenheim Fellow Budd Hopkins. During hypnotic regression performed later, Tomey remembered that she had been regularly abducted by aliens since she was a child of six.

Hypnosis and Hypnotherapy

Before the 1940s, hypnotism existed mainly as one of the minor tributaries of show business. Stage hypnotism was not as lowly as horses that could count, but less honest than the man who kept multiple plates spinning on multiple sticks. People attending hypnosis shows anticipated the novel diversion of a professional hypnotist-performer laying a trance on an audience member (or an accomplice), and then ordering the victim to "feel" extreme cold, or to struggle to lift her arms against invisible weights. Audiences laughed, cheered, and happily threw away their coins to purchase the hypnotists' DIY booklets in the lobby. Hypnotism seemed a pastime of fools and idlers.

Even Freud, a onetime devotee of hypnosis in psychoanalysis, grew disenchanted with it before 1900, suspecting (with good reason) that the memories his subjects conjured while under his hypnotic control had been inadvertently placed there by Freud himself. Some fifteen to twenty years later, physical trauma suffered by soldiers during the Great War inspired some interest in hypnotism's possible role in "bloodless surgery," but it was not until after World War II that serious people began to consider serious applications of hypnotism, primarily to help victims of physical and psychological injury. A respected American psychiatrist named Milton Erickson led hypnotism away from farce and into a relaxed, accessible period of therapeutic "induction," by which suggestions were given to the subject in a low-key way, via something as seemingly simple as, for instance, a handshake that grips the subject's lower arm rather than the hand. The new style of induction hypnotism came to popular venues, as well, led by an American songwriter and radio host named Dave Elman.

The new and improved regard for hypnotism and hypnotherapy continued into the 1950s, concurrent with an American preoccupation with mental and physical well-being that recalled the physical culture fads of the 1920s and '30s.

Serious practitioners of hypnosis, though, had to continually explain what hypnosis is and is not, and struggled to counter pop-culture artifacts the likes of *Abbott and Costello Meet Frankenstein* (1948), in which Dracula effortlessly hypnotizes Lou Costello in order to steal Costello's brain; and a comic 1955 Danny Kaye vehicle, *The Court Jester*, concerning a cowardly royal Fool who is hypnotized (with a finger-snap) into fancying himself a great and confident lover. Then there is *I Was a Teenage Werewolf* (1957), in which an unscrupulous therapist hypnotically regresses a troubled teenage boy to an earlier, primitive stage of human development, with bloody consequences. By 1960, the producers of a sadistic (and weirdly effective) thriller called *The Hypnotic Eye* suggested that stage-show hypnotic suggestion could compel women to go home and mutilate themselves.

The Sting of False Memory

During 1952–53, hypnosis dominated the most celebrated of all hypnotic-regression cases, when a Colorado housewife named Virginia Tighe remembered details of her past life in 19th-century Ireland, as a woman named Bridey Murphy. Whether the amateur hypnotist, Morey Bernstein, successfully regressed Tighe is unknown. Reporters began to dig following the 1956 publication of Bernstein's best-selling book, *The Search for Bridey Murphy*; some concluded that Tighe innocently recalled details from the life of an Irishwoman (named Bridey) who lived nearby when Tighe was a girl. Other investigators suggested that the whole thing was a fraud cooked up by Tighe, Bernstein, or both.

Meanwhile, professional hypnotherapists—credentialed and untrained alike—practiced hypnotic regression with a fervor that, by the mid-1990s, forced the recognition of a dangerous phenomenon: false memory syndrome. Inept hypnotherapists could steer subjects—usually women who claimed to be past victims of incest and other sexual abuse—to memories of *events that never happened.* "Repressed memory" sex-abuse civil-court claims in the U.S. rose from a single case in 1983 to 104 in 1994. U.S. criminal-court cases rose from none or one per year during 1983–89 to a high of twenty-three in 1993. That some defendants (including those tried not for sexual abuse but for medical malpractice and even murder) had been wrongly convicted left fallout that led many among jurists and the public to believe that all hypnotic memory regression is worthless, dangerous nonsense.

Many, if not most, alien abduction accounts arise from memory stimulation encouraged via hypnosis. Advocates of hypnosis say that the process uncovers repressed memory, and brings otherwise unrecoverable detail to abduction narratives. As we have seen, abductee stories can be vivid and convincing. What are we to make of accounts, though, that are the result of false memory? Whether during ordinary recollection or while under hypnosis, many abductees relate tales that are at once believable and unexplainable. Abductee veracity can be difficult to question. On the other hand, hypnosis can implant false memories if the hypnotist purposely or inadvertently gives the subject a prompt—a suggestion of an event that the subject unconsciously embraces as true memory.

By way of example: a 2001 University of Washington memory-and-suggestion experiment—undertaken to demonstrate the dangers inherent in relying on memory regression in criminal prosecutions—successfully suggested (via misinformation and leading questions) to about 40 of 120 subjects that they had met a costumed Bugs Bunny at Disneyland and shaken his hand. The experiment was headed by Elizabeth Loftus and Jacquie Pickrell (who were well aware that

Bugs Bunny is the property of Warner Bros., and not the Disney organization). In a similar experiment headed by Loftus, subjects "believed" that they had been lost in a shopping mall as children. As with the Bugs Bunny experiment, a third of Loftus's subjects recalled something that had not happened, in this case, the trauma of being lost.

Sometimes, false-memory syndrome is an unconscious repression of a frightful, life-altering memory—a kind of psychological self-defense against the horrors of, say, sexual abuse. The syndrome's proponents assume that defensive repression is common, but it is not. False memories can be encouraged by hypnosis and brought to the surface later with trigger words. In other instances, false memory can be created when a subject is eager to please the hypnotist, or satisfy the aims of investigators. If the subject is part of a group claiming a shared negative experience, false memory can be encouraged by a readiness to "explain" one's unusual or "bad" behavior. In other words, *it happened to all of those other people, and then it happened to me, too.*

Cooler Heads

Dr. Ronald Leo Sprinkle (born 1930), Professor Emeritus of Counseling Services at the University of Wyoming, has brought a measured approach to hypnotism-based investigation of alien abduction accounts. A member of the American Society of Clinical Hypnosis, Sprinkle has seen UFOs on multiple occasions, and hosted the Rocky Mountain Conference on UFO Investigation in the 1980s and '90s. Sprinkle's professional background has encouraged him to avoid a temptation to explain away abductee accounts, but rather to, in Sprinkle's words, "emphasize the willingness to explore the personal meaning of these human experiences of spiritual emergence."

In 1968, at the invitation of the Condon Committee (see chapter nine), Sprinkle hypnotized Herbert Schirmer, a Nebraska police sergeant, in order to release the officer's memories of his 1967 capture by extraterrestrials and temporary confinement within an alien spacecraft. Because the Condon Committee's unstated objective was to discredit UFO witnesses and debunk the whole idea of flying discs and similar aerial phenomena, the invitation to Sprinkle amounted to a stunt designed to allow the committee to dismiss Schirmer's claim, saying that committee staff had "no confidence that the trooper's reported UFO experience was physically real."

For his part, Sprinkle felt confident that the trooper "believed in the reality of the events he described." Given that Schirmer had suffered ridicule and physical intimidation back home, and had felt helpless when his wife left him, the belief he expressed during his sessions was more real than even Dr. Sprinkle could have imagined.

Sprinkle founded the Rocky Mountain Conference on UFO Investigation in 1980, to investigate what he calls the "high strange" experiences of UFO witnesses and abductees. To date, he has guided more than five hundred subjects through hypnotic regression.

Chupacabra

Existing in a sideways relationship to alien abduction is the Mexican Chupacabra ("goat sucker"), a creature with roots in ancient Mesoamerican legend linking powerful spirits with a variety of incredible beings. Some Toltec and later Aztec art of the 10th to 16th centuries, particularly friezes and other sculpture, depicts winged beasts suggesting the god Quetzalcoatl, the "feathered serpent" that rules the destiny of humans. In the eyes of many, the images reveal Quetzalcoatl and Chupacabra as one, or as representations of Chupacabra alone.

In the popular Mexican imagination, Chupacabra figures strongly in folklore and oral tradition dating to the 16th century, and the unwelcome arrival of the Spanish conquistadors. Chupacabra, then, has unavoidable connections to the helplessness that accompanies invasion and subjugation. The creature acquired a particular omnipresence in the 1970s to the '90s, when it became a variant of the mutilated-cattle phenomenon. For instance, the legend won considerable acceptance in Puerto Rico early in the 1990s, when the island suffered a wave of livestock killings. By mid-decade, the creature dominated imaginative thought across Texas and Florida; today, most reports come from the U.S.-Mexico border.

Believers describe Chupacabra variously, though most commonly as standing three or four feet high, with gray skin (or hide); a horrid humanoid face dominated by red eyes; and small, kangaroo-like arms. Some descriptions include a spiny back, and witnesses often report wings, a reptilian appearance, and resemblances to warthogs.

The Chupacabra diet favors chickens and other fowl, but also encompasses cows, goats, sheep (particularly lambs), and horses. The creatures feed by utilizing curved fangs against the prey's skull, to drain the blood and brains. This folkloric detail recalls the head trauma suffered by the hapless man discovered near São Paulo in 1988. More popularly, the skull-violating fangs are on prominent view in a well-liked Mexican horror film, *The Brainiac* (1962), in which the title monster is a human transformed into a brain-sucking fiend by a passing comet—an oblique reference to extraterrestrials.

Persistent tales of Chupacabra attacks on humans have a built-in irony, given a relatively common belief that the monsters are not part of the natural world but the result of human meddling in genetics.

Inevitably, a portion of the Chupacabra community believes that the monsters are of extraterrestrial origin, brought to Earth from another world or, less likely, as intelligent engineers of their own destinies. Other accounts cast Chupacabra as organic weapons of alien design, or as the unwanted detritus of extraterrestrial experiments involving earthly fauna.

Chupacabra fever abated in the pop-culture imagination not long after a famed 1997 episode of television's *The X-Files*, "El Mundo Gira" ("The World Turns"). In it, grisly, flesh-eating attacks on people and goats, initially blamed on Chupacabra, are actually the work of a deadly fungus. How mundane!

14

UFOs, Channeling, Quasi-Religion, and Cults

"Salvation Will Come from the Cosmos! I Have Been Chosen, So Pledge Your Lives to Me!"

Most people feel a deep need to believe in something: God, Mother Earth, or quantum physics; the Chicago Cubs, pyramid power, or Charlize Theron; atheism, cold cash, or the scientific method. For many, UFOs promise a reconciliation of Earth's frights and uncertainties. Alien visitors may be wiser than we, and perhaps, via human messengers, they can lead us to the redemption of our souls.

God, salvation, channeling, and UFOs have a long and discomfiting relationship. Since the Arnold incident of 1947, and particularly since the mid-1950s, various persons have appointed themselves the human "voices" of godlike extraterrestrials, or as prophets whose special relationships with the Almighty empower them to lead other, lesser individuals to truth and salvation. Frequently, the otherworldy source of the body- and soul-saving wisdom is unclear: is God Himself engaging in channeling, or do space aliens speak for Him? Perhaps aliens and human prophets are sent to Earth because no human can withstand the sight of God. Or it could be that God and benevolent extraterrestrials are one and the same? Perhaps the creatures that come to Earth in the guise of space aliens are God's angels. Whatever truth exists among the conflations, we are made to understand that intercessors are required.

William Ferguson, for example, a Chicago mail carrier and self-trained relaxation expert, found himself unexpectedly transported to the Sixth and Seventh dimensions in 1938, and subsequently wrote about relaxation techniques. In 1950, Mr. Ferguson earned a two-year sentence for misbranding (fraud), after conducting interstate mail-order sales of a relaxation gadget called Ferguson's Zerret Applicator. Product literature described the device's "therapeutic potency of atoms," which produced "positive Life Energy" and promoted healing. (Ferguson's female associate received a one-year sentence.) Taken to Mars in 1947 by an angel-alien named Khauga, and later to Venus, Ferguson developed his chan-neling abilities, and laid plans for the Second Coming. In 1955, he established the Cosmic Circle of Fellowship, a group that alluded to "rays of life" and "pure universal substance." Ferguson channeled instructions given by Khauga, whom Ferguson identified as the leader of the Universal Brotherhood of the Sons of the Father, a benevolent fraternity comprised of extraterrestrials.

After a Swiss woman named Erika Bertschinger fell off a horse and landed on her head in 1973, she gained the ability to converse with Jesus. As "Uriella," she gathered followers, establishing a formal group, Orden Fiat Lux, in Germany's Black Forest in 1980. Blessed with clairvoyance, she tagged 1998 for the unpleasant arrival of Nazi flying saucers and worldwide natural disasters. Uriella reassured her followers, though, by promising that benign extraterrestrials would lead the group to paradise on Earth.

Tempelhofgesellschaft (Temple Society), a Vienna-based neo-Nazi group established in the 1990s, traces the origins of its members to the planet Aldebaran. Naturally enough, those ancient aliens were Aryan, and later developed links to Sumeria and Atlantis.

Other alien-centric religions have promoted communism, disarmament, crys-tal meditation, and material prosperity. As cheerful as some of that sounds, mes-sages received from aliens caused many cults to become unhealthily preoccupied with Armageddon. A downbeat Texas group, Orville Gordon's Outer Dimensional Forces, prepared for extraterrestrial destruction of Earth by constructing a UFO "Time Ark" base to accommodate the UFO expected to spirit group members to safety. The sect had little tolerance for obstacles, and earned a raid from federal agents after an ODF member planted a pipe bomb at the home of a local politician.

Are alien advisers motivated by nihilism, or is it simply that the joy of cleansing and salvation must be preceded by annihilation? That sober question is leavened, happily enough, by Earthlings channeling messages that are essentially upbeat.

Revelations at Giant Rock

In 1950, a man named Samuel Eaton Thompson met Venusians, who explained to him that Earth's troubles exist because people are born under different astro-logical signs—making them inherently incompatible. George Van Tassel had another idea. A onetime flight engineer with Lockheed, Van Tassel had become preoccupied with religious existentialism before World War II. He thought often of the mystery of mankind's origins, and finally decided to clear his head by radically changing his way of life. In 1947, Van Tassel uprooted himself, his wife Eva, and three daughters, and moved to a spot in the Mojave Desert near Landers, California—and not just any spot, either. Van Tassel was attracted by the world's largest freestanding boulder, a 5,800-square-foot, 100,000-ton behemoth called Giant Rock. Long before white men entered the area, the Rock was considered a holy place by Hopi shamans. Charlie Reche, a homesteader who came to Homestead Valley (later Landers) in the 1880s, was tolerated by the Hopi, and learned a great deal about Giant Rock's spiritual properties. Reche's knowledge slowly spread to the area's other settlers.

Van Tassel became aware of Giant Rock as a young man, around 1930, when he was alerted to the site by a middle-aged, German-born prospector named Frank Critzer. When Critzer allowed Van Tassel to travel to the Rock with him, Van Tassel discovered that the prospector was living beneath the boulder, in a four-hundred-square-foot space hollowed from the Rock's base. Critzer eventually drifted out of Van Tassel's life (and was killed at Giant Rock during World War II, by local police that thought he was a German spy).

In 1952, Van Tassel founded Ashtar Command, a UFO movement based on channeled religious messages sent to receptive Earthlings. Van Tassel believed in the Rock's spiritual quality, and surmised that at least some of that came from the boulder's unique electromagnetic wave forms. Those waves, Van Tassel was convinced, had attracted the attention of extraterrestrials that periodically visited Earth in vast spaceships.

Los Angeles Board of Education photographer Gabriel Green established the Amalgamated Flying Saucer Clubs of America, Inc. in 1959. The group's publication, *Thy Kingdom Come*, espoused a Theosophist philosophy promoting peace and "the spiritual and economic emancipation of man." Green found religious guidance in his associations with Space Brothers from the planet Korender (Alpha Centauri system). He dissolved AFSCA around 1970.

Van Tassel lived with his family in tents pitched near the Rock. He gave August 1953 as the date of his first contact with an alien, a male called Solganda. This alien and his companions (who greeted Van Tassel inside their ship) were non-threatening, and gave Van Tassel the information he needed to begin construction in 1957 on a "cell rejuvenating" electromagnetic device Van Tassel identified as an Integratron. The device also was a time machine capable, Van Tassel said, of sending a user back in time "to take a photograph of Lincoln giving the Gettysburg Address."

Van Tassel described Solganda, companions called Ashtar and Knut, and other aliens as "white people, with a healthy tan." They were, Van Tassel said, about five and half feet tall, "and if they walked down the street, you wouldn't look twice at them." One of the visitors allowed that he was more than seven hundred years old, "in Earth years."

Van Tassel already was interested in channeling as a way to travel beyond one's body; the Integratron promised a more visible exit, to a secure place—whether interplanetary or interdimensional was never clear—where people selected by Van Tassel would find peace, wisdom, and contentment. They would be free from worry, free from harm.

Van Tassel's status as an arbiter determining who would be saved gave his activities a cultlike aspect. Because his personal manner was unassuming, he attracted many people interested primarily in UFOs and alien visitors, rather than otherworldly salvation. In the spring of 1954, Van Tassel organized a UFO convention that attracted scores of people to Giant Rock. Frank Critzer had created a simple airstrip in the 1940s; Van Tassel enlarged it, and for more than twenty years, Van Tassel's saucer conventions attracted buffs that flew their own planes to the site. (Van Tassel claimed to make his living from the "airport" [his word], but the strip was literally in the middle of nowhere.)

A second gathering in 1955 attracted many more people than the first, and by the end of the decade, each Giant Rock convention drew upwards of ten thousand people. Many were simply curious; others had contactee stories of their own. The nuts and bolts of saucer flight attracted saucer buffs, while Van Tassel's ability to channel aliens excited people eager to learn the wisdom of the stars.

During the middle and late 1950s, when contactee accounts were relatively novel, Van Tassel's desert conventions attracted George Adamski, Truman Bethurum, Orfeo Angelucci, and other contactees with exciting stories to relate and books, pamphlets, and photographs to sell. *Variety* columnist and saucer journalist Frank Scully was a special guest at the first convention in 1954.

Before long, Van Tassel and wife Eva opened a forty-seat restaurant, the Come On Inn, to service hungry and dehydrated conventioneers. The annual event welcomed vendors, who came with simple display tables and homemade signs to hawk pamphlets, photographs, "Flying Saucer Shirts," cold drinks, and snacks.

Giant Rock, the desert, and the Rock's Native American pedigree sparked people's imaginations, and offered the lure of a trip more pleasing than a journey to, say, a saucer convention in a hotel ballroom in Oklahoma City. And then there was Van Tassel himself, a square-faced man with regular features, a husky build, and a calm, authoritative voice. If Van Tassel were an actor, Central Casting would have had him play influential businessmen, resolute military officers, or the Secretary of State. He was, in short, an appealing and commanding presence. He channeled for the crowds, occasionally remonstrating the alien presence to insist that more concentration be brought to bear on the communication channel.

When Van Tassel channeled at Giant Rock, he tethered himself to an audio system that altered his voice whenever one of his contacts spoke through him. The channeled messages ran along familiar lines: the importance of brotherly love, and the incipient danger of atomic weapons. A July 18, 1952, channeled message originating with the alien called Ashtar warned that ongoing human research into the hydrogen bomb could only have a bad outcome, not least because hydrogen was one of the key elements of life. Scientists, Ashtar/Van Tassel said, "are tinkering with a formula they do not understand. They are destroying a life-giving element of the Creative Intelligence."

Later in that same July 18 channeling event, Ashtar said, "Your materialism will disagree with our attempt to warn mankind. Rest assured, they shall cease to explode life-giving atoms, or we shall eliminate all projects connected with such. Our missions are peaceful, but this condition occurred before in this solar system, and the planet, Lucifer, was torn to bits. We are determined that it shall not happen again."

Science- and space-focused UFOlogists probably began edging toward the door when they heard the invocation of Lucifer, but Van Tassel persuaded enough people so that he had the means—through monetary contributions from believers—to establish the College of Universal Wisdom, and begin work on construction of his Integratron. The college published a house organ, *Proceedings*, which became useful when Van Tassel wanted to plug his fifty-six-page book *I Rode in a Flying Saucer* (1952) and later publications.

In 1947, religious existentialist George Van Tassel moved with his family to the Mojave Desert, where he dedicated much of his adult life to sharing messages he channeled from benevolent extraterrestrials. In this 1962 photo, Van Tassel shows off his fabulous Integratron.   *Getty Images*

At the beginning of 1978, *Proceedings* reported that Van Tassel had nearly completed construction of the fiberglass and metal Integratron—by this time thirty-five feet high and fifty-five feet in diameter—which resembled a Buckminster Fuller dome. Van Tassel announced that he would be the first to step inside the device. But on February 9, 1978, Van Tassel died of natural causes. He was sixty-eight.

Without Van Tassel's steady presence, the purpose of the Integratron became obscure. Within a few years, the site's outbuildings had been razed by local authorities. In the end, only the Integratron dome remained. In the first decade of this century, promoters organized Retro UFO conventions at Giant Rock. Guests lectured about saucers, astrology, and government conspiracies of secrecy. One enthusiast showed up with a silvered face and mirrored sunglasses. Another wore a gas mask and shin guards. Other attendees wore more traditional costumes;

"space girl" outfits were particularly popular. The conventions' centerpiece was Van Tassel's enormous Integratron dome. Although bereft of scientific equipment needed to make Van Tassel's ambition a reality, the structure, particularly the vaulted, wooden inner dome, is beautiful and impressive. It remains a reasonably popular tourist attraction.

And what of Giant Rock itself? Early in the morning of February 21, 2000, the great boulder spontaneously shed a section of its circumference, revealing an inner rock face as white and pristine as the inside of a coconut.

She Died for the Cause

By the late 1950s, popular enthusiasm for Adamski-like tales of face-to-face contact had waned. Television and tabloid journalism had given contactees a condescending and superficial raking, and mainstream America was nearly done with the idea. Hard-core UFOlogists and buffs continued to be captivated by contactee stories, but growing interest in incidents involving *long-distance* alien-to-human-communication encouraged psychics and channelers (inspired, no doubt, by George Van Tassel) to share their own ET experiences.

Around 1958, LAX ground hostess and former flight attendant Gloria Lee revealed that she first saw UFOs in the early part of the decade, and was contacted in 1952, via automatic writing, by a Jovian named "J. W." An attractive and self-possessed brunette in her thirties, Lee found she could tell her story successfully on the lecture circuit. She told rapt audiences that J. W. had lost his powers of speech, selecting her to act as his "voice," and assemble the story of his life and philosophy. Lee channeled his messages, identifying J. W. as the "etheric space aspect" of an "ascended master" named Djwhal Khul.

Lee was a competent fund-raiser. In 1959, she established the Cosmon Research Foundation, and self-published a quasi-Theosophist book, *Why We Are Here: By J. W., a Being from Jupiter Through the Instrumentation of Gloria Lee*. During a 1960 visit to the Mark-Age Meta Center, a Miami contactee group established in 1956 by Charles Boyd Gentzel, Lee discovered that J. W.—by now calling himself Jim Speed—had assumed human form. (Mark-Age dubbed Gloria "Glo-Ria.") By now, J. W. was concerned about mankind's dangerous play with nuclear weapons, and suggested that salvation lay in an exodus to the stars. J. W. sent Lee plans for a spaceship. Accompanied by a friend named Hedy Hood, Lee dutifully trooped off to Washington, talking up the plans and showing a scale model as she looked for support and funding. Lee's bad luck was all in the timing: this was 1962, when the space race was fed to Americans as a *Life* magazine PR exercise. Few people other than NASA engineers thought seriously about spaceships. Disappointed by the government's disinterest, and self-exiled with Hood to a Washington hotel room, Lee commenced a fast that lasted sixty-six days. She died in the hotel on December 2.

Gloria Lee's death disturbed some mainstream thinkers because Lee said that the fast had been suggested to her by J. W. Her passing had a minor galvanizing effect on the UFO-channeler community, and postmortem messages from Lee were channeled to followers via Mark-Age and a New Zealand channeling group, the Heralds of a New Age. The Heralds combined UFOs with Theosophy and spiritualism, and were one of numerous groups that helped shape what religious historian Robert S. Ellwood described as "part of the birth pangs of the New Age." In that, Lee fashioned herself into a cultural figure of minor but lively importance.

But Lee wasn't done. In a 1963 book, *Gloria Lee Lives! My Experiences Since Leaving Earth*, Lee addressed the faithful by sending her thoughts to a Mark-Age channeler (and temp-agency owner) named Pauline Sharp. New Zealand's Heralds also produced a Lee book of their own in 1963, *The Going and the Glory*.

Just Visiting

A variant of traditional channeling is a "walk-in," by which an extraterrestrial entity occupies a body whose original soul has voluntarily—but not irrevocably—departed. The ET assumes complete control of the body. Although worryingly close to possession, a walk-in is different because the original soul still resides in the body. Rather than possession, then, a walk-in is more like a sub-lease.

The walk-in notion relates to a Theosophical belief that Jesus and Christ were separate souls. According to this line of thought, Christ's soul is more highly developed than Jesus', but because the body of the baby and child Jesus could not contain such a force, Christ's soul was inert during Jesus' early years. As Jesus became a young adult, he vacated his body so that the Christ could "walk in." Similarly, ET walk-ins involved adults, and never babies or young children.

The Doomed Flock of Bo and Peep

The typical person is disturbed and puzzled by suicide. The finality, and the presumed cowardice or courage that allows the act, force us into uncomfortable reflection on our own states of mind and power of will. Suicide pacts carried out by two people are even more intriguing because they allow us to imagine some great passion that bound the victims, and moved them to exit this plane together. Mass suicides—whether inspired by panic, nationalism, or cultish devotion—inspire equal levels of dread, disgust, and fascination.

And then there are those who choose death in order to live.

Much of human social life is a push-pull between autonomy and membership in a group. In moments when a group identity seems important, you give what you are to the group. You may engage in collective behavior that may be productive, destructive, both, or neutral. Devotion is elevated when a group becomes a cult. Although some cultists have passive personalities or low self-regard that make them malleable (and thus desirable as recruits), some others have inflated, even grandiose notions about themselves. People in the latter group may gravitate to a movement's positions of influence, believing themselves chosen or otherwise set apart from common people. The occult writer Brad Steiger considered these egoists and called them Star People. He suggested that they descended from trysts between aliens and humans, or were interplanetary souls reincarnated in human form. Steiger found that an unusual preponderance of these people were women, whom he called Star Maidens.

The behavior of egoists may be explainable, but isn't always excusable. Although one might argue that "aberrant" behavior is relative (that is, what a member of one group labels aberrant may be rational and normal to a member of another group), relativity of perception does not imply *moral* relativism. Murder cultists may regard their crimes as rational, yet those crimes are nevertheless immoral.

Which brings us to two people named Marshall and Bonnie Lu. Under their manipulation of the psychology that underpins cults of personality, and their exploitation of their followers' interest in UFOs and salvation, they facilitated the suicides of thirty-nine people near San Diego during March 23–25, 1997. The group called itself Heaven's Gate. Like some other quasi-religious, UFO-linked cults, Heaven's Gate pursued a supposedly transformative schema intended to elevate members not just to self-realization but, during the end times, salvation. Texas music teacher Marshall Herff Applewhite and a nurse, Bonnie Lu Nettles, established the group—initially called Human Individual Metamorphosis—in 1975.

Typical of many quasi-religious self-enlightenment groups, HIM/Heaven's Gate required members to divest themselves of personal possessions (to the material benefit of Applewhite and Nettles), and surrender their wills to the goals of the group. Use of books, magazines, and television was strictly proscribed. Applewhite (who came to call himself Dō) and Nettles (later known as Ti) supplied the critical information they felt was needed by their followers. The pair expressed, for instance, that space aliens and fallen angels are synonymous. The Virgin Mary was impregnated after being taken aboard a spaceship. Further, Applewhite and Nettles were the divinely protected "two witnesses" bound for martyrdom and resurrection, as introduced in Revelation 11: 3. Revelation 11: 12–13 says, "And they heard a great voice from heaven saying unto them, Come up hither. And they ascended up to heaven in a cloud; and their enemies beheld them. And the same hour was there a great earthquake, and the tenth part of the city fell, and in the earthquake were slain of men seven thousand: and the remnant were affrighted, and gave glory to the God of heaven."

Applewhite and Nettles recognized themselves in this passage. Calling themselves "Bo" and "Peep," they fashioned the Heaven's Gate blend of Christianity and science fiction. Official regulations listed deceit, "sensuality," and negativity as "major offenses." Men and women alike were encouraged to appear androgynous. Male followers had to shave, but they were to move their blades downward only, never up. And then there was this transgression: "Trusting my own judgment—or using my own mind."

A hand-lettered recruitment flyer from the early 1990s was headed with, "UFO's [sic]

• Why they are here.
• Who they have come for.
• When they will leave."

The body of the flyer said, in part, "If you have ever entertained the idea that there might be a real, PHYSICAL level in space beyond the Earth's confines, you will want to attend this meeting."

The group picked up followers in 1993, with a salvation-can-be-yours advertisement placed in *USA Today*, America's national daily newspaper. Yes, the ad said, salvation is possible, but only after a violent dissolution of civilizations. Playing into the self-help movement as well as apocalyptic thinking, Applewhite and Nettles attributed the ad to an apocryphal group, Total Overcomers Unanimous.

The name Heaven's Gate comes from the Book of Genesis. The dreaming Jacob, having surrendered to tiredness on a journey from Beer-sheba

Former music teacher Marshall Herff Applewhite led the Heaven's Gate cult, which promised salvation via a trip to heaven on an extraterrestrial spaceship. This frame grab is from a 1997 video Applewhite recorded to encourage his followers during the cult's final weeks. Over the course of two or three days that March, Applewhite and thirty-eight identically dressed followers packed bags and killed themselves.

© Brooks Kraft/Sygma/Corbis

to Haran, sees a ladder that ascends into Heaven. Angels busily ascend and descend, attending to the Lord's business. The Lord appears at the top of the ladder and says to Jacob, "And behold, I am with thee, and will keep thee in all places whither thou goest, and will bring thee again into this land; for I will not leave thee, until I have done that which I have spoken to thee of" (Genesis: 28:15). Jacob learns that he and his numberless descendants are blessed, and shall "spread abroad" to all points of the compass. Jacob awakes and realizes that he has a great responsibility. Frightened and awed, Jacob says, "How dreadful is this place! This is none other but the house of God, and this is the gate of heaven" (Genesis: 28:17).

The apocalyptic portion of the Heaven's Gate message reflected Christian fundamentalism. (In video lectures, Applewhite referred to the apocalypse as Earth's "respading" or "recycling.") Unknown to his followers, though, was that Marshall Applewhite was a closeted gay who divorced his first wife around 1970, and lost his music professorship at St. Thomas University. He met Bonnie Lu Nettles in 1972, and was attracted to her biblical knowledge and high self-regard. Because they were the witnesses of Revelation ("The Two"), they felt free to flout earthly laws. Credit card fraud involving a rental car landed Applewhite in prison for six months in 1974. He used the time to ponder the role that God had given him. Consistent with Christian thought, Applewhite felt that his body was merely a "vehicle" that carried his soul. But his egoism encouraged him to believe that he and Nettles had origins in what they called the "Level Above Human"; this level was heaven itself, a physical place located in outer space and populated by beings more elevated than ordinary humans. (Applewhite claimed to be two thousand years old.) By spreading God's message, Applewhite and Nettles would elevate themselves and their followers to permanent residency in heaven. Delivery method was via spaceship.

The pair traveled extensively, and began to pick up members. When about twenty people joined almost simultaneously in Oregon in 1975, newspapers and local television took notice. A 1976 book, *U.F.O. Missionaries Extraordinary*, discussed their activities. (The cover blurb of this mass-market paperback reads, "For the first time, Bo and Peep speak freely about their work on Earth.")

Applewhite was his own best salesman, but general public exposure rattled him, probably because of his desire to obscure aspects of his past. For the next few years, he and Nettles reduced their appearances, sending trusted Heaven's Gate members to proselytize in their places. Heaven's Gate carried on, and did not begin to really thrive until the early 1980s, when the group inherited a member's estate.

Somewhat like the Bible's wandering prophets, the Heaven's Gate flock wandered the west and southwest, camping for long periods and adopting a uniform look comprised of coveralls and short hair. Funding from members later allowed the group to purchase residences in Dallas and other parts of the west and southwest.

Bonnie Lu Nettles passed away in 1985, and although her death left Heaven's Gate temporarily rudderless, Applewhite continued to travel and speak. He had wanted to be a New York actor as a young man, and although he hadn't achieved his dream, he had a persuasive oratorical style and a calm, accessible presence that suggested a well-liked middle school science teacher. By about 1990, Heaven's Gate shepherded two hundred members.

Applewhite returned to active preaching, and exploited the relative confinement of indoor quarters to evaluate his members. Those suspected of insufficient zeal were expelled; true believers, as well as those with tangible assets, were retained. Members with computer expertise generated substantial business income that supported the group. While Applewhite encouraged members to make proselytizing videos, he grew increasingly strict, prohibiting drinking and sex. Eight male followers, including Applewhite himself, submitted to voluntary castration.

When astronomers discovered the comet Hale-Bopp in 1995, Applewhite reasoned that the body was a herald of the spaceship sent to take him and the others to heaven. The craft's pilots were space aliens, which to Applewhite were synonymous with fallen angels.

The group shared a final meal at a Rancho Santa Fe, California, restaurant on March 21, 1997. In a banal touch, each member consumed the same innocuous items: iced tea, dinner salad with tomato vinaigrette dressing, turkey pot pie, and cheesecake with blueberries. Then Applewhite and his followers waited a day, until Hale-Bopp reached its closest proximity to Earth. And then inside the group's nine thousand-square-foot mansion, the members of Heaven's Gate began to array themselves on neatly ordered mattresses and bunks, wearing identical blousy black shirts and trousers, shoulder patches ("HEAVEN'S GATE AWAY TEAM"), and black Nike athletic shoes. Applewhite and thirty-eight other believers—twenty-one women and seventeen men—ate a pudding-applesauce mix doctored with vodka and Phenobarbital. Four members had taken the opioid hydrocodone, as well.

Purple shrouds covered the bodies and faces, suggesting that the suicides were accomplished in stages, with members assisting the first victims and tidying up before taking their own lives. Forensic examinations suggested three waves of suicides on March 22 and 23: fifteen, fifteen more, and nine. (Because the bodies had begun to decompose by the time they were discovered, the precise dates of death are not easy to determine; some sources claim the suicides stretched over three days, March 24–26.)

The first person inside the house after the event, a former follower alerted by a letter Applewhite posted a day or two before the deaths, discovered that the heads of many victims had been tied with plastic bags. Some of the flock had carefully packed their suitcases, which stood next to their corpses.

In video shot by the former member, we see a shelf in Applewhite's expansive bedroom, with a few framed pictures. One of them is a neatly matted image of a classic gray, with a large, hairless head; narrow chin; and enlarged eyes.

An angel.

I AM and the Law

Although Guy and Edna Ballard's Theosophy-inspired I AM movement of the 1930s is frequently cited as the first UFO quasi-religion, Guy Ballard's teachings never emphasized extraterrestrials; instead, he claimed to have learned high wisdom from the inhabitants of Earth's etheric plane, an elemental level of existence not usually accessible to ordinary people. That said, Ballard once reported that, during a circa 1930 audience beneath Mount Shasta with the 17th-century master of ancient wisdom, the Comte de Saint Germain, Ballard observed a television set that received broadcasts from the planet Venus.

In 1937, Saint Germain appointed Ballard a messenger to bring the wisdom of the "Mighty I AM Presence" to the world. I AM quickly grew into a religious group partially grounded in alien thought (as interpreted by Ballard). I AM acolytes placed Saint Germain and Christ on equal footing as masters of purified existence.

Ballard identified himself as anointed messenger, charged with utilizing tenets of karma and the apprehensible reality of the divine to reveal the way to re-embodiment. He called the culmination of such a journey "the mighty AM presence." It was, frankly, wondrous: for instance, in his 1934 book *Unveiled Mysteries*, Ballard (writing as "Godfre Ray King") described his meeting with a dozen Venusians who played harp and violin.

I AM put together a million members by 1939, but membership began a steep decline following Ballard's death on December 29 of that year.

In 1940, the U.S. government indicted Edna Ballard and her son, Donald Ballard, for fraud, bringing eighteen charges of false representation of an ability to heal illnesses, and the Ballards' solicitation of money and property from followers. A jury convicted Edna and Donald in 1942, but an important April 1944 ruling by the U.S. Supreme Court absolved the Ballards, writing that followers of religions "may not be put to the proof of their religious doctrines or beliefs." In other words, the issue of whether the Ballards believed in the tenets of I AM must not be left to a court to decide. Freedom of religion is paramount.

Christmas Eve with the Seekers

As we've seen, a notion shared by apocalyptic, end-of-days cults is the presumed specialness of the cult's followers. Cult leaders predict that the world will end, but assure followers that divine action or other intercession will ensure continued physical life. Near the end of 1954 a suburban Chicago housewife-turned-prophet named Dorothy Martin had an epiphany: on Christmas Eve 1954, the world would be destroyed by volcanoes and violent earthquakes. However, spaceships piloted by inhabitants of the planet Clarion stood ready to whisk Martin and her "Seeker" followers to safety. Whether shy or simply concerned she wouldn't be taken seriously, Martin chose Dr. Charles Laughead, a onetime staff physician at Michigan State College, to be her spokesman. (Although fired by MSC in December 1954 for propounding his views about sunken continents to students, Laughead earned newspaper coverage for his claim to be a saucer contactee.)

The Chicago dailies and TV stations dutifully listened to Laughead and reported the story, which excited considerable interest near Martin's Oak Brook home as Christmas Eve approached. Because neighborhood parents soon complained that their children became unmanageable after speaking with Martin, and had trouble sleeping, Oak Park police briefly considered arresting Martin for contributing to the delinquency of minors.

On Christmas Eve, Martin, Laughead, and other Seekers gathered on the sidewalk outside of Martin's home to sing Christmas carols, their eyes flicking frequently toward the sky. Martin and Laughead reminded the waiting travelers that no metal was to be introduced onto the ship. Because of metal clasps, the assembled women removed their brassieres; men cut or pulled the zippers from their trousers. Laughead had to remove the zipper of a man who forgot.

When the spaceships failed to arrive, the group retreated inside the house. In the meanwhile, so many agitated grown-ups arrived to crowd the street that traffic was blocked; rather than arrest Martin for inciting to riot, police took her away and handed her over for psychiatric evaluation.

The unenviable task of facing the reporters fell to Dr. Laughead. He explained, not unreasonably, that the Clarions had probably been concerned about what Laughead called "the mob" of people outside the house; if their ships landed, the onlooker reaction might have been a full-scale riot.

The Christmas Eve prophecy went unfulfilled, but Dorothy Martin unwittingly inspired a mighty contribution to social psychology: a University of Minnesota social psychiatrist named Leon Festinger, and a small group of other psychologists and students, infiltrated the Seekers for two months. The infiltrators listened as Martin spoke to followers about the planet Car, destroyed when the forces of light lost a titanic philosophical battle with Car scientists inspired by Lucifer. Survivors on the side of light settled Clarion and other planets, and now, according to Martin, they dedicated themselves to warning and saving others. In order to be among the saved, a Seeker needed nothing but faith.

At one meeting attended by Festinger and his colleagues, Martin's lecture encouraged informal, small-group discussion, which was followed by a large pink and blue cake decorated with a mother ship and a trio of flying saucers.

There is no way to disprove the reality of the Car war, planet Clarion, or spaceships. Festinger's interest was piqued mainly by Martin's insistence on the doomsday message even after the December 24th deadline had come and gone. The psychologist regarded Martin's certitude as illustrative of cognitive dissonance—the tendency of the human mind to rationalize when deeply held beliefs are empirically revealed to be false (in this case, doomsday was predicted and doomsday failed to happen). To acknowledge that one's deeply held conviction is false can be impossible. Instead, the mind may invest the apparent failure with a counterintuitive significance *that proves the original idea is correct*. The Seekers reacted in this way, explaining that the prophecy went awry because the Clarions worried about the reaction of non-believers, and because Lucifer momentarily gained the upper hand. Nothing about the prediction was incorrect; mere circumstance derailed it. And what if the whole exercise had been a test mounted by the Clarions? *Next* time the prediction will come true.

Festinger was excited by the dynamics of the Seekers, and seized this rare opportunity to field-test his ideas about cognitive dissonance. In 1956, he and a pair of colleagues put together a book called *When Prophecy Fails*. Social psychologists found the book fascinating, and because of an active narrative and explanations of how cognitive dissonance related to politics, economics, and other endeavors, *When Prophecy Fails* found an enthusiastic lay audience. (The book assigns pseudonyms to the Seekers. A 1957 book by Festinger, *A Theory of Cognitive Dissonance*, discusses CD theory in broader terms.)

Prior to gathering the Seekers, Dorothy Martin had investigated Scientology and Theosophy. She committed herself to the climb toward wisdom and self-realization with study at a Dianetics (Scientology) center in Arizona. She later traveled the Andes. By the 1960s, she was in Mount Shasta, California, working with followers at her own institute, the Association of Sananda and Samat Kumara. (Whether people were attracted to the group because of the similarity of "Samat Kumara" to "Kama Sutra" is unknown.) In subsequent decades, Martin slipped easily into New Age thinking. She died in 1992, age ninety-two, in Sedona, Arizona.

The Cosmic Masters Press for Peace

The Aetherius Society is a seminal New Age religion (registered, with status as a nonprofit) very much in tune with latter-day exemplars that share its interests in yoga, spiritual healing, Mother Earth as life goddess, psychic powers, and karma and reincarnation. However, Aetherius is guided, in large part, by peace-loving extraterrestrials known as Cosmic Masters; and by the teachings of Buddha and Jesus Christ—both of whom, Aetherius Society literature tells us, are Cosmic Masters, whose journeys to Earth began on Venus. As the aforementioned karma and reincarnation might suggest, Hindu philosophy has a place in Aetherius thought; much of the Society's activity revolves around the Hindu notion of Prana, the life force that dominates the universe.

The Society takes its name from another Venus-based Cosmic Master, Aetherius, who audibly (but invisibly) contacted a London cabbie named George King (1919–97) in 1954. Aetherius's message to King was this: "Prepare yourself, you are about to become the voice of Interplanetary Parliament." Although King held no interest in extraterrestrials or UFOs, he had already developed a sophisticated interest in yoga, and taught himself the tenets of spiritual healing. Inspired by Aetherius's stated desire for world peace, and by later meetings with an Indian yogi master (who told King to expect "mental rapport with higher intelligences"), King founded the Aetherius Society in 1955, and soon established it in a space above a London health food shop.

Because of the tense Cold War climate of the mid-1950s, George King grew particularly concerned about the dangers posed by atomic weapons, and guided his new organization toward active support of nuclear disarmament. As in Christian doctrine, forgiveness is a virtue; Society literature emphasizes "Oneness and the Divine Spark within all life; God is all."

A newsletter, *The Cosmic Voice*, appeared in 1956. It was followed by a quarterly, the *Journal of Spiritual and Natural Healing*, which metamorphosed into *The Aetherius Society Newsletter*. Today, the Society maintains an Internet presence, with a sophisticated Web site that directs visitors to podcasts and Internet radio programs.

Active mainly in Britain, the United States, New Zealand, and Nigeria, the Society claims a membership of ten thousand; that figure is probably exaggerated upward, with the true number likely to be somewhere in the low four figures. A pair of Temple headquarters, in London and Los Angeles, are handsome but unostentatious. Parallel leadership exists in Britain and America, with newspaper journalist Richard Lawrence working as executive secretary from London and forty-year Aetherius member Brian Keneipp holding the same title in Los Angeles.

Members are activists in the sense that acceptance of Society tenets, and a devotion to the Cosmic Masters, are required for personal salvation. Because the Society neither proselytizes nor actively recruits, Aetherius is unusual among small-membership religious groups. Still, members have faced some rigorous demands. During 1958–61, for instance, the Society held group meetings around the world, on nineteen peaks christened "the Holy Mountains." Pilgrimages and retreats still occur with regularity.

Besides the Masters, important players in human affairs are peace-loving extraterrestrials called Pleiadians; and another, quite different alliance (dubbed the Silence Group by persons other than King), which manipulates influential human beings, multinationally, to obfuscate the truth about UFOs. In August

1958, as a corrective to the latter group, King organized one of the earliest public rallies to demand full government disclosure about UFOs. That rally, mounted in Trafalgar Square, was infiltrated by undercover police, working on an assumption that King's Society functioned as a Communist-front organization. (Scotland Yard's Special Branch, in fact, infiltrated Society meetings and rallies for five years, beginning in the late 1950s, before finally concluding that further investigation would yield nothing.)

During *Mars and Venus Speak to Earth*, a widely recalled live-TV broadcast from BBC2 in 1959, King intrigued home audiences when he went into a trance and channeled a hopeful message from Mars Sector 6—which is not a place but a "Cosmic Adept," a Master.

Rather in the manner Christians await the Second Coming of Christ, the Aetherius Society anticipates the "next Master," who will arrive in a spacecraft to usher in a new millennial age of peace. People that make war will not be destroyed, but transported from Earth to another planet, where they will have opportunities to evolve and develop peaceful spirits.

The Society's main initiative, a "cosmic mission" called Operation Prayer Power, kicked off in the early 1970s. It encourages members to summon positive spiritual energy, for storage in boxlike devices George King called "spiritual energy batteries." Once captured, the energy can be released and sent into the world when needed, as during a hurricane or a civilian crisis in a war-torn nation.

Very little public criticism of the Aetherius Society exists, even on the wide-open Web, though an oppositional blog, pastaetheriussocietymembers.blogspot.com, expresses unhappiness with the "egos" of current Society leadership, and the willingness of those people to welcome "initiates," rather than encourage the spiritually advanced persons favored by King.

Although King passed away in 1997, his videotaped sermons are staples of Aetherius Sunday services.

Opanova and the Daughters of Ummo

It was a happy day in 1960 when a middle-aged Peruvian woman named Juana Pordiavel earned her discharge from a mental hospital. She had become attracted to a younger man, Carlos Opanova, the charismatic leader of a quasi-religious cult he called the Deer of the Sixth Christ. The two married and ran the cult in Peru until 1963, when unwanted government attention prompted them to shift operations to Oruro, Bolivia. An abandoned building became the headquarters of a compound that Opanova dubbed New Heavenly Jerusalem. In 1967, after Oruro authorities aggressively looked into reports of children gone missing near the compound, Opanova and Pordiavel stole away with their followers' cash.

In 1965, two years before the forced abandonment of New Heavenly Jerusalem, a group of Spanish intellectuals led by a Madrid psychologist named José Luis Jordan Peña began a semi-serious campaign to test the limits of everyday belief under the repressive Franco regime. They did this by sending Spanish newspapers, writers, and other vocal sources apocryphal, detailed written messages from Ummites, who had come to Earth in 1950 from the planet Ummo. Situated some 14.6 light years from Earth, Ummo is in the system of the star Iumma, and is home to intelligent beings. Ummo's chief proponent was Fernando Sesma Manzano, director of the Society of Space Visitors. Coincident with a series of saucer sightings near Madrid in 1967, Manzano announced that he had received typed letters and phone calls from representatives of Ummo. Manzano explained that the Ummites wished to mingle secretly with humans and observe cultures across Europe.

This elaborate practical joke (described in detail in chapter fifteen) caught the attention of Opanova, by now settled with Pordiavel in La Paz, Bolivia. The creators of Ummo would not reveal their hoax for another thirty years; to Opanova, the Ummites seemed the gateway to renewed power. He established a new cult that he named the Daughters of Ummo. Opanova prepared a bible that combined José Peña's Ummite fictions with tenets from his own Deer of the Sixth Christ. To keep people interested, Opanova took the name Yiewaka, and announced he had come to Earth from Ummo. Pordiavel renounced the Catholic Church, publicly peed on Communion wafers, and changed her name to Florencia Dinovi Gutiérrez.

Despite Bolivia's stable, democratically elected government and a basic literacy rate above 95 percent, the nation's wealth is unevenly distributed. Peasants who farm are at the mercy of unpredictable weather, and La Paz and other cities are swollen with modestly educated people who have given up on rural life. Partly because of these factors, the Daughters of Ummo attracted recruits quickly. As in Oruro, however, the group became a focus of police investigations of missing, possibly kidnapped, children. (A theory is that the Daughters kidnap to gain new members.) But there was no proof and nobody from the cult was talking. To ensure silence, the cult intimidated members with threats of Ummite hell. (While considering Ummo, Canadian blogger Mike Culpepper wrote, with dry understatement, "An alien hell is something to exercise the imagination. . . .")

Outsiders who expressed too much curiosity about Ummo could expect to receive threatening e-mails and other messages. During the late 1990s, a UFOlogist and amateur investigator named Enzo Daedro received ominous e-mails even after he canceled his e-mail account and opened a new one.

In a summer 2000 group e-mail sent to Daedro and others who "blasphemed the integrity" of Ummo, Opanova threatened to disrupt the hydroelectric power of various Bolivian cities. Plans for a 2033 journey of cult members to Ummo had to be postponed, Opanova said, because the human race remained small-minded.

The Daughters of Ummo continues to operate in La Paz, feeding, clothing, and housing its members. Whether Peña still controls the group is unknown, though odds are good that he does not. Pordiavel/Gutiérrez would have turned one hundred in 2012, so even if she remains on the scene, her ability to lead would be severely diminished. In photos that appear to be from the late 1990s, she is a small, wizened figure with hair dyed jet black, surrounded by the Ummo street vendors whose income still maintains the cult. Recruitment is an ongoing activity, as acolytes buttonhole people on the street, press Ummo literature into their hands, and promise food.

If the group kidnaps children, La Paz police can't prove it.

The Raëlians

When French auto journalist and former singer Claude Vorilhon clambered into the Puy de Lassolas volcano in 1973, he saw a flying saucer that disgorged a friendly, glowing alien. Vorilhon learned that he would shortly hold the secrets of the origins of human life. Further, he had been chosen to be the Earth's Messenger of truth. "Claude Vorilhon" was now a creature of the past. Henceforth, that person would be called "Raël." Inspired by this, Vorilhon/Raël founded the Raëlian movement in 1974. A year later, he traveled to Elohim (an ancient Hebrew word meaning "gods"), a distant planet populated by diminutive humanoids with pale, greenish skin and oversized eyes. During his time on the alien planet, Raël was introduced to Buddha, Mohammad, Confucius, Jesus, and Joseph Smith, the 19th-century founder of Mormonism. Vorilhon learned that although "Claude Vorilhon" had been born of a human mother, he had been sired by an alien.

Today (after a period in Montreal), the Raëlians are based in Geneva, and, according to Raëlian literature, are active in ninety countries. Claimed worldwide membership is one hundred thousand. The group's historical lore is dense and majestic. Thousands of Earth years ago, Elohim on the home planet worried that human beings had the potential to do real damage to Earth and other planets. To forestall that, Elohim already active on Earth denied human beings critical knowledge of human origins, science, and keys for spiritual growth. The Elohim later changed their minds, but the first attempts to educate humanity did not go well: for instance, an attempt at enlightenment mounted by a cadre of Elohim scientists led by an Eloha named Lucifer had disastrous consequences that resonate on Earth to the present day. And then there was a problem with dissident Elohim more dedicated to their own power than helping Earth. The famed Old Testament

Earth's messenger of truth, clone-tech pioneer, traveler to far-distant planets, intimate of the Elohim—all of those are former singer Claude Vorilhon, aka Raël, leader of the worldwide Raëlian movement.   © *Christopher Morris/Corbis*

tale, the account of Noah's ark, is an interpretation of a failed attempt by an aggressive Elohim political party, led by an Eloha named Satan, to destroy humankind. Not long after, the Elohim discovered that they themselves were creations of another, higher race. Elevated by this knowledge, the Elohim resolved to teach and guide humans; Mohammad, Buddha, and Jesus were among the emissaries tasked with carrying out the newly benevolent Elohim agenda.

Much of Raëlian thought is taken from ancient-astronaut theories propounded by rabbinical scholar Yonah Fortner (who wrote about extraterrestrial Elohim in the late 1950s) and writer-translator Jean Sendy (who regarded the Book of Genesis as a fact-based account of alien colonization of Earth). As elaborated on by Vorilhon, humans are descended from alien DNA left on Earth twenty-five thousand years ago. God does not exist; the way to eternal wisdom is an acceptance of the accomplishments of the Elohim, and personal commitments to lives free of strife.

Vorilhon's pronouncement are seldom less than intriguing. He advocates a "geniocracy," a "genius" take on the familiar meritocracy idea of leadership and rule, elected by a "selective democracy" and "backed by military might." Nuclear power, which causes concern in many religions, moved Vorilhon to announce that the detonation of atomic bombs over Hiroshima and Nagasaki in 1945 lifted the curtain on the Age of Aquarius—more ominously referred to by Vorilhon as the Age of the Apocalypse. This ties in neatly with the Book of Revelation, and like Revelation, offers redemption via a savior. In Raëlian thought, the savior is not Jesus but Raël; in other words, Claude Vorilhon. Elohim will come to Earth and save humanity, but only after Raël is recognized as *the* prophet, and is feted with an appropriate temple.

In 1997, Vorilhon and an investor group established Clonaid, a company dedicated to the cloning of human beings. It later called itself "the world's leading provider of reproductive human cloning services." Initially based in the Bahamas, Clonaid quickly suffered the displeasure of that government, and relocated to Las Vegas in 1998. By 2001, Clonaid operated a small lab in Nitro, West Virginia, an industrial town so heavily polluted that it has been a Superfund site since the early 1980s.

Early in 2003, South Korean officials raided the offices of an affiliated Clonaid company, BioFusion Tech, reportedly because of the ethics of human cloning or, alternatively, because of the company's fee-based services. The raid followed closely on Clonaid's December 2002 announcement of the birth of "baby Eve," a cloned human. Because Clonaid spokesperson/CEO Brigitte Boiesslier (a Raëlian bishop) provided neither scientific proof nor the child, media interest fell off quickly. Governments, though, have kept an eye on the company's activities. While Clonaid attempts to work around various countries' laws and ethics, cash flow is maintained by a program of pet cloning. In the meanwhile, Clonaid claims to have created hundreds of human embryos, which have resulted in more than a dozen births of human clones. To date, no proof of such births exists.

The RMX2010, a boxy Clonaid device invented to aid in embryonic cell fusion, has received a skeptical reception from the world scientific community.

The Clonaid Web site appears not to have been updated since 2009, though click-through will take interested persons to the company's Investor Relations page.

The International Raëlian Movement site, rael.org, is up and active, as are discrete Raëlian sites devoted to Raëlian radio, world news, Paradism (the Raëlian political arm working toward a world without work or money), unfounded rumors about the Raëlian movement, and atheism (as of January 2016, this site features a labored "priest" joke about pedophilia).

On a more pleasant note, official Raëlian literature supports the "clitocracy" (women's rights), LGBT activism, and (in a reflection, perhaps, of the Raëlian interest in sensual lives) women's right to go topless.

"The Pureland of God"

After living as a self-described atheist, Hon-ming Chen, a thirty-eight-year-old sociology professor at Taiwan's Chai-Nan Junior College of Pharmacy, experienced a religious awakening. Chen was the product of a nonobservant, working-class Buddhist household. He gave no importance to religion until God—taking the form of green, glowing globes—paid him a visit in 1992. God suggested that Chen had qualities needed to lead people to salvation. Following an unsatisfying and purse-draining experience with a teacher of UFO-based faith, Chen and a small group of followers established the Soul Life Resurgence Association. It grew from one church to four, as an agglomeration of Christianity, Buddhism, Chinese folk religion, UFOlogy, channeling, and broad principles of New Age philosophy. The SLRA became God's Salvation Church in 1993, and predicted an apocalyptic reckoning that Chen called "the Great Tribulation of 1999." In 1995, Chen began to urge the group to follow him to North America, "the Pureland of God," where salvation awaited.

After a few months of church activity in San Dimas, California, early in 1997, Chen settled with his group in Garland, Texas. A church expedition to locate Jesus in Vancouver brought Chen some media attention, and once back in Garland, he announced Christ's imminent return to Earth via spaceship. The momentous event would begin with Christ's appearance on worldwide television on March 25, 1998. Just days later, on March 31, the ships, God, and Christ would arrive on Earth at Garland. Chen's followers confidently declared that when God arrived, He would look like Chen.

Meanwhile, a woman in Taiwan became worried for her daughter, who had followed Chen to the States. Chen still maintained a token presence in San Dimas, and it was there, in the closing days of 1997, that the Los Angeles County Sheriff's Department came for the young woman and reunited her with her mother. The media took their cue from the sheriff, speculating that the young woman was on the verge of suicide, and that Chen practiced abduction, brainwashing, and extortion. CNN reported that Chen traveled in the company of two children identified by him as the reincarnations of Jesus and Buddha.

Chen faced no charges, but God's Salvation Church did manage to raise the hackles of other residents of Garland. The talk of apocalypse brought reporters that seemed to be everywhere. Members of the church purchased some thirty homes in town, but Chen was denied a permit to build what Garlanders suspected was a landing site for God's spaceship. Some locals were put off later by news of a January 1998 road trip to Lake Michigan led by "Teacher Chen." Chen and thirty-two followers decamped at Gary, Indiana, where Chen declared the lake a holy site, and revealed that God's spaceship would land there following the Great Tribulation of 1999, to save survivors. Reporters from Gary and Chicago covered the beachfront event. After that, Chen and his followers drove back to Garland.

The mass suicide of the Heaven's Gate group had occurred in California in March 1997, so reporters in Garland were naturally eager to exploit that angle in interviews with Teacher Chen and other high-ranking church members. The local police, perhaps egged on by the media, spoke publicly about a possible mass suicide of God's Salvation members. Chen countered by revealing that God would appear on television, and later land His spaceship in Garland on March 31.

On March 25, 1998, the day scheduled for God's television broadcast, Garland was a seething mass of police, concerned locals, and snoopy outsiders. The police declared an enormous area surrounding the homes of church members off-limits. At 3513 Ridgeland Drive, Chen and other church leaders held press conferences. The Garland police held press conferences. Everybody waited for God's TV show.

God didn't appear. A dedicated broadcast band set up by the church carried only static. Chen backtracked a little from his TV prediction, and massaged his message about God's arrival, saying that whether God actually appeared on March 31 was irrelevant. A March 27 press release from the church said, "You yourself are God. God will help you become God."

God's spaceship (which Teacher Chen had claimed to see in jet contrails above Garland) failed to appear on March 31. The atmosphere was subdued rather than hysterical. The police were relieved that no one, apparently, was going to commit suicide—though Chen did offer church members an opportunity to stone him to death.

Teacher Chen was discouraged but not defeated. God is within him, he said, as God is within everyone. To demonstrate, Chen stared into the sun for a long moment. (In an academic paper prepared at the University of North Carolina, Charles Houston Prather wrote, "Some reporters seemed less than impressed; one noted that Chen was blinking profusely after the divine demonstration.")

The greater part of Chen's group left him, and many returned to Taiwan. Those that remained settled with Chen in small-town New York State in 1998. The same year, Chen self-published a short book with a long title, *The Appearing of God and Descending of the Kingdom of God: Saving Human Beings by Means of God's Space Aircrafts*.

Further prophecies, including particulars about the international status of Taiwan, a pan-Asian war, and biblical-style floods across the region, failed to come true.

Hoaxes and Other Mischief

Martian Invasions, Shaved Monkeys, and More Tomfoolery

T o UFOlogists, as well as to persons with casual, essentially sympathetic interest in the UFO phenomenon, UFO hoaxes are dispiriting. A hoax, no matter how clever or objectively amusing, gives confirmation to every doubter, to everyone who has listened to a UFOlogist and raised a skeptical eyebrow, to every slug who has looked a believer in the eye and made a dismissive joke about "little green men." Worse (and as we'll see), some widely known hoaxes have been the work of people with serious, vested interests in UFOlogy.

Why They Do It

Plain mischief is behind some false reports of UFOs. Others are manufactured for self-amusement, or faint hope of monetary gain ("Hey, I can sell this video to CNN!"). Some hoaxers long for a million Views on YouTube. Others are moved by dark psychological impulses: not simply the familiar and widely shared wish for recognition as individuals (few of us yearn for lives of complete anonymity), but by desires to embarrass, punish, or humiliate. Such hoaxes may be bluntly sociopathological, or attempts to expose another person's presumed folly. Occasionally, fabricated UFO evidence arrives in the name of scientific research. That happened in April 1971, when a high school sociology class in Maynard, Iowa, created a scorched circle and left other physical evidence that suggested a UFO landing at a local farm. Maynard media inflated the story into multiple sightings, effectively turning a hoax (since known as the Maynard Experiment) into a "real" event. In that instance, hoaxers and the presumably astute providers of news became accomplices.

Although the Web attracts audiences of unprecedented size, UFO hoaxes that gain real traction are relatively rare. But even most that are widely seen (visuals being the key in this overwhelmingly visual age) are seldom widely discussed, and almost none are taken seriously by people whose opinions matter. Still, the very presence of such stuff—*Here's a photo of a UFO that buzzed my school!*—seeps into the cultural groundwater, like runoff, and stays there. Because of YouTube, Facebook, and other platforms and programs, individual hoaxes don't *need* real traction in order to be effective. As one part of a large bunch, the discrete hoax assumes an undeserved, but inevitable, importance, precisely because it contributes to a large total number that is difficult to ignore. Consciously and subconsciously, we begin to feel, *Boy this UFO stuff is a bunch of nonsense.* Even guileless, backyard hoaxers, then, do real harm to serious UFO study.

The visually convincing nature of video and computer technology plays a huge part in the seeming reality of many visually oriented hoaxes. Computer-generated imagery (CGI), motion-control programs, PaintBox, Camera360, and many other programs and applications can turn a hoaxer's concept into apparent reality.

Naturally, trickery predates high-tech. Standouts among early paranormal hoaxes are the Cardiff Giant (New York State, 1869); the Canadian Gorilla (a proto-Bigfoot, 1884); Piltdown Man (c. 1912, Piltdown, Sussex, England); and the Cottingly Fairies (faked photographs made by adolescent female cousins in Britain, 1919–21). Replicas of the Fiji mermaid (monkey head sewn to a fish's body, c. 1840) are in Ripley's museums around the world. People across the globe still believe the veracity of the so-called "Surgeon's Photo" of the Loch Ness Monster (a mock head affixed to a toy submarine, Scotland, 1934). Recent standouts are led by the Pacific Northwest tree octopus (1998); and the pickled dragon (a winged serpent, 2003).

When Wicker Was King

Before flying saucers and other UFOs took their places in Western culture, they did not figure in many hoaxes—reasonably enough. That's not to suggest, however, that the pre-1947 period did not produce any trickery predicated on unidentified flying objects. UFO hoaxes in the United States date to the 1880s, and were concentrated in the west and southwest. The year 1897, which fell at the peak of the so-called airship craze (see chapter four), encouraged pranksters, including a group of locals in Aurora, Texas, who ginned up a tale about a crashed airship—complete with a deceased nonhuman pilot. In Omaha, a pair of idlers attached a wicker basket to a helium balloon, set the basket ablaze, and released the balloon. Meanwhile, a Leroy, Kansas, rancher named Alexander Hamilton insisted that he, his son, and a tenant farmer witnessed the abduction of a Hamilton cow by a hovering airship. According to the older Hamilton, much earthbound tugging on the body of the bawling, levitating cow was insufficient to prevent its kidnapping. A day later, Hamilton and a friend found portions of the cow's miserable remains, and were, according to Hamilton, "greatly mystified." The story was sufficiently colorful to warrant mention in the Yates Center, Kansas, *Farmer's Advocate.* When saucer buffs uncovered the account in the 1960s, further research showed that Hamilton was a member of a local liar's club, and concocted the tale to get a leg up on other members.

Radio and Invasions from Mars

Successful hoaxes ride a foundation of plausibility derived from 1) source and 2) nature of presentation. If the presumed source is an authoritative one, and information is relayed straightforwardly and with confidence, people are inclined to suspend their disbelief. In the history of mass media, no event demonstrates this with as much clarity as the October 30, 1938, radio dramatization of H. G. Wells's *The War of the Worlds*, written by Howard Koch and produced and directed for broadcast by twenty-three-year-old Orson Welles, creator and host of the Mercury Theatre of the Air. Probably inspired by a 1926 BBC broadcast of increasingly violent fictional "bulletins" about labor rioters destroying London, Welles framed a merciless Martian invasion as a series of news bulletins that interrupted "regular programming." By doing so, he redefined the relationship of "new media" (radio) and news, much as the Web, Twitter, and other sources redefine it today.

Available on LP since about 1962 and now easily found on the Web and elsewhere, Welles's *War of the Worlds* (no prefatory "The") quickly became American folklore, partly because tales of nationwide (or, at least, East Coast) panic immediately attached themselves to the tale. But the broadcast did *not* engender panic. An important 2015 book by cultural historian A. Brad Schwartz, *Broadcast Hysteria: Orson Welles's The War of the Worlds and the Art of Fake News*, went to primary sources to discover that the Welles broadcast panicked almost no one, and frightened relatively few. Only a small minority of listeners that became concerned during the broadcast apprehended that the enemy was from Mars; the greater number of worried listeners assumed that the trouble was caused by a terrestrial enemy (Nazi predation in prewar Europe during 1936–38 had already set Americans' teeth on edge), or by natural disaster.

In retrospect, Koch and Welles's creation has far less to do with extraterrestrials and UFOs than with human behavior. But because human behavior—specifically, how we interpret what we see, and what we hope to see—colors every UFO incident, the broadcast remains a uniquely important part of UFO history.

Local variations of the Welles broadcast aired in 1939 (Charleston, South Carolina); 1944 (Chile's Cooperativa Vitaliciaradio network); 1949 (Ecuador's Radio Quito); 1968 (Buffalo's WKBW); 1971 (WKBW); and 1975 (WKBW, again!). Each of the redos provoked the expected laughs and mild upset . . . except for the 1949 Ecuador broadcast, which brought hundreds of citizens into the streets of Quito, and climaxed with the torching of the Radio Quito building. At least half a dozen trapped staffers leapt or fell to their deaths. The blaze spread to nearby structures, and tanks finally had to clear the way for firefighters.

Mr. Scully, Meet Dr. Gee

The everyday citizens of Quito were fooled, but every once in a while, a hard-bitten journalist is as credulous as the general public. In the summer of 1949, author and *Variety* columnist Frank Scully became the victim of a saucer hoax perpetrated by Leo A. GeBauer and alleged Denver oilman Silas M. Newton. In addition to his work as an entertainment journalist, Scully had done a series of books about fun in bed during convalescence, and a collection of celebrity-author profiles. He had no scientific training. Scully included a squib in his *Variety* column about GeBauer and Newton's astonishing adventure: the pair had been present when a dome-shaped saucer crashed outside Aztec, New Mexico, on March 25, 1948. The men approached the wreckage and discovered sixteen small, humanoid corpses peculiarly dressed in antiquarian clothing. (A 1950 FBI report reveals a claim of *eighteen* tiny corpses.) Presumably in no hurry to become laughingstocks, GeBauer and Newton kept their story to themselves. But near an Arizona proving ground not long after, the pair discovered a second crashed saucer, with another sixteen alien bodies. A third crash, at Paradise Valley near Phoenix, left two more humanoid corpses. (Some accounts suggest that the military came upon the saucers first, and that GeBauer and Newton arrived later.)

POPULAR LIBRARY

The Book Everyone Is Talking About

326

BEHIND THE FLYING SAUCERS

Frank Scully

Behind the Flying Saucers, a 1950 book by *Variety* columnist Frank Scully, relates two men's claims about discovering more than thirty extraterrestrial corpses at three saucer crash sites. Although the account was later shown to have been fabricated by the witnesses, *Behind the Flying Saucers* became a significant publishing success. This is the 1951 paperback edition, with the now-famous cover painting by Earle K. Bergey.

Scully told the pair's story in a popular 1950 hardcover, *Behind the Flying Saucers*. Information about the small corpses discovered in the 1947 wreckage at Roswell had not yet seeped deeply into the national consciousness, so Scully's book—perhaps the first dedicated to the saucer phenomenon—was a sensation. The 1951 reprint edition issued by Popular Library enjoyed sales in seven figures.

Frank Scully identified Silas Newton by name but referred to Leo GeBauer as "Dr. Gee." The book's grasp of science is vague but intriguing, with special attention given to unearthly alloys, magnetic propulsion, and supposed magnetic fault zones in the American West; the last, Scully offered, might explain why these sophisticated ships crashed. Scully further claimed that the FBI held more than two hundred pages of classified documents related to the crashes.

From the outset, many people had doubts about Newton and Dr. Gee. A freelance writer named J. P. Cahn looked into the tale and exposed it as a fraud in "The Flying Saucers and the Mysterious Little Men," an article published in the September 1952 issue of *True* magazine. Newton and GeBauer, Cahn wrote, were con artists who had hoped to excite interest in sales of New Mexico oil rights by convincing investors that extraterrestrial technology guaranteed quick removal and refining of the black gold, with plenty of money for all.

In "Flying Saucer Swindlers," an August 1956 follow-up piece for *True*, Cahn elaborated on Silas Newton's credentials, which dated back to 1931 and included pinches for grand larceny, interstate transportation of stolen goods, false stock statements, and conspiracy. No charge against Newton had ever resulted in trial. Meanwhile, Leo GeBauer's past included a suspended sentence for a violation of the Federal Housing Act. Separately and together, Newton and GeBauer had perpetrated swindles in a dozen states. In one particularly absurd con, GeBauer found a mark in Denver and displayed an "oil-finding" machine—a box with an antenna protruding from each end. GeBauer explained that the marble-sized metal balls at the tip of each antenna were plutonium. If true, GeBauer and half of Denver would have been as radioactive as Bikini Atoll. (This particular con cost the eager victim more than $28,000.)

The FBI arrested Newton and GeBauer in October 1952. The pair came to trial in November 1953, charged with fraud and conspiracy. (During the course of the trial, Newton let slip that he hadn't paid income tax for twelve years. A day later, an agent from Internal Revenue was among those seated in the gallery.) Newton and GeBauer earned convictions, and although they looked at thirty-year prison sentences, they received probation, with the caveat that they pay back the many thousands of ill-gotten dollars, plus court costs. At the time of Cahn's second magazine article, neither man had paid a cent.

Silas Newton persevered for another twenty years with uranium swindles and other felonious schemes. The FBI maintained a file on Leo GeBauer until at least 1969, noting that a mark threatened to hurt Leo unless he got his money back.

Frank Scully denied having been the victim of a hoax, and eventually dismissed *Behind the Flying Saucers* as just one book of many with which he had been involved. In *Armour Bright*, his 1963 autobiography, Scully wrote, "Frankly, by now I'm bored with the subject [of UFOs]. Besides, [*Behind the Flying Saucers*] is now out of print, and what author stimulates interest in a book that can't be had for love or money?" In other words, Scully could no longer make a buck off the title, so as he saw it, the question of truth or hoax was pointless.

UFO Crash at Aztec, a 1987 book by William S. Steinman and Wendelle C. Stevens, painted GeBauer and Newton in good lights, claiming that Washington crushed the pair for revealing UFO secrets. Some sources that describe UFO crashes in New Mexico at the time of GeBauer and Newton's Arizona claims suggest that the con men may have stumbled onto real saucer incidents without realizing it. Could the government have wanted to deep-six the New Mexico accounts? One way to do that would be to encourage attention to the patently false GeBauer-Newton claims.

Frank Scully never wrote a second book about UFOs. Original hardcover and paperback editions of *Behind the Flying Saucers* are desirable collectors' items, and the book still has life as a historical curiosity. A trade-paper reprint issued in 2008 by Conspiracy Journal has the original 1951 Earl Bergey paperback cover painting, as well as added text by Stanton Friedman, Scott Ramsay, and other latter-day experts.

And yes, FBI agent Dana Scully of *X-Files* fame was named for the Mr. Scully discussed here.

Electric Razor or Blade?

The weather often grows sultry in Atlanta, Georgia, and drives people to do odd things. Spring and early summer of 1953 brought numerous reports of UFOs. Apparently encouraged, on July 7 a pair of young Atlanta barbers shaved a dead rhesus monkey. (Many accounts give an erroneous date of July 8.) As darkness fell, Edward Watters and Tom Wilson cut off the animal's tail and then gathered the forlorn little body into a car. They drove with friend Buddy Payne to Highway 78 in nearby Mapleton, where all three men scorched the tarmac with blowtorches to simulate saucer exhaust. Watters gave the monkey an artful singe, and then called police. He claimed to have accidentally run his car into the creature after narrowly avoiding a red flying saucer that straddled the road. Two other creatures

Edward Watters (left) and Tom Wilson looked glum while display-ing the shaved monkey corpse they passed off as an extraterrestrial in 1952.   *Getty Images*

quickly entered the saucer, he said, and flew off (leaving a blue glow), but the car struck the third creature and killed it.

The monkey corpse ended up at a local newspaper, where a reporter called the FBI. That agency asked the Air Force Office of Special Investigations (OSI) to investigate. A Department of Defense document that was declassified in 1965 tersely relates, "This animal was first examined by a local veterinarian who stated that he had never seen such an animal before." A subsequent examination by an Emory University zoologist identified the creature as a monkey. The zoologist dryly remarked, "If it came from Mars, they have monkeys on Mars."

Authorities eventually confirmed that the whole story was a hoax resulting from a ten-dollar bet between Watters and Wilson, predicated on a challenge by one or the other that he could not get his picture in the paper. Although the pair had to pay a forty-dollar fine for obstructing a highway, they received some big-league national attention when *Life* magazine sent a photographer to snap pictures as the pair soberly displayed their "alien."

The Elusive Mr. Allingham

Flying Saucer from Mars is a 1954 book by a Briton named Cedric Allingham. In it, Allingham claimed to have witnessed a saucer landing at Lossiemouth, Scotland, and spoken with a humanoid alien that left the craft. A local fisherman named James Duncan also witnessed the landing and signed an affidavit to that effect; the document is reproduced in the book.

The Allingham-Duncan account caught the attention of Scots and others, but both men were elusive when reporters and researchers attempted to contact them for additional information. Duncan seemed to have vanished altogether, and Allingham made only one personal appearance in support of his book (for the pleasure of a UFO club in Tunbridge Wells). Still, supporters of George Adamski and other contactees initially hailed *Flying Saucer from Mars*.

By the 1980s, skeptics concluded that Allingham was British astronomer Patrick Moore, and they were right—partially. Moore did indeed write the book, but the man in the *Flying Saucer from Mars* author photograph (a reedy, musta-chioed fellow posing with a twelve-inch telescope) was Peter Davies, a friend of Moore who passed himself off as Allingham at that Tunbridge Wells appearance. Davies's most significant contribution was his rewrite of Moore's original manu-script, so that the book would have the distinct "voice" Moore desired.

Because of a hugely successful 1979 BBC television program called *The Sky at Night*, Moore (later Sir Patrick) became Britain's equivalent of Carl Sagan—a respected scientist who found popular recognition on television. Moore had interviewed American contactee George Adamski for the BBC's *Panorama* in 1956, following publication of Adamski and Desmond Leslie's *Flying Saucers Have Landed*, and was not overly impressed—except by the ease with which anyone could manufacture a saucer story. Thus was born *Flying Saucer from Mars*.

Moore's good-natured hoax began to unravel when some of his friends and acquaintances confirmed that the telescope in the author photograph of Davies belonged to Moore.

Patrick Moore died in 2012, at eighty-nine. To the end of his life, he maintained that he was *not* Cedric Allingham, and soberly threatened to sue anyone who said he was. Moore's autobiography makes no mention of the book or Allingham.

British folklorist David Clarke concluded a 2012 piece about Moore with the great astronomer's own thoughts about UFOs: "There is nothing I would like better than to meet a Martian, a Venusian, a Saturnian or even a Sirian and my immediate instinct would be to invite him to join me in a *Sky at Night* programme."

Disaster at the Naval Yard

Not long after publication of his 1955 book *The Case for UFOs*, Morris Ketchum (M. K.) Jessup received a highly critical letter. Jessup had speculated in his book that antigravity technology motivated flying saucers from other worlds. The letter he received was written in fractured English and signed by "Carlos Allende." Allende was a Pennsylvanian named Carl Meredith Allen, a drifter who informed Jessup that the book's speculation about extraterrestrial antigravity was redundant and unnecessary because the feat had been accomplished some time ago by human beings. Allen (who most commonly identified himself as Carlos Miguel Allende) cited magnetism as the technological key, writing that "such a form of Levitation [capitalization in original] has been accomplished as described. It is also a Very commonly observed reaction of certain Metals to Certain Fields surrounding a current. . . ."

There is nothing to suggest that M. K. Jessup, an early speculator in theories concerning ancient astronauts, was a hoaxer. However, his eagerness to explain the power source of UFOs led him to take Allen's claims seriously, and perpetuate them. And thanks to subsequent deception perpetrated by Allen, Jessup came to the attention of the U.S. Navy. Allen made handwritten notations in a copy of Jessup's *The Case for UFOs*, using three colors of ink to suggest claims and corrections from three distinct persons with special knowledge of UFOs. The notes elaborated on Jessup's theories about antigravity, and on Allen's special interest in magnetic fields. The notes also claimed that U.S. government experiments with magnetic fields had caused a technological disaster at the Philadelphia Naval Yard on October 28, 1943, when a test of a cloaking device designed to make ships "invisible" to radar, underwater mines, and proximity fuses went wrong. The destroyer USS *Eldridge* (variously described as being at dock and at sea during the event) reacted peculiarly to blasts of strong magnetic fields, becoming "invisible" but leaving much of the crew with brain damage and other physical injuries. (Subsequent speculation by others suggests that the cloaking technology had been taken from/given by UFOs, and even that the experiment's precipitate event was a ray blast sent from a hovering saucer.)

Allen anonymously forwarded the annotated book to the Office of Naval Research (ONR) in the summer of 1955, and early the next year, Jessup received a summons from the navy. He examined the annotated book and identified the scribbles (syntactical and capitalization peculiarities included) as Allende/Allen's. The notes were calculatedly ominous, claiming that Jessup was "CLOSE. TOO CLOSE" to the truth about ancient intelligences on Earth, and "He Knows Something but How Does He know." The notes identify the ancient intelligences as of Lemurian-Muanian origin—brilliant creatures with gills, whose invaluable texts survived untold millennia because the L-M authors had secreted them inside solid rock.

As Carl Allen told the story later, the junior officers at the ONR were sufficiently impressed with the annotated *The Case for UFOs* that the navy authorized a special printing of twenty-five to a hundred copies (accounts vary) of the book and notes, with the annotations reproduced in the original colors. Printing, Allen said, was carried out by the Varo Manufacturing Company, a small electronics firm in Garland, Texas, represented by a man named Austin Stanton.

Allen said that the "Varo Edition" of *The Case for UFOs* was published in 1958. (Purported original editions are typescript and about 8 ½ by 11, with a simple plastic spiral binding; the "book" resembles a training manual or employee handbook.) The edition's introduction is credited to two ONR officers, who provided a rationale for the printing of an edition that virtually no one would ever see: "Because of the importance which we attach to the possibility of discovering clues to the nature of gravity, no possible item, however disreputable from the point of view of classical science, should be overlooked."

According to Allen, Jessup became concerned that the annotations revealed too much, and that he felt uncomfortable as the author of the original book. Jessup died of carbon monoxide poisoning, a probable suicide, in 1959. His death is where the hoax portion of the tale really begins, because Allen began insisting that Jessup had been silenced by Washington.

Allen's address in Kensington, Pennsylvania, became obsolete in 1975, but two years later UFOlogist Jim Moseley traced him to Prescott, Arizona. (We will meet Mr. Moseley again, later in this chapter, vis-à-vis his involvement with contactee George Adamski.) Allen admitted to Moseley that he had faked the annotations to the Jessup book. Although he claimed by this time to have been a witness to the purported calamity aboard the USS *Eldridge*, Allen seemed to Moseley like a man giving a rote recitation of information he had picked up elsewhere. When pressed a little, Allen was unable to demonstrate any knowledge of physics, and after a while Moseley recognized that man and story were the same: threadbare.

Moseley and UFOlogist Gray Barker had carried on a mock feud in their respective saucer newsletters for many years. Rather like the amusingly manufactured Jack Benny-Fred Allen radio feud of the 1930s and '40s, the Barker-Moseley dustup excited interest (within an undeniably small community) and benefited both men. UFOlogists who were gullible, or just enjoyed a good argument, followed the feud closely. Jim Moseley had a nose for the exploitable, and knew that his friend Gray Barker would be intrigued by Carl Allen.

Twenty years after the hand-annotated copy of Jessup's book appeared, Barker conducted an audiotaped interview with Allen. For a while, Barker did a mail-order business in audiotape copies of the interview, but probably came to regret allowing Allen into his life at all. Barker endured a correspondence with Allen, who mailed multiple responses to each one mailed by Barker.

Transcripted versions of the "Varo Edition" of the Jessup book (some with the original three-color scheme) are available from at least two "print on demand" publishers, and the text can be downloaded from numerous Web sites. "Original" copies are typically a 1973 facsimile published by Barker—though what he was working from is a little unclear.

Carl Allen's claims about UFOs receded until 1978, when writers William L. Moore and Charles Berlitz published *The Philadelphia Experiment*, a fanciful retelling of Allen's account. The book was a best seller that inspired books by others, an implausible 1984 Hollywood movie, and a 2012 direct-to-video remake of the same name.

From Here to Obscurity

Howard Menger, a thirty-four-year-old Lebanon, New Jersey, farmer who claimed to have met a female angel as she emerged from a spaceship in 1941, was in the news again during the 1956 Christmas season. On December 29, Menger invited four people to meet a spacewoman—not at a spaceship or other high-tech hideaway, but at a local paint store! The quartet obediently followed Menger to the rendezvous, where they quickly identified the space lady as Connie Weber (later Mrs. Menger), a comely blonde who lived in town,

Menger's ghostwritten 1959 book *From Outer Space to You* gives a Christian-oriented account of his various telepathic and in-person encounters with aliens. The highlight of those is contact number two, which occurred on Okinawa during World War II, after Menger (who had blithely swiped a jeep and gone AWOL) heroically took out three Japanese soldiers without firing a shot. Shaken (and after going AWOL again), he was consoled the following night by a male alien, who offered, "It's too bad about last night."

Menger used his book to answer dozens of frequently asked questions that encompassed propulsion drive to alien breastfeeding. He devoted space to a discourse on disease pathology, and many pages to animal husbandry and soil care. In the book's most exciting section, Menger revealed that he was a reincarnated Saturnian.

From Outer Space to You caused a mild stir, and Menger gave interviews to New York radio host "Long" John Nebel, TV personalities Jack Paar and Dave Garroway, and others that anticipated controversy and some fun. Menger made a few dollars by selling UFO illustrations that he passed off as photos. He had his moment in the sun, but after releasing a record album called *Music from Another Planet*, Menger grew disillusioned with his alien friends—or perhaps other people just grew disillusioned with him. A failed attempt to market a palm-sized "free energy motor" Menger assembled with alien guidance discouraged him. According to a How Stuff Works Web piece credited to "the Editors of Publications International, Ltd.," Menger eventually recanted his saucer tales, "vaguely muttering about a CIA experiment." He passed away in Florida in 2009.

Bad-Luck Saucer

Con artists that mated flying saucer tech-tomfoolery to promises of quick returns for smart investors might prosper . . . for a while. In Baltimore in 1957, a fifty-one-year-old man named Otis T. Carr sold stock in OTC Enterprises, a company he had established two years before. Otis Carr's product was free energy, and when enough investors had come on board, Carr would undertake the final work on his invention, an OTC-XI flying saucer powered by an "electronic accumulator." Once the technology proved itself in a successful demonstration, there would be millions for all.

Carr collected hundreds of thousands of dollars while based in Baltimore. Investors, however, wanted to see a return on their investment, so in 1958, Carr moved his operation from Baltimore to Oklahoma City. A man named Norman Colton handled OTC public relations there, and a contactee named Wayne Sulo Aho became "director of public education," to assist with OTC's day-to-day operations.

UFO-centric investors grew increasingly excited by Aho's status as a contactee, and thanks to work done by Colton, the general public, too, was on board with OTC's saucer/free energy idea. Colton announced the big unveiling for April 19, 1959, at Oklahoma City's Frontier City amusement park. Hundreds gathered to witness the free-energy flight of OTC's saucer. The crowd milled about excitedly and waited.

Neither Otis Carr nor the flying saucer appeared.

When local reporters called at Carr's home, the inventor claimed illness. A day or two later he said the saucer had developed "a mercury leak." When reporters showed up still later, Carr announced that the saucer had been accidentally destroyed by fire.

Space bound 6' diameter prototype of the OTC-X1 Electro-Gravitic Spacecraft awaits first flight test in Oklahoma City. The dawn of the application of free energy and the Third Electrical Age is upon us.

A saucer newsletter, *Thy Kingdom Come*, gave brief coverage to the spurious OTC saucer in 1959. The saucer's "inventors" coaxed hundreds of thousands of dollars from gullible investors.

An open letter from Aho, typed on OTC Enterprises letterhead and distributed to news outlets and flying saucer newsletters, enumerated the troubles, and promised that "all assemblies and circuits will be checked and tested for performance." And then Aho dropped the bombshell: "We are not announcing a flight date and do not plan to announce it in advance." Christopher Columbus, Aho wrote, "had no deadline for sailing the ocean." (The open letter goes on to modestly invoke the patient work of Copernicus, Edison, and Tesla.)

Later in 1959, the state of Oklahoma indicted Otis Carr for illegal stock sales. He was brought to trial and convicted. The court levied a $5,000 fine, which Carr was unable to pay except by working in jail for a dollar a day.

Charges against Wayne Sulo Aho were dropped. PR man Norman Colton may have been the brightest of the bunch: he left Oklahoma before charges could be filed. He later formed a public free-energy company he called the Millennium Agency.

The same year Otis Carr kicked off his saucer scam, 1957, a sixty-year-old grain buyer named Reinhold Schmidt claimed to have entered a UFO in Kearney, Nebraska, to chat with the three men and three women inside. He described the aliens as dark-haired and suntanned, and of average height. They spoke in German, which, Schmidt supposed, was normal enough because he understood the language. The ship's instrument panel bore Arabic and Roman numerals. The aliens "glided" across the deck rather than walked. And in a faintly ominous turn, the visitors asked Schmidt if he knew anything about the U.S. satellite program.

Despite a past prison stretch for embezzlement, and a brief commitment to Minnesota's Hastings State Hospital (formerly the Hastings Asylum for the Insane), Schmidt made some money on the UFO lecture circuit and published a book, *The Kearney Incident Up to Now.* In 1961, a California court found him guilty of swindling a Bakersfield widow out of $5,000 in a mining scheme based on extraterrestrial "free energy crystals." The widow, Eva Newcomb, described for the jury Schmidt's claim that the crystals could heal disabled children.

The Straith Letter

Frequent contactee George Adamski (see chapter twelve) inadvertently convinced many within and without the UFO community that his accounts of hobnobbing with Nordic Space Brothers were hoaxes. Although Adamski remained resolute and stood by his stories, he failed to convince UFOlogists Gray Barker and Jim Moseley.

Late in 1957, the pair concocted a letter to Adamski that they typed on what appeared to be U.S. State Department stationery. The letter, which arrived with a Washington, D.C., postmark, came from R. E. Straith, a functionary with the State Department's "Cultural Exchange Committee." The letter began "Dear Professor Adamski," perpetuating the ill-educated Adamski's fantasy of being an academic. The note was brief, but to Adamski it was bracing acknowledgment of his existence, and more. Based on "a great deal of confirmatory evidence," the letter said, the State Department had concluded that Adamski's accounts were factual. However, the letter included a caveat: "While certainly the Department cannot publicly confirm your experiences, it can, I believe, with propriety, encourage your work."

Adamski was quick to share his vindication with followers and doubters alike. His fans were as exhilarated as he, and some elected not to pursue the matter of the letter's veracity. But when people who had doubted Adamski from the start contacted the State Department, they were told there was no Cultural Exchange Committee and certainly no R. E. Straith. Adamski's supporters finally jumped in, and had no more success in uncovering the elusive administrator. Adamski and his fans concluded that the secret nature of the Cultural Exchange Committee caused the State Department to insulate Straith beneath layers of bureaucracy. Mr. Straith was at State, all right, but Washington kept him beyond the reach of the public.

One Adamskiphobe, Lonzo Dove, smelled a practical joke, and suspected Gray Barker, a fellow known for having an antic sense of humor. Barker always denied having had anything to do with the Straith letter—and anyway, people just couldn't pick up State Department stationery at the five and dime.

Dove persisted, spreading his claim throughout the UFO community and finally preparing an exposé that he submitted to Jim Moseley at *Saucer News* magazine. Moseley declined to publish the piece, disingenuously telling Dove that the thesis was unpersuasive. After Gray Barker died in 1984, Jim Moseley finally admitted that he and Barker had created the letter. A Barker friend, who obtained stationery from a relative working at State, had capped the joke.

George Adamski passed away in 1965 and was spared Moseley's long-delayed confession. As hoaxes go, the Straith Letter was adroit but basic, and did nothing to refute (or confirm) Adamski's claims. FBI agents who informed Adamski that the letter was a fake managed only to provide him with the "secrets and conspiracy" lever he had always wanted. R. E. Straith was a fiction, but for all Barker and Moseley knew, the State Department was full of Straiths, working with files containing precisely the confirmation Adamski longed for.

Billy Meier Has a DellaFavorite

Swiss-born Eduard Albert "Billy" Meier-Zafiriou aka Billy Meier claimed frequent contact with flying saucers and aliens, dating, he said, to 1942, when he was just five. The visitors came from the planet Erra, in the Plejares star system. Their intentions were benevolent, and grounded in concern for undesirable qualities inherited by humans from a common ancestor. Meier went public with all of this in 1970. In the Adamski vein, he described the aliens he encountered as handsome Nordic types. As Meier's celebrity grew in Europe during the 1970s, he wrote books and began a photo catalog where followers could buy his images. His earliest photographs of saucers and good-looking aliens generated some enthusiasm, so Meier added hundreds more as the years went by. Three fuzzy but particularly intriguing photos (catalog numbers 109–111) were offered in 1983. The images showed off a pair of beautiful young female aliens; Meier identified the blonde as Asket and the auburn-haired woman as Nera. Meier explained that the aliens had given their permission to be photographed while Meier was aboard their spaceship in 1975.

Asket's heart-shaped face was dominated by a winsome smile and striking, wide-set blue eyes. She appeared human, although Meier urged buyers to note her elongated, attractively curved earlobes. Redheaded Nera was a somewhat livelier-looking type, with apple cheeks and enormous baby-doll eyes.

In 1998, French computer scientist Luc Burgun and an American debunker of UFOs, Kal K. Korff, announced that the Asket and Nera photos were fakes. Mexican chemical engineer and science writer Luis Ruiz Noguez helped to spread the news that Asket was an American dancer named Michelle DellaFave. Nera was a dancer, too; her name was Susan Lund. When a surprised DellaFave was contacted by the Independent Investigations Group (a volunteer American organization dedicated to rational scientific thought), she confirmed that the women in Meier's photos were of herself and Lund. The images had been snapped from a television screen when DellaFave and Lund were members of the Golddiggers, a perky singing-and-dancing troupe put together in 1968 as an eponymous summer replacement for *The Dean Martin Show*. (Lund was an original member; DellaFave joined in 1969.)

When asked about her earlobes, DellaFave explained that during part of one season of *The Golddiggers* ("about 1971," she said), she wore light blonde side curls that might, perhaps, resemble ear lobes. DellaFave identified Susan Lund, and surmised that Meier had snapped the pictures when *Golddiggers* reruns played in Europe.

Billy Meier offered at least two explanations for all this, and they are tortured. He first claimed that he had indeed taken the photos from a television monitor—inside the spaceship. The ship's magnetic field accounted for the shots' less than sterling quality. When doubters continued to press, Meier explained that DellaFave and Lund were *not* the women he had photographed. The dancers had been inserted later by Men in Black, who wanted the faces of the alien women kept under wraps. Meier's explanation does not seem to account for the longtime presence of DellaFave and Lund in the Meier catalog, but he had a story for that, too. On www.forge-tomori.com, blogger Mori wrote, "[T]he aliens warned [Meier] of the switch but he then forgot about this warning. So he kept selling the forgeries until the photos were exposed in 1998, at which point Meier was able to quickly contact the aliens, be reminded of what he had forgotten, and publish those explanations."

In the mid-1970s, ET-contactee Billy Meier identified singer-dancer Michelle DellaFave (bottom) as "Asket," to support his claim of friendly extraterrestrial contact. DellaFave did not learn of the peculiar deception for nearly twenty-five years.

Hans and Stig Meet the Monsters

A pair of young-adult Swedish hoaxers, Hans Gustafsson and Stig Rydberg, insisted that they witnessed the landing of a disc some sixteen feet in diameter in woods near Helsinborg on December 20, 1958. The day really got interesting when jellylike creatures that apparently intended to drag the pair into the ship pursued them. Rydberg struggled back to his car and scared the aliens away with blasts from the auto's horn.

Swedish military investigators took a hard look at the physical evidence in January 1959 and pronounced the whole story nonsense. Granted, military pronouncements dismiss UFOs with metronomic regularity, but the Swedish military got this one right. Not long before his death in November 1960, twenty-seven-year-old Hans Gustafsson (who got drunk, fell from a boat, and drowned) confessed to his brother that he and Rydberg had cooked up the UFO/near-abduction tale themselves. The brother, perhaps feeling the weight of history's judgment after nearly thirty years, went public with Hans's confession around 1988.

Despite the military's refutation of the adventure, Hans and Stig took to the lecture circuit while their story was hot, enjoying the notoriety, and eventually revealing that aliens invited them aboard *another* ship and gave them a ride.

Hans died young, but he had fun while he could. As for Stig Rydberg, he was the victim of a street beating in February or early March 1984, and died in his apartment, of pneumonia, on March 4. He was fifty-six.

Mysterious Debris at Maury Island

Some sources suggest that ABC-television's *The Invaders* (1967–68)—the ongoing agonies of a saucer witness who can't convince authorities that fiendish extraterrestrials are here—was based on the experiences of Harold Dahl, a local searching for salvage logs near Maury Island in Puget Sound, Washington, on June 21, 1947, three days *before* the nearby saucer incident that made businessman Kenneth Arnold famous. Dahl, his teenage son, their dog, and a pair of crewmen observed a silent, saucer-shaped craft—perhaps momentarily gripped by a mechanical malfunction—dip low and then spray the shoreline with a mysterious substance that suggested chips of metal. Hot debris injured the arm of the Dahl boy and killed the dog. Another five saucers hovered at a higher altitude. The craft departed, and Dahl immediately related his experience to the local harbormaster, Fred Lee Crisman.

A day later, Harold Dahl received a visit from a somber man dressed in black, driving a black '47 Buick, who instructed Dahl to keep quiet about what he had seen. (Some sources date the mysterious man's visit with Dahl as June 24, three days after Dahl's sighting.) Dahl later recalled that the man in black actually said very little. He answered none of Dahl's questions, and seemed oddly impassive. But he did tell Dahl this: "I know a great deal more about this experience of yours than you will want to believe." After that, the man made an implied threat that was barely implied at all.

Meanwhile, Fred Crisman contacted *Amazing Stories* editor Ray Palmer. The Chicago-based magazine wanted the Maury Island story, and commissioned Kenneth Arnold to investigate and prepare a piece. Arnold flew into Seattle and located Dahl, who described the spray as irregularly shaped pieces of metal,

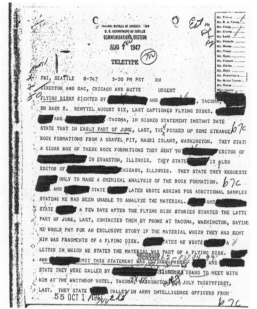

This August 7, 1947, FBI memorandum mentions the Mauri [*sic*] Island sighting, and admits that specialists were unable to identify the "rock formations" supposedly left behind by the UFO. Redacted portions refer to *Amazing Stories* editor Ray Palmer and his interest in the Maury Island story.   *USAF*

thin enough to flutter to the ground. Arnold took a sample and sent it to Palmer. Analysis done at the time (and again, years later) suggested nothing particularly novel about the material's composition, though the stuff didn't exactly seem indigenous, either. (Samples examined during latter-day tests had been stored in Crisman's garage.)

Although Dahl assured Arnold he had snapped images of the UFOs, Dahl never produced a photograph. Further, when Arnold pressed to see the precise spot Dahl had been on June 21, Dahl gave him the runaround. Arnold never saw the site.

Arnold was puzzled later, when Dahl insisted that Crisman had been spirited away on a military plane. Unable to verify that, Arnold nevertheless set up another meeting with Dahl. The meet was to be at Dahl's home, but when Arnold arrived there, he found the house deserted.

Conspiracy Alert

Because of Kenneth Arnold's recent notoriety, and the unresolved mystery of what Arnold saw above Washington's Cascade Mountains on June 24, Army Air Forces Intelligence dispatched two officers to Puget Sound. After conducting interviews, snapping photos, and retrieving what may have been residue from the peculiar spray, Lt. Frank Brown and Capt. William Davidson departed in a B-25—which crashed in a wooded area near Kelso, Washington, killing the officers (two enlisted men aboard parachuted to safety) and destroying the UFO evidence.

Informed by hindsight, UFOlogists working many years later looked hard not just at the crash of the B-25, but at a series of coincidences that, the investigators assumed (or hoped), pointed to a far-reaching conspiracy: Ziff-Davis fired Ray Palmer; potentially fatal engine trouble struck Kenneth Arnold's private plane not long after his time with Dahl and Crisman; a *Tacoma Times* journalist who interviewed Dahl in 1947 died not long after; and *The Tacoma Times* went out of business in 1949. Further, the physical evidence sent to Ray Palmer disappeared during a break-in at Palmer's Chicago office.

Well, Arnold's plane trouble was his own fault: after landing at Seattle, he had closed the fuel valve—SOP after a flight—and forgot to re-engage it during his pre-flight check. The reporter died of natural causes, as people do. *The Tacoma Times* suspended publication because of mid-century economic woes and social changes (such as suburbanization) that hurt many local papers. And Ray Palmer was not dismissed from his job with Ziff-Davis; he quit—because Z-D planned to relocate to New York City when Palmer was preparing to return to his home state, Wisconsin. Further, Palmer's private project, *Fate* magazine, was coming together, and Palmer reasoned (correctly) that he could live without checks from Z-D.

Of all the coincidences, the robbery of Palmer's office is the most intriguing. In its foolishness (who breaks into a science fiction magazine?), it has a bumbling, maybe-it-really-happened Watergate feel. Perhaps the act was related to the Maury Island event, but if so, the thief got very little: just fragments of metal that, as far as Kenneth Arnold was concerned, came from the nearby Tacoma Smelting works. In any event, much speculation surrounds the disposition of the debris, with many accounts of the story spiraling into a convoluted maze of "switched" fragments, double crosses, and people being set up to be killed.

By the late 1960s, after making unsuccessful application for a security job at Los Alamos, Crisman was living in Oregon. His interest in UFOs continued, and he frequently attended UFO conferences. In 1978, Crisman became a peripheral, and innocent, figure in a reopened House investigation of the Kennedy assassination; conspiracy theorists had incorrectly fingered Crisman as one of "the three tramps" seen near Dealy Plaza on November 22.

Dahl simply vanished. According to some accounts, a check of old Tacoma phone books suggested that there had never been a Harold Dahl in the area. Fred Crisman eventually gave Dahl's address to UFO researchers. The researchers managed to contact Dahl by mail around 1967, but later discovered that their correspondence had been answered by *Crisman*.

UFO researchers of varying credibility looked into Harold Dahl more closely. One theory suggested that Dahl had been "invented" by Crisman, an OSS operative during World War II, who later worked for the OSS follow-on organization, the CIA. This point of view adds that Crisman found work at Boeing in 1960 and established himself there as a troublemaker, accusing various managers of being Communists or homosexuals.

Ray Palmer disowned Maury Island in 1958, declaring the whole thing a hoax. But he couldn't say precisely what Crisman had been up to, and he had no explanation at all for the mysterious Harold Dahl.

Youth Will Have Its Day

Adult hoaxers often anticipate monetary reward, or the perquisites of fame. Younger hoaxers, want notoriety, too, but their ability to put one over on adults brings special fun. In 1967, fourteen-year-old Ronnie Hill of Oriental, North Carolina, had a clever idea. On July 21, he snapped a blurry photograph of a figure clad in a spacesuit and with one arm raised in friendly greeting—or perhaps aggressively, as a dark, bell-mouthed object appears to be gripped in the upraised hand. The presumed space traveler has an unusually large, spade-shaped head and painfully thin arms and legs. Behind the figure, apparently at some distance and level with the figure's head and shoulders, is a smoothly spherical shape that Ronnie Hill identified as a spaceship.

The photograph's lower half is comprised of foliage, or perhaps blades of grass; the spaceman stands at the middle of the frame, just above center. Because of the snapshot's fuzziness and visual perspective, scale is at issue. Perhaps the figure is a person in costume, or maybe the visitor is only inches high. In a 1967 letter to Dell Publishing's *Flying Saucers UFO Reports* magazine, Hill described the spaceman as standing three to three-and-a-half feet high. When the boy snapped the photo, the mysterious visitor was about fifteen feet away. The boy added that the craft measured about nine feet in diameter.

Editors at Dell passed the letter and snapshot on to UFOlogist John Keel. Keel shortly located experts willing to vouch for the image's authenticity (though this seems small evidence for an *alien* visitor, even assuming the figure and sphere were real). Some sympathetic examiners saw a resemblance between Hill's spaceman and the spade-headed Flatwoods Monster sighted in West Virginia in 1952 (see chapter ten). Keel wrote about Ronnie Hill's encounter in the January-February 1969 issue of *Flying Saucer Review*. Although Keel later had doubts about the photograph, he was unable to devote sufficient time to a full investigation before his death in 2009.

Around 2011, Fotocat, a credible UFO/IFO investigatory project operated by Vicente-Juan Ballester Olmos, engaged photo expert Andres Duarte to examine the Ronnie Hill image. Duarte mathematically plotted sightlines, angle of sunlight, height-to-distance ratio, and other elements. He concluded that were the photograph real, the sphere would be considerably more elevated. Further, the sphere would dominate nearly half of the frame's area, instead of the small area captured by Hill.

Young Ronnie eventually admitted his prank. The creature was a small doll wrapped in tinfoil, and the spacecraft was an egg. Regardless, Hill's spaceman has survived in UFO lore, inspiring renderings by artists and mention as a "legitimate" sighting in *The Black Book of Flying Saucers*, a 1970 book by Henry Durrant (a pseudonym for Didier Serres).

Ronnie Hill, who smartly copyrighted his photo while still a boy, perpetrated a hoax that has engaged people's imaginations for half a century.

A Perfect Line

Perhaps something was in the atmosphere in 1967, something that, once breathed in, inspired young men to do UFO trickery. Take Chris Southall, David Harrison, and other students at Farnborough, England's Royal Aircraft Establishment, and Farnborough Technical College. The group fabricated six fiberglass discs and placed them in a line stretching 155 miles west to east across southern England, from Bristol to Kent. Each saucer measured about a yard in diameter, and weighed enough to require two men to lift. They were in the classic saucer configuration, with perky center domes rising from the upper fuselages; the saucers had no portholes or other apertures. In a confluence of events that was lucky rather than planned, police stations along the saucers' trail took a barrage of calls on September 4. Shortly, someone realized that the objects had arrayed themselves in a perfectly straight line. What could this mean? Invasion? Hoax? Higher authorities were notified.

In an amusing and possibly deliberate turn, the young men executed their hoax during Rag Week, a period of charitable fund-raising undertaken by students at many UK and Irish universities. But instead of raising money, the saucer hoax caused the government to *spend* it: on a helicopter and crew from RAF Manston (to investigate a saucer found in Sheppey, Kent), a Scotland Yard bomb squad, police from four municipalities, and investigators from the Ministry of Defence.

As a precaution, engineers hauled the saucer discovered by a farmer at Chippenham, Wiltshire, to a dump and blew it up. Elsewhere, a high-ranking engineer at the British Aircraft Corporation examined the saucer found by a paperboy at Somerset. Another saucer—discovered by a letter carrier in Newbury, Berkshire—got a scrupulous going-over from Home Office investigators and USAF scientists attached to the Atomic Weapons Establishment at Aldermaston.

A satellite tracking station was notified when one of the saucers was found at Ascot.

The hoax unraveled when the saucer found on a golf course at Bromley, Kent, was delivered to South London's Bromley police station, where it was X-rayed and found to be, well, nothing.

In a pose that probably was suggested by the photographer, a British police officer presses an ear to one of six saucers fabricated by students and carefully laid across southern England.   *Alamy*

A note appended to Ministry of Defence files declassified in March 2011 describes the saucers as "a very successful practical joke."

What's the Alternative?

In the late 1970s, UFOs enjoyed one of their periodic bursts of mass popularity. Believers and skeptics in Britain had plenty to discuss following Anglia TV's April 1, 1977, broadcast of a documentary called *Alternative 3*. The film "revealed" that Washington and Moscow had for many years conducted joint space-travel research, with the objective of removing a select portion of humankind from Earth before pollution and other vandalism destroyed the planet.

Forgetting for a moment the film's April Fool's broadcast date, and even assuming that the titanic sums needed to finance off-world construction could be hidden from the GAO, Congress, Russia's Ministry of Finance, and similar bodies, and that every one of the tens of thousands of clandestine participants would keep his and her mouth shut, there still were those unpleasant implications of rescue of the select only. Just who *were* those people? The situation conjured pop visions of the heartbreaking lottery at the dramatic core of the film version of Philip Wylie's *When Worlds Collide*, and the middle-aged male idiots gathered in the War Room in Stanley Kubrick's *Dr. Strangelove*. Privileged men can be depended upon to save themselves, to provide for a complement of fecund young women, and select (almost as afterthoughts) scientists, engineers, and other specialists needed to maintain the whole expedition.

Alternative 3 is too polished to suggest the guerrilla-filmmaking "secrets laid bare" tone the documentary attempts to cultivate. Ostensibly spontaneous interviews are clearly scripted, and actors are even noted in the end credits! Well, who pays attention to the credits? Anglia TV had an April Fool's joke that emerged with credibility—largely because it was on television, and thus "real."

Alternative 3 utters not a word about UFOs or extraterrestrials, so the suggestion of high-level secrecy simply angered many Brits, rather than making them frightened. The 1978 U.S. publication of a commissioned book (another "real" medium), *Alternative 003* by Leslie Watkins, threw American conspiracy theorists into a lather because the original documentary had never aired Stateside. And why not? Conspiracy, of course. Given just a little time to percolate, the fabricated flee-the-Earth scenario became conflated with existing notions of human-alien collusion, sex-mad ETs, hybridization, and the ultimate destruction of Earth. In his useful 2013 book *A Culture of Conspiracy*, author Michael Barkun reasons that while all of that said "UFO" to some people, to many others it said just another layer of conspiracy, that is, UFOs are *not* real, but shadow elements within governments encourage us to believe they are—anything to keep us edgy and off-balance, you see.

By 2011, when *Alternative 3* slotted as an official entry at Japan's Yubari International Fantastic Film Festival, the film's fictional aspect wasn't just well known, but applauded.

Oh, That Myron

In the history of American magazines, few publishers exceed the late Myron Fass for sheer industriousness, cynicism, and bald-faced deception. A horror-comics artist in the early 1950s, Fass founded New York-based Countrywide Publications in 1956. His little magazine empire peaked in the 1960s and '70s with one-offs designed to exploit *Jaws*, KISS, Swine flu, and other transitory things; and with regular publication of titles built around martial arts, tabloid shock news, black-and-white horror comics, naked women, and crafts for kids.

The January 1978 issue of Countrywide's *Official UFO* magazine featured a piece called "The Night an American Town Died of Fright," which claimed that Chester, Illinois, had been "destructed" by warlike UFOs on August 2, 1977. The article began, "[T]he news desk has been flooded with reports" that "the entire village of Chester was attacked and burned by a fleet of alien invaders." The piece is dominated by an on-the-spot, first-person account from the Chester sheriff, Luke Grisholm. At about 8 p.m. he saw three "very large" glowing discs in the sky above Main Street. As the objects showed a variety of colors, the engine of Grisholm's cruiser died. A few moments later, the discs veered away from the business district and headed toward Chester's residential area. The car's engine revived, and then Grisholm's radio crackled, "telling me that there was a house on fire by the Route 2 cutoff." The sheriff quickly drove toward the flames he saw in the distance. The discs "were dropping down and each time they did there was a plume of fire going into the sky." Many houses were ablaze. Panicked residents poured into the streets; others crashed their cars. The aliens even took control of the local television station.

The sheriff's office made calls for help to nearby towns and even the governor's office, but got no response. Chester was on its own.

Grisholm wrote, "The papers the next day reported that an Air Force jet had crashed in our town, well, that was simply a lie, we all saw the saucers and what they did to the houses in our town. . . . Our best hope is to get this story out to the public, people have to know that these objects are dangerous, people have to be told."

Because nothing concerning Chester had come across the news wires, and because Chester never had a sheriff, a few reporters who smelled an amusing feature story ambled out that way. When the reporters arrived, they found Chester to be perfectly fine. Quiet, modest, and fine.

On a foggy, chilly December day in 1977, just weeks after the publication of *Official UFO*, KMOV-TV (St. Louis) reporter Al Wiman interviewed residents of Chester. Wiman said he had received a phone call from Bob Nessoff, a New York man who claimed to have worked as a special investigator in the magazine's employ. Nessoff stood by his assertions, but at City Hall, Chester's somewhat bemused mayor told Wiman, "Obviously, there has been not only no mass destruction in the town, but I can't even find any *minor* destruction in the town." Wiman thought that over, and then said that the story's discrepancies suggest that no investigator *ever* visited Chester. The mayor answered, "What you say is correct."

In his on-camera report, Wiman quoted the Chester Police radio log from August 2. The department took two calls that night: a minor traffic accident and "a complaint about a drunk running around a local motel knocking on doors, disturbing guests."

Taking a cue from Wiman, other reporters found Myron Fass in New York and questioned him about the fabrication perpetrated by *Official UFO*. The wily publisher had a ready reply: "The aliens had returned, rebuilt the town, and given the townspeople selective amnesia."

The "Alien Autopsy" Film

Buzz about film footage of a lifeless Roswell extraterrestrial under the knife (and bone saw) of human pathologists began in 1993, when the film's existence leaked—or was leaked—to the UFO community. The prospect was frankly exciting: official military footage of the 1947 postmortem examination of a Roswell alien. The 16mm film belonged to Ray Santilli, a British record producer and film distributor who owned a company called Merlin Communications. Santilli announced his possession of the footage with some fanfare, claiming that he had acquired it for $100,000 from the elderly (and anonymous), ex-Army Air Forces camera operator that had shot it. (The same man, Santilli said, also shot top-secret footage of the first A-bomb "Trinity" test in July 1945 at Alamogordo, New Mexico.)

Santilli hoped to sell television rights for a smart sum, and decided to "tease" the footage with a screening for specially invited opinion makers at the Museum of London. The May 5, 1995, audience numbered about one hundred, and included notables from the worlds of religion and science. According to some accounts of the showing, many in the audience were chopfallen—simply amazed as a surgeon's scalpel cut into the flesh and probed the organs of a deceased humanoid from another world. Others in the audience, though, were skeptical, and suspected that they had been cast as unwitting players in a stunt.

As indeed they had. Santilli built on the initial hubbub generated in London and successfully pitched his footage to America's Fox television network. The autopsy footage—positioned as the heart of a sixty-minute program hosted by latter-day *Star Trek* actor Jonathan Frakes—aired on Fox stations on Monday, August 28, 1995, as *Alien Autopsy: Fact or Fiction?* The show performed strongly in the ratings, pleasing the network and delighting advertisers.

Of course, the centerpiece autopsy was phony.

The procedure supposedly took place at Carswell Air Force Base, near Fort Worth, some weeks after the crash at Roswell. Right off the bat, Santilli's credibility was in question, because his early promotion quoted the old photographer as saying the footage was shot at a dry lake bed near White Sands, New Mexico.

To fill out the program's running time, various experts appear in talking-head cameos. Their presence framed the show and provided some credibility (UFOlogists Stanton Friedman and Kevin Randle were among the guests). The autopsy footage was shot without audio, on grainy, black-and-white film stock. People present in the footage wear surgical gowns and masks. Voice-over narration (added by Santilli) identifies the autopsy physicians as Lloyd Berkner and Detlev Bronk.

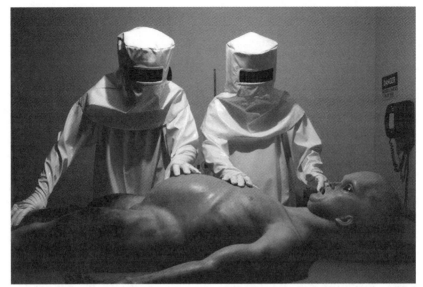

Film distributor Ray Santilli caused a stir in 1995, when he released what he described as long-secret U.S. Army footage showing a 1947 autopsy of an extraterrestrial. Santilli and the Fox television network prospered, but the hoax soon unraveled. Regardless, Santilli mined the whole story for humor in 2006, with a farcical feature film (above) called *Alien Autopsy*.   *Rex*

What We Saw

The autopsy subject is a humanoid biped, hairless from head to toe, lying prone on its back on a table. No external genitalia are visible, but a vertical crease below the pubis suggests a vulva. (On television, digital manipulation blurred the creature's pubic area.) There is no visible navel. The corpse appears pale or chalky, with a head that is large relative to the body. Ears, nose, and jaw are small. The face is dominated by oversized black eyes. The eyes are open at the film's outset, and remain so. The forearms are somewhat longer, relative to the body, than is standard for humans. Each hand and foot has six fingers and toes. The belly is distended, and the right knee and thigh are marked by evidence of trauma and dramatic tissue loss

Radiation or anticontamination suits, with headpieces, disguise the primary human participants. Two people are usually in the room, while a third, wearing a surgical mask, observes from behind a window that, apparently, opens onto a corridor adjacent to the autopsy room. (Because the film stock is overexposed, some critics have erroneously placed the observer inside the room.) A black, rotary phone hugs a wall behind the autopsy table. A microphone, to take the surgeons' remarks, hangs from the ceiling. (Although skeptics claimed that the vintage phone and mic are too modern for 1947, the specific models of both implements had been in use by the early 1940s.)

Red Flags

People familiar with postmortems pronounced the film a hoax almost immediately. They were bothered that although a wall clock suggests a two-hour procedure, the film runs just seventeen minutes. If the footage were genuine, what was going on during the other 103 minutes? Only two walls are visible, which suggests a set rather than a genuine room. A Bunsen burner is included among the equipment—why? The monochrome film became another puzzlement. Although the grainy black-and-white stock suggests the past to modern viewers, its use doesn't jibe with Army practice. In 1947, standard film stock for official Army films was 16mm color. (Although Technicolor had to be filmed with proprietary, very heavy 35mm cameras, other stocks were available in 1947; Ansco Color stock, for instance, was manufactured in 16mm as well as 35mm.) Further, standard 1947 Army filming guidelines for medical-procedures specified *two* cameras, both fixed: one above the autopsy table and the other adjacent. Santilli's alien autopsy, contrarily, was recorded by a single handheld camera, making for focus problems and grossly inadequate "coverage."

Personnel in the autopsy room would have included a still photographer, but no such person is present, either as a figure or in the form of periodic illumination from flashbulbs. (Color Kodachrome film stock was at its peak in 1947, and would have given remarkable still images of the body.)

The autopsy takes place on a plain wooden table overlaid with a sheet, not a proper autopsy table. Examples of the latter are fitted with gutters that manage runoff of blood and other fluids. The pathologists' body language is exaggerated, as if to compensate for the lack of audio. One participant makes a show of using a palpation hammer, which tests reflex reactions. The hammer would have no use during an autopsy. Livescience.com writer Joe Nickell observed, "[T]he person performing the autopsy held the scissors like a tailor rather than a pathologist (who is trained to place his middle or ring finger in the bottom of the scissors hole and use his forefinger to steady the blades)."

The injuries sustained by the alien are inconsistent with the sort of physical trauma (crushing avulsion) expected from an air crash. Except for the right thigh, the body exhibits no visible injuries. Further, the corpse does not suggest the expected "dead weight," but instead seems slight and insubstantial.

American military coding visible on the seventeen-minute print shown at the Museum of London does not match any 1947 codes used by the U.S. Army. When Kodak offered to analyze frames from the film, copyright holder Ray Santilli declined (though he did provide blank "leader" stock that, according to Kodak, could have dated from around 1947). Post-London versions of the autopsy film do not have the coding.

When Santilli displayed the round cans that held the film stock, sharp observers noted a Department of Defense seal. But Santilli claimed that the footage had never reached the U.S. military. How, then, does the DoD seal fit in?

Santelli endured the doubters for some time, explaining that he had culled the footage from a much longer film. Pressed, he finally identified the cameraman as

Jack Barnett. Only two cameramen filmed the Alamogordo A-bomb, however, and neither one was named Jack Barnett.

Everything fell to pieces in 2006, when Santilli produced a comic feature film called *Alien Autopsy*. He continued to insist that an alien autopsy film existed, but that it had physically degraded so badly that he "reconstructed" the autopsy with new footage, retaining original frames where possible. After a while, he gave up that defense altogether, and admitted that the whole enterprise had been a hoax, perpetrated with a simple set and a pair of specially commissioned dummy corpses. If Santilli's admission was difficult for him, he probably felt better while thinking about the money those seventeen minutes brought him: outside estimates suggest $6 million to $10 million.

Lay defenses of the autopsy footage carry on to this day, ranging from reasonable analysis to unhelpful certitude. One defender, posting on YouTube in 2015, wrote, in part, "This is a real autopsie [*sic*] of an alien. I don't give a shit what people say. . . . F__k no way could anyone in those days do a dummy like that"—as if the footage must necessarily have been filmed in 1947!

Another YouTube poster blames the whole thing on Chuck Norris.

CGI Magic

In 2007, a pair of short videos made waves after being quietly posted to YouTube's "News and Politics" section. Crystal clear yet showing the slight shakiness typical of tourist videos, the pieces quickly became YouTube sensations. "UFO Haiti" and "UFO Dominican Republic" were uploaded from two discrete YouTube accounts; "UFO Haiti" runs twenty-two seconds, and shows a pair of illuminated, mostly silent craft gliding above palm trees at sunset, and then directly over the videographer before continuing on toward distant mountains. Roughly circular in silhouette, the craft have four distinct, connected modules. The underside of each module is illuminated by a protuberant white light; the center underside of each carries a larger white lamp. A woman gasps from off-screen as the ships emerge from behind the swaying fronds of palm trees. When in the distance, the ships appear to rendezvous with seven small lights.

"UFO Dominican Republic" aka "UFO Haiti 2 'Dominican Republic,'" runs twenty seconds, and has a "look" similar to "UFO Haiti": the same upward angle, similar palm trees, and the appearance of early sunset. This time, though, the first two craft that appear are in the familiar saucer style, rounded top and bottom and tapering to a narrower center band. Crickets and distant, indistinguishable male voices are heard throughout, and faraway dogs bark during the video's late moments.

"Haiti" and "Dominican Republic" are startling by any standard, and will impress, even thrill, UFO enthusiasts looking at them for the first time. A *Los Angeles Times* reporter named David Sarno became understandably intrigued, and began an investigation. After a false start with a "UFO Haiti" poster who had simply uploaded a shot of her kiss with a boyfriend, Sarno was contacted via Skype by a representative of the original poster—someone calling himself Barzolff814.

Throughout the conversation, Barzolff did not appear on camera, but Sarno could hear him instructing his proxy, a young woman who called herself Sam, about what to say. The reporter had already heard about a fabulous new computer-imaging program, and sure enough, Barzolff had used it: a VUE application that lets the user create total environments, including sky, trees, mountains—and, if the user wishes, UFOs. Not a single visual element of "Haiti" and "Dominican Republic" is real. Each one had been created by Barzolff—who identified himself to Sarno as a professional animator—using a MacBook Pro and 3-D imaging programs that included one from VUE. Both videos required just seventeen hours of Barzolff's time.

Although Barzolff admitted he was doing preliminary work on a feature-length UFO thriller, he insisted that neither "Haiti" nor "Dominican Republic" were viral marketing tools.

Battle in the Stars

Napa County, California, UFOlogist Ed Grimsley maintains an eponymous Web site devoted to UFO battles in our night skies. Grimsley reports that, since his teen years, he has used night-vision technology to observe dogfights among UFOs, as well as aerial battles between UFOs and Earth aircraft. He is stunned by the UFOs' startling aeronautic maneuvers and great speed, and by "what appear to be laser weapons." These aggressive, saucer-shaped UFOs appear in bunches that Grimsley calls "squadrons."

Grimsley worries that extraterrestrials plan to take control of Earth, or evict us altogether. Because the government hides the existence of these craft and battles, Grimsley's Skywatch organization schedules outdoor night-vision viewings of this activity (forty dollars a head) at sites in and around Calistoga, California. Indoor audiences who see his night-vision videos exclaim as if at a fireworks show.

Over the years, Grimsley has progressed to increasingly more sophisticated night-vision goggles. Handily enough, various types of goggles described on the Grimsley home page are available for purchase from Grimsley for between $1,800 and $3,200. The site also sells a DVD, *Ed Grimsley's Night Vision UFO Wars*, for $24.95.

In 2011, Robert Sheaffer, a UFO investigator with the Committee for Skeptical Inquiry, viewed Grimsley's videos. Sheaffer explained to NBC.com newswriter Benjamin Radford that night-vision optics "trade low resolution for high sensitivity. . . . [W]hat looks like a large object may well just be a point of light." Sheaffer added that although night-vision technology reveals light, it is incapable of providing an accurate idea of an object's size. Grimsley and his followers, then, are likely looking at satellites, helicopters, meteors—even bats, birds, and bugs. Sheaffer said that night-vision goggles are not needed to observe night-sky activity; he recommended 10 x 50 binoculars, which reveal airborne objects in better detail.

Besides doing trade in goggles and videos, Grimsley's site solicits donations, some of which go to his "citizens alliance," which pushes back against manipulative governments that lie and encourage their citizens to make war. Another portion of donated money goes to Grimsley's research on water-based automobile fuel that will give one hundred miles per gallon.

Eggs on the Comet

My visit to a popular "alternate news" Web site just days after the dramatic November 2014 landing of the European Space Agency's (ESA) comet probe on the surface of Comet 67P Churyumov-Gerasimenko gave me access to a three-part video in which a person unfamiliar with astronomy and space science expounded on three Comet 67P photographs released by the ESA. The commentator discussed the photos in voice-over (the gentleman did not put himself on screen), using a cursor to draw viewer attention to important areas on the comet's surface. He led our eyes along horizontal "lines," toward evidence of various things he described as "anomalous": supposed laser excavations, various egg-shaped objects with shiny highlights, and a pair of what he called "Saturn objects" rising from the comet's surface on "pedestals." The commentator wondered who had done the excavations, and who left the objects.

Beyond the fact that the person had no scientific training (he hissed "Zzzst!" whenever he mentioned excavation), his use of language illustrated much of the presumption that characterizes the outer fringes of the UFO/extraterrestrial community, and diminishes the importance of credible sightings and other events. As the video poster moved his cursor across the photographs, I saw no lines in the comet's surface—but because he used the word "lines," the easily persuaded might see lines. He introduced the viewer to the shiny objects by describing them as "egg shaped," but later simply called them "eggs," which assumes that they are indeed egg shaped, and not simply a possible misreading of sun and shadow. The commentator is familiar with eggs, so when he saw objects that approximated that shape, the rock or ice fragments he had zeroed in on did not simply appear to be oval—they were eggs, or something akin to eggs. Although the moderator did not articulate specific questions as to the objects' origins, those questions were clear: *Are these objects true, organic eggs? If not, did intelligent hands carefully machine them in an egg shape? Could the objects be sensors? Beacons? Who deposited them on the comet's surface?* (The last question is predicated on the assumption that there is a "who" in the first place.)

Similarly, the "Saturn-shaped" forms (spherical-appearing objects bisected horizontally at midline by what resembles an apron or ring) soon became "the Saturn objects." Their apparent shape reminded the commentator of the planet Saturn, and so they acquired special significance. Once again, inevitable questions, though unspoken, leapt to mind: *Did the Saturn objects come from Saturn? Did beings from Saturn visit the comet on a flyby? Were the Saturn objects the work of intelligences that were cognizant of space and Saturn's shape?*

The commentator regarded the laser excavations as "clearly obvious" rather than as just unsubstantiated guesswork. "Clearly obvious" relieved the viewer of burdensome analysis or doubt. The ESA images of Comet 67P show a surface riddled with bright areas and sharp, contrasting shadows. According to the commentator, the images also reveal the scars of excavation because the excavation itself is "obvious."

The commentator was coy about who or what may have left artifacts on the comet and altered the body's terrain. As suggested above, one inference was that this was the work of an unknown extraterrestrial intelligence. Another was that unknown human agencies had preceded the ESA lander to Comet 67P. In either case, the truth wasn't likely to be shared with the public anytime soon.

The Trouble with Theft

Serious UFO study demands time and dedication, financial support, and an ability to distinguish fact from fancy. Because of that, and because of the particular nature of creative people, a man who retitles another person's UFO documentary or lecture and offers it for unauthorized sale on the Web perpetrates a hoax, and invites approbation and censure from the UFO community. Around 2008, UFO researcher Dennis Balthaser discovered that a self-described UFOlogist named Bill Knell had purloined a Balthaser lecture DVD, *The Roswell Incident: Then and Now*. Knell called it *Aliens Among Us: Stunning Secrets About UFOs and Extraterrestrials*, and pressed it to DVD to sell as his own work. Whatever money coaxed from visitors to Knell's Web site went to Knell, and not to Balthaser. Of course, this kind of base, sneaky-Pete theft is criminal. Balthaser and others whose DVDs had been pirated and sold by Knell contacted the FBI and an FBI partner, the IC3 (Internet Crime Complaint Center). In addition, contact was made with local law enforcement at Knell's Indiana place of residence. Numerous Knell Web sites subsequently shut down, but Knell simply shifted his sales operation to other sites. (In years past, Arizona civil cases brought against Knell and his wife ended with the couple being ordered to make restitution for activity related to credit card fraud and other complaints.)

Knell's scheme plundered the work of about eighty UFOlogists, including Erik von Däniken, Jim Marrs, Linda Moulton Howe, Brad and Sherry Steiger, Whitley Strieber, and other notables. The intellectual property of deceased UFOlogists also was stolen; among those victims were Frank Edwards, Donald Kehoe, CBS newsman Edward R. Murrow, J. Allen Hynek, Long John Nebel, and Paul Bennewitz.

The hammer fell on Mr. Knell in 2010–11, not for piracy but for "neglect of a dependent"—child neglect. His wife also was charged. Local police and investigators with the Indiana Department of Child Services discovered rotted food in the Knell refrigerator, and feces-smeared bathrooms and furniture. Early in 2011, Knell's wife pleaded guilty to three counts of child neglect; she received a sentence of more than four years (suspended) and two years' probation. Later in 2011, Bill Knell accepted a plea deal. Like his wife, Knell avoided jail via suspension of his sentences, but immediately began a ninety-day period of active monitoring. Following that, he was to start a two-year probationary period, during which he was to remain in Indiana, and conduct no business on the Internet.

On the face of it, Knell's brand of UFO hoax may not seem to have explicit relevance to the veracity of UFO reports, but it does, partly because pirates contacted by media in search of "experts" proceed to do an awful job explaining research and thinking that is not their own. In that, the whole UFO community suffers, and the public is deprived of honest insights.

A Saucer a Day

The Internet overflows with more UFO videos than anybody could watch in half a lifetime. More—probably hundreds—are added every day; one site, iUFOsightings, posts a fresh video daily, 365 times a year. How can that be possible? Hint: it can't.

Makers of UFO videos coax viewers with such adjectives as *ultimate, shocking, craziest, kick-ass,* and (of course) *best.* If anything is shocking, it's the gullibility of a lot of people. Obvious mistakes and missteps in spurious UFO videos are easy to discern: craft that cast no shadows; light sources that don't jibe; relative quality of light that seems wrong; issues of scale; UFOs that appear to fly through solid objects; clumsy relative movement of objects in the foreground, middle ground, and background; peculiar color shifts; perspective that seems "off" given the position of the camera; footage that plays against a bed of dramatic music (as if the visual material cried out for a boost). There are many others, but the most damning is probably this one: crystal clarity. Some fabricators forget that when objects recede from our sight, they become less distinct. Fine detail vanishes and colors grow muted. And even when a video UFO's placement suggests a continual close-up view, the craft's visual detail is often unrealistically sharp.

Web content that exposes fraudulent UFO videos can be helpful and a lot of fun, too. Ufotheater.com, for example, maintains a splendid "UFO YouTube Black List" that notes fraudulent UFO-video makers and the particular style and offenses of each. Some technically adept video makers show how fake UFO footage is created, letting you see each step. Others dissect existing videos, demonstrating how the original perpetrators created them. One of the best of the latter is "UFO Over Santa Clarita," a handsome faked video that went viral in October 2012, and that was neatly dissected *by its makers* four months later, in a video called "UFO Over Santa Clarita VFX Breakdown." (The surprise here is that everything in the spurious video is CGI: landscape, sky, clouds, setting sun, lens flares, power towers, automobile interior, driver's hand, UFO—everything.)

Yes, the truth is out there, but you have to look carefully to find it.

Eyes Only: Selected UFO Sightings, 1970–1999

As hoaxers go about their business, other people experience honest UFO sightings. Here are some intriguing ones from a recent thirty-year span.

August 30, 1970: A seven-year-old Vincennes, Indiana, girl spies a UFO at 11:30 a.m. and fetches her father, who examines the object with binoculars. The man later describes the craft as some thirty feet in diameter, with a resemblance to "a garbage can lid with a piece of watermelon on top."

June or July, 1971: While the carrier USS *John F. Kennedy* cruises the Bermuda Triangle at about 8:30 p.m., automatic teletypes in the communications center begin typing lines of gibberish. On deck, seamen witness a glowing, yellow-orange sphere of indeterminate size, hovering above the carrier. The engines of two combat-ready F-4 Phantoms will not turn over, so the sphere remains unmolested for as long as it is present. **Note**: A bosun's mate had to be sedated after this event. Although the sphere's size could not be confirmed, witnesses intuited that it was very large. The ship's communications teletypes functioned normally again after about twenty minutes.

March 8, 1972: Shortly after 9:00 p.m., Coast Guard personnel near Muskegon, Michigan, observe a bright, yellow-white UFO traverse the sky. Simultaneously, a UHF radio band used by the Coast Guard emits long, patterned strings of indecipherable code. **Note**: The object was seen not just by CG personnel but by police officers, FAA officials, and ordinary citizens. Michigan State Police turned the investigation over to the USAF. Air Force personnel cautioned the Coast Guardsmen not to speak of the event.

August 23, 1974: Musician John Lennon and his secretary, May Pang, see a "large flattened cone" with "a large, brilliant red light" (Pang's description) in New York City. The craft is bisected horizontally by a band of white lights. **Note**: Pang called the police, who said numerous other people in the area had reported a similar object. Pang discussed the incident in some detail in her 1983 book *Loving John*.

September 15, 1977: While outside his home at 2:20 a.m. in Paciencia, Brazil, near Rio de Janeiro, bus driver Antonia La Rubia discovers a massive object some 250 feet in diameter sitting in his field. Suddenly frozen by a brilliant light, La Rubia is taken aboard the craft by a trio of four-foot-tall "robots" with elongated antennae. Inside, he sees numerous other robots, and is shown a series of still photos that appear on a mysterious piano-like "box." Some of the images are of La Rubia himself, including one in which he is nude on an examination table. Other photos show farm fields and everyday views of urban Brazil. Two photos are especially disturbing to La Rubia: an image of a barking dog causing a robot to "melt" and a panoramic view of an alien factory. **Note**: For a month after the incident, La Rubia itched and suffered a fever, and had trouble breathing. He later recalled another photograph of himself, with smoke rising from his back.

December 26–27 and 28, 1980: USAF personnel stationed at the Woodbridge, England, RAF base report strange lights near the base, and above nearby Rendlesham Forest—setting off an investigation of what becomes one of the most celebrated stories in UFOlogy. **Note**: For details of the Rendlesham Forest story, see chapter eleven.

December 29, 1980: Two women and a child witness twenty-three single- and dual-rotor military helicopters try and fail to encircle a fiery, diamond-shaped flying object above a forested area near Dayton, Texas. All three witnesses—Betty Cash, and Vickie Landrum and her grandson Colby—return home and subsequently suffer blistered skin, nausea, hair and weight loss, diarrhea, and other symptoms consistent with radiation poisoning. **Note**: The Army denied having had any helicopters in the area on the night in question, and the women's 1981 lawsuit against the U.S. government was dismissed five years later.

July 24, 1981: As many as ten million people see an oscillating, star-shaped object traverse the sky above fourteen Chinese provinces. **Note:** In some accounts, the object is described as "spiral-shaped" rather than starlike. The claim of ten million witnesses has been credited to a U.S. Department of Defense report—though the number is so enormous (and tidy) that it suggests a mere guess. Other sources claim "thousands" of witnesses.

1981–1995: During spring and summer over a period of fourteen years, some seven thousand people (including police and local politicians) in New York's Hudson Valley see neatly arrayed moving formations of lights in the night skies. The lighted objects are silent, and described, in discrete accounts, as delta- or boomerang-shaped, disc-like, and cone-shaped. Many witnesses report having had the sense that the craft tried to "communicate." One witness describes an object two hundred to three hundred feet across. In June 1984, people on the ground at and near the Indian Point nuclear complex at Buchanan, New York, witness UFOs overhead; inside, the plant's security systems are temporarily disrupted. **Note:** Some witnesses claimed to have been abducted, and/or struck by the "missing time" syndrome. In other instances, witnesses said they coaxed a lighted response from UFOs after signaling with flashlights. Those reports are compelling—as well as very similar to events in the 1977 feature film *Close Encounters of the Third Kind.*

February 3, 1983: Pat Norris, a young woman living with her husband and children near Mobile, Alabama, pulls to a stop on a two-lane road off U.S. Highway 90 when the engine of her car begins to act up. In a moment she sees a massive, brilliantly lit object, perhaps a half-mile distant, above a clay and gravel pit. Norris estimates the object to be seventy to eighty feet high and at least two hundred feet across. As the object slowly comes closer, Norris notes that a "chopping wind" lets up; by the time the object is very close, the wind is gone. The craft itself is silent. Through a window circumscribing what Norris later describes as an elevated "deck," she plainly sees twenty to thirty slender, pale humanoids of average male adult height. An open "door" allows Norris to glimpse I-beams and "tubes" and other machinery inside the object. **Note:** After the incident, Norris dreamed of being physically examined. In an intriguing flashback to old-school UFOs, she described the craft's skin as studded with "rivets." This case was investigated on-site by the Aerial Phenomena Research Organization (APRO), which used altered names in its report; "Pat Norris" is a pseudonym.

July 11, 1991: While waiting to see a solar eclipse, many thousands of people in and around Mexico City observe a hovering metallic disc. Video shot by a pair of journalists on hand to cover the eclipse catches the flying object, which is a classic saucer shape with a domed top. **Note:** Because public interest in the eclipse brought countless people outdoors, the Mexico City incident is often cited as the largest mass-witness UFO event to date. After the reporters' video aired on Mexican television, videos shot by nonprofessionals surfaced; in one of those, the disc's trailing edge emits something that appears to disturb the air—clear exhaust or, possibly, an electromagnetic pulse. Skeptics rightfully denounce spurious claims of hundreds of UFOs above the city, and attribute the sighting to optical anomalies caused by the eclipse, or (weakly) to the planets Venus or Jupiter. Contrarily, many enthusiasts make a tenuous connection between the UFO, the eclipse, and Mayan prophecy.

January 4, 1992: A Japanese farmer in Saga Prefecture discovers a pale, tentacled creature "floating" in his cow shed; one of the man's cows is on the floor with a broken leg. Before the farmer can react, the uninvited creature floats out the door and disappears. **Note:** The farmer had been awakened by a barking dog, and reasoned that if he had not arrived in time, his cow would have been mutilated.

March 30–31, 1993: UFOs are spotted by personnel of the Royal Air Force base at Cosford, Shropshire, England. The objects have white lights at the leading edge, and a red light at the trailing edge. Simultaneously, a meteorological officer at RAF Shawbury observes a UFO skim a nearby field, shooting a laser-like beam at the ground. Although the object is silent, the officer can "feel" it in his body, as if he stood next to a mammoth bass speaker. **Note:** UFO researcher Nick Pope contacted the ballistic missile early warning system at RAF Flyingdales, and was informed that a Russian rocket that had placed a communications satellite had reentered the atmosphere very early in the morning of March 31. But because some of the UFO reports had come from military personnel, the rocket theory—though a reasonable explanation for some reports—could not account for every report.

September 16, 1994: Teachers and sixty-two students (age five to twelve) at Ruwa, Zimbabwe's Ariel School witness three moving objects in the sky, and the subsequent landing of one in a nearby field, about a hundred yards from the school. A small humanoid steps into view and explores an area near the craft until noticing the schoolchildren. The creature retreats, and within moments the craft ascends and disappears. **Note:** Leading South African UFOlogist Cynthia Hind visited the school later, to interview headmaster Colin Mackie and meet some of the children. Older students claimed that the "little man" communicated with them telepathically, to express sadness over Earth's environmental problems.

March 30, 1995: A saucer-shaped craft sitting on a road near Groot Marico, western Transvaal, South Africa, is seen by Jan Pienaar, a farmer who rounds a curve during a morning errand and nearly hits the craft with his truck. Pienaar steps onto the road and is held fast by an invisible force. The craft is twenty-five to thirty-five feet high, resting on three pods and looking like "two inverted soup plates with a pudding bowl on top." Pienaar is struck by the "translucent and lustrous" nature of the metallic skin. A dent and a two-foot hole are visible at a top seam, below "seven windows or portholes" that curve across the craft's upper level. The hull coruscates with colors showing the entire visible spectrum. After three or four minutes, the craft rises straight up before taking an oblique course and vanishing. **Note:** Jan Pienaar felt that the craft had landed to effect repairs to its hull. After phoning the police, Pienaar and another farmer, Chap Smit, returned to the site to examine the superheated road surface. The air, Pienaar said, had a scent reminiscent of chloroform.

January 20, 1996: Three young women in Varginha, Brazil, come upon a squat, misshapen creature that they describe as having red eyes, three horns, and a liberal coating of a peculiar sticky fluid. The Brazilian army—already tipped by NORAD to UFO activity in the area—evaluates the women's account and then invents an "explanation" that's ludicrously inadequate. **Note:** For more on this case, including its conspiracy elements, see chapter eleven.

December 11, 1996: Twenty-two witnesses along a 134-mile stretch of Yukon Territory, Canada, gape at a mammoth, diamond-shaped flying object that progresses across the evening sky and visits a campground, a lodge, a gravel pit, and various points above the towns of Pelly Crossing, Mayo, Dawson, Carmacks, and Watson Lake. The craft exhibits a wide, horizontal band of brightly illuminated windows, and sweeps the ground with a broad beam of bright light. **Note:** Witnesses along the 134-mile route observed the object between 7:45 p.m. and 9:00 p.m. The distance and elapsed time suggest an average speed of 107 miles per hour, very slow by UFO standards, but too rapid for sustained flight by any man-made lighter-than-air ship. Triangulation done later suggested that the thing may have been a mile in length. Because of the time of year, some children thought the object must be Santa's sleigh.

March 13, 1997: Shortly before 7:00 p.m., and continuing for the next two or three hours, thousands of ground witnesses in Arizona, New Mexico, and Nevada observe a massive, delta-shaped object soar majestically above towns and desert—sometimes slowly, other times very rapidly. Witnesses describe a horizontal array of six or seven bright lights on the craft's narrow leading edge. **Note:** This protracted incident is now known as "the Phoenix Lights." Descriptions of the lights vary between red and orange; and yellow and white. Witnesses variously recalled the craft as shaped like "sergeant's stripes," a wedge, and a triangle. In 2007, former Arizona governor Fife Symington revealed that he had been among the witnesses.

October 19, 1998: A Chinese J-6 fighter jet is scrambled to intercept a UFO above a military flight-training school at Changzhou, Jiangsu Province. The J-6 (a Chinese variant of the Russian MiG-19) closes to about thirteen thousand feet before the object darts upward. This game of cat-and-mouse, which is instigated and controlled by the UFO, goes on until the jet runs low on fuel and returns to base. Between 100 and 150 ground witnesses see a mushroom-shaped object ringed along its flat bottom portion by revolving lights. **Note:** A French news account published the following month quotes the jet pilot's assertion that the UFO was "just like ones in foreign movies."

February 25, 1999: Fourteen forestry workers in Washington's Cascade Mountains, near Mount St. Helens, witness an elk invisibly lifted from the ground by a disc-shape object hovering above. The craft wobbles after taking the elk inside, and then rises, executes a 360-degree turn, and flies rapidly into the eastern sky, and out of sight. **Note:** Less than a week after the elk abduction, forestry workers discovered the carcass of a pregnant elk, just a few miles from the site of the February 25 incident.

Getting to Where the UFOs Are

Grab Your UFO Spotter's Checklist and Go

UFO literature makes clear that sightings are routinely made across the globe. Besides pondering the objects' origins, UFOlogists wonder why certain parts of the world are more prone to sightings than others. The UFO-heavy site may be as small as a single village or town, or as large as a subsection of a continent. Alien visitors may be keen to learn more about human activity, past and present, as religious monuments, military bases, great cities, and nuclear reactors seem to excite special interest.

Alternatively, visitors may be drawn by natural phenomena, such as weather, bodies of water, geologic fault lines, mountains, deserts, and energy fields.

Among the human animal's wonderful qualities is a willingness to live or travel anywhere on Earth. Because of that hardiness, people are on hand to witness UFO activity in even the most remote parts of the world. Whether accessible or inaccessible, spots that receive regular visits from UFOs will invariably have people on hand to stand witness.

Eyes Only: Global UFO Hot Spots

- **Area 51**: Officially known as Groom Lake/Homey Airport, this highly secure government-owned parcel in the Nevada desert—involved mainly in tests of aircraft and other new military systems—has resonated in the imagination of UFOlogists for decades. Because of claims of saucer tests, visits from extraterrestrials, and other assumptions, Area 51 is a *de rigueur* stop for every UFO enthusiast. (For much more, see chapter eight.) Nevada Highway 375, which runs close to Groom Lake, has a state-approved designation of Extraterrestrial Highway.
- **Arizona**: This state that combines heavily populated urban areas with vast expanses of desert has attracted UFOs since July 1947, mere weeks after the famed Washington State sighting by Kenneth Arnold, which "created" the flying saucer phenomenon. Arizona sightings can be expected to continue near military bases, across the nighttime desert (a locale favored by astronomers and amateur stargazers), and near Tucson, Phoenix, Mesa, and other cities. The state's proximity to Area 51 and the alleged secret underground human-alien

base at Dulce, New Mexico (see chapter eleven), figures in some UFO accounts from Arizona.

- **Bonnybridge, Scotland**: This town in the Falkirk council area is the apparent epicenter of sightings from the town of Stirling to the Scottish capital, Edinburgh. Sightings made by civilians, police officers, and military personnel date to 1942 and continue, with vigor.

- **Brazil**: The UFO history of this enormous South American nation (world's fifth-largest in geographical area and population) goes back to 1947. As with some other UFO hot spots, Brazil exhibits a great variety of topographies, ecosystems, and population densities; sightings have come in from isolated areas as well as cities. Notable cases include the 1966 discovery of the bodies of two electrical technicians near Rio de Janeiro (both men died wearing peculiar lead masks); and the celebrated Varginha event of 1996 (see chapter eleven). Brazilian tales of alien abductions began in the mid-1950s.

- **Canada**: Blessed with picturesque, and remote, forest and glacial areas, the enormous land mass that is Canada came to the fore as a UFO hot spot in the mid-1960s. Sightings have been urban (such as the 1990 Montreal Bonaventure Hotel rooftop sighting) and in the wild (multiple sightings at Harbour Mill, Newfoundland, in 2010). Since the millennium, Toronto, Vancouver, and Terrace, British Columbia (a popular outdoor-activities town) have had increasing numbers of reports.

- **Earth orbit**: If you can get yourself into orbit, you are likely to see unidentified flying objects. Many will turn out to be (after brief consideration) meteorites and other natural bodies, or pieces of man-made space junk. Then again, you may luck out and get a glimpse of the so-called Black Night satellite, a dark, oddly shaped alien invention that has allegedly orbited our world for more than ten thousand years.

- **Elk River, Minnesota**: Home to regular sightings since 1992, this small town north of Minneapolis has seen UFOs in a variety of shapes and sizes, most famously, perhaps, in November 1979, when an unidentified craft crashed into the Elk River mudflats.

- **Kapustin Yar**: The 4th Missile Test Range, a high-security Soviet military and testing base at Kapustin Yar, sits some sixty miles east of Volgograd (formerly Stalingrad). Activated in 1946, the site initially housed captured German V-2 scientists, who worked with their Soviet counterparts on hurry-up development of intelligence-gathering technology and weapons systems. Since 1947, the base has conducted significant tests of rockets, missiles, and nuclear bombs (atmospheric). A significant portion of work is carried out in underground facilities. Fighter wings attached to the base have occasionally tangled with UFOs; a MiG crashed there in 1948 while pursuing a large, cigar-shaped object; and in 1967, another MiG was nearly lost when struck by a light beam emitted by a UFO. Fireballs and red spheres figure in other UFO reports. Alien spacecraft are said to have crashed at the site in 1960 and 1961. Today, Kapustin Yar is popularly known in the West as "Russia's Roswell" and "Russia's Area 51."

- **The M Triangle, Russia**: This remote, forty-square-mile area in Russia's Ural Mountains about six hundred miles east of Moscow has produced reports of the paranormal for three generations. Perhaps inspired by local folklore and natural phenomena, some of the accounts seem explainable enough. But repeated accounts of luminescent humanoids; odd, dancing lights; anomalous sounds; and indecipherable symbols that appear in the sky suggest an environment unusually attuned to the unorthodox.

- **Myrtle Beach, South Carolina**: This attractive beach community attracts thousands of tourists every year, some of whom come to see UFOs. The "Grand Strand" area, which includes Myrtle Beach, Little River, and Cherry Grove, is a longtime attractor of mysterious flying lights; many Myrtle Beach reports taken by MUFON and NUFORC are dominated by the color orange: "orange orbs," "orange circles," "orange fireballs," "orange spheres," "orange lights." Skeptics invariably mention Shaw AFB in Sumter, South Carolina (about a hundred miles northwest of Myrtle Beach), which regularly conducts night maneuvers off the coast.

- **Nullarbor Plain, Australia**: As its name suggests, the lonely Nullarbor Plain has no trees—or very few, anyway. It is an arid and semi-arid expanse of some 750 miles, traversed by excellent highways, and thus accessible to hardy locals and visitors. On January 20, 1988, a "bright light" dogged the car of the Knowles family, landed on the roof, filled the cabin with noxious gray mist, and then lifted the car from the road. Inside, the Knowles' panicked speech audibly slowed. Much to their discomfort, the Knowles became the most famous people in Australia. Skeptics suggested the family had seen the rising sun, dust devils, and an electrical storm. Other notable cases from the Nullarbor Plain: authorities discover a crashed UFO and deceased alien (1977); flying lights buzz a truck and rock it (1992); a craft parked at a highway berm lifts off when approached by car (1992); two women driving across the Plain enter a fugue state, experience discomfort in their vaginas, and see visions of small blue humanoids (2006).

- **Pacific Coast Highway (PCH; California State Route 1)**: California's most picturesque highway runs up the coast from San Diego to Redwood National Park, north of San Francisco. Although broad and busy in Orange County and near Los Angeles, the route has considerable stretches that are relatively quiet. UFO sightings on and near the road date back at least to World War II, and encompass lights, fireballs, spheres, discs, and saucers. Some sightings have been explained as jets and test firings from Vandenberg AFB, located 130 miles up the coast from Malibu. A portion of UFO activity near the highway is linked (by some) to secret underwater saucer bases—a stimulating notion that has yet to be proved. Intense speculation focuses on Sycamore Knoll, a contoured, 2.5-mile-wide underwater shelf about two thousand feet below the ocean's surface, northwest of Malibu. According to some UFOlogists, Google Earth images suggest a carefully plotted oval "roof" supported by pillars, and a wide, dark entrance, suggestive of a purpose-built underwater base. But complementary images from other sources show a natural formation above a fault line. The "pillars," when viewed from side angles, are vertical striations in rock, and the presumed "entrance" is a shallow concavity that leads nowhere. The oval roof is rock in an oval shape.

- **San Clemente, Chile**: This municipality located in the Chilean Andes 150 miles south of Santiago has produced hundreds of UFO reports since the mid-1990s. In 2008, the Chilean government designated a nineteen-mile mountain path as a "UFO trail," reflecting interest in UFO hot spots at Colbun Lake, El Enladrillado (a supposed landing pad built from volcanic rock), and the Reserva Nacional Altos de Lircay. Altitudes in this district located 150 miles south of Santiago can top eighty-two hundred feet, and portions of the area are accessible only on horseback.

- **San Luis Valley, Colorado**: Located about 110 miles southwest of Pueblo, this eight-thousand-square-mile basin sits about seventy-six hundred feet above sea level. Although aquifers have created wetlands and even lakes, and local farmers grow potatoes and other crops, the Valley is generally arid. Lacking ground light, the area has seen UFOs for decades. During the summer and fall of 2014, authorities in Hooper, Crestone, and other nearby Valley towns struggled to keep up with a steady flow of UFO reports. During the same period, local ranchers complained of missing or mutilated cattle.

- **Sochi, Russia**: Since 2009, the skies above the Black Sea resort that hosted the 2014 Winter Olympics have been very active with UFOs—hundreds of them, according to residents. A considerable portion of local speculation revolves around nearby Bytkha Mountain, a peak that had sacred significance to Paleolithic settlers, and later to Geniokhs and Ubykhs. Some in Sochi insist that the mountain houses a secret saucer base. Others suggest that the peak is the epicenter of a "galactic hub" or "vortex" that allows UFOs to sideslip the vast distances of space as they shuttle between their home planets and Sochi.

- **Stephenville, Texas**: UFO reports here date to January 8, 2008, when Stephenville residents saw mammoth flying objects "as big as a football field," and even larger. According to some sources, even the Bush Ranch (yes, *those* Bushes) came in for a buzzing. (UFOlogist Scott Waring claims that George W. Bush himself flew the largest of the Stephenville UFOs.) Simultaneous reports came from towns close to Stephenville: Dublin, Cisco, Alexander, and Comanche. Following international media coverage, the U.S. military explained that residents had seen F-16 fighters from nearby Carswell Field, an airbase attached to the Naval Air Station at Fort Worth. (The initial number of F-16s cited by Carswell, four, later grew to ten.) During the course of the exercise, the F-16 pilots dropped flares suspended by parachutes. Heat from the flares caused the chutes to rise. UFO sightings at Stephenville have continued to the present day.

- **Wycliffe Well, Australia**: This town in north-central Australia has been a center of UFO activity since World War II. The frequency of sightings speeded up in the 1990s, with regular observation of rectangles, squares, spheres, and cigar shapes, flying solo, in pairs, and in groups. Local lore says that if the curious stay up all night at Wycliffe Well, they will almost certainly spot a UFO. Some UFOlogists credit the great number of sightings at Wycliffe Well to "ley lines": hypothetical straight lines that trace mountains, great rocks, fault lines, and other landforms, as well as sacred sites, ancient monuments, and ancient burial grounds. The theory holds that the lines generate power from magnetic fields.

- **The Welsh Triangle**: Vivid accounts of UFOs around St. Brides Bay at Pembrokeshire, Wales, date to 1952. Witnesses have observed cigar-shaped objects, discs, and ovoids. Many sightings involve humanoids of various shapes and sizes; some of the creatures reveal a propensity to peep in windows. Physical evidence has included scorched grass and earth, and unusual metal objects. At least one Triangle event (June 1977) involves Men in Black. In a declassified document released in 2012, someone at a 1995 Ministry of Defence meeting ventured that aliens visiting the Triangle could be indulging in "tourism." Speculation about underground bases, ley lines, and physical embodiments of Welsh folk tales persists.
- **Your own backyard**: Anything can happen. So keep wondering, keep watching.

UFO Spotter's Checklist

Few experiences are as remarkable as an encounter with a UFO, from a distance or close up. Although your sense of wonder will be stimulated, it is important that you note and recall as much about your experience as possible. Memory-training exercises have applications in everyday life, and are particularly useful during and after UFO sightings.

- You are likely to be unable or disinclined to take notes as the event unfolds. Hence, the checklist below. Study it, or custom craft your own, and upload it to your smartphone, tablet, or notebook. For immediate note-taking or sketching, pencil and paper are good ideas.
- Record details of your sighting as soon as you are able.
- Vis-à-vis your safety during a sighting, be aware of your surroundings. Be mindful of dead ends, cliff edges, uneven terrain, low-hanging tree limbs, bodies of water, and other potential hazards.
- Remove yourself from the scene at any indication of electricity, heat or fire, unusual cold, gas or haze, "disturbed" air, or other phenomena with a potential to do physical damage.
- Do not stare into lights, particularly if they are flickering or rotating.
- Do not make your presence known. Do not assume that the UFO, and its occupants (if any), are "friendly."
- If you are detected, assume a neutral, unthreatening demeanor. If your departure seems prudent, execute it promptly and calmly.
- If occupants leave their craft to reveal themselves, be wary if they approach you. If the occupant extends a hand, or a hand gripping a device, retreat. Do not allow the occupants to step into your blind spots, and never allow them to get behind you.

- If you make your sighting at long distance, ask yourself if people in the area were apt to have been flying model planes or drones. If you live near an airport or military base, consider the possibility of routine flyovers or weather balloons. In rural areas, hot air balloons are not uncommon.
- Did the sighting take place near routes likely to be monitored by police or traffic helicopters? Is there an air show nearby? Were you near a park that encourages kite flying? Did your sighting occur on the Fourth of July or other holiday/celebration?
- Are there nearby businesses that might have engaged searchlights or advertising blimps? Did your sighting occur near parkland or a nature preserve with large populations of birds?
- Remember that laser pointers are common, and can be seen over considerable distances, particularly against low clouds and distant windows.
- If your sighting occurred near a body of water, consider that the Moon or lights of conventional aircraft may have reflected off its surface. Distant ships and boats will be lighted after dark; likewise, buoys, channel markers, and remote water-treatment plants.
- Ground lights from distant cities and towns may create odd effects, especially against partial clouds.
- Check with your local weather service or observatory for lightning or ball lightning, ice crystals, heat inversions, convection, unusual cloud formations, meteors, meteor showers, comets, an eclipse, visible planets, or other natural activity on the date of your sighting.
- Remember that the night sky is apt to reveal satellites, and the occasional satellite or booster reentry.

Although the checklist allows for estimates of speed, size, altitude, and distance, those things are extremely difficult to judge, particularly when an object is sighted against a "blank" sky that offers no reference points that might suggest relative size. Even experienced pilots routinely err in these estimations.

UFO Spotter's Checklist

Witness

- [ ] Name
- [ ] Gender
- [ ] Age
- [ ] Present occupation
- [ ] Occupational/professional training
- [ ] Address
- [ ] Eyeglasses
- [ ] Contact lenses
- [ ] Prescription medication
- [ ] Non-prescription medication
- [ ] Sole sighting to date
- [ ] One of multiple sightings
- [ ] When and where were others?
- [ ] Your physical state immediately prior (ill, well, tired, etc.)
- [ ] Your distance from object
- [ ] How you arrived at the scene (automobile, motorcycle, boat, walking, etc.)
- [ ] Any obvious effect on automobile or other machines?

Location of Sighting

- [ ] Nation
- [ ] State or province
- [ ] County, district, or province
- [ ] City or town
- [ ] Zip code
- [ ] Sighting at or near your home
- [ ] Compass reading
- [ ] GPS reference
- [ ] Notable buildings, structures, or establishments nearby
- [ ] Military base
- [ ] Armory
- [ ] Military proving grounds
- [ ] Police station
- [ ] Fire house
- [ ] Airport
- [ ] Observatory
- [ ] Aerospace campus
- [ ] Television station(s)
- [ ] Radio station(s)
- [ ] Newspaper office
- [ ] Factories and heavy manufacturing
- [ ] Power plant
- [ ] Power relay station
- [ ] Power lines
- [ ] Power towers
- [ ] Nuclear reactor
- [ ] Schools
- [ ] Colleges or universities
- [ ] Hospitals
- [ ] Farms or ranches
- [ ] Food-processing plant
- [ ] Bridges
- [ ] Tunnels
- [ ] Dams
- [ ] Major roadways
- [ ] Zoo
- [ ] Sacred sites (burial grounds, etc.)
- [ ] Monuments
- [ ] Other

Duration of Sighting

- [ ] ___ seconds
- [ ] ___ minutes
- [ ] ___ hours
- [ ] Sighting interrupted and then resumed
- [ ] Not sure

The Object

- [ ] Altitude
- [ ] Distance
- [ ] Shape
- [ ] Bell
- [ ] Boomerang
- [ ] Bullet
- [ ] Cigar
- [ ] Circle
- [ ] Cluster (individual shapes difficult to discern)
- [ ] Cone
- [ ] Cross
- [ ] Cylinder
- [ ] Delta
- [ ] Diamond
- [ ] Disc
- [ ] Dome
- [ ] Egg
- [ ] Fireball
- [ ] Football
- [ ] Hat (flat top, flat bottom)
- [ ] Irregular
- [ ] Light bulb (widest at top)
- [ ] Manta
- [ ] Missile
- [ ] Orb

- ☐ Organic
- ☐ Pancake
- ☐ Point of light
- ☐ Polygonal (pentagon, etc.)
- ☐ Rod
- ☐ Saturn (bisected horizontally)
- ☐ Saucer
- ☐ Sphere
- ☐ Star
- ☐ Teardrop (widest at bottom)
- ☐ Top
- ☐ Triangle
- ☐ Trident
- ☐ Wedge
- ☐ Shape changed/shifted
- ☐ Other
- ☐ Size (approximate inches, feet, or meters)
- ☐ Outer material (steel, alloy, plastic, etc.)
- ☐ Color(s)
- ☐ Black
- ☐ Blue
- ☐ Charcoal
- ☐ Gray
- ☐ Green
- ☐ Metallic
- ☐ Red
- ☐ Silver
- ☐ White
- ☐ Yellow-white
- ☐ Other (specify)
- ☐ Unchanging combination of colors
- ☐ Shifting/changing colors
- ☐ Speed/speed range
- ☐ Bursts of acceleration
- ☐ Sounds (whir, hum, engine noise, etc.)
- ☐ Silent
- ☐ Windows
- ☐ Portholes
- ☐ Hatches or doors

- ☐ Antennae or other mounted extrusions
- ☐ Visible occupants
- ☐ Number of visible occupants
- ☐ Illuminated
- ☐ Glow
- ☐ Cornea or ring
- ☐ Exterior lights
- ☐ Direction(s) of travel
- ☐ Dramatic changes of angle or elevation
- ☐ Trail left behind (exhaust, electrical disturbance, etc.)
- ☐ Angle of elevation
- ☐ Chased by another object(s)
- ☐ If yes, what chased it?
- ☐ Landed/touched down
- ☐ If yes, how long did it remain on the ground?
- ☐ Two objects
- ☐ Three or more objects
- ☐ If two or more, did the objects fly in tandem, or in formation?
- ☐ Primary object releases other objects
- ☐ Other objects joined the primary object
- ☐ Noticeable odor
- ☐ Organic
- ☐ Non-organic
- ☐ Sweet
- ☐ Sour
- ☐ Sickly
- ☐ Nauseating
- ☐ "Hot" or "electrical"
- ☐ Object appeared to perform a specific task
- ☐ Task
- ☐ How did the object disappear from your sight?
- ☐ Did the object return?

Immediate Environment

- ☐ Time of day
- ☐ Weather (sunny, windy, fog, haze, sleet, etc.)
- ☐ Did the weather affect the object?
- ☐ Did the object affect the weather?
- ☐ Did the weather change during the encounter?
- ☐ Visible moon
- ☐ Visible planets
- ☐ Other aircraft (identifiable and otherwise) in the vicinity?
- ☐ Urban
- ☐ Industrial
- ☐ Suburban
- ☐ Semi-rural
- ☐ Rural
- ☐ Beach or waterfront
- ☐ Terrain (trees, foothills, river, etc.)
- ☐ Animals nearby
- ☐ If yes, what species, and did they exhibit reaction(s) to object?
- ☐ Effect on vegetation (flattening, crushing, burning, wilting, etc.)
- ☐ Crop circles nearby
- ☐ Unusual sounds before and after object presented itself (humming, crackling, etc.)
- ☐ Unusual heat or cold

Hynek Close Encounter Classification

(See chapter ten for details)

- ☐ CE1
- ☐ CE2
- ☐ CE3
- ☐ CE4
- ☐ CE5
- ☐ CE6
- ☐ CE7

Occupants/Creatures

- ☐ None
- ☐ Visible while aboard object
- ☐ Visible after leaving object
- ☐ Bodily configuration
- ☐ Human
- ☐ Humanoid
- ☐ Non-humanoid (avian, reptilian, insectoid, winged, quadruped, "blob," etc.)
- ☐ Head size and limb lengths matched typical human proportions
- ☐ Number of fingers
- ☐ Number of toes (if visible)
- ☐ Male
- ☐ Female
- ☐ Males and females
- ☐ Unknown or indeterminate gender
- ☐ Height (typical human height, shorter, taller)
- ☐ Weight
- ☐ Anomalous facial features (over-sized eyes, nose slits, small mouth, etc.)
- ☐ Skin tone
- ☐ Skin texture
- ☐ Hirsute
- ☐ Hair color
- ☐ Hair length
- ☐ Hair texture
- ☐ Hairless
- ☐ Attire (uniforms, headgear, foot-wear, varied attire, no attire)
- ☐ Demeanor
- ☐ Friendly
- ☐ Wary
- ☐ Frightened
- ☐ Disinterested
- ☐ Neutral
- ☐ Mischievous

- ☐ Aggressive
- ☐ Menacing
- ☐ Indeterminate or unknowable
- ☐ Sexual contact (if multiple occupants/ creatures)
- ☐ Communicative
- ☐ Audible speech (English and any other human language)
- ☐ Audible, indecipherable organic sounds
- ☐ Audible "artificial" or "mechanical" sounds

- ☐ Touch
- ☐ Telepathy
- ☐ Symbols
- ☐ Music
- ☐ Patterns of light
- ☐ Patterns of color
- ☐ Non-communicative
- ☐ Miscellaneous anomalous creatures (Bigfoot, Sasquatch, Chupacabra, ghosts, etc.)

Abduction

- ☐ Invited aboard craft
- ☐ Forced aboard craft
- ☐ Nature of craft's interior (bulkheads, machinery, etc.)
- ☐ Interview/conversation
- ☐ Physical examination

- ☐ Sexual violation
- ☐ Blood drawn
- ☐ Tissue samples taken
- ☐ Photographed
- ☐ Released at point of abduction
- ☐ Released elsewhere

Documentation

- ☐ Additional witness(es) able to give first-person corroboration
- ☐ Physical evidence (burned vegetation, metal objects, etc.)
- ☐ Digital photo (camera, smartphone, or tablet)
- ☐ Film photo
- ☐ Video
- ☐ Film footage
- ☐ Audio recording
- ☐ Police report
- ☐ Did you prepare (or asked to have prepared) a sketch or other illustration?

Report Made to Authorities

- ☐ Local police or sheriff
- ☐ Federal law enforcement
- ☐ Local airport

- ☐ Fire department
- ☐ FAA
- ☐ Military

Report Made to UFO Group

- ☐ BUFORA
- ☐ CUFOS
- ☐ FUFOR
- ☐ MUFON
- ☐ NICAP

- ☐ NICUFO
- ☐ UFOIRC
- ☐ Other (specify)

Report Made to Media

- ☐ Newspaper
- ☐ Television/cable television
- ☐ Radio (traditional, satellite, podcasts, Internet)
- ☐ Facebook, blog, or other Internet post
- ☐ Magazines (general-interest or specialty)
- ☐ Websites and Web forums
- ☐ No report made

Aftermath

- ☐ Examined by doctor or nurse
- ☐ Hospitalized
- ☐ Partial amnesia
- ☐ Missing time
- ☐ Muscle strain
- ☐ Broken bones
- ☐ Marks on body
- ☐ Bruises
- ☐ Wounds
- ☐ Welts
- ☐ Bite marks
- ☐ Bumps or ridges
- ☐ Implant(s)
- ☐ Impression marks
- ☐ Burns
- ☐ Singed hair
- ☐ Depression
- ☐ Anxiety
- ☐ Fatigue
- ☐ Fever
- ☐ Chills
- ☐ Vertigo
- ☐ Nausea or vomiting
- ☐ Rash
- ☐ Patchy hair
- ☐ Pregnancy
- ☐ Spontaneous abortion or miscarriage
- ☐ Childbirth
- ☐ Other (specify)
- ☐ Unsettling dreams
- ☐ Encounters with Men in Black (MiB)
- ☐ Voluntary hypnosis/hypnotic therapy/hypnotic regression

Eyes Only: Selected UFO Sightings Since 2000

Thanks to the Internet and smartphones, the number of UFO reports made since the millennium is almost literally uncountable. What once might have been termed a flood of fresh UFO information, pre-Internet, has become something larger and metaphysical: a great, overtly challenging force. For instance, NUFORC, for the brief period of August 7–22, 2011, posted approximately 350 new reports. Another leading UFO organization, MUFON, maintains and posts a running log of UFO reports coming into that organization—averaging sixteen each day. If every sighting from the last decade and a half could be added to a haystack, and each of us had a pitchfork, we'd be pitching hay for the rest of our lives. But because we're curious, we try to process as many UFO accounts as possible.

For whatever reasons, the preponderance of reports made since 2000 have an obvious sameness: clusters or formal formations of lights, usually orange (though sometimes red or white) that show themselves for less than a minute before zooming out of sight. Amazing, too, how many recent accounts begin with, "I stepped outside for a cigarette . . . ."

Here is a sampling of recent reports that are somewhat more engaging.

January 5, 2000: Four police officers and three civilians in St. Clair County, Illinois, spot a large, silent V-shaped craft, as it follows one course, and then another, and then still another, at about 4:00 a.m. The first witness, a civilian, says the object is "as big as a house." That witness, and subsequent ones, agree that the craft's perimeter is illuminated by white lights, and by a red one on the underside. **Note:** The UFO community quickly regarded the "St. Clair Triangle" as a major event, generating discussion sufficient to inspire a pair of cable-TV pseudo-documentaries (Discovery Channel, 2000; Sci-Fi, 2004). ABC-TV news anchor Peter Jennings hosted a 2004 UFO-investigation special that prominently featured the St. Clair Triangle. Despite this attention, many who studied the reports, and checked them against known aircraft activity on January 5, concluded that the witnesses saw a lighted advertising blimp operated by the American Blimp Company.

August 23, 2001: Forty-five miles off the New Jersey coast, a recreational fisherman observes a metallic cylinder that hovers a thousand feet above the Atlantic, and fifteen hundred feet above his boat. The cylinder has two equal sections that counter-rotate against each other. Although the fisherman discerns no engine noise, the mid-afternoon air is charged with an audible electrical hum. The boat's GPS and compass systems go off-line, and small fish (the witness calls them "bait fish") become agitated and swim to the surface. **Note:** In the time the fisherman needed to dash below and grab his camera, the cylinder departed. GPS, compass, and fish shortly returned to normal.

Never assume that your encounter with an extraterrestrial will be free of threat. If you're unwary, you could be in for a disagreeable experience. Just ask Gloria Castillo, clutched here by one of Paul and Jackie Blaisdell's cabbage-heads in *Invasion of the Saucer-Men* (1957).

January 11, 2002: At 4:30 a.m., a male camper at Point Mugu (California) State Park (located about a dozen miles northwest of Malibu) observes a bright light hovering a hundred feet above the Pacific, moving back and forth in synch with two lights visible beneath the water. After half an hour, the elevated light accelerates into the sky and disappears; the pair beneath the water dive out of sight.

April 26, 2003: A "missile" shooting a focused blue beam from its nose streaks across the sky above Delta, British Columbia, Canada. The witness watches as the object ascends from about five hundred meters to "several kilometers" in just a couple of minutes, before disappearing over the Pacific.

December 6, 2003: Eight people on a bus traveling between Salta and Puna, Argentina, get a close-up look at a luminous "device" measuring more than three hundred feet across, resting on thirty-foot struts in the middle of the Tin Tin road. The witness who ventures closest, a La Poma farmer named Julio Espinosa, watches thin, brightly glowing "strange beings" exit the object. One jumps into a bramble bush, apparently to examine it and take samples. After twenty minutes, Espinosa returns to the bus to tell the others about the creatures. **Note**: The news story published in Salta, Argentina's *Diario El Tribuno* (January 11, 2004) says nothing about how much longer the object remained on the road, or how and when it departed.

April 15, 2004: A low-flying flashing object showing red, green, and blue is observed moving east to west over Tabriz, a city in northwestern Iran, by a woman named Saina Haghkish. **Note**: Iran's state news agency, IRNA, suggested that the witness saw a spy or communications satellite. This event is often discussed as one of a series of sightings over Iran during April 12–15 or, alternatively, April 12–21. An Iranian astronomer, Sa'dollah Nasiri-Qeydari, insisted that Haghkish and others saw the planet Venus.

September 9, 2005: A big-headed humanoid with red eyes, and standing less than two-and-a-half-feet tall, is seen by villagers at Huay Nam Rak, Mae Chan District, Thailand. Sawaeng Boonyalak and others observe as the creature blithely explores a rice field. After about an hour, the creature floats into a tree and then ascends into the sky, "into the bright light." **Note**: No footprints were discovered in the rice field. Later elaboration claimed that the creature was preceded into the field by "floating fire." Witnesses could not agree about whether or not the creature had arms.

January–March 2006: Numerous witnesses report glowing discs flying above Aliso Viejo, in California's San Joaquin Valley. Accounts describe the objects as about a yard in diameter, and festooned with flashing lights. One witness recalls the disc as a "glowing Nerf football." In a separate incident, a cab driver is so startled he runs his car up a curb. The staff of an Aliso Viejo restaurant is scared to come outside. **Note**: In March 2006, the *Los Angeles Times* interviewed Aliso Viejo resident Gaylon Murphy, a cardiovascular surgeon; and Steve Zingali, a facilities engineer from Mission Viejo. The two friends created the foam-board and carbon fiber saucers in their garages, pursuing a hobby that became a side business: flight-ready saucers, with lithium batteries, remote control, and forty mph capability, for a thousand dollars apiece.

October 14, 2008: From an ideal vantage point on the Canadian side of Niagara Falls, the manager and other staffers with the Sheraton on the Falls Hotel observe a very large, triangular object slowly fly west, toward the hotel, about five hundred feet above Horseshoe Falls. Each of the craft's three edges is marked by a trio of white lights; a single red light illuminates the object's underside. As the object continues west, a wide, white beam of light originating at the underside plays across the water. The witnesses are startled when the beam suddenly shines at *them*. **Note:** The hotel manager and other employees described the craft as being about 250 feet long. *See next entry, May 15, 2009.*

May 15, 2009: Seven months after the manager and other staffers at the Sheraton on the Falls Hotel (at Niagara Falls, Ontario, Canada) witness an enormous, triangular craft slowly fly above the Falls, a security staffer tells the manager that numerous employees encountered two "extremely odd-looking" men on May 14. Employees remember very pale men, of identical height and attired in identical black trench coats and black hats. The strangers had come to the hotel looking for the manager. The manager and hotel security review May 14 surveillance tapes of the inside front entrance, and quickly locate the two visitors. Later on the fifteenth, a female staffer meets with the manager to describe the men further, recalling not just the identical clothing, but large blue eyes that never blinked; and a complete lack of facial hair, including eyebrows. The woman remembers that both men appeared to wear wigs. More significantly, she reports having had the uncomfortable feeling that the strangers could read her mind. **Note:** Although hotel staffers present on May 14 informed the men that the manager was not in that day, the men roamed the hotel nevertheless, buttonholing employees and asking to see the manager. Aerial Phenomenon Investigations (API), a D.C.-based UFO research group, could not resolve the October 2008 Niagara Falls sighting, or explain the later presence of the Men in Black.

December 10, 2009: After being taken from his Indiana apartment at 4:30 in the morning and physically examined by four or five "Reptilians," a man realizes that a barbed implant has been placed in his penis. **Note:** In the report he prepared for MUFON, the victim expresses great (and repeated) worry about his penis, which he refers to as "my johnson."

September 13, 2010: While on a night training exercise with Special Forces recruits at Camp Mackall, North Carolina, about thirty miles southwest of Fort Bragg, a veteran instructor observes a pair of F-15 Eagle fighter jets flying at about ten thousand feet, in rapid pursuit of an enormous triangular craft flying at two thousand to three thousand feet. The object is "gunmetal or carbon black" and the size of "an NFL football stadium." Each corner of the silent ship is marked by a pale blue light. The craft proceeds north for about two minutes and disappears behind a tree line—only to show itself again, this time moving south. By now, a third Eagle has joined the other two. All four craft disappear behind trees to the witness's southwest. **Note**: Besides the primary witness, the craft was observed by an assistant instructor and fifteen Special Forces trainees. Although the instructor searched local newspapers for accounts of the object, he found none.

Mid-June 2012: A security guard working a construction site near Yuba City, California, spots a brightly illuminated white object traveling above treetops about six hundred yards away. Binoculars and night-vision apparatus give the man a clear view of the object's "classic" saucer shape. The fuselage has illuminated points of red, blue, and green. Because the saucer illuminates the trees, the witness is able to estimates its diameter as between fifty and a hundred feet. **Note**: The witness observed the object for five minutes, and then left to fetch a friend. When the two returned, the object was gone.

December 28, 2013: While looking from his window in a Hong Kong hotel, a traveler named Jack Watson sees "something" in the distance, and is shortly visited by an alien. The creature is "big green. . . . ten feet tall and five feet wide." When it pulls Watson from bed, they dance. **Note**: In the account taken and posted by ufoevidence.org, Watson revealed that "the alien was actually quite good at dancing and as I like to try new things we had sex." Welcome to the Internet.

March 20–22, 2014: A farmer who discovers an alien in his barn at New Paltz, New York, is surprised when the creature stays for three days. **Note**: A witness photograph provided to MUFON reveals the head of a classic gray (large cranium; dark, oversized eyes) as it peers from around the doorway of a dilapidated hay barn.

November 15, 2015: International Space Station astronaut Scott Kelly posts a nighttime image of India as that country appears from space; the photograph's upper-right corner is dominated by an elongated object that suggests a cylinder with a pod at each end; or a cylinder with a bright light(s) at each end. Kelly, who may not have noticed the object, makes no mention of it in his accompanying tweet. **Note**: The UFO Sightings Daily blog described the object as cigar-shaped, with a metallic body measuring about eighty feet in length. The blog deduced that when Kelly snapped the photo, the UFO was between 500 and 650 feet from the Space Station. Other sources ventured that the object is a reflection on Kelly's window; or, more persuasively, one of the many hunks of equipment that festoon the Station's exterior. *Forbes* magazine suggested that the object is the Station's High Definition Earth-Viewing System (HDEV).

January 2, 2016: Shortly before dawn, a man living in Tempe, Arizona, observes a saucer-shaped "mother ship" disgorge at least three flying discs. Visible for about thirty minutes, the four craft appear to play keep-away with military helicopters on the scene. The mother ship displays yellow-white illumination that changes to green, blue, red, and orange. Finally, the smaller craft ascend back to the mother ship via "ropes" of light. **Note**: Although the witness saw no physical engagement with the saucers, he observed jet fighters on the scene, as well as copters.

Afterword
Where Do We Go from Here?

Exploration, Knowledge, and the Future of UFOlogy

Here Comes Planet X

A January 20, 2016, *Washington Post* story began this way:

> Astronomers at the California Institute of Technology announced Wednesday that they have found new evidence of a giant icy planet lurking in the darkness of our solar system far beyond the orbit of Pluto. They are calling it "Planet Nine."

Besides reminding everybody that little Pluto is no longer the ninth planet—and aggravating those who insist that it *is*—the announcement generated excitement in the lay community, and cautious optimism among scientists. After detecting anomalous, possibly gravity-influenced motion of dwarf planets and other bodies in the faraway Kuiper Belt beyond Pluto, Caltech astronomers Mike Brown and Konstantin Batygin surmised the existence of "Planet Nine." Brown and Batygin described the planet as two to four times the diameter of Earth, with five to ten times the mass; by way of contrast, planet number eight, Neptune, is seventeen times the mass of Earth. Neptune lies 2.7 billion miles from Earth; on average, Planet Nine's orbit takes it twenty times farther from the sun than Neptune's path. A "year" on Planet Nine passes in ten thousand to twenty thousand Earth years.

The writers of the *Post* article, Joel Achenbach and Rachel Feltman, displayed an instinctive grasp of the romance inherent in Caltech's scientific announcement by weighting their lede with the words "giant," "lurking," "darkness," and "far beyond." A less discretionary word choice, "our," is nevertheless the lede's most significant: "our solar system," the reporters wrote. Planet Nine is in our solar system. Something amazing is apparently out there, and it is part of *us*.

X = Trouble

Just a day or two after the Caltech announcement, professional journalism's pulpy faction (Britain's *Daily Express* is one culprit) referred to Planet Nine with an alternate, more ominous name, "Planet X." (Remember *The Man from Planet X*? He brought out the worst in the Earthlings that discovered him). In a goofy turn, sensationalist newspapers and Web sites conflated Planet Nine with the wholly imagined Planet Nibiru, alleged by the late, self-taught archaeologist Zecharia Sitchin to be the longtime home of the Annunaki, "space-faring overlords" that traveled to Earth ages ago, to dominate human affairs. (Author Jim Marrs perpetuates the story today.) Elements of the UFOlogical fringe jumped on board, reminding everybody about Nibiru's collision with Earth, predicted in the mid-1990s by a Wisconsin woman named Nancy Lieder to happen by April 2016. (An earlier date given by Lieder, May 2003, came and went without Nibiru showing itself, and nothing happened in April 2016, either—but you probably already knew that.)

Conspiracy theorists who had no truck with Nibiru pasted their own ideas onto Planet Nine, struggling to gain traction with the claim that a thirty-year span of deaths of astronomers—by accident, disease, and simple old age—is really a string of assassinations engineered to hide the apocalyptic truth about Planet Nine.

If your special concern is extraterrestrials from Planet X, Nibiru, or elsewhere, Altamonte Springs, Florida's UFO Abduction Insurance Company sells specialized policies for $19.95, with a $10 million payout, and double indemnity if "the aliens insist on conjugal visits," and if "the aliens refer to the abductee as . . . THE OTHER WHITE MEAT" [capitalization in original]. To collect, abductees need only provide "proof of abduction and return." Approved claimants are paid a dollar a year for ten million years, or until they die. The gentleman behind this civic-minded idea, tax attorney Mike St. Lawrence, explained, "After carefully reviewing my homeowner's policy I discovered that I, like many other Americans, was not covered."

Planet Nine, Planet X—whatever the name, as far as some people are concerned, the giant world that may orbit on the outer fringes of our solar system is really Nibiru, home to aggressive aliens.   *Alamy*

Blue Book Returns

The seminal days of UFO study returned to the fore in January 2015, when the 130,000 pages of declassified Project Blue Book documents mentioned in this book's introduction came to the Web. While conducting research, I looked at thousands of those declassified Blue Book pages—admittedly not tens of thousands, but thousands, nevertheless. Between 1947 and 1969, Blue Book took 12,618 UFO reports. Of that number, Blue Book determined that 701 must remain "Unidentified." (Vintage CIA documents released to coincide, rather too cutely, with the 2016 reboot of *The X-Files* reveal that agency's conviction that some UFO cases must "remain unexplained.")

Blue Book document pages (preserved as paper-to-microfilm transfers executed in 1975) are now digitized. Researchers can locate particular documents by dates, location of the original incident, and by microfilm-roll number. To call up specific cases is time consuming but rewarding, not only when the payoff is an account of a well-known case, but when a heretofore anonymous case gets another moment in the sun. Researchers will be best rewarded by visiting bluebookarchive.com and theblackvault.com.

Individual pages are "rough," with smeared or thickened typescript; speckles and other "dirt" (probably from damage to the microfilm); and evidence that many original document pages had been wrinkled or otherwise poorly handled. Some documents had been "reversed" when preserved as photostats at some time during their life as paper; those digitized pages are white typescript on a black background, and virtually all are unreadable. Some other documents are too faded to be legible, suggesting that in such instances only carbon copies remained in the Blue Book paper files. In the main, though, the archived documents are readable—and thus remarkable conduits into UFO history.

A relative few pages show the handwritten notes of whichever Blue Book staffer happened to take a phone call, or spoke with someone who stopped by in person. Other pages are comprised of official Blue Book witness questionnaires and original correspondence (with the mailing envelopes), from witnesses.

Many Blue Book document pages consist of newspaper clippings, witness sketches, scientific computation, phone-call memos, and photographs. Pages from the *Congressional Record* are scattered throughout. Blue Book investigators could be catholic in their tastes, and even tossed in the occasional cartoon. As the little saucer pilots in a 1965 drawing (document page MISC-PBB2-238) hover above Earth, Pilot 1 says, "I'm sure I saw some 'people' down there!!" Pilot 2: "You aren't going to start those silly rumors again, are you?"

Longtime UFOlogists oriented to primary-source research were already well familiar with Blue Book's overall record of denial, and expected little in the way of latter-day revelations following the documents' move to the Web. Further, because many of the documents had been declassified before 2015, UFO researchers had carefully examined a good portion years ago, when the pages were far less easy to get to, but were nevertheless available to the persistent. No "shocking and new" revelations came to light after January 2015. The news value of the 2015 Web dump arose from the papers' new, and relatively easy, accessibility.

Many, perhaps most, of the documents are marked by physical redactions: black bars designed to obscure certain words, phrases, and sections. The documents have been declassified for a long time because declassification posed no general danger. But even declassified government papers may contain information that, even many years later, should not be released. In 1995, an executive order established the Interagency Security Classification Appeals Panel (ISCAP),

UNCLASSIFIED

HEADQUARTERS
637TH AIRCRAFT CONTROL AND WARNING SQUADRON
505TH AIRCRAFT CONTROL AND WARNING GROUP
Moses Lake Air Force Base
Washington

23 May 1949

SUBJECT: Project "SIGN".

TO: Chief of Staff
         United States Air Force
         Washington, 25, D.C.
         Attn: Director of Intelligence, Requirements Division

1. At 1330 a call was received from the Hanford Area (Concrete) that a Flying Saucer was over the East 200 area approximately 4 (four) miles east of the Hanford Atomic Plant, Washington. The operator at Hanford stated that the Disk was standing still and then took off in a south-easterly direction at a speed greater than that of a jet fighter. The available aircraft was called for by the Hanford operator and the aircraft was scrambled. The Hanford operator cleared the aircraft into their prohibited area (authorization coming from the Assistant Chief of the Security Section at Hanford). The scopes were instructed to search the southern sector with no results. Crew personnel and the controller searched the sky, visually, and noted a round, white or silver object traveling in a north easterly direction at a speed greater than that of jet fighters at approximately 10,000 to 15,000 feet. The base weather section was then contacted to see if any weather ballons were sent up and they reported in the negative. Base weather section stated that they do not utilize weather balloons. At 1420 an F-82, Gertrude 20, pilot Gardner was airborne and reported in to Torch controller. A target, number 81, was being tracked in the east-south-east sector by Torch at this time and the ADCC instructed the controller to intercept it in hopes that it might be a Disk. Target 81 faded in radar contact just after (approximately 5 minutes) Gertrude 20 was airborne. The controller was able to give two vectors before target 81 faded. Radar contact with the fighter was spotty, so poor that a coherent track on the fighter was impossible. At approximately 1425 Hanford reported falling bits of paper in their area (in the vicinity of the Rattlesnake Mountains). The Hanford operator described the papers as being approximately 6 inches square, red on one side and green on the other. The fighter was then sent to the vicinity of the Rattlesnake mountains to examine the area for the papers.

UNCLASSIFIED

The declassified Blue Book documents produced no world-shattering revelations, but they do offer insight into the course of the bureaucratic mind, and a legitimate concern for national security. This May 23, 1949, USAF memo describes a flying saucer's unwelcome interest in the Hanford Atomic Plant, in Washington State. Hanford had been visited since 1945, and by the spring of 1949—as the Soviets secretly prepared to reveal their atomic bomb—such overflights gave Air Force personnel sleepless nights.   *USAF*

to codify classification systems of government documents and provide redaction codes (justification and reasoning) for removal of information "contained in records under 25 years old"; and "contained in records over 25 years old." Redaction codes pertinent to older documents provide for protection of intelligence sources; removal of information useful for the manufacture of weapons of mass destruction; information that could compromise the security and efficacy of cryptologic systems and weapons systems; information posing potential harm to the president and vice president; information likely to embarrass or harm foreign governments; information whose release is in defiance of international treaties or other official agreements; removal of tactical and operational details of U.S. war plans with application to present-day plans; and information related to U.S. plans for civil defense.

Redacted portions of Blue Book documents appear to relate mainly to changes from CONFIDENTIAL to DECLASSIFIED. Names, addresses, telephone numbers, and other personal information about long-ago witnesses are left intact.

Particularly intriguing redactions suggest investigators' willingness to alter their initial findings. MISC-PBB2-339, for example, has a black bar redacting what was a few words, or a brief sentence in the "Conclusion" box of a 1965 report. Immediately below, handwritten in capital letters, is this: "UNIDENTIFIED."

Of course, information that is *not* redacted is generally far more illuminating than what has been excised. The summary page of Blue Book's further investigation (1956) of the 1947 Kenneth Arnold sighting (document MAXW-PBB2-750), for instance, practically vibrates with official disinterest, reading:

> The report cannot bear even superficial examination, therefore, must be disregarded. There are strong indications that this report and its attendant publicity is largely responsible for subsequent reports [made by others].

Another page from the Arnold document, MAXW-PBB2-756, has no typescript, only mathematical computations scribbled by UFOlogist/USAF consultant J. Allen Hynek—computations that led Hynek to declare Arnold's statements about the objects' speed and size "mutually contradictory." So although Blue Book's Arnold documents bring no revelations, and no firm evidence of cover-up, we nevertheless begin to grasp that even in its early days, Blue Book moved beyond the objectively scientific and into issues of culture and opinion.

The USAF closed Project Blue Book because 1) the project had not demonstrated that unidentified flying objects posed a threat to the United States, and 2) Blue Book had outlived its usefulness as a public relations tool designed to assuage American unease about "flying saucers." As we've seen in chapter nine, interludes of conscientious work done by Blue Book uncovered many spurious accounts, and many innocent misapprehensions. Good investigation also confirmed incidents that defied understanding. But in the end, of course, the pretense of the government's willingness to pursue the facts was allowed to dissolve. Blue Book went away.

The State of UFOlogy

The vistas offered by the Worldwide Web were unimagined during Blue Book's day—a time of land lines, typewriters, scratch pads, the U.S. mail, and in-person interviews. Now, UFOlogists and the merely curious can locate each other with simple keystrokes. UFO-related news, such as the apparent discovery of Planet Nine, flashes around the world in hardly more than a heartbeat.

The Web has been invoked many times in this book. It stands as the medium—and the socio-cultural driver—that is the signpost to the present state of UFOlogy. The Web is unarguably a blessing, but because UFO study remains a marginal discipline, UFOlogists are especially vulnerable to the energetic nonsense made possible by the Web's unregulated nature. Pleasure and real knowledge are afoot on the Web, and if you wish to explore UFOs in the context of hard science, history, and legitimate cultural study, you're in luck. But as we've seen, a great deal of UFO Web content amounts to junk thinking characterized by faulty reasoning and egged on by silliness, fakery, snark, and old-style humbuggery. The hazard is that all of those things deliver a disreputable sort of fun that easily commands everyone's attention—including the attention of media people that go for entertainment whenever they need background for the (now-rare) UFO feature article or TV-news segment. Faced with opportunities to contact a sober astronomer or, alternatively, the fellow from the Web who insists the Mars Rover photographed a squirrel (Google it), a feature writer or segment producer may struggle to resist the siren call of Squirrel Guy. That sort of decision encapsulates a portion of the external threat to UFOlogy. Government disinterest and scarce funding for institutional research are other external factors that loom large.

Internally, danger is posed by the continual, frankly dreary infighting among individuals and UFO factions, which exposes UFOlogy's lack of standards and discipline. If UFOlogy expects to grow into general respectability, it must move beyond things that are of interest only to UFO insiders, particularly arguments—posted to the Web, for all to see—about who in the field is an alleged idiot and who is not.

Worse, UFOlogy has been hijacked. Far too many dubious ancillary topics clamor for attention: Bigfoot; time travel; Nazis in the Antarctic; the Bermuda Triangle; crop circles; quasi-religious UFO cults; the Illuminati; alternate dimensions; the JFK-alien connection; chakras, auras; and alien implants. The never-ending flow of alien abduction accounts is now less concerned with science than with personal accounts reflective of the childlike "I me mine" emphasis that drives Facebook and other social media. A resurgence of interest in ancient astronauts flushes science so that a racialist faction preoccupied with DNA links to extraterrestrial Aryans can have its say. And science takes it on the chin again when the metaphorical mic is handed to little Paul Reveres eager to warn of secret alien bases peppered here and there on Earth, or on nearby planetary bodies.

Hard science needs to be the chugging core of UFO study, but because hard science is, well, *hard*, too many UFO enthusiasts—particularly wide-eyed newbies—avoid it. Certainly, the so-called mainstream media are not interested. Hard science isn't easily comprehended by lay-persons, and it sure isn't sexy (except during occasional cable-TV talking-head remarks from young, unusually good-looking astronomers or physicists). There *is* real romance in science—not the instant-gratification kind, but the sort that develops during years of serious study. But we are an increasingly impatient society in love with action, artificial emotiveness, and the certitude that relieves us of the obligation to think. We don't have time for years of *anything.*

Unfortunately, segments of the UFO establishment buy into this cultural pique. MUFON, which performs valuable work as

This "Project 10073 Record Card" dated November 7, 1957, gives the bare details of a UFO flyover at Walker AFB, located just a few miles south of Roswell, New Mexico. Like the Hanford atom plant, Roswell attracted UFOs for years.   *USAF*

a repository of UFO news and research, nevertheless tops its glossy home page with the words, "AS SEEN ON"—followed by the logos of CNN; the History Channel and that network's tabloid-style H2 spinoff; the National Geographic Channel; the Travel Channel; the Science network; Syfy; and the Discovery Channel—as if cable television confers intellectual value and scientific legitimacy.

In a 2014 article for *New York* magazine's Daily Intelligencer Web page, journalist Mark Jacobson lamented the flat attendance—just four hundred souls—at the annual MUFON convention, a get-together that drew four thousand to five thousand registered attendees, year in and year out, a generation ago. The relative lack of present-day interest suggested to Jacobson that UFOlogy had become passé. He proposed that "the simple flying disc from far, far away has become a quaint, almost nostalgic specter."

If that is indeed the case, UFOlogy is realizing that nostalgia is death to any undertaking that wishes to move forward. Nostalgia can never compete with the new, and yet UFOlogy remains wedded to stories and controversies of the past. Roswell never goes away. The Condon Committee still raises hackles. Barney and Betty Hill are discussed as if their experience happened last week instead of a half century ago. Rendlesham Forest, George Adamski, Mothman, the Shaver Mystery and hollow Earth, Kenneth Arnold, Captain Mantell's P-51 crash, the Lubbock Lights—all of those and the rest of the fascinating, fundamental history of UFO study have acquired an outsized importance, as if UFOlogy now exists only to frame the ghosts of those past people and events.

A Lifeline

The U.S. government and military have devoted decades to debunking UFOs and UFO study, painting reasonable believers not simply as crackpots, but as persons of no consequence. That's the ultimate, scarily metaphysical insult: because UFOlogists don't matter, their ideas are non-ideas. Washington, the

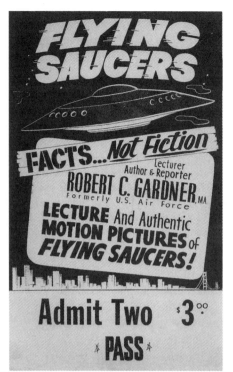

"FACTS . . . _Not Fiction_." The UFO landscape boils with people claiming to offer the straight story; in the early 1950s, UFO investigator and lecturer Robert C. Gardner was one of many. The discussion continues. Who can determine which tales are genuine and which are fabrications? Well, _you_ can. The human mind—which is apparently of great interest to extraterrestrial visitors—is a splendid instrument. When we use it with discernment, it will light our paths to the truth.

armed services, and other Beltway players remain ready to dismiss serious UFO study right out of existence.

We do not suggest a conspiracy here. To the contrary, we suggest discrete systems (the political system, the military system, and others) in pursuit of discrete goals. As with any system, the goal of political bodies and the military is self-perpetuation. If Washington guides us toward governance, the governance is incidental. When the military protects us, the protection is ancillary. Contrary to what we're expected to believe, the systems exist simply . . . to exist. If the activities of one system overlap with the activities of another, the confluence isn't evidence of concerted cooperation in the service of a master plan. It's just overlap.

Yes, but _why_ is there no conspiracy? Because a system that allows another system too close to its inner workings begs to be compromised and revealed. And when that happens, the continued life of the unwary system is jeopardized.

UFOlogy's real adversary, then, is UFOlogy itself. By tolerating scattershot research and speculation, by indulging the fringe, by seeking legitimacy in crumbs thrown by cable television, and by failing to function as a unified force, UFOlogy exposes its vulnerabilities while forgetting that it, too, is a system.

To ensure meaningful, long-term survival, UFOlogy needn't adopt the brute survivalist thinking that drives the military and similar systems. UFOlogy can endure and prosper by reclaiming its original focus on unidentified flying objects. Tune out the noise. Ignore the trivial. Forsake the foolish. Insist on civility and scientific integrity. Welcome the thoughtful and the trained. Look to the skies and reflect on the intelligent life that surely is out there. Devote all momentum to the gathering of facts, because only facts lead to the truth.

There are no squirrels on Mars.

Bibliography

Declassified Documents, Project Blue Book

Thousands of pages reviewed. Particular information gleaned from:

AFR-200-2 (initial report, Barney and Betty Hill, 1961)
MAXW-PBB2-750 (Kenneth Arnold case, 1956)
MAXW-PBB2-756 (Kenneth Arnold case, 1956)
MISC-PBB2-238 (flying saucer cartoon, 1965)
MISC-PBB2-339 (saucer-case conclusion, 1965)
NARA-PBB2-1290 (DC-3; Montgomery, AL; July 24, 1948)
NARA-PBB86-1156 (Project Grudge, 1961)
NARA-PBB86-1157 through 1161 (USAF memo re obstacles to accurate UFO reports, 1967)

Books

Adamski, George. *Flying Saucers Have Landed*. British Book Centre. New York: 1953.
———. *Inside the Space Ships*. Abelard-Schuman. New York: 1955.
Allingham, Cedric (pseudonym of Patrick Moore and Peter Davies). *Flying Saucer from Mars*. British Book Centre. New York: 1955.
Angelucci, Orfeo. *The Secret of the Saucers*. Amherst Press. Amherst, WI: 1955.
———. *Son of the Sun*. DeVorss & Co. Los Angeles: 1959.
Annan, David. *Movie Fantastic: Beyond the Dream Machine*. Bounty Books. London: 1974.
Arnold, Kenneth and Ray Palmer. *The Coming of the Saucers: A Documentary Report on Sky Objects That Have Mystified the World*. Amherst Press. Amherst, WI: 1952.
Ash, Brian. *The Visual Encyclopedia of Science Fiction*. Harmony Books. New York: 1977.
Asimov, Isaac. *Extraterrestrial Civilizations*. Crown. New York: 1979.
Austen, Jake, ed. *Flying Saucers Rock 'n' Roll*. Duke University Press. Durham, NC: 2011.
Barker, Gray. *The Silver Bridge*. Saucerian Books. Clarksburg, WV: 1970.
———. *They Knew Too Much About Flying Saucers*. University Books. New York: 1956.
Barker, Gray and Ruth Anne Leedy. *Serpents of Fire: German Secret Weapons, UFOs, and the Hitler/Hollow Earth Connection*. New Saucerian Books. Point Pleasant, WV: 2014.
Barker, Gray, ed. *The Book of Adamski*. New Saucerian Books. Point Pleasant, WV: 2014.

Barkun, Michael. *A Culture of Conspiracy: Apocalyptic Visions in Contemporary America*, 2nd edition. University of California Press. Oakland: 2013.

Barson, Michael. *"Better Dead than Red!"* Hyperion. New York: 1992.

Bennett, Colin. *Looking for Orthon*. Paraview Press. New York: 2001.

Berlitz, Charles and William L. Moore. *The Roswell Incident*. Grosset and Dunlap. New York: 1980.

Bethurum, Truman. *Aboard a Flying Saucer*. DeVorss & Co. Los Angeles: 1954.

Beukes, Lauren. *Maverick: Extraordinary Women from South Africa's Past*. Oshun Books. Johannesburg: 2004.

Blumrich, Josef F. *The Spaceships of Ezekiel*. Bantam Books. New York: 1974.

Boyne, Walter J. *The Influence of Air Power upon History*. Pelican. Gretna, LA: 2003.

Brandenburg, John E. *Death on Mars: The Discovery of a Planetary Nuclear Massacre*. Adventures Unlimited Press. Kempton, IL: 2015.

Brosterman, Norman. *Out of Time: Designs for the Twentieth-Century Future*. Abrams. New York: 2000.

Brown, Len. *Mars Attacks*. Abrams ComicArts. New York: 2012.

Bruni, Georgina. *You Can't Tell the People: The Cover-up of Britain's Roswell*. Sidgwick & Jackson. London: 2000.

Bugliosi, Vincent. *Reclaiming History: The Assassination of President John F. Kennedy*. W. W. Norton. New York: 2007.

Bullard, Thomas E. *The Myth and Mystery of UFOs*. University Press of Kansas. Lawrence: 2010.

———. *UFO Abductions. The Measure of a Mystery, Volume 1: Comparative Study of Abduction Reports*. Fund for UFO Research. Bloomington, IN: 1987.

Burt, Harold E. *Flying Saucers 101*, 2nd edition. Alien2U Publishing. San Diego: 2012.

Cantril, Hadley. *The Invasion from Mars*. Princeton University Press. Princeton, NJ: 1940.

Christopher, Paul. *Alien Intervention: The Spiritual Mission of UFOs*. Huntington House. Lafayette, LA: 1998.

Cicero. *The Nature of the Gods*. (Translated by P. G. Walsh.) Oxford Paperbacks. Oxford: 2008.

Clark, Jerome. *The UFO Book: Encyclopedia of the Extraterrestrial*. Visible Ink Press. Detroit: 1998.

———. *The UFO Encyclopedia: The Phenomenon from the Beginning*, 2nd edition. Omnigraphics. Detroit: 1998.

Clark, Mark. "Scenes from a Marriage: The Sexual Politics of I Married a Monster from Outer Space." *Science Fiction America*. David J. Hogan, ed. McFarland & Co. Jefferson, NC: 2006.

Cochman, Charles, ed. *Mars Attacks: 50th Anniversary Collection*. Abrams ComicArts. New York: 2012.

Cook, Nick. *The Hunt for Zero-Point: Inside the Classified World of Antigravity Technology*. Broadway Books. New York: 2002.

Cooper, Gordon and Bruce Henderson. *Leap of Faith: An Astronaut's Journey into the Unknown*. Harper. New York: 2000.

Cooper, Milton William. *Behold a Pale Horse*. Light Technology Publishing. Flagstaff, AZ: 1991.

Corn, Joseph J. and Brian Horrigan. *Yesterday's Tomorrow: Past Visions of the American Future.* Summit Books & the Smithsonian Institution. New York: 1984.

Corso, Philip. *L'Alba di una Nuova Era.* Pendragon. Bologna: 2003.

Corso, Philip and William J. Birnes. *The Day After Roswell.* Simon and Schuster/ Pocket Books. New York: 1997.

Couffer, Jack. *Bat Bomb: World War II's Other Secret Weapon.* University of Texas Press. Austin: 1992.

Crawford, David, ed. *38 Messages from Space: The Wilbert Smith Archives Remixed.* CreateSpace Independent Publishing Platform. Seattle: 2008.

Cremo, Michael A. and Richard L. Thompson. *Forbidden Archaeology: The Hidden History of the Human Race.* Bhaktivedanta Institute. San Diego: 1993.

Däniken, Erich von. *Chariots of the Gods? Unsolved Mysteries of the Past.* Econ Verlag. Dusseldorf: 1968.

Davies, Paul. *Are We Alone?* Basic Books. New York: 1995.

Dick, Robert. *Auto Racing Comes of Age: A Transatlantic View of the Cars, Drivers, and Speedways, 1900–1925.* McFarland & Co. Jefferson, NC: 2012.

Di Fate, Vincent. "Where Do Little Green Men Come From? A Speculative Look at the Origins of a Pop Culture Icon." *Science Fiction America.* David J. Hogan, ed. McFarland & Co. Jefferson, NC: 2006.

Druffel, Ann. *Firestorm: Dr. James E. McDonald's Fight for UFO Science.* Wild Flower Press. Columbus, NC: 2003.

Edwards, Frank. *Flying Saucers—Serious Business.* Lyle Stuart. New York: 1966.

Eichar, Donnie. *Dead Mountain: The Untold True Story of the Dyatlov Pass Incident.* Chronicle Books. San Francisco: 2013.

Ellwood, Robert S. *Islands of the Dawn: The Story of Alternative Spirituality in New Zealand.* University of Hawaii Press. Honolulu: 1993.

Evans, Hilary and Robert Bartholomew. *Outbreak! The Encyclopedia of Extraordinary Social Behavior.* Anomalist Books. San Antonio: 2009.

Filer, George A. III. *Filer's Files: Worldwide Reports of UFO Sightings.* Infinity Publishing. West Conshohocken, PA: 2005.

Ford, Brian. *German Secret Weapons: Blueprint for Mars.* Ballantine. New York: 1969.

Fort, Charles. *The Book of Charles Fort (The Book of the Damned, New Lands, Lo! and Wild Talents).* Holt. New York: 1941.

Fowler, Gene and Bill Crawford. *Border Radio.* University of Texas Press. Austin: 2002.

Fowler, Raymond E. *The Andreasson Affair.* Prentice-Hall. Englewood Cliffs, NJ: 1979.

———. *The Watchers 2: Exploring UFOs and the Near-Death Experience.* Wild Flower Press. Columbus, NC: 1996.

Friedman, Stanton T. *Flying Saucers and Science.* New Page Books. Pompton Plains, NJ: 2008.

———. *Top Secret/Majic.* Marlowe & Co. New York: 1996.

Friedman, Stanton T. and Don Berliner. *Crash at Corona: U.S. Military Retrieval and Cover-up of a UFO.* Paragon House. New York: 1992.

Fry, Daniel. *Atoms, Galaxies, and Understanding: Cosmology in Its Simplest Form.* Understanding Publishing. El Monte, CA: 1960.

——. *Steps to the Stars*. Understanding Publishing. El Monte, CA: 1956.

——. *The White Sands Incident*. New Age Publishing. Los Angeles: 1954.

Fuller, John G. *Incident at Exeter*. Putnam. New York: 1966.

——. *The Interrupted Journey: Two Lost Hours Aboard a Flying Saucer*. Dial Press. New York: 1966.

Gallop, Alan. *The Martians Are Coming! The True Story of Orson Welles' 1938 Panic Broadcast*. Amberley Publishing. Stroud, United Kingdom: 2011.

Gelernter, David. *1939: The Lost World of the Fair*. The Free Press. New York: 1995.

Good, Timothy. *Above Top Secret: The Worldwide UFO Cover-up*. Morrow. New York: 1988.

——. *Need to Know: UFOs, the Military, and Intelligence*. Sidgwick & Jackson. London: 2006.

Gordon, Stan. *Silent Invasion: The Pennsylvania UFO-Bigfoot Casebook*. Stan Gordon Productions. Greensburg: PA: 2010.

Gosling, John. *Waging the War of the Worlds*. McFarland & Co. Jefferson, NC: 2009.

Green, Christopher. *Overpowered! The Science and Showbiz of Hypnosis*. The British Library. London: 2015.

Green, William. *Rocket Fighter*. Ballantine. New York: 1971.

Greenberg, Martin, ed. *Travelers of Space*. Gnome Press. New York: 1951.

Greenewald, John Jr. *Beyond UFO Secrecy*. The Black Vault. Los Angeles: 2002.

Greer, Steven M. *Extraterrestrial Contact: The Evidence and Implications*. Crossing Point. Afton, VA: 1999.

——. *Hidden Truth, Forbidden Knowledge*. Crossing Point. Afton, VA: 2006.

Haines, Richard F. *CE-5: Close Encounters of the Fifth Kind*. Sourcebooks. Naperville, IL: 1999.

——. *Observing UFOs*. Nelson-Hall. Chicago: 1980.

Haines, Richard F., ed. *UFO Phenomena and the Behavioral Scientist*. Scarecrow Press. Metuchen, NJ: 1979.

Haley, Leah. *Unlocking Alien Closets: Abductions, Mind Control, and Spirituality*. Greenleaf Publications. Murfreesboro, TN: 2003.

Hall, Richard H., ed. *The UFO Evidence (Unidentified Flying Objects)*. National Investigations Committee on Aerial Phenomena. Washington, DC: 1964.

——. *The UFO Evidence: A Thirty-Year Report, Volume II*. Scarecrow Press. Oxford: 2001.

Heiser, Michael S. *I Dare You Not to Bore Me with the Bible*. Lexham Press. Bellingham, WA: 2014.

Hesemann, Michael. *The Fatima Secret*. Dell. New York: 2000.

Hewes, Hayden and Brad Steiger, eds. *UFO Missionaries Extraordinary*. Pocket Books. New York: 1976.

Hill, Paul R. *Unconventional Flying Objects: A Former NASA Scientist Explains How UFOs Really Work*. Hampton Roads Publishing. Newburyport, MA: 1995.

Hind, Cynthia. *UFOs over Africa*. Horus House. Madison, WI: 1997.

Hoagland, Richard C. *The Monuments of Mars: A City on the Edge of Forever*. North Atlantic Books. Berkeley, CA: 1987.

Hobana, Ion and Julien Weverbergh. *UFO's [sic] from Behind the Iron Curtain*. Souvenir Press. London: 1974.

Hogan, David J., ed. *The Fifties Chronicle*. Legacy Publishing. Lincolnwood, IL: 2006.

Hollings, Ken. *Welcome to Mars: Politics, Pop Culture, and Weird Science in 1950s America*. North Atlantic Books. Berkeley, CA: 2014.

Holy Bible, King James Version, 14th printing. Holman. Nashville: 1996.

Holy Bible, New International Version. Zondervan. Grand Rapids, MI: 2013.

Hopkins, Budd. *Art, Life, and UFOs*. Anomalist Books. San Antonio: 2009.

———. *Intruders: The Incredible Visitations at Copley Woods*. Random House. New York: 1987.

———. *Missing Time: A Documented Study of UFO Abductions*. Richard Marek. New York: 1981.

Hornish, David. *The Modern Hobby Guide to Topps Chewing Gum: 1938 to 1956*. Lulu Press. Raleigh, NC: 2013.

Howe, Linda Moulton. *An Alien Harvest: Further Evidence Linking Animal Mutilations and Human Abductions to Alien Life Forms*. Linda Moulton Howe Productions. Littleton, CO: 1989.

———. *Mysterious Lights and Crop Circles*. Paper Chase Press. New Orleans: 2001.

Howlett, Mike. *The Weird World of Eerie Publications*. Feral House. Port Townsend, WA: 2010.

Hughes, Robert. *American Visions: The Epic History of Art in America*. Knopf. New York: 1997.

Hynek, J. Allen. *The UFO Experience: A Scientific Inquiry*. Regnery. New York: 1972.

Jacobsen, Annie. *Area 51: An Uncensored History of America's Top Secret Military Base*. Little, Brown. New York: 2011.

Jessup, M. K. *The Case for the UFO*. Citadel Press. New York: 1955.

———. *The Expanding Case for the UFO*. Citadel Press. New York: 1957.

Johnson, DeWayne and Kenn Thomas. *Flying Saucers over Los Angeles*. Adventures Unlimited Press. Kempton, IL: 1998.

Joshi, S. T. *H. P. Lovecraft: A Life*. Necronomicon Press. West Warwick, RI: 1996.

Jung, C. G. *Flying Saucers*. MJF Books/Fine Communications. New York: 1997.

Kaufman, Marc. *First Contact*. Simon & Schuster. New York: 2011.

Kean, Leslie. *UFOs: Generals, Pilots, and Government Officials Go on the Record*. Harmony Books. New York: 2010.

Keel, John. *The Mothman Prophecies*. Saturday Review Press. New York: 1975.

———. *Operation Trojan Horse*. Putnam. New York: 1970.

———. *The Perspicacious Percipient: How to Investigate UFOs and Other Insane Urges, Selected Writings*. New Saucerian Books. Point Pleasant, WV: 2015.

———. *Searching for the String: Selected Writings*. New Saucerian Books. Point Pleasant, WV: 2014.

———. *Strange Creatures from Time and Space*. Fawcett Gold Medal. New York: 1970.

Keene, Carolyn ("house" name for Harriet Stratemeyer Adams). *The Flying Saucer Mystery. Nancy Drew Mystery Stories 58*. Grosset & Dunlap. New York: 1980.

Keyhoe, Donald. *Flying Saucers from Outer Space*. Henry Holt. New York: 1953.

Kick. Russ, ed. *Everything You Know About God Is Wrong: The Disinformation Guide to Religion*. Disinformation Books. New York: 2007.

King, George. *The Twelve Blessings*. Aetherius Press. Los Angeles: 1995.

Klass, Philip J. *The Real Roswell Crashed-Saucer Coverup*. Prometheus. New York: 1997.

———. *UFO Abductions: A Dangerous Game*. Prometheus. New York: 1989.

———. *UFOs Explained*. Random House. New York: 1975.

———. *UFOs—Identified*. Random House. New York: 1968.

Kloetzke, Chase with Richard M. Dolan. *Admissible: The Field Manual for Investigating UFOs, Paranormal Activity, and Strange Creatures*. Richard Dolan Press. Rochester, NY: 2014.

Koch, Howard. *The Panic Broadcast*. Avon. New York: 1970.

Korff, Kal K. *The Roswell UFO Crash: What They Don't Want You to Know*. Prometheus Books. Amherst, NY: 1997.

Leir, Roger. *The Aliens and the Scalpel*. Granite Publishing. Columbus, NC: 1999.

———. *Casebook: Alien Implants*. (*Whitley Strieber's Hidden Agendas*). Dell. New York: 2000.

Lewis, James R. *UFOs and Popular Culture*. ABC-CLIO. Santa Barbara, CA: 2000.

———, ed. *The Gods Have Landed: New Religions from Other Worlds*. State University of New York Press. Albany: 1995.

——— and Jesper Aagaard Petersen, eds. *Controversial New Religions, Second Edition*. Oxford University Press. Oxford: 2014.

Lindemann, Michael, ed. *UFOs and the Alien Presence: Six Viewpoints*. Wild Flower Press. Columbus, NC: 1995.

Longerich, Peter. *Heinrich Himmler*. Oxford University Press. Oxford: 2012.

Lusar, Rudolf. *German Secret Weapons of World War II*. Neville Spearman. London: 1959.

Mack, John E. *Abductions: Human Encounters with Aliens*. Scribners. New York: 1994.

Magilow, Daniel H., Kristin T. Vander Lugt, Elizabeth Bridges, eds. *Nazisploitation! The Nazi Image in Low-Brow Cinema and Culture*. Continuum. London: 2012.

Maloney, Mack. *UFOs in Wartime*. Berkley Books. New York: 2011.

Marinetti, Filippo Tommaso. *Critical Writings: New Edition*. Günter Berghaus, ed. Farrar, Strauss & Giroux. New York: 2008.

Marrs, Jim. *Alien Agenda: The Complete Untold Story of the Extraterrestrials Among Us*. HarperCollins. New York: 1997.

Marshall, D.J. and F. V. G. Royce. *"Griff" on the Gremlin*. Pilot Press. London: 1943.

Maxwell, Charles. *The World's Greatest War: Its Inception and Progress*. Leslie-Judge. New York: 1915.

McLaren, Carmen. *UFO Conspiracy*. Schiffer. Atglen, PA: 2011.

Menger, Howard. *From Outer Space to You*. Saucerian Books. Clarksburg, WV: 1959.

Menzel, Donald H. *Flying Saucers*. Harvard University Press. Cambridge. MA: 1953.

——— and Ernest H. Taves. *The UFO Enigma*. Doubleday. New York: 1977.

——— and Lyle G. Boyd. *The World of Flying Saucers*. Doubleday. New York: 1963.

Metzger, Bruce M. and Roland E. Murphy, eds. *The New Oxford Annotated Bible*. Oxford University Press. New York: 1991.

Michel, Aimé. *The Truth About Flying Saucers*. Criterion Books. New York: 1956.

Miller, Timothy, ed. *America's Alternative Religions*. SUNY Press. New York: 1995.

Mitchell, Edgar. *The Space Less Traveled: Straight Talk from Apollo 14 Astronaut Edgar Mitchell*. Pen-L Publishing. Fayetteville, AR: 2012.

Moffitt, John F. *Picturing Extraterrestrials: Alien Images in Modern Mass Culture.* Prometheus Book. Amherst, NY: 2003.

Moseley, James. *Jim Moseley's Book of Saucer News.* CreateSpace. Seattle: 2014.

Moseley, James and Karl T. Pflock. *Shockingly Close to the Truth.* Prometheus Books. Amherst, NY: 2002.

Mullaney, Dean, ed. *The Golden Age Superman: Sunday Pages 1946–1949.* IDW Publishing. San Diego: 2014.

Nadis, Fred. *The Man from Mars: Ray Palmer's Amazing Pulp Journey.* Jeremy P. Tarcher/Penguin. New York: 2013.

Narváes, Peter, ed. *The Good People: New Fairylore Essays.* University Press of Kentucky. Lexington: 1997.

Nelson, Buck. *My Trip to Mars, the Moon, and Venus.* Quill Press. West Plains, MO: 1956.

Nicholls, Peter. *The Science Fiction Encyclopedia.* Doubleday/Dolphin. Garden City, NY: 1979.

Patton, Phil. *Dreamland: Travels Inside the Secret World of Roswell and Area 51.* Villard. New York: 1998

Piccard, George. *Liquid Conspiracy.* Adventures Unlimited Press. Kempton, IL: 1999.

Picknett, Lynn and Clive Prince. *The Stargate Conspiracy.* Berkley Books. New York: 1999.

Pliny the Elder. *Natural History, Books 3–7. (Pliny's Natural History Volume II).* Translated by H. Rackham. Harvard University Press. Cambridge, MA: 1942.

Pohl, Frederik. *Chasing Science: Science as Spectator Sport.* Tor. New York: 2000.

Ponce de Leon, Charles L. *Self-Exposure: Human-Interest Journalism and the Emergence of Celebrity in America, 1890–1940.* University of North Carolina Press. Chapel Hill: 2002.

Prelinger, Megan. *Another Science Fiction: Advertising the Space Race 1957–1962.* Blast Books. New York: 2010.

Randle, Kevin. D. *Roswell Revisited.* Galde Press. Lakeville, MN: 2007.

Randle, Kevin D. and Donald R. Schmitt. *UFO Crash at Roswell.* Avon. New York: 1991.

Randles, Jenny. *UFOs and How to See Them.* Sterling. New York: 1992.

Redfern, Nick. *True Stories of the Real Men in Black.* Rosen Publishing. New York: 2014.

Rickard, Bob and John Michell. *The Rough Guide to Unexplained Phenomena.* 2nd edition. Rough Guides. London: 2007.

Rife, Philip L. *It Didn't Start with Roswell: 50 Years of Amazing UFO Crashes, Close Encounters, and Coverups.* iUniverse/Writers Club Press. Lincoln, NB: 2001.

Roberts, A.R. *From Adam to Omega: An Anatomy of UFO Phenomena.* iUniverse. Bloomington, IN: 2012.

Rose, Bill. *Flying Saucer Technology.* Midland. Hersham, Surry, UK: 2011.

Ruppelt, Edward. *The Report on Unidentified Flying Objects.* Doubleday. Garden City, NY: 1956.

—— and Chet Dembeck. *The Uncensored Truth About UFOs.* Chet Dembeck. Baltimore: 2012.

Rutledge, Harley. *Project Identification: The First Scientific Study of UFO Phenomena.* Prentice-Hall. Englewood Cliffs, NJ: 1981.

Saler, Benson, Charles A. Ziegler and Charles B. Moore. *UFO Crash at Roswell.* Smithsonian Institution Press. Washington, DC: 1997.

Schuessler, John. *A Catalog of UFO-Related Human Physiological Effects.* [Self-published]. 1996.

Schwartz, A. Brad. *Broadcast Hysteria: Orson Welles's War of the Worlds and the Art of Fake News.* Hill and Wang. New York: 2015.

Scully, Frank. *Behind the Flying Saucers.* Henry Holt. New York: 1950.

Shermer, Michael. *Why People Believe Weird Things: Pseudo-Science, Superstition, and Bogus Notions of Our Time.* MJF Books. New York: 1997.

Showalter, Elaine. *Hystories: Hysterical Epidemics and Modern Media.* Columbia University Press. New York: 1997.

Steinman, William S. and Wendelle C. Stevens. *UFO Crash at Aztec.* UFO Photo Archives. Tucson, AZ: 1987.

Straub, Peter, ed. *Lovecraft: Tales.* The Library of America. New York: 2005.

Strieber, Whitley. *Communion.* Beech Tree Books. New York: 1987.

———. *The Grays.* Tor. New York: 2006.

Stringfield, Leonard S. *Situation Red: The UFO Siege.* Doubleday. New York: 1977.

Sturrock, Peter A. *The UFO Enigma: A New Review of the Physical Evidence.* Warner Aspect. New York: 1999.

Thomas, Gordon and Max Morgan Witts. *Enola Gay.* Stein and Day. New York: 1977.

Thomas, Paul. *Les Extraterrestres.* Plon. Paris: 1962.

Trench, Brinsley Le Poer. *Secret of the Ages: UFOs from Inside the Earth.* Panther Books. St Albans, England: 1976.

Tumminia, Diana G., ed. *Alien Worlds: Social and Religious Dimensions of Extraterrestrial Contact.* Syracuse University Press. Syracuse, NY: 2007.

Vallée, Jacques. *Anatomy of a Phenomenon: Unidentified Objects in Space—A Scientific Appraisal.* Henry Regnery. Chicago: 1965.

———. *Dimensions: A Casebook of Alien Contact.* Contemporary. Chicago: 1988.

———. *Messengers of Deception: UFO Contacts and Cults.* Ronin. Berkeley, CA: 1979.

———. *Passport to Magonia: From Folklore to Flying Saucers.* Henry Regnery. Chicago: 1969.

Vallée, Jacques and Chris Aubeck. *Wonders in the Sky: Unexplained Aerial Objects from Antiquity to Modern Times.* Jeremy P. Tarcher/Penguin. New York: 2009.

Van Tassel, George W. *I Rode in a Flying Saucer: The Mystery of the Flying Saucers Revealed.* New Age Publishing. Los Angeles: 1952.

Wallace, Amy, David Wallechinsky, and Irving Wallace. *The Book of Lists #3.* Bantam Books. New York: 1983.

Waller, William H. *The Milky Way: An Insider's Guide.* Princeton University Press. Princeton, NJ: 2013.

Warren, Bill. *Keep Watching the Skies! The 21st Century Edition.* McFarland & Co. Jefferson, NC: 2010.

Watson, Nigel. *UFO Investigations Manual.* Haynes Publishing. Yeovil, Somerset, UK: 2011.

Wilkins, Harold T. *Flying Saucers on the Attack.* Citadel Press. New York: 1954.

Wilkinson, Frank G. *The Golden Age of Flying Saucers.* New Paradigm Press/Lulu. Raleigh, NC: 2007.

Williamson, George Hunt and John McCoy. *UFOs Confidential: The Meaning Behind the Most Closely Guarded Secret of All Time*. Essene Press. Corpus Christie, TX: 1958.

Wilson, Colin. *Alien Dawn: An Investigation into the Contact Experience*. Virgin. London: 1998.

———. *Dreaming to Some Purpose*. Century. London: 2004.

———. *The Outsider*. Gollancz. London: 1956.

———. *World Famous UFOs*. Parragon Plus. Bath, England: 1996.

Magazines and Journals

Angelucci, Orfeo. "California Soul Rush Days." *Talk of the Times*. July 1958.

"Are You Up-to-Date on UFOs?" *Popular Mechanics*. January 1966.

Blish, James. "Tomb Tapper." *Astounding Science Fiction*. July 1956.

Brown, Ted and Kelly Everding. "Two by Colin Wilson: Alien Dawn and the Books in My Life." *Rain Taxi*. Winter 1998.

Cahn, J. P. "The Flying Saucers and the Mysterious Little Men." *True*. September 1952.

———. "Flying Saucer Swindlers." *True*. August 1956.

Cuoghi, Diego. "The Art of Imagining UFOs." Translated by Daniela Cisi and Leonardo Serni. *Skeptic*. July 2004.

Dickinson, Terence. "The Zeta Reticuli Incident." *Astronomy*. December 1974.

Ferris, Timothy. "The Playboy Interview: Erich von Däniken." *Playboy*. August 1974.

Folger, Tim. "Journeys to the Center of the Earth." *Discover*. July/August 2014.

Ginna, Robert and H. B. Darrach Jr. "Have We Visitors from Space?" *Life*. April 7, 1952.

Gladych, Michael. "The G-Engines Are Coming!" *Young Men*. November 1956.

Grisholm, Luke. "The Night an American Town Died of Fright." *Official UFO*. January 1978.

Hogan, David J. "Wernher von Braun, Rocketeer." *Outré*. No. 15–18, 1999.

Hoversten, Paul. "Operation Highjump." *Air & Space*. July 2007.

Hsu, Hua. "We Are 'Sheeple,' and Our Overlords Lizard Aliens. (Who Came from Inside the Earth)." *New York* magazine; www.nymag.com. November 17, 2013.

Hynek, J. Allen. "Are Flying Saucers Real?" *Saturday Evening Post*. December 17, 1966.

Keel, John. "Kenneth Arnold and the F.B.I." *Flying Saucer Review*. August 1987.

Lemonick, Michael D. "Life Beyond Earth." *National Geographic*. July 2014.

Martinez, Yleana. "A Long Tall Texas Tale." *American Journalism Review*. May 1, 1993.

Masaaki, Aniya. "Compulsory Mass Suicide, the Battle of Okinawa, and Japan's Textbook Controversy." *Asia-Pacific Journal*. January 2008.

Montague, W. T. "Why Grinding-Wheel Chips Solidify." *American Machinist*. February 5, 1914.

Niven, Larry. "The Warriors." *Worlds of If*. February 1966.

Oberg, James. "The Failure of the 'Science' of UFOlogy." *New Scientist*. October 11, 1979.

Randles, Jenny. "Alien End Game?" *Fortean Times*. March 2013.

Rojcewicz, Peter M. "The 'Men in Black' Experience and Tradition: Analogues with the Traditional Devil Hypothesis." *Journal of American Folklore*, number 396. April–June 1987.

Schwarz, Berthold. "Berserk." *Flying Saucer Review*. January–February 1974.

Shermer, Michael. "Patternicity: Finding Meaningful Patterns in Meaningless Noise." *Scientific American*. December 2008.

Sherwood, John. "Gray Barker: My Friend the Myth-Maker." *Skeptical Inquirer*. May–June 1998.

———. "Gray Barker's Book of Bunk: Mothman, Saucers, and MiB." *Skeptical Inquirer*. May 2002.

Shostak, Seth. "Should We Keep a Low Profile in Space?" *New York Times*. March 27, 2015.

Speigel, Lee. "Once-Classified UFO Files Now Searchable Online." *Huffington Post*. January 27, 2015.

Swift, Earl. "What Really Happened in Area 51?" *Popular Mechanics* (popularmechanics.com). September 12, 2011.

"That Time Subterranean Aliens Killed 60 People in New Mexico." *The Huffington Post*. April 20, 2014.

"UFOs for Real? *Newsweek*. October 10, 1966.

"Water's Interstellar Origins." *The Week*. October 31, 2014.

Newspapers

Achenbach, Joel and Rachel Feltman. "New Evidence Suggests a Ninth Planet Lurking at the Edge of the Solar System." *Washington Post*. January 20, 2016.

"Air Force Order on 'Saucers' Cited; Pamphlet by Inspector General Called Objects a 'Serious Business'" *New York Times*. (United Press International story) February 28, 1960.

"Britain Is Alarmed by Burlesque Radio 'News' of Revolt in London and Bombing of Commons." *New York Times*. January 17, 1926.

Broad, William J. and David E. Sanger. "U.S. Ramping Up Major Renewal in Nuclear Arms." *New York Times*. September 21, 2014.

"Chile's UFO Trail Touts Intergalactic Ties." *Sydney Morning Herald*. August 22, 2008.

"Chinese Air Force Pirate Chases UFO." Agence-France Presse (AFP). November 5, 1998.

Doan, Lynn. "It Came from the Planet Garage." *Los Angeles Times*. March 18, 2006.

"Doctor Claims World Will Upheave, Not End." *Pittsburgh Post-Gazette*. December 17, 1954.

"Floating Mystery Ball Is New Nazi Air Weapon." *New York Times*. December 14, 1944.

"Flying Saucer Stalled Truck, Says Farmer." (Capetown, South Africa) *Die Bruger*. March 31, 1995.

Fox, Margalit. "Budd Hopkins, Abstract Expressionist and U.F.O. Author, Dies at 80." *New York Times*. August 24, 2011.

Glading, Jo Astrid. "'Martians' Get Warmer Welcome This Time." (Hendersonville, NC) *Times News*. October 30, 1988.

Gutteridge, Nick. "Revealed: Special Branch Tailed UFO Cult Leader for Five Years over Fears He Was Communist." *Sunday Express*. July 28, 2015.

Hawksley, Rupert. "Britain's Roswell: The Truth Behind the Rendlesham Forest UFO Incident." *The* (London) *Telegraph*. February 16, 2015.

Herschel, John [spurious byline; actual writer: Richard Adams Locke]. "Great Astronomical Discoveries Lately Made by Sir John Herschel, L.L.D., F.R.S. &c. at the Cape of Good Hope." *New York Sun*. August 25–29 & 31, 1835.

Huppke, Rex W. "For Some, Clinton Would Be Out-of-This-World Candidate." *Chicago Tribune*. April 7, 2015.

Kass, John. "Space Raiders from Planet Nine Won't Be Friendly." *Chicago Tribune*. January 22, 2016.

Levy, Claudia. "Philip Klass, 85, Dies; Aviation Journalist, UFO Debunker." *Washington Post*. August 11, 2005.

McQuiston, John T. "U.F.O. Fan Ruled Unfit for Trial in Long Island Murder Plot." *New York Times*. November 14, 1997.

"Militia Leader Killed, Deputy Wounded During Attempted Arrest." *Arizona Republic* (Associated Press story). November 6, 2001.

Murphy, Jody. "Alien Claims Took Toll on Derenbergers." *Parkersburg* (WV) *News and Sentinel*. June 11, 2011.

"Oh, That Bird It Was Seen Again." *Point Pleasant* (WV) *Register*. November 25, 1966.

"Pedro Ferriz Santa Cruz, a Pioneer of Mexican Television, Dies." (Mexico City) *Excélsior*. March 9, 2013.

"Pursuit of 'Saucers' Changes Scientist's Life." *Spartanburg* (SC) *Herald-Journal*. (Associated Press story). November 23, 1977.

Sage, Adam. "Salut, Earthlings." *Times of London*. February 5, 2003.

Sarno, David. "It Came from Outer Space." *Los Angeles Times*. August 22, 2007.

"Scientists Consider UFO Data Amazing." *Cape Girardeau Southeast Missourian*. November 19, 1973.

Strauss, Steve. "Radio's Bell Is Sound Example for Entrepreneurs." *USA Today*. June 15, 2015.

Tizon, Tomas Alex. "Seeking UFOs, Deep Underground." *Los Angeles Times*. March 28, 2008.

Travis, Alan. "Alien Invasion Hoax Fooled MoD, Archive Papers Reveal." *The* (London & Manchester) *Guardian*. March 2, 2011.

Turner, Ralph. "Mason Bird-Monster Presumed Gone Now." *Huntington* (WV) *Herald-Dispatch*. November 22, 1966.

———. "That Mothman: Would You Believe a Sandhill Crane?" *Huntington* (WV) *Herald-Dispatch*. November 19, 1966.

Vartabedian, Ralph and W. J. Hennigan. "Dusting Off the Nuclear Arsenal." *Chicago Tribune*. December 11, 2014.

Zolfagharifard, Ellie. "'I Saw Men Walking on Mars in 1979': 'Former Nasa [*sic*] Employee' Claims There Was a Secret Manned Mission to the Red Planet." (London) *Daily Mail*. November 28, 2014.

Pamphlets

Arnold, Kenneth. *The Flying Saucer as I Saw It.* Self-published: 1950.
Stringfield, Leonard S. *Inside Saucer Post . . . 3-0 Blue.* Self-published (Civilian Research, Interplanetary Flying Objects). Cincinnati: 1957.

Newsletters

Flying Saucer News. August 1961.
Thy Kingdom Come No. 8. Amalgamated Flying Saucer Clubs of America, Inc. March–April 1959.
U.F.O. Investigator Vol. II, No. 10. December–January 1963.

Papers

Bae, Young K. "Prospective of Photon Propulsion for Interstellar Flight." Space Technology and Applications International Forum II, 2012. Albuquerque, NM: 2012.
Brummett, William E. and Ernest R. Zuick Jr. "Should the USAF Reopen Project Blue Book?" Master's thesis. Air Command and Staff College. Auburn Alabama: 1974.
"Calculated Altitude Performance, Model P-51D." North American Aviation, Inc. Inglewood, CA: February 6, 1946.
Goldberg, Leo and Lawrence H. Aller. "Donald Howard Menzel: A Biographical Memoir." National Academy of Sciences. Washington, DC: 1991.
Hallet, W. H. Marc, with Richard W. Heiden. "A Critical Appraisal of George Adamski, the Man Who Spoke to the Space Brothers." Paris: 2015.
Lindell, Jeffery A. "A Historical and Physiological Perspective of the Foo Fighters of World War II." Indiana University Folklore Institute. Bloomington: 2012.
Prather, Charles Houston. "Chen Tao—God's Salvation Church: Past, Present, and Future." University of North Carolina. Greensboro, NC: 1999.
Puthoff, H. E. "Synopsis of Unconventional Flying Objects: JSE Review." Institute for Advanced Studies. Austin, TX: 1997.
Quintanilla, Hector. Book proposal, *UFOs: An Air Force Dilemma* aka *UFOs: A $20,000,000 Fiasco.* 1974.
"Speed vs. Altitude, P-51B with 1650-7 Packard Engine." Flight Test Engineering Branch. Wright Field, Dayton, OH: May 20, 1944.
"Typical Layout for Balloon Test Flight." United States Air Force. Washington, DC: 1950.
"United States Air Force Projects Grudge and Bluebook [*sic*] Reports 1–12." National Investigative Committee on Aerial Phenomena. Washington, DC: June 1968.

CD Collections

Atomic Platters: Cold War Music from the Golden Age of Homeland Security. Book: *Atomic Platters*. Text by Bill Geerhart and Ken Sitz. Bear Family Records. Hambergen, Germany: 2005.

Brain in a Box: The Science Fiction Collection. Book: *Brain in a Book*. Text by David Garland et al. Rhino. Burbank, CA: 2000.

Pulp & Pop Culture Box Vol. 1. RockBeat Records/S'more Entertainment. Sherman Oaks, CA: 2013.

Websites

www.abomb1.org

www.abovetopsecret.com

www.adamskifoundation.com

www.aetherius.org

www.af.mil

www.air-and-space.com

www.airlines-inform.com

www.aliencontactandhumanevolution.com

www.alienjigsaw.com

www.aliensandchildren.org

www.alienscientist.com

www.alien-ufos.com

www.allpar.com

www.amberclouds.com

www.americanantigravity.com

www.answeringgenesis.org

www.archive.org

www.armaghplanet.com

www.astro.caltech.edu

www.astronautix.com

www.astrosurf.com

www.badufos.blogspot.com

www.biblehub.com

www.biblestudytools.com

www.bibliotecapleyades.net

www.billymeierufocase.com

www.binarydecoder.info

www.binnallofamerica.com

www.blueblurrylines.com

www.bluebookarchive.org

www.boeing.com

www.brumac.8k.com

www.buffalohistoryworks.com

www.businessinsider.com

www.calphysics.org

www.capecentralhigh.com

www.chicagomag.com

www.cia.gov

www.classicufo.com

www.claudelafleur.qc.ca

www.coasttocoastam.com

www.conspiracyarchive.com

www.conspiracytheorytruths.blogspot.com

www.conspiracy-watch.org

www.cufon.org

www.cufos.org

www.cuttingedge.org

www.dailygrail.com

www.darkgovernment.com

www.davidgleason.com

www.davidicke.com

www.debunker.com

www.designation-systems.net

www.disinfo.com

www.dotsub.com

www.doubtfulnews.com

www.drdavidclarke.co.uk

www.edgrimsley.com

www.educatinghumanity.com

www.educationforum.ipbhost.com

www.elfis.net

www.enchantedlearning.com

www.enterprisemission.com

www.excludedmiddle.com

www.fabiozerpa.com.ar

www.fastwalkers.com

www.fineartamerica.com
www.flatwoodsmonster.com
www.floridaufonetwork.com
www.flyingmag.com
www.fmsfonline.org
www.fodors.com
www.fold3.com
www.forgetomori.com
www.forteantimes.com
www.fortean.wikidot.com
www.fotocat.blogspot.com
www.freedomofmind.com
www.freekurtis.org
www.galacticconnection.com
www.geektimes.ru
www.geni.com
www.gethampshire.co.uk
www.ghostradio.wordpress.com
www.gizadeathstar.com
www.goodyearblimp.com
www.gpposner.com
www.greyfalcon.us
www.hardevidence.info
www.history.mfnc.nasa
www.hoaxes.org
www.howstuffworks.com
www.huffingtonpost.com
www.human-science-research.blogspot
    .com
www.hyperphysics.phy-astr.gsu.edu
www.ibtimes.com
www.icar1.homestead.com
www.imdb.com
www.indianinthemachine.com
www.integratedsciopsychology.net
www.inventors.about.com
www.io9.com
www.theironskeptic.com
www.iufosightings.com
www.japanfocus.org
www.jeremiahproject.com
www.jjbenitez.com
www.jimmarrs.com
www.johnemackinstitute.org
www.jpl.nasa.gov
www.kalisanidiot.blogspot.com
www.latest-ufo-sightings.net
www.lhup.edu/~dsimanek
www.listverse.com
www.livescience.com
www.lockheedmartin.com
www.lucernevalley.net
www.markdice.com
www.mentalfloss.com
www.metmuseum.org
www.metrocosm.com/map-of-ufo
    -sightings
www.motherboard.vice.com
www.motherjones.com/politics
www.mothmanfestival.com
www.museumofflight.org
www.mysteriousuniverse.org
www.nationalufocenter.com
www.nbcnews.com
www.newsandsentinel.com
www.nicap.org
www.northbynorthwestern.com
www.noufors.com
www.npshistory.com
www.nuforc.org
www.openminds.tv
www.openminds.tv/roswell
www.originalgolddiggers.com
www.paranormality.com
www.pastaetheriussocietymembers
    .blogspot.com
www.patheos.com/Library/
www.paul.rutgers.edu
www.philipcoppens.com
www.phys.org
www.physics.smu.edu
www.popularmechanics.com
www.project1947.com
www.prorael.org
www.prufospolicedatabase.co.uk
www.rael.org
www.raelianews.org
www.realityuncovered.net
www.redstarfilms.blogspot.ca
www.rense.com
www.richarddolanpress.com
www.roswellfiles.com

www.roswellproof.homestead.com
www.sacred-texts.com
www.sanandaseagles.com
www.sciencedaily.com
www.sciencedirect.com
www.science.howstuffworks.com
www.sciencelearn.org.nz
www.scientificamerican.com
www.seacoastnh.com/History
sjhstrangetales.wordpress.com
www.skeptic.com
www.skepticreport.com
www.skeptoid.com
www.skyatnightmagazine.com
www.skylaire.com
www.slappedham.com
www.solstation.com
www.space.com
www.spiritscienceandmetaphysics.com
www.spitfireperformance.com
www.splcenter.org
www.stanford.edu
www.stantonfriedman.com
www.stopabductions.com
www.sufoi.dk
www.techcrunch.com
www.techtimes.com
www.temporaldoorway.com
www.terribleminds.com
www.theblackvault.com
www.thecid.com/ufo/
www.theforbiddenknowledge.com
www.thehollowearthinsider.com
www.thenewearth.org
www.thenightsky.org
www.thereisnogod.info
www.therendleshamforestincident.com
www.theufochronicles.com
www.thewellarmedwoman.com
www.thinkaboutitdocs.com

www.topsecretwriters.com
www.translate.google.com
www.trilateral.org
www.tvtango.com/listings
www.ufoabduction.com
www.ufocasebook.conforums.com
www.ufodigest.com
www.ufogrid.com
www.ufoinfo.com
www.ufologie.patrickgross.org
www.uforesearchnetwork.com
www.ufos-aliens.co.uk
www.ufosightingsdaily.com
www.ufos-scientificresearch.blogspot
   .com
www.ufostoday.com
www.ufotheater.com
www.ufotrail.blogspot.com
www.ufotruthmagazine.co.uk
www.ufo2001.com
www.ufoupdateslist.com
www.ufowatchdog.com
www.undebunkingufos.blogspot.com
www.unexplainedaustralia.com
www.unexplained-mysteries.com
www.universetoday.com
www.unmuseum.org
www.venturebeat.com
www.vintageufo.blogspot.com
www.virtuallystrange.net/ufo/
www.v-j-enterprises.com
www.voyager.jpl.nasa.gov
www.walesonline.co.uk
www.war-ofthe-worlds.co.uk
www.waterufo.net
www.weeklyworldnews.com
www.whofortedblog.com
www.wwiiaircraftperformance.org
www.youtube.com/watch?v=
   cmPiZv4q4Ms

Index

Page numbers in **bold** indicate a photograph or other image

THE FAQ SERIES

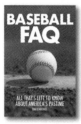

Prices, contents, and availability subject to change without notice.

Nirvana FAQ
by John D. Luerssen
Backbeat Books
9781617134500......................$24.99

Pink Floyd FAQ
by Stuart Shea
Backbeat Books
9780879309503...................$19.99

Elvis Films FAQ
by Paul Simpson
Applause Books
9781557838582......................$24.99

Elvis Music FAQ
by Mike Eder
Backbeat Books
9781617130496......................$24.99

Pearl Jam FAQ
*by Bernard M. Corbett and
Thomas Edward Harkins*
Backbeat Books
9781617136122..........................$19.99

Prog Rock FAQ
by Will Romano
Backbeat Books
9781617135873......................$24.99

Pro Wrestling FAQ
by Brian Solomon
Backbeat Books
9781617135996......................$29.99

**The Rocky Horror
Picture Show FAQ**
by Dave Thompson
Applause Books
9781495007477......................$19.99

Rush FAQ
by Max Mobley
Backbeat Books
9781617134517..........................$19.99

Saturday Night Live FAQ
by Stephen Tropiano
Applause Books
9781557839510......................$24.99

Seinfeld FAQ
by Nicholas Nigro
Applause Books
9781557838575......................$24.99

Sherlock Holmes FAQ
by Dave Thompson
Applause Books
9781480331495......................$24.99

The Smiths FAQ
by John D. Luerssen
Backbeat Books
9781480394490...................$24.99

Soccer FAQ
by Dave Thompson
Backbeat Books
9781617135989......................$24.99

The Sound of Music FAQ
by Barry Monush
Applause Books
9781480360433...................$27.99

South Park FAQ
by Dave Thompson
Applause Books
9781480350649...................$24.99

Bruce Springsteen FAQ
by John D. Luerssen
Backbeat Books
9781617130939.......................$22.99

Star Trek FAQ
(Unofficial and Unauthorized)
by Mark Clark
Applause Books
9781557837929.......................$19.99

Star Trek FAQ 2.0
(Unofficial and Unauthorized)
by Mark Clark
Applause Books
9781557837936...................$22.99

Star Wars FAQ
by Mark Clark
Applause Books
978480360181......................$24.99

Quentin Tarantino FAQ
by Dale Sherman
Applause Books
9781480355880...................$24.99

Three Stooges FAQ
by David J. Hogan
Applause Books
9781557837882......................$22.99

TV Finales FAQ
*by Stephen Tropiano and
Holly Van Buren*
Applause Books
9781480391444......................$19.99

The Twilight Zone FAQ
by Dave Thompson
Applause Books
9781480396180......................$19.99

Twin Peaks FAQ
*by David Bushman and
Arthur Smith*
Applause Books
9781495015861.......................$19.99

The Who FAQ
by Mike Segretto
Backbeat Books
9781480361034....................$24.99

The Wizard of Oz FAQ
by David J. Hogan
Applause Books
9781480350625....................$24.99

The X-Files FAQ
by John Kenneth Muir
Applause Books
9781480369740...................$24.99

Neil Young FAQ
by Glen Boyd
Backbeat Books
9781617130373........................$19.99

Frank Zappa FAQ
by John Corcelli
Backbeat Books
9781617136030......................$19.99

HAL•LEONARD®
PERFORMING ARTS
PUBLISHING GROUP

FAQ.halleonardbooks.com

0316